How the War was Won

The Second World War is usually seen as a titanic land battle, decided by mass armies, most importantly those on the Eastern Front. Phillips O'Brien shows us the war in a completely different light. In this compelling new history of the Allied path to victory, he argues that in terms of production, technology and economic power, the war was far more a contest of air and sea supremacy. He shows how the Allies developed a predominance of air and sea power which put unbearable pressure on Germany and Japan's entire war-fighting machine from Europe and the Mediterranean to the Pacific. Air and sea power dramatically expanded the area of battle and allowed the Allies to destroy over half of the Axis's equipment before it had even reached the traditional "battlefield." Battles such as El Alamein, Stalingrad and Kursk did not win World War II; air and sea power did.

Phillips Payson O'Brien is Director of the Scottish Centre for War Studies and Reader in History at the University of Glasgow.

CAMBRIDGE MILITARY HISTORIES

Edited by

HEW STRACHAN, *Chichele Professor of the History of War,*
University of Oxford and Fellow of All Souls College, Oxford
GEOFFREY WAWRO, *Professor of Military History, and Director of the*
Military History Center, University of North Texas

The aim of this series is to publish outstanding works of research on warfare throughout the ages and throughout the world. Books in the series take a broad approach to military history, examining war in all its military, strategic, political and economic aspects. The series complements Studies in the Social and Cultural History of Modern Warfare by focusing on the "hard" military history of armies, tactics, strategy and warfare. Books in the series consist mainly of single author works – academically vigorous and groundbreaking – which are accessible to both academics and the interested general reader.

A full list of titles in the series can be found at: www.cambridge.org/militaryhistories

How the War was Won

Air–Sea Power and Allied Victory
in World War II

Phillips Payson O'Brien
University of Glasgow

CAMBRIDGE
UNIVERSITY PRESS

CAMBRIDGE
UNIVERSITY PRESS

University Printing House, Cambridge CB2 8BS, United Kingdom

One Liberty Plaza, 20th Floor, New York, NY 10006, USA

477 Williamstown Road, Port Melbourne, VIC 3207, Australia

314-321, 3rd Floor, Plot 3, Splendor Forum, Jasola District Centre, New Delhi - 110025, India

79 Anson Road, #06-04/06, Singapore 079906

Cambridge University Press is part of the University of Cambridge.

It furthers the University's mission by disseminating knowledge in the pursuit of education, learning and research at the highest international levels of excellence.

www.cambridge.org
Information on this title: www.cambridge.org/9781108716895

First published 2015
First paperback edition 2018

A catalogue record for this publication is available from the British Library

Library of Congress Cataloging in Publication data
O'Brien, Phillips Payson, 1963–
How the war was won: air–sea power and Allied victory in World War II / Phillips Payson O'Brien, University of Glasgow
    pages cm.
Includes bibliographical references and index.
ISBN 978-1-107-01475-6 (Hardback)
    1. World War, 1939–1945–Campaigns.   2. Air power–History–20th century–
Case studies.   3. Sea power–History–20th century–Case studies.   4. World War,
1939–1945–Aerial operations.   5. World War, 1939–1945–Naval operations.
I. Title.   II. Title: Air–sea power and allied victory in World War II.
D743.025 2014
940.54´4–dc23   2014027836

ISBN 978-1-107-01475-6 Hardback
ISBN 978-1-108-71689-5 Paperback

CONTENTS

FIGURES

MAPS

TABLES

ACKNOWLEDGMENTS

This book was only made possible by the extraordinary support of my family and friends. Over the past few years they have been a source of companionship and comfort, there both to inspire and cajole me in equal measure. My parents, William and Nancy, have not only provided me a home and refuge, they imparted to me their love of ideas and discussion. My sisters, brothers and nephews, Elizabeth, Sarah, Bill, Jamie, Sam, Andrew, Sam and Ben, are rocks of support and wonderful friends, and have listened with great patience to what must have seemed to them endless reports of the process of writing this book. My Aunt Anne and Uncle Ray, who is missed constantly, were also great sources of comfort and happiness. I am more grateful to my family than they will ever know.

Throughout this process many colleagues at Glasgow University, past and present, have impressed me with their penetrating intellects and provided me with great cheer and companionship. Simon Ball, Evan Mawdsley, William Mulligan and Peter Jackson all possess a profound knowledge of World War II and have shared that with me with unstinting generosity. I was fortunate to have each one of them so close at hand during different parts of the writing process. They are all excellent historians and dear friends. I must also thank Matthew Strickland and Stuart Airlie for Kino Club – always a high point of the social calendar – and Cian O'Driscoll for countless morning coffees and breakfasts. Other excellent historians at Glasgow whom I have been privileged to have as colleagues (past and present) include Marina

Moskowitz, Simon Newman, Alex Marshall, Alex Bamji, Sonke Neitzel and Graham Cross. I must also say how blessed I have been with tremendous students over the years, many of whom provided intellectual sustenance at different times during the writing and many of whom have become close friends. Angela, Katherine, May (and Ed), Tony, Sigbjorn, Eilidh, Joe, Dani, Chris, Tim and Marzia – Thank You. Finally thanks very much to my special subject students of 2013–14, World War II devotees all.

In the greater Glasgow community there are some others upon whom I came to rely for their support. Roddy Neilson and Anne Parker know the meaning of friendship, and I am in their debt. Helen Ball, except for her preposterous decision to abscond to sunnier climes, always makes me smile. Maurizio and Esther have prepared more healthy and tasty meals for me than I can count. I am blessed to have some friends in Sicily whom I would like to visit even more than I do. Fabio, Simona and Marco – eating pasta norma with you has led to some of the happiest moments I experienced during this writing process. Vittoria, I cannot thank you enough for your friendship and for introducing me to your delightful (and growing) family in Catania. Even though I met Jon Parry many years ago in Cambridge, he has become Sicilian in my mind and during his visits I have learned many historical and epicurean truths. In America I must mention Randall, Alison, Alexander and Michael Heather. Your home in Yorktown Heights feels like my own when I am lucky enough to visit. Finally, thanks to Steve Fraidin and Lori Kramer who, though coming relatively late into this narrative, allowed me to share an excellent trip to the Highlands of Scotland and a number of New Year's Eves with them.

I also received some important institutional support in the creation of this book. Glasgow University, as well as providing an intellectual home, was generous in its allocation of research leave and research funding. The Carnegie Fund for the Universities of Scotland and the Naval Historical and Heritage Center in Washington, DC both provided research grants which allowed me to press on more quickly with the research. I would also like to thank the National Institute of Defense Studies in Japan for hosting me twice and allowing me to develop some of the early ideas for this book. Finally, many thanks go to Michael Watson, Rosalyn Scott and everyone at Cambridge

University Press for their effort and professionalism. I hope they are pleased with the final product.

Finally, I must always thank Zara Steiner, who through her patience many years ago imparted a wisdom and integrity about historical writing that I try my best to live up to today.

ABBREVIATIONS

Adm   Admiralty Papers, National Archives (UK)
AFV   armored fighting vehicles
Air   Air Ministry Papers, National Archives (UK)
ASW   anti-submarine warfare
Cab   Cabinet Papers, National Archives (UK)
CBO   Combined Bomber Offensive
CCS   Combined Chiefs of Staff
COA   Committee of Operations Analysts
DEI   Dutch East Indies
ETO   European theater of operations
FDR   Franklin D. Roosevelt Papers, Hyde Park, NY
FO   Foreign Office Papers, National Archives (UK)
IJN   Imperial Japanese Navy
JCS   Joint Chiefs of Staff
JIC   Joint Intelligence Committee
MAP   Ministry of Aircraft Production (UK)
NARA   National Archives and Records Administration (USA)
NAUK   National Archives United Kingdom, Kew
NAUS   National Archives United States, College Park, MD
OKW   Oberkommando der Wehrmacht
Prem   Prime Minister's Papers, National Archives (UK)
RM   Reichsmarks
SD   State Department Papers, National Archives (USA)
UKSBS   United Kingdom Strategic Bombing Survey
USAAF   United States Army Air Force

USN   United States Navy

USSBS   United States Strategic Bombing Survey Papers, National Archives (USA)

War   War Department Papers (UK)

WD   War Department Papers (USA)

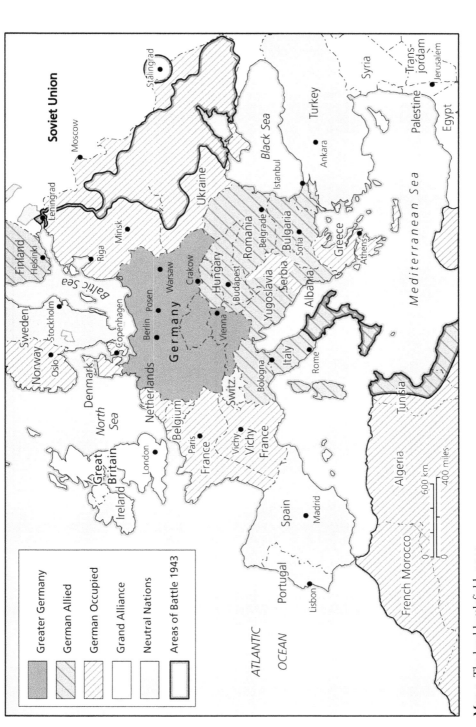

Map 1 The land battlefield, 1943

Map 2 The air–sea super-battlefield, 1943

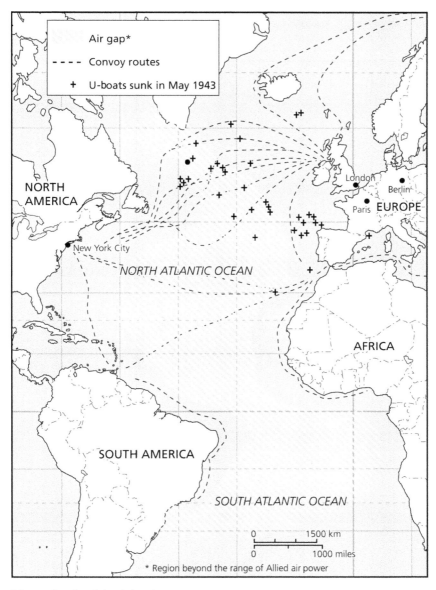

Map 3 Battle of the Atlantic, 1943

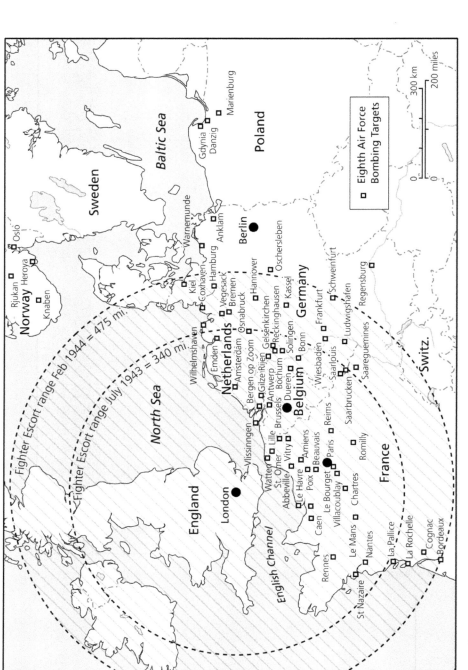

Map 4 Strategic air war in Europe, 1943

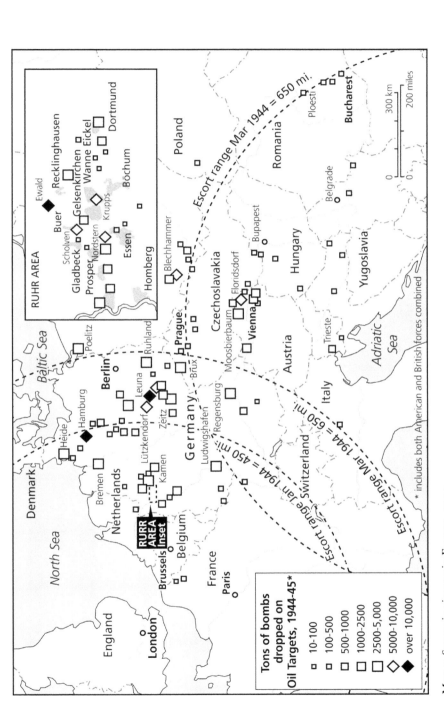

RUHR AREA

Ewald
Recklinghausen
Buer
Gelsenkirchen
Wanne Eickel
Dortmund
Scholven
Gladbeck
Prosper
Nordstern
Krupps
Böchum
Essen
Homberg

Poland

Escort range Mar 1944 = 650 mi.

Ploesti
Bucharest
Romania

300 km
200 miles

Belgrade
Yugoslavia

Blechhammer

Budapest
Hungary

Czechoslovakia
Floridsdorf
Moosbierbaum
Vienna
Austria

Trieste
Adriatic
Sea

Baltic Sea
Poelitz

Ruhland
Brüx
Prague

Berlin
Leuna
Hamburg
Zeitz
Lützkendorf
Regensburg
Italy

Heide
Germany
Ludwigshafen
Escort range Mar 1944 = 650 mi.

Bremen
Kamen
Switzerland

Netherlands
RUHR AREA inset

Belgium
Brussels
France
Paris

North Sea

Denmark

England
London

Escort range Jan 1944 = 450 mi.

* includes both American and British forces combined

Tons of bombs dropped on Oil Targets, 1944–45*

- 10–100
- 100–500
- 500–1000
- 1000–2500
- 2500–5,000
- 5000–10,000
- over 10,000

Map 5 Strategic air war in Europe, 1944

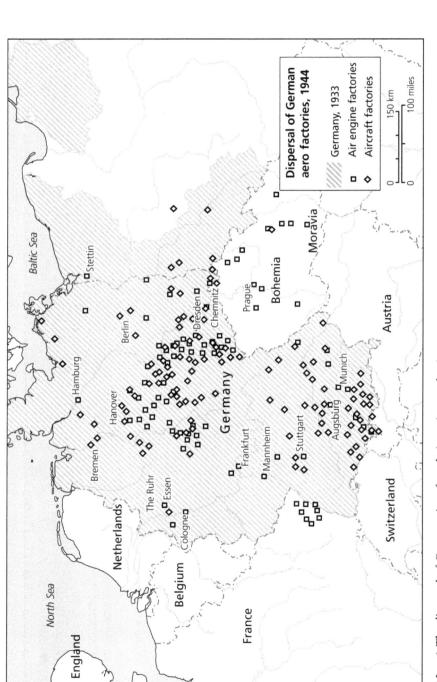

Map 6 The dispersal of German aircraft and air-engine production

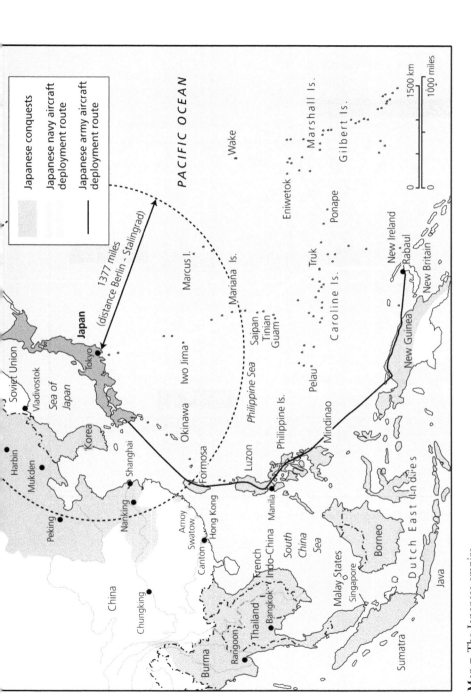

Map 7 The Japanese empire

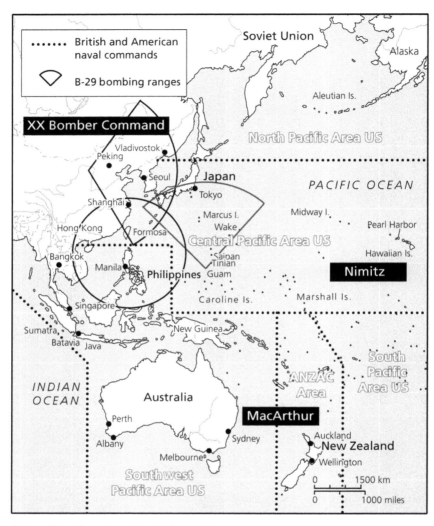

Map 8 The three American drives to Japan

INTRODUCTION

There were no decisive battles in World War II. This might seem a strange thing to say as the war is usually viewed through the prism of its famous engagements. As this book was being completed, the seventieth anniversaries of El Alamein, Stalingrad, Kursk and Midway have been remembered. It has led to a great deal of reflection on this pivotal period of the war.[1] Each battle is usually discussed with superlatives which invariably include how it changed the course of the war or was responsible for leading the Allies to victory.

El Alamein, the famous tank battle in the Egyptian desert in October and November 1942, between Bernard Montgomery's British 8th Army and Erwin Rommel's Afrika Corps, is most remembered in the United Kingdom and parts of what was the British Empire. The destruction of most of Rommel's panzers, which started the German retreat from North Africa that would culminate in the surrender of a large German force in Tunisia in May 1943, is depicted as a crucial marker heralding German defeat.[2] In the words of Winston Churchill, it may not have represented the beginning of the end, but it was "the end of the beginning." Later he would say that before El Alamein the British never had a victory, and after they never had a defeat.

The Battle of Stalingrad, which ended in February 1943, was discussed globally. Newspapers in Europe, the English-speaking world and Asia all reported the widely held view that Stalingrad constituted a devastating blow to Nazi power.[3] In fact, of all the battles of the war, Stalingrad, more than any other, is described as the decisive defeat for Germany.[4] The surrender of the entire German 6th Army in February

1943, with the loss of its equipment, as well as corresponding losses in other German and German-allied armies fighting in support of the 6th Army, are seen as causing irreparable damage to Germany. It left no doubt that the USSR would survive and allowed the Americans and British to change the way that they planned for the end of the war.[5]

The Battle of Kursk on the Eastern Front, which started with the German offensive codenamed "Citadel," on July 5, 1943, is often described as the "greatest" battle of the war or the largest tank battle in human history.[6] With somewhere between 7,000 and 8,000 tanks involved in the fighting, and possibly more than 2 million men, Kursk is seen as the last time the Germans could mount a serious offensive. When their advance ended on July 16, the German army was placed in a state of permanent retreat that would culminate in the capture of Berlin less than two years later.

These superlatives make for dramatic reading, but the truth is, within the context of German production, the losses suffered during each battle were small and easily replaceable. For instance, the German army lost at most 350 armored fighting vehicles (AFV) during the first ten days of the Battle of Kursk, when the fighting was most intense.[7] During all of July and August 1943 on the Eastern Front the German army lost 1,331 AFV.[8] Yet, during 1943 as a whole, Germany produced just over 12,000 AFV. This means that the Germans lost less than 3 percent of the AFV they built in 1943 during the Battle of Kursk, and only 11 percent of annual AFV production during all of July and August. El Alamein was even less damaging. At the start of the battle on October 23, 1942, Rommel's famous Panzerarmee Afrika had 249 German tanks.[9] By November 4, 36 of these were left. The Germans thus lost just over 200 AFV in two weeks.[10] Within the context of German AFV production, El Alamein barely registered. Just looking at the war on land, therefore, it has to be said that it was the daily attritional loss of equipment that mattered more than any great battle. Individual battles might raise the daily loss rates by a few percentage points, but in and of themselves, they destroyed modest amounts of equipment.

Even more surprising, however, is the minuscule percentage of overall German munitions output that these "great" battle losses represent. One thing that has to be understood about the war is that land armaments were only a small part of munitions output for Germany and Japan – and the USA and UK as well. In 1943 AFV comprised only

7 percent of German weapons output. This means that the losses of AFV during the high point of the fighting at Kursk represented an inconsequential 0.2 percent of German armaments production for the year – and those of El Alamein just a little more than 0.1 percent. Even the losses at Stalingrad, which will be discussed later, were small enough that German production could make them up quickly.[11]

The idea that battle losses represented great blows to German power seems, at best, exaggerated. Far more important to German and Japanese defeat was the engagement of their air and sea weaponry. This is what really constituted national effort in World War II. Industrially and technologically, the war was primarily a competition of aircraft development and construction. In Germany the construction of airframes, air engines, and the weapons and machinery needed to power and arm aircraft made up at least 50 percent of German production every year of the war, and at certain times reached up to 55 percent. In the UK the percentage was even higher. Other elements of the air and sea war took up large percentages of construction, from warship building and merchant shipbuilding, to anti-aircraft artillery (the vast majority of which was used in an anti-aircraft role and not in a ground war role as it is sometimes believed) and all the technological developments that went into the war in the air and sea. In all cases, at least two-thirds of annual construction during the war went to air and sea weapons, and in some cases, such as that of Japan, the proportion was considerably higher. When it came to weapons development, the design, testing and production of air and sea weaponry was also of a much higher order, completely outstripping the cost of developing weapons for the army – which were relatively cheap.

If air and sea weaponry dominated all stages of production, seeing how it was destroyed also leads invariably to the conclusion that battles or the land war as a whole tell only a relatively small part of the story of World War II victory and defeat. Giving just two examples in 1943 demonstrates how both Germany and Japan were losing huge numbers of aircraft outside combat on non-operational duties such as deployment flights. When we look at the losses in 1943 for the Japanese navy (which possessed half of all Japanese air power), what we see is that non-combat losses were a much more crippling drain than those lost in action. (See figure 1.)

This helps put an event like the Battle of Midway into context. Of all the great encounters of World War II, Midway probably comes

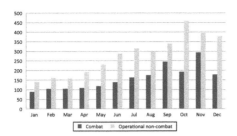

1 Japanese naval aircraft losses, 1943
Note: The exact figures were 3,355 operational non-combat aircraft losses and 1,907 combat losses.
Source: USSBS, Fukamizu Interview, Appendix B. Fukamizu had access to excellent statistics of Japanese naval aircraft losses, and reproduced some invaluable charts for the USSBS, including a monthly breakdown of losses for the entire war.

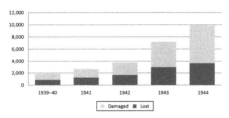

2 German aircraft: non-operational lost and damaged, 1939–44
Source: Spaatz MSS, 116, GAF Aircraft and Aircrew Losses, 1939–1945.

closest to a decisive battle – though even in this case the phrase is too dramatic. Why Midway mattered more than El Alamein or Kursk is that replacing the equipment losses after the battle was considerably more difficult. This had nothing to do with Japanese aircraft losses, which were not especially damaging at Midway since most of the experienced pilots survived.[12] Instead it was the loss of four aircraft carriers, which could not be replaced for a number of years.

German aircraft losses outside combat also became astonishingly large in 1943 and 1944. A digest of Luftwaffe losses on a weekly basis indicates that destruction of aircraft in non-operational duties almost doubled between 1942 and 1943. (See figure 2.) Such losses were much higher than those suffered by the Luftwaffe supporting the German army in any land battle, except perhaps those in western Europe from the summer of 1944 onwards.

The only way to make sense of losses like these is to understand how Anglo-American air and sea power were starting to put unbearable pressure on Germany and Japan's entire war-fighting system. Air and sea power were decisive because they multiplied exponentially the physical space and conceptual possibilities of the area of battle. This allowed the British and Americans to start destroying Axis equipment long before it ever reached what we have traditionally described as the battlefield. The area of this air and sea battle might be termed a "super-battlefield." It was not only thousands of miles in length, it was thousands of miles in breadth – covering an area that dwarfed the land war (see Maps 1 and 2). The Germans, to counter the threat of strategic bombing, were forced to station expensive equipment from Romania to Norway and from Poland to south-western France, while at the same time flooding Germany itself with aircraft and anti-aircraft weaponry. The Japanese, meanwhile, had to deploy forces from New Guinea to northern China, and from Burma to the Alaskan islands. On the other hand, these air and sea super-battlefields actually offered opportunities to both Germany and Japan. The German U-boat war against trade in the Atlantic forced the Allies to deploy forces from the North Sea to the Gulf of Mexico and caused such a fright in American and British minds that they devoted a large slice of their production in 1942 and 1943 to combating the threat. The Japanese, on the other hand, failed completely to realize the potential of engaging American production in this way and kept their naval and air forces geared towards a battlefield-centric understanding of warfare.

One of the great advantages of the super-battlefield that was created by air and sea power was that it allowed for a much more efficient destruction of German and Japanese equipment. There were three different phases during which this could be achieved, best termed "pre-production," "production" and "deployment." One of the key arguments of this book is that victory and defeat in the war must be analyzed from this perspective.

In the end it is the relationship between the air–sea super-battlefield and the better-known traditional land battlefield that is the primary distinguishing characteristic of "modern" warfare. What happened in the great land battles made almost no difference in the air–sea war. These battles, except in exceptional circumstances, were fought over territory of little or no economic value, the loss or gain of which made relatively little difference to equipment development or production. Moreover, the amount of equipment destroyed during the great land battles was actually rather small within the context of overall production and could be easily replaced. However, the struggle throughout the air–sea super-battlefield determined the outcome of every land battle in the war. In the first case it determined the vast majority of World War II munitions production. It then limited, in some cases most severely, the types of each weapon that could be built and, just as important, the amount of built equipment that was able to reach the fighting area. Finally, when it came to the land battles, the ability to control or deny control of the air space over the fighting almost always proved decisive.

The existing vision of victory and defeat in World War II

One of the main purposes of this book is to discuss how the British and Americans came to engage and destroy the greater part of German and Japanese production through the application of air and sea power, and thereby win World War II. It is also to show how air and sea power combined to keep the results of production away from the battlefield as well as determining the course of battles (through its action or absence). By de-emphasizing the importance of land battles, it will pull the focus of the war away from the Eastern Front (as well as the fighting in North Africa and Italy).[13] This is in no way an attempt to denigrate the enormous sacrifices that the USSR made in the fight against Nazi Germany. It is instead an attempt to move away from the traditional notion of the land battle as the greatest focus of national effort or commitment.[14]

So many books and articles have been written which address the question of victory and defeat in the war that it is impossible to discuss them all in detail. However, if there is one constant, it is that the war in Europe was won and lost on the Eastern Front. Paul Kennedy recently published a book on the key adaptations that led to Allied victory in World War II. He ranges widely over the global war, but it is obvious what he considers to be crucial. He describes the Eastern Front war between Germany and the USSR as "clearly *the* campaign of all the major struggles of the 1939–45 war."[15] In 2000, Michael Burleigh, in his thoughtful and engaging history of Nazi Germany, began his chapter on Barbarossa by saying: "The greatest military conflict of modern times erupted amid scenes of utmost normality."[16] This has become so much the orthodoxy that in 2010 Burleigh actually expressed frustration with what he sees as the extraordinary focus on the Eastern Front as the decisive theater of war. "So much emphasis has been put in recent years on the clash of the totalitarian titans (four out of every five German fatalities occurred on the Eastern Front), not least by British historians of Germany and Russia, that one might imagine that the British were not engaged in a shooting war at all."[17] The core reason for this extraordinary consensus is the underlying assumption that manpower in land armies is the determining measure of national effort. Geoffrey Roberts has claimed that 80 percent of the "combat" in the European war occurred on the Eastern Front.[18] Keith Lowe, while writing a book specifically about the bombing of Hamburg in 1943, feels it necessary to state that during 1943 the USSR was doing most of the "fighting."[19]

This vision of the war has dominated the overall narrative for decades.[20] In 1992, writing a historiographical summary piece, Joan Beaumont said it was a "universal view" among western historians that the Eastern Front was the fundamental reason Germany lost the war.[21] At approximately the same time, two large one-volume histories of World War II were released: Gerhard Weinberg's *A World at Arms: A Global History of World War II* and Peter Calvocoressi, Guy Wint and John Pritchard's *Total War: The Causes and Courses of the Second World War* (this last book was a revised edition of a survey first published in 1972). Both make it clear that the USSR was responsible for doing the heavy lifting in the defeat of Germany.[22]

The best overall general military history of World War II published recently is Williamson Murray and Allan Millett's *A War to be Won: Fighting the Second World War*, released in 2000. Though Murray and Millett see regular improvements in the fighting qualities of all the Allies in the war, it is particularly the USSR that develops the fighting power needed to destroy Nazi Germany. By 1943–4 the Soviets were superior to any other force in the world and capable of dealing the most crushing blows to the Germans.[23]

The view of the dominance of the Eastern Front is found in more popular books about victory in the war such as those written by Max Hastings.[24] Andrew Roberts is even more explicit in his belief that it was the USSR that shouldered the dominant load in victory over Germany.[25] When writing a book devoted to British and American grand strategy, he feels it necessary to mention the supremacy of the Eastern Front.[26] Roberts echoes one of the most important groups of American foreign policy scholars of the past fifty years, the

"Revisionists," on the origins of the Cold War. This group partly base their arguments on the understanding that the USSR contributed far more to the destruction of Germany than did the USA and UK. They argue that it was the supposed reluctance of the United States and United Kingdom to carry their full burden in the war against Germany that validates the Soviet need to dominate eastern Europe after the war.[27]

If the outcome of the land war on the Eastern Front is usually seen as decisive, historical views on the importance of the air war are mixed. There continues to rage an argument about the effectiveness of strategic bombing, that is, the use of air power against targets that were chosen specifically because of the damage to the enemy that would result in advance of any battle, such as factories, cities and transport systems. One large group has dismissed the entire Anglo-American strategic bombing effort as a minor contribution to ending the war, including very well-known air power theorists such as Robert Pape.[28] Others who have minimized the impact of the strategic bombing campaign include Gian Gentile, John Ellis and Stewart Halsey Ross.[29] Some economic historians also tend to downplay the importance of bombing in bringing about the end of the war.[30] Certainly, a number of general histories of the war assume that the strategic air campaign was mostly ineffective and at the same time morally reprehensible.[31]

If there is one relative constant in the strategic air power discussion it is that before the spring of 1944 the bombing efforts that were made by the British and Americans were a failure. The view given is based around the assumption that strategic bombing did little to damage German production while at the same time resulting in large losses. Paul Kennedy titled his section on the subject "The Allied Bombing Offensive and its Collapse, Late 1940 to Late 1943."[32] If anything this idea has been reinforced recently, such as in histories written by Gordon Corrigan and Antony Beevor.[33] Of the two, Beevor's book is a textbook example of a battle-centric history of victory and defeat in the war.[34] Even very recent books that are slightly more complimentary to the impact of strategic bombing are still careful to say that at best it played only a complementary role in ultimate victory, with the land war considerably more important.[35]

This stress on the failures of the campaign in 1943 is to be found in some of the best books about the air war in general. Max

Hastings, in his history of Bomber Command, discusses the RAF's impact on German production and morale in 1943 (and 1944 for that matter) in damning terms, believing that it did little to help win the war.[36] Tami Davis Biddle discusses 1943 mostly in terms of losses to American bombers.[37] Ronald Schaffer actually says little about strategic bombing in 1943, but portrays American efforts as too costly and remarks on how they shifted away from their earlier focus on daylight precision attacks towards a more British-like plan for attacks on large areas.[38] Michael Sherry also discussed the 1943 Combined Bomber offensive in terms of its failures and shortcomings.[39] Only a few surveys tend to say anything positive about strategic bombing in 1943; these include Weinberg, and Murray and Millett.[40] There is one book that takes a different line from almost any other, and that is Adam Tooze's *The Wages of Destruction*. In this book Tooze argues that the British area bombing of Germany in 1943, which is almost always seen as failure by those with a detailed knowledge of the air war, did real damage to German production.[41]

If 1943 is overwhelmingly seen as a failure, the view of the impact of strategic bombing in 1944 is considerably more divided. Here it is important to mention the work done immediately after the war by the United States Strategic Bombing Survey. This body, which included some of the great economic minds of the twentieth century such as John Kenneth Galbraith, was established by President Franklin D. Roosevelt to provide a detailed study of the role of strategic bombing in ending the war.[42] On the one hand, it collected a huge amount of data from German and Japanese primary sources, data which remains invaluable, if underutilized, to this day. So much data was collected that the large bulk of it never made it into the summary reports, but appears in the thousands of pages of subsidiary subject reports which are often ignored. This data, if not the analyses, has generally stood the test of time.[43] Even research done specifically to try and refute the data of the USSBS has found only relatively small areas of difference.[44]

The survey also conducted tens of thousands of pages of interviews with German and Japanese subjects from high policy makers to ships' captains. These interviews contain fascinating observations and obfuscations, but also invaluable insights into what equipment the Germans and Japanese built and how it was destroyed. In the end there was so much material collected and so many different reports written that the USSBS could be used to support almost any position on the efficacy of strategic bombing.[45] That needs to be said, because it is often assumed that the USSBS claimed clearly that strategic bombing was decisive in winning the war in Europe – when its conclusions were far more nuanced, or confused (depending on your opinion), than that.[46] Its real claim was that air power in its totality was what mattered. This included both tactical and strategic air power and ranged from defending convoys in the North Atlantic to supporting Allied armies in the field. It never claimed that strategic bombing won the war.[47] In fact, the USSBS was rather critical of strategic bombing as a whole in 1943 and dismissive about its impact in damaging German morale throughout the war. The USSBS's summary conclusions specifically on the strategic bombing of Germany would represent a minority view among those studying the subject today.[48]

The USSBS had a far more positive view of the impact of strategic bombing in 1944. For them the key development was the plan to target German oil production, in particular factories within Germany that were converting coal into high-octane aviation fuel. The United Kingdom also, somewhat begrudgingly, set up its own strategic bombing survey.[49] This effort was on a much smaller scale, and actually took a great deal of data from the American effort. Interestingly, as the RAF had led the way in attacking German cities in 1943 and 1944, the UK Bombing Survey was particularly critical of area attacks, seeing them as causing only minor damage to German production. On the other hand, the UKBS, under the intellectual control of Solly Zuckerman, came out strongly in favor of the transportation campaign being decisive in the second half of 1944.[50]

These two campaigns have continued to be the focus of those who believe that strategic air war played a major role in Allied victory in 1944.[51] A number of works claim that one or the other showed that the best way to use strategic air power was now being better understood, but that it just occurred too late in the war for its effects to be registered in isolation. One group, often from an American point of view, clusters around Carl Spaatz's campaign against oil. This goes back to the American official history of the USAAF in the war, but includes others.[52] Another group gives far more credit to the campaign against German transportation which started in the second half of 1944.[53] The great problem for the proponents of strategic air power at this time is that Germany was also collapsing on the battlefield, so that the effects of bombing are difficult to single out within the overall context of German failure.[54]

If there is one way to summarize the views on strategic air power, it would be to look at one of the truly great historians on the subject, Richard Overy. Overy has produced much important work on the war in general, not just bombing. In his book *Why the Allies Won*, he argues that Anglo-American strategic bombing did play a material role in defeating Germany. On the other hand, he is careful to show that the Russian contribution was more important.[55] "The Soviet Union bore the brunt of the German onslaught and broke the back of German power. For years the western version of the war played down this uncomfortable fact, while exaggerating the successes of Democratic war-making."[56] Before that, in his first book on the air war, Overy was far from enthusiastic about the impact of strategic air power.[57] However, in *War and Economy in the Third Reich*, published in 2002, he claims that in 1944 bombing reduced German military equipment output considerably.[58] Interestingly, in his more recent book *The Bombing War*, published in 2013, he has partly reverted to his earlier position. In this great achievement of scholarship, he argues that strategic bombing in 1943 accomplished relatively little in terms of both production losses and damage to German morale (its two greatest targets).[59]

Overy's evolution is a useful way to summarize the view on the impact of strategic air power on Germany. The more constant refrain is to stress the failures of the campaign, especially in relation to the importance of the Eastern Front. In particular, strategic bombing in 1943 is portrayed as a great failure. On the other hand, some argue that there also seem to have been some significant improvements by 1944 which did have a real impact on the way that Germany conducted the war. However, almost everyone views the land war as much more important in German defeat.

When it comes to the use of strategic air power against Japan, the debate is less developed than that for the war against Germany. A number of books on the war in the Pacific focus on the destruction wrought by the B-29s under the command of Curtis LeMay, without making an assessment of how important it was in American victory or simply implying that because of the destruction it must have played a significant role in compelling Japanese surrender.[60] On the other hand, Ronald Schaffer, who was interested in the ethical question, and is critical of the impulses which drove the American campaign, argues strongly that American bombing "contributed immensely" to compelling Japan to surrender.[61]

The USSBS was noticeably less coherent about the bombing of Japan. It ended up becoming mired in an inter-service rivalry between the American navy and air force.[62] Some of their findings argue that strategic air power was crucial to Japanese defeat, and others implied that it was more of a contributory factor. The summary report even made a case about strategic bombing damaging Japanese morale, after having dismissed such notions about Germany.[63] Also, some of the arguments about transportation are based around what would have happened more than what did. The problem that the bombing survey had, as it acknowledged, was separating out the impact of strategic bombing from the hammer blows the Japanese economy had received before bombing had begun – in particular the destruction of Japanese trade which had already peaked before LeMay devastated Tokyo.[64]

The somewhat contradictory nature of their conclusions left one of their military advisers, Major General Orville Anderson of the USAAF, to file a separate summary in which air power was given a more concrete role in achieving victory.[65] The American official histories are likewise lacking in clarity. They do discuss the enormous damage inflicted by the B-29s on Japanese cities after March 1945, but they also admit that tying this destruction directly in to a collapse of Japanese production is difficult.[66] Other works, like that of Sherry, tend to minimize the economic impact of the attacks.[67] Still others seem relatively uninterested in the economic effects of LeMay's bombing, preferring to use the destruction involved as part of a larger discussion on the morality and aims of strategic bombing.[68] Richard Frank, in his excellent history of the end of the war in the Pacific, implies that strategic air power was poised to decide the war against Japan, as technology and force structure were about to change to allow the USAAF to move away from LeMay's general destruction of Japanese cities back to the specific destruction of individual targets.[69] In many ways the best shorter summary of the campaign has come in Murray and Millett's A War to be Won. They catalogue the destruction meted out to Japanese cities and industries, the effect of which was massive. On the other hand, they stop short of saying that this is what made the Japanese surrender.[70]

There is one other disagreement on the war in the Pacific, and that is on the different drives towards Japan. While American air and sea power are widely recognized as of decisive importance in Japanese defeat, there is disagreement on the way that power was used. During the course of the war the United States developed three different campaigns aimed at Japan (though this is usually unfairly reduced to two). The best-known two were the Southwest Pacific drive headed by Douglas MacArthur and directed towards the liberation of the Philippines, and the Central Pacific drive under the command of Chester Nimitz, which was eventually aimed at the Mariana Islands. The third, which can be overlooked, is the USAAF's campaign from China, which envisaged driving Japan out of the war primarily with strategic bombing from the Asian mainland. There has been a lively discussion over the effects of the Southwest and Central Pacific drives, which revolves about the question of whether both were necessary to defeat Japan.[71]

In summation, certain views have prevailed in the portrayal of victory and defeat in World War II. In most narrative histories of the war in general, the land campaigns are seen as decisive in the victory over Germany – in particular the fighting on the Eastern Front. In such histories the strategic air campaign, as well as the war at sea, are seen as at best active subsidiaries, and in many cases, of little consequence in German defeat. When it comes to those with a strong interest in the air war, there is a general consensus that the strategic air campaign of 1943 was a failure. The picture for 1944 is more diverse, with some arguing that strategic air power, in particular the campaigns against German oil production and transportation, were important in German defeat while others continue to argue strongly that strategic air power was still subsidiary. When it comes to the war against Japan, there is a general assumption that strategic bombing played a crucial part in bringing about the end of the war, though the analysis can be based on levels of destruction alone.

Air and sea power and the control of mobility

Although battles will not be ignored, this is not a book about tactics or brilliant generalship or bravery in the face of the enemy. It will instead address many of its central questions from the point of view of equipment production and destruction. In particular it will describe how air and sea weapons were prioritized, allocated and used. The first two chapters will outline the overriding economic and strategic importance of air and sea power in World War II. Chapter 1 will show how air and sea weaponry dominated war production in Germany, Japan, the USA and the UK. The similarity in economic profile between the four nations is compelling, and shows how little effort each expended on the land war. It will also show, contrary to a widely held view in the European historiography, that Japan was a much greater economic power than is normally understood. From 1942 to 1944 the Japanese produced at a level almost identical to that of the USSR, only with superior technology and without any meaningful support from its closest allies. Chapter 2 will then outline why the prioritization of air–sea power made sense through describing the process by which it destroyed Axis equipment. The three stages of equipment destruction before it reached the battlefield will be outlined in more detail.

Chapter 3 examines the interwar period and the war itself until the fall of 1940 – the end of the first stage of the Battle of Britain and the re-election of Franklin Roosevelt. This earlier period was actually one in which only a hazy notion existed of the way in which air and sea power would be effectively employed in the war. Chapter 4 will introduce the key British and American grand strategists who made the crucial choices about how the air and sea war developed. These include the war leaders, Winston Churchill and Franklin Roosevelt, and also their service chiefs of staff. Chapter 5 returns to the description of the war, covering the period from November 1940 until the United States entered the war in December 1941. This vital period saw some important choices which materially affected how the air and sea war would be fought in 1942 and 1943, but on the other hand, showed how far things still had to progress. Chapter 6 will examine the crucial grand strategic choices made in the war in 1942 and 1943. These concerned how much Anglo-American equipment should be deployed against Germany and how much against Japan, and then how that equipment should be used in theater. Churchill, Roosevelt and their military chiefs all had different ideas on how the war should be fought, and the air and sea war as developed was necessarily a compromise between them.

The final five chapters will analyze how air and sea power crushed German and Japanese resistance from the end of 1942 onwards. Chapter 7 focuses on the war at sea, in particular the Battle of the Atlantic in 1942 and 1943. One of the important points here is the need to look at the war at sea, not as a battle of submarine against convoy, but as a battle by the British and Americans to get their merchant ships into convoy. Chapters 8 and 9 will cover the war in Europe in 1943 and 1944, contrasting the war in the air to the war on the land. It will describe the different campaigns waged by the British and Americans against German power and describe the process that led to German collapse. The Germans were forced first to switch the Luftwaffe away from the battlefield, and when this could not stop air attacks, saw their production go into irretrievable decline. Chapter 10 will discuss a similar process in the war against Japan to the end of 1944. The three different American campaigns to defeat Japan will be analyzed, and the decisive importance of the capture of the Mariana Islands underscored. Chapter 11 will start with the war against Japan in 1945, showing how the cut-off of raw materials and the earlier bombing of specific Japanese industries was already leading to a collapse in Japanese production before the United States turned to the incendiary bombing of Japanese cities. It will then cover how Germany and Japan tried to fight when they had completely lost the air and sea war. Finally the chapter will end with a discussion of the ethicality of strategic bombing in general and of the dropping of the atomic bomb in particular – the most extreme example of the dominance of air power.

Many familiar parts of the war narrative will be covered only briefly. While the Eastern Front is discussed in parts of different chapters, it will seem woefully under-represented to those who believe that German power was really broken by the Soviet Union. The role of Italy has also been deliberately minimized. This will be contentious in some circles.[72] From 1943 onwards, Italian production was only important as part of an overall German economic empire. It was not being used in any specifically Italian fashion. Also, even with the collapse of the Mussolini regime, the Germans remained in control of northern Italy, and all the raw materials and industrial plant therein. The United States and Britain, in control of the south, deprived Germany of little that was necessary for the Reich to wage its air and sea death struggle.

Within the Anglo-American world, the role of different parts of the British Empire may also seem under-represented. While the Canadian role in the Battle of the Atlantic is mentioned, on the whole the British Empire's contribution to the air and sea war is folded into that of the United Kingdom. This is partly out of the need for simplicity, but it is also grounded in reality. Except for the construction of smaller naval vessels and vehicles in Canada, the production of the vital equipment used in the defeat of Germany was undertaken in the United Kingdom (or for the United Kingdom in the United States). Also, it was the British decision-making structure that controlled the allocation and usage of this equipment, and as such they dominated the British Empire's war effort.

Finally, what might be most unusual is that this book on World War II will spend little time discussing combat or human bravery and cowardice – the meat and drink of most war histories. That is a deliberate decision. While the experience of combat is one of the crucial human experiences to be found in war, when it comes to World War II it was not important in understanding victory and defeat. There were great acts of courage and cowardice, sacrifice and atrocity on all sides. In the end, the war was won because the Allies had far more powerful and effectively equipped armed forces than did the Axis, and this equipment, particularly air and sea weapons of war, kept the Germans and the Japanese from moving.

Bravery did not win or lose World War II. Air and sea power did.

1 THE DOMINANCE OF AIR AND SEA PRODUCTION

The German state-sponsored histories of World War II, published in English translation as *Germany and the Second World War*, are remarkable achievements of scholarship. Fair-minded and detailed, they present a thorough picture of Germany at war. In one of the sections on war production the authors seemed surprised that Germany's economic effort was geared much more towards aircraft production than land armaments. They then pose a question:

> If it is true that the Second World War was ultimately decided on
> the battlefields of eastern Europe, by the clash of German and
> Soviet tank armies, then the question arises why the share of
> firepower and mobility of land forces was so conspicuously small
> in Germany.[1]

It is a central question, but it is also misdirected in its assumptions. Instead of Germany spending a "conspicuously" small amount of effort on the land war, the Nazi state's efforts in this area were absolutely typical of all the major powers, with the exception of the Soviet Union. The economies of four of the five great industrial and technological powers that fought World War II were geared by large majorities towards the production of air and sea weapons. Germany, Japan, the United Kingdom (with the British Empire) and the United States all devoted between 65 percent and 80 percent of their economic output to the making and arming of aircraft, naval vessels and anti-aircraft equipment. In all cases aircraft were the single largest element of production, ranging from 30–35 percent of US munitions output to more than 50 percent in the case of the United Kingdom. When one adds the costs of developing and arming aircraft to the costs of constructing airframes and engines, these percentages jump to slightly below 50 percent for the United States and to more than half for Germany and the United Kingdom. In all, construction of air weapons also received first priority in the allocation of industrial workers and in being supplied with crucial raw materials such as aluminum. In many ways it is the allocation of aluminum that really shows the high priority given to the air war. It is common to refer to a nation's steel production as somehow indicative of its ability to wage a modern industrial war. On its own, this is highly deceptive. Aircraft, with few exceptions, could not be built of steel; they required aluminum. Aluminum, with its non-corrosive, lightweight and high strength characteristics, was the only material, other than wood, that could be used to construct modern airframes, and during the war all the major powers channeled the vast majority of the metal to this purpose. By 1944 well over 70 percent of German, Japanese, British and American aluminum production went into aircraft construction. As such, aluminum production is at least as important as steel production in demonstrating a nation's ability to produce the weapons needed to fight a modern war.

Throughout the course of the war, all of these countries, even Germany, devoted a larger percentage of their munitions output to naval vessels than to armored fighting vehicles (AFV) such as tanks and self-propelled artillery.[2] For the United States, United Kingdom and Japan this was a constant for every month of every year of the war. For Germany this was the case for the entire war up until the end of 1943, when the percentage of German munitions made up of AFV surpassed naval construction for the first time. The one clear exception to this rule was the USSR, which built very few naval vessels in the war, and whose production of aircraft, while prodigious, was relatively ineffective when compared with the air forces of the other powers. To show just how dominant air and sea construction was for the different powers, we should survey them briefly.

Germany

More than any of Hitler's closest political allies, Albert Speer, his Minister of Armaments from 1942 to 1945, remains a perplexing figure. There have been debates about both his economic and ethical choices.[3] Though Speer could clearly be charming – he won over one of his prosecutors during the Nuremberg trials – his attempts to distance himself from the regime of Adolf Hitler, which he served so enthusiastically, smell more of self-preservation than revelation.[4] Once released from Spandau Prison after serving twenty years for crimes against humanity, he set out to build a firewall between his actions and the truly evil deeds of the Nazi regime.[5] One of his favorite tricks was to stress the difference between his industrial activities and those of Heinrich Himmler's SS. In the book *Infiltration*, Speer argues that the SS was so jealous of his power in the economic sphere that they set about creating their own industrial empire (which of course committed the most diabolical crimes).[6] During his research for *Infiltration* in German archives, he decided to calculate how much of Germany's industrial effort in June–July 1944, when war output peaked, was devoted to aircraft construction. In doing this, he was definitely not trying to enhance his reputation as a managerial genius, because his ministry had only taken over Luftwaffe production in March 1944. The first time he even attended the German fighter production board was on May 26 of that year, and until then he was probably in charge of a minority of German armaments output.[7] While doing his research, Speer calculated that during the summer of 1944 aircraft construction alone made up 53.7 percent of all German war production.[8]

To many this might seem like an extraordinarily high figure, but there certainly is supporting evidence that it was broadly correct. When the Reichsmarschall and head of the Luftwaffe Hermann Goering was interrogated at the end of the war he said this:

Q. It has been said that as much as 55 percent of German war production went towards production for the Luftwaffe. Is this correct?
A. That is probably figured a little too high but undoubtedly the air force had swallowed up a large part of it ...
Q. Do you think that even more than 55 percent should have been put into that part of your total war effort – as distinguished, for example, from your land effort?
A. I would not say that. But I do believe very definitely that in the years 1940 to 1943, we should have invested even more in the air force.[9]

The dominance of the Luftwaffe in German production is not always recognized by western historians and this has caused problems.

One article written just after the war ended, and which was based on incomplete wartime assumptions, was by Raymond Goldsmith.[10] Goldsmith assumed, entirely incorrectly, that 60 percent of German production went towards the land war, when in fact it was little more than half this. His drastic overestimation of the value of land armament production has subsequently been used to overestimate the value of Soviet wartime production vis-à-vis Germany.[11]

The history of the German war economy has developed greatly since the war. Some of the most important areas of discussion involve the level of efficiency, or not, that the Nazi state brought to military production. After the war it was fashionable to discuss the slow pace of German production before 1942, which was blamed on the Nazi state's reluctance to confront the German people with a decline in living standards. This played a role in the argument put forward for a while that Germany went into the war with a "Blitzkrieg" economy, which provided for armaments in breadth but not depth. In the past few decades this notion has been challenged robustly.[12] The view that now appears is that the German state was committed to high levels of war production from early on in the conflict, but inefficiencies in the system meant that it took a while before steep production rises could occur.[13] When the rises did start, one of the interesting points was the specific role that Speer, or Speer-inspired reforms, played in the acceleration.[14] Until very late in the war, Hitler possessed great confidence in Speer and this was the reason why, structurally, the armaments minister held great power within the regime.[15] In *Germany and the Second World War*, Speer's efforts are given some praise for rationalizing production and using plant more efficiently.[16] However, this kind of praise is now more the exception than the rule, as others, such as Overy and Tooze, are more likely to play down Speer's role and put the stress on reforms that were started before he took office.[17] Whatever the reason, it is important to see how much progress was made in the last few years of the war. To some, this wartime growth in German production plant and know-how was the reason West Germany was able to rise phoenix-like from the ashes of World War II defeat.[18]

From late 1941, according to Speer, Luftwaffe production was given highest priority, even while army production was slated to be cut.[19] This picture is supported by others. Karl Saur, another controversial figure, was at the center of Germany's industrial war effort from

March 1940 when he became Technical Director to Fritz Todt, Hitler's Minister for Weapons and Munitions before Speer. After Todt's death, Saur continued working for Speer, somewhat uneasily, and was eventually put in charge of aircraft production in 1944. Saur claimed that, from his perspective, Germany never had clear armaments priorities and that effort could be redirected quickly and dramatically. When he came to office in 1942, just as the war on the Eastern Front was in a crucial phase, three of the four highest priority weapons were part of the air–sea war. "Dr. Saur emphatically denied that there were any 'absolute 1, 2 and 3' priorities in German war production until March 1944. He claimed that, in early 1942, aircraft, Tiger tanks, flak guns . . . and U-boats stood in equal degree of priorities"[20]

From that point on the air war continued to dominate. "On 7 March 1942, locomotives were given an equal rating. V-Weapons were added in the summer of 1943. With the exception of locomotives, the priorities remained the same until . . . 1 March 1944. Thereafter, fighter aircraft held a definite first priority." The high priority for aircraft construction caused real resentment in the army, though the Luftwaffe considered it natural. According to General Eckhard Christian, who served at Hitler's side for much of the war as the dictator's Luftwaffe liaison, "At an early date it had been decided that air-power was the decisive factor in the war. The Luftwaffe's influence was so great, on the one hand, in the land and sea fighting, that people were compelled to face facts."[21]

The largest element in Luftwaffe construction dominance was the building of airframes and aircraft engines. The USSBS put the relative percentage of war construction that was devoted to building just aircraft at between 40 and 45 percent depending on the month and year. Other sources support this. In the summer of 1944, Speer's ministry, under the leadership of Hans Kehrl, produced an analysis of German war production in 1943 and 1944, and estimated that the true percentage of effort Germany spent building aircraft during these peak years of its armament production was "between 40 percent and 50 percent."[22] The German histories of World War II mentioned earlier also chart the percentage of German effort spent just on aircraft construction as averaging approximately 40 percent, with highs of 46.1 percent in the beginning of 1942 and 45.9 percent in the middle of 1944 contrasting with lows of 36.3 percent at the end of 1942 and 35.7 percent at the end of 1943.[23]

At the same time it is remarkable how little of Germany's effort went into land armaments. The USSBS, relying on German internal documents, describes the amount of German production devoted to AFV as follows:

> Production of panzer vehicles represented only a small part of the German armament industry. At the beginning of the war and until the end of 1942 the value of panzer output was less than 4 percent of total armaments. Even though in the last two years of the war it increased enormously – more rapidly than the production of total output – the value of panzer production in 1944 was only slightly more than 8 percent.[24]

The value of this relative increase is supported by the internal study of the German economy in early 1944 which claimed that, even with the large increases in panzer production, spending on aircraft was still at least five times as large as the spending on all types of vehicles for all of the branches of the German armed forces.[25] And it should be noted that this percentage was calculated during a special period, the last few months of 1943, when aircraft production in Germany was at one of the lowest percentages that it reached during the war.[26]

However, aircraft in and of themselves were only part of the expense on the air and sea war. The Luftwaffe's aircraft had to be armed with weaponry and supplied with ammunition. Ammunition production, following aircraft construction, was actually the second largest category of German munitions output. In 1943, when the amount spent on aircraft construction was approximately RM 10 billion, the amount spent on ammunition was RM 6 billion.[27] The amount spent on all weapons (from small arms to artillery pieces) was RM 2.5 billion, while that for all vehicles was only RM 2 billion. Thus all weapons and ammunition spending combined was only about 85 percent of aircraft construction spending. A similar percentage was discovered by the USSBS. They calculated that, in May 1943, 40 percent of German effort was spent on aircraft, 26.5 percent was spent on ammunition and 7.9 percent was spent on weapons, while in July 1944, when production peaked, 48.3 percent of German production went to aircraft, 24 percent to ammunition and 9.3 percent to weapons.[28] It does seem that, from 1942 to the end of the war, between 33 and 35 percent of German production was devoted to ammunition and weapons. While the army usually received a small majority of

Table 1 *Germany: weapons production distribution by armed service and quarter,*
1942–4

	1942				1943				1944			
	1	2	3	4	1	2	3	4	1	2	3	4
Army	48	52	51	50	49	53	53	55	58	56	56	58
Luftwaffe	6	7	5	8	8	7	8	9	7	10	10	10
Navy	22	17	16	15	14	11	10	10	10	9	7	7
Anti-aircraft	24	24	28	27	29	29	29	26	25	25	27	25
CAS[a]	52	48	49	50	51	47	47	45	42	44	44	42

Note: [a] Combined air–sea, made up of the Luftwaffe, navy and anti-air allocations.
Source: USSBS, European Report 3, p. 284.

Table 2 *Germany: ammunition production distribution by service and quarter,*
1942–4

	1942				1943				1944			
	1	2	3	4	1	2	3	4	1	2	3	4
Army	27	44	54	59	67	67	64	63	66	68	68	69
Luftwaffe	30	25	23	21	15	15	12	15	14	12	10	7
Navy	12	10	6	5	4	4	4	3	3	4	4	4
Anti-aircraft	31	21	17	15	14	14	20	19	17	16	18	20
CAS[a]	73	56	46	41	33	33	36	37	34	32	32	31

Note: [a] Combined air–sea, made up of the Luftwaffe, navy and anti–air allocations.
Source: USSBS, European Report 3, p. 284.

Germany's weapons output and a slightly larger one of ammunition, it sometimes received a smaller portion and its overall majority was only modest. Tables 1 and 2 show the quarterly allocations. The upshot of this situation was that the Luftwaffe was receiving on average about 5 percent of Germany's overall munitions output annually through its allocation of weapons and ammunition (this is not even considering the extremely large allocations to its anti-aircraft forces). If you combine this with the amount of effort spent building aircraft, it supports the claims of Speer, Goering and others that between 50 and 55 percent of Germany's war production was devoted to the aircraft end of the Luftwaffe.

Now Germany's expensive effort in anti-aircraft munitions must be discussed. The building of anti-aircraft weapons and ammunition was a point that Hitler personally stressed throughout the war.[29]

Field Marshal Keitel, the deservedly much-maligned head of OKW, and one of Hitler's most devoted and best-paid servants, described in great detail Hitler's belief that flak had to be one of Germany's highest production priorities. According to Keitel, in the winter of 1941–2, it was Hitler's "farsightedness" that caused the German dictator to place flak so high up the production priority list.[30] By 1944 Hitler was going to great lengths to support this effort. According to Dr. R. A. Fleisher, the director of Henschel, which produced aircraft and a range of equipment for the German army, the great flak construction program of that year involved 300,000 workers working 24 hours a day on three shift patterns.[31] To show just how important Hitler believed this program to be, as late as November 1944 he forbade the Wehrmacht from conscripting any workers from the anti-aircraft industry.[32]

Tables 1 and 2 make clear that Germany devoted almost 10 percent of its entire productive effort to the construction of anti-aircraft weapons and ammunition from 1942 to 1944. And the overwhelming majority of this construction was spent on anti-aircraft weaponry based in Germany defending the Reich from the Anglo-American strategic bombing offensive. On 1 November 1943 Germany deployed 13,500 heavy and 37,500 light anti-aircraft guns on all fronts. Of these, only 1,850 heavy (or 13.7 percent) and 6,200 light guns (or 16.5 percent) were deployed on the Eastern Front including the USSR, Poland and the Baltic States, with those remaining all deployed against Anglo-American forces.[33] By January 1945 the number of German anti-aircraft artillery deployed in the east had dropped in percentage points to only 10.3 percent of heavy guns and 13.3 percent of light guns. The overwhelming majority of the remaining guns were deployed against the British and American air forces.

Combining its anti-aircraft effort with its enormous aircraft construction effort would have consumed at least 60 percent of Germany's munitions output (and sometimes more) – but there is one final element that needs to be considered: the effort Germany put into building naval vessels. The amount of effort devoted to naval construction, whilst always smaller than that for the Luftwaffe or army, was still considerable. At certain times in the war, Hitler personally placed a very high priority on naval construction. Field Marshal Erhard Milch, who controlled Luftwaffe production from 1940 until it was folded into Speer's ministry in March 1944, was one of the most important figures in the German war effort, though he figures far less prominently in most narratives of the war than generals such as Guderian or Manstein.[34] He claimed that, at the outbreak of the war, Hitler actually wanted to make new naval construction Germany's highest munitions priority and that it was "ne plus ultra" in Hitler's mind.[35] At the end of the war Hitler's opinion seemed not to have changed much. In his last clear priority instruction, given to the Armaments Ministry in January 1945, U-boats were given the highest priority rating, equal to fighter planes, flak and anti-tank weaponry. Panzers, on the other hand, were nowhere to be found.[36]

The actual percentage of munitions output that went to the navy was modest, though until the summer of 1943 it remained at around or just over 10 percent of German output. In 1941 and 1942 it was well over 10 percent, as the U-boat war remained an important element in Hitler's global strategy.[37] At the same time that the German army was invading the USSR, Hitler was calling for more resources to be poured into U-boat construction.[38] As late as the first quarter of 1943, 11 percent of German war output was made up of submarine production. The figure then declined steadily in the second half of 1943, after Germany had lost the Battle of the Atlantic. The catastrophically high number of U-boats being sunk in the Atlantic in May 1943 made it clear to Grand Admiral Doenitz that the Germans could no longer rely on the bulk of their submarines, the Type VIIs and XIs. German U-boats were withdrawn from much of the Atlantic in June, and in July Hitler gave high priority to the construction of completely new classes of submarines, most famously the type XXI.[39] These new vessels represented a great leap forward in submarine design and were far superior to Allied vessels. They were built with streamlined hulls that allowed them to reach 18 knots under water and they had snorkels so that they could recharge their batteries and take in oxygen while submerged. However, until these new boats could be properly designed and built, German naval construction as a percentage of output declined. By the second quarter of 1944 naval construction was down to 6.1 percent of German output and in the third quarter reached its lowest point of the war, 4.5 percent. At this point the relative effort Germany spent building submarines leapt sharply, as the newly designed U-boats went into full production. In the last quarter of 1944, 8.1 percent of German armaments construction was made up of U-boats and in the first quarter of 1945 it was 7.5 percent.

While U-boat construction dominated within naval production in Germany, there were other elements to consider. Even with the focus on building U-boats, the Germans spent a great deal of effort maintaining their on-water vessels in shipyards.[40] Also, as Tables 1 and 2 show, the navy received on average about 10 percent of German weapons production and 4 percent of its ammunition production – which, combined, would have amounted to about 2 percent of Germany's overall munitions production. Looked at as a whole, German construction effort for the navy, except for a period of approximately a year from the second half of 1943 to the summer of 1944, would have been at least 10 percent and perhaps as high as 15 percent of overall munitions output.

It should also be kept in mind that the dominance of air–sea construction in the German war economy was not limited to cost or raw-material allocation. The percentages for these were reflected in other metrics such as cash flow and numbers of industrial workers. In February 1942 there were 1.7 million workers in the aircraft industry and by March 1944 this figure had jumped to 2 million.[41] Eventually, according to Speer, this figure reached 2.33 million workers, more than all the workers employed building all the weapons and ammunition for the army.[42] This is a remarkably high figure, and it may surprise some that it was equal to, if not slightly larger than, the number of American workers building aircraft. The dramatic difference in per capita aircraft output in the United States and Germany was mostly influenced by the air war at this time and helps illustrate just how air power really decided the war.[43]

The other armed services had smaller workforces. In August 1944, Speer claimed in a speech that all finished army production involved 1.9 million workers and that for the navy was being done by 500,000.[44] Also, workers building aircraft and aircraft engines were overwhelmingly skilled workers, some of the very best in the German workforce.[45] The Luftwaffe was also superior in financial services. During the war the Wehrmacht and Luftwaffe created private companies, in essence banks, to control the outflow of their expenditures. By 1945 the army's bank had disbursed RM 3 billion to firms while the Luftwaffe's had disbursed 4 billion.[46]

Coming to one overall percentage for how much Germany devoted to air and sea weapons over land is not possible, owing to the month by month and year by year shifts. It is possible, however, to

Table 3 *Germany: munitions production, divided by type, July 1944*

	Percent
Aircraft	48.3
Ammunition	24.0
Weapons	9.3
AFV (panzers)	7.8
Naval vessels	4.5
Motor vehicles	2.4
Half-tracks	1.6
Powder	2.1

Source: USSBS, European Report 3, p. 145.

give a detailed picture of one month, July 1944, when German munitions output peaked for the entire war. A range of figures exist for this month which allows for some interesting comparisons. First we have the overall categories (see Table 3). Using the third quarter breakdowns for ammunition and weapons production given earlier, these different categories were divided as follows. Of ammunition production, 68 percent, or 16.3 percent of overall production, would have gone to the army and 32 percent of the ammunition production, or 7.7 percent overall, would have gone to the Luftwaffe, navy or anti-air services. Of weapons production, 56 percent, or 5.2 percent of overall production, would have gone to the army and 44 percent, or 4.1 percent of overall production, would have gone to the Luftwaffe, navy or anti-air services. While these calculations leave the approximately one-third of anti-aircraft production that was not engaged against the Anglo-American bombing effort in the air–sea column, they also give the Luftwaffe and navy no credit for the motor vehicles they would have received at this time. Using these breakdowns, and splitting the use of powder between the services in the same way as ammunition, Germany was devoting 66 percent of its armament production to an air–sea war when its munitions output reached its maximum level. As this period represented an historic low in U-boat construction, it is safe to say that during the last three to four years of the war, weapons and ammunition for the air and sea war made up at least two-thirds of German munitions output.

This two-to-one advantage in air–sea production cost actually significantly *understates* the amount of effort put into the air–sea war. First, the development costs for aircraft and naval vessels were exponentially higher than those for land vehicles. Two of the best-known and moderately successful German AFV designs made during the war, the Panzer V (Panther) and Panzer VI (Tiger), moved relatively quickly from the design to the production stage. The Panther, which was arguably the most successful German AFV of the war, though it did have a number of teething problems, was first conceived of in March 1942.[47] By November prototypes were already in production and the first combat-ready models were ready for the Battle of Kursk in the summer of 1943. The time from conception to production was fourteen to fifteen months. The design process for the Tiger tank was even quicker. A direct result of the shock the Germans felt when they first encountered the Soviet T-34 after the commencement of Barbarossa in June 1941, the Tiger was designed, tested and in production in approximately one year, between late 1941 and late 1942.[48]

Aircraft, on the other hand, took many years to design, involved many more workers and cost many times more. Dr. Kurt Tank, the president of the Focke-Wulf aircraft company, estimated that it took Germany three and a half to four years to bring an aircraft from design to production, or three times as long as that for the Panther or Tiger.[49] Two of the most expensive German aircraft design programs of the war, those for the HE-177 four-engine bomber and the ME-210 two-engine fighter, are among the least known because, even after the enormous expense involved, neither program produced a plane that was capable of fulfilling its mission. The ME-210, which was supposed to be Germany's successor to the ME-110, was cancelled after great expense before ever going into full production.[50] Even then, its cost to that point was the equivalent of five thousand aircraft, or as much as Germany's annual expenditure on AFV during any year of the war. The HE-177 is a slightly better-known failure. (See Figure 3.) First planned in 1937, it could have been the German equivalent of the famous four-engine B-17 and B-24 American bombers or the British Lancaster.[51] However, it experienced a number of design problems, the greatest being the fact that, because its four engines were actually built into the wing in two linked front-to-back casings instead of being spaced separately, the plane tended to explode.[52] In January 1944 Hitler referred to the plane as "garbage."[53] The overall cost of the HE-177 program, while undoubtedly vast, is difficult to ascertain. However, details of construction man hours are available. It took approximately 18,000 man hours to build one HE-177 when the bomber went into

3 Aircraft development was extremely expensive, even for flawed aircraft. One of Germany's most expensive weapons development projects of the war was for the HE-177 four-engine bomber, seen here. The enormous propellers were supported by two linked engines each, which often caused the plane to explode.

operational construction after some of the problems had been resolved.[54] The only vehicle comparable was actually the V-2 rocket, which took 20,000 man hours once it had been brought into full production. As a counter-example, one of Germany's two great piston-engine fighters of the war, the FW-190, took 3,700 man hours each for construction.[55] Milch described the disastrous state of the HE-177 that he found when he took over Luftwaffe construction.

> As far as I remember it must have been after 1940. Then nothing more was done about it. 1941: the aircraft were standing about, were not flown, and nothing was done to them. The Heinkel firm had a bad conscience, they knew there was something wrong with the aircraft, but they didn't know the cause of the crashes and accidents and when I took the affair over at the end of 1941 ...
> I immediately fetched the aircraft out again in January 1942 and sent it to Rechlin to be flown there. We immediately had accidents: engines catching fire, then the wings simply burned away behind the engines, the wings broke off and the people crashed. Usually they couldn't get out of the aircraft. Then the engines were taken in hand: I immediately stated that a new design would be made of the same aircraft, but with four single engines. The Fuhrer sent for me and asked why we had those two engines at all. "I gave the orders long ago that the aircraft were to have four engines." He said that he was of the opinion that what Goering always called the "welded-together engines" were no use. I said: "I am of the same opinion." According to my technical knowledge – I was once technical director of Deutsche Lufthansa, and I had a very great deal to do with technicalities there – I still knew too little about the

vibrations which might arise in it, and of course the fires were
another question ... The Daimler-Benz engines were not clean:
they always dripped a lot of oil and had a whole lot of other leaks
as well. If ever an injection valve broke, the stream of fuel would
pour straight down there, and that caused the fires ... The flying
was continued; suddenly the wing of another aircraft broke, but
without there having been any fire. Nobody knew what was the
cause of that. There were continual investigations and then
I demanded that several wings were subjected to breaking tests.
Those showed that the wing was wrongly calculated. It was too
weak. Then the spaces were reinforced with spars ... and so that
question was settled. Then suddenly crashes occurred again – I lost
100 men killed in the experiments at that time – and it turned out
that at a certain speed the wing profile was wrong. In the ordinary
way one would have said: "Scrap the whole aircraft. Build
another!" But this was war and we had to tackle the problem ...[56]

Even successful aircraft designs were remarkably expensive.
Perhaps the most technologically impressive German aircraft achievement of World War II was the design and production of the ME-262 jet
fighter. The world's first combat-effective jet, the ME-262 was conceived in 1939 but didn't enter service until 1944. Its design process
ended up being contentious and expensive. Not only was the technology employed completely new in a combat plane, the German leadership, including but not limited to Hitler, could not make up its mind as
to the plane's purpose.[57] At one point, enraged by the growing Anglo-
American strategic bombing raids on Germany, Hitler ordered that it
be designed as a dive-bomber, so that it could strike back at the United
Kingdom.[58] He even wanted it nicknamed as the "Blitz" bomber to
make its purpose clear.[59]

Many in the Luftwaffe, however, were determined to see the
ME-262 designed as a fighter. In the end, such disagreements and the
technological complexity of producing the world's first combat-ready
jet aircraft delayed full-scale construction. It wasn't until the spring of
1944 that it reached twenty to thirty a month.[60] From that point on,
though, enormous efforts were put into ME-262 construction as the
plane was seen as one of the few weapons that could challenge the
Anglo-American strategic bombing campaign. Plans were drawn up
to increase construction to a grand total of 1,334 by the end of 1944.
The effort put into this program was enormous. Frederick Seiler, the

chairman of the board of the Messerschmitt Corporation at the end of the war, claimed that, by 1944, the plans for construction were so large that up to 4 million workers were needed to reach full production.[61] Needless to say, the Germans were never able to get close to this number, but Seiler believed that at its high point construction of the ME-262 involved up to 1.3 million workers, which alone would have been close to the number working on all army munitions – and if true meant that the Germans probably had more people employed building aircraft in 1944 than did the Americans. However, the production facilities for this revolutionary new aircraft were often in awkward positions such as caves and hollowed-out mountains or of inefficient layout to shelter them from Anglo-American bombing attack.[62] Considering how many workers were involved, the actual output of the plane was very small, with approximately 1,400 ever completed.

Then there were the famous V-weapons programs, in particular the V-2 rocket. The exact costs of the development of the A-4 rocket program, which was named the V-2 (or vengeance weapon) when it went into service, are also not completely clear. One thing is known, however, that as an army program, the costs of the V-2, even though it was definitely part of the air war, were borne by the army and not the Luftwaffe. One of the reasons that the Luftwaffe actually developed the much cheaper V-1 cruise missile was that it was worried that the army's enormous investment in the V-2 would exclude the air force from the pilot-less aircraft offensive. Certainly the costs of the V-2 put it in a special category for Germany's war effort. Albert Speer, who pushed construction of the V-2 in 1943 because, as an army program, it was actually under his control, believed that when production for use first began, the unit cost was RM 1 million per rocket, but then reduced to the still extreme RM 250,000–300,000 per unit.[63] In relative terms he estimated that the expense of building one V-2 was the equivalent of constructing six fighter aircraft.[64]

In 1943, once Hitler was persuaded of the V-2's potential to strike back against Anglo-American strategic bombing, the weapons system was given a special priority rating, entitling it to first choice for any material it needed.[65] By the end of the war, the amount of effort put into designing and building the V-2 has been estimated in two different ways. The USSBS calculated that it cost an equivalent amount to the construction of 24,000 aircraft. If this is correct, the V-2 would have cost more than Germany's entire expenditure on AFV from

1942 to 1945. Michael Neufeld, who has written the best book on the subject, compares the expense of the A-4 program in Germany to that of the Manhattan Project in the United States.[66] He estimates that its total cost was approximately RM 2 billion, or $500 million. As this was about one-quarter the cost of the Manhattan Project and the German war economy was approximately one-quarter of the American, the relative costs borne by the two were equal. It must also be pointed out that, as part of the air–sea war, the V-2 was used to attack British or Anglo-American forces or civilian targets almost exclusively. Not a single V-2 was fired to the East; all but a handful of the 3,000 fired were targeted either at Great Britain, mostly to hit London, or at Belgium, Holland and France to try to damage the British and American forces that were getting their supplies through ports such as Antwerp.[67]

The V-2 fiasco also revealed one of the major systemic shortcomings for Germany in the air–sea war: the German military rarely collaborated with Germany's scientific community. This meant that while the Germans often concentrated a great deal of resources on headline-grabbing technological developments such as the V-2 rocket or the jet-powered aircraft, they rarely kept up in the incremental technological developments that were needed to fight the war. On the other hand, the Luftwaffe for much of the war had a very poor relationship with the German aircraft industry and provided little in the way of "leadership or guidance" to those who were actually building its aircraft.[68]

Of course, the Nazi state was responsible for many of these shortcomings. German science blossomed during the tolerant Weimar Republic, but under the racist and anti-Semitic Nazi dictatorship, many of Germany's finest scientific minds, most famously Albert Einstein, left for the United States and Great Britain where they would do important work against the country of their birth.[69] Yet, as the war went on and the Germans found themselves being suffocated by Allied air and sea power, the assumption of German racial superiority made it very difficult for the Germans to admit to themselves that they were falling technologically behind the Allies.[70]

In the end it is clear that fighting the air–sea war, particularly the former, was the dominant preoccupation of Germany's war economy. At least two-thirds of German weapons production, even excluding the V-2, went to air, sea and anti-air weapons. Moreover, the development costs of these weapons in money, raw materials and scientific expertise were exponentially higher than for land weapons and the time involved in the design process was years longer. Although the average German fighting man may have been in the army, the average German was far more involved in the war in the air and on the sea.

Great Britain

In the summer of 1940 Great Britain supposedly found itself fighting for its existence. The shockingly quick collapse of France, following hot on the heels of the German capture of Norway, Denmark, Holland and Belgium, completely altered the strategic and productive assumptions which had driven the British government since the outbreak of World War II in Europe. The upshot was that the British government had to readjust its war production priorities dramatically and immediately. The first thing was to set up a priority system with three distinct classes: 1(a), 1(b) and 2.[71] Class 1(a), which until the end of 1940 received overriding precedence, contained the four groups of weapons considered vital to British survival, three of which were part of the air war against Germany. They were fighter, bomber and training aircraft, bombs, and anti-aircraft equipment. The only non-air equipment to be part of this list was the relatively inexpensive category of small arms and small-arm ammunition.

The shift ended up being decisive until the war was almost over. It marked the moment when aircraft construction not only became the highest priority item, but became the greatest focus of war production, making up approximately half of British war output. Prior to this, aircraft construction had become the largest element in British construction, but not decisively so. In 1938, for the first time, the RAF surpassed the Royal Navy in total government rearmament expenditure by £66 million to £63.2 million. This small advantage increased even further in 1939 when the RAF was allocated £109.9 million for rearmament expenditure and the Royal Navy received £82.9 million, with the army lagging behind at £67.6 million.[72] However, the shift that started in 1940 was decisive.

As a whole British World War II munitions production, even with all its shortcomings, is a story of substantial achievement in terms of both quantity and quality. With the exception of the United States, the British ended up building a wider a range of air, sea and land equipment than any other power. Qualitatively British equipment was often superior to that of the Germans, particularly when it came to air defense and the war at sea, which gave them crucial advantages.[73] In the air, not only did they build one of the best fighters of the first half of the war, the Spitfire, a British-designed engine also ended up powering the best fighter in the war, the P-51 Mustang. The British were able to build and deploy an effective, heavy four-engine bomber, the Lancaster, long before the German equivalent, the HE-177, could enter service. They were even able to design and construct a plane as innovative and important as the wooden-framed Mosquito, which ended up causing numerous headaches for German air defense. On the sea, they built a full range of vessels from aircraft carriers to battleships through to numerous small anti-submarine vessels, as well as submarines themselves. These ships were of high quality, some with advanced design features such as the reinforced steel aircraft carrier deck, and were able to operate in all theatres in the world by 1945.[74] On land, the production of British AFV was always in moderate proportions and their quality is best described as solid but not spectacular. Finally, the British were able to provide technological support to their weapons systems with high-quality radar and radio sets in a way that easily surpassed all but the Americans. The Germans, on the other hand, not only had the aforementioned problems designing a truly effective heavy bomber, they had a limited range of naval construction once the war started, focusing overwhelmingly on submarines. The Germans also could never design and build enough modern radar equipment. The Japanese, meanwhile, almost abandoned the construction of AFV during the war and were themselves also unable to develop an effective heavy bomber. The Soviet Union, meanwhile, hardly built a naval vessel of note and its aircraft, while plentiful, were restricted in quality, range and effectiveness.

The vision of Britain as a "great" power before and during the war is one that has evolved in the past few decades. For a while it was fashionable for many to dwell on British decline and stress the limited nature of the United Kingdom's contribution to victory when compared with the USSR's huge role in the land war and the United States' enormous output of munitions. In the past few decades, however, the trend has been moving strongly against this view. Historians such as Brian McKercher and John Ferris have argued that, in the interwar years, the United Kingdom remained the world's pre-eminent force.[75] More recently, David Edgerton, in *Britain's War Machine*, has pushed this argument to the limit, portraying Great Britain as perhaps the most impressive performing power of World War II. While this argument is probably overstated – Edgerton's claims about the relative merits of certain British aircraft and warships are sometimes debatable – the thrust of his argument is extremely important. Not everything the British made in the air and sea war was the best or even close to it, but the fact that they were able to make what they did across such a wide range of technologically advanced weaponry was one of the remarkable achievements of World War II.

Not only was British construction impressive in its scope, what sets it apart is also the speed and degree of its mobilization when compared with others. The shock of the summer of 1940 meant that the entire country was almost completely deployed in the war effort. In 1940 and 1941 the United Kingdom significantly out-produced Germany in the crucial weapons of war, and the British economy reached "full" production in 1943, while it took the other powers until 1944 to reach the highest extent of their munitions production. One of the places where the dominance of air and sea construction within the British economy can be seen is in the examination of worker allocation.

Manpower concerns were some of the greatest issues confronting the Churchill government during the war. The United Kingdom itself (without the resources of the British Empire) was the smallest nation of the great powers in terms of population. Yet it had to fill all three branches of the armed services and the different munitions and productive industries. This gave manpower questions an even greater urgency within the British mind. As Churchill and others made perfectly clear to the Americans right after the re-election of Franklin Roosevelt in 1940, the British believed that the era of mass infantry armies was at an end. This was a belief stemming from both self-interest and diminished expectations. Unlike the Roosevelt administration, which had relatively vague, if hopeful, notions about a post-war world, the British government, at least as long as Winston Churchill was in power, knew exactly what it was fighting for – the preservation of the British Empire. The British therefore approached the war intellectually from a very different point of view from the Americans. While Roosevelt and his advisers were primarily concerned with beating Germany and Japan and then working out what they wanted in the post-war world, the British knew what they wanted, and worked continually to tailor the method of victory to suit their needs – hence the reliance on air power.

An air-centric construction policy served the basic need of preserving the British Empire by reducing human casualties and by switching the losses to machines. During the entire war Bomber Command lost 47,130 aircrew on operational duty, fewer than the British army lost in the first few days of the Battle of the Somme in World War I.[76] Casualties in the British army, particularly in 1944 and 1945, were also kept remarkably low by World War I standards. From D-Day until the surrender of Germany, 30,276 soldiers of the British army were killed or subsequently died of their wounds during the fighting in France, Belgium, Holland and Germany.[77] British air casualties, while they were high in percentage terms considering the number of men who actually went into combat in aircraft, were relatively small when compared with the absolute number of men who died in land combat.

By relying on machinery staffed by a smaller number of highly skilled pilots and aircrew as opposed to more mass infantry and armored units, the British were better able to contend with one of their constant worries during the war, the shortage of industrial workers in British industry. British manpower requirements led to a constant conflict between the needs of the armed forces and the needs of the factories, so much so that there were regular fights and commissions set up to try to cope with the problem. In the end, the RAF almost always triumphed.

Starting in 1941 the United Kingdom was suffering from what was called "a famine of men," and the government instituted some of the most rigid population controls placed on any of the combatant nations during the war.[78] Of course, even this statement distorted the issue. The British government mobilized its female population in the workforce, including major war industries such as aircraft production, much earlier and more efficiently than the Germans. (See Figure 4.) By 1942 British man and woman power was almost fully deployed, which meant that it was the distribution of workers within the system that showed industrial effort and priority. "In the later years of the war manpower budgeting had become a very powerful instrument. It was, in fact, the only method the War Cabinet ever possessed of determining the balance of the whole war economy by a central and direct allocation of physical resources among various sectors."[79]

4 British men and women building aircraft engines. Britain made much more efficient use of its working population, of both sexes, earlier than the Germans, which was one of the reasons they out-produced Germany during the Battle of Britain. The workers here are building the famous Merlin engine, which, when placed in the airframe of the P-51 Mustang, created the best fighter plane of the war.

It was in this struggle for manpower in 1942 and 1943 that the dominance of air and sea construction within the British economy can best be seen. In the United Kingdom, workers for industrial construction were allocated to production through their assignment to one of three supply departments: the Ministry of Aircraft Production (MAP), the Admiralty and the Ministry of Supply. The first two are self-explanatory, but the third not only controlled all the production for the army, it was in charge of all ordnance and weapon production,

Table 4 *United Kingdom: production manpower by ministry, July 1, 1942*

Ministry of Supply	1,656,000
Ministry of Aircraft Production	1,514,000
Admiralty (supply)	814,000

Source: Hancock and Gowing, *British War Economy*, p. 449.

much of which was dispersed to the Royal Air Force and the navy. Table 4 shows the workers controlled by each branch on July 1, 1942. Although it is not possible to calculate what proportion of the Ministry of Supply-controlled workforce were involved in production for the air and sea war, more than 60 percent of the workforce at the time was building equipment just for the Royal Navy and the RAF, and a significant percentage of the rest would have been as well. Furthermore, in the debates over worker allocation that went on during the coming year, it was the RAF and navy that triumphed. On July 10, 1942, the Minister for Aircraft Production, John J. Llewellin, sent a memo to the War Cabinet basically arguing for aircraft production to receive a significant injection of manpower.[80] The MAP had been promised an extra 45,000 workers per month in the spring of 1942, but had received only 27,000. To reach their required levels, the minister asked that other major areas of the war economy, including coal, shipbuilding, the Royal Army Ordnance Corps and the Merchant Navy, be denied access to MAP personnel. To attract workers, the aircraft industry then started paying the highest average wages in the UK.[81]

It was the start of a rather brutal fight over workers that went on for well over a year. In July 1942 the different branches of production submitted their demands for additional labor for the coming year. The Ministry of Supply and the Admiralty were quite modest in their demands, while the MAP was wildly ambitious. Even though all the demands had to be cut, in the end the MAP ended up with an extra 307,000 workers and the Admiralty 104,000, with the Ministry of Supply actually being forced to reduce its number of workers by 186,000.[82] (See Table 5.) By the end of 1943, therefore, the MAP actually controlled more workers than the Ministry of Supply, while the Admiralty figure had crested 900,000. In relative terms the number of British workers involved in air and sea construction (including those

Table 5 *United Kingdom: demands and allocation of new workers, 1942–3*

	July 1942[a]	December 1942[b]	July 1943[b]	December 1943 (actual)[c]
Ministry of Supply	148,000	−78,000	−165,000	−186,000
MAP	603,000	503,000	205,000	307,000
Admiralty (supply)	186,000	111,000	111,000	104,000

Notes:
[a] The demands issued by the different branches for additional workers for 1943.
[b] The allocations made by the War Cabinet.
[c] The actual number of workers gained (or lost).
Source: Postan, *British War Production*, p. 225.

Table 6 *United Kingdom: production manpower by ministry, December 1943*

Ministry of Supply	1,470,000
Ministry of Aircraft Production	1,821,000
Admiralty (supply)	918,000

Note: Calculated by using the starting figures in Table 4 and then adding/subtracting the workers allocated as shown in Table 5.

who were working on air and sea munitions for the Ministry of Supply) would have surpassed 70 percent. (See Table 6.)

This shift can be seen in the debates over British production priorities during the same period. From the summer of 1940 until the end of 1941, the air war had retained its position as the top priority for British munitions production. The reality of this priority was not only established by government decision, it was reinforced by personality. The appointment of Lord Beaverbrook to head the Ministry of Aircraft Production in May 1940 gave the priority teeth, as he was one of the true political heavyweights in the government.[83] He held the job until May 1941, and to begin with, his determination to maximize aircraft production was so resolute that other areas of the economy suffered.[84]

When Beaverbrook left the MAP in May of 1941 for the Ministry of Supply, there was actually a growing public debate over armaments priority. A group of tank enthusiasts started arguing that British forces in North Africa were too poorly provided for with AFV and that greater effort should be spent pushing their construction.[85] This led the government to place tanks on the highest priority level.

On July 29, 1941, when the government was facing a vote of confidence, Churchill addressed the question publicly in the House of Commons. In his speech, Churchill made particular mention of his personal role as Minister of Defence as apart from that of Prime Minister. In his discourse, being Minister of Defence allowed him personally to draw up the armaments plans for the three different services at the beginning of the manufacturing year, a crucial power without which he believed he could not stay in charge of the British war effort.[86] However, having established his dominance in setting production targets, he then went on to downplay the existence of any strong priority system for British armament manufacture.

> I may say, while I am on the point, that much of this talk about difficulties of settling priorities is a back number. The whole business of priorities has undergone a complete transformation. We have no more of these arrogant absolute priorities in virtue of which one Department claimed all that there was of a particular commodity and left nothing for the lesser but indispensable needs of others. Although the 1A priority is still maintained largely for psychological reasons, for certain particular spheres of production such as aircraft, and tanks now, it is no longer exercised in the crude manner of the last war or in the early months of this. The method of allocation of labour, materials, and facilities has modified and to a large extent replaced the scale of priorities.[87]

The implication was that the allocation of raw materials to the manufacture of different munitions was a flexible process, in which no hard and fast priority would limit the output of another area. What occurred subsequently was that some other areas of production had their priorities raised to the high level already accorded to aircraft. In November 1941 there was a new priority direction that included a range of other outputs, from barrage balloons to cranes to fire-fighting pumps.[88] Yet, the reality of these changes was that aircraft production continued to dominate, and in many ways strengthened, as the country shifted from the manufacture of single-engine fighters to the manufacture of the much heavier and more expensive four-engine bombers such as the Lancaster.

In 1940, when Britain was faced with the prospect of the Battle of Britain, fighter production leapt to the front of the queue and the results were impressive. Not only did the British significantly raise

Table 7 *United Kingdom: RAF production plans, October 1940–July 1942*

Name of program	Date	Target size	Heavy bombers	Percent heavy bombers
Hennessy "target"[a]	October 1940	37,973	1,572	4.1
Revised "target"	July 1941	50,776	6,971	13.7
"Bomber"	December 1941	56,205	9,748	17.3
"Consolidated"	July 1942	80,993	15,534	19.2

Note: [a] The Hennessy scheme was a production plan drawn up with the assistance of Lord Beaverbrook's personal adviser, Mr. Hennessy of the Ford Motor Company.
Source: Postan, *British War Production*, pp. 475–8.

fighter production in the last six months of 1940, they significantly out-produced the Germans in this vital category. During the last six months of 1940, the United Kingdom produced almost 3,000 single-engine fighters while the Germans produced almost 1,000.[89] It was one of the reasons the Battle of Britain was over as quickly and decisively as it was.[90] However, in 1941, when the government began looking for ways of taking the war to Germany, bomber production began to be emphasized more strongly. It was the main reason that wartime aluminum production rose enormously in the United Kingdom (using access to the British Empire, particularly bauxite in Guiana and electricity in Canada).[91] Overall, aluminum production more than quadrupled, from 8,000 tons per month in 1939 to 33,000 tons per month in 1944.

This allowed not only a large numerical leap in RAF aircraft production, but also for the construction of the much larger four-engine bombers which needed considerably more aluminum. Table 7 shows the main plans set forward for the RAF from October 1940 through July 1942. Although the Consolidated plan ended up being beyond British capabilities (or strategic need), even with significant amounts of US lend-lease aircraft, what stands out is the extraordinary assumptions about how large the RAF needed to be and how much of it needed to be heavy bombers. While the last target could not be met, British construction did conform to the shape of the Consolidated program in terms of percentage of heavy bombers. (See Table 8.) In weight and cost terms, therefore, British output of aircraft climbed much more than the 30 percent numerical increase that occurred between 1941 and 1944.

To see how air-centric the British were, it is interesting to compare their aircraft and AFV production with that of Germany. (See Table 9.) This ratio significantly underplays Britain's prioritizing of aircraft construction over armor, for, as is well known, not only were the British building larger numbers of heavier planes than the Germans in the last three years of the war, British tanks were actually lighter than their German counterparts. We know from German figures that the greater expense of aircraft meant that they spent approximately five to eight times as much on aircraft as AFV each year, and the British ratio of production was even more lopsided in favor of the air. It is also important to notice that when war production peaked in 1943, the British actually decided to reduce the amount of effort that they were putting into the construction of AFV.

In March 1943, the Defence Committee approved a large program of tank construction for that year and the next.[92] The plan

Table 8 *United Kingdom: aircraft production, 1940–4*

Year	Overall	Heavy bombers	Percent heavy bombers
1940	15,049	41	0.12
1941	20,094	498	2.4
1942	23,672	1,976	8.3
1943	26,263	4,615	17.5
1944	26,461	5,507	20.8

Source: Statistical Digest of the War (London, 1951), p. 152.

Table 9 *United Kingdom and Germany: AFV and aircraft production, 1940–4 (first six months)*

Year	United Kingdom			Germany		
	AFV	Aircraft	Ratio	AFV	Aircraft	Ratio
1940	1,399	15,049	1–10.7	1,643	10,826	1–6.6
1941	4,841	20,094	1–4.1	3,790	11,776	1–3.1
1942	8,611	23,672	1–2.7	6,180	15,556	1–2.5
1943	7,476	26,263	1–3.5	12,063	25,527	1–2.1
1944	2,474	14,607	1–5.9	8,929	17,040	1–1.9

Note: The calculation for AFV includes all tanks and self-propelled guns, and that for aircraft includes all models such as fighters, bombers, transports and trainers. *Sources:* USSBS, European Report 3, pp. 276–9; *Statistical Digest of the War*, pp. 148, 152.

was to produce, excluding all light vehicles, 8,400 tanks in 1943 and 10,700 in 1944. However, as 1943 went on, and the pressure of all of Britain's production requirements increased, the decision was made to slash the tank program. By July a decision was made to reduce the 1943 program by 2,350 tanks and the 1944 program by 800.[93] British thinking had started to see the drawbacks to large tank formations by this time. Both the Minister for Production, Oliver Lyttelton, and the Chief of the Imperial General Staff, Sir Alan Brooke, believed that new models of anti-tank weaponry made modern tanks much more vulnerable than before.[94] Along with these doubts, there was a worker shortage in British AFV-producing factories, which cut into production significantly.[95] By January 1944 that year's production schedule, which only eight months before had been 10,700, was cut in half to 5,280.[96] All this was happening as the British were gearing up to re-enter the continent through an invasion of northern France.

At the same time, Churchill was pressing for as many aircraft as possible. In January 1943 he chaired a meeting of the War Cabinet precisely to find ways to increase aircraft production. "The Prime Minister said that he was disappointed to find that the programme was not larger. We had frequently been promised in the past that the year 1943 would see the great increase in aircraft production. The new programme, however, was only five-sixths of that previously put forward, and only envisaged an output of 2 percent per month throughout the year. He thought that a higher target should be set, so that there would a constant incentive to achieve more."[97] For the rest of the year, as tank production was being slashed, the Churchill government did everything possible to try to meet its aircraft targets. The official historian of British war production, Michael Postan, describes just how British aircraft production attained the level of half of all British production.

> Aircraft production therefore continued to enjoy the first claim on resources which it had acquired in the dramatic summer months of 1940. In the course of 1941 it had to share its claims with a number of other urgent war-stores, but its total demands, especially after the introduction of the bomber programme at the end of 1941, were so great as completely to outweigh the burden of the others. It would not be an exaggeration to say that throughout

1942 aircraft production was by far the largest single claimant to additional factors of production, and more especially to labour. Its requirements under the bomber programmes for more than a million additional men and women and for an intake for the first five months of 58,000 per month, were of course greatly exaggerated and could not possibly have been met. Yet even in October 1942, after the requirements had been pruned by the Lord President and the Minister of Production, they still amounted to 208,000 for the second half of the year, which was more than the comparable requirements of the other supply departments together.[98]

The final area that must be discussed is Britain's very large effort in naval construction. That Britain spent large amounts both before and during the war on ships is hardly surprising. In fact, the only time that aircraft construction actually was threatened with losing its overriding pre-eminence in British armaments production was when the war against the U-boats in the Atlantic Ocean seemed to be going in Germany's favor. In the late autumn of 1942, following the most brutal period of the Battle of the Atlantic, brought about by the massive numbers of merchantmen sunk by the Germans after the United States entered the war, the British bomber construction program had to be "slightly" reduced in favor of anti-submarine vessels and weapons. Yet, even these aircraft reductions were significantly smaller than reductions in other areas of British war industry.[99]

Certainly the British, who entered the war with a relatively small number of destroyers and smaller vessels when compared with 1914, needed to exert real effort to increase these numbers so as to be able to convoy most merchant shipping across the Atlantic. From 1940 through the end of 1943, the United Kingdom produced 176 destroyers and 160 corvettes and frigates.[100] This production proved decisive for, as the Battle of the Atlantic showed, the key step in transporting trade across the Atlantic remained arranging merchant ships into convoy. The dramatization of the war at sea often focuses on the battle between the convoys and the U-boats. This is certainly great theater, but it distorts the real picture. The vast majority of ships that were sunk in the Atlantic were sailing unescorted. Though there were some famous encounters between U-boat wolfpacks and convoys, the reality was that once ships were in convoy, their odds of crossing the Atlantic safely were extremely high.[101] To build these ships required an enormous workforce, as the numbers of industrial workers controlled by the Admiralty testifies. The 914,000 workers in Admiralty-controlled munitions production, while half as many as those working in aircraft production, were probably equal to the numbers producing for the entire army.

Of course, the question of naval armaments also raises the issue of the limits of British munitions production. The focus on smaller, trade-protection craft meant that Britain did produce a relatively small number of larger vessels – and those vessels were certainly not the best of their types in the world. During the war the United Kingdom finished five capital ships, four battleships of the King George V and the Prince of Wales classes. Despite claims for their supposed excellence, these 35,000 ton, 14-inch gunned vessels were considerably outclassed by German (Bismarck Class, 45,000 tons and 15-inch guns), Japanese (Yamato Class, 62,000 tons, 18-inch guns) and American (Iowa Class, 45,000 tons, 16-inch guns) capital ships designed and built at the same time.[102] The situation for construction of aircraft carriers was similar. During the war the British were significantly out-produced in carrier numbers by the Japanese, and Japanese carriers were able to carry considerably more aircraft. Also, the Japanese were able before the war began to design truly effective carrier aircraft, something that eluded the British throughout the war as they had to rely on American supplies of carrier planes to be combat-effective in the Pacific.

Taken altogether, though, what stands out is British achievement in the air and sea production war. This is the case independently of munitions production that came in from the British Empire. Production from the empire, particularly Canada, was helpful but was only a small percentage of UK home production.[103] The United Kingdom mobilized more quickly than any other power, deployed its workforce with more ruthless efficiency, and produced a large number of high-quality aircraft and naval vessels. This was a remarkable achievement in the air–sea war, and occurred despite the fact that the British could never match American production, and that Germany, once it was fully mobilized and controlled all of Europe's human and mineral resources, had the fundamentals to produce considerably more – and would have, had it not been for the strategic bombing campaign.

United States

Franklin Roosevelt is often closely connected with the United States Navy in the historical mind.[104] Having served as Assistant Secretary of the Navy under Woodrow Wilson, and being a keen sailor, Roosevelt often unconsciously referred to the USN as "us" and the US army as "them." His sentimental love of the fleet and the sea, which was real, did not, however, make him prioritize the production of naval vessels over other munitions. When it came to World War II, Roosevelt could be as unsentimental as Stalin. He decided before the United States even joined the fighting that complete dominance in the air was the key step to achieving victory, a position that he stuck to doggedly and which crucially determined the kind of war that the United States fought.

It was not the case that Roosevelt had highly developed notions about how aircraft should be used – he did not. Instead he believed that overall control of the air, to be gained by sheer numbers of aircraft, was the United States' first industrial priority. Before the war this was manifested in him calling for the construction of more planes than the USAAF had ever imagined. As France was falling in May 1940, the President called for the United States to increase its annual production of aircraft to 50,000 and to maintain a front-line force of the same number, with the USAAF deploying 36,500 aircraft and the US Navy 13,500.[105] It was a plan outside of American capacity and military planning, made partly so that Roosevelt could transfer many of these aircraft to those still fighting the Nazis, and the actual production figures for 1941 were significantly below these.[106]

Yet, the fact that the United States actually went on to build 299,293 planes during the course of World War II has led some to assume that it simply built masses of all weaponry in order to swamp Germany and Japan.[107] This is not true and we need to be careful not to over-exaggerate the ability of the United States to produce everything it wanted during the war.[108] Certainly it had the ability to produce more than any other power, partly owing to the fact that it could organize its industry in terms of raw material access, industrial plant location and design, and transport, without any real consideration of the air power of its opponents. This advantage allowed it, for instance, to build considerably more aircraft than Germany with approximately the same number of industrial workers, 2 million, or than the United Kingdom, which employed only 10–15 percent fewer people in the aircraft industry.[109] The famous Willow Run factory which Henry Ford had constructed for the production of B-24 Liberator bombers was built on an enormous scale without concern for air attack, which allowed for the remarkable production rate of 650 aircraft a month from the one facility, or more four-engine bombers in two months than Germany was able to build in the war. The largest plant directly sponsored by the USAAF was the enormous Dodge aircraft engine plant built outside Chicago at a cost of $173 million. It had a huge (and unprotected) floor space of 6,430,000 square feet which made this one factory as large as all the aircraft engine factories in America combined before 1942.[110] At the same time the Germans were being forced both to bury their factories underground and to scatter them so that the loss of one would not cripple the production of all. However, even with these crucial advantages, American production, while prodigious, did fall far below the expectations put forward for it at the beginning of the war. And that meant that the United States had to make crucial choices in 1942 – all of which favored its ability to fight an air–sea war over land battles. (See Figures 5 and 6.)

The best place to start is during the strategic discussions of Arcadia, the conference held in Washington, DC between Roosevelt, Churchill and their advisers almost immediately after the Japanese attacked Pearl Harbor. On January 3, Roosevelt sent a formal letter to Henry Stimson, Secretary of War, calling for the production of 60,000 aircraft in 1942 and 125,000 in 1943. The target for tanks was equally bold at 45,000 in 1942 and 75,000 in 1943.[111] Even with this plan, which was referred to at the time as the "Victory Program," American effort in aircraft construction would have been a very large percentage of the country's construction output, about 30 percent in 1942. The plan continued the spending ratio that the United States had adopted going into the war, as its production of aircraft and aircraft equipment in 1941 consumed about 28 percent of its munitions spending.[112] The cost per unit of an American aircraft, as it was for the German or British, was considerably higher than for land vehicles. The American figure was in fact about to become even higher because of the development and production of the massively expensive four-engine B-29 Superfortress bomber.[113] (See Figure 7.) This one weapons program, for the most advanced and effective bomber of the war, had a development and production cost of between $3 billion and

5 B-24 production. More Liberators were produced than any other four-engine bomber during the war. Because there was no need to worry about air attack, the Americans laid out enormous, rational factories that produced far more per worker than German facilities.

6 Another example of American production on a massive scale. These are nosecones for A-20 attack aircraft being assembled in Long Beach, California in 1942.

3.7 billion.[114] The equivalent cost of the Manhattan Project was $2 billion.[115] In other words, the B-29 cost approximately six times as much as the German development and production costs of the A-4/V-2 rocket program.

On the other hand, the "Victory Program" called for balanced spending between a land, sea and air war.[116] Roosevelt made that

7 Production of the B-29. This was the most expensive weapons program of the war, costing more than the atomic bomb project.

explicit in February 1942, according to Donald Nelson, the chairman of the War Productions Board, when he said aircraft should be first priority but almost all other categories of munitions production were to be pressed on with with equal commitment.[117] In February 1942, the expectation was that spending on all ground equipment would actually be slightly higher than that for all air equipment, with shipping a respectable third. The army was determined to maintain this balance.[118]

This is where it gets interesting, especially in the light of the sometimes grandiose assumptions about American production. By the summer of 1942, it was clear that, even with all these efforts, Roosevelt's goals for all areas of munitions production were inflated – by a very large margin. The fact that the United States had already started utilizing its spare capacity before Pearl Harbor meant that Roosevelt's expectations about how much production could quickly be increased were far too optimistic.[119] Certain commodities, such as aluminum, were also in shorter supply than expected (a sign of how German success in the Battle of the Atlantic held out the possibility of reducing American war materials in the pre-production phase).[120] As things were developing, all targets were going to be missed by at least 20 percent and many by much more. It was here that Franklin Roosevelt made his most important and crucial military intervention during World War II. When, in August, he digested the reports that aircraft production in particular was going to fall considerably below expected targets, the President instructed Nelson to send him a report clearly describing how many planes could actually be built in 1942 and 1943 – and Nelson replied in rather stark, and somewhat exculpatory, terms.

On January 3rd of this year you announced an aircraft program
objective of 60,000 planes for 1942. This has subsequently served
as our directive, toward the attainment of which every effort has
been made. Although many of our associates have from the first
indicated that they considered it unlikely that we could reach this
figure, I have, nevertheless, felt it would be unwise to advise you of
their doubts until the time had arrived ... that time is now.

Under the existing conditions of aircraft priority assignments,
manufacturing facilities, and material supplies available to aircraft,
it is probable that our 1942 deliveries will not exceed 48,000
planes.[121]

Moreover, Nelson pointed out that unless drastic action was taken
then, aircraft production in 1943 would fall far below Roosevelt's
intended target of 125,000. It was this double blow that compelled
the President to send a letter to the Army Chief of Staff, George
Marshall, on August 24, instructing him to order the head of the Army
Air Force, General Henry (Hap) Arnold, to draw up a plan for air
dominance.

I wish you would ask General Arnold to submit to you his
judgment of the number of combat aircraft by types which should
be produced for the Army and our Allies in this country in 1943 in
order to have complete air ascendancy over the enemy.

This report should be prepared without consideration for
existing schedules or production possibilities or any other
competing military requirements. I am asking for this because
I would like to know what the theoretical requirements are to get
complete control and domination of the air.[122]

So much of this letter stands out – the first being Roosevelt's
clarity. Roosevelt normally preferred not to give direct orders if possible. By nature, when dealing with both civilian and military leaders,
he favored working through suggestion and guidance as opposed to
precise orders. Furthermore, he knew that in telling Marshall to have
these plans drawn up without regard to other construction priorities, he
was treading on sensitive ground, as the general had previously lobbied
him to increase spending on AFV construction in place of other programs.[123] To hammer his point home, three days later Roosevelt sent
Marshall another letter on air production, this time with Nelson's
appraisal of the possible shortfall.[124]

This began a three-month standoff between Roosevelt and Marshall, who had the, not always committed, backing of Arnold and Ernest King, the Chief of Naval Operations and Commander in Chief of the US fleet. Roosevelt originally had in mind a production target of 131,000 aircraft in 1943, 100,000 of which would be combat and transport planes of different types, with the rest trainers.[125] However, this was far beyond American capabilities, and by October he had scaled his request down to 107,000 aircraft, which was what he had been told could be achieved if the US gave aircraft construction the absolute first priority for all needed materials. The Joint Chiefs of Staff seemed shocked that the President was determined to put so much effort into aircraft construction and responded with a plan of their own, originally calling for 85,000 aircraft and then, partially trying to appease the President, one calling for 100,000 aircraft of all types. Marshall went to great lengths to change Roosevelt's mind. He lobbied Harry Hopkins, one of the few people whom Roosevelt trusted, to try and persuade the President to back down.[126] Marshall told Hopkins that, by building at full capacity and giving everything possible to aircraft construction, the 107,000 aircraft in total might not even be built in 1943, and doing so would have disastrous implications in other areas of the economy, which could lead to cutbacks in the amount of equipment that could be sent to America's allies (he knew that Hopkins was keen to send as much aid as possible to the USSR).

Hopkins, of course, was far too sensitive to Roosevelt's feelings to side with Marshall, and cemented his close relationship with the President by arguing that Roosevelt should stick to his guns.[127] He warned the President that the Joint Chiefs might try to pull the wool over his eyes, by defining the President's instructions to mean that, by the end of 1943, US construction should have reached a monthly rate equivalent to 107,000, not a grand total of 107,000 for the year. Roosevelt's response was clear and decisive. On October 29, he instructed Nelson to do whatever he needed to do to fulfill Roosevelt's plan.

> This aircraft program (for 1943) will provide for the production of a minimum of 107,000 planes total, of which 82,000 shall be combat type. This program for aircraft, aircraft engines and their components will be given highest priority and whatever preference is needed to insure its accomplishment. The Army, Navy and other

governmental agencies are to cooperate to the fullest in the furtherance of this program.

I want to reiterate that this directive calling for 82,000 combat planes and 25,000 non-combat for the calendar year does not mean production on a monthly basis at the end of 1943 at a rate equal to one-twelfth of the above planes, but that it does call for the production, or in other words actual delivery, of 82,000 combat planes and 25,000 non-combat planes between January 1, 1943 and December 31, 1943.[128]

It was a crucial decision, reorienting American construction in 1943 and the first part of 1944 towards the construction of aircraft over all other armaments. It certainly led to a significant change in the munitions spending of the American government and some massive cuts in army production.[129] In terms of the size of the US army, it was the key driving force to slash its eventual size to a hundred divisions. This might sound like a lot, but in 1941 and early 1942 the United States was planning on an army of two hundred divisions or even more.[130] In a matter of months, to protect aircraft construction, the US army had lost half of its planned strength.

In 1942, as the production crisis in the second half of the year showed, the United States found it impossible to build the munitions that it planned (and budgeted) to construct. Overall spending for munitions for the year, which was supposed to be $41.7 billion in February, had dropped significantly to $29.3 billion by November. In December it would fall even further. The difficulty in retooling America's factories to build the needed aircraft was a major part of this problem. In 1943, instead of calculating the cost of what was spent in the different areas, the War Production Board calculated the value of the production that actually emerged – and it was a surprisingly small number. For all of 1942, the United States produced military equipment with a total value of $8.6 billion.[131] The production crisis of 1942 ended up being far more real than anyone had guessed.

In terms of the air–sea war, the value of American production showed that, even in 1942, before ground equipment such as AFV had their production targets slashed, more than 70 percent of American construction was going to aircraft, naval vessels, merchant ships, or their combined supporting machinery and weapons. (See Table 10.) However, even this imbalance was not enough. Roosevelt's extra pressure to build aircraft and merchantmen saw a further shift towards air

Table 10 *United States: combat munitions expenditures, 1942, by quarter (in millions of dollars)*

| | Quarter | | | | | |
	1st	2nd	3rd	4th	Total	Percent
Air munitions	515	740	953	1,174	3,382	39.3
Ground munitions	279	475	728	950	2,432	28.2
Naval munitions	300	431	587	738	2,056	23.9
Merchant vessels	100	164	220	251	735	8.5
Total					8,605	

Source: FDR PSF 172-2, War Progress Report, October 2, 1943, p. 12.

Table 11 *United States: combat munitions expenditures, 1943, by quarter (in millions of dollars)*

| | Quarter | | | | | |
	1st	2nd	3rd	4th	Total	Percent
Air munitions	4,190	5,096	6,058	7,839	23,183	43.1
Ground munitions	2,872	3,169	3,442	4,168	13,651	25.4
Naval munitions	2,408	2,789	3,202	3,828	12,227	22.7
Merchant vessels	940	1,146	1,219	1,390	4,695	8.7
Total					53,756	

Note: In this case the figures for January through August are exact values, while those for September through December are projected values.
Source: FDR PSF 172-2, War Progress Report, October 2, 1943, p. 12.

and sea weapons. In October 1943, hard figures were released for the value of product turned out through August of that year, complete with the projections of monthly schedules through the end of the December. (See Table 11.) By this time, air–sea weapons now made up 75 percent of the value of all American weapons output. Just aircraft, without their weapons and ordnance, made up about one-third of the output. As the 1943 year-end summary report from the War Productions Board described the situation heading into 1944: "aircraft will dominate munitions production this year, accounting for one-third of total production. Month to month gains in munitions output will be dictated by what happens in the airplane group."[132]

Why Roosevelt's interjection in the second half of 1942 ended up being so important was that, even with this significant shift in favor of air construction, the United States still came nowhere close to meeting his end of year targets. Instead of the 107,000 aircraft the

President wanted in 1943, at the end of the year only 85,423 had been built, and only 54,094 were combat types for the army and navy.[133] So, even with the intense pressure the President put on the production process, the United States was only able to build 66 percent of his target for combat aircraft. Had the priority situation favored by George Marshall gone into operation, American construction of combat planes would have been approximately 40,000 for the year. This amount, while seemingly large, would not have allowed the US to operate with the air superiority that it did in the European and Pacific theaters. It would have been a much bloodier and less successful year.

As it happened, Roosevelt's 1943 program was then transferred over to 1944, when the annual target for that year was set at 107,425 aircraft in total, with 83,250 being combat types.[134] This figure was even more daunting than it first seemed, as construction of heavy bombers now included significant runs of the awesomely expensive B-29. The President's production goals could only be achieved by raising the percentage spent on aircraft. In the first half of 1944, this figure went up to more than one-third, while spending on land equipment was reduced even further.[135] Even then, production that year was 10,000 behind target, as 96,356 aircraft were produced, 74,141 of which were combat planes.[136]

The other side of this story is the relative decline in American ground equipment production from 1942 into 1944, in particular for AFV but including other sectors as well. The decline of the tank as an element of American production was unmatched. Originally AFV production was planned to be a little less than 10 percent of overall American munitions output. By November 1942, the AFV program targets were actually slashed by 55 percent, reducing the planned percentage in this category to approximately 5 percent.[137] Halfway through 1943, it was decided to cut AFV production even further. The War Production Board wrote on September 18:

> Tank and Tank Destroyer schedules have been cut again. New production forecasts for 1944 call for one-quarter fewer tanks and self-propelled guns on tank chassis than were scheduled as of June. From a monthly average of 3,700 in the second quarter of this year, the combined programs have already dropped to 3,100 this month. They head on downward to fewer than 2,100 a month in the second half of 1944.[138]

This decline in relative effort extended into 1945. During December 1944 and January 1945, AFV construction came in at 3.8 percent of American munitions production.[139]

Before leaving the subject of AFV, the development cost question should be addressed for the United States as well, for in this case the gap during the war was larger than for any other power. The amount of money that the United States was willing to spend on developing aircraft was prodigious, not only on the exceedingly expensive B-29, which put all other plane development costs in the shade, but on other aircraft such as the B-31 which never got beyond the prototype phase. By 1945 the air force's own budget just for research and development had reached $800 million.[140] At the time the monthly cost of American combat vehicle construction of all types was less than $200 million.[141] In 1942, the United States had started designing one of the best tanks in the world, the M-26, which was given the name Pershing.[142] However, resistance to its development within the army meant that it was pushed along at a slow pace and it was starved of resources. It was not until 1945 that the Pershing was deployed to fight in Germany, where it quickly showed itself as at least equal to both Panthers and Tigers. Unlike aircraft construction, pushing new and powerful AFV was never a major priority of American munitions construction during the war.

In 1944, the exact figures for different classes of armaments production are available in a slightly different form than earlier. Figures for ammunition, guns and fire control, and communications and electrical equipment are not divided up into their different allocations to the army, navy and air force. Still, it is clear that the dominance of aircraft and naval vessel production remained unmatched. (See Table 12.) The cost of aircraft and ships was more than six times higher

Table 12 *United States: war production, 1944 (in billions of dollars)*

Munitions class	Cost of production
Aircraft	18.9
Ships (including merchant)	14.1
Guns and fire control	3.4
Ammunition	6.7
Combat and motor vehicles	5.3
Communications and electrical equipment	4.3

Sources: Hopkins MSS, 24, Increased War Production for 1945, J. A. Krug, January 16, 1945, p. 6.

than the cost of all combat and motor vehicles, and double the cost of all of these added to all ammunition and gun production. It is important to note how much was being spent on shipping as late as this. The U-boat war turned decisively in favor of the British and Americans in the late spring of 1943, and after the successful D-Day landings in Normandy in 1944, the United States' need for more landing craft was reduced. In 1945, the expectation was that shipbuilding would receive a significantly smaller percentage of American munitions production. However, from 1942 to 1945, American shipbuilding, both naval and merchant, had made up a larger percentage of munitions production than had land weapons.

Like the British, the Roosevelt administration's strategic plans started with the basic assumption that the United States needed to have a shipping dominance that went hand in hand with its air supremacy. In 1942, two developments coincided to cause spending on naval and merchant shipping actually to rise in production percentage during the year, while that for aircraft fell and that for land equipment was slashed (see Table 10). In the Atlantic, the extremely high losses of merchantmen along the American East Coast from January to July, and in the Pacific, the very high damage caused to American naval vessels by the brutal fighting with the Japanese from Pearl Harbor through the start of the Guadalcanal campaign, pushed shipping construction higher up the priority list.[143] In February 1942, the plan was to spend $7.1 billion on naval vessels of all types during the year.[144] By November, the planned yearly construction was $7.8 billion. Spending on merchant vessels also rose considerably, from a February expectation of $1.9 billion to a November plan of $2.1 billion. This figure for merchant ships is particularly telling. Once the decision was made in 1942 to reduce the relative effort spent building AFV and increase that on merchant shipping, spending on the latter remained consistently much higher than on the former until the end of 1944.

Taken as a whole, American naval construction during the war, in relative terms, reached staggering proportions. By 1945, almost 100,000 vessels of different types had entered into service in the US Navy. These included 8 battleships, 13 heavy cruisers, 2 large cruisers, 33 light cruisers, 17 fleet aircraft carriers, 9 light aircraft carriers, 77 escort carriers (another 37 were built and given to the British), 349 destroyers, and more than 85,000 smaller vessels ranging from landing craft to destroyer escorts.[145] One of the signs of the navy's high priority was that, from early in the war, naval construction received a higher steel allocation than army production. If aluminum was the key metal for determining maximum aircraft production, steel production was most important for the construction of most land weaponry or naval vessels. By April–May 1942, the navy's allocation of steel had surpassed the army's (including the US Army Air Force).[146] In November 1942, when the amounts spent building naval vessels and naval construction targets were being raised in real terms, it was decided to slash American tank output targets by 55 percent. The main reason given was that the necessary steel would not be made available for AFV building.[147] From that point onwards, the navy increased its munitions output at a higher growth rate than the army, until American munitions production peaked in 1944.[148]

Vessels of different types could actually be dramatically moved up the production priority list if need be. In 1943, anti-submarine escort vessels and landing craft all had their production targets increased markedly. A few developments in the war pushed this shift along. The intensification of the submarine war in the Atlantic in the first five months of 1943, plus the American push for a seaborne invasion of France in 1944, seem most important. In January 1943, the Joint Chiefs of Staff requested the War Production Board "to take every step possible immediately to accelerate and expand the construction of escort vessels."[149] This was actually a remarkable request as in that month the USA was already spending almost as much on constructing anti-submarine vessels, $144 million, as the combined budget for battleships, cruisers, aircraft carriers, destroyers and submarines, which was $163 million.[150] By August 1943, however, in response to this pressure, monthly American spending on anti-submarine vessels had leapt to $325 million, while that for battleships, cruisers, aircraft carriers, destroyers and submarines had increased more modestly to $187 million. The increase ended up being so prodigious, in fact, that the USA found itself with many more anti-submarine vessels than it needed in 1944 and had to cut back their construction markedly.

Construction of landing craft was likewise highly prioritized, though this time it was in the second half of 1943. During the first six months of that year, the United States spent on average $69.3 million per month on landing craft. By March–April 1944, the monthly average had jumped to $205 million. In April 1944 the monthly spend on landing craft was $214 million, while that on all combat ships was $276 million.[151] To put these figures into even greater perspective, the United States spent only $134 million monthly producing all of its combat vehicles in April 1944.[152]

To sum up American construction, the overwhelming bias in favor of air and sea weapons was clear throughout the war, and it grew markedly between late 1942 and early 1945. The cost of building aircraft and naval vessels meant that the air–sea war was always going to take up a majority of American munitions production, but this advantage was made much more pronounced by Franklin Roosevelt who, in October 1942, ordered the Joint Chiefs of Staff and the War Production Board to prioritize aircraft construction over all others. Throughout the war, American spending on aircraft alone made up approximately one-third of its munitions output, and when you add all the supporting weapons and ordnance, the air war took well over 40 percent of American effort. The sea war, on the other hand, came second, but always outpaced the amount of effort put into the war on land. The construction of naval vessels and merchant ships combined made up more than 30 percent of American effort, and regularly received higher priority than the construction of land armaments.

In the end there were many more similarities than differences in the way in which the United States and the United Kingdom fought the production war. Both favored the production of machines over the use of personnel in uniform, and both chose overwhelmingly to build air and sea weaponry over all others. Although American and British grand strategy can be faulted in many ways, this reliance on production made their armed forces the most modern in the world and that is reflected in their relatively low casualty rates.

Japan

If there was one nation more than any other that fought an extreme air–sea war in terms of production, it was Japan. Almost from the moment Pearl Harbor was attacked on December 7, 1941, the Japanese focused their economic efforts on the production of aircraft and naval and merchant vessels over land armaments. Even though Japan was still on the offensive, by March 1942 its losses of ships and aircraft began to exceed new production.[153] The army's response by the end of that year was to dramatically reduce the production of AFV, using much of the effort that it had expanded in that area to build anti-aircraft artillery. Major General Joichiro Sanada, who was chief of Japan's War Ministry Strategic Preparations Division, described the impact of this decision, as well as the true impact of a modern air–sea war, in matter-of-fact, if grim, detail.

> [I]n the latter part of 1942, plans were made to concentrate production on anti-aircraft weapons and ammunition at the expense of tanks ... and artillery. Hence in '43, '44, and '45 very few tanks were produced. The divisions were adversely affected through the shortage of divisional artillery weapons. In the summer of 1943 a plan was put into effect to withdraw the artillery weapons from Manchuria to equip and maintain divisions fighting in the Pacific. It took quite a while to accomplish this. The bulk of these weapons were finally destined for Okinawa, Philippines, Iwo Jima and Japan. However, due to submarines and airplanes much of this equipment was lost or not delivered to proper destination. For instance, only one-fourth of that destined for Iwo Jima ever arrived, most of the balance being sunk.[154]

Later he added that Japan had only been able to ship ten tanks into the Philippines before the American invasion in late 1944, and most of those had been destroyed by American aircraft before they could even be used against American troops.

Japanese production is sometimes overlooked in the history of the war, as it is assumed that it was the least developed of the great powers. Again, this is only immediately defensible if AFV and land vehicles are considered (incorrectly) to be the most important elements of World War II production. To see just how lopsided Japanese production was in favor of air–sea equipment, we need only look at the amount spent producing different classes of armaments. (See Table 13.) In total Japan spent 19,598 million yen on aircraft, naval vessels and merchant ships between 1942 and 1944, and only 1,004 million on all motor vehicles (which includes AFV). In percentage terms the difference between Japan's air–sea war and land war seems even more remarkable. (See Table 14.) Land vehicles and equipment hardly register within the context of Japanese war production in 1943 and 1944, while aircraft, naval vessels and merchant ships, completely independent of the weaponry and ammunition needed to operate them, made up

Table 13 *Japan: war production, 1941–4 (by expenditure) (in millions of yen)*

	1941	1942	1943	1944
Merchant ships	403	544	1,411	1,665
Navy ships	1,014	1,112	1,476	2,099
Navy ordnance (all)	972	1,540	2,551	4,638
Army ordnance (all)	956	1,262	1,586	2,107
Motor vehicles	691	427	309	270
Aircraft	1,081	1,843	3,687	5,024

Note: The ordnance figures given for the army and navy include the ammunition made for each of the air forces as well.
Source: USSBS, Pacific Report 53, pp. 203–4.

Table 14 *Japan: war production, 1941–4 (by percentage of effort)*

Percentage of construction	1941	1942	1943	1944
Merchant ships	8	8	13	10
Navy ships	20	17	13	13
Navy ordnance (all)	19	23	23	30
Army ordnance (all)	19	19	14	13
Motor vehicles	13	6	3	2
Aircraft	21	27	33	32

Source: USSBS, Pacific Report 53, pp. 203–4.

60 percent of overall production. Illustrating how relatively unimportant land weapons were, the large Japanese armies in China were ordered to make do with whatever they could produce locally. The famous Kwantung Army based in Manchuria, for instance, was basically self-sufficient after 1942, receiving only aircraft and certain "minor" equipment from the Japanese homeland.[155] The different armies in China created an internal barter economy between themselves, securing supplies through trading the raw materials and finished products to which they each had access.[156] Beyond the loss of aircraft involved, therefore, the land war in China was not a great drain on Japanese munitions produced in the home islands.

However, outside land production, the Japanese story from 1942 until the summer of 1944 was one of surprising success.[157] Japan became a first-class manufacturing nation of aircraft and naval/merchant shipping. For instance, it was forced to regularly upgrade the construction priority that it gave to aircraft production, and in 1943 it established its first Ministry of Munitions specifically to increase the production of aircraft.[158] In early 1944, owing to its losses of aircraft and the decisive battles which were expected to begin soon, the building of new aircraft was given absolute highest priority in the war economy. According to Lt General Saburo Endo, chief of the Cabinet Bureau's research department, at this point Japan switched to the "immediate, all-out production of aircraft."[159] The overall production increase between 1942 and 1944 was more than 300 percent, which is impressive considering some of the innate inefficiencies of the Japanese production system – including the complete division of army and navy aircraft production which led to an excessive multiplicity of aircraft models.[160]

However, even with this extraordinarily lopsided production schedule, the Japanese were eventually overwhelmed by American equipment. This picture, reinforced by testimony such as that by Sanada, is one that most Eurocentric histories of World War II would endorse. It is commonplace for many European historians to reduce the war against Japan to a sideshow when compared with the great war against Germany. John Keegan's six hundred page history of the war devotes only a hundred pages to the war against Japan.[161] Antony Beevor's history devotes at most 20 percent to the war in Asia and the Pacific.[162] As such, they are following a lead set down by British and American planners in 1941, when they decided on what has come to be known as the Germany-First policy. This strategic concept was based on the assumption that Germany was so much more powerful than Japan industrially that in any war with both powers, Germany would have to be confronted first by the overwhelming mass of Anglo-American production. Only once Germany had been defeated should a large percentage of production be switched to the Pacific, as Japan had no possibility of victory with Germany out of the war. Such a belief was bolstered by intelligence estimates about what Japan was building and could build in relation to Germany. However, these estimates ultimately proved to be wide of the mark. Not only were the Germans not producing the masses of equipment that the British and Americans thought they were in 1940 and 1941, the Japanese ended up being able to produce far more than expected. Japan, in terms of production, was in many ways the most surprising of major air–sea powers in World War II.

Though this might come as a shock to a generation of historians fixated on the land war in Europe, Japan's production and position in World War II was approximately equal to that of the Soviet Union.

Unlike the Germans, Americans and British, both were unable to make all kinds of weapons efficiently, so had to concentrate on smaller ranges of technology. Both also had very similar production profiles in terms of raw materials and weight/value of finished production. This is not always understood because Soviet industrial strength going into World War II was more developed than Japan's. However, with the loss of much of western Russia and Ukraine in 1941 and early 1942, the Soviet Union was denied a great deal of its industrial base. At the same time, the Japanese empire, by expanding into the Dutch East Indies (DEI) and other resource-rich areas, was significantly augmented in resource terms. This meant that Soviet and Japanese access to crucial raw materials was relatively similar during the crucial years of war production, 1942 through 1944. (See Table 15.) The difference that occurs in 1944 is a result of the collapse of the Japanese economic system brought about by the American air and sea offensive, which effectively sundered the trading lanes between the Japanese home islands and their far-flung empire.[163] Before that, however, what stands out is the similarity in the resource access profiles. Soviet production of iron ore was a little higher, but Japanese production of aluminum was superior. As very little of the equipment built before 1941, except for major naval vessels, actually was in use in the years 1942 to 1945, the similarity of resource access meant that, in terms of overall production, what the Japanese

Table 15 *Japan and USSR: production of certain raw materials, 1942–4*

	1942	1943	1944
Steel ingots (millions of metric tons)			
Japan	8.0	8.8	6.5
USSR	8.1	8.5	10.9
Coal (millions of metric tons)			
Japan	118	117	107
USSR	75	93	121
Iron ore (millions of metric tons)			
Japan	7.7	7.5	6.1
USSR	9.7	9.3	11.7
Aluminum ingot (thousands of metric tons)			
Japan	105	144	110
USSR	52	62	82

Sources: USSBS, Pacific Report 53, p. 112 for Japanese steel ingot production. For Soviet production, see Ellis, *The World War II Databook* (London, 1993), pp. 274–6.

Table 16 *Japan and USSR: AFV production, 1942–4 (individual units)*

	1942	1943	1944
Japan	1,191	790	401
USSR	24,446	24,089	28,963

Note: The Japanese figure is the combined total of medium tanks, light tanks and self-propelled guns. It does not include armored cars or other types of combat vehicle.
Source: USSBS, Pacific Report 53, p 221. For Soviet production see: Ellis, *The World War II Databook*, p. 277

and Russians built was close, if very different in individual units. Basically, what the USSR devoted to the construction of AFV Japan devoted to the production of naval and merchant shipping.

It will come as no surprise that in AFV terms the USSR built more than thirty-two tanks for each one constructed by the Japanese. (See Table 16.) However, when it comes to naval vessels, the situation was completely reversed. Japanese production of shipping during the war was impressive. Merchant and naval vessel construction received half of all the finished steel Japan produced between 1943 and 1945.[164] Between 1942 and 1944, the Japanese finished the construction of one battleship (of the enormous 64,000 ton Yamato Class), 13 aircraft carriers, 5 cruisers, 55 destroyers and 99 submarines.[165] As a point of comparison, the United Kingdom in these years completed 2 battleships (combined displacement of 70,000 tons), 6 aircraft carriers, 15 cruisers, 141 destroyers and 111 submarines.[166] Beyond the obvious British superiority in destroyer construction and Japanese superiority in aircraft carrier construction, these production profiles were quite similar. And, when compareing what Japan built in naval terms with what the USSR produced, the result is as equally lopsided a picture as in AFV construction, though this time in Japan's favor. During the entire war from 1941 to 1945, the USSR commissioned only 2 cruisers, 25 destroyers and 52 submarines.

The balance in Japan's favor in terms of merchant ship construction was even greater. During the war from 1942 to 1945, the Japanese produced 3,392,814 tons of merchant shipping, 986,159 tons of which were fuel tankers.[167] Production in the United Kingdom during the same period, completed almost entirely without any real damage from strategic bombing which severely hindered Japanese production during the last year of the war, was only 14 percent higher.

Between January 1, 1942 and June 30, 1945, 3,874,000 tons of merchant shipping was completed in the UK.[168] Without bombing the Japanese might have actually out-produced the British in merchant shipbuilding. On the other hand, it is not clear whether the USSR built any merchant shipping during the war as it was completely reliant on the cargo delivered by the Americans and British. To sum up, an equivalent amount of steel to that employed by the Russians in the land war was used by the Japanese to build naval and merchant vessels. The difference was not one of industrial strength, but one of different construction allocation.

Finally we have aircraft, the key component of World War II production for all powers. Before analyzing this, it is worth noting that the USSR's production was only made possible by lend-lease shipments of bauxite, the key ore that was refined into aluminum. As Table 15 shows, between 1942 and 1944, Soviet access to domestically produced bauxite was severely limited. Yet, without bauxite, aircraft production in the USSR would have been almost impossible. During the war all the major powers used the vast majority of their aluminum to build aircraft, severely restricting its use in other areas. By November 1942, 60 percent of American aluminum was completely given over to the production of aircraft, a figure that would eventually rise to more than 80 percent.[169] In Germany the situation was similar. In 1944 Albert Speer claimed that 80 percent of German aluminum was also being expended in the production of aircraft.[170] The Soviet Union, however, was desperately short of aluminum. When Harry Hopkins paid his first visit to Josef Stalin in July 1941 to ask the Soviet dictator what the country needed to keep fighting in light of the German invasion, the number one priority he was given was immediate aluminum shipments so that the Soviet Union could build more aircraft.[171] From then until the end of the war, the United States poured aluminum into the Soviet Union. By 1943 it was providing the Soviets more of the metal then was actually allocated to the entire United States Navy.[172] By the end of the war, the United States had transferred almost 75,000 tons of processed aluminum and almost 195,000 aluminum bars and ingots to the USSR, 98 percent of which came under lend-lease.[173] Only because of this enormous infusion of aluminum was the USSR able to out-produce the Japanese in aircraft between 1942 and 1944, though the numbers are closer than people often realize, and the Japanese even increased production by a larger number and at a higher rate. (See Table 17.) It is

Table 17 *Japan and USSR: aircraft production, 1942–4*

	1942	1943	1944
Japan	8,861	16,693	28,180
USSR	25,436	34,845	40,246

Note: These figures include all types of aircraft including trainers.
Source: USSBS, Pacific Report 53, p 222.

here that one of the interesting comparisons between Japanese and Soviet construction appears to support Japan as a more advanced industrial and technological power. If the Russians out-produced the Japanese in individual units, the Japanese out-produced the USSR in terms of technological quality. There is something absolutely perplexing about the lack of damage that the USSR was able to inflict despite having so many planes. From early 1942 onwards, the Eastern Front was, even during the height of the Kursk campaign, a minority front for the Luftwaffe. For the rest of the war, between 80 and 70 percent of the Luftwaffe, numerically, was always deployed against the British and Americans. And loss rates for the Luftwaffe fighting against the British and Americans were much higher, even considering that the best pilots and equipment were sent to the west. The Luftwaffe on the Eastern Front was therefore made up of the less-skilled German pilots, often flying out of date technology that had proved to be ineffective during the Battle of Britain in 1940 – such as the JU-87 (Stuka) dive-bomber and the HE-111.[174] Yet, even with the Soviets' overwhelming numerical superiority the loss rates they were able to inflict on the Luftwaffe were modest to say the least.[175] Much of that seems to be down to two elements: the relatively poor performance of Soviet aircraft and the weakness of their pilot-training schemes.

The Japanese, on the other hand, did a far more impressive job in the air war. As Pearl Harbor demonstrated, by 1941 they had trained a superb naval air wing into one of the most dangerous striking forces in the world. Technologically, the Japanese had designed the famous Mitsubishi A6M (Zero/Zeke) fighter which entered active service in 1937. It was not until 1944 that the Russians were able to bring out a fighter that could have fought with the Zero, namely the Yak 3, but even that aircraft was severely restricted in range (one of the most important characteristics of any aircraft) when compared with the Zero. Also in 1944, when the Yak 3 was introduced, the Japanese brought out the Nakajima I-84 (Gale/Frank), one of the most impressive piston-engine fighters of the war. The Frank not only had greater speed than the Yak 3, it had four times the range and much greater firepower. It was able to bring down B-29s at the height of America's strategic bombing offensive against Japan.

The Frank was not alone, however. The Japanese were also able to design and produce two other excellent piston-engine fighters by the end of the war, the navy's Kawanishi N1K George and the army's Ki-100. (The latter never received a formal American nickname.) However, in this case the production records of both were limited because of the collapse of Japanese economic activity brought on by American air and sea power. Both were ready for full production only months after the fall of the Mariana Islands in 1944, which effectively severed Japanese access to the raw materials of the southern empire and severely restricted the flow of materials from China and Manchuria. The upshot was that few of these classes could be built. Certainly any comparison of aircraft, both in terms of design and operation, would point to Japan being a more advanced technological power than the USSR.

While Japan was unable in the end to cope with American production and technology, it showed much greater industrial power than many Eurocentric historians of the war have realized, and its technology in the air–sea war was superior to that of the USSR. Under wartime conditions, it was estimated by the United States that the Japanese were able to double the size of their GDP between 1937 and 1944.[176] Japan also had to operate during the war without the support of its main ally, while the USSR received raw materials and finished goods on an enormous scale, material without which its aircraft construction would have been severely reduced. Japan tried desperately to fight a modern air–sea war, but in the end it was overwhelmed.

2 THE AIR AND SEA WAR AND THE PHASES OF EQUIPMENT DESTRUCTION

Saburo Sakai was one of the most skilled fighter pilots of World War II. In 1942, when at the controls of his Mitsubishi A6M Zero (known to the Americans as the Zeke), a highly maneuverable, fast and long-ranged fighter, he reputedly shot down up to sixty American aircraft in a little more than nine months. As a member the Japanese navy, he could also count on flying with some of the best-trained and most experienced pilots to be found anywhere in the world. Two of his closest friends were Toshia Oto and Hiroyoshi Nishizawa, both among Japan's other legendary fighter aces. On August 8, 1942, however, Sakai's luck ran out.[1] Flying out of the famous Japanese base in Rabaul, he was part of a mission sent to attack American forces which had just appeared off the island of Guadalcanal. As a round trip of 1,300 miles, this was an extremely long-range flight, even by the standards of the Zero. When Sakai reached Guadalcanal, he ended up attacking a large force of new American Avenger torpedo bombers. The tail gunner of one shattered Sakai's cockpit, causing an explosion of glass and metal which ripped into his face and body.

Remarkably, Sakai made it back to a Japanese airstrip, but was so severely wounded that he was sent home. He lost the sight in one of his eyes, so when he felt strong enough to resume duty, he was sent to train the ever-growing number of pilots that modern war demanded from Japan. By the summer of 1944, however, he felt he could no longer serve in a non-combat capacity. When it was clear that the United States was going to assault the Mariana Islands, which many Japanese realized was the linchpin of their home defense, Sakai, even with only one good eye, persuaded his superiors to allow him to return to action. Along with his good friend Nishizawa, he was charged with leading a force of thirty aircraft from the Japanese mainland to the island of Iwo Jima, from where they would be in range of Saipan and Tinian.

Sakai knew that trying to deploy his unit of recently trained pilots over the open ocean posed great dangers. It was the rainy season, and the Japanese had had to slash practice flying time for their new pilots because of severe fuel shortages and the need to make up losses. The new pilots thus lacked the basic skills needed to make the flight in stormy weather. Sakai described the predicament:

> Our experience in such matters had been tragic. Early in 1943, several squadrons of Army fighter planes, manned by pilots who had absolutely no experience in long-distance flying over the ocean, left Japan for a base to the south. En route, they encountered severe weather conditions. Almost every plane disappeared in the endless reaches of the Pacific.[2]

When, on June 16, Sakai's flight encountered bad weather during their first attempt to reach Iwo Jima, the whole unit had to turn back for Japan. Three more times between June 17 and 19, Sakai and Nishizawa tried to guide their fellow fighters to Iwo Jima, but each time the weather proved too much for the new pilots. Finally, on June 20, the weather cleared enough for them to complete the journey, though the inexperienced pilots were forced to stay close on the tails of the veterans. When the flight finally reached Iwo Jima, the runway they were supposed to land on looked too precarious for their new recruits. Nishizawa ordered a change in plans and directed the newer pilots to a safer and simpler landing strip on another part of the island.[3]

The amazing thing about this whole experience was that most of the new Japanese fighters made it to their deployment points – albeit five days late, which meant that they missed the Battle of the Philippine Sea which was ending just as they landed. Having Sakai and Nishizawa to shepherd them kept down losses. At this time many deployment flights, in both the Japanese army and navy, were suffering losses of 25–50 percent. Lt General Torashiro Kawabe was one of the most senior commanders in the Japanese army with a detailed knowledge of the air war. He was the head of the Japanese army's Bureau of

Aeronautics from August 1944 to April 1945, at which time he was promoted to be Deputy Chief of Staff for the entire army. At the end of the war, he ended up representing the Japanese army and was sent to meet with Douglas MacArthur to coordinate Japan's surrender. When Kawabe took over the Bureau of Aeronautics, the Japanese army was redeploying huge numbers of its aircraft from the Japanese home islands to the Philippines, to await the expected American invasion. However, what he discovered was that only a small fraction of the planes sent were in combat-ready condition by the time they landed (if they were lucky enough to actually arrive at all).

> ... At that time, although we didn't have any to spare, I feel that the production was more or less adequate. But of the planes produced in the home country, we couldn't have one hundred percent of them in action at the destination.
>
> Q. What percent could you have, normally?
> A. I can't express it exactly in figures, but it was a very small figure. One of the reasons for that low percentage of planes reaching the destinations which were operational was that, unlike the United States, the maintenance of bases enroute was very poor. Had we been able to set up good bases fast like the United States did, our losses would have been much smaller; but as it turned out, only a very small percentage actually became operational at the destination.
> Q. Well, roughly 10 or 25 percent?
> A. The ones that actually engaged in combat after they left for there, I would guess around 10 percent.[4]

The German experience at the same time was only marginally better. Right after the war Speer and his friend, the highly decorated Luftwaffe pilot Werner Baumbach, were asked to explain why, when German aircraft production was rising sharply in the first half of 1944, this did not result in larger deployed Luftwaffe forces.

> Q. One thing is not clear to us. While the June production was 1,664 fighters, why were there not more than 500–550 planes at the west front during those critical days?
> A. (Speer) More were sent. 2,000 planes were sent which Galland had intended for the defense of homeland production. You never saw them because they had been destroyed in transit flights and on the ground, some by insufficient training...It is our opinion that at the

end about 25 percent of the production was lost during transit flights because of bad training. Is that right Baumbach?

A. (Baumbach) I don't know, but the figures were very high, if not even higher.

A. (Speer) I have seen 8–10 machines land at one drome and 4 crack up.

A. (Baumbach) The loss in transit flights of fighters were 3–4 times as high as ferrying bombers. That is caused mostly by training.[5]

This figure of 25 percent of aircraft being lost in the deployment phase was corroborated immediately after the war by the chief technical director of the Focke-Wulf Company, Dr. Willi Kaether. On April 24, 1945, he was asked to explain why Germany's increased production in aircraft did not result in larger forces in the field. His explanation was identical to that of Speer and Baumbach.

In February 1944, at the time of the decision to launch a vast fighter aircraft expansion program Goering expressed great concern about obtaining the necessary personnel to go with it. Lack of pilots was a great handicap. Not only were pilots lacking in numbers, but the state of their training deteriorated constantly. A situation was reached where the training schedule was reduced to 40 hours. The direct result was an aircraft wastage rate of 25 percent, caused by pilot error.[6]

What both the Japanese and Germans were experiencing by 1944 was a modern air and sea war which saw huge quantities of their equipment being destroyed long before ever reaching combat. It illustrates why the United States and the United Kingdom were absolutely correct to devote so much of their economic strength to producing air and sea weaponry, while Germany and Japan had no alternative but to spend so much of their national production trying to keep pace. The deployment disaster with which Germany and Japan were wrestling was the result of constant pressure being placed on their economic and military systems by the Americans and British. To start with, this constant pressure meant that both nations were struggling to train unexpectedly large numbers of new pilots. Additionally, fuel shortages brought on by Anglo-American attacks meant that these newer pilots were given far fewer hours of flight time before being sent on deployment. The lack of fuel also meant that the engines of the planes they were flying were given far shorter test runs so that fewer faults could be discovered before deployment. Moreover, transportation problems meant that maintenance facilities at the deployment areas were poorly provided with spare parts and the right personnel. And yet this was just one way in which air and sea power destroyed war machinery before it reached combat.

A key reason it was so important to destroy German and Japanese production before it reached the battlefield was because equipment destruction on the battlefield was, until rather late in the war, considerably smaller than equipment output. In the Introduction the battles of Kursk and El Alamein were mentioned, but it was the same with other famous engagements. In the Pacific specific series of days could matter more, because of the relatively high cost of large naval units, especially when combined with the cost of the aircraft needed both to launch from them and to protect them. Aircraft carrier battle groups, including a wide range of ships from the carriers themselves to destroyers, frigates and supply vessels as well as hundreds of aircraft, represented one of the most expensive concentrations of industrial production seen during the war. When they came into contact and ships were sunk, therefore, the cost could be steep, particularly when the ships sunk were aircraft carriers which effectively destroyed many of the aircraft they carried. During the Battle of Midway, which stands out in this regard, Japan lost four of its large aircraft carriers as well as hundreds of its naval aircraft. The lost carriers, the *Kaga*, *Akagi*, *Soryu* and *Hiryu*, represented two-thirds of Japan's large aircraft carrier force at the time, and could not effectively have been replaced for eighteen months. The loss of carrier aircraft also seemed severe, estimated at 257 aircraft during the course of the three-day battle.[7] However, as Japan built 8,861 aircraft of all types in 1942, this loss represented approximately 3 percent of annual aircraft output of the time – or ten days' worth.[8] Counting just naval aircraft, the damage done at Midway would have been approximately twenty days' worth of construction. On the other hand, as carrier battles were so expensive, they were also rare. After Midway, American and Japanese carriers met in direct combat only twice more for a total of three days (the Battle of the Eastern Solomons, August 24, and the Battle of the Santa Cruz Islands, October 26–27) during the rest of 1942.

The numbers of aircraft that Japan lost in straight head-to-head fighting during this phase, while considerable, were not something that the Japanese economy could not replace. The Japanese navy lost

901 naval aircraft fighting the Americans between August 1, 1942 and January 1, 1943.[9] This figure was little more than 10 percent of Japanese aircraft production for the year. The total was only moderately higher than Japanese non-combat naval aircraft losses at the same time, which came in at 680.[10] So, even at this early point of the war in the Pacific, before American air and sea pressure had caused the Japanese to lose more equipment before it reached the battlefield than during the fighting itself, non-battle losses were considerable.

Even the carrier battle that caused the single greatest loss of Japanese aircraft during the entire war, the Battle of the Philippine Sea, simply paced Japanese construction at the time. This battle, which saw so many young, recently trained Japanese pilots confront much more experienced and better-trained American flyers in what came to be known as the "Marianas Turkey Shoot," resulted in appalling Japanese losses. During the two days of fighting, from June 19 to 21, 1944, the Japanese fleet lost 395 carrier aircraft and 31 float planes from all causes including combat and crashes.[11] Naval aircraft losses suffered in combat during all of June 1944 were 789, the highest monthly loss total for Japan of the entire war.[12] In comparison, Japanese production of all combat planes in June 1944 was 1,809.[13] Of that, approximately half would have been naval aircraft. As a way of showing just how important pre-battle losses were in the war against Japan at this point, in 1944 the Japanese navy lost a total of 3,635 aircraft during operations. At the same time it lost 6,675 aircraft outside combat.[14] The pressure of the air and sea war against the Japanese now meant that so many Japanese aircraft were being effectively destroyed before reaching their deployment areas that only a relatively small percentage of Japanese aircraft losses were caused in combat. Only by looking at the totality of equipment losses that occurred through a series of different phases which were regulated by Anglo-American air and sea power can we understand how victory in World War II was achieved.

Pre-production destruction

One of the most efficient methods of destroying equipment, if also very difficult to quantify, is by preventing it from being built in the first place. This "pre-production" destruction of German and Japanese military equipment came through a multi-layered effort that involved some of the most famous campaigns of the war. In basic terms it involved depriving the Axis powers of the raw materials, workers or necessary economic systems needed to produce war material, thus keeping equipment which should have been built from ever coming into existence. Probably the single most devastating example of this was the combined American submarine and air attack on Japanese raw material shipments.

The large empire that Japan had assembled by the middle of 1942 had access to a vast amount of raw materials – enough to dramatically increase Japanese weapons production. As hardly any of these resources were located in Japan itself, they had to be shipped over sea and land before they could be processed into the weapons of war by factories in the home islands. Two of the most vital raw materials were oil and bauxite from the Dutch East Indies. Japan's attack on Pearl Harbor was prompted by the need to have access to both, in particular oil, after shipments from the United States had been embargoed by Franklin Roosevelt. In the short term these strategic needs were very well met. The oil installations in the Dutch East Indies were captured almost entirely intact in early 1942, giving Japan access to more oil than it would need to fight the war.[15] In 1942 Japan was able to ship 1,779,000 kiloliters from the Dutch East Indies, a figure that rose to 3,534,000 kiloliters in 1943.[16] It was then that Japan's oil situation went into disastrous decline. This was due not to any problem in production but to a sustained attack on Japanese shipping. At first a successful submarine campaign waged by the United States Navy began seriously affecting oil shipments starting in September 1943.[17] In the summer of 1944, after the fall of the Mariana Islands, this was combined with a USN and USAAF air campaign to sever almost completely the shipping lanes between the Dutch East Indies and Japan. The losses that Japan suffered in tanker tonnage were catastrophic. Plenty of oil was available for shipment to Japan well into 1945; it was simply impossible to make the journey.[18] In 1944 only about 50 percent of the oil destined for Japan, or approximately 1,800,000 kiloliters, ever reached the home islands.[19] By April 1945, the shipping link between Japan and its southern empire was completely broken.[20]

In the same way that oil was cut off, so were Japanese imports of bauxite, needed to maintain the impressive increase in Japanese aircraft production from 1942 to the middle of 1944. The original plan of the Japanese government was to import a million tons of bauxite a year from the Dutch East Indies and the Palau Islands, almost entirely to support aircraft construction in the home islands.[21] In 1943 the plan was well on its way, as 820,430 tons arrived safely in the home islands.[22] Had the eventual target figure been reached – and the issue was never one of access to the raw materials, rather one of shipping – Japanese aluminum production would have come close to matching Germany's. Japan had the capacity to produce approximately 400,000 tons of aluminum a year if the bauxite was available for refining, but thanks to the shipping crisis, in the end it only produced a maximum of 225,000 tons.[23] Shutting off access to oil and bauxite prevented many thousands of Japanese aircraft from being built.

On the other hand, probably the most famous pre-production campaign of the war was considerably less successful. This was the attempt by the RAF to destroy German production by depriving it of workers through the area bombing of German cities. This campaign is often mistakenly referred to as "morale" bombing – but this is a simplification. It was also aimed at destroying production. One of the motivating factors behind the campaign was the hope that it would either de-house, demoralize or outright kill so many Germans that the economy would grind to a halt and, perhaps, the German people would themselves find a way to dispose of the National Socialist government. Because of its overt attempt to attack civilians, British area bombing became contentious during the war, and has been heavily debated since.[24] It will be discussed in greater detail later, but a quick overview would show that, in terms of denying the Germans war production, this campaign, which was very expensive for the United Kingdom to undertake, had at best modest effects. Almost all of the Germans with a knowledge of war production claimed after the war that area bombing was the least effective strategic bombing campaign that they faced. The United States Strategic Bombing Survey was actually kinder than most and estimated that overall German production (not just munitions) would have been reduced by 9 percent in 1943 and 17 percent in 1944.[25] However, the impact of this reduction specifically on munitions would have been considerably less as the Germans reduced civilian production to make up the shortfall. The United Kingdom Strategic Bombing Survey made even further investigations into the impact of area bombing on German munitions production. This survey was considerably more negative in its conclusions about the impact of area bombing than the American one. After studying the manufacturing

industries in the twenty most heavily bombed German cities, it concluded that war munitions production was brought down by only small
amounts in 1943 and 1944. During 1943 it estimated that war production was reduced on average by 2.8 percent and in 1944 by only
1 percent.[26]

While these estimates are not to be read as gospel, it does seem
that area bombing was not a particularly successful way of preventing
German equipment being built. However, strategic air power did hold
out other far more effective options for pre-production destruction.
Maybe the most important of these was the transportation campaigns
of 1944 and 1945 against both Germany and Japan. Ripping up
Germany's transport network, primarily its rail network, but also its
river and canal traffic, prevented equipment from being built through a
number of means, including depriving German factories of power
through halting the supply of coal throughout the economy.[27] Attacks
like these help explain why German production peaked when it did.[28]
There was no other reason, even with the loss of territory Germany
suffered in the summer and fall of 1944, why German production
should have fallen significantly at this time. Even with these losses,
German stockpiles of raw materials were so large that not only could
production have continued to rise, it could have maintained that pace
for at least another year and a half.

The final area of pre-production losses did involve the loss of
workers, though in a different way. The destruction caused by strategic
bombing in Germany and Japan was so great that millions of workers
had to be redeployed from different productive areas of the economy,
to repair and clean-up duties.[29] For instance, Germany's hydrogenation
plants, which converted coal into aviation-grade fuel, became the
subject of regular attacks in the spring of 1944. When these started,
their survival was considered so important that the German government assigned 150,000 workers to their constant repair and upkeep.[30]
On August 3, Speer addressed a conference of Gauleiters in Posen, and
mentioned how shifting workers away from direct construction was
harming output.

> For it is obvious that, in this complicated, individualized work of
> removing air raid damage, it is unfortunately necessary to employ
> for the most part only German workers. We estimate the loss of
> armament potential due to air attacks at an average of 30 percent

of our total armament capacity. In other words, we should be able to produce 30 percent more than the figures already given to you, if we could regain air superiority at home...[31]

Germany's rail network caused even more worker reallocation. When the campaign against it became intense in late summer 1944, up to 2 million workers were devoted to keeping Germany's rail network and oil production operational. Field Marshal Milch described how, by the summer of 1944, repairing bomb damage to Germany's oil system and transportation network (which he deemed communications) had become one of the overriding priorities of the German worker.

> There are two targets which are vulnerable in Germany: the synthetic oil plants, and communications. The invasion in the North of France would never have been so successful if communications had still been working properly. Then the Allies completely destroyed the area to the left of the Rhine in Germany, then completely destroyed the area to the right of the Rhine as far as the Ems, then as far as the Weser, then as far as the Elbe, and did it so systematically that we could no longer carry on any transport. We took a million workers out of the armament factories in order to put them on repair of communications, but it was too late to win the race. We already had 800,000 people on the job and wanted to repair the lines again with 1,800,000.[32]

By 1944 American and British air and sea power were clearly reducing the amount of weaponry being built by a very large amount. They were severely restricting the flow of raw materials throughout the Japanese and German empires so that factories could not produce to capacity. The destruction of energy resources, meanwhile, meant that factories could not operate to full efficiency. Moreover, the brutal campaigns waged against Japanese and German civilians played a real role in holding down output through increased absenteeism, lethargy, depression and the shifting of workers into repair positions.

Production and destruction

Destroying war equipment at the place where it was being built was one of the great ambitions of interwar air policy in both the United

States and Great Britain. Both developed plans to obliterate the factories that produced their enemy's weapons of war in either their component or assembly phases. For the USA this became a particularly
important task as American technology made it seem that the USAAF
could hit targets accurately in daylight.

Considering the amount of attention paid to direct production
destruction before World War II, the successes in this area were modest
initially. Early the British in the war suffered very high losses flying in
daylight, and rarely hit any of their intended targets, so by 1942 they
switched to more area bombing, which worked by concentrating a large
number of bombers over a considerably larger target.[33] The USAAF,
however, mostly planned its 1943 campaign against Germany around
the notion of destroying specific areas of production, most famously
Germany's ball-bearing and aircraft industries. Though these attacks
are usually portrayed as failures, the destruction they caused compares
well with that of the more famous battlefields. This is particularly the
case with the attacks on German aircraft production. Two raids in
1943 caused significant losses in German fighter output: the August raid
against Regensburg, a center of ME-109 (or BF-109) production, and an
October raid that completely destroyed an FW-190 plant in Marienburg
(figure 8).[34] The losses caused were far larger than those which occurred
in the skies over Kursk or even Sicily. Field Marshal Milch, who was in
charge of German aircraft production until March 1944, calculated that
these raids were mostly responsible for a 25 percent reduction in

8 A B-17 after one of the more successful American strategic bombing attacks of
1943, an attack on the Focke-Wulf assembly plant in Marienburg. Though
successes like this were not common in 1943, when they did occur they destroyed
a larger amount of Luftwaffe production than more famous battles such as
Kursk or El Alamein.

German output.[35] He stated that German fighter output was expected to have reached 2,000 units a month by the end of 1943, but was kept to approximately 1,000 by the raids on German airframe production. It was the best example in 1943 of a significant amount of German equipment being destroyed before it reached the field of battle.

> During June/July [1943], however, the heavy raids – mainly American, but also English – started, which had as their chief target the air-frame industry. As a result we were not able to produce more than those 1,000 fighters a month from August 1943 until February 1944. The additional number which we would have produced was destroyed. According to the programme, by January 1944 we should have reached the figure of 2,000 fighters a month. . .[36]

The view from within the German fighter aircraft industry supports Milch's outlook. The August attacks on ME-109 production at Regensburg destroyed more aircraft than an entire average month's losses on either the Mediterranean or the Eastern Front. Messerschmitt himself, while trying to minimize the impact of the raids, said that they "only" inflicted a 30–40 percent loss of production for approximately a month.[37] However, he also admitted that the dispersal plan that was put in place after the August raids reduced Germany's potential output by 50 percent until well into 1944.[38] Even assuming this is slightly overstated, the total effect on German output of ME-109s in the last six months of 1943 would have been the loss of between 2,000 and 3,000 aircraft.

The Focke-Wulf production losses, even with the complete destruction of the Marienburg plant, were less dramatic. As Marienburg was a final assembly yard, the main destruction was of aircraft actually being assembled at the moment of the raid.[39] It seems that approximately one hundred aircraft were destroyed there, and that no assembly could take place for another four months. Dr. Kaether, the chief technical director of the Focke-Wulf company endorsed these figures.[40]

However, these direct attacks did damage Focke-Wulf production by leading them to undertake large-scale dispersion as well.[41] By the spring of 1944, the German aircraft industry was dispersing 27 main productive factories into 729 separate plants.[42] There was an important change in the type of dispersal in 1944 as well. Earlier dispersals aimed to move the plants out of the supposed range of American and British bombers. The new plants, however, were still to be built above ground in normal industrial buildings. In early 1944 the dispersals were ordered to be below ground or into concrete-based structures specifically designed to protect the production facilities from bomb attacks. Milch described the shift as follows:

> When I took the thing over at the end of 1941, my first step was to give the order to disperse from the factories immediately, and out of a floor space of 12 million square meters, 4 million were moved further out, but not below ground. The decision to do that was only made at the beginning of 1944. It was then said that there would be buildings below ground and concreted ones, similar to the big U-boat shelters on the Channel coast. The reason for the long delay was the persistent belief that the war would end victoriously. Goering always believed there would be no large-scale bombing, and always tried to deny the possibility.[43]

Dispersal caused real problems for the Luftwaffe in more areas than just lost production. These facilities were considerably less efficient in output per worker than larger, more rationally ordered ones. A major problem was that the new factories, built with great haste, produced aircraft with more structural flaws. Goering believed that this was a particular problem that came to haunt the Luftwaffe in 1944. The quality of aircraft built in the dispersed factories "suffered considerably. It happened, for instance, that the fittings at the assembly were not accurate enough and similar things. Sometimes it was just that the fittings on the wing section were rough, in other cases the two landing wheels were different."[44]

Another area in which destruction of German production in 1943 was almost as successful as the aircraft attacks was in finished metal production, both steel and aluminum. The USAAF estimated after the war that German steel ingot production in 1943 was reduced by 13.7 percent and in 1944 by 25.2 percent.[45] In 1944, Speer's ministry estimated that crude steel production was reduced by 6.4 percent in 1943 by the combined impact of all bombing.[46] The situation was similar for aluminum production. In 1943 there were some modest successes. Most importantly, in July of that year the Giulini aluminum processing factory in Ludwigshafen was hit.[47] This one attack reduced

German annual production of alumina by 27,000 tons (or of finished aluminum by 13,000 tons). However, in 1944 the damage inflicted was considerably higher. Two major plants, the Luftschiffbau Zeppelin and the Lautawerk plants at Lausitz, were almost completely destroyed, with significant damage being done to other factories. It was estimated that by December 1944 the aircraft industry was deprived of 25,000 tons of finished aluminum through these attacks, which was enough to provide for the construction of 7,000 aircraft.[48]

Going back to 1943, it would be fair to say that the total number of German aircraft, mostly fighters, destroyed because of factory destruction, relocation and aluminum losses would have been at least between 5,000 and 6,000. This estimate is in line with strategic bombing survey calculations and the differences between German intended and actual outputs. The USSBS estimated that between July 1943 and December 1944 German aircraft production was reduced by 18,492 units because of strategic bombing, of which number 14,353 were fighters.[49] This all makes sense when one looks at how the rise in German aircraft construction stopped immediately in July 1943, and levelled off, with some noticeable declines, until February 1944 (see Figures 41 and 43 in Chapter 8.)

Japanese aircraft factories were also some of the first targets of American strategic bombers. Though the American bombing against Japan has become famous (or infamous) for the incineration of Japanese cities, at first, as in Europe, they expended most of their effort to try and destroy specific industrial targets.[50] Admiral Soemu Toyoda, who became commander in chief of the combined fleet in May 1944 after Admiral Koga was killed, believed that the bombing was one factor, but certainly not the most important, in the halving of naval aircraft construction between 1944 and 1945.[51] In the case of the Mitsubishi Corporation, the builder of the Zero fighter and many other types of aircraft from bombers to trainers and reconnaissance planes, the bombing of two specific plants did reduce production significantly. Their main airplane engine factory in Nagoya was heavily damaged on December 13, 1944 and their main airframe factory was hit on December 19. These raids were crucial in cutting all Mitsubishi aircraft production by one-third.[52] For those in charge at Mitsubishi, these raids were devastating. They destroyed any illusions they had about the future of the war, and for the first time they admitted there were feelings of "helplessness and hopelessness."[53]

These Nagoya raids also set off a chain reaction within Japanese munitions production which reduced construction across the board. According to Teijiro Toyoda, they caused a dispersal of industry into smaller plants which was not a success – because of the increased bombing of small towns.

> The destruction of the two Mitsubishi plants in Nagoya was remarkably complete and the loss of those plants was very important to us. You know that the growth of the Japanese aircraft industry had been remarkably rapid and as a result relies heavily on small and home industries. Besides the precision attacks, your destruction of the little plants in the smaller cities hit by bombing reduced our productive power greatly.
>
> Q. What steps did you take to overcome the destruction of the little plants and industries?
> A. The small plants were scattered all over the country in an attempt to avoid destruction. However, when you attacked our transportation facilities and bombed the small cities in which so much transportation had been established, our production was dealt a fatal blow.[54]

When it came to other areas of munitions production, the results of direct air attacks are not always the easiest to measure. Finished metal production, such as the conversion of iron ore to steel or bauxite into aluminum, was certainly reduced by bombing, though the direct air attacks always seemed less effective than the campaign to stop the pre-production transportation of the raw materials. In the end the attacks specifically on Japanese factories destroyed a large amount of military equipment before it could be produced. Though most Japanese with an intimate knowledge of their economic situation believed that the American campaign to isolate transportation of materials in and out of Japan did relatively more damage, the direct attacks, particularly on the aircraft industry around Nagoya, weakened Japan's ability to resist significantly.

However, the USAAF soon abandoned these kinds of industry attacks in favor of the wholesale destruction of Japanese cities. Much of the motivation behind this move was to make the USAAF's role in the defeat of Japan more obvious.[55] The ensuing firebombing of Tokyo, the most destructive air raid of the war in human terms, ushered in a change which saw the Americans obliterate huge parts of most of Japan's cities. However, the production benefits of this shift are not easy to calculate. Earlier industry attacks, combined with the almost total severing of Japanese trade, meant that Japan's production was already in terminal decline when this targeting shift occurred.

What is clear is that while destruction of specific production areas in the war was not as effective as pre-war analysts had expected, it did play an important part in the destruction of German and Japanese munitions. Combined with all the pre-production losses, these raids not only destroyed as much German and Japanese equipment as many famous land battles, they caused industrial dispersal and worker reallocation, all of which cut significantly into German and Japanese output. There was no one magic bullet amongst all the effects, but together, they were devastating.

Deployment and destruction

Returning to the subject at the start of this chapter, we need to consider the losses of equipment that occurred during deployment – after it had been produced, but before it was used against the enemy. This is one of the most important but least understood ways in which the air and sea war weakened the fighting strength of the Axis powers – particularly as the war progressed. By 1943 and 1944, these deployment losses were some of the most debilitating being suffered by Germany and Japan, and by late 1944 they were catastrophic. The single most expensive example was the enormous loss of German and Japanese aircraft while being deployed. It is interesting to note that this even affected Germany's highest priority and most advanced aircraft program in the last year of the war. In 1944 and 1945, great efforts were put into building and deploying the ME-262 jet fighter as Germany's last, best hope to win back air control over the country's production systems. However, insufficient pilot training, a lack of fuel and maintenance shortfalls meant that more than half of the 1,400 ME-262s that Germany was able to build were destroyed outside of combat owing to poorly trained or equipped pilots, lack of fuel or inadequate support facilities.[56]

For Japan this problem began earlier than for Germany, because of the immense geographic size of its empire, which encompassed an area many times that of the Reich. As the Japanese expanded their defensive perimeter across the Pacific Ocean in the first six months of the war, it meant that pilots on their first deployment often had to take extremely long flights over the open ocean for thousands of miles. Had the Japanese been able to ship all of their new planes to forward bases using carriers, this could have been controlled. However, as preserving Japanese carrier strength became important after Midway, they were used less frequently to deploy aircraft. After 1942 the Imperial Japanese Navy (IJN) regularly flew about half its planes to their deployment bases, using carriers to transport the other half.[57] The army, on the other hand, with no regular access to carriers, seems to have flown far more of its aircraft directly. In many cases that left many pilots needing to fly all the way from Japan to a forward deployment thousands of miles away.

These pilots had to fly themselves over distances many times larger than that from Berlin to Stalingrad. (See Map 7.) For instance, to deploy an aircraft to Rabaul on the island of New Britain, Japanese army pilots had to fly from Kyushu to Formosa and then to the Philippines and from there to Rabaul.[58] Many of the new pilots, who were not used to long flights over the open ocean, disappeared before reaching Formosa.

Major C. Takahash of the Japanese army's aircraft supply section and Captain T. Takeuchi who was in charge of the department that kept statistics for the section, both stated that from early on in the war, 50 percent of Japanese army aircraft were not reaching their deployment points. As the Japanese empire contracted, the situation if anything seemed to get worse.

Q. You have stated that ferrying losses averaged 50 percent throughout the war. Was the figure really that high during the early stages?

A. Yes, early in the war the haul down to the southern areas was much longer and any number of things occurred enroute. Later, when the haul became shorter, engine failures between Kyushu and Formosa accounted for heavy losses. Another factor was the decline in effectiveness of maintenance personnel. Virtually all the best technicians were sent to forward areas, got stuck there and could not return.[59]

The Japanese navy, maintaining the strict separation of the services that was such a problem for Japanese war-making, had an equally difficult deployment procedure. Under its system, new navy pilots being deployed to Rabaul usually left from the Yokusuka base in Honshu. They were first sent to Saipan with a possible stop in Iwo Jima. If they were lucky enough to complete this route, they then had to fly over completely open ocean to the large fleet base at Truk in the Caroline Islands and from there to Rabaul.[60] Even those Navy pilots who made it to Truk, therefore proving that their planes were in good working order and their flying skills were relatively strong, often disappeared before reaching Rabaul. Captan C. Kanai, who was in charge of the IJN's Southeast Air Depot based in Rabaul, said that 5 percent of the aircraft which took off from Truk never reached their forward destination.[61]

Aircraft losses may have been the most dramatic, but it was also the case that significant amounts of equipment for the land war could also be destroyed while it was on its way to deployment. This highlights one of the more modern ways that air power was used by the British and Americans when compared with the other powers. On the Eastern Front, for instance, neither the Germans nor the Russians spent much effort interdicting the flow of supplies from the factories to the front. Instead, the overwhelming focus was on using air power in a tactical sense of battlefield operations or attacks on troop concentrations close to the front lines. For the Germans, this meant a great simplification of their defensive thinking in the east, and it also allowed the USSR much greater freedom of action in planning its assaults. This phenomenon led many German soldiers with experience of fighting in the east to assume that this was somehow a "normal" way of warfare when compared with the extraordinarily different experience of protecting supply lines in the west.[62]

Major General Erich Dethleffsen was a decorated and vastly experienced Wehrmacht officer who served continually on the Eastern Front from 1941 to 1945, except when recuperating from injuries. As a staff officer for the 4th Army in 1944, he had intimate experience of German supply problems. He said there were few attacks on German reinforcements heading to the front until very late in the war. When asked directly what percentage of reinforcement trains heading to the Eastern Front were damaged or destroyed before reaching their destinations, he replied "infinitesimal."[63] Other officers with an intimate knowledge of transporting German supplies support this view. General Gehrke Peters was named transportation chief of "Central Germany" from 1942 to 1945. In this role he was responsible for coordinating the transportation of all army, Luftwaffe and German navy supplies on road and rail, reporting directly to the overall transport chief for the armed forces. Peters described a very different supply/reinforcement situation on each front. In the west, trains had to be stopped far from the front and troops and supplies they carried sent on by road to avoid air assaults. Troops heading to fight against the Normandy invasion sometimes had to be de-trained as far away from the fighting as Germany itself, to protect them on their way to combat.[64] Even then they could suffer destructive attacks long before they reached the front. By 1945 attacks on the transport system in the west were considered so destructive that 80–90 percent of the expected supplies could not get through. In the east, even at this late date, the situation was thought to be "much better."[65] The Quartermas-ter General of the Wehrmacht from the time of the July 1944 plot against Hitler until April 1945, Major General Toppe, also claimed that there was a very different supply situation in the west and east until almost the end of the war.[66] When asked about the situation on the Eastern Front in early 1945, he stated that Russian attacks on German supply lines caused almost no damage.

> Q. How did the situation look at the East front as far as transportation and communications systems were concerned?
> A. There were no difficulties at the East front as far as transportation and communication systems were concerned.
> Q. Until when?
> A. Until the end.

The situation in the west was very different, with whole shipments disappearing. Field Marshal Keitel claimed that in the last part of the war, whole trains of AFV vanished while trying to deploy their cargo.

> Every 50 or 100 km. that a tank has to run on the road under its own power to the zone of operations constitutes needless wear and tear. We, therefore, used rail transport to bring them up as far as possible. Due to the large destruction of our transportation needs, the [sic] whole train of tanks were often "lost"; nobody knew where they were and, consequently, they did not reach the front. In the east, we were able to move the tank on the railroad to within twenty miles of the front.[67]

For the Japanese, the destruction of land forces while being deployed was in many ways an even more difficult task because of the air–sea war. Reinforcing their troops scattered over thousands of miles of Pacific islands called for convoys of vulnerable shipping which, as the war progressed, were besieged by submarine, surface vessel and aircraft attacks. The scale of the deployment task they had undertaken was made clear as soon as the fighting broke out on Guadalcanal in August 1942. Needing to rush forces into hold the island, in September the Japanese started shipping into the island two of their best fighting divisions, the 38th based in Hong Kong and the 2nd based in Java. Each had to be transported more than 3,000 miles to reach their destination.[68]

In the eyes of many Japanese, it was the toll taken on the convoys heading to Guadalcanal, not the fighting on the island, which really decided the course of the battle. Lt General Shuichi Miyazaki, who served as chief of staff to the Japanese 17th Army during the fighting on Guadalcanal, was one of these.

> The biggest problem was the loss of ships. Actually the bombing of troops and troop concentrations on the ground was not much of a hindrance because, although the bombing scared everybody and made lots of noise and had an effect on morale, the actual destruction was not great. The biggest problem was the loss of our capacity to move these troops to the fighting areas. I myself was bombed and I still have a fragment of bomb in my back.[69]

Later in the war the losses suffered trying to reinforce other islands were even larger. The Japanese started trying to beef up the defenses of the Mariana Islands in 1944, when they realized that the Americans might attack them next. Many of the convoys carrying these reinforcements were destroyed either wholly or in part.[70] Even weapons being deployed by submarine could be destroyed before arrival. For instance, the Japanese decided to deploy their notorious chemical and biological weapons Unit 731, based in Manchuria, to the islands, complete with porcelain canisters of bacteria-laden fleas.[71] Thankfully, the submarine carrying this horrific cargo, and many other Japanese vessels trying to bring material to the Marianas, were sunk.

Major General Inichiro Sanada, who served on the army's General Staff and in the War Ministry from 1941 to 1945, said that in 1943 a plan was made to withdraw almost all the artillery pieces in Manchuria to supply army forces fighting in the Pacific islands. Most of this equipment was eventually assigned to the Philippines, Iwo Jima or Okinawa. However, a majority of it was lost in transit.[72] In the specific case of Iwo Jima, 75 percent of the equipment dispatched never reached the island.

By 1944 only a minority of the war-making potential of Japan and Germany was actually able to be put into "battle." Pre-production, production and deployment losses meant that this equipment was either never built or never reached theater to be used to destroy Allied military forces. The reduction of Japanese and German transport and raw material systems meant that the basis of their production was limited long before the factories of finished production were involved. The attacks on these factories not only destroyed production, but led to mass redistributions of industrial workers, and in some cases an inefficient and expensive dispersal of production. Even when equipment was produced, it was often destroyed before being put into combat. This could happen because the pressure of the air war so diminished German and Japanese pilot training that the human raw material was not up to the task. Also ships and trains carrying the equipment to the fields of battle were destroyed en route. Gauging an exact percentage for all of this crucial pre-battlefield destruction is impossible. However, being cautious, it seems that in 1943 at least a quarter of Japanese and German potential and actual construction was destroyed before battle, and by 1944 this figure would have been well over 50 percent.

Air and sea power and the determination of the land war

On September 20, 1944, Major General F. W. von Mellenthin arrived in Alsace to take over as Chief of Staff to the German Army Group G.[73] Mellenthin was one of the most experienced German commanders of the war, having fought in Poland, France in 1940, the deserts of North Africa in 1941 and 1942, and on the Eastern Front from Stalingrad through the summer of 1944. What he encountered in Alsace, however, was the kind of tactical air power that he had never experienced previously. Two days after he arrived he observed his first German counterattack against an American position.

> The morning of 22 September was shrouded in fog so our tanks were protected against the dreaded fighter-bombers which dominated the battlefields of the West. At first the attack of the

111th Panzer Brigade against Juwelize went well, but as soon as the sky cleared the "Fabos" [German slang for fighter-bombers] swarmed down on the panzers. American artillery kept up a heavy fire, and their tanks put in a vigorous counter-attack. The result was that the 111th Panzer Brigade was virtually destroyed and at the end of the day was left with seven tanks and eighty men.

This was hardly a promising introduction to Army Group G; it was clear that American air power put our panzers at a hopeless disadvantage, and that the *normal* principles of armored warfare did not apply in this theater. (Emphasis added.)[74]

What stands out is Mellenthin's use of the word "normal." His experience of the war to this point had been one in which German armor had maintained relatively good mobility, even in the face of Anglo-American or Russian tactical air power. By the late summer of 1944, however, he was fighting in an entirely different world.

In discussing the role of air power in shaping land battles during World War II, a great deal of focus has been placed on tactical usage – the direct attacks of aircraft on enemy ground forces.[75] Some actually believe that it was the effectiveness of tactical air power over strategic that was the most important lesson of the war, one that remains true to this day.[76] On the other hand, some German and Japanese military men described Allied tactical air power, particularly before 1943, more as a great inconvenience than as a war-winning weapon.[77] There certainly were teething problems in the first part of the war.[78] However, in 1944, German and Japanese equipment losses became considerably higher than in earlier years. One of the key factors in this was a great loss of mobility. At some point in 1943 both Germany and Japan lost any prospect of air and sea control over the battlefield, and despite desperate efforts they could never win it back. As such they lost freedom of movement, particularly during the day. Troops engaged could still fight ferociously in well-designed defensive positions, and inflict great casualties on the Allied forces, but it became increasingly difficult to supply them and, when their lines were broken, it became much more complex, if not impossible, to extricate them.

Until well into 1943 the Luftwaffe was usually able to provide the Wehrmacht some protection over the space of combat, which allowed German land forces mobility going forward and, crucially, when being pushed back. Even after the surrender of their forces at

Stalingrad and in Tunisia in 1943, the Germans were able to extricate troops from perilous situations such as the Soviet breakthrough in Ukraine in early 1943 or from Sicily in August 1943 because there was enough Luftwaffe support in the area, if not to control the air space over combat, at least to contest it. For Japan this transition had started a few months earlier. Throughout 1942, during the struggle of Guadalcanal, the Japanese were able to contest with the Americans for air, and also sea, control around the island. This allowed them to both resupply their forces and, when needed, evacuate a good number of them. However, after this brutal struggle, the Japanese were never again able to seriously contest air superiority over the area of fighting for more than a few days or even hours. The fighting during the famous island campaigns that followed could be horrible in its intensity, but the Japanese defenders stood no chance of victory – their only strategic role was to inflict as many casualties as possible on the American forces before being killed.

One of the best ways to measure the change in the fighting on the ground caused by this lack of mobility is by looking at German and Japanese casualties. Military casualties in terms of battlefield deaths for the Germans and Japanese through 1943 were not high by World War I standards. In fact, during the first four years and three months of World War II (the length of World War I), German casualties were almost 15 percent fewer than those of 1914–18. German military deaths from all causes between September 1, 1939 and November 30, 1943 were 1,776,670,[79] while those during World War I as a whole were just over 2 million.[80] Moreover, the casualties suffered by the Germans in World War II came from a considerably larger population base. In 1914 Germany went into the war with a population of approximately 68 million. In September 1939 the Reich, including Austria and the Sudetenland, had a population of approximately 80 million. In terms of overall population, therefore, German casualties during the first four years and three months of World War II were running at a rate only 72 percent as high as during World War I.

It is hard to argue, from this, that manpower losses were somehow crippling for the Germans before 1944. From 1942 into 1945, General Walter Buhle was in command of the OKW section in charge of personnel.[81] In this role he was responsible for seeing that the Wehrmacht's needs for troops were met. He claimed that, in manpower terms, German armed forces remained remarkably constant during that

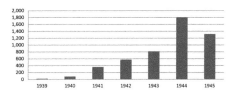

9 Germany: military deaths from all causes, 1939–45 (in thousands)
Source: Overmans, *Deutsche Militärische Verluste*, p. 239.

time, at about 9 million in total, only declining markedly near the end of the war.[82]

However, in 1944 and 1945 the Germans experienced a dramatic leap in casualties, losing more men killed in 1944 alone than they lost during the entire time between 1939 and 1943. In 1945 these losses continued at this extreme pace, with the Germans losing almost as many men between January and April of that year as they lost in 1942 and 1943 combined. The difference between 1944 and earlier is stark, as shown in figure 9.

Japanese battle deaths before 1944 were also modest when compared with what came afterwards. Though it seems impossible to find exact figures on a year-by-year basis, the main battles for the islands of the Pacific became many times more expensive in human lives for the Japanese as the war developed. Japanese casualties during the fighting over Guadalcanal were actually rather modest considering that fighting on the island went on for more than six months. Samuel Morison claims that the Japanese lost 14,800 killed in operations, with approximately 1,000 taken prisoner.[83] Moreover, as American air dominance at this time was far from complete, the Japanese, in an impressive operation, were able to evacuate 11,706 men from Guadalcanal in early February 1943.[84] Later island campaigns, however, were fought under conditions of almost total loss of air and sea control. As such the casualty rates were much higher and were suffered in much shorter time periods. Once American troops made it ashore, the fate of the Japanese island defenders was sealed, as they could neither be resupplied nor reinforced nor could they move easily around their defensive positions.

By late 1943 the Americans were able to assault the Gilbert and Marshall Islands under conditions of air and sea dominance. Even though the Japanese fought skillfully and fanatically, their garrisons were destroyed in a few days with almost total loss of life. On Betio, the tiny (291 acres) island on the Tarawa atoll that the Japanese had fortified, the entire garrison of more than 4,500 troops was wiped out in four days.[85] In July 1944, during the struggle over the Mariana Islands, the Japanese navy committed every ship and plane that it could to contest air and sea control with the United States. It actually committed as many fighter aircraft to try and control a few small Pacific islands as the Luftwaffe had on the entire Eastern Front at the same time. Nevertheless, the Japanese lost control of both air and sea and the island garrison was marooned. On Saipan they lost approximately 30,000 military personnel killed or missing in three weeks of fighting, twice as many men as lost on Guadalcanal in less than 15 percent of the time.[86] From that point on Japanese casualties continued to skyrocket. During the fighting to stop American attempts to retake the Philippines, Japanese military casualties probably exceeded 300,000 in less time than it took the United States to take Guadalcanal.

The loss rates for German land equipment accelerated in a similar fashion after 1943. Through early 1944 they were not crippling by any reasonable standard, but lagged considerably behind production. However, in the summer of 1944, army losses shot up so that in only a four-month period between July and October they far outstripped production for the first time. Looking at the numbers of the most numerous types of panzers being accepted into the German army in 1944 – Panzer IVs and Panthers – the dramatic nature of this change is clear.[87] (See Figures 10 and 11.) Many of these panzers were lost in two of the defining land campaigns of the summer of 1944: the collapse of Army Group Center on the Eastern Front and the fighting in France after the Normandy landings. German losses were so high in those engagements because, for the first time in the war, the army was

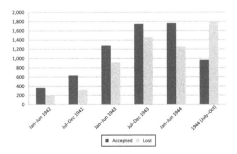

10 Germany: Panzer IVs accepted into service and lost, 1942–4, in six-month intervals

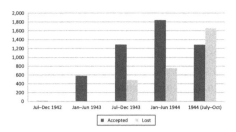

11 Germany: Panzer Vs accepted into service and lost, 1942–4, in
six-month intervals

fighting without any effective air cover. The battlefields had, effectively, been stripped of German fighter planes, which were desperately
needed in the skies over Germany itself.

This shift of German air power away from the land battlefield
began in 1943. During the first half of the year, the Germans built
up three large air forces, one in each of the theaters fighting three
quite distinct battles. On the Eastern Front, after the fall of Stalingrad,
a large force made up of one-quarter fighters and three-quarters ground
attack or transport aircraft was assembled to support the Kursk attacks;
in the Mediterranean, a force that was about equally split between
fighters and bombers was deployed to try to halt the invasion of Sicily;
and in the Reich/on the Western Front, a force that was about three-
quarters fighters was deployed primarily to fight against the Combined
Bomber Offensive. In overall percentage terms, 45 percent of the
Luftwaffe was on the Eastern Front, 33 percent was in the Reich/on
the Western Front and 21 percent was in the Mediterranean.

However, that was the last moment when the Luftwaffe
dispersed itself so fully. With Russian successes on the Eastern Front,
an invasion of Sicily and Italy, and a Combined Bomber Offensive
against German cities and industry, a decision was made that the last
was the greatest threat to German power, and thus began a decisive
shift in deployment. By December 30, 1943, 54 percent of all aircraft
were in Germany/on the Western Front, and by December 30, 1944 this
figure had jumped to 67 percent. In terms of fighters, by far the largest
portion of German aircraft production in 1944, the shift away from the
Eastern Front and Mediterranean was even more pronounced. In the
second half of 1944, 80 percent of German fighters were deployed
facing Anglo-American bombers or Anglo-American armies on the
Western Front. (See figure 12.) What this meant was that German land

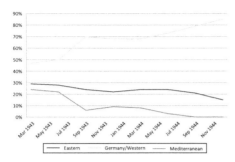

12 Germany: fighter deployment (all types) by percent and front, May 1943–
November 1944
Source: Air 40/1207, "German Air Force First Line Strength during the
European War, 1939–1945."

armies during the great battles of 1944 had to operate in conditions
where the Allies controlled the skies over the Wehrmacht on all fronts.
The few German planes left on the Eastern Front no longer regularly
flew air patrols in large formation, but instead acted in a ground attack
role.[88] These operations left the skies open to the Red Air Force and
drastically reduced the mobility of German land forces. During the
fighting in France, though the Luftwaffe did try to intervene with much
greater force, the result was the same. No matter how many fighters
they committed – and at different times they did commit many
hundreds or even more than a thousand at one moment – they simply
could not dent Anglo-American air supremacy. The German army
could and did continue to fight bravely and stubbornly on the defensive. However, it could move only with great difficulty, and once its
lines were penetrated, more often than not it was left to surrender in
place or walk away and leave its equipment.

Even Hitler came to realize that the crisis facing his army
everywhere in the summer of 1944 was the result of a shortage of
fighters for the battlefield.[89] In one of his interminable monologues in
late July 1944, just after the attempt by Von Stauffenberg to assassinate
him, he claimed that if only Germany could build up a mass force of
2,000 fighters, it could tip the balance in the war. Just looking at
German production figures, such a hope did not seem unrealistic. In
August 1944 alone Germany produced 3,020 fighters of all types.[90]
Yet, their constant attrition, both in combat and from non-combat
actions, meant that Hitler's hope remained unfulfilled. Indeed, it is
remarkable, considering that German production of fighters grew

markedly in the first seven months of 1944, that the number on active deployment remained flat. Goering explained this through a combination of high operational and non-operational losses (he generally believed that Germany was losing one fighter through non-combat operations for each one it lost in combat).[91] The non-operational cause that he talked about in most detail was the collapse of the German transport system.[92] This meant that planes with damage that could be repaired could neither be transported to a repair site nor receive the necessary spare parts to enable it to be repaired at its deployment base. The Reichsmarschall also believed that the decline in pilot quality was responsible for the growing losses suffered while deploying Luftwaffe aircraft for the first time.[93] Like the Japanese, new German pilots were not properly prepared to cope with bad weather, and many were lost when encountering storms during their deployment.

In the end, if one combines all the losses that occurred before the battlefield – during pre-production, production and deployment – with those that happened on the battlefield, the paramount importance by 1944 of air and sea weaponry in determining the outcome of World War II is clear. Not only did air and sea weapons make up the vast majority of what was being built on all sides, they were responsible for the enormous equipment losses suffered in combat itself.

3 THE AIR AND SEA WAR TO NOVEMBER 1940

In December 1940, after the most dramatic phase of the Battle of Britain had ended, Maurice Hankey wanted to discover just how much damage German bombing had done to British production. The long-time secretary to the Committee for Imperial Defence, Hankey had joined the War Cabinet when World War II commenced.[1] In this role he had argued strongly, and increasingly unsuccessfully, in favor of a strategic bombing policy aimed at destroying Nazi Germany's access to oil. He also regularly argued against any bombing aimed at the destruction of German morale, viewing it as fruitless and counterproductive.

Not surprisingly, Hankey was eager to find out the precise damage that the Luftwaffe had inflicted on British industry. He asked the Ministry of Home Security to send him data on individual bomb hits on different sectors of the British economy. On December 11, the ministry replied. During the three most intense months of the Battle of Britain, when the United Kingdom was supposedly fighting for its very survival against the all-powerful and victorious Luftwaffe, exactly seventeen German bombs had caused "severe" damage (the highest damage rating) to Britain's aircraft and aero-engine production, electricity services, gas supplies, water industry, oil infrastructure and all food service industries –*combined*.[2] Even more remarkably, the highest priority target of Luftwaffe bombers during the battle, Britain's docks and harbors, had not been hit by a single bomb that did "severe" damage.

Even considering bombs that did "substantial" damage, the next highest category provided by the Ministry of Home Security, the Luftwaffe had failed miserably to find its targets. The different sectors listed above had received exactly seventy five "substantial" bombs hits.[3] Description of the damage inflicted by this remarkably small number of bombs made clear that British production had barely been affected by German bombing. The aircraft industry, which had received ten of the seventeen severe hits, had had a few disruptions: "There have been no cases of damage which are catastrophic to the industry; but there have been a few cases where certain factories have been severely damaged and their production has experienced a serious but nevertheless temporary setback. In the majority of cases, however, it will be seen that the damage has been negligible and slight."[4] On the other hand, the damage that had been done to Britain's docks and harbors was inconsequential in terms of reducing output.

> Attacks on docks and harbours, since the outbreak of enemy action have been numerous. Although the plant and equipment of the London Docks have been damaged, at no time have the docks and their outer basins been rendered unserviceable. In the Liverpool area, only one of the numerous docks was seriously damaged, but, even here, the dock basin still remains serviceable. At Southampton extensive damage was inflicted on one relatively unimportant dock.[5]

For Hankey such a report would have prompted mixed emotions. In four months of air attacks the Luftwaffe, supposedly the most powerful air force in the world, had been able to drop fewer than a hundred bombs that did real damage to its intended targets. What it showed was that, even in late 1940, strategic air power used in any fashion offered little realistic prospect of damaging an enemy. If the Luftwaffe's bombs could make so little impact, what difference would it make if one chose to attack large cities versus specific industries? At the time, the reality of the ridiculously small amount of damage inflicted by the Luftwaffe on Great Britain as a military and industrial power was not dwelt upon. The Germans wanted to make it seem that they had come close to victory, while the British people, politicians and RAF wanted to give the impression that they had succeeded in fighting off a powerful and destructive enemy with their typical pluck and courage. It was in everyone's interest to stress the idea of Britain withstanding a great German

"Blitz." Nothing could be further from the truth. The Battle of Britain was a battle that the Germans had absolutely no chance of winning, during which they did little damage, and which they lost quickly.

The most important thing to take from the Battle of Britain was that, even well into the second year of the war in Europe, neither the air weapons nor the air doctrine had been developed that could actually "win" a modern war. When it came to the war at sea, both the United Kingdom and the United States had only a partial understanding of how victory would be achieved, and still needed to make major advances in doctrine and equipment before this could happen. Very little that had come out of the interwar period had proved particularly useful, and by 1945 most interwar period technology and doctrine would seem like dusty old antiques.

The interwar years

There has been a tendency recently to describe the interwar period, particularly the 1930s, as an era of militarization.[6] It is an interesting argument to make, though it is important to place this idea in context. When compared with the World War I era, military spending spiked quite late. Hitler's Germany witnessed its marked increase in investment for war starting in 1936.[7] For the British and Americans there was a significant military build-up, though it began even later, especially when compared with World War I. As Zara Steiner has shown in her definitive account of international politics in the 1930s, British rearmament, while meaningful, was based on the assumption that Germany would not be ready for war until 1942, and Talbot Imlay has also described the strong British desire to strictly limit any continental commitment as late as 1938.[8] Therefore, British military spending was extremely modest until 1936 and only significantly accelerated in 1937. So the build-up began only two and a half years before the war started, whereas the spike in military spending before World War I started in 1909, five years before the conflict.[9] (See Figure 13.) Also, as a percentage of government expenditure, military spending through the 1930s remained far below that of the pre-World War I period. In the five years before 1914, spending on the army and navy averaged approximately 40 percent of UK government spending, a figure that

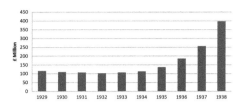

13 UK: defense spending 1929–38 (£ millions)
Source: Mitchell, *British Historical Statistics* (Cambridge, 1988), pp. 590–1.

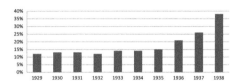

14 UK: defense spending as percentage of government expenditure, 1929–38
Source: Mitchell, *British Historical Statistics*, pp. 590–1.

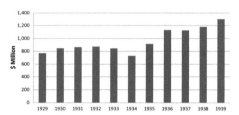

15 USA: defense spending, 1929–39 ($ millions)
Source: O'Neil, *Interwar US and Japanese National Product and Defense Expenditure* (June 2003). Available online at www.analysis.williamdoneil.com/CIM_D0007249.A1.pdf.

was never reached in the later period before 1939 – even with the RAF added to the mix. (See Figure 14.)

In relative and absolute terms, the American build-up through 1939 was also modest. Defense spending between 1936 and the end of 1939 went up by less than 15 percent. (See Figure 15.) Moreover, as a percentage of government expenditure, defense costs declined moderately between 1932 and 1939 as Roosevelt's New Deal significantly expanded the scope of the federal government. (See Figure 16.) It is important to see how relatively low British spending was before 1937 when compared with that of the United States. For much of the 1930s, one British pound was worth approximately five US dollars.[10] However, this American over-spending was not part of any special

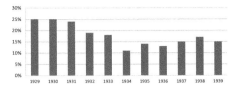

16 USA: defense spending, as a percentage of government expenditure 1929–39
Source: O'Neil, *Interwar US and Japanese National Product.*

build-up of force, but was partly the result of the political nature of American defense spending, always relatively inefficient among the great powers. The United States as a rule tended to support too many military establishments, such as naval bases, as a means of dispensing largesse to local constituencies.[11] Overall, US military spending between 1929 and 1935 was 50 percent greater than British expenditure – though if anything the US maintained smaller armed forces.

Returning to the build-up that began in 1937, many of the weapons constructed at this time, particularly aircraft, were of dubious value, as the war in Europe quickly demonstrated. Of the Anglo-American aircraft that would prove decisive in the war in Europe, only two were actually in production before the outbreak of fighting in September 1939: the Spitfire and the B-17. In terms of development, only three had taken their first flight before September 1939. (See Table 18.)

If the planes that were built during the interwar period build-up were poor designs that were quickly replaced by wartime construction, air power theory at the time was of little more use.[12] The three giants of air power theory after World War I are usually agreed to be Giulio Douhet, William "Billy" Mitchell and Air Marshal Hugh Trenchard. Their writings provide very little of use in understanding the air war in World War II.

Douhet's most famous work, *The Command of the Air*, was published in 1921, just after World War I ended. As such it is extremely vague. In general terms, Douhet made some important points about the flexibility of aircraft, the growing range of which would be transformative to warfare.[13] However, when it came to actually attacking a strategic target, he had a completely unrealistic idea of what could be achieved. He believed that it was important that all targets should be destroyed fully in one raid – even italicizing this line. "The guiding

Table 18 *British and American aircraft: first flight and production years*

Plane	First flight	Production
Spitfire	1936	1938
Lancaster	1941	1942
Mosquito	1940	1941
P-38	1939 (Jan.)	1941
P-47	1941	1942
P-51	1940	1942
B-17	1934	1936
B-24	1939 (Dec.)	1941
B-25	1940	1941
B-26	1940	1941
F-4U (Corsair)[a]	1940	1942
SBD (Dauntless)[a]	1940	1940
F-6F (Hellcat)[a]	1942	1943
B-29[a]	1942	1943

Note: [a] In the Pacific, none of the aircraft that would play a major role in defeating Japan were in production in 1939.
Source: Craven and Cate (eds.), *The Army Air Forces in World War II*, vol. I, p. 109.

principle of bombing actions should be this: *the objective must be destroyed completely in one attack, making further attack on the same target unnecessary.*"[14] Such complete destruction proved almost impossible in World War II, until the development of the atom bomb.

Douhet also prophesied inaccurately in a number of other crucial areas, as the war would attest. He underestimated the ability of defensive forces against aircraft, and urged that bombing be met by counter-bombing not fighter aircraft.[15] Most problematic, however, is that he said nothing useful about what kinds of targets should be attacked. He did seem to favor strategic attacks over tactical, but within strategic simply generalized. As he added in the later edition of the book published in 1926: "In view of the carrying capacity and range of modern aircraft and the efficacy of present destructive materials, these advantages are such that a country *in possession of adequate air forces* can crush the material and moral resistance of the enemy; that is to say, that country can win *regardless of any other circumstances whatsoever.*"[16]

The point of these excerpts is not to mock Douhet – far from it. There was an important kernel of truth in his ideas, which hardly anyone else was arguing at the time. However, as a useful guide to how air power would be used in World War II, Douhet lacked any utility.

William "Billy" Mitchell was somewhat more useful than Douhet. His "book," *Winged Defense*, published in 1925, was a collection of separate articles that had previously been published in the *Saturday Evening Post*.[17] Mitchell has been hailed as a genius and the founder of the American air force.[18] He was certainly an enthusiastic self-publicist, and after his early death was lionized in the Walt Disney film *Victory through Air Power*.[19]

Mitchell's most famous fights were with the US Navy, and in this sense the real focus of his work was tactical. He liked to stress the vulnerability of war machinery, such as naval vessels, to air attack.[20] From a tactical point of view, he was the most important air power theorist of the interwar period, and the war in the Pacific and the Atlantic represented a broad vindication of his ideas about the superiority of aircraft to naval vessels. Another of Mitchell's important notions, though he seemed to move in the opposite direction as he aged, was that bombers were indeed vulnerable to attacks by other aircraft. He at first strongly supported the construction of fighter aircraft as a means of defense – as he believed that other ground-based anti-aircraft weaponry would prove useless.[21] However, like Douhet, his thoughts on the strategic use of air power were maddeningly vague. Mitchell would talk of different important "targets," but never describe what they were. Moreover, like Douhet, he seemed to believe, particularly in his later works, that destroying targets with the use of strategic air power would be much easier than it turned out to be. It was as though air power was so advanced it would find a way to win, even if that way to win could not actually be described. As he stated in the conclusion of *Winged Defense*, "The influence of air power on the ability of one nation to impress its will on another in an armed contest will be decisive."[22] An interesting point – but it was not much help in understanding the coming air war.

Air Marshal Hugh Trenchard was the only one of the three still alive during World War II and, while he had retired from RAF command, he tried to intervene in arguments over RAF doctrine. He came out of World War I convinced that air power had to be used offensively and that, while it could do important material damage, it was even more powerful as a psychological weapon.[23] During the interwar period he codified these ideas in a series of doctrines which were influential in RAF education. He carried these notions into World War II, when he was perhaps the strongest advocate of using strategic air power to attack German civilian morale. His specific role in persuading the RAF to go down this route during the war is unclear, and it is doubtful that his interventions were decisive, but at least he was the most famous advocate of the area/morale bombing of German cities that the RAF finally adopted. He began his lobbying for such a campaign almost immediately after the Germans crossed the border into Poland.[24] In June 1941, he was asked to present his views on the subject to the Air Staff.

> In his [Trenchard's] opinion, everything turned on the difference between the German and British mentality. Reports from all sources, in particular from men of Continental countries with an intimate knowledge of the German character, emphasized that the German civil populations stood up, in general, very badly to the strain of repeated bombing attacks. Their morale was noticeably reduced by those. On the other hand, the inhabitants of British towns that had been badly bombed had shown remarkable capacity for enduring repeated bombing.
>
> Weakening of morale had an important effect in industrial output. Experience in this country had shown that the effect of this, aided by the damage to essential services caused by indiscriminate bombing in a town, was far greater than that caused by the aimed bombing of factories...
>
> His recommendation was therefore that German morale should be made the primary target for our bombers.[25]

There are so many peculiar elements of this interjection. By June 1941 the German civil population had not been bombed repeatedly anywhere, so it is hard to see how the first judgment had been made. Moreover, Trenchard seems to have interpreted the failure of German strategic air power (as would have been the case of all strategic air power in 1941) to mean that the problem was not the ability to hit, but in choosing what to hit. It sums up the weakness of all early air power theory.

Doctrinally, therefore, the RAF and US Army Air Force had very much to devise their plans as they went along. By 1939 they had developed two subtly different mind-sets, both with major shortcomings. Throughout the interwar years the Americans had seriously considered the direct bombing of German cities and civilians to break their morale.[26] However, by the end of the 1930s the Americans were much more focused on the idea of attacking specific economic and industrial targets. The technological success stories of 1930s strategic air power for the United States, the development of the four-engine B-17 bomber and the Norden bombsight, had given the Americans a real and somewhat misguided sense of confidence that they could hit specific targets with great accuracy. First successfully tested in 1935, the B-17 was put into regular production in 1937 and could efficiently carry a heavy load further than any other plane of its era.[27] The Norden bombsight, a device first developed for the US Navy and later adopted by the air force, was ordered into large-scale production in 1933, and when placed in the B-17 gave the Americans (too much) confidence that they could hit specific targets.[28] When it came to the specific targets to attack, however, American thinking was still uncertain.[29] In fact, it was not until 1941 that a sensible list of priority targets for an attack against Germany was developed by the new Air War Plans Division.[30]

The RAF in some ways had the opposite problem. If the Americans knew how they wanted to use strategic air power but not what to attack, the British had a huge number of plans about what to attack but almost no means to adequately deliver the necessary blow. Like the Americans, the British had discussed precision bombing in the interwar period. The RAF regularly trumpeted its abilities to hit targets in papers with wide government circulation. In its preparatory memoranda for the Imperial Conference of 1930, the Air Staff of the RAF made some remarkable claims about its ability to hit individual houses while dropping bombs within a few yards of their intended targets.

> In some air operations taken in 1927, on the north-west frontier of India, the hostile elements were established in some small villages on the hillsides closely adjoining friendly villages which it was important not to hit. Of these operations the Chief Commissioner of the North-West Frontier Province has stated: "The Royal Air Force by their operations and by correctly picking out not only the villages of the guilty, but the very houses of those most deeply concerned, leaving untouched the property of the well-disposed, have dispelled the idea that we would be unable to pick out a small village, and still less any individual houses, as targets."
>
> In quoting this example the Air Staff do not intend to suggest that such a degree of accuracy is obtained in all operations. It may, however, be mentioned that the average of the results in *all*

bombing squadrons in the annual training trials, *including the results obtained by young pilots and airmen in their first training season*, show that, from the height suitable for bombing trial objectives, on the average, one-half of all bombs dropped fall within a circle of 53 yards radius. For a low-flying attack the radius of this circle would be 26 yards. (Emphasis in original.)[31]

However, when it came to actually delivering such attacks against large industrial or civilian targets, the RAF was considerably more circumspect. When war started in 1939, the RAF had basically reacted to the indefinite understanding of the use of air power by developing sixteen different plans, some containing a number of separate options, in case Great Britain found itself in a war with Germany. Some were sensible conceptually, others impractical, but very few of them could actually have been attained with anything like the force available at the time. The plans were:[32]

WA. 1: Plan for attack on the German Air Striking Force and its maintenance organization (including aircraft industry).

WA. 1(b): Action against certain major aerodromes in the north-west corner of Germany.

WA. 2: Plans for reconnaissance in cooperation with the Navy in Home Waters and the Eastern Atlantic.

WA. 3: Plans for close cooperation with the Navy in convoy protection in Home Waters and the Eastern Atlantic.

WA. 4: Plans for the attack on German military rail, canal and road communications.

WA. 4(a): Attack on road and rail communications in W. Germany in a concentration period.

WA. 4(b): Attack to delay a German invasion of southern Holland, Belgium and France.

WA. 5: Plans for attacking German manufacturing resources:

WA. 5(a): The attack on German war industry.

WA. 5(b): The attack on the Ruhr and its effects on the military lines of communication in Western Germany.

WA. 5(c): Attack on Germany's war resources of oil.

WA. 6: Plan for attack on Italian manufacturing resources.

WA. 7: Plans for counter-offensive action in defence of seaborne trade in cooperation with the Navy.

WA. 7(a): Attack on Wilhelmshaven.

WA. 7(b): Limited attack with air forces alone on Wilhelmshaven.

WA. 8: Plan for attack on especially important depots or accumula-
tions of warlike stores other than air in enemy country.

WA. 9: Plan for putting the Kiel Canal out of action.

WA. 10: Plans for the destruction of enemy shipping and facilities in
German ports: Precedence to be given to the Baltic.

WA. 11: Plan for attack on Forests.

WA. 12: Plan for attack on German fleet or a section thereof at sea.

WA. 13: Plan for attack on enemy's headquarters and administrative
offices in Berlin and elsewhere.

WA. 14: Plans for dropping propaganda leaflets.

WA. 15: Plans prepared in concert with the Naval Staff for operations against enemy shipping by "M" mine.

WA. 16: Buoyancy mine attack against German waterways.

The main problem the British had, other than deciding which one of
these plans might actually damage Germany, was that most of them
were practically unattainable. When the war broke out, RAF Bomber
Command possessed mostly Wellington, Whitley and Hampden
bombers, aircraft that would make up the majority of its force until
November 1941.[33] These bombers were slow, could carry only a small
bomb load and could not fly high enough for their own protection.
Even the subsequent classes of British bombers, the Sterlings and
Manchesters, were deficient machines. The Halifax bomber was a
noticeable improvement on these, but even it had problems bombing
from altitude. It was not until the Lancaster bomber arrived in numbers
that the British had a true weapon for strategic bombing.[34]

Moreover, the lead British fighter of the time, the Hurricane,
was a sturdy but limited aircraft. It certainly did not have the range to
escort British bombers from the United Kingdom to Germany and
back. As a result, had the British sent any kind of bomber force over
Germany on a regular basis, it would have been met by the best fighter
aircraft of the time, the ME-109, with little or no help from escorting
fighters – and would have been massacred.

Before leaving this point, however, it is important to mention
some areas where British and Americans did make important advances
in the interwar years, as this indicates how they would eventually
defeat the Germans and Japanese. One of the key advances was in the

integration of important technological developments. Both before and throughout the war, the British and Americans, with some noticeable hiccups, integrated scientific developments relatively smoothly into the military process. Scientists were given much greater high-level access and American and British military officers often worked side by side in scientific institutions to try to understand, and even aid, the weapons development process.[35] The situation for Germany and Japan was very different. Whereas Churchill and Roosevelt took the greatest interest in scientific developments and indeed often consulted with different experts, Adolf Hitler, and even his Luftwaffe head, Hermann Goering, rarely sought out scientific advice.[36]

The defeat of the Axis was not simply down to their being out-produced in quantity when it came to air and sea weapons; it had just as much to do with being out-produced in quality. Starting before the war, the British and Americans had established some important technological advantages, and during the war they would establish many more. They were able to conceive of, design, test and, crucially, produce their air and sea weapons in such a way that the Germans and Japanese in the end could no longer meet them as equals. This does not mean that in every area American and British air and sea weaponry was superior to that of their enemies. However, in vital areas of advanced technology they were almost always able to develop and produce better weapons more quickly.

One of the crucial British and American advantages, which started before the war and then expanded significantly after 1939, was in detection technologies. The ability of the Allies to develop workable radar and sonar sets gave them a great advantage in the air and sea war. Radar is the use of electromagnetic waves to detect objects in the air, on land and on the surface of the sea. Research into radar had been undertaken widely in the interwar period; however, the British became the most focused on developing a workable system. The fear that German air power could be used to attack targets on the British mainland pushed the British to centralize and support radar developments with greater urgency in the five years before the war started. In 1934 the Air Ministry established a committee, dubbed the Tizard Committee after its chairman, Sir Henry Tizard, to investigate British air defense. At its first meeting, in January 1935, the possibility of using radar to detect incoming air attack was discussed.[37] However, it took the brilliance of Sir Robert Watson-Watt, the head of the Air Ministry's

Bawdsey research station, to really push the project along.[38] Watson-Watt envisaged series of linked radar stations on England's eastern and southern coasts which could provide a continual check for all incoming enemy aircraft.

The system that the British put into operation in 1939, called Chain Home, was an extremely important development in the history of war. Though it certainly had its flaws, it could usually detect German aircraft from far enough away to give the British enough time to get their own fighters into the air. The detection distance varied according to different variables such as the height of the approaching aircraft, but under ideal conditions, Chain Home by 1940 was capable of finding German aircraft flying at 500 feet altitude more than 100 miles away.[39] Not only were the linked radar stations capable of detecting Luftwaffe aircraft, but the British had come up with an efficient system to feed all the information into a central fighter command hub, from which the defense of British airspace could be coordinated.[40] Even though British radar was not, simply as a form of detection, the best in the world, their entire radar system was far more advanced than that of the Germans when the war started and would be for the first two years of the war.

Moreover, the British and Americans pushed forward with important radar advances. For the rest of the war, the western Allies continually improved and refined their detection systems, particularly in the field of radar, providing absolutely crucial advantages at certain important stages of the war. The Allies' key advantage was in the development of short-frequency (sometimes called microwave) radar. The shorter the electromagnetic wave that could be produced by a radar set, the greater the ability of that wave to detect an object. Shorter waves concentrated more power on a target, allowing for the detection of even small objects while yielding much less reflected power from nearby ground or water.[41] It was also much more difficult for an enemy to jam a shorter wave, and jamming was regularly attempted as the war developed.

The problem faced by all powers was coming up with a workable and practical system to generate short-wave radar. Eventually, a crucial breakthrough was made by two researchers at the University of Birmingham, named John Randall and Henry Boot. They devised a brilliant mechanism for amplifying the electrons of electromagnetic waves in relatively small circular chambers – a mechanism that they named the cavity magnetron. This has been called the most "significant academic invention" of the war by one noted historian.[42] This British cavity magnetron, which was superior to a similar device being developed in the United States at the same time, was given to the Americans during the Tizard Mission of 1940, a scientific mission sent by the British government to alert the United States to numerous British technological advances and thus persuade the Americans that the British could continue to fight.[43]

Yet, despite the importance of these interwar advances, the British and Americans went into World War II with few of the weapons and only a vague idea of the doctrine needed to fight a modern air war. They would have to make much of it up as they went along.

Sea power in the interwar years

If a proper understanding of air power was hampered by the lack of any real knowledge on the subject, it was perhaps the reverse for sea power. World War I had broadened the technological possibilities of sea power to include craft operating under the water or flying over it. The submarine and naval air power (either carrier- or land-based) were factors that had to be included in interwar period naval planning. The difficulty was deciding how these new technologies should be integrated into the material and doctrines of the British and American fleets.

British policy during the interwar period was markedly successful in one area: it severely limited the capital shipbuilding of possible enemies. The naval arms control process set down during the Washington Conference of 1921–2, so derided in some quarters, very much served British interests. It kept Japanese capital ship construction under control until 1935 when Japan withdrew from the system during the London Conference. German capital ship construction was ruthlessly controlled by the Versailles system until the Anglo-German Naval Agreement of 1935 allowed the Germans to construct a fleet 35 percent as large as the Royal Navy. By 1939 this meant that neither the Japanese nor the German navy represented a serious threat to the Royal Navy in finished capital ship construction.[44]

As such, the threat to the British at sea would come from submarines or aircraft. For the British perhaps the most pressing problem was how to combat enemy submarines. World War I had demonstrated the threat that underwater attacks posed to Britain's seaborne trade as both British stomachs and British factories needed outside supply to keep functioning. The history of the development of British anti-submarine capabilities in the interwar years represents one of the only (moderately) successful examples of preparation for the actual fighting that would occur. One of the key moments for this was the development, and then successful incorporation into naval craft, of ASDIC, the first effective sonar system.[45] Starting in 1932, the Royal Navy began installing ASDIC on all new escort vessels, including destroyers.[46] Going into the war British ASDIC sets could detect submerged German submarines at up to 2,000 meters distance, weather permitting.[47] However, there were still potential problems for British anti-submarine forces to face, such as when the Germans switched to night-time, surface attacks by packs of submarines. Recent research has shown that British training and doctrine were aware of this tactic.[48] As long as the British had enough ASDIC-equipped escort vessels to run large convoys across the North Atlantic, the merchant ships had a very high chance of reaching their destination.[49] Once these convoys were augmented by continual air support, losses stopped almost entirely.

This highlights another of the problems of stressing the militaristic aspects of the UK in the 1930s. The British actually had relatively few anti-submarine vessels on hand in 1939. What World War I had shown was that a proper defense against a submarine offensive involving even a relatively small number of German submarines required a great number of anti-submarine escort vessels. It was not a question of the relative number of escorts to submarines, but instead a question of the relative number of escorts to the merchant ships that needed to be protected as they crossed the Atlantic. As both World War I and World War II would demonstrate, any unescorted merchant ship sailing in a submarine-patrolled area was in danger, even if there were only a handful of submarines on operational duty. The greatest massacre of merchant shipping ever in the Atlantic – the sinkings off the US East Coast during the first six months of 1942 – was accomplished with fewer than twenty submarines on duty at any time.[50]

So, while the British had some understanding of what would be needed to win a trade war, they did not, however, build enough of the right kind of ships in the interwar period to put this understanding into full action. That meant that there were far too many unescorted merchant ships on the high seas for the first few years of the war.

When it came to naval air power, the British likewise were relatively slow in starting construction of modern aircraft carriers. This is indicative of the general fact that while aircraft carriers were to become recognized as the new, decisive form of capital ship in World War II, there were precious few of them built in the interwar period. There were also almost no aircraft that could be flown from carriers at this time that could inflict significant damage. The British laid down only a single new aircraft carrier between 1919 and 1935,[51] but thereafter they went on a comparative binge, laying down six between 1936 and 1939.[52] These were solid ships that represented an interesting, but logical and limiting, choice for a navy that might well do a great deal of fighting close to the European mainland where large formations of land-based aircraft could attack. They were built with considerably heavier side and flight deck armor than their American or Japanese counterparts. This certainly did make British carriers more robust, and their ability to withstand direct hits, including those from kamikaze, was impressive.[53] However, at the time the war broke out, they had yet to be completed, and the Royal Navy possessed only one modern vessel that had actually been built as an aircraft carrier, the *Ark Royal*.[54]

The aircraft deployed on British carriers at this time were primitive. Much of the blame for the weakness in British naval aircraft has been laid at the feet of the interwar period governmental decision to give all air power decisions to a separate Air Ministry, thus denying the Royal Navy its own self-controlled and equipped fleet air arm.[55] The Royal Navy would not regain formal control over its own air forces until 1939. The Swordfish torpedo-bombers, Skua fighter-bombers, and Roc and Sea Gladiator fighters with which Britain entered the war had barely evolved beyond World War I technology. It was not until they were re-equipped with American carrier aircraft years later that the Royal Navy could be said to possess a modern striking force. Furthermore, British naval air doctrine was also not advanced. The British continued to see aircraft as support forces to the main battle line.[56]

The American position when it came to submarine and anti-submarine warfare was, if anything, less satisfactory than the British. The United States Navy was considerably slower in equipping its vessels with sonar to fight a modern sea war. By September 1939, it had equipped only sixty ships.[57] Moreover, American training and tactics in anti-submarine warfare were considerably behind those of the Royal Navy. When it came to naval air power, the United States had a force of some striking power – partly assembled by chance. The USN possessed the two largest carriers in the world, the *Lexington* and *Saratoga*, which could launch a total of approximately 150 aircraft between them. However, these ships were only constructed because the United States wanted to reuse two battlecruiser hulls laid down as part of the 1916 naval program. In the 1930s the USN demonstrated some real foresight in aircraft carrier development. There were some important design changes in American carriers, allowing them to carry more aircraft and giving them range.[58] The USN also started to push the notion of mobile base operations in the Pacific, operations that would give them an important head start when it came to planning the great campaigns over that vast ocean.[59]

On the other hand, the USN still had a long way to go in realizing the crucial role that naval air power would play in the Pacific. When it came to fighting at sea, the aircraft carrier still remained, in American eyes, a secondary vessel to the battleship.[60] Between 1930 and 1939, the United States started the construction of only four fleet carriers (*Enterprise*, *Yorktown*, *Hornet* and *Wasp*) and one smaller carrier, *Ranger*. Because there were relatively few new aircraft carriers, the navy was still unsure about how they should be employed.[61]

When Roosevelt began pushing for money for the USN to construct new vessels, the navy continued to opt for a battleship-centric fleet until Pearl Harbor. Between 1937 and 1939 the United States started the construction of six large battleships (two of the North Carolina Class and four of the South Dakota).[62] Once the war in Europe started and before the Japanese attack on Pearl Harbor, the USN was given authorization to build a further eleven battleships, six of the Iowa Class and five of the mammoth Montana Class.[63] As it was, only four of the Iowa Class were ever completed and the rest cancelled when it became clear during the war that the aircraft carrier was now the decisive weapon. If only the USN had known this before it would have started more than the two aircraft carriers it laid down between 1937 and November 1941, the *Hornet* in 1939 and the *Essex* in April 1941. It was still thinking in terms of a capital ship duel in the Pacific.

The aircraft carrier was considered useful primarily as part of this capital ship engagement, or in the attacking of stationary targets such as canals and naval bases.[64] At the same time, carriers were still a secondary funding priority for the Americans (and the British and Japanese) as far more money was plowed into capital ship construction and refurbishment.[65]

Certainly the United States did not possess the most powerful carrier air striking force in the world when the war started. In fact, if any navy had the right to claim that title, it would have been the Japanese.[66] Because of their superior naval aircraft, and their intense training and tactical understanding, the Japanese had a more effective strike force, as they showed during the first few months of the war, although, like the Americans, they only had a limited number of aircraft carriers. Moreover, while American naval aircraft were more advanced than their British counterparts, they were hardly war-winning machines. Two of the three main aircraft that flew during the Battle of Midway, the F4F Wildcat fighters and TBD Devastator torpedo-bombers, were functional aircraft with some major flaws.[67] Only the SBD Dauntless dive-bomber was better than Japanese aircraft of the same class.

Like the USAAF, the United States Navy had a long way to go before it possessed the needed doctrine and technology to win World War II. It would have to develop those during the fighting. These weaknesses shown by the Americans and British during the interwar period did not mean that Germany or Japan had progressed significantly further. In naval terms, the German fleet had almost none of the vessels needed to restart an effective trade war against the United Kingdom. The surface fleet, which had a few excellent individual units on the stocks (*Bismarck* and *Tirpitz*), was still mostly a paper force, to be properly completed (or actually improperly, as would have been the case had it been completed) in 1947 under the name Plan Z.[68] Plan Z demonstrates how naval aviation had not yet penetrated German naval thinking, as the German fleet in 1947 was to be composed of ten of the largest and most powerful battleships in the world, but only four aircraft carriers. Even the U-boat arm of the German navy, which would eventually wage a relatively cost-efficient economic war against the UK and USA, had few units that were ready to go in 1939. When the war began, the German navy had only twenty-two U-boats available that could effectively operate in the North Atlantic.[69] At the same time German construction of U-boats was running at between two and four units per month.

As for the Luftwaffe, there was one clear success story. The Germans had developed perhaps the best strategy for the tactical support of ground forces by aircraft then in existence. Their aircraft mix, from the ME-109 to the JU-87, was well constructed to support ground forces by attacking enemy forces directly or providing air cover over the battlefields. On the other hand, German strategic air power was in some ways less advanced than its American and British counterparts. German bombers (the two-engine HE-111, JU-88 and DO-17) were shown to be almost entirely ineffective as strategic bombers against even light opposition. They were also some distance from building an effective four-engine bomber, which was a necessity if high amounts of ordnance were to be dropped on a target. As a counterpoint, the Luftwaffe had made some important advances in strategic bombing, being ahead of the Allies when it came to devising a blind-bombing radar.[70] However, in the end, as the Battle of Britain would demonstrate, the Luftwaffe had neither the bombers needed to launch a strategic air campaign nor a fighter with the necessary range to protect the bombers.

The Japanese situation is likewise mixed. The successful attack on Pearl Harbor launched by Japanese navy aircraft carriers on December 7, 1941 might make it seem that the Japanese had the most highly developed notion of the uses of naval air power. They certainly did have the best carrier airplane in existence at the time, the Mitsubishi Zero (see Figure 17). However, the Japanese success should

17 Mitsubishi A-6M2 "Zero" fighters being prepared for launch from the aircraft carrier *Shokaku* during one of the battles off Guadalcanal in 1942. In early 1942 the Zero was the best naval aircraft in the world, and a key reason for Japanese successes. However, the Americans soon countered with better plane designs of their own, while the constant combat around Guadalcanal caused extremely high Japanese pilot wastage.

not obscure the point that until then the Japanese navy, like the American, still believed that the outcome of the war in the Pacific would be determined by battleships. Indeed, that would be the only way that they could have seen the results of Pearl Harbor, in which four battleships were sunk or seriously damaged, as a great victory. This would hardly have been the case if the Japanese believed that the aircraft carrier was the naval weapon that would win the war. When it came to the use of land-based air power, either strategic or tactical, the Japanese were not as advanced as the Germans, British or Americans.

In the end, the United Kingdom, United States, Germany and Japan all left the interwar period with only a hazy notion of what a modern air and sea war would be like. They had developed, even in prototype stage, only a small amount of the weaponry that would be needed to fight the war to its conclusion. Moreover, when it came to having a doctrine by which that weaponry should be used, large gaps remained. The strategic use of air power was widely recognized as crucial, but its ability to quickly achieve results was overestimated, while the difficulty of determining its proper targets was underestimated. For the United Kingdom and the United States, in the air and sea war, this meant that they would have to make much of it up as they went along.

From September 1939 to November 1940

When the Germans crossed the border into Poland on September 1, 1939, this period of faulty planning and preparation came face to face with the reality of combat. Though it could be argued, rightly, that in political terms World War II began in 1937 when Japanese forces invaded China, the modern air and sea war did not commence until the war in Europe began. The war in China involved modest amounts of aircraft on the Japanese side and very few on the Chinese. Naval power, likewise, was a secondary consideration.

However, the war in Europe brought together armed forces with thousands of planes and hundreds of naval vessels. To begin with, the British believed that their preparations for the war had been mostly vindicated. It was decided not to risk attacking Germany with the RAF's strategic bombers, as this would have led to a German retaliation in kind. It was thought far better to keep the power of the RAF as a deterrent to German actions. To some in the British government, including the Secretary of State for Air, Samuel Hoare, it was assumed that Hitler's immediate goals would be limited, if for no other reason than the Germans wouldn't want to risk fighting a strategic air war against an RAF that had a superior bombing force.[71] Hoare, who was in regular contact with Trenchard, also believed the latter's view that German morale would break under the strain of British bombing, which would preclude a direct German attack on France or the United Kingdom.[72]

Early air engagements further strengthened this conviction in the basic superiority of British aircraft (even if they undermined the notion of a straightforward strategic bombing campaign on either side). At the end of October 1939, Hoare confidently wrote to Lord Lothian in Washington, DC that British fighters could "walk round" German bombers.[73] On the other hand, it was becoming clearer that British Bomber Command was equipped with aircraft that would have a hard time damaging the German economy.[74] Before the German invasion of Norway in April 1940, the RAF hardly dropped a bomb in anger.[75]

If there was one member of the British defense establishment (if such a word can be used) who pushed for a more aggressive economic war against Germany, it was Maurice Hankey. Hankey was convinced from the beginning that the best way to attack German power was to strike at Germany's Achilles heel, its oil supply. Although Germany only consumed one-fifteenth as much oil as the United States on a per capita basis, its domestic production of crude oil was grossly insufficient. German sources were able to provide only 7 percent of its peacetime needs.[76] At the start of the war, the majority of German oil, up to two-thirds, had to be supplied through importation. Another quarter of their oil needs was met by the synthetic production of oil involving hydrogenation, coal-tar distillation and Benzol plants.[77] However, in 1939 this domestic production was still limited and German stocks of oil were far below intended targets, with only six months' supply available at wartime usage rates.

With the outbreak of war, German options for imported oil became extremely limited, with the still-productive Romanian and Soviet oilfields being the only close sources of fuel. If Soviet supplies of oil to Germany were guaranteed by the Nazi–Soviet pact, Hankey believed that Britain should do everything possible to deny the country access to Romanian oil. His belief in the effectiveness of attacking Germany's oil position was profound, and he pushed hard to put some plans into action.[78] He pressed the Foreign Secretary, Lord Halifax, to put pressure on the Romanian government to reduce oil exports to Germany, and he even went so far as to place large British orders for Romanian oil to reduce further the amount that could be shipped to the Germans.[79] Before the fall of France, Hankey was prophesying that the Germans would soon move to militarily dominate the Balkans, to assure a supply of crude that could not be cut off by British sea power and that was not dependent on the whims of Soviet Russia. However, he complained that the RAF was unwilling to consider his plans in this area, including using air power to stop all Danube River traffic (much of the oil was sent by river barge) or even the wholesale destruction of Romanian oil rigs.[80]

As with many of the plans for the strategic use of air power at this time, the real fly in the ointment was not so much the underlying economic assumptions, as the relative difficulty of achieving the plan's objectives. Amongst its many different war plans, the RAF had discussed attacking both German domestic oil production and its foreign supply. Just before the invasion of France, the Air Ministry updated WA. 5(c), "The attack on German war resources of oil."[81] It determined that the best way to attack Germany's oil supply at this point was to attack the points of creation in Germany itself, the domestic refineries and synthetic plants. It considered ten plants to be particularly vital, with the Leuna works, Germany's largest synthetic oil-producing plant, being singled out for attention. Strategically, this plan was sound and well reasoned; the problem was the relatively small force that was believed to be necessary to carry it out.

For instance, it was assumed that the Leuna works, which were believed to be heavily defended, could be completely destroyed with ten sorties of thirteen bombers. Together, the ten largest refineries and synthetic oil-producing plants in Germany were thought to be vulnerable to destruction by a combined fifty-one sorties of thirteen aircraft each (or half the aircraft that would be used during individual raids by 1942).[82] The total number of accurate bomb hits needed to achieve this goal was thought to be 493, a figure that was considered achievable if 7,645 bombs were delivered through the raids. Again, as the Battle of Britain would show only a few months later, reaching the figure of 493 direct hits would take exponentially more bombs.

While the war in the air seemed unthreatening to begin with, the war at sea actually appeared to be under British control. German submarines inflicted little damage on British merchant or equipment shipping. Not a single one of the half-million men or 89,000 vehicles shipped from Britain to France were lost en route.[83] Moreover, merchant ships carrying supplies from North and South America into the British Isles suffered only small losses from submarines.[84] Where the U-boats did exact a toll on the Royal Navy was in the sinkings of some major combat units. On the evening of October 13, 1940, the German submarine U-47, commanded by Gunther Prien, sank the British battleship *Royal Oak*. A few weeks earlier U-29 had sunk the British carrier *Courageous*, discovered by chance when the carrier was sent out on anti-submarine patrol.[85] The fact that the British had sent an aircraft carrier out on such a ridiculous mission for a vessel of its type helps demonstrate how little understanding there was of the proper use of naval air power in the interwar period. While these losses and others caused some public outrage and shock, they were certainly manageable and in no way threatened British naval supremacy in European waters.

There were two lessons about modern sea power that did become apparent before the invasion of France. The first was that the aircraft represented both an entirely new threat and a new weapon for the British. German air-dropped magnetic mines and direct seaward attacks on British vessels became a constant headache for the Admiralty. On the other hand, British aircraft patrolling off the coast demonstrated their usefulness in locating U-boats and protecting shipping. From that moment on, finding an aircraft with the range to cover more of the sea lanes became a constant preoccupation of the Admiralty.

The other lesson was the extreme difficulty of launching a true combined operation involving the landing and supply of ground forces. For many decades naval enthusiasts had boasted about how the flexibility of sea power gave one nation the ability to threaten another anywhere along its coast. Admiral John (Jackie) Fisher, the First Sea Lord during much of the build-up of the Royal Navy before 1914, liked to boast of the Royal Navy's ability to land a force only miles from Berlin. The reality was very different. The British landings at Gallipoli in 1915 demonstrated that getting ashore was only a small part of an amphibious operation. Both ferrying in supplies and expanding the beachhead were much more difficult than the initial landing. The results of the, partly Churchill-inspired, Norway fiasco for the British in April 1940 made this point even clearer.[86] The Germans, through great daring, were able to seize the main Norwegian towns from Oslo to Narvik in a series of attacks on April 7–9. However, their navy was so severely damaged in these operations that the Royal Navy was soon able to exert sea control in Norway's offshore waters, and British troops were landed to try and capture Narvik, above the arctic circle, and, more crucially, Trondheim, which was located almost halfway up the Norwegian coast.

These troops were unable to take their objectives, even with British sea control, because the Germans used land-based aircraft and seized the Norwegian rail system, which allowed them to transport supplies to their own men and threaten British forces and ships. Sea power without air control was of little value. Throughout the operation, the Luftwaffe, using land-based aircraft much closer to the scene of conflict, was able to exert far more control over the area fighting than the RAF, which had to fly from the UK itself, or the fleet air arm flying from British carriers.[87] Using naval air power to support ground fighting was a new concept, and it posed huge risks that would not be solved until 1943, when the USN showed that overwhelming force was needed to make it effective.[88] This meant that British naval units near the Norwegian coast were operating without control of the airspace above them and under constant threat of attack from German submarines as well. Considering this, the Royal Navy acquitted itself extremely well; it was just that the longer it stayed in Norwegian waters supporting the British raid, the greater the danger it was in. The heavy cruiser HMS *Suffolk* was almost sunk by a German dive-bomber and then, tragically, the aircraft carrier HMS *Glorious* was sunk. The loss of the *Glorious* shows how far the understanding of naval air power still had to go. One carrier, with a small escort, was caught by German surface vessels. It should never have happened. By May any British attempt to remain in Norway was at an end.

The German invasion of Holland, Belgium and France in May 1940, however, quickly moved the focus away from Norway, though in the short term it certainly did not make things more comprehensible. Success for certain equipment on the battlefield, such as the famous JU-87 (Stuka) dive-bomber, seemed to reinforce the notion that bombing could be extremely accurate. The Air Ministry even urged the Admiralty's Air Division to switch over to dive-bombing in light of German success.[89]

The air war over France, Belgium and Holland was a shocking development. Both the Germans and the Allies deployed significant, but very different forces (numerically the Luftwaffe was 50 percent larger in terms of combat aircraft than the force used to support the invasion of the USSR one year later).[90] Excluding all support aircraft such as those used for reconnaissance and transport, the Luftwaffe had almost 3,000 combat planes (fighters and bombers) assigned to operations when the offensive started.[91] The French air force, though it had some excellent planes under construction, had only one-third as many combat aircraft as the Germans.[92] The RAF had access to a sizeable operational force of more than a thousand aircraft. However, they kept most in the UK for home protection or in case they decided to launch a strategic bombing campaign against Germany itself.[93] A little over 400 RAF aircraft were sent to France and Belgium, which meant that over the battlefield, the Germans had more than a two to one advantage.[94]

Doctrinally the Germans also were considerably more advanced than the Allies. They used their aircraft and ground troops together to punch large holes in the French and then British lines, keeping the panzers moving and not allowing the Allies to settle. Much more so than any other air force, the Luftwaffe had developed a close air support system that allowed its aircraft to work with German armored spearheads – which allowed for an unprecedented level of mobility on the battlefield.[95] Experience during both the Spanish Civil War and the invasion of Poland had given the Luftwaffe invaluable lessons, and crucially logistical experience, which allowed it to keep its air wings functioning in support of the advancing armies. During the invasion of France, even when the German armored spearheads were dangerously far ahead of their supporting infantry, Luftwaffe support allowed the panzers to keep moving and prevented the French and British organizing a coherent resistance.[96]

French doctrine, however, was only just begining to catch up. Throughout the interwar period, serious shortcomings in French air planning meant that proper coordination of French ground and air power was still a long way off. It was not until just before the Germans invaded that the French started to realize what a modern tactical air war would involve.[97] The upshot of all of this was that the Luftwaffe ruled the skies over the battlefields of France, allowing the German army to shatter the combined Franco-British ground forces of approximately equal size.[98]

Yet, in the end, the Luftwaffe's tactical performance caused a huge overestimation of German air strength, particularly when it came to strategic bombing. Gone was Hoare's confidence about the ability of RAF fighters to see off German bombers (as Hoare was gone himself, dispatched as ambassador to Francoist Spain), and in its place was a view of the Luftwaffe as a huge and growing enemy with enormous striking power. This assumption was key to shaping the perceptions then, and our perceptions now, of the subsequent air battle that came to be known as the Battle of Britain.

Easily one of the most quoted statements of the entirety of World War II was Winston Churchill's tribute to the Royal Air Force in 1940, that never was "so much owed by so many to so few." In a sentence the impression of a plucky and grossly outnumbered RAF fighting against enormous odds was written into granite. Unfortunately, this impression simply wasn't accurate. To begin with, Churchill had been speaking on August 20, 1940, before the large Luftwaffe bombing raids really commenced. His statement was therefore a prophecy of an upcoming struggle not a statement of reality. Secondly, Churchill was basing his vision on faulty assumptions about German numerical strength.

At the time of the French surrender, British intelligence estimates made the Luftwaffe out to be a force of unparalleled strength. One of the major problems was that they assumed each German air unit had considerably more aircraft than it did. On July 12, 1940, it was estimated that the Luftwaffe had 11,730 combat aircraft of all types available for use.[99] A little less than half this number, 5,400, were thought to be deployed in operational *gruppen*, with the remaining 6,330 kept in reserve to be "immediately" available (within twelve hours) to make up combat losses. By type, the disparity between British assumptions of German strength and the Luftwaffe's reality was stunning. Even taking into account German losses suffered between July 12 and August 13, 1940, the British had created an enemy in their minds far more formidable than that which existed. In terms of operational aircraft, those actually deployed to front-line units, the British assumed the Germans had double the strength that they actually did. (See Table 19.) Moreover, the Germans were thought to be able to replenish the Luftwaffe at a far higher rate than

Table 19 *United Kingdom: government assumptions and the reality of Luftwaffe strength, 1940*

	Air Ministry assumptions (July 12)	Luftwaffe reality (August 13)
Bombers	2,550	988
Dive-bombers	500	311
Fighters	1,550	1,171
Coastal	400	108
Other	400	131
Total	5,400	2,709

Sources: Bungay, *The Most Dangerous Enemy: A History of the Battle of Britain* (London, 2000), p. 418, and Air 20/4076, Statement A, July 26, 1940.

was conceivably possible, given the assumption of the amazing number of 6,330 aircraft, including 4,110 bombers and 1,740 fighters, for the "immediate" reinforcement of front-line units.[100] When it came to building new aircraft, British intelligence likewise painted an extreme and misleading picture of German capabilities. In May 1940, the Air Ministry estimated that Germany was producing 1,300 airframes (1,000 of which were combat aircraft) and 2,500 engines per month.[101] In reality, the 1940 monthly average of front-line German fighter and bomber production was a combined 401.[102] No wonder Churchill suggested the British were so few.

Although the Germans had more aircraft than the British, the RAF actually had quite a similar number in the category that mattered most – fighters. On July 1, 1940 Fighter Command deployed 640 aircraft, mostly Hurricanes and Spitfires, and on September 1, it deployed 648.[103] However, these were only a fraction of the fighters that the British had available. When intelligence estimates were recalibrated after the first month of the Battle of Britain, it was still assumed that the Germans outnumbered the RAF by at least two to one. On October 11, 1940, it was estimated that the Germans had 3,050 operational bombers and dive-bombers (with another 4,280 immediately available for deployment), and 1,900 single- and twin-engine fighters operational (with another twenty immediately available for deployment).[104] In reality, the figures were 1,808 bombers and 1,464 fighters operational on September 29, 1940.[105] The RAF, on the other hand, had more fighters than the Germans operational or immediately available for deployment: 1,981. Additionally, these fighters were operating with the force multipliers of Britain's excellent radar defense system and the greatly increased relative range and flying time that came with the combat occurring in the skies over the United Kingdom. The RAF was bound to win.

The gross overestimation of German aircraft superiority also helps explain just why some believed that a German invasion of the United Kingdom was feasible. In fact, the planned German combined arms invasion, codenamed Operation "Sealion," was preposterous. The Germans would have had to successfully land a large invasion force of infantry and panzer divisions, with little special training or planning, in Great Britain when the latter had clear naval superiority. The German plan was to put ashore 120,000 men with all of their equipment in the first three days.[106] British planning assumed that the Germans would have to land in a number of places, and take a major harbor at the beginning of the landing process, in order to disembark such large armored formations.[107] Even had they reached shore using such primitive landing craft as refitted river barges, this force would have run out of supplies quickly unless the Germans were able to establish a workable convoy system, again with hardly any vessels suitable for such an operation and without naval control in the English Channel.

The need for the Germans to gain air superiority to have even a glimmer of success for "Sealion" was well understood in the British government. Alexander Cadogan, Permanent Under-Secretary of State for Foreign Affairs through the entire war, wrote in a private letter in September that "I should have thought that he would be rash to try unless he obtained air superiority, which he most emphatically has *not*. He has troubled London a good deal lately with night bombing (which has not given him any military advantage)."[108] For this reason, some, such as Hankey, desperately wanted the Germans to attempt "Sealion," anticipating a crushing German defeat.[109] As it is, the Germans wisely decided not to, and this has caused a debate as to whether they were ever serious in their intentions.[110]

As for the battle that was fought, the attempt by the Luftwaffe to gain control over the skies of southern Britain, it was over quickly and decisively. As a plan for strategic bombing, the Germans actually made a number of sensible choices which, had they been accomplished, would have done real damage to British production. They opted for two distinct targets. The first was British air strength, through attacks on both its bases and its sources of production. The second was a transport campaign that aimed to stop the flow of raw materials and supplies around Britain by wrecking British harbors and ports. These priorities, as laid out on June 30, 1940, were:

a) By battle against the enemy air force, its ground organization and the aircraft industry, to create the prerequisites for an effective campaign against enemy import and supply lines, for an undisturbed continuance of German supply and the German war economy, and thereby to protect the German living area.
b) By war against import harbors and their facilities, commercial and warships, to destroy English service of supply.[111]

Of the two, the destruction of the RAF was the vital first step as the following section emphasized with underline.

> As long as the enemy air force is not crushed, the prime principle of air warfare is to attack the enemy formations at every favorable opportunity that offers itself, by day or night, in the air and on the ground, without regard to any other mission.[112]

As the Anglo-American strategic bombing campaign would demonstrate in 1944, such a two-step plan could be damaging. Once the Luftwaffe was ground down over Germany and the German transport system was heavily damaged, German production began plummeting, even when sufficient raw material stocks were there to maintain it at a high level.[113] However, in 1940 such a plan was impossible for the simple fact that it would have been inconceivable for the Luftwaffe to "crush" the RAF. The mathematics were all wrong.

The Luftwaffe went into the battle planning on effectively knocking out RAF resistance in four days.[114] Yet, right from the beginning German losses were higher than British, as they were bound to be. Between July 10 (the date that the British gave for the start of the battle) and July 31 the Luftwaffe lost 185 fighters and bombers while the RAF lost 91 fighters.[115] Throughout the entire Battle of Britain, the loss rate was only marginally less in the British favor. In the end the Germans lost 1,887 aircraft of all types and RAF Fighter Command lost 1,023.[116] On the other hand, during the period of battle, the British production of fighters was considerably higher than Germany's.

Between July 1 and December 31, 1940 Great Britain constructed 2,779 fighters while the Germans built 3,106 during the entire year.[117]

The British were pressed occasionally in the area of pilot losses, but again this was always going to end up in the RAF's favor. Going into the battle the RAF had considerably fewer trained pilots than the Germans. However, as the battle was primarily fought in the skies over the United Kingdom and British aircraft loss rates were smaller, pilot losses ran at a rate of two to one in the RAF's favor.[118] Finally, the British also showed superior adaptive qualities during the battle. Their ability to upgrade their radar analysis made German attempts to attack the UK more dangerous as time went on.[119]

In that sense the Battle of Britain really lacked all drama in terms of its outcome, despite the attempt of filmmakers, authors and politicians to claim otherwise. Certain moments, such as "Alder Dag" or the first week in September when Luftwaffe attacks seemed to stretch British defenses to the point of breaking, can be presented as occasions when the outcome was in the balance.[120] This would be inaccurate. Even had the RAF been forced to stop defensive flights for a few days, it would have made little difference in the battle. At different times during the strategic bombing of both Germany and Japan, each of the Axis countries stopped flying defensive operations for periods because of high losses or the need to use their aircraft in other ways.[121] In neither case was that specific period the one that destroyed the country's economy.

The failure of Germany to do any substantial damage to British production became apparent quickly to those with knowledge of the true state of affairs. The Minister for Aircraft Production, Lord Beaverbrook, was given great leeway to raise British fighter production during the Battle of Britain. Although he was aware of how serious the British public thought the German attack was, he was personally dismissive of its real impact. "The German air offensive is at present the thing that occupies the public's mind to the exclusion of almost everything. Yet, looked upon as a serious military operation its effect is small. Production in the aircraft factories is affected more by the sirens than by the bombs and not much by either."[122] Even those who tended to be more pessimistic by nature than Beaverbrook were surprised by how little real damage seemed to be done to the British war effort. Lord Halifax wrote in a private letter in October that: "Life in London, though noisy at times – particularly at night – is not too bad. The spirit of the people of every class and condition remains beyond all praise and there is really surprisingly little interference with work despite the weight and frequency of the air attacks."[123]

What the Battle of Britain really showed is just how far the reality of strategic air power still was from meeting the expectations of its greatest advocates. This was true for all air forces at the time. No one had the machines capable of delivering the necessary accuracy or weight of attack needed to seriously damage the productive capacity of another country. No one possessed a fighter aircraft with the range necessary to protect the existing bombers deep into another country and to return. And, crucially, both the Germans and the British possessed enough modern fighters to make any incursion of unescorted bombers far too damaging to continue, except under conditions when the hitting of specific targets would have been practically impossible. In that sense, the Battle of Britain was won by the many over the few.

As well as allowing for the Battle of Britain, the fall of France, temporarily, transformed the war at sea in the North Atlantic. If the fundamental tenets of air power seemed very much up for debate in 1940, the war at sea in the Atlantic was revealing itself to be a war with some clearer lessons. In particular, it taught that three elements were crucial to defeating the German submarine threat: convoy, ship speed and air cover. The importance of the convoy, herding merchant vessels into large groups where they could be protected by anti-submarine vessels, was a lesson learned during World War I. In World War II the importance of convoy was, if anything, even more pronounced and demonstrated early on.

The trade war in the Atlantic can sometimes be seen as a contest between submarine and convoy, with running battles between U-boats and the escort ships whose job it was to protect merchantmen.[124] However, the overwhelming number of merchantmen that were sunk in the war were sailing alone and without escort.[125] The struggle was therefore to build and man enough escort vessels to provide convoy protection. This fact helps explain the great peaks and troughs that punctuated the war in the Atlantic. Until the fall of France, the German U-boat attack on escorted trade was small beer indeed. Up until the end of May 1940, a total of 503 British, Allied or neutral merchant vessels were lost as a result of enemy action in all waters of the globe.[126] Of these, only 36 were sunk while in convoy.[127] After May 1940, the overall rate of merchant sinking shot up dramatically, though the basic fact that ships in a convoy were relatively safe, and a small percentage of overall losses, remained. The change at this time led to it being christened the first "Happy Time" by the Germans. The capture of the French and Norwegian coastline, including their naval bases and air facilities, meant that German U-boats could exit and enter their home ports with much greater ease. On the other hand, the ability of the Royal Navy to provide convoy protection was weakened owing to the relatively small amount of naval construction undertaken in the interwar period.

Those who like to talk about the militarization of Britain in the 1930s would have to admit that when it came to building escort vessels, the United Kingdom proceeded at a leisurely pace, especially when considering how World War I had demonstrated just how vital they were. When the war in Europe started, the Royal Navy had only forty destroyers assigned to the different commands whose first priority was convoy duty.[128]

The upshot of this was that after the fall of France, when the Germans could deploy their submarines easily into the North Atlantic, the navy was in a far inferior position when compared with that of 1917–18. As a means of comparison, six months after the Germans had started unrestricted submarine warfare in 1917, the Royal Navy had at its disposal in home waters 449 vessels that could take part in convoy protection in some form, including 170 that were specifically devoted to escorting convoys through the particularly dangerous areas of the North Atlantic.[129] In March of 1940, six months after the Germans had announced unrestricted submarine warfare during World War II, the Royal Navy only had 135 vessels capable of providing any kind of convoy protection in home waters, though many of these had to be used in other duties. Just comparing destroyers, the most powerful type of escort ship, the difference between 1917 and 1940 is clear. In 1917 the Royal Navy had 277 destroyers fighting the U-boats, in March of 1940 they had 96.[130]

The relatively small number of British escort vessels made the war at sea much more difficult because, even though there were considerably fewer U-boats at sea in early 1940 than in 1917, those U-boats had a much larger pool of unescorted merchantmen to attack. In this first "Happy Time," the Germans could usually find merchantmen that they could attack with little fear of reprisal. Between July and October

1940, the U-boats sank 217 unescorted or inadequately escorted merchantmen while suffering only two losses from convoy escorts.[131]
During 1940 as a whole, 992 British or Allied merchant ships were lost
at sea anywhere on the globe, only 203 of which were sunk while in
convoy.[132] In percentage terms, of the 17,882 merchant ships that
sailed with convoy escort into and out of the UK in 1940, only 101,
or approximately 0.6 percent, were lost to German U-boats.[133]

   Therefore the first immediate need of the war at sea was for the
British to gain possession of more escort vessels. This was done by
ramping up home construction and through the hand-over of American
equipment. The American transfer of fifty World War I destroyers to
the British in September 1940 is sometimes seen as a mixed blessing.[134]
They were given to the British by Roosevelt as a stop-gap measure after
the fall of France. However, because of American domestic politics they
could not simply be handed over, and in exchange the British signed
over leases to a number of different naval bases in the western hemisphere, including Bermuda. The destroyers themselves were in need of
major renovation before they could operate with convoys, and their
reputation as submarine hunters was mixed. However, focusing on
their individual prowess misses the story. Their number allowed for
an expansion of convoys in 1941, which was a crucial element in the
failure of the German submarine effort in that year.

   The other area that needed an immediate increase was British
production of anti-submarine vessels. The British went to great lengths
to try to make up for their lack of production in the interwar years. In
the 1939 War Emergency Act, and the 1940 naval building program,
the government began construction on 120 destroyers of different
classes and 85 corvettes – all of which were completed.[135] It was these
vessels, more than pre-war construction, which would be the key to
winning the war against German U-boats in 1942 and 1943.

Anglo-American relations to November 1940

Franklin Roosevelt watched the unfolding war in Europe with greater
unease than most of his fellow Americans. There is a large historiography about American and Rooseveltian reactions in this period, in
particular focusing on the internationalist–isolationist debate.[136] Before
the fall of France, the Americans, at least to British eyes, seemed

unprepared. The British ambassador to the United States, Lord Lothian, described the country in September 1939 as being as ready for war as the United Kingdom was under the Baldwin government.[137] It was a view that was probably shared by many in the American armed forces, who believed that they had been deprived of the necessary funds for a military build-up to that point. Also, while there was a great deal of shock in the country about the outbreak of war, in particular the Nazi–Soviet pact, there was little desire to take part in a European conflagration. Again, as Lothian described the situation in February 1940 in a letter to Halifax, the American determination to avoid war was

> due partly to the historic isolationism based on Washington's warning against foreign entangling alliances. But it is also due to the fact that American public opinion has been educated in the last twenty years to believe that its participation in the last war was a profound mistake; that its entry then had been induced by astute British and French propagandists, supported by the buccaneers of Wall Street who wanted to make gigantic profits for themselves; that all the world's troubles since have sprung from the Treaty of Versailles, which is believed to have been passed by crooked statesmen of the old war in defiance of American idealism, and which has now been lifted into a kind of symbol of European wickedness; that Europe is incorrigible so that under no circumstances whatever will it do any good either to America or to Europe itself that the United States should once more entangle itself in Europe's internal problems.[138]

Franklin Roosevelt was acutely aware of and rather distressed by this widely shared view in his country. Privately he was a passionate supporter of the British and French in their war with Nazi Germany. However, always mindful of public opinion, publicly he was careful to stress the non-interventionist convictions of his administration. The first sign that Roosevelt was willing to substantially change America's position of neutrality happened in May 1940.

The collapse of France hit Roosevelt very hard, and reinforced his notion of the importance of air power. Some of the most detailed reports he heard about the fighting in France came from the American ambassador in Paris, William Bullitt.[139] Bullitt, who had a rather grandiose view of his own importance in the unfolding drama, described in lurid detail the devastation wrought by the Luftwaffe during the assault. His telegrams, sometimes more than one a day, spoke of wanton assaults on both civilians and military targets and left Roosevelt in no doubt that the aircraft was the decisive weapon in the war. On May 14, he wrote that "I have talked with eyewitnesses of the German bombings in Belgium and Luxemburg, including the Archduke Otto and Back, Foreign Minister of Luxemburg. Neither men, women, nor children are being spared and the tales of horror pass belief."[140] Later that same day he said in another telegram that this was one of "the most terrible moments of human history. France would fight on but the French soldiers, brave as they were, could not stand against simultaneous attacks by tanks on the ground and bombs and machine gun bullets from the air."[141] He also said that the French government told him directly that, if they were to have any hope of survival, they needed as many planes as possible from the United States.[142] It was a plea that Roosevelt received directly from the British as well. On May 15, 1940 Winston Churchill began his first telegram to FDR as Prime Minister with a claim that the Germans had a "marked preponderance" in the air and this was making a deep impression on France's ability to resist.[143] A few days later Churchill stated that Britain's greatest need was the immediate dispatch of as many P-40 fighter aircraft as possible from the United States.[144]

Roosevelt, who was already prejudiced in favor of building aircraft, seems to have been deeply affected by the statements from both Bullitt and Churchill about the effectiveness of air power. On May 16, he called for the United States to increase its annual production capacity for aircraft hugely to 50,000, so as to be able to field an AAF force of 36,500 planes and a USN air corps of 13,500.[145] As was typical of Roosevelt, the exact purpose of such a massive force was not explained, nor was it probable that FDR had clear notions about the use of air power: it was as though he wanted enough planes not to wage one kind of air war, but to wage all kinds of air war. The number was so large that it would allow for the transfer of masses of planes to the British. Even the American ambassador to the United Kingdom, Joseph Kennedy, who was normally not the most sanguine about Britain's ability to resist Nazi Germany at this point in the war, told the RAF that the United States would supply them with as many planes as they would need to take the war to Germany. He even mentioned the retooling of the automobile industry to make aircraft, which would be one of the decisive shifts in the production war.

Kennedy said that he understood that General Motors had taken the job in hand amongst others and that Ford also had joined in. If that is the case then we are going to have a real supply of aeroplanes, almost along the lines of what we originally contemplated. The training of 50,000 pilots also in America ... ought by the middle of next year to give us such a Force as to lay Germany flat, which would be very enjoyable.[146]

To transfer all the new aircraft, and other supplies, to Great Britain, Roosevelt needed a legal shield. Again immediately after the disaster in France, he started the negotiations that would conclude in the famous Destroyers for Bases deal, by which the United States would transfer not only warships, but B-17 bombers and ammunition to the UK in exchange for leases on British Empire bases in the western hemisphere.[147] The importance of keeping open the North Atlantic remained undimmed, and was considered the necessary prerequisite for any sustained flow of material from the United States to Great Britain. Of course, before the upcoming presidential election Roosevelt could not sell any of this to the American people as simply direct aid to the United Kingdom. When he first publicly spoke of the agreement, in September 1940, the president claimed that the deal created benefits for the United States similar to the Louisiana Purchase![148] It was an important but incomplete change. It was not until Roosevelt's re-election that the planning for a combined Anglo-American air and sea war could begin.

4 GRAND STRATEGISTS AND THE AIR AND SEA WAR

When Franklin Roosevelt died in April 1945, his closest war-time collaborator during the previous three years was devastated. He wrote in his private diary, beginning with a sentiment of general grief that could have been written in a mainstream newspaper. "This world tragedy deprives the Nation of its leader at a time when the war to preserve civilization is approaching its end with accelerated speed, and when a vital need for competent leadership in the making and preservation of world peace is at least seriously prejudiced by the passing of President Roosevelt who was a world figure of heroic proportions."[1]

Then Admiral William Leahy, Chief of Staff to the Commander in Chief of the Army and Navy of the United States, went in an entirely different direction, one that makes him stand out within the functioning of the American government, and the creation of American grand strategy, during the war. "His death is also a personal bereavement to me in the loss of a devoted friend whom I have known and admired for thirty-six years, since we first worked together in World War I." Three days later, after Leahy had accompanied Roosevelt's body to its interment in Hyde Park, New York, the President's family estate, the admiral was once again overcome with grief. At the end of the burial he wrote about "a long day that was for me full of sad memories, and that also for me probably was my last visit to the home of my friend who will live in history as one of our greatest Presidents. He was a great gentleman and a true friend."[2]

Neither George Marshall, Henry Arnold, Ernest King, Henry Stimson, Cordell Hull nor any other figure that influenced American grand strategy, with the possible exception of Harry Hopkins, could have honestly called Franklin Roosevelt a "true friend." Even Hopkins, who lived in the White House to be close to Roosevelt for two years, was more of a paladin than companion. This position gave Leahy enormous power, power he exercised but was careful never to call his own. However, his role in the American war effort has, mistakenly, been downplayed when compared with the others, especially Marshall.[3] After his appointment as Roosevelt's military Chief of Staff in July 1942, Leahy met with the President practically every day that he was in Washington, DC, dined regularly with the Roosevelt family, and spent holidays with the President either in Hyde Park or fishing. During much of 1944, when Roosevelt was either too tired to work (he spent much of the spring in Bernard Baruch's estate in South Carolina) or busy with the presidential campaign, Leahy ran a great deal of the American war effort. Much of what is known as the Churchill–Roosevelt correspondence in 1944 was actually the Churchill–Leahy correspondence.

What makes Leahy so important is that, thanks to his close knowledge of Roosevelt's intentions, it is through him that we can best see how the President's own views on the air and sea war evolved during the war. Unlike the other military chiefs of staff, Marshall, King and Arnold, who operated more as advocates for a certain policy, Leahy acted as Roosevelt's interpreter of policy. It was he who discussed the options privately with the President in the White House and, more often than not, he who transmitted the President's decisions to the rest of government. They were also two of only a handful of men who made the real decisions about the grand strategic questions for British and American air and sea weaponry. From 1941 onwards, these decisions were really in the hands of eleven men. British strategic planning was dominated by only one civilian, Prime Minister Winston Churchill, and the different service chiefs, Field Marshal Alan Francis Brooke (later Lord Alanbrooke), Air Marshal Charles Portal (affectionately called Peter and later ennobled as the 1st Viscount Portal of Hungerford), Admiral Sir A. Dudley Pound and his successor as First Sea Lord, Admiral Sir Andrew Cunningham (known by his nickname ABC and later ennobled as 1st Viscount Cunningham of Hyndhope).[4] They all attempted to steer the Prime Minister in different directions and worked out the details with their American counterparts and British subordinates, which determined where the different air, sea and land efforts would be made. It is interesting to see how little influence other members of the Cabinet had over grand strategy. The Foreign Secretary, Anthony Eden, was at the heart of World War II diplomacy but was not a major player in determining strategic war campaigns. Labour members of the Cabinet, in particular the Deputy Prime Minister Clement Attlee and the Minister of Labour Ernest Bevin, had huge impact on British domestic policy, in many ways far greater than Churchill's, but were not part of the strategic discussion in any meaningful way.

Unlike among the British, there was one civilian in the United States who did play a major role in strategic policy, at least in 1941 and 1942, and that was Harry Hopkins. As long as he was fully trusted by Franklin Roosevelt, and healthy enough to discharge his duties, Hopkins acted as the eyes, ears and voice of the President. As in Britain, members of the Cabinet who one would think would matter in strategic decisions about war fighting were often kept at arm's length by Roosevelt and his service chiefs. Neither the Secretary of State, Cordell Hull, nor the Secretaries of War and the Navy, Henry Stimson and Frank Knox, were particularly influential in making the major strategic choices. Only James Forrestal, who succeeded Knox in May 1944, had real influence over Roosevelt and the service chiefs, but by the time he took his position most of the major decisions had already been made.

The eleven men who did make the real choices operated under enormous strain during the war. Two of them died (Roosevelt and Pound), two of them almost died (Hopkins and Arnold), one of them had a clear depressive breakdown (Churchill), while Ernest King and Alanbrooke seemed on edge for much of the time. Only Leahy, Marshall, Portal and Cunningham served from 1942 to 1945 in moderately good health, though even they had their moments. In a later chapter the particular debates that they had will be discussed in more detail. However, understanding their general outlook on the air and sea war will help provide a foundation for understanding how the war was fought to eventual victory.

Roosevelt and Churchill

Winston S. Churchill and Franklin D. Roosevelt are two of the most discussed personalities in history.[5] Their roles as war leaders have been the subject of numerous books and articles, to say nothing of plays, television shows and films. Their relationship has been analyzed from almost every perspective and almost all of their correspondence has been published, making it almost impossible to say anything new about them. Their personal relationship was the most important one of the war. Both during and for a while after the conflict, it was common to stress their common purpose and close personal connection. More recently, a group of historians has put stress on the tensions in their relationship – in particular over the future of the British Empire.[6]

There are strong elements of truth in both portrayals. Within the history of wartime alliances, the Roosevelt–Churchill relationship was remarkably close, and they communicated on an intimate level that has rarely happened between the leaders of such large global powers. This always should be remembered, particularly now when the stress is often on the more tempestuous side of their relationship. On the other hand, they viewed the world very differently, and this did lead to real, and in some ways growing, problems. Churchill was in many ways fighting for the past. He definitely wanted to forestall change, to maintain for as long as possible the British Empire as one of the world's few "superpowers." His policies in the war, though they might seem erratic or at least unpredictable, had this as their guiding principle. He famously said in 1942 that he had not become the king's First Minister in order "to preside over the liquidation of the British Empire."[7] Roosevelt, on the other hand, was fighting for change, even if he wasn't entirely sure what that future change would be. He certainly kept his more specific intentions very much to himself. As Leahy said of American war aims (and he would have known better than anyone other than Roosevelt), no other American really had a clue. "There were times when I felt that if I could find anybody except Roosevelt who knew what America wanted, it would be an astonishing discovery."[8] He wanted passionately to destroy Fascist Europe and militarist Japan and replace them with what he considered more progressive systems, certainly something closer to New Deal America. He put a great emphasis on crushing "imperialism," by which he meant systems that were not only non-democratic but also not evolving in a democratic way (thus in his mind excepting the USSR, which he believed was dictatorial but heading in the right direction). When it came to the non-European world, Roosevelt believed that the United States and the United Kingdom should play a guiding but not controlling role, therefore putting him at odds with the British Empire as constructed. The President did not go to war to save the British Empire – in many ways he went to war to ease the process of its dissolution.

If there was one issue that early in the war best showed the difference between the two men it was their assumptions about India.[9] For Roosevelt, India was on an unstoppable course to becoming an independent nation, and so he believed that Indian nationalism should be encouraged as part of the war effort. In early 1942 he seemed willing to act as a negotiator between the British government and Indian nationalists, as part of a plan that would end British rule in the country.[10] In March, he even sent Churchill a telegram in which he suggested, either helpfully or maliciously, that India should be seen as in a historical equivalent to the American colonies between 1776 and 1783.[11] Churchill, on the other hand, worked feverishly to postpone any change in the relationship between India and the British Empire. Although he almost certainly realized that the future would lead to greater Indian autonomy, at the least, he wanted to keep that day at bay for as long as possible.

When it came to the air and sea war, they did share many basic similarities. Both were determined to have a strong numerical superiority in machines and both believed that winning the air and sea war was the crucial predeterminate to victory on land. That said, there were important differences between them on how to achieve this victory, differences that came from their ultimate purpose in fighting World War II. Churchill, in trying to maintain British greatness, was determined to keep the number of British casualties as low as possible and therefore had an aversion to large land battles.[12] He was far more willing to let air and sea power act before committing a large British Empire force to fight in northwest Europe. Roosevelt, on the other hand, wanted to show the United States' commitment to the future by having American soldiers fighting on the ground as soon as possible.

Roosevelt may have been the greatest politician elected President of the United States, and he brought his immense, if at times waning, skills in this area to the conduct of grand strategy. Though there has been a great deal of nonsense written about how Roosevelt supposedly knew about the Japanese attack on Pearl Harbor ahead of time, and was willing to leave American military personnel unprotected to solidify the case for war, it certainly is true that he was determined to get the United States involved in World War II before the Japanese attack. From the moment of his re-election in November 1940, he pursued a policy that can best be described as acting as a non-combatant ally of the United Kingdom. Three days after being re-elected, he called for a plan whereby half of all US war production would be sent to the United Kingdom.[13] In this he worked extremely hard, and sometimes in direct opposition to the desires of his service chiefs, to send as much aid as possible to Great Britain.

When it came to his grand strategic assumptions, pinning Roosevelt down to one policy, or even set of policies, is not the easiest thing to do. In 1942 he was a forceful and impetuous war leader, and this meant that he determined US policy in many areas. He definitely favored the construction of air and sea weapons over ground equipment when it came to military construction. Two weeks after the attack on Pearl Harbor, he instructed Marshall to draft a strategy memo on the course of the war which gave first mention to the creation of an air war against Germany and Japan.[14] Later in 1942 he overruled his service chiefs in imposing targets for aircraft construction that made the building of planes easily the highest priority in American construction – and led to steep declines in AFV building. He certainly was a strong supporter of a strategic air war against Germany, though he was never particularly specific about how that war should be fought.[15] When it came to shipbuilding, he was quite farsighted in seeing the need for a host of smaller vessels, including both landing craft and anti-submarine vessels, the construction of which he started pushing for early in 1942.[16]

On the other hand, he was determined from the moment the USA entered the war to get American ground forces into combat quickly, even if it subverted any proper planning for an air and sea war. Thus Roosevelt became the driving force, again over the skepticism of his service chiefs, pushing for an American invasion of North Africa in 1942. This was a crucial decision as it not only closed down other arcs of strategic advance, it meant that the Mediterranean as a theater now became one that rivalled northwest Europe in Anglo-American minds for the next two years. In the Pacific, he also sometimes acted impulsively. At one time he seemed to order so many men and machines to go to protect Australia that it would have made any significant 1942 build-up in Europe impossible.[17]

Internationally, he was also determined to obtain as much aid as possible for the United Kingdom, the USSR and China, even if it hampered the speed of America's own air and sea build-up. Roosevelt seemed determined that the wartime alliance, of which he sat at the apex, would endure afterwards to control global security. Again, being Franklin Roosevelt, he was not particularly concrete in his plans as to how this would be achieved, but his intentions were clear. Thus, to him, it was extremely important to maintain close relations with the three other warlords, Churchill, Josef Stalin and Chiang Kai-Shek. This seems to have shaped many of his assumptions about how the air and sea war should be fought. In the Pacific, he was definitely part of the group that believed America should aim to open up a road to China as soon as possible and to use China as the major base from which the war against Japan would be prosecuted to its victorious conclusion.

When it came to supporting the USSR, Roosevelt not only made the delivery of aid one of his highest priorities, he was willing to risk ruptures with the British government when he believed the latter was letting Stalin down.[18] In 1942, when it was clear that the British would resist any quick invasion of France, Roosevelt ordered Marshall and King to study whether the USA could invade without British support.[19] He even proposed a suicidal invasion of France if it looked like the USSR might collapse.[20] Ever the practical politician, Roosevelt did seem to believe that the USA and the USSR were not as far apart ideologically as many of the extremists in both countries suggested, and that after the war the two countries could cooperate. As he told Secretary of the Navy Knox, Soviet communists were considerably more reasonable than American communists.

> The Soviet people in Moscow are said to have little liking for the American Communists and their methods – especially because it seems increasingly true that the Communism of twenty years ago has ceased to exist in Russia. At the present time their system is much more like a form of the older Socialism conducted, however, through a complete dictatorship combined with an overwhelming loyalty to the cause of throwing every German out of Russia.[21]

On the surface, Roosevelt seemed a strong supporter of the Germany-First policy. He clearly believed that the Nazi state was the more formidable enemy of the United States and reassured the British from early on that the United States would direct a large majority of its efforts towards Europe. On the other hand, he did not envisage a mere holding operation in the Pacific (even when he used that exact phrase). On May 6, 1942 he specifically spelled out his intentions for the Pacific to the Joint Chiefs, Hopkins and Stimson, in a farsighted memorandum.

> The whole of the Pacific area calls, at the present time, fundamentally for a holding operation...
>
> Defense of all essential points in the Pacific Theater is the primary objective. This defense calls for offense in two areas – attacks upon the Japanese lines of communication and the bombing of Japan proper from the east and west.
>
> The objective of this defense strengthened by offensive actions is to destroy or damage as many Japanese naval vessels, merchant ships and airplanes as possible. In this regard, it is essential to maintain destruction or damage of a much larger number of Japanese ships and planes each month than they can replace. In other words, combat against Japanese ships and planes must be sought out in order to hasten the attrition of Japanese arms.[22]

The "holding" operation that FDR was calling for was not only well thought out and expressed, it would also require a very large commitment of American force. The United States would be expected to send enough ships and aircraft to the Pacific to sink Japanese forces at a high rate, and at the same time begin approaching the Japanese mainland through both China and the Pacific islands, so that it could be strategically bombed. It was basically everything but the invasion of the Japanese homeland itself.

If the Roosevelt of 1942 was energetic and decisive, the Roosevelt of later in the war seems ever more circumspect and tired. Also, he played only a minor role in operational strategy, and as the war became more one of fighting than of planning, his interjections became less crucial.[23] The arrival of Leahy meant that the President corresponded less frequently with his chiefs and wrote fewer strategic memos of this type. Instead his wishes were communicated through his new Chief of Staff and, crucially, the other chiefs were often instructed to go through Leahy before approaching the President. This was something that the British understood as well, as Churchill would approach Leahy with tricky issues that he didn't want brought directly to Roosevelt.[24] Moreover, Roosevelt seemed to become physically less powerful as the war developed. His illnesses lingered and his holidays lengthened. Beginning in the second half of 1943, in particular after the conferences in Cairo and Teheran, he seemed to tire far more easily.[25] He could still raise himself to intervene strongly if concerned, such as in his desires to keep relations amicable with Stalin and Chiang-Kai Shek, but when it came to the specifics of the war, as long as success was being achieved he did not intervene nearly as often or as forcefully. In 1944 this tendency not to intervene only grew as the impending presidential election took up more of his decreasing strength.

Churchill's influence over British strategic policy remained far more hands-on during the entire course of the conflict. Of course he had a far more difficult job than Roosevelt. In the first place, he was definitely not one of the greatest domestic politicians of his era. Had World War II not come about, he would be known as one of the great "almost" figures of British political history, with a long career involving many different major Cabinet positions, but also a record of distrust that kept him from ever reaching the top. When the war broke out, however, both his experience and energy were desperately needed, so much so that his shortcomings were overlooked.

As a war leader, Churchill had a number of evident talents. In a political culture that often prized the ironic or understated, he had an ability to capture a moment or a mood with directness. His speech about the Battle of Britain, given before the battle really started and based on faulty intelligence, helped define British resistance both at the time and in the decades after the war. The line that "never has so much been owed by so many to so few" is one of the few unforgettable phrases of the entire conflict.

Churchill also knew his limitations as a war leader, particularly domestically, and worked amicably within a coalition government in this area – even if it ended up being disastrous for himself politically. He gave different Labour ministers, particularly Clement Attlee and Ernest Bevin, huge scope to influence British life to aid the war effort. The latter, in production terms, wielded enormous power through his control of the workforce. Through this, Britain was able to produce a large amount of war materials and fight the air and sea war in an advanced manner.

What Churchill has been most criticized for as a war leader, however, most bitterly by those who had to work with him during the war, was his supposed erratic and impulsive nature which led him to latch on to fanciful and dangerous plans. In Alanbrooke's diary this is a constant complaint. When Admiral Cunningham took over as the First Sea Lord in October 1943, he was advised by Alanbrooke's predecessor, Field Marshal Sir John Dill, not to give in to Churchill's notions. "In council with – shall I call him the Minister of Defence? – you will have great difficulty in controlling your hackles! Perhaps it will be best if you don't attempt to control them entirely."[26] After taking office, Cunningham soon started complaining about what he believed was Churchill's childishness and stupidity.[27]

It is impossible, even in private, to imagine the American Chiefs of Staff speaking about Roosevelt in this fashion, and that partly points out one of the great difficulties for Churchill as a war leader. He lacked a Hopkins or a Leahy, someone whom he trusted to act as his protector and buffer. He did have Hastings "Pug" Ismay, who had been secretary of the Committee for Imperial Defence just before the war, and became Churchill's chief secretarial officer during it.[28] But Ismay was an unassertive and plodding man who had few opinions or, if he did, was rarely able to articulate them. Churchill's political colleagues, on the other hand, were also rivals, most of them aiming to succeed to the top job themselves. He did have people he trusted, such as Brendan Bracken or Lord Cherwell, but they were not at the heart of the strategy-making apparatus.[29] As such, Churchill often felt besieged by those both within the British government and outside who tried to alter his plans.

And plan he did, though perhaps not as erratically as it seemed to some of his contemporaries. Churchill's strategic notions almost all involved campaigns that deliberately avoided large commitments of land forces. For this reason, under his leadership aircraft and naval construction always seemed to win the lion's share of British effort. When it came to large-scale operations, until almost the moment the troops went ashore on D-Day, Churchill tried to delay an invasion of France. It has been argued that his faith in the British army being able to beat the Germans on land had been severely undermined by 1942, and that he never fully recovered from this.[30] He also saw no geopolitical need for an invasion of France. Believing from the moment the Japanese attacked Pearl Harbor that the UK would now be on the winning side, Churchill wanted the United Kingdom to emerge from the contest with as small losses as possible. As such he saw no reason to attack the Germans where they were strongest, but wanted to whittle them away at the edges, letting strategic air power damage their morale and economic might while the USSR faced the majority of the German army.[31] It is debatable whether this policy was deliberately aimed at weakening the USSR for the post-war world, though that has been the view of many.[32]

In 1942 and 1943, Churchill led the charge to concentrate the ground fighting in North Africa and the Mediterranean. In this he showed admirable determination and, when he was supported by Alanbrooke and Portal, was able to triumph over the American plan, championed mostly by Marshall, to attack France much sooner.[33] In some ways, however, he was moving away from a more modern conception of warfare in doing so. In 1941 and early 1942, Churchill more commonly referred to the need to engage German air power as a major part of his strategy. When he first met with Stalin, in August 1942, he tried to justify his focus on the Mediterranean by telling the Soviet dictator that it would open up new areas from which to attack German air power, including the strategic bombing of German production.[34] By the second half of 1943, however, this argument had mostly disappeared and he talked almost entirely in a battle-centric manner about the need to divert German divisions from the Eastern Front and France.[35]

When the Americans forced the British to plan the invasion of France for the spring of 1944 (codenamed Overlord), Churchill fought them so strenuously that he had what is best termed a depressive collapse in Cairo.[36] Even as late as April 1944, as the American and British armies were preparing for the Normandy assault, Churchill described his strategic concepts to the American General A. C. Wedemeyer, who was passing through London on his way to becoming Mountbatten's deputy in the South East Asian Command.

> The P.M. [Churchill] did state that if he had been able to persuade the Chiefs of Staff, the Allies would have gone through Turkey and the Balkans from the south and into Norway on the north, thus surrounding the enemy and further dispersing his forces. He added, however, that the die is cast and that we must carry Overlord through vigorously to a successful conclusion. I told him that I liked very much to conjecture on what might have happened if we had taken the bulk of the half million men and the 8000 airplanes that we employed in Mediterranean operations and moved them to the British Isles for an invasion in April 1943. It told him that we would have been undertaking our operations when Germany was

so terribly committed and overextended against the Russians, and I sometimes felt that we would have by this time created a vast airdrome in France from which we could bomb, with fighter protection, Germany's most vital installations. He replied in a dramatic manner that he would personally assume the responsibility before God for the decision to do Torch and the operations which immediately followed. It was amusing, I can assure you, and at two-thirty in the morning I went back to the hotel, chaste and enlightened.[37]

Churchill's desire to avoid a large direct land battle extended to the Pacific, particularly after the fall of Singapore to the Japanese. Before that time British strategists were intent on a major commitment to the war in the Pacific, particularly in terms of ships and aircraft. The surrender of Singapore, on the other hand, almost completely eliminated this desire and the British opted for a very defensive attitude based around protecting India. They, quite adeptly as it turned out, rebuffed American pressure to commit large forces to invade Burma and reopen an efficient land route to China. Becoming involved in a large land war that would have stretched into China was in no way something the British could have undertaken at the time without a huge diversion of effort. On the other hand, Churchill did continue to push some aggressive action, though by a more circuitous route. In August 1943 he latched upon the notion of a landing in northern Sumatra (DEI) which was relatively lightly defended. Conceptually, there was actually a great deal to be said for such a move: if successful, it would have stopped the flow of oil from the DEI. On the other hand, it was an operation that was probably beyond British capabilities in the Pacific at the time, specifically in regard to landing craft and naval air support. So Churchill's different planning was not nearly as erratic as it seemed to those around him. He was looking for campaigns that Britain could fight with air and sea weaponry primarily. If the ideas seemed disconnected, it was in their location and number, not their intention.

The Americans: Leahy, King, Marshall, Arnold and Hopkins

While discussing the different service chiefs from a national perspective provides a partially prejudicial narrative (in many cases American and

British service chiefs actually agreed along service lines against fellow countrymen in different branches of the armed forces), nationality also provides an important element of strategic and structural separation. Also, personal relationships played a material role in shaping decision-making. The Leahy–Roosevelt relationship went back to 1915, when Roosevelt, who was serving as Assistant Secretary of the Navy in the Wilson administration, was a mostly unknown Democratic politician with a valuable last name. Leahy, a young officer with a finely developed political nose, took over command of the Secretary of the Navy's personal dispatch boat, and through that, the two men became friends to the degree that Leahy actually visited with Roosevelt at both his Hyde Park and Campobello homes.[38] Unfortunately, there is a perplexing neglect shown by historians towards Leahy's powerful role in the making of World War II strategic policy.[39] Mark Stoler, who has written by far the best works on the American Joint Chiefs of Staffs during the war, is one of the few who comment intelligently on his power and influence.[40]

Through this contact Roosevelt obviously derived a high opinion of Leahy's organizational skills and personal loyalty. In 1937 he named Leahy as his Chief of Naval Operations, which meant that the admiral was in charge during the build-up of American naval vessels that began at that time. When Leahy retired in 1939, Roosevelt rewarded him with the Distinguished Service Medal and made him governor of Puerto Rico. At the time the President told him: "Bill, if we have a war, you're going to be right back here helping me to run it."[41] Instead of allowing Leahy to enjoy the pleasures of Puerto Rico for too long, after the fall of France in 1940 Roosevelt once again showed his great confidence in the man by making him the ambassador to Vichy France, the most important American diplomat in occupied Europe.[42]

All of this was the table-setting to what came later. After the Pearl Harbor attacks, Roosevelt recalled Leahy as soon as it was diplomatically convenient, and made him his military Chief of Staff in Washington, a position that made him the second most important American in deciding the grand strategy of the war. Unlike Marshall, King or Arnold, Leahy quickly entered into Roosevelt's inner circle. He took up residence across the street from the White House in the Hays-Adam Hotel and was one of only three men to have an office in the new East Wing (the other two were Harry Hopkins and James

Byrnes).[43] The British delegation in Washington was quick to understand his powerful position in the White House. Brigadier Vivian Dykes, who was the British secretary to the Combined Chiefs of Staff, discussed Leahy's appointment with his US counterpart Walter Bedell-Smith and was told "that Admiral Leahy will almost certainly become a super-Chief of Staff for the Americans – a Pug Ismay, but senior instead of junior."[44] A few weeks after he took up his new post, the British embassy, which was always sensitive to power in Roosevelt's court, paid Leahy the ultimate compliment by treating him as the most important guest during the funeral service for the Duke of Kent, which attracted the cream of Washington society.[45] However, what mattered more to Leahy was how Roosevelt viewed him, and the President made it clear from the beginning that he wanted Leahy beside him whenever possible. In early September 1942 he went away with the President for a two-night stay at "Shangri-La," Roosevelt's favorite retreat in the Catochin Hills.[46]

Moreover, as the war went on and Roosevelt became less energetic, Leahy became more and more a gatekeeper controlling access to the President. He was the only man in constant contact with all the different strategic elements of the American government, from the State Department to the Joint Chiefs to the President himself. The only way for the Joint Chiefs of Staff to get major decisions from Roosevelt, such as whether the United States should push for the invasion of southern France under the Anvil plan, was through Leahy using his influence with the President.[47] He also clearly played a role in deciding what information the rest of the Joint Chiefs of Staff would be told on issues of diplomacy. It was Leahy who often decided what elements of Churchill's correspondence with Roosevelt would be sent to the other chiefs.[48] This power was one that Marshall, at least, feared. He complained at different times that Leahy was not letting him know important decisions, such as the decision to break off diplomatic relations with Finland in 1943.[49]

This continual access to the President stands in stark contrast to the other American military chiefs. It also means that his power has been severely underestimated. His relative silence during major arguments has been remarked upon as if to imply he didn't influence events.[50] This is a fundamental miscalculation. Leahy's power was such that he did not need to argue with the other chiefs; all he needed was the support of the President, which he had in spades. Even traveling to

18 Franklin D. Roosevelt's inner circle. This picture is indicative of the special
place that Harry Hopkins and William Leahy had in the President's eyes.
Here they are celebrating FDR's birthday with him in the air on January 31, 1945.
The fourth man is the plane's pilot. Marshall, King and Arnold traveled in
another plane.

something like the Casablanca Conference in January 1943 showed the
difference. Leahy was always berthed in Roosevelt's own railway car or
personal plane (See Figure 18.). The other chiefs were given a completely separate railway car or plane.[51] Marshall and Roosevelt had a
professional relationship, and it seems that they met together alone
only a few times during the entire war. King, whom Roosevelt valued,
was also kept at arm's length personally, and later in the war the
President showed real irritation at what he thought was King's heavy-
handedness in the Navy Department.[52] Arnold, meanwhile, had even
less access to Roosevelt and suffered a number of heart attacks during
the war which kept him away from the President for long periods of
time. The President seemed to value a number of things which explain
why he kept Leahy close. The admiral was not a prima donna; he was,
while intelligent, not a showy intellect; and, perhaps most importantly,
he was extremely discreet. For instance, like Field Marshal Lord Alanbrooke, who filled a somewhat analogous role with Winston Churchill,
Leahy kept a diary. However, it was a rigidly controlled piece of
recollection in which the American was the model of discretion. While
Alanbrooke was petulant, gossipy and opinionated on almost every
page, Leahy only rarely ventured a personal view. When he did, however, it clearly mattered to him – and through that we can see how he
guided Roosevelt in a certain direction.

Although Leahy became Chief of Staff in July 1942, it was not
until September 9 that he gave in the diary a clear indication of the

direction in which he would like to push American grand strategy. It came after his description of a meeting between himself and a Chinese military delegation. "I have an idea that Great Britain will not give any useful assistance to a Burma expedition at the present time, and it is my opinion that from the long distance American viewpoint of essentials in our own war effort, the opening of the Burma Road and the support of China should have a very high priority."[53] It was one of a number of mentions in his diary where Leahy clearly expressed a desire for the United States to prioritize operations in the war against Japan.[54] While he recognized that Germany was a stronger economic enemy, he was never a "Germany-Firster" in strategy. He was worried that Japan, if allowed to prepare its defenses while American effort was directed at Europe, would be extremely difficult to fight and would take years longer to conquer. Furthermore, he was acutely aware of the future importance of China, and showed constant frustration with what he believed was British reluctance to send appropriate forces into the war against Japan.

The other member of the Joint Chiefs of Staff to agree with Leahy on this priority was, not surprisingly, Ernest King. King's desire to concentrate more effort in the Pacific at the expense of the war against Germany was widely acknowledged both during the war and after. Alanbrooke thought he was a fanatic on the subject. He certainly was willing to dissemble wildly to obtain more resources for the Pacific, as he did at the time of the Casablanca Conference in January 1943. King's desire, however, was more basic than that of Leahy. The latter seemed motivated by a number of considerations: the future of China and the real threat that Japan posed if it was allowed to establish a firm defensive perimeter, as well as the desire to have the United States carve out a policy in the region that was distinct from the British Empire. For King, on the other hand, the desire to send more force to the Pacific was about the need for a singular success for the United States Navy. Deeply suspicious of the British and of the American army, if more respectful of the former and less so of the latter than people realize, King wanted an area of independent action where the United States Navy could shine. He even tried to make it impossible for the British to take part in the final assault against Japan, to keep them from gaining any credit for victory in the Pacific.[55] In the Atlantic he believed the American fleet would always be duelling with the Royal Navy for prominence, and would probably lose the public relations battle owing to British craftiness. Any war in Europe would also certainly end with a large American army in Europe, and once again the navy would be over-shadowed. In the Pacific, however, the American navy would be the vital service.

As King wrote in a series of pungent, handwritten notes after the war:

> One should recall that the British have been managing world affairs for well over three hundred years, that is, since the defeat of the Spanish Armada in 1588. Meanwhile they had seen many changes during this period but they seemed to carry on just as they had been doing and they entered into World War II with the same idea in mind. However after Dec. 7 1941, a great change took place since it was the United States who had the forces, the material and especially the money. The U.S. also had the basic idea that the situation in the Pacific required some attention and effort and should carry on at the same time as assistance was being given to the British and the other Allies against the Nazis and Fascists in Europe where the British thought they had their own ideas "sewed up."[56]

A few lines later he added:

> The British were able to convince some people in the U.S. – especially the Army that the British course of action was the best to follow. Since most U.S. people did not want to leave Japan a free hand to "round-up" the entire Pacific – that is where I came into the picture – when I was ordered to command the United States Fleet – and I naturally did everything I could to go after the Japanese. That is where I ran afoul of the British with their contrary basic idea and the U.S. Army whose leaders did not understand *sea power*. But I seemed to be able to carry on against the "enemy" in spite of my troubles getting attention focused on the Pacific. (Emphasis in original)[57]

When the United States Navy had complete control of the waters around Japan, something that they had been inexorably establishing since the capture of the Marianas, King wanted to ensure that the British fleet was kept as far away as possible from the final victory to make sure that the USN's superiority was recognized.[58]

Whether King's bitterest enemy was the Japanese, the British or the American army would be difficult to say. Of course, it was this aggressive spirit that made King attractive to Roosevelt in the first place. A trained naval aviator, he never entered Roosevelt's inner circle in the 1930s.[59] The President seemed wary of his heavy drinking (King once developed a cocktail known as the King's Peg which was a lethal combination of brandy and champagne), but he did respect his undoubted drive and aggression. In the wake of the Pearl Harbor attacks, King was thought by both the President and the Secretary of the Navy, Frank Knox, to be the dynamic force the American fleet needed to get it back on its feet. To the President's later chagrin, he actually created the most powerful position in the history of the USN for King, making him both the commander in chief of the United States Fleet (all ships in the navy) and Chief of Naval Operations, and therefore also in control of all the onshore naval bureaucracy.[60]

From this position King exercised enormous power over the fleet for the rest of the war. Compared with the other service chiefs, he kept his main theater commander, Admiral Chester Nimitz, on a very short leash. Where Marshall usually gave Eisenhower a free hand in deciding strategy in Europe and Arnold allowed Generals Eaker and Spaatz latitude to design their own strategic air campaigns, King was constantly meeting with Nimitz and pushing the Texan down certain strategic routes, even rebuking him strongly when he thought the commander of the Pacific Fleet had erred. On the other hand, King's immense influence also contributed to at least one major disaster. Perhaps his greatest shortcoming was his reluctance until the summer of 1942 to support the convoying of merchantmen along the American seaboard. He was, rightly in my opinion, strongly criticized for this, which was partly responsible for the enormous loss in merchant shipping that the Allies suffered in the first six months of the year – the highest merchant shipping losses for the entire war. One of the reasons for this blunder was clearly that King wanted to keep as many ships as possible in the Pacific. And it was in that region that he developed the most sophisticated air and sea strategy of World War II: the Central Pacific drive against the Marianas. At the time of American entry, and for almost all of 1942, the intended direction of the American drive through the Pacific was a long slog up through the Dutch East Indies, to the Philippines and then on to the Asian mainland and China. It was a perimeter strategy that would have involved high losses in equipment and personnel.

King, starting in December 1942 and before anyone else at the top of American decision-making, understood the importance of a Central Pacific drive. Unlike the American air force, which imagined basing heavy bombers in China to assault Japan, he realized that the Marianas offered even closer and easier to supply bases from which the newly designed super-bomber (known as the B-29) could bombard Japan. Moreover, taking the Marianas isolated Japan from the oil and other resources of its southern empire as fully as (and considerably less expensively than) physically invading those territories. It is here that the relationship between King and Leahy shows how important the latter would be in the making of American grand strategy. King set out trying to win his way through sheer mendacity – he decided to cook the books.[61]

If King was relatively successful in achieving his greatest aim in the air and sea war, Marshall and Arnold were considerably less so. Of the two, George Marshall remains the most difficult to judge. Opinions on the man during World War II were so wildly divergent that it is hard to believe at times that the different observers were talking about the same individual. Alanbrooke clearly thought Marshall was an empty, if finely tailored, suit. He constantly remarked on what he believed to be his basic stupidity and inability to grasp simple strategic concepts.[62] King, in contrast, often thought Marshall was a devious plotter, protecting the interests of the army in various underhanded ways.[63] On the other hand, the soon-to-be Air Marshal Sir John Slessor, who visited Washington, DC on a crucial mission in 1941, believed Marshall was a great man and by "head and shoulders" the most impressive officer within the US army.[64] Within the army there was enormous respect and affection for Marshall, and Eisenhower, for one, constantly treated him with considerable deference. Certainly, from the point of view of history, Marshall is, more than any other member of the Joint or even Combined Chiefs of Staff, seen as the greatest figure of them all. Roosevelt, meanwhile, came to see him as invaluable in running the US army and kept him in Washington, DC when it was originally expected that he would be sent to Europe to serve as supreme commander during the invasion of France in 1944. At the same time, Roosevelt and Marshall also maintained a rather distant relationship. The President seemed far more interested in sea power and aircraft construction than in large land armies, and so rarely expressed strong opinions about Marshall's area of expertise – except to always overrule him and call for cuts in ground equipment building. When Marshall was appointed Chief of Staff of the army in 1939, he at first found his access to the President to be quite restricted.[65] Roosevelt personally never seemed particularly comfortable with the stiffer, more formal Marshall.[66] When the President tried to add an air of intimacy to their relationship by referring to Marshall as "George," the general blanched.

If there is one major correction that needs to be made about Marshall, it is to de-emphasize his importance within the overall strategy of World War II. In terms of both the production that was under his direct control, and his own plans for the defeat of Germany and Japan, it could be argued he was actually the least important and effective of the Joint Chiefs of Staff. In Europe he was mostly concerned with setting as early a date as possible for a land invasion of northwest Europe. In that policy he was thwarted for at least a year and a half. He contemplated plans for an invasion as early as the second half of 1942, and seemed really determined to press ahead with an invasion in 1943 at the latest.[67] To realize these plans, he wanted the United States to concentrate on the build-up of American forces in the United Kingdom under Operation Bolero. To make sure that Bolero was given the highest priority, he was instinctively skeptical of any large-scale commitment of American ground forces in other areas such as North Africa or the Mediterranean. In 1942 he was reluctant at first to support the invasion of North Africa, codenamed "Gymnast", and disagreed with the President when Roosevelt first started supporting it.[68] In 1943 he was one of the most vocal opponents of any commitment of forces to invade Italy. He saw some advantage to an invasion of Sicily as there were already a large number of American forces in the theater, but he showed no desire to widen operations to include an invasion of the Italian mainland itself.[69] Instead he wanted the British and Americans to throw everything possible into an invasion of France in 1943. He lost every one of these strategic arguments.

When it came to the specifics of the air and sea wars, Marshall was also relatively detached. The US Army Air Force was allowed to develop American strategic air power doctrine on its own, with little input from the army's Chief of Staff. Instead Marshall viewed air power mostly from a tactical point of view. When Ira Eaker presented the first complete plan for the strategic bombing of Germany in 1943, Marshall wondered whether it was wise to devote so much force to the effort and instead favored the diversion of aircraft to more tactical roles.[70] His focus on the support of ground forces usually led him to argue for greater production of land vehicles. In 1942, when it was becoming clear that the United States would not be able to build everything that it had planned, he argued for the prioritizing of different armored vehicles.[71] A few months later, he was the leader of the Joint Chiefs in their arguments with the President over the latter's clear preference for maximum aircraft construction.[72]

When it came to the wider question of theater priorities, Marshall was always the most assertive of the Germany-First lobby. In 1942 he warned regularly against the deployment of too much US force to the Pacific. In May 1942, he told the President that operations in Europe were so important that he (Marshall) doubted whether the United States should even try to hold the Japanese in the Pacific. He summarized his overall strategic priorities as follows:

> While I agree that we must *hold* in the Pacific, I do not concur that this is our "basic strategic plan." My view, and I understood it to be your decision prior to your visit to England, was that our major effort would be to concentrate immediately for offensive action against Germany from the British Islands...Hence, the urgency of "Bolero." Only by a complete and whole-hearted acceptance by all concerned, British and American, and by the exertion of every practicable effort on the part of all, can "Bolero" have any chance of success.[73]

Marshall thus wanted strict limits on the numbers of army air and ground units sent to the Pacific. He resented sending reinforcements to the Pacific when the fighting on Guadalcanal descended into expensive attritional warfare. As for the overall strategic direction of the Pacific campaign, he was the most committed member of the Joint Chiefs in favor of a strategic thrust towards China.[74] Even in late 1944 he was pushing for a large commitment of ground forces to China as part of the overall defeat of Japan. In these areas he was usually outmaneuvered by Ernest King, who understood far earlier than Marshall the way that victory would be achieved in the Pacific.

In the end, Marshall was probably the least influential member of the Joint Chiefs when it came to the ultimate victory over Germany and Japan. He controlled the smallest equipment pool in terms of production cost and showed the least interest in the fundamentals of the production war. He lost most of the strategic arguments in

1942 and 1943, only seeing success in Europe in 1944, and never really contributing to the crucial campaigns that saw Japan defeated.

In contrast to this, the man who actually had control over a huge amount of American production was the member of the Joint Chiefs of Staff who is often considered the least powerful, Henry "Hap" Arnold. A graduate of the West Point class of 1907, Arnold quickly gravitated towards military aviation. He was in the first class of trained army aviators, having been taught the craft by the Wright brothers themselves. During World War I, he first played a role supervising aircraft construction before shipping out to Europe just before the armistice.[75] In the interwar period his great energy and flair for showmanship (he undertook a number of long-distance flights that received public coverage) helped him rise to the top. When the Army Air Corps was created in July 1941, he was chosen to be its first commanding general. When the Joint Chiefs of Staff was assembled, he naturally sat in as the Chief of Staff of the air force. As such, he was in an extremely powerful position in which to shape American strategy in this area. After the war Leahy said that the Joint Chiefs "generally accepted his [Arnold's] views on air strategy as correct."[76]

Arnold was known as an energetic and forceful officer who, when healthy, spent a great deal of time traveling – visiting both front-line units and production facilities.[77] He also took a very close interest in technical innovations in his aircraft.[78] He was instrumental in persuading the British to provide the United States with their early jet engine technology and personally pushed along the construction of the United States' first generation of jet fighters.[79] He was also a relatively early and enthusiastic backer of fitting the airframe of the P-51 Mustang with the British-designed Merlin engine, which was responsible for creating the greatest fighter aircraft of the war. However, Arnold's health during the war was not always good. He missed both the Trident Conference in 1943 and that at Yalta in 1945 because of heart conditions, the latter because of a serious heart attack that kept him out of service for months. Because of this, his colleagues and subordinates could play an important role in shaping Army Air Force doctrine. At different times Robert Lovett, the Assistant Secretary of War for Air, assumed a number of Arnold's duties.[80] Interestingly for a civilian, Lovett built up personal relationships with RAF officers such as Air Marshal Harris. Maybe Arnold's greatest talent was in choosing the right subordinates for major commands. The American air force fielded one of the most successful slates of commanding officers during the war, including Carl Spaatz (one of Arnold's particular favorites), Robert Kenney, James Doolittle and Curtis LeMay. Even Ira Eaker, who has a more mixed reputation, was a man of real ability. In that sense, Arnold passed the most important test of any senior officer, which is appointing the right people to major commands.

Arnold also was willing to commission expert groups to study serious subjects and report back with recommendations. He was directly responsible for the creation of the Committee of Operational Analysts (COA), which developed the first sophisticated American strategic air force doctrine. While most officers in the USAAF, including Arnold, had an implicit belief that air power would be decisive in modern warfare, the specifics of this decisiveness were lacking.[81] When the war started, it was quickly shown that achieving victory through the air was going to be far more difficult in reality than the rather grandiose air power theorists of the interwar period had assumed. Arnold personally seemed convinced that "precision" bombing as he conceived it would be more effective than "area" attacks. However, when it came to what specifically should be bombed, he was rather vague – except for the proviso that he believed that destruction of Germany's ability to manufacture aircraft should be a definite high priority.

Arnold was clearly a Germany-First advocate when it came to the deployment of American force.[82] He tried to ensure that as many as possible of the bombers sent to Europe were deployed to the UK to attack Germany. He appointed the COA to give the USAAF some intellectual coherence in deciding what to target so as to maximize damage to the German economy.[83] The COA was the brains behind the American end of the Combined Bomber Offensive, and provided the United States with its first considered strategic air power theory. It was the COA, for instance, that first seriously discussed attacking Germany's ball-bearing production as a way of limiting its overall munitions production. Again, it is a sign of the flexibility of Arnold's leadership that he was willing to cede so much authority in this area.

When it came to the Pacific, Arnold believed that strategic air power could be decisive against Japan and he was an early advocate of using Chinese bases to bomb the Japanese mainland.[84] He was willing to divert a great deal of air force effort, including the first deployment of the wildly expensive B-29 bomber, to prove his point in Asia. One problem with his analysis was his assumption about Japanese production – he did not understand how many aircraft they could construct when fully mobilized. As such, at first he seemed to believe that a smaller number of American aircraft could do the job. In the end he comes across as a sensible and rational member of the Joint Chiefs, who appointed good people to fulfil major tasks, stressed training and technological development, and made few bad choices. Within the context of World War II grand strategy making, that is a noted achievement.

Before leaving the Americans, there has to be discussion of the most unusual man who influenced the Anglo-American air and sea war, and that was Harry Hopkins. Hopkins' authority rested entirely on the close confidence that Roosevelt placed in him. The frail, often ill, chain-smoking Hopkins was the most important person in Roosevelt's political life. He had a feline understanding of the President's moods and, more often than not, he delivered the results that Roosevelt wanted. He was also entirely dependent upon Roosevelt's favor for his position in life. Only in 1943, when caught between the President and the demands of his new wife, did he not put Roosevelt first. His decision to move out of the White House ended up seriously denting his political power. Before that, however, he wielded enormous influence.

Leahy, who had very sensitive antennae when it came to Roosevelt's preferences, stated that in 1942 the President trusted Hopkins "implicitly."[85] This trust, which stretched back to the early days of the New Deal, had earned Hopkins the jealousy of many in American politics, as well as the reputation of a forbidding and powerful backroom operator. His most important biographer, Robert Sherwood, who worked closely with him during the war and became very fond of the Iowan, described him in his diary as "faintly ominous" when they first met.[86]

Roosevelt obviously prized Hopkins. Unlike Hull and Stimson, who were given posts with ostensibly far greater authority, he was entirely Roosevelt's creature – and therefore was bestowed with more real power. It was Hopkins whom the President sent on truly important diplomatic missions to the United Kingdom and the USSR to negotiate with Churchill and Stalin. Hopkins also carved out an important position of influence within the military. His relations with Marshall were particularly close. It seems that Hopkins' influence with Roosevelt played a key role in securing the army Chief of Staff position for Marshall.[87] The general repaid him by being extremely solicitous of the latter during the war. When Hopkins fell ill, Marshall made sure that he had the best healthcare the government could provide and made available to him the special facility set up in White Sulphur Springs, West Virginia.[88] Hopkins also had a close relationship with Arnold, with whom he collaborated on numerous occasions in the 1930s.

It was definitely in the early stages of the war, from December 1940 through the end of 1942, that Hopkins' influence was at its greatest. Almost immediately after Roosevelt's re-election in November 1940, the President decided to send him to the United Kingdom both to assure the British of American support and to ask the British what equipment they most needed to keep up their resistance to Nazi Germany. This trip was a great success. Though at first somewhat confused as to who Hopkins was, Churchill and other British policy makers such as Lord Beaverbrook quickly realized that they were dealing with a man who had great influence with Roosevelt and therefore treated him as a prized asset.[89] When Slessor arrived in Washington in 1941, he described Hopkins as a "fanatic" about aid to the UK.[90] When the British needed help getting equipment built or allocated, they often turned to Hopkins, who ended up as the de facto controller of lend-lease.[91] When the situation in India threatened to expose Anglo-American differences on what the war was about, Churchill turned to him to try to persuade the President not to intervene on the subcontinent.[92] Eventually the British became so grateful for Hopkins' support that they planned to name their next generation of light tanks after him.[93]

He filled a similar role for the USSR. When Germany invaded in June 1941, Hopkins was quickly dispatched to the UK and then sent onwards to meet Stalin, arriving in Russia on July 27.[94] It was the beginning of a relationship in which Hopkins became one of the few Americans that the Soviet dictator apparently trusted. From that point onwards, if the Soviets felt an immediate need for important equipment they often went directly to Hopkins. In March 1942, for instance, Maxim Litvinov, the Soviet ambassador to the USA, made a special request to him for a large supply of cargo-carrying aircraft.[95] And Hopkins usually worked hard to get these needs met. In response to Litvinov's letter, he put pressure on Lovett to meet the Soviet request. By April this pressure had led the Army Air Force to allocate an additional thirty cargo planes to the USSR, even though they were in short supply at this crucial time.[96]

His perceived impartiality on the equipment issue, and his closeness to Roosevelt, were the reasons why Hopkins was made chairman of what could have been a powerful committee, the Munitions Assignment Board (MAB). The MAB was set up to make final determinations on where vital equipment would be sent, with the assumption that such decisions would be difficult but crucial. It was made up of both American and British officers, and began functioning regularly in 1942.[97] It dealt with some serious issues at first, such as the allocation of high-octane fuel, which was necessary to power aircraft.[98] It also dealt with a wide range of seemingly less important but actually vital supplies, such as radio receiver sets and copper wire.[99]

In fact it was in the allocation of equipment that Hopkins made some interesting policy interjections. In the summer of 1941, he urged the British to use American-supplied B-24 Liberator bombers to bomb Germany instead of in a maritime role to protect trade.[100] While in no way trying to pass himself off as an expert in strategic bombing, he did generally push for the aerial bombardment of Germany over some other options.[101] Like Roosevelt, Hopkins also was a believer in giving aircraft the number one construction priority for American production. When the issue erupted in the second half of 1942, he advised the President privately to ignore the JCS objections and simply order that aircraft construction should trump all other considerations.[102] It was a sign of his status at the time that Roosevelt, on the same day that Hopkins wrote to him, did order his aircraft production targets to be met.[103]

When examining the war, Hopkins was also important because of his understanding of domestic politics. His basic instinct was always Germany-First, though he was aware that many Americans felt an instinctive need to make a major effort against Japan.[104] Of all the Americans in the decision-making elite, he was clearly the most solicitous of Soviet needs and saw the war in Europe as pre-eminent because of the need to keep the USSR fighting. He certainly seemed less involved with the specifics of the war in the Pacific, though he was also sensitive to the political implications of that conflict. He wanted the British to at least seem to be doing more in the theater, to provide a counterbalance to those who were arguing that the USA was simply doing the UK's fighting in Europe, and receiving no support in return in Asia.[105]

Gradually during the course of 1943, however, Hopkins' power seemed to wane owing to ill health and a decline of confidence from the President.[106] In his private papers, for instance, there are considerably fewer examples of the British and Russians making direct appeals to him (though certainly such appeals did still occur). The reason for the loss of Roosevelt's confidence is somewhat perplexing and doesn't show the President in the best light. One idea is that when Hopkins fell in love, got married and moved out of the White House, Roosevelt felt betrayed.[107] It was also true that Hopkins' illnesses kept him physically away from the President and out of regular contact for long periods, which also reduced his usefulness. Finally, the growth in professionalism of the JCS under Leahy's leadership meant that Hopkins' special position became less necessary to the functioning of the war effort. And that was the great weakness in Hopkins' status. Possessing no actual authority, the loss of his usefulness to the war effort and to Roosevelt, severely undermined his position. Yet, in the crucial years of 1941 and 1942, he played an extremely important role in shaping the air and sea war to come.

The British: Alanbrooke, Portal, Pound and Cunningham

In 1943 the American delegation to the Casablanca Conference marveled at what they saw as the great coordination amongst the British service chiefs. To them, Alanbrooke, Portal and Pound (see Figure 19) provided a mutually supporting field of fire for British policies, compared with Marshall and King who were interested in rather different objectives. This united front, however, hid the fact that the British Chiefs of Staff were in many ways more divided in their views of how World War II would be won.

In writing the history of the British chiefs of staffs during the war, Alanbrooke stands out, though not necessarily for good reasons. With Pound dying in 1943 and Portal refusing to cash in and write a biography after the war, only Alanbrooke's story was told in detail, in one of the most entertaining, if petulant, diaries of a major war leader that has ever come to light. Born to two hypochondriacal Anglo-Irish parents resident in France, there was something rather un-English about Alanbrooke's character.[108] During World War I he served in the artillery, where he excelled at organizational tasks. During the

19 Churchill and his service chiefs (from left to right: Portal, Pound and
Alanbrooke) meeting on the *Queen Mary* while traveling to the USA for the
Trident Conference in May 1943. Whilst they often disagreed strongly, when
negotiating with the American chiefs the British usually presented an effective
united front. Figure 27 shows the *Queen Mary* in wartime painting in New York
Harbor.

interwar period, he rose steadily through the ranks, serving in a wide
variety of different locations, from training commands to the Imperial
Defence College, to serving as the army's officer in charge of air
defense. When World War II began in Europe in 1939, Alanbrooke
was commander of II Corps which was deployed to France. During the
disastrous collapse of Anglo-French defense in May 1940, he handled
his corps skillfully and saved many of his men, who were evacuated at
Dunkirk. Back in Britain, he was given the Southern Command, in
charge of the army in the areas that the Germans were most likely to
invade, and then became Commander in Chief Home Forces. At this
time, the serving Chief of the Imperial General Staff was Field Marshal
Sir John Dill, whose relationship with Churchill became increasingly
strained. Once Dill accompanied the Prime Minister to Washington,
DC in December 1941, it was decided that he would remain in America
as the United Kingdom's senior military representative.[109] Alanbrooke
was chosen to replace him as Chief of the Imperial General Staff on
Christmas Day 1941.

An army man to his bones, Alanbrooke's conception of grand
strategy was almost entirely based on land conquest, with air and sea
power support units that were to do everything possible to aid the
ground troops. He had little concept of an economic, air or sea
war.[110] Because of this, when he analyzed the grand strategy of the
war, he often proceeded to use troop numbers as the key indicator of
effort, and equipment solely as a means of supporting these numbers.

His is a difficult personality to like. With the desire to categorize people that is typical of those with limited imagination, Alanbrooke seems to have made up his mind very early on between those who were either stupid, dangerous or erratic and those who were brilliant and far-sighted. Most people, including Marshall, Eisenhower, Churchill and King, fell into the first camp, while a lucky few, such as Montgomery, were in the latter. Disagreeing with Alanbrooke was sure to be seen by him as a sign of a lack of intelligence, which seems to have been particularly the case for George Marshall. Both Marshall and Alanbrooke had a rather low opinion of the other's intelligence, but for Alanbrooke, pointing out Marshall's supposed stupidity was a regular event, especially when the two disagreed about strategic priorities: "A very disappointing wire from American COS – Marshall absolutely fails to realize what strategic treasures lie at our feet in the Mediterranean and always hankers after cross Channel operations. He admits that our object must be to eliminate Italy and yet is always afraid of facing the consequences of doing so. He cannot see beyond the tip of his nose and it's maddening."[111] Much of his bile was reserved for Churchill, for not recognizing Alanbrooke's strategic genius. When Churchill first conceived of an operation to capture northern Sumatra, Alanbrooke reacted as if the Prime Minister had lost his mind. In his diary on August 23, 1943, he first began complaining about American behavior, but quickly turned to Churchill.

> But when you add to it all the background of a peevish, temperamental prima donna of a Prime Minister, suspicious to the very limits of imagination, always fearing a military combination of effort against political dominance, the whole matter becomes quite unbearable! He has been more unreasonable and trying than ever this time. He has during the sea voyage in a few idle moments become married to the idea that success against Japan can only be secured through the capture of the north tip of Sumatra! He has become like a peevish child asking for a forbidden toy![112]

In retrospect, the problem in accepting any of Alanbrooke's judgments is that, while he was successful in winning his way in 1942 and the first half of 1943, his assumptions almost always proved wrong. It was he, for instance, who led the British charge for a full-scale invasion of Italy in 1943 in the hope of forestalling, and maybe even preventing altogether, an invasion of France. His argument in favor of the Italian operation was two-fold: first, that Italy would collapse and this would be a real blow to Axis power, and secondly, it would lead to a large redeployment of the German army from the Eastern Front to Italy.[113] He also seemed to believe that the conquest of Italy could be achieved relatively quickly.[114] However, his thinking was not only flawed, it was limited. He never understood how Italy could be used to attack other facilities vital to German production, such as Ploesti, and, moreover, never seemed to understand how small Italy was within the context of the German war economy (and that all that really mattered to the Germans economically was in the far north of the country). It was indicative of his general lack of interest in the air and sea war. When it came to strategic bombing he showed little engagement, and only complained against those who, he believed, thought it would be too effective.[115]

When it came to the war at sea, again Alanbrooke showed a limited understanding of modern warfare. During discussions about the war in the Atlantic, he seemed to accept what Dudley Pound told him, even though he was constantly worried about Pound's health and mental acumen. When it came to the war at sea in the Pacific, Alanbrooke was out of his depth. He obviously thought this war (in the form of its great protagonist – Ernest King) was a sideshow when compared with Europe. Yet, even though he believed that almost any force sent to the Pacific before the surrender of Germany was a waste, he allowed King to completely out-maneuver him on the issue. When, at Casablanca, King produced his false figures which deliberately understated the amount of effort that the United States was sending to the Pacific, Alanbrooke never bothered to check their accuracy.[116] At Trident, when King outlined the Central Pacific strategy which would have required a great deal of air–sea effort, Alanbrooke again accepted his presentation without fully understanding what it meant for the allocation of American equipment.

Maybe the best way to sum up the different views is by looking at Alanbrooke's description of his own and those of the other grand strategists during the Trident Conference in May 1943. Trident was the crucial conference in laying out the plan for winning World War II in both Europe and the Pacific. Alanbrooke summed up the different perspectives he encountered:

(a) King thinks the war can only be won by action in the Pacific at the expense of all other fronts.
(b) Marshall considers that our solution lies in the cross Channel operation with some 20 or 30 divisions, irrespective of the situation on the Russian front, with which he proposes to clear Europe and win the war.
(c) Portal considers that success lies in accumulating the largest air force possible in England and that then, and then only, success lies assured through the bombing of Europe.
(d) Dudley Pound on the other hand is obsessed with the anti-U-boat warfare and considers that success can only be secured by the defeat of this menace.
(e) AFB [Alanbrooke] considers that success can only be secured by pressing operations in the Mediterranean to force a dispersal of German forces, help Russia, and thus eventually produce a situation where cross Channel operations are possible.
(f) And Winston??? Thinks one thing at one moment and another at another moment...[117]

Of these notions, Alanbrooke's was the most incorrect. Operations in the Mediterranean played almost no role in making a cross-Channel operation possible and drew only a limited amount of force from the Eastern Front. However, it is unlikely that Alanbrooke spent any time worrying about that.

Alanbrooke's criticisms of Portal, which were actually far fewer than those of Marshall, King or Pound, may have been motivated by envy with respect to a more able man. Portal was intellectually the most impressive performer of all the Combined Chiefs of Staff. Churchill had referred to him as the "star" of the RAF when he was named Chief of Air Staff in 1940.[118] He was highly decorated for a series of World War I, assignments during where he excelled at flying and coordinating reconnaissance aircraft.[119] In the interwar period he rose steadily, and played a crucial organizational role during the dramatic expansion of the RAF during the late 1930s. In 1940, during the fall of France and the Battle of Britain, he served as the head of Bomber Command, though the force under his control was not yet equipped with the number or types of aircraft that could do much damage to the German war effort. After that he moved into the air staff where he remained, working extremely long hours, for the rest of the war.

In this position he excelled in many areas, crucially in getting along with his American counterparts. Leahy, who was extremely impressed with Portal's performance during the different conferences, believed that the Briton was in total control of his subject.[120] Arnold was extremely fond of him personally and professionally. The Englishman did a wonderful job of impressing Arnold when they first worked closely during the latter's visit to the UK in April 1941.[121] From that point on, the American was happy to collaborate with Portal and the two reached many agreements on issues such as technology transfer and theater command.[122]

Within the UK's power structure, Portal's diplomatic skills were also valuable. He had a way of seeming to agree with people, but at the same time pressing his own argument. Typical of this was a meeting in June 1941 when the RAF air staff met to discuss the future direction of Britain's strategic bombing campaign.[123] Air Marshal Trenchard, the godfather of the RAF, had written a memorandum on the need to target German morale. Portal seems never to have been convinced about the superiority of a morale-driven campaign. He supported its adoption later when it seemed like the most feasible option open to the UK considering the equipment on hand. At this meeting, however, he allowed Trenchard to give a long treatise based on the presupposition that German morale was noticeably weaker than British morale. After hearing Trenchard, and gently asking him to leave, Portal steered the conversation to an interesting conclusion. While seeming to support the principle of a morale campaign, it actually undermined its centrality in favor of other options, in particular those having to do with the mobility of equipment – both British and German.

> CAS [Portal] asked the D. Of Plans to draft a paper for submission to the Chiefs of Staff and the Defence Committee asking for approval of the plan. This should bring out that the Battle of the Atlantic had overriding priority when a suitable target presented itself, but that the principal objective of the bomber force should be the morale of the German people linked with the attack of suitable transportation targets, particularly in the neighbourhood of the Ruhr. The paper would have to be carefully drafted to secure political support in the Defence Committee.[124]

Besides demonstrating his diplomatic skills, this kind of summation was indicative of the flexibility with which Portal approached strategic bombing. He certainly was convinced that the direct bombing of Germany was the best way for Britain to carry on the war, even before US entry. While this focus might be ridiculed at times by Alanbrooke, it was almost certainly the right policy if Britain actually wanted to engage with the German economy – directly or indirectly. In September 1941, Portal believed that the RAF's plan for the strategic bombing of Germany was being threatened. Churchill had circulated a minute which indicated that British aircraft should first and foremost be used in a tactical manner to support the army and that strategic air power alone would probably not be a decisive weapon against Germany.[125] In response Portal gave a defense of strategic bombing, in particular of the morale bombing against German cities.

> Since the fall of France it has been a fundamental principle of our strategy that victory over Germany could not be hoped for until German morale and German material strength has been subjected to a bombing offensive of the greatest intensity ... Production has been planned to conform with this strategic conception and we are deeply committed to it.
>
> I feel duty bound to restate these facts, because I find them hard to reconcile with your minute of 27th September... the bombing offensive, on the scale on which we hope to wield it in 1943, as a weapon calculated, if not to break Germany, at least to reduce her strength to the level at which our armoured forces could hope to intervene successfully on the continent. If this is a gross over-estimation of the power of the bomber and if the most we can hope to achieve with our bomber force is a heavy and growing annoyance, then, as I see it, the strategic concept to which we have been working must dissolve and we must find a new plan...
>
> The effect of bombing on morale depends, I believe, on the weight of attack. Light attacks may well stimulate morale, but this can scarcely be said of attacks on the Coventry model. Judging from our own experience it is difficult to believe that any country could withstand indefinitely the scale of attack contemplated in the Air Staff plan. Civilian casualties alone would be a major feature. German attacks on this country over the past year have caused the death or serious injury of 93,000 civilians. This result was achieved with a small fraction of the bomb load we hope to employ in 1943.[126]

It is interesting to see Portal giving this positive argument in favor of civilian/morale bombing, because he often seemed to have doubts about giving pre-eminence to such a targeting priority. Throughout the war he showed a belief that targeting German transportation or oil targets was actually more important than area bombing cities.[127] Even in documents that seemed to clearly endorse the bombing of cities, he had included specific provisos that transportation targets could receive priority.[128] When the Americans released the report of the COA in 1943 which called for the bombing of German ball-bearing production, Portal was obviously intrigued.

Beyond strategic bombing, Portal did show a need to support British interests globally. Before the fall of Singapore, he favored the deployment of large numbers of aircraft to the Far East. When, immediately after the Pearl Harbor attack, Arnold told Portal of his doubts whether the Philippines could be held, Portal asked for the aircraft that were being "poured" into Australia to be sent to Singapore to hold that position.[129] In 1943, when the British were pressing for a general commitment of effort in the Mediterranean, and in particular a campaign in Italy, he supported the position for subtly different reasons. The war in Italy, in and of itself, didn't seem to be a great objective of his. He certainly didn't envisage launching a large strategic air offensive from there. However, a successful attack into Italy, he believed, might very well bring Turkey into the war on the side of the Allies, as this would open up a new air front against German resource production and would therefore stretch German power considerably more.[130] As he said during the British planning meetings preceding the Trident Conference in May 1943:

> [He] thought the case for developing the main effort against Italy was somewhat weak. Two alternative operations had been put forward. Our ability to carry out the first, the attack on the Heel of Italy, was dependent on certain conditions which might not materialise. It was doubtful whether the second operation, the capture of Sardinia, would in effect make any real contribution towards the collapse of Italy, particularly during the coming winter. He felt that the Italians would not stand for another winter in the face of a full-scale bomber offensive and that, while we should capture the Toe of Italy, we could rely primarily on air attack to bring about the Italian collapse. Meanwhile, he felt that there was much more to be said for the capture of the Dodecanese

and straining every effort to bring Turkey into the war in the autumn. Such policy would inevitably provoke a German reaction and so draw off forces from the Russian front, while it would, at the same time, open up strategic possibilities in South-East Europe.[131]

In one way, however, Portal's flexibility of mind could lead him to be, perhaps, too deferential. In the second half of 1944 he seemed very much to believe that the strategic bombing campaign against German synthetic and natural oil production was paying great dividends, certainly greater than that being attained by the area bombing of German cities. However, his thinking in this area brought him into conflict with Arthur "Bomber" Harris, the head of Bomber Command. Where Portal was flexible in his approach to strategic air power, Harris was dogmatic. He had decided that the area bombing of German cities was the proper strategy and attacked, usually with crude insults, any other usage of air power, from American industry assaults to raids on the German transportation system.

Portal obviously appreciated Harris' drive and determination, but was also concerned by his inability to tolerate different points of view.[132] In late 1944, therefore, when Portal started to doubt the usefulness of Harris' continuing destruction of German cities, he was faced with a tricky situation. He sent to Harris a series of letters that were alternately cajoling and critical, trying to persuade the head of Bomber Command to spend more effort attacking Germany's fuel supplies.

> The essence of the immediate task before the Allied strategic bomber forces is *to put out and keep out of action the 11 synthetic plants in Central Germany.* These are producing 70 percent of the enemy's current supplies of aviation and motor spirit. There is no doubt in my mind that their immobilisation and the continued immobilisation of the major producers would represent by far the greatest and most certain contribution that our strategic bombers could make to the achievement of an early decision in the German war...
>
> For these reasons I am profoundly disappointed that you still appear to feel that the oil plan is just another "panacea". Naturally, while you hold this view you will be unable to put your heart into the attack on oil. (Emphasis in original)[133]

It was in many ways a tragic situation for Portal. He had come to the proper conclusion about the best way to attack German strength, striven his best to try to persuade an officer under his command to accept this view, but in the end could do nothing if that officer refused to change. And Harris was not for turning. Portal, even for all his evident conviction, could not enforce a change that he honestly was convinced was right on all levels. In this case Dresden would pay the price for his diplomacy.

If Portal was the most open-minded and flexible of the chiefs of staff, Admiral Sir Dudley Pound was probably one of the most focused, if in a very subdued manner. Until 1943, when he died, one of the constant comments about him was his apparent lack of energy. This was certainly due in part to the fact that there was a tumor growing in his brain, which made him progressively weaker. Alanbrooke regularly pointed out when he thought Pound had slept through important meetings.[134] Leahy also had a rather restrained opinion of him.

> Sir Dudley Pound, whose post as First Sea Lord roughly
> corresponded to that of our Admiral King, was quiet and reserved.
> I did not know then that he was in poor health. Pound was an
> experienced sea officer, but entered the staff discussions only when
> they involved the employment of the British Navy, about which he
> expressed very positive opinions.[135]

However, Pound had certain important talents. He understood the vital necessity of protecting trade in the Atlantic, didn't intrude into areas outside his expertise and, remarkably, could work well with Ernest King. Though King was suspicious of British naval officers as a general rule, he seemed to make an exception with Pound. In 1942 the two men worked closely and even exchanged vessels between theaters. King remarked after the war how, in February 1942, Pound offered the Americans twenty British anti-submarine vessels for the Pacific.[136] Considering the disaster in merchant shipping losses that was occurring in the Atlantic at the time, it was a generous offer.

Pound was a product of the World War I Royal Navy at its zenith. A battleship captain during that war, he commanded HMS *Colossus* during the Battle of Jutland and at one point in the interwar period, he took command of the Battlecruiser squadron. He was named First Sea Lord in June of 1939, and his performance in this role during the war has received mixed reviews. For some, he demanded too much control but couldn't stand up to Churchill when it mattered.[137] When it came to the larger grand strategic questions faced by the Combined Chiefs of Staff (CCS) during the war, Pound did seem the most detached of all. However, when it came to the question of sea power and trade warfare in and out of the British Isles, he often got his way.

Earlier in the war, Pound showed some real fight, particularly in his disputes with the Royal Air Force. He was well aware of the crucial importance that aircraft would play in defeating the German submarine threat in the Atlantic and he used his good relations with King to request more American aircraft for the Atlantic on a number of occasions.[138] In 1942 he fought what he termed the "Battle of the Air" to try to force the RAF to devote more aircraft to the Coastal Command fight against the U-boats.[139] The force that Pound had in mind was massive. He estimated in March 1942 that the RAF needed to deploy 1,940 aircraft of different types to fight the U-boats at sea (that is, not including heavy bomber attacks on U-boat ports or production facilities).[140] At the same time, the Luftwaffe had 1,766 aircraft on the entire Eastern Front. For the next six months there was a continual round of arguments between the navy and the RAF about aircraft deployment. In the end Pound was able to secure a 10 percent increase in the number of squadrons given to Coastal Command, as well as thirty new Halifax bombers and, crucially, thirty additional B-24 Liberator bombers from the United States.[141]

This was indicative of the general success that Pound had in keeping the Battle of the Atlantic near the top of the priority list for both equipment production and allocation. At the Arcadia Conference the maintenance of the North Atlantic trade route was reconfirmed as the number one strategic goal of both the United States and the United Kingdom.[142] When shipping losses in the Atlantic then skyrocketed, the resulting shift in American and British construction priorities was weighted heavily towards the creation of new merchant and anti-submarine shipping.[143]

Pound's death in 1943 brought a far more active sailor, Andrew Cunningham, to the post of First Sea Lord. Unlike Pound, Cunningham had dash and was a fine seaman, something which impressed Leahy greatly. Cunningham reciprocated the admiration, seeing Leahy as an important "steadying" influence over American policy making.[144]

On the other hand, Cunningham's more assertive personality probably weakened the Royal Navy's position, as it drove a real wedge between himself and Ernest King. The two seemed to get on each other's nerves. One of the last things King ever wrote was a response to Cunningham when the latter referred to him in his memoirs as rude and overbearing.

> I believe that I recall the incident which prompted Andrew Cunningham to write in his book that I was "rude and overbearing."
>
> Sometime during the summer of 1942 when he was head of the British Admiralty delegation in Washington, he came into my office on a matter which had to do with Allied convoys versus Nazi U-boats. He wanted to know specifically if I couldn't spare one or more additional divisions of destroyers or other escort type vessels to help the situation in the North Atlantic crossings.
>
> That morning I had read in the newspapers about the British press sounding off to the effect that most of the convoy escorting was being done by British and Canadian ships and that we (the U.S.) weren't helping out as much as we could and should. At that time we were using every available escort vessel. We were escorting tankers from the West Indies and Cargo ships from the Eastern Atlantic up to Freetown and on up to the very entrance to the English Channel. We were also busily engaged in setting up the "Torch" operation. Meanwhile we were very busy in the Pacific.
>
> I therefore interpreted Cunningham's query as a "needle" directed at me – and I was indeed very abrupt (rude) with him- and purposely so![145]

In grand strategic terms, the switch from Pound to Cunningham in October 1943 did not make a great difference, as most of the important decisions had been made by this point. Nor does it seem that Cunningham changed the direction of any policies that were already in place. The Battle of the Atlantic was very much in hand and would not flare back into action until almost the end of the war when Schnorkel-equipped German submarines threatened to once again reopen Germany's war on trade. In the Pacific, Cunningham's appointment probably only complicated matters as the real question was to what degree the Royal Navy would be allowed to participate in the final assault on Japan. When the British Pacific Fleet was deployed to fight during the assault on Okinawa, to begin with they were held at arm's length by the American navy.[146] If Pound had still been in charge, King would likely have been more accommodating.

5 UNDERSTANDING THE AIR AND SEA WAR FROM DECEMBER 1940 TO MARCH 1942

On July 28, 1941 two of the most important political figures of World War II first met; Josef Stalin, dictator and warlord of the Soviet Union, and Harry Hopkins, one of the few people in the world who was trusted by Franklin Roosevelt. It was an informal meeting in Moscow that took place against the dramatic background of the ongoing German invasion of the Soviet Union. For Hopkins, it represented one of the more remarkable moments of an already remarkable career. A man both endearing and vaguely sinister, by 1941 he had become Franklin Roosevelt's second voice.[1] Hopkins was clearly impressed with the Soviet dictator, who to him seemed both calm and knowledgeable.[2] Stalin certainly turned on his special kind of charm and devoted a great deal of time to cultivating Hopkins. He had a personal air-raid shelter set aside for the visiting American, and made sure that it was liberally stocked with champagne, caviar, chocolates and cigarettes.[3] Stalin also praised Roosevelt extravagantly, figuring that would please both the President and his intimate.

Hopkins had two overriding goals for the meetings. The first was to assure Stalin that Roosevelt and Winston Churchill, whom Hopkins had just left in London, were committed to supporting the Soviet Union in its life and death struggle with Nazi Germany. The second was to ask Stalin to list what the Soviet Union needed to help it resist the German invaders.[4] The dictator was clear that the greatest threat posed by Germany was not its army – he expressed great confidence in Soviet tanks and stated that, if allowed time, Soviet numbers should prove telling. The greatest threat to the continued resistance of the USSR was the strength of the Luftwaffe. Hopkins summarized Stalin's views on the subject for Roosevelt: "He [Stalin] emphasized the fact that Germany has a strong and powerful air force, and that their present production of planes was probably between 2500 fighters and bombers per month, but not more than 3000 a month."[5]

Hopkins wanted to know both what the Soviet Union needed to stabilize the military situation immediately and also what it would need for a long war. In both cases Stalin was unequivocal: the Soviet Union needed equipment to fight an air war. Anti-aircraft weapons were the immediate priority. Stalin wanted medium-caliber anti-aircraft guns (somewhere between 20 and 37 mm in caliber) and asked for 20,000 pieces, an astronomical sum for 1941. For long-term needs, the Soviet Union's first two priorities were high-octane aviation fuel and, crucially, as much aluminum as it could be given. The USSR had very little bauxite, and without that precious ore it would not be able to build aircraft. Stalin told Hopkins, "Give us anti-aircraft guns and the aluminum and we can fight for three or four years."[6]

So much of this meeting helps us understand World War II at this crucial juncture. There was no time for diplomatic pageantry. Both men shared a desperate need to defeat Hitler and got right down to the basic question of the priorities for American aid. Also, both accepted without much discussion that air supremacy was the *sine qua non* for Soviet resistance. Both Stalin and Hopkins, neither of whom had a particularly sophisticated understanding of modern war at this time, believed that the Red Army needed to counter the superiority of the Luftwaffe if the USSR was going to have a chance of survival. This conviction started a process which saw the United States supply the USSR with almost an entire air force, both completed aircraft and aircraft designs, and enough raw materials for the Soviets to construct ten of thousands more aircraft on their own.[7]

By 1941, much had changed from the beginning of the war. There was now a growing, if still far from complete, understanding of how air power could be used. Air power's decisive tactical nature had been shown in the fall of France, and this meant that Hopkins, speaking for Roosevelt, was more than amenable to providing the USSR as much support in this area as possible. When it came to strategic air power, there was also a great deal of worry. Hopkins tried to glean from Stalin how much of the Soviet Union's production would come within range of German bombers if the Wehrmacht reached Moscow and Leningrad (the American estimated 75 percent).[8] It was indicative of how air and sea power dominated the President's thinking, and became the tool by which he eventually caused American entry into the war.

This was also the time when perhaps the first sophisticated strategic air power debate occurred. Within the UK, when it was shown that there was still a desperate imbalance between what was actually achievable with the existing aircraft and air technology, and what actually would work in damaging German production, there was an intense discussion of what should be targeted in Germany and how. The war at sea also showed real progress as the Royal Navy recovered from the crisis that set in after the fall of France. Even though the Germans now had access to submarine bases in western France and Norway, which gave them unimpeded access to the Atlantic Ocean, the threat was, to a large degree, mastered. In that limited sense, it was a crucial period in causing the eventual defeat of the Axis.

The Roosevelt administration joins the air and sea war

Roosevelt's exact thinking in 1941 is still elusive. On the one hand, there are those who believe that he was determined to get the United States into the war by whatever means, Machiavellian or not, that lay at his disposal.[9] He thus broke international and national law to help Britain and the USSR, tried to goad the Germans into firing on American warships on the high seas, and when all this failed, ended up forcing the Japanese into attacking the United States by embargoing the sale of oil to Japan.[10] On the other hand, some say that Roosevelt, for all his reassuring words towards the British (and there were many), was always careful to avoid promising American entry into the war.[11] Instead of planning for an inevitable American entry, he was gearing his efforts towards helping the British as a non-combatant. They point out that as late as November–December 1941, he was still not able to call for a declaration of war.

Anyone who reads Roosevelt's writings and descriptions of his interactions will not be surprised at these two very different pictures. A consummate political animal, Roosevelt had a way of putting those he was with at the moment at great ease and persuading them that he agreed entirely with them, while at the same time avoiding a clear-cut commitment to do what they really wanted.

When Air Vice-Marshal (later full Air Marshal) John Slessor arrived in Washington, DC on November 8, 1940, he received the full Roosevelt treatment. Slessor, one of the more cerebral RAF officers of his generation, came to Washington to discuss RAF aircraft production in America, something close to Roosevelt's heart.[12] The President made sure that the Englishman was given access more similar to that of a visiting head of state than of a military officer on a technical mission. Henry Morgenthau, the Secretary of the Treasury, established contact before Slessor even reached the United States.[13] When he arrived, Slessor was met by Roosevelt's intelligence chief, William Donovan, who had personally organized his accommodation and then took him out to a nightclub. Donovan had already arranged meetings between Slessor and perhaps the most pro-British member of the Cabinet, Secretary of the Navy Frank Knox, as well as with the Roosevelt himself. Slessor was frankly overwhelmed at the reception. As he told Portal in a letter: "I am astonished at the apparent importance which the Americans attach to this visit."[14]

In his meetings with Roosevelt, Slessor was treated with the jocular faux-intimacy that appeared when the President wanted to establish warm personal relations. To show his common cause with the United Kingdom, Roosevelt openly mocked Irish diplomats in front of the British officer:

> ... he [FDR] told me with evident relish about his interview that morning with Aiken, the Eire War Minister who was in Washington trying to get money and arms. FDR said he thought he was "the most ghastly fellow I have ever met". He had evidently thoroughly enjoyed himself, had told Aiken he knew his record (and recounted it to him), and said that this was no time for the old Irish political game of twisting the lion's tail, and no-one who did that need expect any help from the USA. Aiken blustered and sweated and must have had a miserable time. The President suggested to him that Eire should declare a 50 mile "chastity belt" off their West coast, the Irish to patrol it with surface and aircraft and fire on any belligerent warship. Aiken said they had not the craft to do it, and FDR said he'd supply them.[15]

When it came to fully committing the USA to the war, Roosevelt played his normal game. He persuaded the Briton that he was "fired with the one intense determination to see the Axis beaten."[16] On the other hand, during an April 7, 1941 meeting, when Slessor asked the President to see if he could increase the pace of US heavy bomber construction, Roosevelt claimed that he needed to be cautious because of public opinion. "The President said I must remember that US was not yet actually at war, and it was extraordinarily difficult to get the tempo of national effort necessary to full production when one is officially at peace. "[17]

Roosevelt's personal reticence stands out now, and stood out then for Slessor, because most of the Cabinet officials who were in touch with the British were far less cautious in their formulations. Knox, maybe the most interventionist member of the Cabinet, was so pro-British that he had been "openly preparing the Navy for intervention for some time and is determined to get into the war as soon as he can."[18] The Secretary of War, Henry Stimson, was "old and rather tired", but was still "fired with an almost religious conviction as to the essential need to defeat Hitler." Above them all, though, stood the enigmatic but enormously influential Harry Hopkins.

> Harry Hopkins is almost a fanatic on the subject of aid to Britain and his recent visit to England has given him a real insight into our problems and point of view. There is no doubt that he is a most valuable friend. He is, however, a sick man; on his own admission he is a hopeless administrator; he is an untidy man, and his desire to "keep things fluid" in respect of the organization of defense is typical of what I think is an ingrained characteristic of this country – the love of doing things "off the record."[19]

This was an astute observation, and one that a number of British policy makers were to make. As soon as Roosevelt was re-elected, one of his first moves was to send Hopkins to Britain in January 1941 to see how the United States could best aid the British war effort.[20] Although Winston Churchill was at first ignorant as to Hopkins' position, after one weekend together the British Prime Minister telegraphed Roosevelt thanking him profusely for sending him the Iowan.[21] He soon calculated that Hopkins had far more real power than high American Cabinet officers such as Morgenthau, and in fact avoided dealing with them.[22] It is not always clear whether the British praise for Hopkins, which was laid on with a trowel as 1941 went on, was a result of genuine affection or of political calculation, but certainly Churchill's sentiments were echoed widely. Lord Halifax, the replacement for Lord

Lothian who had died not long after Roosevelt's re-election, and Maurice Hankey both viewed Hopkins as a crucial figure. To them he was a true friend of Britain, and Hankey even asked Halifax to show one of his war situation memoranda to Americans he could trust, someone of a "Harry Hopkins type."[23]

Maybe the best example of Hopkins' importance in British minds in 1941 is the rather fawning way that Lord Beaverbrook treated him. Beaverbrook was a man with a keen sense of power and an extraordinary belief in his own rightness, a common trait amongst extremely rich newspaper owners, and he quickly seems to have decided that Hopkins was the key man in the American government. He flattered Hopkins without mercy, such as in the telegram, which he sent after the famous Churchill–Roosevelt summit in Newfoundland (Argentia) that resulted in the Atlantic Charter: "You have shown such faith in us, you have held such confidence in our people that you have sustained our courage in the darkest hours and amidst the most terrible attacks. Every one of us recognises the influence that you spread through this country and we look to you for leading and guidance in the future."[24] Right after the Pearl Harbor attack, Beaverbrook urged Roosevelt to place Hopkins in overall control of American wartime production.[25] A few weeks later, during the Arcadia Conference, he even started passing information to Hopkins that he knew could be used to subvert Churchill's stated position, so as to shape the conference's agreements more in the American direction.[26] In the end, it can be said that Hopkins was, second only to the President, the most important American formulating strategic policy for the United States in 1941 and early 1942. From the moment of his first visit to the UK in January 1941, he played a crucial role in pushing for American entry into an air and sea war against Germany.

At this time Roosevelt directed that the embargoes placed on American trade with the USSR, which had been in place since the Soviet invasion of Finland, be lifted.[27] He also allowed for a much greater sharing arrangement with British and British Empire scientists.[28] It was also in January 1941 that Roosevelt ordered the American service chiefs to meet with their British counterparts to discuss global strategy in case the United States formally entered the fighting.[29] The importance of these staff conversations in determining the eventual grand strategy that was used in the war was relatively insignificant. None of those who would take the real decisions from the second half of

1942 onwards was part of the formal negotiating team, with the possible exceptions of General Joseph McNarney and Slessor, who took part as the RAF's representative.[30]

When it came to the specifics of air and sea power, the conclusions reached in March 1941 by the combined staffs, known as ABC-1, were so broad as to be almost meaningless. The first two points delineating the general strategic concepts were:

(a) Application of economic pressure by naval, land and air forces and all other means, including control of commodities at their source by diplomatic and financial measures.

(b) A sustained air offensive against German military power, supplemented by air offensives against other regions under enemy control which contribute to that power.[31]

Perhaps the best-remembered part of the conclusions was the policy that came to be known as Germany-First or Europe-First. The negotiators clearly stated that in the case of a global war, the United States and the United Kingdom should consider the Atlantic/European theater "decisive," and that operations against Japan in the Pacific should be conducted only to facilitate the main effort against Germany.[32] The actual war plan that was decided during the negotiations bore little resemblance to the air and sea war that actually took place. Most mentions of air power were either defensive or tactical, to protect Allied positions or to support ground forces in the battles against the German army.[33] Moreover, Germany-First was very much the rule. Important American naval forces would be transferred from the Pacific to the Atlantic. It was still a battleship-centric understanding of sea power. The largest American deployment was a three-battleship force which would be sent from Hawaii to the Atlantic to take over protection for Gibraltar.[34] This redeployment from the Pacific to Gibraltar was something accepted by Roosevelt, as Knox sent him a gung-ho letter on the subject on March 20.[35] That being said, in American eyes the Mediterranean was to remain a secondary theater. Knox told Roosevelt that the Gibraltar deployment was to help protect convoys from South America, Africa and the Caribbean – and would not be used in the Mediterranean. If the British wanted to press on there, the United States would play a secondary role.[36] Instead, the Americans would plan on a major build-up of power to attack Germany directly in northwest Europe.

When it came to the war in the Pacific, the United States was to assume a defensive posture, though one completely different than it would face when the war actually broke out. ABC-1 assumed that the Malaya–Philippine line would be held by the British and the Americans. Ernest King summarized the agreement as follows: "Military strategy in the Far East to be defensive. US Pacific Fleet to be employed against Japanese economic power and to support defense of Malay barrier by diverting Japanese strength from Malaysia."[37]

If the strategic elements of ABC-1 ended up being mostly irrelevant, the structural ones remained. The staff conversations did result in the establishment of a permanent joint staff of British and American officers. They also laid the groundwork for future intelligence cooperation. As such, it is the assumptions of ABC-1 that stand out. Its mindset was about when, not if, the United States would enter the war. Many in the British government and armed forces at this time assumed that all the moves being sanctioned by Roosevelt at the time were tantamount to a pledge to enter the war sooner rather than later.

If there was one area in the air and sea war that Roosevelt pushed most at the time, it was in the production and transfer of American aircraft to Britain. His plan as laid out in March 1941 was for American production to be able to support a 30,000 aircraft force: 12,000 for the USAAF, 12,000 for the RAF and 6,000 for the USN air force.[38] In reality it was a plan designed to maximize the aircraft to be made available to the UK, as the USAAF at the time did not want or have plans for a 12,000-plane force.[39]

The stories that Roosevelt was told at the time further reinforced his prejudices in favor of air power. He was sent a detailed account of a combined German–Italian dive-bombing attack on the British fleet in the Mediterranean.[40] In response, he seemed particularly determined to increase the supply of American heavy bombers to Britain. Not only did he tell Slessor that this was one of his highest priorities, he directed specific orders on the point to the US army.[41] And in May he told Stimson to make sure that American heavy bomber production was raised to 500 units per month, specifically so that they could be given to the British.[42] This was actually a remarkably high rate at the time, considerably larger than either the British or the Germans ever were able to achieve during the war. The British were only producing on average 41 heavy bombers per month at this time, and even in their peak year of production, 1944, they would only average 459.[43] The Germans built almost exclusively smaller two-engine bombers in 1941, and even then their average monthly construction for all bombers was 336.[44]

This stress on sending more heavy bombers to the United Kingdom continued for the rest of the year. In October Hopkins told the President that he believed the USAAF was trying to keep too many four-engine bombers for itself.[45] According to Hopkins, the army could send an additional 100–150 heavies without endangering American security. That same day, Roosevelt sent a letter to Stimson asking him to send 100–150 bombers to Britain as soon as possible.[46] The President also spoke extremely indiscreetly to a number of different Britons about obtaining more American air support for the UK. When Hugh Dowding was reassigned to Washington, DC in 1941, Roosevelt urged him to keep pressing the American military to provide more equipment for the RAF.[47] In April 1941, during a meeting with Slessor, he discussed ways that he could circumvent US law so as to help the United Kingdom.[48] The British took Roosevelt's private statements very seriously indeed. Hankey wrote in March 1941 that the President's re-election in 1940, should now be seen as the most important event that had taken place in the war since the fall of France.[49] In June 1941, Halifax told Churchill that Roosevelt was firmly convinced that the United States had to enter the war.[50] The question was how to do it and keep public opinion on side.

Certainly some British diplomats started acting far more aggressively at this time, as though the United States was just about to enter the war. It does seem that, in 1941, American interest in controlling Spain grew, in particular with the American government starting to use oil shipments as a carrot and stick to control Spanish behavior.[51] Samuel Hoare, then British ambassador to Spain where he excelled at paying bribes to Spanish officials, was in close contact with Beaverbrook, Halifax and Hankey.[52] In February of 1941, he started to contemplate the use of American power to further British interests in his new area. He proposed to Churchill that the United States now be urged to take Spain and Portugal under their control as part of an extended Monroe Doctrine.

> [It] is undoubtedly the time for us to press on with an Anglo-
> American offensive in the economic field ... I feel sure that with
> your great capacity for grasping big possibilities you will see the

immense advantage of making by means of economic guarantees a kind of extension of the Monroe Doctrine over the Iberian Peninsula and the Atlantic coast of Africa. There is a chance of doing this and it is worth trying for it. I believe that the Americans and we could buy the peninsula for 20 or 30 millions-worth of economic help.[53]

This kind of planning for a post-war world in which the United Kingdom would be the victor along with the United States was not limited to Hoare. Halifax began pressing for a form of political union between the United States and the United Kingdom.[54]

The invasion of the Soviet Union by Germany in June 1941 added even greater urgency to Roosevelt's desire to get American aid to those fighting the Nazis.[55] His most ardent interventionist Cabinet members started pressing for action right away. Knox wrote to him the day after the invasion commenced claiming that it represented a great opportunity for the United States to fully enter the conflict by pre-emptively attacking Germany.

> Since I left here Friday, the Russian–German war has begun and I feel very deeply that I ought to say to you that, in my judgement, this provides us with an opportunity to strike and strike effectively at Germany. Hitler has violated his own resolution not to engage in two wars at once on two separate fronts. The best opinion I can get is that it will take anywhere from six weeks to two months for Hitler to clean up on Russia. It seems to me that we must not let that three months go by without striking hard – the sooner the better.[56]

A few weeks later Knox promised the President that the navy would hand over any equipment needed by the USSR as soon as possible – all they needed was a list.[57]

While Roosevelt was far too sensible to commit such sentiments to paper, he did take the opportunity to place Knox and, inevitably, Hopkins in charge of increasing American war production. On July 9, he formally ordered Knox to set up a committee with Stimson and Hopkins to plan a report, to be kept confidential of course, on how to raise American production capacity so that it would clearly be larger than that of Germany, Japan and other possible enemies combined.[58]

Hopkins was, if anything, even more committed to getting aid to the Soviet Union and Stalin, with whom he was very "impressed."[59] He was one of the few people at the time to believe firmly that the Russians would successfully resist the German invaders, as long as they received the right support.[60] This made him particularly exasperated with his own countrymen, who he believed did not understand how much aid the Russians and British needed. During Argentia, he ridiculed the supposedly selfish attitude of the Americans in front of the British delegation.[61]

It was also during Argentia that the strength, and limitations, of Roosevelt's commitment to help the British were fully revealed. This meeting, which occurred between August 9 and 12 in Placentia Bay in Newfoundland, involved both Roosevelt and Churchill, vital members of their governments such as Hopkins and Beaverbrook, and most of their Chiefs of Staff. The British left somewhat disappointed with the commitment of the President. They had come to believe his earlier words as a guarantee that he would get the United States in the war soon. However, as the meetings went on, and it was clear that Roosevelt and the rest of the American delegation were shying away from firm commitments, frustration crept in.[62]

For instance, the British went into the meeting determined to acquire as much American munitions production as possible, with particular emphasis on US aircraft. The RAF told the Americans that they were aiming for an operational force of 10,420 aircraft at any one time, including 4,090 heavy bombers and more than 3,000 fighters, which would have involved the RAF receiving almost all American production.[63] However, during the conference the British received mostly promises and symbolic satisfaction. The American chiefs, led by Marshall and Stark, spent much of their time discussing the mechanisms whereby equipment would be transferred to the British, and refused to commit the United States to handing over exact amounts.[64] Arnold, who arrived at the conference hoping to maintain at least 50 percent of American production for the USAAF, felt that the Americans had defended their position relatively well. Roosevelt himself spent most of his time helping devise a statement of common purpose with Churchill, eventually known as the Atlantic Charter, which sounded high-minded but obligated the United States to do little. Such cautiousness surprised the British, and Churchill seemed to become depressed at how far the United States was from providing the wholehearted support he desired.[65]

However, the British simply did not have a good handle yet on Franklin Roosevelt. After Argentia, the President took even more steps behind the scenes to use American power to support the United Kingdom.[66] He remained determined to craft a policy that would lead to American entry into the war against Germany, or at least the provision of such enormous quantities of war material to the UK that the British Isles would remain unconquerable.[67] But he still needed a pretext. On the way to Argentia, he gave a summary to his military advisers which laid out his strategic thinking. After the meeting, Arnold wrote a summary of the President's intentions. It is clear just how invested in the air and sea war Roosevelt had become and how he believed it posed the best opportunity for the United States to join the fighting against Germany.

> Our line of responsibility extends to the east of the Azores and East of Ireland. The Azores to be considered as part of the Western Hemisphere. Although the responsibility includes Iceland, it is not to be considered part of the Western Hemisphere.
>
> The United States has a definite responsibility for insuring the safe transport of goods made in this country across the ocean. Our responsibility covers the safety of any and all naval vessels which may be crossing the ocean. If any commercial craft, foreign or domestic, tie onto these capital ships, that is perfectly OK with us, but if any hostile craft, surface, air or submarine comes within shooting range of such a convoy of ships, we must assume that they have hostile intent. There is no way for the crew of our capital ships to know whether such hostile craft are going to attack those ships which may be accompanying us, or our warships themselves. Accordingly, it would be too late to start shooting after the attack had started. *We must start shooting first.*
>
> If Japan goes into Thailand the United States will not be overly concerned, but if it goes into the Dutch East Indies, then we are vitally interested and must do our utmost to get them out.
>
> We are vitally interested in doing everything possible towards providing for delivery of aircraft in England. We should establish such metereological and radio stations in the Arctic as to make ferrying possible during the winter months. We should aid England by taking over such training for them as to cut down transportation necessary for returning ferry pilots after delivering the planes to England.

It is desired to put 10,000 soldiers in Iceland even if we have to undergo considerable difficulties in the United States. Marines can be withdrawn as the Navy sees fit...

We will increase forces in the Philippines so that there be some "bite" to any ultimatum which we may send to Japan – in general, B-17s and P-40s, tanks and antiaircraft guns.

The general plan for Russia was to give them as little as possible in order to keep them satisfied with token forces of one kind or another. (Emphasis added)[68]

It is a fascinating series of reflections. The last comment about the USSR stands out, and was probably made by the President to appeal to his audience of military men, who were considerably more skeptical of the USSR than was he. Not only was the United States not planning on sending the USSR only token forces at the time, but without Hopkins or Sumner Welles in the room with him, Roosevelt probably felt uncomfortable speaking of the importance that he attached to the survival of that country. The most important part was just how dramatically the President was expanding the American zone of operations in the Atlantic, with what seemed to be the express hope of sparking off a confrontation with Nazi Germany. By pushing the boundaries of American patrolling to a line stretching from Iceland to the Azores, Roosevelt was effectively telling the Germans that much more than half of the North Atlantic was to be off limits to their operations and thus fully safe to ship war goods into the UK. If the Germans allowed their submarines to operate inside this area, war with the United States was sure to ensue.

The statements about the Pacific also show that Roosevelt was quite willing to go to war to keep the Japanese from attaining a protected supply of oil in the Dutch East Indies. However, the tone of his remarks, and later what he would say during the conference itself, made it seem that his real expectation was that war would be avoided in the Pacific and that the United States would be free to pursue one against Germany – when and if the Germans would oblige the American President by attacking American forces. This may have been because Roosevelt, like Churchill at this time, still underestimated the Japanese and found it hard to grasp that they might win major engagements against the Americans and British.[69]

In that sense, Roosevelt remained entirely committed to getting the United States into the war against Germany; he just desperately wanted the Germans to provide him the political cover necessary to do so. His most dramatic move in this attempt was to make most of the North Atlantic an American lake. On September 12, in response to a request from Admiral Stark to push the American zone far to the east of Iceland, only about 400 miles from the coast of Scotland, Roosevelt wrote that he "wholly approved" of the change.[70] He was thus committing the United States to protecting at least 80 percent of the ocean distance between New York City and London. The area where the Germans could now attack merchant shipping without risk of involving American warships was so reduced that the British could provide strong convoy support and air cover for almost every ship in the area.

Knox, for one, clearly told the British that such a large American zone was established specifically to cause a shooting war between the United States and Germany – and he regretted the fact that it had not quickly led to a dramatic confrontation. In October 1941, he sent a personal letter to his British counterpart, the First Lord of the Admiralty, A. V. Alexander.

> Personally, I have been surprised at the seeming avoidance by the Germans of any attack upon the convoys escorted by our vessels. I can hardly understand this save only on the basis that German commanders have been given specific orders to avoid such contacts. Of course, such a situation cannot long continue, but while it does last, it certainly affords a reason for congratulations in that the tonnage reaching British ports from the Americas safely has gone up in such a gratifying fashion.[71]

On the few moments when the Germans took Roosevelt's bait and started exchanging fire with American warships in the Atlantic, the President demanded as much information as possible.[72] On September 4, the USS *Greer*, an American destroyer, came across a German submarine in the American zone near Iceland and started to track it.[73] The Germans responded by firing a torpedo, leading to the *Greer* dropping depth charges before the vessels lost contact. In October, two USN vessels, the *Kearney* and the *Reuben James*, were attacked by German submarines while escorting convoys, and the latter ship was sunk with the loss of 115 crew members.[74] This second attack was the more important as it compelled Congress, over the objections of the isolationists, to approve the arming of merchantmen for their own protection.[75]

Roosevelt was particularly interested as to whether he could claim that the Germans had fired first during these incidents. He even instituted a shoot-on-sight policy after the October engagements.[76] Interestingly, after these exchanges, the Germans mostly bowed to American pressure and stopped attacking merchantmen sailing in the vast area of the Atlantic Ocean that the United States now claimed. It took Japan to push the United States into the war.

The Japanese decision to attack Pearl Harbor was very much connected to the actions of Franklin Roosevelt (intentional or not).[77] The Japanese military and government had been debating the merits of a southwards move to take over the Dutch East Indies since the 1930s.[78] The discussions picked up steam in 1940 when Germany conquered the Netherlands and France.[79] It was the only place where Japan could acquire the crucial raw materials it needed, particularly oil, but also bauxite, to assure its economic independence. Until the summer of 1941, the debate over the southward move was dragging the Japanese government in different directions.[80] The freeze that Roosevelt put on Japanese assets – plus the embargo on sales of American oil, in response to the Japanese move into French Indochina – was a severe shock to the Japanese.[81] In a matter of months, the stalemate in the Japanese government was broken and the decision was made to seize the raw materials.

Although musing on the precise contents of another person's soul is fraught with danger, especially when that person is Franklin Roosevelt, it does seem that the President definitely wanted the United States to enter the war. To do so he was willing to contravene legal standards both internationally and nationally. However, he was not willing to fire the first shot – and while he gave a clean and loaded pistol to the Germans and paraded countless targets in front of them, in the end it was the Japanese who pulled the trigger.

British air and sea power in 1941

While Roosevelt was trying to get the United States into the war, the British had to fight it, alone, until June 1941. Considering the fact that Germany had access to the productive resources of the entire European continent for that year, the British performance during the air and sea war was impressive. For most of the year, the British were able to control the sea lanes in and out of Europe and demonstrated that they were the Luftwaffe's most deadly enemy.

The most important campaign at sea was the war against German submarines. The other areas that receive comment, such as the sortie of the *Bismarck* or the war between the British and Italian navies in the Mediterranean, were relatively unimportant within the context of victory and defeat in the war. In particular, the *Bismarck* and other German surface ships were assets that held no prospect of shaping the outcome of the war. In an era of aviation, surface vessels sailing on their own were anachronisms. Moreover, individual units of any type of equipment in World War II, even something as large as a battleship, were not crucial. It was the ability to replace and replenish production that mattered. From that point of view, German surface vessels only caused a tiny amount of damage, and once sunk could not be replaced. Just by way of comparison, between the outbreak of the war and the end of 1941, German submarines sank 4,779,068 tons of merchant shipping, while German surface vessels of all types sank 360,146 tons.[82] Even had the *Bismarck* been lucky enough to survive its famous sortie, and headed out once or twice more, its impact on the war's course would have been negligible.

While the Mediterranean theater will be discussed in more detail later, in 1941 its role in the defeat of German production was also limited. The number of German ships sunk in the area in that year was insignificant. In the four months between June and September 1941, the Germans lost five ships there with a combined tonnage of 15,496.[83] Also, the fighting in the Mediterranean posed no threat to German production beyond battlefield destruction. The war in the Atlantic, on the other hand, was crucial because it was one of the few campaigns where Germany could actually wage truly modern war by destroying production in either its pre-production or its deployment phase. Victory in it for Britain was the necessary precondition of victory in the war for the Allies.

In 1940, convoys were once again shown to be the vital first step in the protection of merchant shipping, and in 1941 the Royal Navy was able to increase dramatically the number of properly equipped escorts available for convoy protection. Drawing mostly upon British construction, but also making as much use as possible of the fifty older American destroyers received from lend-lease, the number of British anti-submarine vessels fitted with Asdic more than doubled. Almost 100 extra destroyers and approximately 175 extra corvettes became available for operations.[84] A fleet considerably larger than the anti-submarine forces with which Britain entered the war was added in less than 12 months. With many fewer unescorted vessels to attack, German submarines were forced to go directly after the convoys themselves, with the result that their own losses grew rapidly. In March 1941, after the Germans lost five U-boats in two weeks, they were forced to abandon close surface attacks.[85]

Greater numbers of escorts were probably the most important development in the war at sea, but the British were also making crucial strides in other areas. The importance of air support for convoys became much better understood. Aircraft that could patrol the areas around convoys not only provided greater vigilance on behalf of the protective force, they could attack U-boats on the surface with great effect. The problem in 1941 was gaining access to enough aircraft with the range necessary to do the job. It was an issue that often brought the Royal Navy and the RAF to loggerheads. It was also an area where British access to American aircraft was vital. If there were two aircraft that were recognized as crucial in 1941, they were the Catalina flying boat and the B-24 Liberator. Both aircraft possessed exceedingly long operational ranges for the time. The Catalina had a range of about 600 miles and the Liberator an impressive 750 miles, which was hundreds of miles more than their British counterparts, the Hudsons, Whitleys, Wellingtons and Sunderlands.

Very long range (VLR) Liberators were the most coveted. Once fitted with Asdic and depth charges, they proved to be a devastating anti-submarine platform.[86] They could either patrol directly above a convoy or they could be used to scout ahead. The latter kept German U-boats submerged during the day, depriving them of speed and drastically reducing the radius of their operational range. The first all-VLR Liberator squadron was activated in June 1941, and was part of the process of significantly reducing the area of the Atlantic in which the U-boats could operate in relative safety. The notion of a "gap" that was without air cover now entered the lexicon of the sea war, most famously the Iceland "gap," which represented a stretch of sea that was too distant from land to receive air cover until later in the war. (See Map 3).

In trying to obtain more Liberators, the Admiralty was willing even to subvert the wishes of Harry Hopkins. For political and strategic reasons (and as a sign of his real power at the time), Hopkins had been urging the British to use all the heavy bombers they received from the United States to bomb the German homeland. During Argentia, Pound brought this up in a clever fashion, through a request for additional Catalinas. In a meeting of American and British service chiefs, not attended by Roosevelt or Churchill, Pound pleaded for more of the flying boats.

> He [Pound] commented on the excellent performance of
> the Catalinas ... in the Coastal Command, but said it was a "rude
> shock" to find that practically none were to be delivered in the
> next few months. The need for Catalinas, he indicated, was
> increased by the probability that no more Liberators ... might be
> given to Coastal Command. This probability was the result of the
> representations made by Mr. Hopkins to have the Liberators taken
> out of Coastal Command and used to bomb Germany.[87]

This was one of the few times that the American service chiefs were united in agreement with their British counterparts. To them, Hopkins had no authority to direct the British to use aircraft in any specific fashion, and they let Pound know it.

This one success did not stop the Admiralty from trying to wheedle extra Catalinas as well. In September 1941, the British asked the Canadians to forgo a shipment of fifty Catalinas that they were due to receive from the United States so that they could be given directly to the Royal Navy.[88] Just a few days before Japanese bombs fell on Pearl Harbor, the Admiralty intensified its efforts. The last letter from the First Lord of the Admiralty to the American Chief of Naval Operations before news of the bombing broke was to ask for at least sixty more Catalinas to patrol the British coast.[89]

One more area where the Admiralty was successful was in persuading the RAF to direct a huge number of its raids against U-boat targets, from the nearly indestructible U-boat pens, to the assembly factories, to the mining of German harbors. (See Figure 20.) Arthur Harris, who was prone to exaggeration but did have a point in this case, argued that from April 1941 to March 1942, half of all British strategic bombing raids were directed towards thwarting Germany's naval power – with much of the effort wasted.[90] However, if the direct raids were particularly ineffective, the overall impact of the expansion

20 Concrete German U-boat pens at Brest, France. Despite great
effort in 1942 and 1943, all attempts to destroy these pens by direct bombing
proved fruitless.

of air support for the war at sea in 1941 was profound. While convoys
without air support continued to provide a high chance of survival for
merchant ships, convoys with air support provided almost complete
protection.

Finally, there was one other British advance: a proper understanding of the importance of convoy speed in traveling across the
Atlantic safely. Because of a submarine's relatively slow speed, it was
discovered that ships that could maintain an unbroken pace of more
than 12 knots were almost invulnerable to attack. This was even the
case for unarmed merchantmen. In March 1941, the Admiralty began
studying the possibility of completely removing ships of at least
12 knots speed from convoys and letting them sail on their own.[91]
Though large steps in this area were not yet taken, by early 1942 the
Admiralty had come to the conclusion that ships of at least 15 knots
speed were best left to sail alone.[92]

Taken altogether, the British by the end of 1941 had a very
good idea of how the war in the North Atlantic would be won. If they
built merchant ships with increased speed, made sure to place the
slower ones in well-protected convoys, and then provided the convoys
with air cover, German U-boats would be able to do little to damage
Allied production or equipment deployment.

If the war at sea in 1941 was developing in promising ways, the
war in the air presented a more complex picture. When it came to
strategic air power, the British were still riven by basic differences of
opinion. The main problem was that it was now becoming clear how
little damage could be inflicted by the bomber force at hand, and how

far air forces still were from realizing the more grandiose assumptions of interwar period strategic air power enthusiasts. For much of 1941, the British debate was over what to target in the German productive system. At the end of 1940, the key target was oil. The RAF evaluated the possible effectiveness of a strategic bombing campaign against German domestic production of oil, mostly synthetic, and the shipping of oil to the Reich from Romania – now a German ally.[93] The analysis made clear that if they could significantly reduce German oil production, it would be an important blow. The plans also showed that it was Germany's synthetic fuel production, based around nine major factories, which provided the best target. All of this would prove correct in 1944. In December 1940, Portal argued that German oil production should now be the primary target of British strategic bombing.[94] At the time Ismay, who was close to Churchill, was the most vociferous opponent of the plan, and argued for a campaign against German cities aimed at weakening morale and damaging munitions production. However, the oil campaign won out and destruction of Germany's synthetic production of fuel, as well as sabotage operations against Romanian oil production, was moved up the priority list.

It was here, however, that the plan revealed its great problem. As the RAF planners well realized, the important thing was to fully destroy these plants, and this showed how far air power still was from meeting the lofty expectations of its supporters. German oil facilities had to be bombed during a clear day, which gave the attacking aircraft at least some chance of placing their explosives close enough to the target to damage it. However, not only did the weather have to cooperate to allow such attacks, but operating during the day left British bombers, which had relatively weak defensive armament, open to more effective attacks by German fighters and flak. As such, any successful campaign against oil by the British was potentially extremely costly, and the chances of success were small.

The greater danger that the British faced if they wanted to continue to bomb Germany in daylight can be seen in the very different loss rates Bomber Command suffered in 1940 and 1941.[95] In 1940, 1.9 percent of Bomber Command aircraft sent on sorties at night were lost, and the figure for 1941 was 2.5 percent. Flying in daylight was about two and a half times more dangerous. In 1940 Bomber Command lost 4.6 percent of aircraft sent on daylight sorties, and the figure for 1941 was an unsustainable 6.1 percent.

Also, these dangerous daylight raids seemed to be making little difference. Judging the effectiveness of strategic bombing during the war was never easy, but early on it seems to have been particularly problematic. In 1940 and 1941, many of the British attempts to analyze the impact of their attacks were based on impressionistic reports that overemphasized the accuracy of their bombing.[96] Because of this there were initially some grotesquely optimistic assumptions about the damage caused to German oil production.[97] By March 1941, however, it became clear to many that German oil production did not seem to be hampered in any material way, and that continuing to focus on oil as a primary target was achieving little but costing a great deal.[98] Crucially, Portal started expressing real doubts over the effectiveness of the daylight oil campaign.[99] By April he had circulated a paper calling for greater attacks on Germany's transportation system, in particular attacks on the railway system in occupied France.

This helped kick-start a serious debate over British strategic bombing policy that would continue for a year. Trenchard threw his weighty hat into the ring in May 1941 when he circulated a memorandum on the state of the air war.[100] Most interestingly, he was willing to admit how few bombs even a modern bomber could deliver on target. By his estimate, no more than 1 percent of all bombs dropped could be expected to land close enough to a specific target to damage it, so that 99 percent of the effort put into precision bombing attacks was lost.[101] His solution to this problem was to make German cities as a unit the main targets, as their large areas meant that almost all the bombs dropped on them would be bound to hit something. Trenchard argued that such a campaign should have first call on British bombers, and that using them on targets outside Germany, even German preparations for an invasion of the UK, would be a waste.[102]

The Chiefs of Staff met on May 30, 1941 to discuss Trenchard's paper, and while it was clear that it had some impact, it was also clear that it was far from being widely supported.[103] One of the weak points was that Trenchard wanted absolute priority in both production and allocations given to the bombing of Germany. Neither the army nor navy wanted to have their needs so dramatically sacrificed in this way. Within the RAF there was also less than wholehearted support for Trenchard's vision, as was shown when he addressed the

Air Staff on June 2.[104] It was at this meeting that he gave a full exposition on his belief that German morale was considerably more fragile than that of the British, and needed to be targeted directly.

The arguments in favor of area bombing against German cities were attacked from a number of different directions. Not surprisingly, Maurice Hankey stood ready to take up the challenge. He had little time for arguments in favor of attacking civilian morale and seemed unconvinced that German morale was in any way weaker than its British counterpart.[105] In fact, he ridiculed Trenchard's notion by making claims about both past behavior and the German population in the war so far. "If history is any guide, therefore, we have to assume that the German peoples possess great powers of endurance, resistance and recovery. Indeed, no-one who lived through the Great War, or who has read either the British or the German accounts of it, could form any other conclusion."[106]

Moreover, Hankey argued that any campaign directed against cities as targets was bound to fail, as most Germans did not live in the large cities.[107] However, if he made a strong case critiquing the underlying assumptions behind the area bombing of cities, his plan was only to keep doing what had been done before (without much success). Once again he argued that attacks on Germany's fuel production should receive the highest priority.[108] At this time, however, there were few people who would argue strongly for the continuation of a policy that seemed to have delivered so few results. Also Hankey was clearly losing influence. He had never been close to Churchill, and the more he watched the Prime Minister, the more skeptical he became about his war leadership. Hankey was part of a faction that believed Churchill was becoming increasingly dictatorial whilst surrounding himself with "yes men."[109] This made it even more unlikely that his opinion would be supported, and by September 1941 oil was downgraded as a priority target, to be replaced by the transportation policy favored by Portal.[110]

Portal's vision also included attacks focused on German cities, not because they were cities, but because they were "centres of communication."[111] The British experience had shown that, when railways were damaged, this had a greater impact on production than direct attacks on factories, and the assumption should be that this would be the same for Germany. Additionally, German transportation centers, as they were located in larger cities, could be attacked by British bombers at night, so that the many bombs that were sure not to hit the target would at least fall on something definably German. "Sir Charles Portal said that he was rapidly coming round to the view that ... the transportation system in Germany should now be our primary target. Reports of the recent air bombardment of Germany's industrial towns tended to prove the value of such attacks."

Moreover, such a campaign could be waged from high altitude at night, which it was hoped would reduce British losses. Portal believed that German night fighters would probably never gain dominance over the heavy bomber. "Science could not turn night into day, and it was unlikely that the night bomber would have to face the attacks of more than one fighter at a time."[112] It was interesting to see that at this time Portal was supported by Sir John Dill, the army Chief of Staff. Dill seemed considerably more interested than his successor, Alanbrooke, in the discussion over the use of strategic air power. Together, Portal and Dill were able to turn what seemed to be a Chiefs of Staff decision in favor of a Trenchard-like policy of bombing German morale, into one that was actually directed at German transport. In the June 1941 report to Churchill, the Chiefs of Staff, after praising morale bombing as the way forward, concluded: "As a short-term bombing policy, we should attack transportation targets so as to achieve dislocation, coupled with maximum direct attack on morale."[113]

It was a subtle appeal to a Prime Minister who was clearly having doubts about following any strict policy on strategic bombing. Churchill had started to express his unease about the effect, or more likely the lack thereof, that the bombing of Germany was having. When he heard from the Chiefs of Staff that they favored a transport campaign, he felt it lacked flexibility and scope. Instead, in a personal minute, he argued that there should be no clear priority for targeting that would have precedence for more than a month.[114] Though the Chiefs of Staff quickly tried to squelch such a haphazard policy, it was indicative of Churchill's mind when it came to air power. He never seemed particularly attached to, or particularly opposed to, any specific target. He also showed a healthy skepticism of the more dramatic claims of air power enthusiasts. On October 7, 1941, not long after British strategic air policy had been changed to focus on German cities as a way of damaging transport and morale, Churchill sent the following minute to Portal:

We all hope that the air offensive against Germany will realise the expectations of the Air Staff. Everything is being done to create the bombing force desired on the largest possible scale ... I deprecate however placing unbounded confidence in this means of attack, and still more expressing that confidence in terms of arithmetic...Even if all the towns of Germany were rendered largely uninhabitable it does not follow that the military control would be weakened or even that war industry could not be carried on.

The Air Staff would make a mistake to put their claim too high. Before the war we were greatly misled by the pictures they painted of the destruction that would be wrought by air raids.[115]

Although Churchill has been roundly criticized by many of his contemporaries for altering his strategic outlook too often and too dramatically, his instinct in this case was more right than wrong. The problem was that for all the different ideas being thrown back and forth, no specific strategic air policy had shown itself to be terribly effective. Neither the German bombing of British harbors and London nor the British attempts to attack Germany's oil supplies or transportation network had yielded noticeable results. By the end of 1941, the British were still a long way from being able to influence German production in any way before it reached the battlefield.

However, on the battlefield, the British played a crucial role in significantly weakening the Luftwaffe forces that were available to support the German invasion of the Soviet Union. German air support for Operation Barbarossa was, within the framework of other major German operations, surprisingly weak. Because of the previous heavy losses suffered against the British and the French, the Luftwaffe that supported the German invasion had only little more than half the planes it had available to support the invasion of France and the Low Countries in May 1940.[116] It was also noticeably smaller in terms of combat planes than the force used during the Battle of Britain. The Luftwaffe maintained a force of between 2,130 and 2,330 bombers and fighters in the east during the first three months of Barbarossa. (See Table 20.) This was a very small force considering the size of the front. During the Battle of Britain the Luftwaffe had deployed 10–20 percent more aircraft than this in a much smaller area. On August 13, 1940, after the battle had been underway for a few weeks and many German

Table 20 *Germany: Luftwaffe deployment on the Eastern Front, June and September 1941*

	June 28, 1941	September 27, 1941
Bombers (all)	1,323	1,341
Single-engine fighters	829	629
Twin-engine fighters	181 (estimated)	160 (estimated)
Total (approx.)	2,333	2,130

Source: Air 40/1207.
Note: This table is based on official Luftwaffe Quartermaster General Reports. The 1941 figures did not provide theater breakdowns for two-engine fighters until December 1941, but when they did, about 20 percent were on the Eastern Front (70 out of 402 twin-engine fighters were on the Eastern Front on December 28, 1942). In my estimate of approximate aircraft numbers on the Eastern Front I have doubled this to 40 percent.

aircraft had been lost, the Luftwaffe still had 2,470 bombers and fighters deployed against Great Britain.[117] Yet even this force was considerably smaller than that deployed as part of the invasion of France and the Low Countries only a few months earlier. At the end of March 1940, when the Germans were preparing to invade, the Luftwaffe had 3,987 bombers and fighters available for operations, a force almost twice as large at that used to invade the USSR.[118] Again, this extremely large force was operating in a much smaller area of operations.

Even in the week that Barbarossa was launched, the Luftwaffe had 1,117 aircraft deployed attacking Britain or in the Mediterranean, with an unknown additional number in the Reich on home defense missions.[119] This figure represented a low point for the year, as in the coming months the Luftwaffe was forced to shift even more of its forces to fight the British. On December 27, 1941, when the fighting outside Moscow was reaching a crescendo and long before the USAAF had appeared in any numbers in Europe, the Germans had deployed almost a hundred more aircraft to fight the RAF than they had on the Eastern Front. (See Table 21.)

In simple production terms, the UK in the second half of 1941 played a major role in limiting the number of aircraft the Germans could send east. The British also provided a significant amount of their own form of lend-lease aid to the USSR at this crucial time.[120] Certainly through their efforts in drastically weakening the

Table 21 *Germany: Luftwaffe deployment on Eastern and Western Fronts,*
27 December 1941

	Eastern Front	Western Front/Mediterranean
Bombers (all)	981	597
Single-engine fighters	512	721
Twin-engine fighters	70	332
Total	1,563	1,650

Source: Air 40/1207.

Table 22 *United Kingdom: night-time bombing effort, June 1–10 and*
July 1–10, 1941

	June 1–10, 1941	July 1–10, 1941
Number of bombers	237	1,664
High explosives (tons)	354	1,643
Incendiary bombs(no.)	14,490	138,400
Lost aircraft	4	55

Source: FDR MSS, PSF 3.
Note: This table comes from an intelligence report sent to Roosevelt to show
him how much more effort was being put into the air war since the German
invasion of the USSR. Beardall to FDR, July 22, 1941.

Luftwaffe on the Eastern Front and helping the USSR with emergency
aid, the British played a major role in saving Moscow from the clutches
of the Nazis.

If the air war against Britain materially affected the Eastern
Front, the Eastern Front also changed the air debate that was going on
in Britain. It added greater urgency to the notion that something
noticeable needed to be done to damage Germany. It was at this time
that the move to more night-time bombing, which was less dangerous
and allowed for the dropping, effective or not, of heavier bomb loads,
received further support.

In the first ten days of July 1941, British night bombing jumped
by between 500 and 1,000 percent (depending upon variable) when
compared with the first ten days of June. (See Table 22.) The relatively
small losses suffered on these raids and the need to seem active
helped push along the process of re-evaluating strategic air policy. In
September 1941, when announcing that attacks on German oil facilities would be suspended, Portal stated that Berlin would be made a

major target when practicable.[121] However, when, in early November, raids over Germany caused high losses of the new, expensive and still scarce four-engine bombers, it was decided to scale back operations as a whole. In the meantime, the RAF would wait until it had built up a proper striking force of four-engine bombers and it would debate how to use such a force.[122] Discovering exactly how the British were going to use their strategic bombing force would have to wait.

6 GRAND STRATEGY IN ACTION: PRIORITIZING THE AIR AND SEA WAR

Ernest King was a committed note-taker. He liked jotting down his impressions in almost stream of consciousness form as a way organizing his thoughts. In December 1942 he was planning for the momentous meeting of American and British grand strategists scheduled for January 1943 in Casablanca. As a note-taker, King had to be careful with his commander in chief, Franklin Roosevelt. Roosevelt was wary about people writing down his statements in meetings and discouraged the habit. Therefore, King often recorded Roosevelt's opinions, and his own, after meeting with the President, which has left us with a fascinating record of American grand strategy that December.

On December 12, King produced a series of notes, somewhat random, certainly not pre-structured, which provides a tantalizing glimpse into his view of the Pacific war at the time and, crucially, some of Franklin Roosevelt's views. When it came to the President, he recorded one very interesting point – the amount of American effort that the President wanted sent to the Pacific war in the coming year.

> December 12 [1942]...
> Distribution of war effort. Overall – Cominch thinks it is
> about time to take stand to establish percent to be in Pacific
> somewhere between 20–35 – this will include China front
> (Burma) – situation does not remain static.[1]

This was an extremely important moment for King, as he was determined to make sure that the war against Japan received as much

American production as possible. On the other hand, he was perfectly content to keep the British out of the region as much as possible. In 1942, as will be shown below, the war in the Pacific, surprisingly to some, had received the majority of American war construction. The political necessity of maintaining the American position in the region after Pearl Harbor and the great Japanese successes in early 1942 meant that the United States sent far more to the Pacific than it should theoretically have if it was truly fighting a policy of Germany-First. However, as 1942 was ending, King knew that the strategic thrust of the war was turning towards Europe.

King's specific role in deciding grand strategy in the war has sometimes been unfairly characterized (for both good and ill). He was without doubt rude and unpleasant, and had an irrational suspicion of both the British and the American army. However, he was also very intelligent and willing to imagine air and sea operations that were beyond most of his colleagues. Had he not been in charge of the United States Navy during the war, the course of the conflict would have been very different. In 1942 and 1943 there were three distinct decisions that needed to be taken, and air and sea power were instrumental to all of them. King ended up triumphing in two. The basic decision was how much Anglo-American force should be deployed against Germany and how much against Japan. Once that had been decided, the next question was how that force should be used in theater to destroy the military power of the Axis. When it came to Europe, King, as will be shown, was more than happy to take a back seat. However, when it came to the Pacific, he turned himself into the driving force in the war to defeat Japan. This chapter will not only cover the foundational question of Germany-First in Anglo-American thinking. It will also delve into the question of how best to engage German power, which bedeviled British and American grand strategists in 1942 and 1943, leading to some of the most acrimonious splits in the alliance.

The (partial) myth of Germany-First

For the British, this seeming American indecision about Germany-First in 1942 was troubling – after the fall of Singapore. With German air and sea weaponry threatening the United Kingdom on a daily basis, it is not surprising that Churchill and the British government argued strongly for a Germany-First policy. The only time the British contemplated the dispatch of a significant striking force to the war in the Pacific was before the Japanese capture of Malaya which culminated in the British surrender at Singapore in February 1942, an event that Churchill called the greatest disaster in British military history. Before then, the British had envisaged the deployment of more than simply a defensive force to the Pacific. The desire to protect as much of the British Empire as possible, and not to allow the dominions of Australia and New Zealand to believe that the United States alone was responsible for their defense, meant that the British planned to send a large amount of their air and sea production to the Pacific. The Admiralty, supported by a memorandum written by Pound, was preparing in January 1942 to remove a large majority of the Royal Navy's battleships and aircraft carriers from European waters to go to the Indian Ocean.[2] At this time they were even willing to countenance the switching of American forces from Europe to the Pacific. In January 1942, Churchill willingly agreed to divert the deployment of 21,000 American soldiers, complete with all their equipment including their air cover, from the United Kingdom to the Pacific.[3]

However, the loss of Singapore, coming hot on the heels of the sinking of HMS *Prince of Wales* and *Repulse*, snuffed out the desire for a major British commitment in the region and marked the beginning of the end of the UK as a meaningful power in East Asia.[4] Having suffered such a blow to imperial prestige, the British opted for a completely defensive and very cheap strategy, based around the protection of India. Indeed, much of the strategy of the Churchill government from this point on in the European theater, in particular the doggedness with which Churchill and others fought for a major commitment of Anglo-American force in the Mediterranean, was based around the maintenance as much as possible of British rule in the Indian subcontinent – having realized that their position in the Pacific had changed substantially. It was one of the reasons that Anglo-American differences over the war against Japan became some of the most difficult and contentious of the wartime alliance.[5]

Examples of how little the British were willing to expend in the Pacific abound (at least in the period after the fall of Singapore and before the surrender of Germany). In that entire period, British and Indian army casualties in British major operations – stretching from repelling the Japanese invasion of India to reconquering Burma – were

11,969 dead.[6] As 1942 turned into 1943, what few British forces remained directed towards Japan were reduced further. In the summer of 1943, forty-eight ships of the British Eastern Fleet were detached and sent to the Mediterranean to support the invasion of Sicily.[7] At that point the entire British naval commitment to the Pacific would have been about 1 or 2 percent of British naval power as a whole, as the fleet was composed of one antiquated battleship (*Ramilles*), no aircraft carriers, four cruisers, one submarine flotilla and a handful of destroyers.[8] When it came to air power, again, the British were unwilling to commit any of their best front-line forces until after the Germans surrendered. In December 1943, the number of RAF aircraft of all types that were operational for the Eastern Command was 464.[9] Moreover, these were overwhelmingly much less expensive fighters. As the best British bomber, the Lancaster, did not have the range to hit any major Japanese targets even if based in American facilities in China or the Marianas, Bomber Command paid little attention to the war against Japan. They even assumed that the only way they could play a meaningful role in that conflict would be if the Americans lent them some B-29s.[10] Again, while it is impossible to come up with one percentage that would encapsulate the amount of effort the British put into the war against Japan before the summer of 1945, it would certainly be below 5 percent in production value – perhaps considerably below.

Therefore, with the British full commitment to a Germany-First strategy from February 1942 onwards, it was left to the United States to determine how much effort should be expended in the Pacific. For the rest of 1942, the United States fought what can only be termed two different and approximately equal wars, against Germany and Japan – with, if anything, a bias in favor of the war against Japan. For Roosevelt, the Japanese successes destroyed one of the underlying assumptions behind Germany-First. Both before and immediately after American entry into the war, there was a belief (held by both Roosevelt and Churchill) that the Japanese could be confined geographically approximately where they were in late 1941. Certainly they assumed that the strategic defensive line based on Malaya, the Philippines and the Dutch East Indies could be held by the Allies. In one of the earliest American strategy memoranda drawn up under Roosevelt's direct orders, the second highest priority for the United States, after providing for the security of Great Britain, was to "reinforce the Philippines, Dutch East Indies and Australia to further the security of China and

Southwest Pacific."[11] Both the British and the Americans also assumed that Japanese production, particularly of air and sea weaponry, would be far below reality.[12]

The great Japanese successes, however, made the assumption of a clear Germany-First policy strategically, and perhaps even more importantly, politically dangerous for the United States. The truth was that Japan was a greater power than almost everyone assumed then, and the shock of their success caused the scrapping of all pre-war American assumptions. Roosevelt certainly took a keen interest in the Pacific for the rest of 1942, often ordering the dispatch of large American forces to the region. In April he even seemed to opt openly for a Pacific-First strategy. Later, he pressed for extra equipment to be sent first to Australia and then later to support the fighting in the Solomon Islands. Marshall, a committed backer of Germany-First, came to doubt that the President shared this strategic outlook. That is why King's note is so revealing – for perhaps the only time in the war, Roosevelt gave a specific percentage to the amount of the American war effort that he wanted to be sent against the Japanese, "somewhere between 20–35" percent.

The relative application of American force during the war has been discussed by many historians. For a while after the war, most assumed that Germany-First was American policy, even in 1942. Roosevelt's decision to support the invasion of North Africa was thus seen as necessarily limiting the resources that the United States could send to the Pacific.[13] Some, often based in Europe, seem to assume that Germany was the greatest enemy and that the United States committed considerably more force to the war in Europe than to the war in the Pacific.[14] Others, however, have pointed out the flaws in this point of view. The weaknesses in the Germany- or Europe-First argument have been attacked, sometimes successfully, sometimes too dramatically. Mark Stoler, by far the most important historian who has delved into this question, has demonstrated that, particularly in 1942, the United States followed more of a "Pacific-First" strategy than anything else.[15] This is an extremely important corrective to those who seem to blithely assume that Germany was a much greater enemy who tied down considerably more American resources – which is part of a general assumption by some that the war in Europe was by far the greater conflict. On the other hand, some revisionists go too far in assuming that the United States maintained this position, or at least one of strategic parity, throughout 1943 and 1944.[16]

In fact, the American application of force, both strategically and in terms of production, was a changeable feast and the most important dividing line was that between the different American services. The American army was the greatest proponent of the Germany-First policy. Marshall in particular believed that the war would only be won by the quickest possible invasion of northwest Europe and also that the build-up of forces for such an event should be the first task for American production. He was supported by those in the army in other important positions of power, such as Dwight Eisenhower (when he was the Director of Plans) and Thomas Handy, the army's Assistant Chief of Staff for Operations.[17] The army believed that essential supplies to the USSR and the UK should receive a higher shipping priority than reinforcements for the southwest Pacific or even Hawaii.[18] Even though Marshall was unsuccessful in his push for an invasion of northwest Europe in 1942 and 1943, he was able – partly because of Roosevelt's decision to support the North African invasions, which led almost unconsciously to a major Mediterranean commitment in 1943 – to make sure that most combat troops were sent to Europe after 1942. However, for the first year of the American war effort, army troops (including those in the USAAF) were split almost equally between Europe and the Pacific. In 1942 a grand total of 972,450 army troops were sent to overseas bases.[19] Of these, 54 percent, or 524,714, were sent to different "Atlantic" operations – the largest group being the 224,413 sent to different parts of northwest Africa. On the other hand, a still substantial 46 percent of army personnel, or 447,736, were sent to different Pacific areas, the single largest group being the 144,509 sent to Australia.

In 1943, this relative state of equality was ended for the army as many more troops were sent to the European theater. On a monthly basis, well over 60 percent of army troops (including those in the USAAF) were sent to Europe or North Africa.[20] What this meant was that in January 1944, the US army overseas deployment was 65 percent against Germany and 35 percent against Japan. The specific regional breakdown was as shown in Table 23.

In 1944, with the build-up for the Normandy landings and then the need to reinforce the American ground and air forces in Europe after D-Day, this swing towards the war against Germany became even more pronounced. For much of the year, approximately 80 percent of the American troops deployed in any month were sent to Europe. In

Table 23 *USA: army personnel overseas by theater, January 31, 1944*

Theater	Troop numbers (thousands)
European (includes UK/Iceland)	953
North Africa/Mediterranean	622
Total against Germany	1,575
Asiatic (includes China/India)	102
Central Pacific	219
South Pacific	208
Southwest Pacific	328
Total against Japan	857

Source: Lubin MSS, Stevens to Lubin, March 31, 1944.
Note: There was also a figure recorded for "all others" of 292,000 that is impossible to assign to the war against either Japan or Germany.

September 1944, the highest percentage of the war was recorded when 84 percent of all army forces deployed overseas were sent to Europe – most sent directly to the continent, bypassing the UK entirely.[21] Even in January 1945, Europe was receiving many more army troops than the war in the Pacific, when 71 percent of the troops shipped overseas were directed to the war against Germany and the rest to the war against Japan.[22]

To try to sum up the army deployment in the war against Germany versus that against Japan in one statistic is meaningless, but it would be safe to say that between the summer of 1943 and early 1945, approximately three-quarters of US army personnel were devoted to the war against Germany – with one proviso. Overseas deployments tell only part of the story for army personnel. The US army always retained a substantial proportion of its personnel, sometimes a surprisingly large amount, back in the United States, a long way from the fronts or even supporting the fronts. At the end of February 1945, for instance, when overseas deployments were at their height, the army's total strength was 8,095,000, of which 2,822,000 (35 percent) were still in the United States.[23]

Troop numbers alone, however, give only one picture of American effort – and a less important one if the primacy of production is considered. If army effort in terms of war equipment deployment is considered, a slightly different picture emerges. For instance, the US Army Air Force made up approximately one-quarter of the figures given above for overall army deployments. A complete breakdown of army personnel by sector for September 1944 is given in Table 24. The

Table 24 *USA: army personnel overseas, August 1944*

Sector	Number	Percent
Air force combat	466,572	11
Air force service	593,878	14
Ground forces combat	1,484,940	35
Ground forces service	496,111	11
Service forces	1,139,123	27
En route	92,366	2
Total overseas	4,272,990	100

Source: Lubin MSS, Stevens to Lubin, September 19, 1944.

one-quarter of personnel who were devoted to the air forces actually controlled considerably more production than the three-quarters in all other services.[24] Just to compare, at the time when this deployment balance was tabulated, the monthly spend on building aircraft for the United States, $1,663 million, was almost twelve times larger than the equivalent monthly figure for combat vehicles, $144 million.[25]

When it came to the US Army Air Force, there was a distinct disconnect between the rhetoric of strategic deployments and the reality on the ground in 1942. The USAAF, at least in terms of its major figures such as Arnold, Spaatz and Eaker, was strongly Germany-First by nature. The Air War Plan drawn up and endorsed by Arnold in August 1942 was one of the most precise documents produced at the time within the US strategic structure that argued that the war on Germany should receive the dominant share of the American war effort.

> 1. To win this war by defeating both Germany and Japan we must insure the retention of the United Kingdom as an operating base and should retain Great Britain as an actual ally.
> (A) Germany is the nearest and most powerful threat to Britain's security...
> 3. Our forces are incapable of accomplishing a decisive strategic offensive against both Germany and Japan simultaneously.
> (A) We must, therefore, retain our original concept of the strategic defensive in the Pacific pending the defeat of Germany.[26]

It was a refrain that Arnold continued for the rest of the war. However, the deployment situation of the air force never matched the preponderance put forth in this strategy until 1943. In 1942, much as for the army in general, there was no set priority for aircraft deployments. Aircraft, which were still relatively small in number for the US Army Air Force, were deployed as produced on a seemingly need-to-have basis. Since the Pacific seemed to be in crisis for much of the year, in numerical terms the USAAF actually had more aircraft deployed to the Pacific than in Europe/North Africa for much of the time. Table 25 gives the complete breakdown for August 1942 at exactly the moment when the USAAF was arguing for the overriding importance of the war against Germany Even in the category of the most expensive aircraft, the four-engine B-17 and B-24 bombers, which were supposed to be used primarily to bomb Germany, the Pacific had the majority of deployment. There were 198 four-engine American bombers either deployed or en route to the different Pacific theaters, while 193 were deployed in the war against Germany. On October 14, 1942, the relative balance in aircraft between the Pacific and Europe remained basically unchanged, with 1,938 aircraft of all types deployed or en route to the Pacific and 1,577 directed towards the war against Germany.[27]

Entering 1943 the USAAF was determined to correct this balance and place far more force against Germany. At this point, those who argue that the United States was no longer following a Germany-First policy are clearly wrong, at least when it came to American air

Table 25 *USA: USAAF deployment of aircraft by type and region, August 21, 1942*

	Bombers	Fighters	Transport	Total
Against Japan				
Alaska	78	147	0	225
Hawaii	57	205	0	262
South Pacific	54	89	0	143
Australia	243	383	0	626
India/China	26	166	0	192
Total	458	990	0	1,448
Against Germany				
Middle East	125	69	0	194
UK	106	328	104	538
Atlantic	22	68	0	90
Caribbean	96	223	0	319
Total	349	688	104	1,141

Source: Hopkins MSS, 125, "Location of Combat Airplanes of the Army Air Force," August 21, 1942.
Note: These figures combine both those deployed and those en route to the different areas.

Table 26 *USA: USAAF aircraft outside continental USA (ready for combat),*
March 6, 1943

	Heavy bombers	Medium bombers	Light bombers	Fighters	Transport	Total
Germany	541	389	208	1,970	246	3,354
Japan	329	227	13	1,139	150	1,858

Source: FDR MSS, PSF 83, Memorandum from Stratemeyer to FDR, March 11,
1943.
Note: This is an important report, made for the President after a specific request.
The heavy bombers were broken down between B-17s and B-24s, the medium
bombers between B-25s and B-26s, the light bombers between A-20s, A-24s and
A-36s, the fighters between P-38s, P-39s, P-40s, P-47s, P-51s and Spitfires (manned
by US crews), and the transport aircraft were C-47, C-53 and C-60.

power. During the first six months of the year, large numbers of
aircraft were sent to the UK to begin the strategic bombing of Germany
and to North Africa to support operations there and in the Mediterranean. By April 1943, a dramatic shift in deployment had occurred and
the USAAF had almost twice the combat strength directed towards the
Germans as it did towards the Japanese. (See Table 26.)

By the middle of the year the USAAF had more than twice as
many aircraft fighting Germany as it did against Japan. Moreover, the
USAAF deployment of heavy bombers had also swung even more
decisively towards the war against Germany. In July 1943 the USAAF
had 1,341 B-17s or B-24s deployed in theater against Germany (UK,
Middle East, North Africa) and only 234 deployed against Japan in the
southwest Pacific or India/China.[28]

Looking forward, the USAAF was planning on further increasing the relative share of its combat forces fighting the Germans. The
plan was that by the summer of 1944, the ratio in favor of the war
against Germany was to be more than three to one. On July 1,
1943 Thomas Handy, Marshall's Chief of Staff for Operations,
informed the War Production Board about the present state of air
deployment and the expected position by the summer of 1944. (See
Table 27.)

There is one, quite interesting, exception that needs to be
mentioned when it comes to USAAF effort at this time, and this was
the extremely expensive B-29 bomber. The original contracts for development of the B-29 had been drawn up in 1940, when Germany was
considered by far the greatest threat to the United States.[29] One of the

Table 27 *USA: USAAF air groups deployed and expected to be deployed, July 1943 to July 1944*

Area	July 1, 1943 (actual)	January 1, 1944 (estimated)	July 1, 1944 (estimated)
Europe/Africa	69.5	120.5	159.0
Pacific/Asia	32.5	39.5	47.5

Source: WD Special Staff, RG 165, Handy to War Department Procurement Review Board, July 12, 1943.

primary reasons behind production of the bomber was to give the USAAF the ability to bomb Germany from bases in Iceland. However, when the United States did enter the war, the USAAF, and Arnold in particular, began to see the B-29 as a weapon that would be directed towards the Pacific theater. Arnold's great hope, which he spelled out in a late 1942 war plan, was that these long-range planes could be based in China, from where they could supposedly singlehandedly drive Japan to defeat.[30] However, this is not a sign of his weakening in terms of a fundamental Germany-First plan. It was more that he was not expecting enough B-29s to be available in time to play a decisive role in the war against Germany. By the end of 1943, he was assuming he would only be able to deploy 144 B-29s against Japan.[31] At the same time, he envisaged more than 3,000 heavy and medium bombers to be deployed in the strategic bombing of Germany.

So, one might say that the United States army and USAAF followed Franklin Roosevelt's strategic direction pretty closely. Between 1943 and 1944, they did deploy somewhere between 65 and 80 percent of their effort, as defined by equipment and personnel allocation, to the war against Germany. But, of course, there was the USN, the ship and aircraft allocation for which was still in the hands of Ernest King. King had no intention of devoting anything like 70–80 percent of his available resources to the war against Germany; if anything he wanted to devote more than 80 percent of his resources to the war against Japan, and that is why he pulled off the greatest strategic bluff of World War II – what could be termed the Casablanca percentage. King's performance at Casablanca was much commented on by the British. He was accused of being surly and aggressive. To some historians his behavior was puzzling.[32] Certainly he seems to have spent little time coordinating positions with Marshall so that the American delegation has been criticized for being disunited. For King this was not a failure, as he was not united with Marshall in wanting to focus on Europe.

What King wanted to do was make sure that in 1943 and 1944 he could determine how much of the American naval effort should be devoted to the Pacific. At the same time, he knew the percentage that Roosevelt believed was suitable. Therefore, at Casablanca he told a whopper – and got away with it. The afternoon meeting between the Combined Chiefs of Staff on January 14, 1943, the first day of formal meetings at Casablanca, began with an opening for which King had clearly prepared. At first, Marshall laid out Roosevelt's thinking, without telling Pound, Portal and Alanbrooke that it came from the President.

> GENERAL MARSHALL outlined the broad problem facing the Combined Chiefs of Staff as the allocation of resources between the two major theaters of war – the Atlantic (which included for this purpose the Mediterranean) and the Pacific. He suggested as a concept on which to work that this broad allocation should consist of 70 per cent in the Atlantic theater and 30 percent in the Pacific theater.[33]

King then stepped in with his whopper.

> ADMIRAL KING said that according to his estimates we were at present engaging only 15 percent of our total resources against the Japanese . . .[34]

Of course, at the time, the United States was, if anything, spending slightly more than 50 percent of its resources against Japan, and when it came to the United States Navy in particular, this figure was well over two-thirds. Even adding in the British, this percentage would have been far too low. King had to know this, though interestingly this percentage was never challenged either by the British or by Marshall or Arnold. In fact, Alanbrooke and the British, who were worried by the thrust of American thinking, moved the talk away from hard percentages to general concepts.[35] As the conference went on, the British chiefs seemed reluctant to challenge King on the Pacific question at all, and focused on attacking Marshall's plan for an invasion of France in 1943.

There is one record surviving of King mentioning the creation of the percentage, in 1951 when he was relatively close to death. In a letter he stated that the 15 percent calculation was "my own estimate and was not challenged by any member of the Conference."[36] The key thing for King was that by combining his estimate with Marshall's stated desire to use 30 percent of Anglo-American strength against the Japanese, he could reasonably claim that he had sanction for the United States Navy to focus almost entirely on the Pacific. This conceptual change seemed to be understood by Arnold, who was also in the room that day. He never mentioned the percentages idea specifically, but he did describe the agreement on future strategy that came out of the day's discussion as: "Assuming that Germany is the principal enemy, what dispositions and troops are necessary for Pacific to maintain pressure against Japan."[37] Earlier specific doctrines had talked about holding a defensive position in the Pacific.

In that way, King became the great victor of Casablanca and felt free to continue with the deployment of American naval power which he overwhelmingly directed towards the Pacific. Now, simply talking about it at Casablanca could not have secured such independence for King to deploy so much force against Japan. That was just the first step. There were two other things that were working strongly in his favor. The first was the stout British opposition – a strategic outlook shared by both Churchill and Alanbrooke – to an invasion of France and their support for a Mediterranean-based strategy in 1943. Such an invasion, which was originally given the codename "Round-Up," could only happen if the build-up of US army equipment in the UK, codenamed "Bolero," was given absolute first priority (as the army wanted). However, the British were quite happy for US army forces to be diverted to North Africa and the Mediterranean, thus undermining one of the major pillars of Germany-First. The second matter in King's favor was the crucial influence of William Leahy.

By the time of Casablanca, Leahy had been Chief of Staff to Roosevelt for half a year and was beginning to flex his muscles. He was convinced that the allocation of Anglo-American air and sea weaponry would determine the course of grand strategy during the war.[38] Whilst never as innately suspicious of British motives as King (who was dogmatic on the subject), Leahy had come to believe that the United States and Britain were fighting the war with two distinct agendas.[39] In particular, he became convinced that the Churchill government was not fighting to defeat the Germans and Japanese as quickly as possible – but instead that they were primarily concerned with protecting British strength, maintaining the empire, and safeguarding Britain's global position after the war.[40] From early in his role as Chief of Staff, this was revealed (ever so subtly) in his expressed doubts that the British would provide real support to the war against Japan.

One of the areas where Leahy was very much in sync with his friend and commander in chief, Franklin Roosevelt, was in the amount of time he spent focusing on China.[41] The future of China was a massive concern in American minds, and for much of the war the President and his chiefs spent more time discussing the Chinese question than developments in Europe.[42] For both Roosevelt and Leahy, the future of China was one of the two most important strategic questions to be determined by the war, the other one being the fate of Germany. Both men constantly, and entirely unsuccessfully, pressed the British to make a major effort in Burma to reopen a land road to move supplies into China. Without that, the Allies had to rely on a hugely expensive air-cargo system. It is unlikely that Churchill, or the British Chiefs of Staff, had a real notion of just how suspicious their reluctance to expend any force in the India/Burma theater, and thus protect China for the future, appeared to the Americans. Leahy's first diary discussion on the topic of the relative balance in the American war effort, made after he had become Roosevelt's Chief of Staff, was on September 9, 1942: "I have an idea that Great Britain will not give any useful assistance to a Burma expedition at the present time and it is my opinion that from the long distance American view point of essentials in our own war effort, the opening of the Burma Road and the support of China should have very high priority."[43] Over the next month he would twice more remark in his diary that he believed that the United States should concentrate more on the war against Japan.[44] When it came to the Casablanca Conference, however, Leahy seemed to believe that the British had acquiesced into taking part in aggressive action in Burma as a way of winning American acceptance for shelving an invasion of France in 1943. Because Leahy fell ill and could not actually attend the conference (undoubtedly one of the reasons that the American delegation seemed so disorganized to the British), this impression was gained by his conversations with Roosevelt, Marshall and King. "It appears that our British Allies were forced to accept the necessity for some aggressive action against Japan in the Southwest Pacific and in Burma. In Europe the American plan to invade France via the Channel in 1943 failed of acceptance by Great Britain and a decision to take combined aggressive action against the Mediterranean Islands was substituted therefore."[45] Certainly Leahy and the Americans did not define Germany-First to mean "Pacific-nothing" on the part of the British.

This set off what seemed to be a decisive chain of events which led to Leahy's wholehearted support for King's massive use of USN force in the Pacific in 1943 and 1944. Right after Casablanca, Leahy took charge of coordinating American grand strategy. He either attended or chaired many of the crucial meetings where American priorities were laid out and, starting in April, when it was agreed that another major conference would take place in May (Trident), he oversaw the drafting of the American position papers. Crucially he was also involved in war production policy and the making of American foreign policy – while always spending much more time with Franklin Roosevelt than anyone else, except possibly Harry Hopkins. Leahy's position at the nexus of American policy even caused Marshall once to complain to him of being kept uninformed about crucial foreign policy information.[46]

This was also the time when Leahy's earlier assumptions about British action in Burma turned out to be correct. By April it was becoming clear that at least for 1943, the Americans could expect little in the way of British support in the war against Japan, and that if aid to China was going to get through, the United States would have to carry it alone. Leahy wrote in his diary on April 6: "accompanied by General Marshall, Admiral King, General Arnold and Mr. Hopkins, conferred with the President in regard to possibilities of a campaign in Burma to open a road to China. It appears that Great Britain does not wish to undertake a campaign against Japanese troops in that area ..."[47] By early May these suspicions had taken deep root for Leahy.

> At noon the President held a conference in his study with the Joint Chiefs of Staff and Mr. Hopkins. This conference was called to discuss impending visit to Washington of the Prime Minister of Great Britain and his military advisors....
>
> General Marshall informed us that unless some active steps are taken in Northern Burma without delay our air ferry service of material to the Chinese Army will be destroyed by Japanese attacks on landing fields. It appears that the present situation of Chiang Kai Shek is critical with a possibility of the collapse of his whole movement, which if it should happen would be seriously detrimental to our prospects of success in the war against Japan.

> It has become increasingly apparent of late that Great Britain
> does not wish to take the aggressive [? word missing] against
> Burma and that China has no confidence in British intentions or
> British ability.
> There have recently been many indications of a Japanese attack
> on India which probably accounts for the reluctance of the British
> to engage in a Burma campaign.[48]

This one entry encapsulated all of Leahy's fears about the difference between American and British policy both during and potentially after the war. To Leahy the British were governed mainly by imperial concerns, particularly India, and would only fight where they believed their interests would benefit. If this meant that the United States would have to go it alone in the Pacific, both to defeat Japan and to save China, so be it. Leahy did not feel somehow betrayed, but he certainly made sure that enough American force was sent to the Pacific to ensure that the United States' interest in the region was protected. And, as he was one of the firmest believers in the United States about the supremacy of air and sea power, it was aircraft and ships that he pressed for most of all.[49]

Leahy's view, and that of other Americans, was that Trident would be a test of British commitment to playing a significant role in the Pacific war, in particular in providing support to China. In the final summation of American policy, agreed to on May 8, the second highest priority for the Americans was, after getting the British to agree to a cross-Channel invasion in 1944, to obtain a British commitment for a major operation in Burma (codenamed "Anakim"). If the British didn't, the United States should feel free to send whatever it wanted to the Pacific theater. "If Anakim proves impossible, due to lack of British support or other reasons, and no adequate alternative can be agreed upon, the United States will expand and intensify its operations in the Pacific, in order to counteract the advantage which Japan gains by Allied failure adequately to support China."[50]

At Trident itself, the British walked into this trap, only partly aware of the gravity of their actions. In his memoirs of World War II, Churchill speaks openly about the British heading to Trident determined to thwart American plans for aggressive action in Burma.[51] During the meetings Churchill listed supporting China as Britain's sixth highest priority, and even then was probably being disingenuous.[52] At other meetings, while different Americans from Roosevelt downwards spoke of the need for aggressive action in Burma, the British response was to delay and prevaricate. Alanbrooke seems to have become particularly depressed at this time. In his diary he mentions a special meeting of just the British service chiefs held during Trident, dedicated to finding a way to thwart American pressure to become involved in Burma, pressure that he saw as coming from Leahy.

> 9.00 to 11.30 COS [Chiefs of Staff] meeting during which we had to decide the attitude we would take to resist American pressure to do impossible operations in Burma in order to satisfy Chinese and public opinion. 11.30 to 1.30 Combined COS at which we reached a complete impasse with a suggestion by Leahy that we should send in separate reports. They were still pressing for a full scale advance from Assam into Burma...[53]

In the end the British opposition to doing anything else significant in the Pacific region in 1943 provided the final impetus that King needed, under Leahy's protection, to allow him to make sure that the United States Navy placed its overwhelming strength almost entirely against the Japanese. In summarizing the state of the war at the end of 1943, Leahy not only wrote off the impact of any British efforts in Burma in 1944, he saw the American navy as the key component that would bring Japan to its knees in 1945, regardless.[54] By this time, the navy had devoted at least 90 percent of its combat forces to the war against Japan, placing almost all of its great warships, with their expensive air support components, in the Pacific in 1943 and 1944. Furthermore, the US Marine Corps was entirely devoted to the war against Japan.

After the war, both King and Samuel Morison bristled at the notion that the war in Europe was an afterthought to the USN, though it is hard to see why. In June 1944, for instance, the USN was involved in two massive amphibious assaults at exactly the same time, the D-Day assaults on Normandy and the amphibious landings on the Marianas: Saipan, Tinian and Guam. Because of the timing, there was no way for vessels to be transferred from one theater to the other. For D-Day, the United States Navy was content to allow the British to provide most of the large naval vessels so the American force involved was modest. During the assault phase of Operation Neptune, the codename for the beach landings themselves, the USN vessels on hand or in reserve to support the operation comprised three older battleships, three cruisers, thirty-four destroyers, six frigates and twenty-five minesweepers.[55]

On the other hand, the naval forces for the Marianas invasion were enormous. King himself boasted of having more than six hundred ships assigned to operations (not including landing craft).[56] He had allocated Admiral Nimitz enough warships for two major fleets. There was the carrier strike force, under Raymond Spruance, which was based around fifteen aircraft carriers (seven large fleet carriers and eight light carriers), seven battleships, eight heavy cruisers, thirteen light cruisers and sixty-nine destroyers.[57] Then there was the landing force, intended to carry the 127,571 troops for the different assaults and provide them with fire support, which alone contained 535 vessels of all types.[58] On June 14, the second day of preparatory bombardment, when many ships had been sent off with the carrier force to prepare for the Japanese main fleet's arrival, there were still eight battleships, six heavy cruisers, five light cruisers and twenty-six destroyers assigned to attack Saipan and Tinian.[59] The supply tail for this force was correspondingly enormous. All fuel and other perishable supplies needed for the operations sailed with the fleet – only ammunition was left behind as it was thought too dangerous to transfer it while at sea.[60] It is actually difficult to find one table with all the different major American warships that took part in these various operations. Roskill, in the British official history, has calculated that in total these forces contained "fourteen battleships, fifteen large and medium aircraft carriers, ten escort carriers, twenty four cruisers, about 140 destroyers and escort vessels..."[61]

In the end, trying to sensibly compare the American naval forces involved in the Normandy and Marianas operations is almost impossible because there was one enormous difference that in production terms changes any equation: the enormous size of the American naval air force in the Pacific. For instance, the carriers that took part in the Marianas operations alone held a total of 956 aircraft of different types.[62] At the same time, the USN had even more aircraft deployed on land bases throughout the Pacific. The growth of the American navy's air arm is one of the most impressive production and allocation stories of World War II. In the end, 69,118 aircraft were built for the navy between 1941 and 1945.[63] This made up about one-quarter of overall American aircraft production of 299,293.[64] The growth of this force meant that it alone became one of the largest air forces in the world in 1943. In November of that year, President Roosevelt asked for a tabulation of all American and British forces deployed overseas and in combat areas. He was told by the Joint Chiefs that on November 22, the US Army Air Force had 8,245 combat aircraft deployed, with the US Navy having approximately 30 percent as many (both shipboard and based on land) at 3,266.[65] Interestingly, the relative percentage difference between the navy and air force was actually supposed to narrow significantly during the coming year, so that by July 1944 it was expected that the USN would deploy just over 45 percent of the number of combat aircraft deployed by the USAAF – a total of 5,633 for the former and 12,483 for the latter. When it came to aircraft in stock (not those deployed to forward battle areas), in September 1943 the United States Navy was not that much weaker than the RAF or USAAF. At that time, when it came to completed aircraft actually in the possession of the different services, the USN had 8,901, the USAAF had 11,471 and the RAF had 13,035.[66]

By the summer of 1944, therefore, the USN deployed an air force that was the third most powerful in the world, after the US Army Air Force and the Royal Air Force. Its closest comparator would actually have been the Luftwaffe, which at this time was, in terms of numbers and equipment, quite similar to the USN. In the summer of 1944, when the USN was reaching a total deployed force of around 5,000 aircraft, the Luftwaffe had a similar number. Moreover, while the USN had relatively few of the four-engine aircraft that had pride of place for the USAAF and the RAF, the Luftwaffe itself had hardly any. Like the USN, the Luftwaffe was using single-engine aircraft (primarily adapted FW-190s) to do much of its attacking – when it could afford to.

Almost all American naval aircraft were deployed in the Pacific. In June 1943, just after the battle of the convoys in the Atlantic had reached its peak, the United States Naval Air Arm had 21 very-long range, 191 long-range and 6 medium-range aircraft deployed throughout the entire Atlantic theater.[67] These 218 aircraft comprised significantly less than 10 percent of the aircraft under the navy's command. For the rest of the war, this figure seems to have increased little, while the number of aircraft deployed to the war against Japan skyrocketed, as more and more aircraft carriers were added to the American Pacific Fleet. As with ground forces, it is impossible to choose one percentage and say that, in 1943 and 1944, the USN devoted this much of its effort to the war against Germany. However, it would be safe to say that, considering aircraft and naval vessels together, at a minimum

90 percent of the USN's fighting power was in the Pacific – and it could easily have been 95 percent or more.

Because of this extraordinary imbalance, it is impossible to say that the United States ever fought a clear policy of Germany-First. The US army and air force definitely did in 1943 and 1944, when they deployed somewhere between 70 percent and 80 percent of their force against Germany. However, with the navy doing the exact opposite, albeit more so, and having access to about 40 percent of American overall war construction, the United States as a whole fought relatively similar equipment wars against both Germany and Japan.

Grand strategy and the engagement of German production

On January 17, 1943, as the Casablanca Conference was ongoing, Winston Churchill sent a telegram to the Cabinet in London describing the developments so far. After complaining about Ernest King's obsession with the Pacific war, he pointed to a great difference within the American delegation as to the direction of the war against Germany. Churchill was keen to push the Americans to accept a Mediterranean-based strategy in 1943. He knew that George Marshall was his greatest roadblock in this matter, and he told the Cabinet that the head of the American army remained keen on an invasion of France at the expense of Mediterranean operations. On the other hand, Churchill judged, Roosevelt now seemed "strongly in favor of the Mediterranean being given prime place. He also seems increasingly inclined to Operation HUSKY [invasion of Sicily] which he suggested to me last night should be called BELLY and I advised BELLONA."[68]

The difference between Marshall and Roosevelt over just how focused the British and Americans should be on invading Europe is one that Churchill had skillfully played on in 1942. He had been able to win Roosevelt around to the notion of a North African invasion in place of a build-up of force in the United Kingdom.[69] By the summer of 1942, Roosevelt, who was keen to send American troops into combat against the Germans as soon as possible, had swung strongly behind an invasion of North Africa.[70] Although Marshall remained dubious as to this operation's ultimate usefulness, he dutifully went along, but at Casablanca, he was not keen to see the Mediterranean theater once again become the focus in 1943 and fought hard to turn attention back to an invasion of France. Churchill, however, once again fought his corner fiercely and successfully.

After Casablanca, however, when all eyes turned to operations in 1944, Churchill would see his hopes for greater commitment to the Mediterranean whittled down, not only at Trident but at subsequent meetings in August in Quebec (Quadrant) and at the end of the year in Cairo (Sextant) and Teheran (Eureka).

At Trident, Churchill first ran into an American delegation that had been well prepared and unified by Leahy. The US chiefs were determined to press ahead with Overlord in 1944. Their main worry was not that Britain would actually be willing to veto the operation, but that Churchill might somehow persuade Roosevelt to agree to some operation in Italy that would draw off more American resources and lead to the cancelling or delay of the invasion of France. Marshall seems to have become particularly worried about Churchill's abilities to bamboozle the President. Whilst preparing for Quadrant, he even drew up a memorandum to make sure that Roosevelt was not tricked by the British Prime Minister into making any kind of statement that would commit the United States to a major effort in Italy.[71]

During Trident, the American delegation was determined to obtain a commitment to an invasion of France in the spring of 1944. In the end they certainly believed they had triumphed.[72] The text that was sent to Roosevelt and Churchill at the conference's conclusion explicitly endorsed this concept with a plan to have twenty-nine divisions invade France (Overlord) in May 1944.[73] The British commitment to Overlord, however, was still not deep. With preparations underway for the Quebec Conference in August 1943 (Quadrant), the British chiefs once again began pressing for a much greater effort in Italy. It was here that the other great believer in the Mediterranean strategy, Alanbrooke, started to integrate more sophisticated notions of production into the analysis. Alanbrooke's argument was that events on the Italian battlefields were intrinsically linked to the success of Overlord, that success in the Mediterranean was the necessary precondition for the success of Overlord.

Quadrant itself followed a predictable path. The British, led by Alanbrooke, pressed for a major effort to capture much of northern Italy to help guarantee success for Overlord. The Americans countered by saying that nothing could be agreed to that would hinder the build-up for Overlord. The final document was a clear acceptance of the

21 A photograph of the grand strategists at the first Quebec Conference (Quadrant), August 1943. In the front row, Churchill and Roosevelt sit with the Canadian Prime Minister, Mackenzie King. Behind them the service chiefs are interacting in a typical way. While Pound and Leahy, Marshall and Sir John Dill, and Portal and Arnold seem relaxed, King and Alanbrooke do their best to ignore each other.

supremacy of Overlord over the Mediterranean, which seemed, for a while at least, to have settled the major Anglo-American difference. Pound, who died not long after Quadrant, and who of all the British chiefs seemed the least interested in the Mediterranean, wrote immediately after Quadrant that the conference had been a real success because the Americans were now convinced that the British were committed to the invasion of France.[74] (See Figure 21.)

Unfortunately, Pound's expectations about the future were soon undermined. Almost immediately after leaving Quebec, Churchill started to once again push for operations that would, at the least, delay Overlord significantly. He approached the President about this first in September.[75] When neither Roosevelt nor anyone else in the United States structure was willing to budge, however, it seemed to destabilize Churchill greatly. He started complaining to colleagues about the American outlook and, somewhat bizarrely, even expressed his doubts to Stalin. In October, he wrote to Eden, who was in Moscow for talks with Stalin, and complained bitterly about the future prospects for Overlord, saying that the Americans and the Soviets (the latter of whom were more convinced of the need for an invasion of France than even Marshall) were pushing the British into an operation that would definitely be bloody and very possibly a colossal failure:[76] "now we are getting into a position most dangerous and painful, where we are gripped by our two Allies and forced into vicious and perilous dispositions." In November 1943, when Churchill and Stalin met face to face, Churchill actually tried to interest the Soviet dictator in his Italian plans and hinted that Overlord might be delayed. He was more than happy to criticize the American position to try and ingratiate himself with Stalin: "The Prime Minister said that he was half American and he had great affection for the American people. What he was going to say was not to be understood as anything disparaging of the Americans and he would be perfectly loyal towards them, but there were things which it was better to say between two persons." He then told Stalin that a great opportunity had been wasted in Italy by American plans for Overlord and their desire that the British take some action in Burma. This meant that the Italian campaign had been denied new troops and, crucially, landing craft were being diverted to the UK and the Pacific, landing craft that could have been used in the Mediterranean. He said straight out that the Americans were ignoring the Mediterranean because they did not want to have a British supreme commander in the region. Churchill was playing a dangerous game – and one that had little chance of success. Stalin would have none of it. He told Churchill that from the Soviet perspective, Overlord must have priority, and anything that delayed it would be a major blow to Soviet expectations and confidence in the alliance.

This kind of exchange with Stalin was a sign that Churchill was reaching a crisis. He had profound doubts about Overlord and remained absolutely convinced that a major exertion of force in the Mediterranean was very much in British interests. However, both the Americans and Soviets were telling him, with unrelenting force, that Overlord must go ahead in May 1944. Things reached a head during the great series of meetings that ended the discussion, the conferences in Cairo (Sextant) and Teheran (Eureka). At Cairo and Teheran, Churchill, while professing great commitment to Overlord, made another effort to delay the operation from May until July or even later.[77] In a rather impolitic fashion considering both American and Soviet suspicions of his intentions in the Mediterranean, he argued rather oddly for a delay of the invasion of France until at least Rhodes could be taken by amphibious assault. He still seemed convinced that the battlefield casualties that the British and Americans were going to suffer in France would be prohibitive. However, he was alone in this belief, as Leahy recorded laconically in his diary for November 28, 1943.

> In the late afternoon the President, the Prime Minister, and Marshal Stalin, with their Military Staffs held a plenary meeting where it developed that the one important question before us here is settlement of a date for the promised Anglo-American invasion of France. Mr. Churchill wants a sufficient delay to permit the occupation of Rhodes and other islands in the Aegean Sea. Stalin wants to fix upon the earliest possible date that is practicable and the President is in agreement with Marshal Stalin.[78]

In the end, Churchill's position helped push Roosevelt and Stalin closer together.[79] He was able to use the need to fully prepare for Overlord and its sister assault in southern France (Anvil) as a way of reducing the commitment of equipment to any Burma operation in 1944, but this was a hollow victory. His fears about the losses the British would suffer in any invasion of France remained, and after Cairo he seems to have had a nervous collapse.[80] He was kept under enforced bed rest at Tunis, where he had stopped off on his way back from Cairo, and suffered from a number of different complaints, some of which, such as heart palpitations, headaches and an inability to relax, were almost certainly stress-related.

The British attempt to focus on the Mediterranean is not particularly surprising to anyone who has read about the grand strategy debates in World War II. The British triumph in diverting American efforts away from France and towards Italy and the Mediterranean in 1943 is widely acknowledged. The impact on air and sea equipment of the campaign that was fought will be discussed in Chapter 7. However, it would be interesting to examine the different British perceptions from the point of view of German equipment production and destruction. The Mediterranean did open up the possibility for significant destruction of German production in the pre-battlefield stage; it is just not clear that Churchill and Alanbrooke were concerned with this advantage.

Churchill spent a great deal of time trying to interest the Americans in making a major effort in the eastern Mediterranean, in particular to bring Turkey into the war on the Allies' side. Again, instead of seeing this as a way of attacking Germany, it was presented as a more traditional means of fighting a land war and with an eye on the post-war settlement. He began seriously to try to persuade the Americans of the merits of such a move in November 1942 during a late night, well-lubricated discussion.

> His mind now turns to Turkey which he believes can be brought into the war at almost any moment providing tanks and modern materiel can be made available for her forty five divisions. This he will undoubtedly urge since he visualizes Turkey as a convenient bridge between a usable Mediterranean and Russia. He believes also that Turkey, when properly armed will erupt to the Balkan Area creating a situation of the greatest difficulty for Germany...he seems to be growing colder to the idea of Round-Up except as a final stroke against a tottering opponent. As you know, the Pacific to him seems very far away...[81]

The most interesting issue, from the point of view of this study, is just how Churchill believed a large Mediterranean campaign could destroy German production. In 1943, he had a battlefield-centric vision of the Mediterranean as a way to defeat Germany. Indeed, at this time his belief in the effectiveness of strategic bombing seemed weak. On May 20, 1943, during Trident, Churchill hosted a British Empire delegation meeting in the White House with high-ranking representatives from Canada, Australia, India, New Zealand and South Africa – and without American participation. He started with an overview of the state of the war at present. His analysis of the strategic bombing of Germany, which was meant to be positive, showed that he had real doubts as to its achieving one of its main goals, the degradation of German morale.[82] "He did not pretend to pronounce upon the effect of air attack on the enemy's morale. Some thought it would harden them as it had hardened us. Others took to the contrary view. All he would say was that we intended to go right through with it and let the experiment provide proof of its effect." At the same time, Churchill expressed deep concern about the possibilities of a landing in France anytime in the near future. "The French shore bristling with cannon, secured by currents, and having the protection of a 30-foot tide and unduly flat beaches, must be regarded as a deadly coast. If the Germans could oppose an attack with an active mobile force, we might meet with disaster. He for one did not want a dozen simultaneous disasters." The answer, for Churchill, was to press forward with a campaign into Italy. As expressed, however, he saw no advantages for this from the use of air power to attack German power or production, and instead, as usual, visualized it as a land campaign, the great advantage of which would be the destruction of German divisions on the battlefield.

> How, then, could we help Russia? There could be no better way than to knock out Italy. If we could do this we could gain many advantageous positions from which to press forward the fight. We should gain access to the Balkans, where 34 enemy divisions including 26 Italian, were contained by the activities of the Yugoslav guerrillas...Italy, by her defection, caused the withdrawal of her Divisions from the Balkans, a gap would be caused which the Germans could only fill by withdrawals from the Russian Front...

It was a World War I analysis of World War II. There was no discussion of relative allocation of German aircraft, or of planning different campaigns around damage not just to armies, but to German production and supply. There were real economic targets, in particular Romanian oil production and southern German industrial production, which could have been opened up for attack by different Mediterranean campaigns aimed at, for example, northern Italy or Turkey. However, that did not seem to be what was driving Churchill on at this point. His conception of victory and defeat had become more focused on the battlefield at this time – and he wanted to carefully determine on which battlefields British troops would fight.

Alanbrooke mentioned the strategic advantages to be gained by a greater effort in the Mediterranean a number of times, particularly in the preparations for and proceedings of Quadrant. He wrote once in his diary how important it was that airbases in northern Italy were captured, to allow for the strategic bombing of aircraft manufacture in southern Germany.[83] It was an identical position to the central British Chiefs of Staff document put together at the time which argued for a large assault to take most of northern Italy. The plan they called for was an offensive to take major bases starting with the Pisa–Ravenna line, but then moving up to the Lombardian plain around Milan.[84]

The argument given was mostly built around weakening the Luftwaffe to allow for the Overlord assaults. It was claimed that 65 percent of German fighter aircraft production occurred in bases that would be much easier to attack from northern Italy and, moreover, that German air defenses in this region were unprepared and undeveloped. At Quadrant, Alanbrooke made exactly the same point, specifically mentioning the need to reduce German fighter numbers,[85] but to the Americans, what he seemed to be arguing for was a significant delay to Overlord. However, after Quadrant, Alanbrooke avoided mention of the air power benefits of an Italian campaign, and at the same time, usually reserved special criticism in his diary for those, like Harris, who he believed were too reliant on air power in their conception of victory. As he wrote on October 13, 1943:

> Bert Harris of Bomber Command came to see us this morning . . . According to him, the only reason why the Russian Army has succeeded in advancing is due to the results of the bomber offensive!! According to him I am certain that we are all preventing him from winning the war. If Bomber Command was left to itself it would make much shorter work of it all![86]

The truth of the matter is that this Quadrant performance seemed to be very much aimed at persuading the Americans. It is interesting to note that both Churchill and Alanbrooke, when not talking to the Americans and trying to bolster their case, tended to downplay the effectiveness of strategic bombing in general, and from the Mediterranean in particular. The one time Churchill and the British Chiefs of Staff fought strenuously against an increase of force in the Mediterranean began in August 1943 when Arnold suggested a build-up in Italy of strategic bombing forces.[87] Most telling was a minute that Churchill wrote in November 1943 when he actually complained that too many aircraft were being deployed to Italy, and soaking up too high a percentage (one-third to be exact) of the supplies available in the theater.[88] It would be far better, he argued, to transfer more ground troops in to fight a land war. When the British COS analyzed the question, they too stated that too many aircraft were in the region and blamed Eisenhower for asking for too many planes.[89]

Portal provided an interesting contrast to Churchill and Alanbrooke. His 1943 focus was squarely on the strategic bombing campaign from the UK, and the Mediterranean never seemed to him the potentially decisive theater that it was for the other two. In the preparations for Trident, Portal was openly skeptical of a major push in Italy and argued that if a great effort were to be made in the Mediterranean theater, then the focus should be on bringing Turkey into the war. That would provide an outlet for strategic air power to be used against German energy supplies.

> Sir Charles Portal thought that the case for developing the main
> effort against Italy was somewhat weak. Two alternative
> operations had been put forward. Our ability to carry out the first,
> the attack on the Heel of Italy, was dependent on certain
> conditions which might or might not materialize. It was doubtful
> whether the second operation, the capture of Sardinia, would in
> effect make any real contribution towards the collapse of
> Italy ... Meanwhile, he felt that there was much more to be said
> for the capture of the Dodecanese and straining every effort to
> bring Turkey into the war in the autumn. Such policy would
> inevitably provoke a German reaction and so draw off forces from
> the Russian front, while it would, at the same time, open up
> strategic possibilities in South-East Europe.[90]

During Trident, Portal made that case openly to the Americans, pushing to get Turkey into the war so that the Romanian oil facilities at Ploesti could be bombed.[91] During Quadrant, he also dutifully supported Alanbrooke with his argument in favor of securing bases in northern Italy.[92]

And yet, beyond these mentions, it is hard to find Portal really integrating himself well into the Churchill–Alanbrooke Mediterranean strategy. He spent most of 1943 coordinating the Combined Bomber Offensive (CBO),[93] and certainly spent little of his time outside these conferences pressing for a Mediterranean strategy. In fact, towards the end of the year he deliberately repudiated the value of bases in northern Italy in a note to the Prime Minister stating that he now believed he had "considerably overstated" their value.[94] Added together, these different perspectives point out one of the basic flaws of the British Mediterranean strategy: as conceived, it was aimed overwhelmingly at a battlefield notion of World War II. There were different strategic cases that could have been made about using the Mediterranean to put real pressure on German production, but these were mostly undeveloped and ineffective. Without them, the strategy was one of simply marking time.

Before moving on, there is one other grand strategy question that should be examined: the feasibility of an invasion of France in 1943 – the stated American position in 1942 and during Casablanca. This has received some debate over the years.[95] While this discussion cannot be replicated in depth here, one major point should be made. In terms of Anglo-American air and sea equipment, there would have been more than enough to invade France in 1943, if the Mediterranean operations had been scaled back and the Pacific relegated to holding operations. One of the arguments in favor of the Mediterranean strategy was that there simply was not enough equipment (to say nothing about ground troops) available for such an operation. Upon reflection, this argument is rather weak, and part of the problem is that it does not comprehend that arguing for a Mediterranean strategy and empowering Admiral King to base the American fleet overwhelmingly in the Pacific was what really killed off any chance of an invasion of France in 1943.

Actually, had the USN been forced to commit to a Germany-First policy, the United States and the UK could have supported a 1943 invasion of France with a larger naval force than that which was in use in 1944. During the D-Day landings, the invasion was supported by a combined Anglo-American fleet of six battleships, twenty-three cruisers, eighty fleet destroyers, twenty-five smaller destroyers and a large mix of coastal craft.[96] When the British and Americans invaded Sicily in July 1943, they were supported by 6 battleships, 15 cruisers and 119 destroyers of all types.[97] Adding only a relatively small portion of the American navy in the Pacific in the summer of 1943 would have allowed for a far larger naval support force than that on hand for D-Day. By way of comparison, the USN launched a major amphibious assault on the Gilbert Islands (most famously Tarawa) in November 1943. That force was composed of (at least) thirteen battleships, eighteen cruisers, forty-two destroyers, six large aircraft carriers, five light aircraft carriers and eight escort carriers.[98] Even in the case of landing craft, which is one of the least understood aspects of World War II grand strategy, there would have been enough to do a landing in France in 1943. When Neptune was launched, there was a total of 4,126 landing craft employed, approximately 1,100 of which were the crucial LSTs and LCTs which were needed to land AFV.[99] For the Sicily landings, the British and Americans used 1,734 landing craft.[100] Yet the United States, because of Casablanca, had changed its landing craft allocation plans completely in 1943. In late 1942 the plan was to give priority to the invasion of France, and everything else would be sacrificed to that end. Once Casablanca had killed off a landing in France before 1944, the United States started shifting landing craft to the Pacific.[101] From that point onwards, the plan was to send more American landing craft to the Pacific than to the European theater of operations (ETO) for the rest of 1943.[102] By April 1943, however, US plans had changed so that the allocation for the ETO was only 70 percent of that for the Pacific.[103] While the Sicily operation was ongoing, the United States was using even more landing craft in the Pacific in the conduct of two campaigns, namely the battle led by MacArthur which was aiming for Rabaul, and Nimitz's drive in the central Pacific which was just about to begin. For the landings in the Gilberts in November 1943, for instance, there was landing ship capacity enough to place two divisions, the 2nd Marine and the 27th US Army, ashore at one time.[104] Considering that German defenses were considerably weaker in France in 1943 than in 1944, the forces on hand would have been able to place five divisions ashore on the first day.

When it came to aircraft, had the British and Americans focused outright on an invasion of France in 1943 they would have had sufficient air cover. One of the problems with the push for the Mediterranean campaign was that while it did end up destroying a significant amount of German equipment in combat, it also caused the diversion of a massive number of Anglo-American aircraft.

The RAF had stationed a large number of aircraft in the Middle East and Mediterranean since 1941. In 1943 their deployments reached at least two thousand aircraft. In April 1943, the exclusively British or British Empire air forces in the region, the Middle East Air Command and the Malta Air Command, had 1,298 and 185 aircraft on hand respectively, 1,026 and 155 of which were available for operations.[105] At the same time, the Northwest Air Command, a mostly bombing force that was composed of both British aircraft from the older Eastern Air Command and American aircraft from the 12th Air Force, had 1,758 aircraft in total, 1,357 of which were operational.[106] In the summer of 1943 these numbers were increased as both British and American squadrons were removed from the UK, much to Harris' great anger, to support the Sicily operation. In the end, there were 3,462 aircraft deployed in support of Husky.[107] This number was maintained throughout the summer, even after high losses. When the time came for the assault on the Italian mainland at Salerno, the Mediterranean Air Command had 3,280 operational aircraft.[108]

In one area, however, the RAF almost always gave highest priority to UK deployment, and that was with their finest heavy bombers, in particular the Lancaster. The bombing forces sent to Africa or the Mediterranean in 1943 were overwhelmingly less successful models such as Beauforts, Blenheims and Wellingtons.[109] The same could not be said of the American air force, which deployed large numbers of its best aircraft to the region. In April 1943 the imbalance between American aircraft in the Mediterranean area and in the UK was extreme, when there were more than twice as many aircraft in most categories in the 12th Air Force (North Africa) than in the 8th Air Force (UK). On April 27, the 8th Air Force had only 371 aircraft of all types available for combat, 165 of which were the heavy and medium bomber class of B-17s, B-24s, B-25s and B-26s.[110] On the same date, the 12th Air Force had 1,053 aircraft ready for combat, 302 of which were heavy or medium bombers. By July 1943, the USAAF deployed 472 heavy bombers (B-17s and B-24s), 706 medium bombers (B-25s and B-26s) and 179 light bombers (A-20s) in North Africa or the Middle East.[111] Such a force would have increased the striking power of the USAAF that was already in the UK, which at the time was made up of 879 heavy bombers and 448 medium bombers. When it came to fighters, for much of 1943 there were considerably more than twice as many US aircraft assigned to the war in the Mediterranean than to the strategic bombing forces in the UK. In March 1943, for instance, there were 532 USAAF fighters either deployed in or on their way to the UK. At the same time there were 1,438 American fighters in North Africa or the Middle East. If the USAAF had been concentrated in the UK, therefore, its striking power would have been immensely improved. Moreover, the USN had its own force of thousands of aircraft that could have been added to the mix. In September 1943, it alone had 78 percent as many completed aircraft in its possession as the USAAF (8,901 to 11,471). Therefore it not only could have deployed almost 3,000 for actual operations, it could have sustained that number even in the face of heavy losses.

Also, attrition of aircraft in North Africa, because of the less developed infrastructure and the more difficult conditions, was considerably higher than in any other theater of war for the American air force. Between May 1 and December 31, 1942, the monthly attrition rate for all American aircraft in North Africa was a very high 15 percent, while that for those based in the UK was only 4 percent.[112] To put the North African figure in context, American aircraft serving in the southwest Pacific, another more difficult region for maintenance, suffered only a 9 percent monthly attrition rate. It meant that numerical losses were higher in North Africa than in any other theater of war while the fighting went on there. During all of December 1942, the USAAF lost 225 planes in operations in combat theaters.[113] Of these, by far the largest number were in North Africa (91), with the next being among those based in the UK and Iceland (61) and then the southwest Pacific (45).

So, had the RAF, USAAF and even USN naval air wing been concentrated for an invasion of France and not dispersed to North Africa and the Mediterranean in 1943, they could have mustered an overwhelmingly large force. One estimate put the combined operational size of such a force at 8,000 aircraft (which presumably didn't include any aircraft from the USN).[114] This seems reasonable as the three services in September 1943 had a combined total of 33,407 completed aircraft actually on hand, while just the RAF and USAAF had 24,056.[115] Also, there were at this time 19,355 aircraft actually in the process of being built for the three services, so they could have made up even extreme loss rates during any invasion. Overall, the force available for front-line operational duties in the summer of 1943 might have been slightly smaller than that which was used in June 1944 to support Overlord. The total aircraft operational to support the D-Day landings was 11,590.[116] However, the Luftwaffe itself would have been unable to contend with such a force, and moreover German aircraft production was still significantly below 1944 levels, so that it is impossible to imagine how they would have been able to contest Anglo-American air dominance over any invasion attempt. All in all, the British and Americans had the equipment needed to seriously attempt an invasion of France in the summer of 1943; they just decided to disperse their efforts in a number of different theaters. The two men most responsible for that were Ernest King and Winston Churchill.

7 WINNING THE SHIPPING WAR

SC 42 is one of the better-known convoys of World War II. Its story is told in many of the histories of the Battle of the Atlantic.[1] SC were the code letters that the Admiralty assigned to convoys that were sent from Nova Scotia to the United Kingdom and 42 was the sequential number given to the convoy as it left port.[2] SC 42 was therefore traveling on the most important trade route of the war during one of the most important times in the conflict, September 1941. It was a large convoy composed of sixty-four merchant ships with a combined total of 500,000 tons, many of which were old, slow bulk carriers carrying raw materials for Britain's factories, such as lumber, iron ore and phosphates.[3] However, for such a large convoy it had a relatively small, if seasoned, escort force of one destroyer and three corvettes, all Royal Canadian Navy (RCN) vessels. There were also two other destroyers training in the North Atlantic at the same time which could conceivably be called upon if the convoy ran into trouble.

And run into trouble it did. As SC 42 had a top speed of only 7 knots, it was ideally suited for U-boat attacks. The importance of convoy speed had become well understood by the summer of 1941. U-boats of the Type VII class could only travel at 8 knots while submerged, so a convoy of this speed or lower could be hunted by German submarines which could remain hidden until the last possible moment. On September 9, 1941, as SC 42 was running very close to the east coast of Greenland, it crossed paths with a large U-boat wolfpack, codenamed *Markgraf*, at first composed of eight boats. On that evening, when the U-boats could operate on the ocean surface free from air attack and able to reach high speeds, *Markgraf* started to rip into SC 42's flesh. Sometimes darting between the mostly helpless merchant ships, the U-boats sank seven vessels the first night.[4]

There was a brief respite during the following day, when the escorts severely damaged one of the U-boats. When the sun set, however, the attacks started once again. By this time, even more U-boats, which were being fed news about this plodding, vulnerable convoy, had joined the fight. During the course of the evening they sank another seven vessels, most spectacularly the fuel tanker *Bulysse*, which exploded in a ball of fire that cooked the night sky. The escorts, at least, had one success that night. U-boat 501 was so damaged by a depth charge attack that it was driven to the surface, astonishingly appearing just next to RCN corvettes *Chambly* and *Moose Jaw*.[5] The captain of the German boat was so close to the Canadians that he was able to leap across to their ship and surrender. The Canadians were able to get a boarding party on to U-501, but the Germans had damaged everything of intelligence value and the ship was rapidly sinking so they abandoned it to the depths.

If the U-boats had been able to continue their attacks for a third night, the convoy would have suffered even more misery, but on the 11th a huge infusion of additional escorts from the Royal Navy arrived, including five destroyers, two corvettes and two sloops. Now properly protected, SC 42 was able to travel almost unscathed the rest of the way to the UK, losing only one more merchant ship off the Scottish coast near the Outer Hebrides.

The story of SC 42 is typical of how the war at sea is often viewed by the public and in some histories. And yet, what is important about SC 42 is how atypical it was. It was one of the few times in World War II that a convoy suffered such heavy losses and it was one of the main reasons that September 1941 was an atypical month of the war at sea. It was the first month of the entire Battle of the Atlantic when significantly more merchant ships were sunk in convoy than among those without escort, and looking at the war as a whole, only one other month, March 1943, had a more pronounced gap. Moreover, SC 42 was also unusual in that it had a very small escort considering its slow speed and large number of ships. After the disaster, the number of escorts on such convoys was significantly raised.[6]

It helps summarize the story of the greatest British (and Canadian) victory of the air and sea war: the victory over German

22 Admiral Karl Doenitz inspects U-boat 94 in St Nazaire, France, 1941.
Head of the German submarine fleet, Doenitz was in charge of the most modern
campaign that Germany could wage against Anglo-American power. His failure
by May 1943 was the real beginning of the end of German power.

submarines which became almost total by June 1943. In many ways
this marked the end of any possibility for Germany to win the war. The
Battle of the Atlantic, as both Hitler and Doenitz realized, was one of
the most important offensive actions Germany could undertake. It was
the only "modern" campaign that it was waging at the time. Not only
did it force the Allies to devote an extremely large share of their
national wealth and power to fighting the campaign, it also allowed
the Germans their greatest opportunity to destroy Anglo-American
equipment before it reached the battlefield. The merchant ships sunk
often contained finished war munitions or, in the case of SC 42, raw
materials needed to keep British war production going. In the end,
victory for the Allies was made possible by the British pushing the
boundaries of modern warfare fully. It required technological superiority, for example with radar and sonar, superb operational analysis of the
science of convoy speed and size, great shipbuilding resources, excellent
training and, eventually, a significant air component. (See Figure 22)

It even required them to triumph over the obstinacy of
Ernest King.

The shipping crisis of 1942

In March 1942, such an all-encompassing success seemed far away.
Winston Churchill, for one, was a worried man. His elation in the
immediate aftermath of the Japanese attack on Pearl Harbor had
drained away after a series of military reverses. The fall of Tobruk,

the sinking of HMS *Price of Wales* and *Repulse* and the surrender of Malaya and Singapore were a series of body blows, each of which added to the Prime Minister's gloom. However, the thing that most frustrated him was the enormous loss of merchant ship tonnage, including many valuable tankers laden with precious fuel, in the waters off the American East Coast. To Churchill this was an appalling and unnecessary crisis, and he did what he often did at this time when he had a serious point to make to the American government: he approached Harry Hopkins.

> I am most deeply concerned at the immense sinkings of tankers west of the 40th meridian and in the Caribbean Sea. In January, 18 ships totalling 221,000 dead-weight tons, were sunk or damaged; in February the number rose to 34, totalling 364,941 dead-weight tons; in the first 11 days of March 7 vessels, totalling 88,449 dead-weight tons have been sunk. Yesterday alone 30,000 tons were reported as sunk or damaged. Thus, in little over two months, in these waters alone, about 60 tankers have been sunk or damaged, totalling some 675,000 dead-weight tons. In addition to this several tankers are overdue.[7]

In no way was Churchill being alarmist.[8] In the first months of 1942, the Germans sank more merchant ships than in any other six-month period during World War II. Between January and June of that year approximately 526 vessels, or 2,832,000 tons of American, British and neutral merchant shipping, were lost in the region that took in the American eastern seaboard and the Caribbean.[9] This was the single greatest shipping disaster for the Allies during the war. In what was known as the first "Happy Time" for the U-boats after the fall of France in 1940, merchant ship losses ran at a pace only half that experienced during the first six months of 1942.[10] The losses in this latter period were far larger even than those suffered by British and American merchant ships in all theaters of the war during the first six months of 1943, which is often considered the great crescendo of the U-boat war in the Atlantic.[11]

Throughout the war and after, Churchill maintained that control of the Atlantic was the "dominating" strategic consideration for the British and the Americans.[12] This fact had been recognized by both countries since they began serious staff conversations in 1941. The

ABCD agreement, which started not long after Roosevelt's re-election, acknowledged the primary importance of shipping in the Atlantic. This was also something that the United States recognized in the Rainbow war plans of 1941.[13] During the Arcadia Conference, the meetings in Washington, DC between Churchill, Roosevelt and their staffs in December 1941 and January 1942, the pre-eminence of the trade war in the Atlantic was re-emphasized. In the summary strategy memo to which the two leaders agreed at the end of the meeting, it was clearly stated that the defeat of Germany was the first priority of the Alliance, and in order to do achieve this, the first priority in terms of communication was the shipping lanes between the United States and the UK.[14]

They were right. Any discussion of the air–sea victory of the United States and the United Kingdom must start with control of the movement of supplies and raw materials across the Atlantic Ocean. It was the greatest example during the war of where the Axis made a serious, and at times successful, attempt to use air and sea power to destroy British and American production before it reached the battle-field. If the Germans could ever have severed the supply links between the USA and the UK, they might have won a European war, or at least forced a negotiated peace. Not only would it have been impossible to build up the kind of force in the UK necessary to attack Germany, German industrial muscle would have outclassed Russian production and driven the USSR (which also would have been denied much of its lend-lease supplies including aluminum and thus its ability to build aircraft) out of the war. As this crisis unfolded, Marshall even wrote to Roosevelt, saying that its outcome would determine all American strategic planning. "This problem is with us daily and hourly. The carrying capacity of our shipping is a controlling factor in all strategic plans upon which equipment and other items are based."[15]

If the strategic argument in favor of controlling shipping in the Atlantic was widely understood, it was also widely realized that the first step was to place merchant ships, particularly the slower ones, into convoys with sufficient escorts. As had been seen time and time again in 1940 and 1941, properly escorted merchant vessels had a considerably smaller chance of being sunk than those without escort, even when they were outside the range of patrolling aircraft. During the entirety of World War II, more than twice as many merchant ships were sunk by German U-boats when sailing out of convoy than when sailing under escort protection. (See Figure 23.) When it came to the disastrous merchant ship sinkings in early 1942, the difference between those lost sailing on their own and those lost whilst in convoy swelled to three or four to one between January and June. (See Figure 24.) And this highlights why Churchill was particularly distraught. He knew this was a crisis that need not have occurred, at least not with nearly the ferocity that it did. When his earlier pressure bore little fruit, he pressed Hopkins again in July with a damning report. "I send you my own personal return of shipping losses for the first six months of one nine four two [*sic*]. It is all very serious, particularly the remorselessly increasing losses of American and American controlled shipping."[16]

To Churchill the answer to the problem was simple. More anti-submarine vessels must be redeployed from other theaters, including the Pacific, to the Caribbean and American seaboard. Churchill

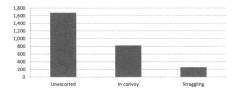

23 Allied merchant ships sunk by German submarines, 1939–45.
Source: Grove (ed.), *The Defeat of the Enemy Attack on Shipping*, vol. 1b, Table 13.
Note: Those down as straggling had originally been in convoy but had to drop out because of mechanical problem, damage, etc. This was a particularly vulnerable class of merchant vessel, and it is a sign of the overall success of the convoy effort that so relatively few were lost this way.

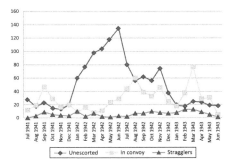

24 Allied merchant ships sunk by German submarines, July 1941–June 1943.
Source: Grove (ed.), *The Defeat of the Enemy Attack on Shipping*, vol. 1b, Table 13.

believed that the United States government had already committed to making the Atlantic and the war against Germany the greatest priority, so this redeployment should not have been problematic. As early as April 1941, the British assumed that the Americans were in complete agreement on the need for convoys in the Atlantic and were planning on utilizing them as soon as they joined the fighting.[17] Therefore, in 1942 as the crisis was unfolding, Churchill believed it made sense to switch American vessels from the Pacific to the Atlantic.

> The situation is so serious that drastic action of some kind is necessary, and we very much hope that you will be able to provide additional escort forces to organize immediate convoys in the West Indies–Bermuda area by withdrawing a few of your destroyers from other services, even if this means temporarily weakening your destroyer strength in the Pacific...[18]

A few days after writing this to Hopkins, Churchill pressed Roosevelt directly to order King to transfer ten American destroyers to the Atlantic for convoy duties.[19] To aid the Americans in this switch, he even offered to send British escorts to help them set up a proper convoy system in US coastal waters. British repair and maintenance of naval vessels at this time had improved significantly, so that there were now far more British ships available for escort duty than ever before.[20] Nor was this the only time the British assumed the United States would agree to take escort vessels from the Pacific to the Atlantic to support the strategic policy it agreed to at this moment in the war. The British Admiralty in early 1942 acted under the assumption that the United States was about switch some of its invaluable destroyers from the Pacific to the Atlantic.[21]

What the British completely underestimated was the tenacious resistance to any such move by Ernest King. In purely logical terms, King should have seen the acute need to protect trade in the Atlantic. His earlier experience had made it clear how vital escort vessels would be in that theater. For much of 1941, he had been in command of the Atlantic Fleet, and was responsible for planning American convoy operations.[22] It was under his command that ships of the Atlantic Fleet such as the USS *Greer* started engaging with German submarines. He was therefore as well acquainted as any American officer with the great need for anti-submarine vessels in Atlantic waters. By the time he left the Atlantic Fleet in December 1941, as he pointed out rather proudly in his private papers, he had constructed a detailed set of plans to fight against German submarines.[23]

However, with the formal American entry into the war in December 1941, King was promoted to a unique position of strength over all of the USN. On December 17, 1941, Roosevelt, who admired King's aggression, named the admiral both Chief of Naval Operations and Commander in Chief of the United States Fleet. King was not only the direct line commander of every American warship, he controlled the entire naval bureaucracy. He was therefore directly or indirectly responsible for much of the disaster that occurred off the American coast in early 1942, though this was soft-pedalled immediately after the war. Both the American and British official histories place most of the blame on a general lack of American preparedness. In ascribing blame, Samuel Morison spoke of the navy as a whole, but never mentioned King.[24] Roskill was content to echo Morison.[25] King's greatest biographer, Thomas Buell, also ascribes blame generally to a shortage of American escort vessels, and quotes King as saying that he would very much have liked to have employed a convoy system in the Caribbean and along the eastern seaboard; he just didn't have access to enough shipping.[26] In other descriptions, King bears a significant amount of the responsibility for the disaster. Williamson Murray and Allan Millett claim that King "botched" the campaign in 1942.[27] Others say it was a systemic failing because the United States did not have enough of the right vessels.[28]

King himself was particularly sensitive to any criticism that he was responsible for this shipping disaster in the first half of 1942. In his papers are a number of different justifications of his behavior. Rather pathetically for such an aggressive character, he even accused the stenographers of the JCS for improperly recording his thoughts at the time, leading to the impression that he was not devoted enough to fighting the trade war in the Atlantic.

> The available records of the JCS, at least for the first six months [of 1942] were rather sketchy until the secretary and his deputies had been trained in extracting the meat or kernel of what the top officers were saying. Even later, the two or three other secretaries would often not get the import or gist of what was being said, because it is hard work to get the sense, and at the same time, keep pace in handwriting.[29]

If there was one consistent theme in King's attempts to defend himself it was that the Roosevelt administration had not provided the navy with enough of the right kind of warship to fight the U-boat threat. Not only had Roosevelt handed over fifty American destroyers to the British in 1941, he also favored the construction of anti-submarine vessels which were too small to cope with the powerful German submarines.[30]

King's defensiveness is not surprising – and not convincing. Even with the systemic failures of the American navy in not preparing for a submarine war in the North Atlantic, there was no reason for such a massacre, and the scale of the losses is to a large degree because of King's allocation of American warships. This allocation was the result of preference and not necessity. While the United States Navy was certainly pressed for warships at this time, it had more than enough to provide a basic convoy system in home waters – if this theater was really going to be given the highest priority for the USN. After the war, the navy prepared data on the number of vessels it had on hand capable of anti-submarine warfare on June 30, 1941 and June 30, 1942. In each case it was considerable. In 1941, there were 281 such ships, including 176 destroyers (the most effective vessel), available to be deployed.[31] In June 1942, there was more than double this number, with 527 vessels on hand which were capable of anti-submarine operations, of which 190 were destroyers. Yet King was willing to have only a small number sent to the Atlantic, the supposedly dominant theater. In April 1942, Admiral Adolphus Andrews, who was commander of the eastern sea frontier which ran from Maine to Florida, had no destroyers allocated to him to escort merchant vessels, only small coastguard cutters.[32] The US Navy in the Pacific, on the other hand, had almost all American destroyers under its control. Though Nimitz certainly had to be careful with their allocation, he was, for instance, able to detach ten destroyers from the main body just before the Battle of Midway and assign them to the defense of the Aleutians.[33]

Therefore, to have instituted a convoy system in the Caribbean and along the American East Coast would have involved the transfer of a modest number of vessels from the Pacific to the Atlantic. It would not have required a wholesale stripping of the Pacific force. As will be seen, King was fully aware of the latest developments in convoy warfare, particularly the need to separate ships by speed. Moreover, there were actually very few German submarines in American waters.

If King had taken basic steps, the number of sinkings could have been significantly reduced.

King, however, did everything possible to make sure such a transfer did not take place. For instance, he fought obstinately against the appointment of a single officer to take control of all anti-submarine efforts in the Atlantic.[34] Although this was something being pressed by both the British and many Americans, King recoiled at the notion of any high-profile appointment that was sure to increase pressure on him to devote more effort to the Atlantic.[35] On the other hand, he kept pressing Roosevelt to make the war against Japan a greater priority than the war against Germany. In March 1942, he wrote a strategy memorandum for the President which argued that the defense of Australia was the most important priority for the United States as it would be intolerable for a "White Man's" country to fall to the Japanese.[36] Moreover, he told Roosevelt that the defense of the Pacific needed to have a higher priority than Bolero, the plan to build up force in the United Kingdom to attack Germany.[37] Again, for a while, King seemed to have great influence on Roosevelt, so much so that in May Marshall, who was determined that the United States should focus on Germany-First, assumed that the President had changed strategic priorities so that the defense of Australia ranked higher than Bolero.[38]

King also deliberately pressed Nimitz, Commander in Chief of the Pacific Fleet and therefore in charge of the warships that would have had to be redeployed to the Atlantic, to take offensive action in the Pacific quickly, to make sure that as many American vessels as possible were engaged in that theater. His desire for aggression in the Pacific led him to rebuke Nimitz in February 1942. Nimitz favored a cautious strategy at the time, and suggested that the remaining battle-ships in the Pacific be used to convoy merchant shipping.[39] It was certainly an unorthodox, one might say highly pessimistic, strategy, but had it been used, it would have freed up some smaller escorts for other duties, including those in the Atlantic. King, however, was furious with such a notion. "Your Pacific Fleet not repeat not markedly inferior in all types to forces enemy can bring to bear within operating radius of Hawaii while he is committed to extensive operations in Southwest Pacific...Cannot readily accept use of battleships for escorting convoys as suitable employment because it is passive in character."[40]

Instead of transferring vessels from the Pacific to the Atlantic to institute convoys, King played for time until new construction could make up the difference. He started looking for other scapegoats or explanations. In March 1942, he asked the army to enforce black-out restrictions on the East Coast, claiming that it was the well-illuminated American cities that were helping the U-boats sink so many merchant ships.[41] He even dabbled in the use of decoys to try to lure German submarines into traps,[42] supporting the use of dummy vessels to entice unsuspecting German submarines to the surface to sink them.[43] In April, he persuaded Knox, who was never able to stand up to him, to issue a preposterous statement that the submarine threat would be under control by May 1, a claim so ludicrous that Hopkins complained to the President.[44] In particular, he seemed to want to temporarily pass over the main responsibility for combating German submarines to the USAAF.

One of King's tactics was to lobby for greater strategic bombing against both German U-boat bases and production.[45] He seems to have at first persuaded Roosevelt that this was one of the most important steps to be taken to stop the crisis. In March 1942, Roosevelt went out of his way to tell Churchill to make the bombing of German submarine bases and manufacturing an extra-special priority.[46] Churchill took the President's recommendation very much on board.[47] The British Air Ministry, however, was rather skeptical about whether this would make much of a difference in the short term, and wanted more aircraft to patrol over the trade routes.[48] It certainly didn't want King to dictate the direction of its bombing campaign.

King also called for the USAAF to provide almost all the aircraft needed to maintain anti-submarine patrols in the Caribbean and off the American East Coast during the first six months of 1942.[49] He did believe that combating the U-boats would require an enormous number of planes; it was just that he seemed reluctant for the USN to provide them. He told Marshall in June 1942 that to properly protect shipping from the Gulf of Mexico to the Canadian border would require 1,500 aircraft.[50] He had used the need for some of these aircraft to justify the navy's requests for more medium bombers of the B-25 and B-26 class, which were highly prized in 1942. However, Arnold, for one, was suspicious that King had no intention of using such aircraft in the war against the Germans, and later asked for written guarantees from the navy that they would do so.[51] Arnold was undoubtedly right. King was willing to spare hardly any navy aircraft to patrol off the American seaboard. The Eastern Seaboard command had no aircraft assigned to it in December 1941.[52] By April 1942, when the sinkings were rising inexorably, the number of navy aircraft in this theater had only increased to a meager eighty-six.

As with escorts, the question of aircraft deployment was one of choice, not necessity. There were more than enough planes on hand in 1942 to play a major role in escorting merchant shipping off the coast of the USA, they were just deployed in other theaters, including the Pacific. In this way, the USAAF shared a desire with King not to deploy its prized assets for trade protection. It prioritized supporting armies in the field and the build-up for a strategic bombing campaign. The USAAF conducted an audit of the location of all of its combat aircraft in August 1942. At that time there were 2,579 American combat aircraft deployed in units capable of directly engaging the enemy (in other words, they were not being used for training or being ready to be shipped to theater).[53] Of these, 1,448 were deployed against the Japanese and 1,131 against the Germans. Of the 1,131 deployed against the Germans, only 399 were deployed in Atlantic or Caribbean bases, and many of these were being prepared for shipment to the European theater.

King's obstinacy in refusing to allocate the necessary resources to protect trade was remarkable considering the anger it caused. Not only the British were appalled by what was happening in the Atlantic, the Royal Canadian Navy was left fighting almost singlehandedly in the western Atlantic, and at times had to keep 90 percent of its vessels on active duty.[54]

The American army was also outraged. George Marshall regularly brought to the attention of the President the need to have more shipping in the region if the United States was to fulfill its strategic obligations.[55] However, his relationship with King made it difficult for him to influence the admiral. Marshall had a warm regard for King's predecessor, Admiral Harold (Betty) Stark (King believed it was too warm a relationship), but the new head of the navy could not be reasoned with quietly. By June 1942, Marshall was forced to confront King directly in a short memorandum that spelled out the disastrous situation as it appeared to the army.

The losses by submarines off our Atlantic seaboard and in the Caribbean now threaten our entire war effort. The following statistics bearing on the subject have been brought to my attention.

Of the 74 ships allocated to the Army for July by the WSA, 17 have already been sunk.

22 percent of the Bauxite fleet has already been destroyed.

20 percent of the Puerto Rican Fleet has been lost.

Tanker losses have been 3.5 percent per month of tonnage in use.

We are all aware of the limited number of escort craft available, but as every conceivable improvised means have been brought to bear on this situation, I am fearful that another month or two of this will so cripple our means of transport that we will be unable to bring sufficient men and planes to bear against the enemy in critical theaters to exercise a determining influence on the war.[56]

In the end, King won his general campaign, though at significant cost to the Anglo-American war effort. It was not until July 1942 that Roosevelt bent to the pressure he was receiving from the British and the US army and directly ordered King to institute a convoy system in the Caribbean and along the American East Coast. In this order Roosevelt summarized the situation admirably, and his figures go a long way to show just how important an earlier introduction of convoy could have been.

You will note that in the Canada–Greenland area, where very few merchant ships are sailing independently, three were lost between May 17th and June 27th, and five sailing under escort were lost in the same period. On the other hand, off the US Atlantic Coast, thirty-three merchant ships sailing independently were lost and only four were lost under convoy in the same period.

So also in the Gulf of Mexico – thirteen ships sailing independently were lost and only one under escort.

In the Caribbean sixty-nine sailing independently were lost and ten under escort...

I think it has taken an unconscionable time to get things going and further I do not think that we are utilizing a large number of escort vessels which could be used...[57]

Roosevelt's understanding of the situation was correct: convoys in these areas would have staved off much of the shipping disaster – as it was actually inflicted by very few German submarines. For instance, in

May 1942 only six German submarines in the Caribbean were responsible for the sinking of forty-one merchant ships with a combined tonnage of 219,867, the highest monthly total in any area at any time during the whole of World War II.[58] Targets were so plentiful that this small number of U-boats had to strictly ration the number of torpedoes they fired to make sure that they didn't run out.[59] During the entire campaign in American waters, the Germans never had more than twelve U-boats deployed at any one time.[60] Had there been more American escorts made available in the Atlantic during early 1942, losses caused by this relatively small number of submarines would have been considerably less and there would have been nothing like another German "Happy Time." Only one convoy that was protected by American escorts during the first four months of 1942 suffered significant losses.[61] During the entire massacre between the middle of January and the end of July 1942, 360 ships were sunk in American waters. Of these, only 11 were in convoy at the time, and one was a straggler than had fallen behind.[62] When convoys were eventually extended to the East Coast of the United States in the summer of 1942, merchant ship sinkings plummeted immediately. In July only three merchant ships were sunk along the American eastern sea frontier area – and these were the last ships sunk there during the entire year.[63] The U-boats had to look elsewhere.

Before leaving this section, this massacre of merchant shipping, when compared with what came afterwards, can be used to help explain the relative importance of production and strategy over intelligence in the defeat of the U-boats. It is common in many of the narratives of the war at sea to attribute great importance to Ultra decrypts in defeating the submarines.[64] 'Ultra' was the designation given by British intelligence to the information gleaned from the supposedly undecipherable German radio and teleprinter communications system. It is the most famous example of an intelligence success in the war and was called 'Ultra' because the security clearance needed to access the information was kept strictly limited, much more so than earlier clearance levels used by the British state. These decrypts supposedly allowed the Admiralty to plan convoy routes in such a way as to avoid submarine attacks. Harry Hinsley, maybe the most important historian of intelligence, makes some remarkable claims. He believes that without Ultra, which allowed for the re-routing of convoys, the Battle of the Atlantic might have been lost.[65] At another time he claimed that Ultra was responsible for saving 1.5 million tons of shipping in the second half of 1941 through the re-routing of convoys.[66]

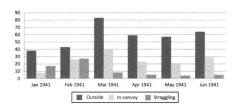

25 British, Allied and neutral merchant ships (all tonnages) lost through enemy action outside convoy, in convoy and straggling.
Source: Grove (ed.), *The Defeat of the Enemy Attack on Shipping 1939–1945,* vol. 1b, Table 13.

These are dramatic, probably overstated, claims. On the one hand, it is probably untrue that at any time during the war the British were in danger of losing the Battle of the Atlantic. On the other, Hinsley makes the fundamental mistake of not differentiating between merchant ships sunk in convoy and those sunk outside of convoy. In the first six months of 1941, while sinkings were high, they were still primarily sinkings outside of convoy. At this time, 344,000 tons of merchant ships were sunk sailing independently, only 147,000 tons were lost in convoy, and another 66,000 were lost straggling behind.[67] (See Figure 25.) The idea that somehow this figure for convoy losses would have gone up by 750 percent without Ultra seems questionable.

Ultra was an important, but ultimately subsidiary player in the war at sea.[68] It was only after the summer of 1942, when Allied shipping production limited German options, that the great battles occurred between large U-boat packs and convoys. However, by this point, it was relatively well known where the convoys were going to be attacked – in the air gap in the North Atlantic that Allied air cover could only reach with the use of escort carriers. Furthermore, the understanding of how to defend convoys had progressed to the point that it was actually useful to the Allies for the Germans to attack convoys. These attacks sped up their victory on the seas.

The benefits of the U-boat campaign for the German war effort

One of the means of analysis used in this book is to examine the campaigns of World War II in terms of equipment deployed and equipment destroyed independent of the manpower involved. A successful campaign can be said to be one which diverts or destroys far more resources than it takes to fight. By this notion, the German U-boat campaign, even after the withdrawal of the submarines from the American coast, can be considered a partial success. This was because the reaction to the massacre of merchantmen up until July 1942 caused the British and the Americans to deploy a great deal of their resources, much of them in inefficient ways. The two most potent examples of these deployments were the exaggerated import-ance given to the construction of escort vessels and merchant shipping from the second half of 1942 until the end of 1943, and the percentage of the Anglo-American strategic bombing campaign that was devoted to the bombing of U-boat targets, many of them the invulnerable U-boat pens.

The production shift was one that was greatly aided by King's decision to wait for new construction to protect merchantmen rather than using the forces already at his disposal. In the summer of 1942, the United States actually experienced a significant crisis in production.[69] The early, extremely optimistic, munitions targets set out early in that year were shown to be completely unattainable. Beginning in August 1942, it was clear that targets would have to be reduced substantially in many areas. Now, in overall terms of this book, the most important outcome of this crisis was Roosevelt's direct intervention in favor of the construction of aircraft over all other munitions. However, the Presi-dent was also reorienting the entire focus of American production towards an air–sea war at this time. He probably felt that his order to King in July to enforce convoy operations along the American coast had paid dividends immediately with the rapid decline in sinkings. This development served to reinforce all of his previous experience. During World War I, when he served as Woodrow Wilson's Assistant Secretary of the Navy, the future President was deeply impressed by the import-ance of having enough escort vessels to provide convoy protection. Now, when he was confronted by a production decision in which tough choices were going to have to be made, he was decisive in recognizing their importance.

In August 1942, when the production crisis first called for Roosevelt's strong intervention, he laid out his ideas in a memorandum for Marshall. It was clear that shipping and protecting American supplies was Roosevelt's primary concern.

I am receiving almost daily a variety of military requirements for 1943 and 1944. These come from the Army, Navy, Maritime Commission and our Allies. While the most important of these requirements is the proposed increase of the Army, there are others which affect our production as much, if not more.

Furthermore, I believe that our production schedules in certain respects, particularly concerning combat aircraft and escort vessels, are probably too low and need to be revised . . .

What I should like to see is a fresh and realistic look at 1943 overall requirements from a strategic point of view. This implies that certain assumptions must be made on which estimated requirements for United States forces of all types in the various probable theaters of war, by number and general composition, are determined. It naturally follows that these assumptions must include judgments as to the strength of our Allies in 1943 and the probable strength of our enemies. *The ability to transport and supply those forces overseas, of course, is an essential factor in determining our requirements.* (Emphasis added)[70]

Roosevelt was being partly disingenuous with his senior army commander. He was determined to prioritize aircraft and naval construction over land power. The proposed increase in the size of the American army, as his disputes with his Joint Chiefs would show, was one of his lowest priorities for the American military. To British observers, in fact, Roosevelt's call in the late summer and fall of 1942 for the reprioritizing of American production in this way was a deliberate attempt to limit the size of the American army.[71] The British Prime Minister's thinking at the time was almost identical to that of the American President. In September and October 1942, Churchill lobbied Roosevelt, once directly and once again through Hopkins, to build even more escort vessels, claiming that this was the Allies' number one construction priority. He even wanted to give them priority over landing craft, which were also a growing bottleneck at the time.[72] At the same time, Churchill believed that Anglo-American tank production could be cut significantly without any decrease in real fighting strength.[73] He also thought that in 1943, increasing German U-boat construction would open up an even more dangerous chapter in the war, and in a personal letter to Roosevelt in October 1942 (see below), he pointed to the success of the convoys belatedly formed off the American coast to make his point.[74] The problem that the British had was that because of earlier British industrial mobilization, there was considerably less scope for the United Kingdom to build more escort vessels. This did not stop the government from trying, and for one of the only times in the war, naval construction rivaled aircraft production in priority at this time.[75] Considering that there was so little scope for production increases in the UK, the improvements that were realized were impressive, particularly in destroyers, which in 1942 and 1943 were being produced at the absolute maximum that the British economy could construct. According to Postan:

> The building of destroyers was to be continued to the limit of capacity...Under the wartime "emergency" programmes there were by the end of 1941 some 118 destroyers in various stages of construction. To these in the course of 1942 there were added forty-two...During 1942, seventy-five destroyers were completed and some 107 were still in hand at the beginning of 1943. An additional forty-three were authorized even though the capacity of the shipyards was so fully engaged that there was little chance of their being laid down or completed before the end of the war.[76]

Therefore, as Churchill well realized in his October 1942 letter, if there was going to be a huge increase in ship production, it was going to come from the intervention of the American President. It was a particularly fortuitous time for him to make the case, as Roosevelt was already locked in the dispute with his Joint Chiefs over production priorities. What eventually came out of the President's intervention was the clear prioritization of aircraft and escort vessels/merchant ships, and a remarkably steep decline in all AFV construction and other ground force equipment in favor of aircraft and escort vessels. The aircraft situation was discussed earlier, and while that was clearly the first priority, it is fascinating to see just how the German submarine threat had shaped the second. In October 1942, Roosevelt told the heads of the different American production bureaus to build an additional seventy escort vessels in 1943.[77] In November 1942, he gave explicit orders for an overall construction plan of 330 destroyers and other anti-submarine escort vessels by the end of 1943, a remarkable number.[78]

It took a little while, however, for the production of escort vessels to be greatly accelerated. On January 2, 1943, the Combined Chiefs of Staff once again requested that American and British construction of escort vessels be greatly accelerated.[79] At the same time, there were great efforts being made to standardize the construction of these vessels in Britain, America and Canada. The increases in spending to build extra escort vessels accounted for approximately $1.5 billion. In April 1942, the amount that the American government was planning to spend on building minor combat vessels (which were mostly escort vessels) in 1943 was $3.3 billion.[80] By December 1942, this figure had grown to $4.8 billion. The extra effort put into construction was equally impressive in number of units to be built. In June 1942, planned combined destroyer construction for 1942 and 1943 was to be 177 units. By December this was raised by about 15 percent to 202.[81] The rise in destroyer escorts was much larger than even this. In June 1942, the United States was planning on building 181 destroyer escorts in 1942 and 1943; by December this figure had risen by more than 40 percent to 260.

The increase in the spending on vessels for the war against the submarines meant that in the second half of 1942 their construction surpassed that of large warships for the first time. American spending on battleships, cruisers and carriers averaged $62 million in the first quarter of 1942, $73 million in the second quarter and $71 million in the third. On the other hand, spending just on anti-submarine vessels independent of destroyers averaged $44 million in the first quarter, $74 million in the second and a very large $97 million in the third.[82]

The increases in merchant shipping because of the 1942 disaster were just as impressive. In both April and June 1942, the American plan was to construct approximately 19 million tons (dwt) of all merchant vessels in 1942 and 1943 combined.[83] By December 1942, this figure had been raised by almost half to 28 million tons. Monetarily, the increase was from a $4.5 billion spend on merchant vessel construction in these two years to a $6.3 billion dollar expenditure – a rise of $1.8 billion. It was the only area in the late 1942 spending review to have a real increase in spending (all other disputes were about how to prioritize a smaller budget).[84]

Such increases in expenditure were made possible by drastically reducing the percentage of war production spending on equipment for the army. During 1942 as a whole, the US army's share of American war production planned for 1943 was cut in half to allow for the greater prioritization of spending on the air force and the navy. In

February 1942, the United States government had expected to devote approximately 35 percent of its production budget to army needs (independent of the air force). By December 1942, this percentage had dropped to about 20 percent.[85] The cut in all combat vehicle construction was the most dramatic as it fell in 1943 planned terms from $14.4 billion in February 1942 to only $5.9 billion in December – a decrease of 60 percent.

The decline in the spending on ground force equipment was mirrored in a general reduction in the number of combat units that were to be raised. During and immediately after Arcadia, as expressed in the Victory Plan of 1942, the United States was planning for a ground force of 169 infantry divisions and 90 Armored Battalions by December 1943, and an enormous 213 infantry divisions and 113 Armored Battalions by July 1944.[86] Because of the large reductions that were forced on the army to allow aircraft and naval construction to be protected, a decision was made that the United States would plan on only a hundred division army in 1943.[87] This was a tiny force by earlier standards, but amazingly one with which the USA persisted throughout the rest of the war.

In new construction alone, King's policy of starving the Atlantic Fleet of escort vessels in early 1942 paid handsome dividends for the British and American navies, in both monetary cost and unit numbers. The construction that came off the slips in 1943, which had been greatly accelerated and increased because of the disaster in early 1942, was prodigious: 128 new destroyers were commissioned for the United States Navy in 1943 alone. Even more directly connected to the submarine menace, the United States commissioned for its own navy or handed over to its allies (overwhelmingly the British) a remarkable 295 destroyer escorts in 1943.[88]

The other area where the British and the Americans ended up employing extra resources to combat the German submarine threat in 1942 and 1943 was in the growing strategic bombing campaign. Within this expensive campaign that was being waged against Germany, anti-submarine targets received a high priority. For the first six months of 1942, the USAAF was devoted entirely to different anti-submarine operations.[89] When it started to launch attacks against the European continent in the fall of 1942, this situation did not change materially. Through June of 1943, attacks against German U-boat forces, either in production yards, in their bases or even at sea, remained the "primary concern" of American strategic bombing forces.[90] At first Churchill, if not the Admiralty, seemed to share American enthusiasm for this campaign. In late March 1942, he boasted to Roosevelt about the success that the British bombers were having against U-boat targets.[91] Yet, even with all this effort, it is not likely that the USAAF strategic bombers made a great deal of difference. In particular, when it came to the bombing of U-boat pens, which were made of excellent German concrete sometimes 12 feet thick, it seems that almost no material damage was done.

Unfortunately this was not realized at the time, which is why the campaign continued for so long. In fact, the backers of strategic air power, who were so used to assuming that their campaigns would be effective, drastically overstated the effect of the bombing while it was ongoing. Ira Eaker, the first commander of the 8th Air Force and one of the greatest American advocates of strategic air power, told Arnold in late November 1942 that he could cripple Germany's U-boat operations from France using American bombers to attack their bases.

> The bombing which we have done of the submarine bases has been even more effective than we had hoped for with the force we had available...
> I am now more firmly convinced than ever that if we had ten heavy groups we could eliminate a large part of the submarine activity now launched from the five principal bases on the Brest peninsula. At the time I saw you in Washington you may remember I told you and the President that we could guarantee with ten groups to eliminate 60 percent of the submarine menace in the Atlantic, since 85 percent of it was launched from these five bases and we could render then unusable with an Air Force of that size. I can tell you now that all the facts growing out of actual missions definitely support that estimate.[92]

Arnold seems to have been persuaded by such bravado, which is why attacks on German submarine pens remained such a high American priority. In a memo on strategic policy he drew up for the Joint Chiefs of Staff, he highlighted American policy in this area, and contrasted it with British policy which was focused on using air power to attack German submarines at sea. His analogy was colorful, though in hindsight it looks rash.

The British have concluded that "the most rapid, effective and
permanent means of reducing the submarine menace is considered
to be direct sinkings by surface and air attack." ... We cannot
accept such conclusions. If flies infest a community, this menace is
combated by destruction of breeding places, not by giving each
citizen a fly swatter with which to kill a fly.[93]

In this case Arnold was certainly in the wrong, while British
skepticism was certainly right. If there was one great opponent of
the bombing of submarine installations it was Air Marshal Harris.
Beginning in late 1942, Harris began to complain strongly that the
intense American effort to bomb submarine facilities, including the
"impermeable" submarine pens, was a great waste of resources.[94] He
regularly lobbied Portal and the Americans to stop attacks on the
U-boat pens, which he considered impervious.[95] Of course, being
Harris, his solution was to abandon almost all defensive efforts and
expend resources on attacks on German cities, which he assumed
would lead to a collapse in German submarine production.[96] He
wanted to withdraw much of the air protection devoted to convoys
and switch these resources to strategic bombing. His monomania led
him to take a basically correct position on the inability to bomb
German U-boat pens and turn it into one that would have made
things worse.

Coastal command should be re-named the High Seas Air
Command and its operations control should revert to the Air
Ministry. Much of the force in it would then become available for
the destruction of the centres of U-boat production, without in any
way jeopardizing essential sea routes, and in the knowledge that the
scale of the U-boat attack on these routes would begin thereafter
rapidly to decline.[97]

While Harris failed in his campaign for almost no trade protection, it is quite clear that the British were less supportive of the
bombing of German submarine installations than were the Americans.
During 1943 as a whole, approximately half of the bombs dropped by
the USAAF based in Britain were on German submarine targets.[98] The
figure for the RAF was approximately 20 percent. As the British were
still dropping many more bombs on German targets than were the
Americans at this time, their decision prevented the anti-submarine

campaign from completely wasting Allied air resources. Yet, overall, it was still a large outlay of effort that made very little difference.

In the end, it is the totality of the reaction to the U-boat threat which demonstrates why it was worthwhile for Germany to fight the campaign, even if it held out almost no prospect for victory. In the first place, it was the only major campaign that allowed the Germans to destroy British and American production before it reached the field of battle. It is not easy to calculate the value of the military supplies sunk by German submarines during 1942 and the first half of 1943. Many of the ships sunk during the massacre off the coast of the United States and in the Caribbean in the first six months of 1942 were carrying raw materials, such as fuel and bauxite, destined for war production. It is interesting to note that while this was going on, American production was much smaller than expected, in some cases approximately one-third below targets. In particular, American aircraft construction in early 1942 came in far below projections, leading to the production crisis that started in August. According to George Marshall 22 percent of the bauxite transporting fleet was sunk at this time. At the same time Donald Nelson was telling Franklin Roosevelt that total aircraft construction in 1942 would come in at only 48,000 instead of the 60,000 requested by the President – a 20 percent shortfall. It is therefore entirely possible that the German navy destroyed at least twice as many American aircraft in the pre-production phase in 1942 as the Luftwaffe was able to do in combat in 1942 and 1943.[99] Also, in the second half of 1942 and the first of 1943, when German submarines concentrated on shipping between the United States and the UK, a great deal of military equipment was sunk before it reached American and British armed forces in Europe or North Africa. The American War Production Board estimated that in the first quarter of 1943, when sinkings on this route were at their high point, approximately 5 percent of the military supplies destined for the American army went down in the Atlantic.[100] This figure, if accurate, would have meant that the U-boats destroyed more American army equipment in 1942 than the German army.

Beyond that, the damage wrought by a small number of German submarines in early 1942, much of which was the result of conscious choices, resulted in many *billions* of dollars being spent on both escort vessels and merchant ships in late 1942 and 1943. Spending on each was increased by at least a combined figure of $3.3 billion in late 1942 ($1.8 billion extra for merchant ships and $1.5 billion extra for small naval vessels). These billions, especially for the huge number of new escort vessels, were to a large degree wasted, even if that wasn't realized when they were allocated. By the summer of 1943, it was clear that a drastic over-production of escort vessels had been undertaken. In September 1943, the United States Navy informed the President that they were planning on cancelling the construction of a whopping 405 different destroyer escort vessels, the loss of which would not imperil seaborne trade in any way.[101] The British situation was analogous, but on a smaller scale. They were also building a large number of escort vessels in the second half of 1943, a six-month period which saw them complete far more in terms of warship tonnage than in any other equivalent six-month period of the war.[102] Many of these warships would not have an enemy to fight.

Finally, the German U-boat threat caused the diversion of a large amount of British and American strategic air power during 1943, when the strategic bombing of Germany first threatened to produce real results. Half of the bombs dropped by the American strategic bombers based in the UK and one-fifth of those dropped by the British were directed towards submarine-based targets. Much of this effort was aimed at destroying German U-boat pens, which proved to be practically indestructible. This enormous outlay of Anglo-American strength paid almost no dividends and was caused by approximately 10 percent of German production in 1942 and the first half of 1943, not a bad exchange by any stretch of the imagination.

The battle of the submarines and the convoys

In August 1942 an important development occurred in the pattern of Allied merchant ship losses. For only the third month since the war began in 1939, and for the first time since the United States joined the war, more merchant ships were sunk whilst traveling in convoy (sixty) than were sunk when sailing independently (fifty-six).[103] It was an important indication of where the trade war was now heading, and where it would end disastrously for the Germans in the spring of 1943. (See Map 3).

When a proper convoy system was finally introduced off the American East Coast and in the Caribbean in the summer of 1942, the U-boat war finally entered the phase where the direct fighting between submarines and convoys would decide its outcome. The withdrawal of German U-boats from North American waters left Admiral Doenitz with two options. He could send boats out to less vital trade routes to seek out the ever shrinking pool of unescorted merchant shipping that could be attacked with little risk. This was done off the coast of South America and Africa. A large number of merchant vessels, the great majority of which were unescorted, were torpedoed off the coast of Venezuela and the shores of West Africa between August 1942 and May 1943.[104] However, these sinkings were of only limited value in damaging the Anglo-American war effort. Not only were they often older ships, they were carrying cargo on trade routes that were not vital to Allied war production or armed forces supply.

The other option was to attack directly the convoys that were bringing the vital supplies from North America to the United Kingdom. On the surface, the Germans now had some real advantages when compared with earlier in the war. The U-boat crews possessed some of the most skilled military men in Germany and they had developed a strong esprit de corps.[105] However, the real advantage that they seemed finally to have was numbers. German production, which had grown significantly since 1939, now meant that Doenitz had access to the large force that he had always coveted. On November 10, 1942, there were 220 German U-boats in operational service.[106] By 1943, there were more than 400 U-boats in active service or on trials, and in July of that month there were 240 actually on operations. (See Figure 26.)

Churchill, who was well aware of this growth in German submarine strength, painted a bleak picture of the future in the Atlantic in a personal letter written in October 1942, which was delivered to Roosevelt in November. He started by discussing what he believed was the most important issue of the war.

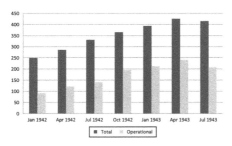

26 German U-boat strength, total and operational, January 1942–July 1943. *Source:* Roskill, *The War at Sea*, vol. II, Appendix K, p. 475.

First of all, I put the U-boat menace. This, I am sure is our worst danger. It is horrible to me that we should be budgeting jointly for a balance of shipping on the basis of 700,000 tons a month loss ... the spectacle of all these splendid ships being built, sent to sea crammed with priceless food and munitions, and being sunk – three or four a day – torments me day and night...

Next year there will be many more U-boats and they will range far more widely. No ocean passage will be safe. All focal points will be beset and will require long-range air protection. I expect all convoys will have to have anti-U-boat escorts, and often auxiliary aircraft carriers throughout the greater part of their journeys, and fast convoys will have to be arranged for the ships at present routed independently. How are we to find craft for this?

Nothing is more clearly proved than the efficacy of the convoy system. The marvellous recovery of your Atlantic shore is one proof. The immunity hitherto enjoyed by the vast and numerous troop convoys with ample escorts is another. We are doing all we can to strike at the U-boat bases and U-boat plants, and you are proposing to base strong bomber forces here to multiply our effort. All the same it is *Escorts* that we need, even more than merchant ships. We want both, but I am all with those who say "A ship not sunk in 1943 is worth two built for 1944".[107]

It was a fascinating evaluation of the trade war in the Atlantic, at times insightful and prescient, at others overly pessimistic. However, the letter also indicated that the British had come a long way down the road to understanding just how to defeat the submarine.

In fact, even for all their increased strength, the Germans were now facing an enemy with a superb grasp of the war at sea, and one that had in its possession a trained and equipped force that was able to put this understanding into action. By 1943, the Royal Navy had reached a state of technological and intellectual maturity when it came to fighting German submarines. The notion of the importance of convoys in general had been realized by the British early in the war. Convoys needed, not only escorts, but wherever possible air support. Now, however, there was also a highly developed understanding of the importance of other elements, such as ship speed, convoy size and air support, when it came to anti-submarine operations.

The speed issue was one that had been apparent to the British, if only partially understood, much earlier in the war. German submarines, like all of this type of vessel at the beginning of the war, were relatively slow. The Type VII, which was still the mainstay of the German U-boat fleet into 1943, had a top speed of less than 8 knots when submerged. It simply could not properly track fast merchant ships unless it could attack while on the ocean surface, where it had a top speed of about 17 knots. When the British government in early 1941 felt confident enough to start asking the United States for large amounts of war supplies, one of the most important requests was for fast merchant ships.[108] At the same time, the Admiralty and Churchill discussed separating out faster merchantmen and allowing them to proceed in specialized, high-speed convoys.[109]

The key speed that needed to be reached to provide a great deal of protection to merchant ships was 13 knots or greater.[110] Ships that could maintain such a pace were at a very low risk of being sunk, even if completely without protection. It was estimated that independents were three times safer if they could travel at 14 knots rather than at 12 knots. If they could go considerably faster than this, they were practically invulnerable. The large, fast, pre-war cruise liners that could cross the Atlantic carrying passengers were a particular example of this. Famous ships like the *Queen Mary* or the *Queen Elizabeth*, which traveled at up to 30 knots and were used to ferry many thousands of troops, were often sent completely unescorted across the Atlantic in 1942 and 1943.[111] (See Figure 27.)

When the United States entered the war, this lesson was one of the first that the British tried to pass along to Ernest King. The American noted in March 1942 how

27 The famous liner *Queen Mary* carrying American troops back from Europe in 1945. Understanding the proper role of a ship's speed was an important British success during the Battle of the Atlantic. Fast liners such as this were allowed to travel on their own, without escort, as German submarines could never move quickly enough to launch an attack.

> Captain Bittleston of the British Admiralty has raised some
> interesting questions in connection with the allocation of tankers
> to various important routes on which these vessels move. He
> states that the Admiralty experience indicates that vessels capable
> of a speed of 15 knots or better, operating in the North Atlantic
> from the Atlantic seaboard to the UK, if running alone, are
> practically speaking, immune from submarine attack, but that
> ships ... should be in convoys where the speed is necessarily
> 11 knots or less.[112]

When presented with such a tried and tested plan of allocation, King
dissented. He argued, in essence, that separating out the faster and
slower ships would be too much work.[113] One can only hope that this
was not due to his distrust of the British – but once again his judgment
is called into question.

In the second half of 1942 and early 1943, this speed issue was
now being understood even more exactly. It actually helped govern the
construction of American and British merchant ships.[114] In 1942 the
British were hoping that their new merchant vessels would be able to
maintain a speed of 11 knots whilst in convoy, a pace which would
certainly still have given German submarines a chance of attacking
them, but one which would have significantly reduced the odds of such
an attack succeeding. However, it was not until 1943 that these ships
could be used to their full potential. The use of substandard coal, the
employment of too many firemen who were not trained sufficiently and
therefore could not keep the engines working at maximum efficiency,
and the weighing down of many merchantmen with anti-torpedo
devices such as nets and chains meant that many ships were steaming
at less than 10 knots throughout 1942 and into 1943. This situation
was much the same with the famous "Liberty" ships built in American
shipyards in 1942 and 1943. These vessels, which were partly based on
the British-designed Sunderland cargo ship, were mass-produced at a
remarkable pace and in very large numbers.[115] They were designed
with a speed of 11 knots in mind, one which would have provided them
with a natural advantage in crossing the Atlantic. The Americans
ended up calculating the safety difference of convoys in 1943. They
determined that even for relatively slow ships, an extra knot or two
could provide a large boost in protection. One American calculation
was that increasing the speed of a convoy from 7 knots to 9 knots gave

the ships involved an extra one-third as much protection from German submarine attack.

This simple fact of speed differential should also help correct one of the other misunderstandings about the war at sea, and that is the relative uniformity of merchant tonnage. The tonnage that the Germans were able to sink for much of the war was older, unescorted vessels or ships that were taking part in slower convoys. The loss of such vessels, while serious, was being made up by new construction that was considerably faster, such as the Liberty ships (See Figure 28.). The tonnage of these newer, faster vessels was worth considerably more than the tonnage of older, slower ships. Not only could they bring goods and supplies across the Atlantic more quickly, they were inherently safer. For instance, between October 1942 and May 1943, the faster convoys (those averaging around 9 knots) suffered a 50 per-cent smaller casualty rate than slower convoys (those averaging around 7 knots), even when they were attacked at approximately the same rate.[116] It was a sign of just how the war at sea was becoming unwin-nable for the Germans. By March 1943, two-thirds of the 510 merchant ships that were being deployed in the Atlantic were capable of making at least 10 knots.[117] At this point, what the Germans were doing was thinning the merchant ship herd of its weakest members.

Another area where convoy tactics were improving markedly was in the understanding of the importance of convoy size. There had been an ongoing discussion about the optimal number of merchantmen and escort vessels since the introduction of the convoy system. In 1943 this discussion was answered decisively in favor of the larger convoy, that of sixty vessels or larger.[118] The key person in this devel-opment was the Nobel Prize-winning Professor P. M. S. Blackett, who headed the Admiralty's Operational Research Section in 1942 and 1943.[119] The basic reasoning behind Blackett's discovery was that the determining factor in merchant ship losses for any convoy was not the relative number of escort vessels to merchant ships, but instead the number of escort vessels to submarines attacking. The perimeter of a larger convoy was not much greater than that of a smaller one, so the escorts assigned to protect a larger convoy would have more freedom of action to confront attacking German submarines.[120] As more escorts could be assigned to defend larger convoys, they were much more effective against U-boat attacks. (See Figure 29.)

28 "Victory" ships laden with goods bound for American armed forces. Though these specific Liberty ships were bound for the Pacific, the majority were used in the Atlantic to ferry supplies to Europe.

Experience has shown that hitherto in an attack on a convoy the *average* number of ships sunk depends only on the number of U/Bs [U-boats] attacking and the number of escorts defending the convoy. It does not depend noticeably on the size of the convoy. This is because the perimeter on which the escort forces move increases very slowly with the size of the convoy...[121]

29 A large Atlantic convoy organized in 1943. By this time, the British had developed a superb understanding of how factors such as size and speed provided protection to convoys.

Such reasoning allowed for interesting intellectual developments. Instead of seeing convoys as means of just protecting trade, the convoys themselves could be turned into vehicles to destroy submarines. For much of the war there was one group, interestingly led by Churchill, which argued for the creation of specialized hunter-killer groups of anti-submarine vessels. Such groups would be unencumbered from convoy duty and sent out to try to find submarines. While conceptually this might sound sensible, it ended up being an almost total failure. Submarines were simply too difficult to locate on their own, and these hunter-killer groups achieved little. On the other hand, by 1943, the convoy itself could be turned into the hunter-killer group – by appearing to be an enticing prey. Periodically, or so the reasoning went, a different convoy, preferably a large one, could be escorted by twice the usual allotment of escort vessels.[122] The submarines that attacked such an over-escorted convoy would be facing extreme danger. In March 1943, Churchill informed Roosevelt that the British had discussed using a convoy on the politically important, yet extremely dangerous, route from the UK to Russia as "bait" to draw the Germans in.[123] Taken together, the improved understanding by the British of the roles of convoy size, speed and escort numbers gave them a distinct advantage as 1943 progressed and the Germans were forced to attack the convoys directly.

The final areas which now swung decisively towards the Anglo-Americans in the war at sea were ones of production. The number of escorts available in 1943, if never enough to please the pessimists in the Admiralty, grew significantly. On August 1,

1942, the main Admiralty command that could dispatch vessels to fight German submarines, the Western Approaches Command (Londonderry, Liverpool and Greenock), had a combined force of fifty-four destroyers and sixty-seven corvettes. On January 1, 1943, they had fifty-five destroyers and eighty-nine corvettes.[124] This figure was augmented after the successful Operation Torch landings in North Africa allowed the transfer of more anti-submarine warfare (ASW) vessels to the Atlantic. Overall, in April 1943, there were 500 different vessels available for anti-submarine duty under British operational control in Atlantic and UK waters.[125] Moreover, this force was soon to be supplemented by a large number of vessels being constructed in American shipyards. During 1943, the United States commissioned for its own navy or handed over to its allies a remarkable 295 destroyer escorts (which the British classified as corvettes).[126]

If the anti-submarine vessel numbers were increasing, so was their overall technological effectiveness. If there was one area where the war at sea was considerably more expensive than the war on land (excepting aircraft), it was in technological development. Fighting on water, a substance upon which human beings cannot walk, has always made sea warfare technologically more sophisticated than that on land. Until the development of aircraft, and in some cases long after, warships represented the most technologically complex and expensive creations of the human mind. The war at sea in the North Atlantic represented another of these intense epochs of technological competition. The introduction of new weapons and counter-weapons occurred regularly from 1941 to 1943.[127] The Germans developed better magnetic and inertia pistols for their torpedoes, "Metox" search receivers which allowed their submarines to detect Allied radar and avoid attacks, and, belatedly, better radar equipment themselves.[128] The Allies, overwhelmingly the British, countered with a huge number of different innovations such as the Hedgehog anti-submarine mortar, significantly improved depth charges, and vastly improved radar sets. (See Figure 30.) When it came to developing radar, the British were considerably ahead of the Germans, and produced sets with much higher frequency and in much greater numbers.[129] Doenitz was entirely aware of this British radar superiority by 1943, and considered it a key factor in the eventual defeat of the U-boats.[130]

If there is one British weapon that exemplifies the way in which this war at sea was advancing the development of modern warfare, it is

30 An example of British technical innovation was this forward-firing mortar, nicknamed Hedgehog, which first entered service in 1942.

31 Another invention was the Leigh-Light, an ingenious weapon which used radar to track a U-boat on the surface at night, with a light that would only shine just as the aircraft was about to attack.

the famous "Leigh-Light" aerial attack aircraft.[131] These were converted Wellington bombers that used radar to detect submarines that could not be seen. When one was detected, the aircraft would approach and, when close, illuminate the submarine with a powerful searchlight, allowing for immediate air attack. (See Figure 31.) By the summer of

1943, these attacks involved effective acoustic Mark 24 air-dropped torpedoes, known as Fido.[132] At this point, the air–sea war had become much more advanced than anything on land. Targets were being located by radar and attacked by "fire and forget" weapons. Modern warfare had arrived.

It should be noted that there was one service that had not yet fully benefited from improved technology and equipment, and that was the Royal Canadian Navy. The Canadian contribution to the war at sea has not always been recognized and remains controversial.[133] However, they undertook a great deal of the convoy efforts in the Atlantic in 1942 and 1943, and showed some important tactical awareness and growth.[134] The British had a somewhat patronizing view of the Canadians, and when the battle in late 1942 turned to a direct U-boat–convoy confrontation, the Admiralty asked Churchill to pull the Canadians (and the Americans) from the mid-Atlantic gap.[135]

Finally, the use of aircraft in all their forms against the U-boats was to prove the last nail in the coffin of the German submarine war. The importance of aircraft, particularly the long-range B-24 bombers, had been recognized since 1941. Some German officers believed that it was the Liberators in 1943 that caused the eventual withdrawal of Germany's submarines from the North Atlantic.[136] One of the British complaints against the American plans to directly bomb U-boat bases was that many of these bombers could be more profitably used patrolling the sea lanes and protecting convoys.[137] For much of 1942, British Coastal Command, which was in charge of using land-based aircraft against German submarines, actually had only a modest force. On January 1 of that year, Coastal Command had only 127 aircraft in total, 10 of which were Liberators.[138] By January 1, 1943, however, it had three times that number, 40 of which were Liberators. Moreover, British technological and doctrinal developments meant that these aircraft were far more effective in attacking German submarines. (See Figure 32.)

In 1943, therefore, the use of long-range, land-based aircraft had slowly squeezed the area in the North Atlantic where the U-boats could operate with some measure of safety.[139] (See Map 3.) By the spring of 1943, the United States was making Liberators available in sufficient numbers so that only a few hundred contiguous miles of the Atlantic Ocean could not be patrolled by them. This area, known as the Greenland Air Gap, was where Doenitz concentrated the majority of his submarines in the first half of 1943.

32 A long-range B-24 Liberator of RAF Coastal Command attacks a U-boat during the Battle of the Atlantic. If caught on the surface like this, U-boats were in great peril. This one was destroyed in minutes.

In the end it was the layered and multifaceted campaign against the U-boat that really stands out in the Battle of the Atlantic. By 1943 they could be tracked and attacked in many different ways, while their targets were being shepherded in much more efficient convoys. Picking out one specific element for special mention misses the point – it was the totality of improvements that spelled doom for the U-boats. This totality of effort stands in stark contrast to what the Germans did themselves. To begin with, they did not improve their basic submarine technology between 1939 and 1943, so that the boats built at this time showed few performance advancements. Also, the Germans never were able to combine other elements of trade warfare (particularly from the air) in efficient ways with their U-boats, leaving the submarines to fend for themselves. Because of numerous factors including aircraft range problems, lack of coordination (and the German navy would say lack of interest), and general economic and technological weakness, the Luftwaffe and the navy were never able to work out a system for mutual cooperation in the war against the convoys.[140] Between January 1942 and May 1943, the U-boats sank a total of 8,049,243 tons of merchant shipping, while German aircraft sank 814,702 tons.[141]

The outcome of this battle between the submarines and the convoys was never in doubt. The Germans did have a few successes against specific convoys. In March 1943, forty U-boats were concentrated against two specific convoys, the slow convoy SC 122 and the faster HX 229.[142] A number of unusual factors combined to create a mini-disaster. Extremely bad weather meant that land-based air cover was severely restricted so the convoy had to proceed for much longer without air support. The rough seas also hampered the escorts and caused disorganization between the convoys. As the slower convoy left first, the two masses of ships eventually met up, causing a chaotic herd of shipping which, along with the bad weather, left many ships straggling behind (stragglers behind convoys were always in a particularly dangerous situation). Eventually the U-boats were able to sink twenty-one vessels with a combined tonnage of 141,000 – at the cost of one U-boat sunk.

Yet, this specific result would not be repeated. In March 1943, not only did the United States agree to dispatch even more Liberators to patrol the Atlantic, the first of a very important class of naval vessel, the escort aircraft carrier, USS *Bogue*, appeared with a convoy.[143] This class of ship effectively closed the air gap for any convoy so protected. These air developments, with the continued improvement in the effectiveness of the convoy escort vessels, led to an immediate change in U-boat behavior. In April 1943 it was noticed by the Admiralty just how tentative the German U-boats had become when attacking convoys.[144] And the Germans had reason to be worried: very few escorted merchantmen were sunk in April for every U-boat lost, just three for each submarine. And this ratio was set to get worse for the Germans.

May saw all the technological, production and intellectual developments in the trade war put into use with devastating effect. The Germans had a mass of submarines ready to intercept shipping in the North Atlantic. On May 1, Doenitz had four main U-boat groups, with about sixty submarines, poised on both sides of the Greenland Gap.[145] At the same time, there were a number of large convoys moving back, with sufficient trained escorts, well supported by land-based aircraft and the escort carrier *Bogue*.[146] The result was a massacre – of the U-boats. For the month as a whole, thirty-four merchant ships, with a combined tonnage of 163,507 tons, were sunk in the North Atlantic.[147] Of these, twenty-six were lost in convoy. On the other hand, U-boat losses had skyrocketed. By May 22, the Germans had lost thirty-three U-boats and for the month they lost forty-one.[148]

It was perhaps the best example of technology integration in the war. Naval vessels with new offensive weapons worked with carrier- and land-based aircraft and new detection technologies to deprive German submarines of any possible sanctuary. If the submarines were below the surface, they could be detected by sonar and attacked by new weapons such as the Hedgehog forward-throwing mortar or air-carried depth charges. Those on the surface could be

Table 28 *Methods of U-boat sinkings, April and May 1943*

Surface escort vessels only	16
Surface escort vessels and carrier air power	2
Surface escort vessels and shore-based air power	4
Shore-based air power as part of convoy escort	10
Shore-based aircraft not with convoys	3
Shore-based air patrol (Bay of Biscay and Norwegian coast)	9
Shore-Based air power—Other	3
Carrier-based air power	2
Submarine patrols	2
Mine	1
Other/unknown	4
Total	56

Source: Roskill, *The War at Sea*, vol II, p. 377.

detected by air- or sea-based microwave radar sets and blown to bits. The sheer variety of ways by which the U-boats were sunk in April and May 1943 shows how completely and successfully the new systems had been integrated. (See Table 28.) In Doenitz's own words, it was the many layers of Allied ASW options that overwhelmed the U-boat.

> The overwhelming superiority achieved by the enemy defense was
> finally proved ... The convoy escorts worked in exemplary
> harmony with the specially trained "support groups". To that must
> be added the continuous air cover, which was provided by carrier-
> borne and long-range, shore-based aircraft, most of them equipped
> with new radar. There were also new and heavier depth charges
> and improved means of throwing them. With all this against us
> it became impossible to carry on the fight against the convoys.[149]

The U-boats had nowhere to hide.

These losses were so high that the Admiralty realized that Doenitz's crews had been decimated. In June they wrote this appreciation of the May battles. "The large number of U-boat sinkings in May, at comparatively small cost to the Allies, must have had a very demoralizing effect on the U-boats and the German High Command must have realized that such heavy losses could not continue without bringing disaster to the whole U-boat campaign."[150]

Before the month was out, Doenitz had decided to abandon the North Atlantic – which for all intents and purposes meant that Germany was definitely going to lose World War II. If the submarines were going to come back to the Atlantic, they were going to have to do so in completely new boats with far more advanced equipment – which both Hitler and Doenitz were desperate to see happen. Though the Germans would eventually design and build new Type XXI and XXIII U-boats for precisely this purpose, they ran out of time before the new boats could be used effectively. Anglo-American air power limited German construction so that only one Type XXI would put to sea for operations before Germany's surrender.[151] The Germans would continue to fight for two more years, inflict a huge amount of damage and, at times, mount successful operations – but all it was doing was forestalling the inevitable.

8 THE WAR IN EUROPE IN 1943: STRATEGIC BOMBING AND THE LAND WAR

On the morning of August 17, 1943, a clear and sunny day with superb visibility, the 100th Bombardment Group of the USAAF's 8th Air Force, 4th Air Division took off from the United Kingdom to attack the Messerschmitt aircraft works in Regensburg, Germany.[1] They were commanded by one of the more driven officers in the American air force, a fast-rising colonel named Curtis LeMay. This was a much more dangerous mission than any that the pilots in the unit had tried before. Raids by the 8th Air Force had previously been aimed mostly at German U-boat facilities on the coast, many in France – raids for which they could receive fighter escort for their entire time in the air.

In this raid, however, the twenty-one B-17s of the 100th Bombardment Group were placed "lowest and last," flying at 17,000 feet at the absolute end of the 4th Air Division's bomber stream as it headed deep into Germany. Regensburg was located in southeast Germany, approximately halfway between Nuremberg and Munich. Until the 100th reached the skies over Holland, they met no opposition. Finally, at 10.17 in the morning, when the B-17s reached the Dutch town of Woensdrecht, they encountered German flak. Ten minutes later, whilst nearing the German border, the first Luftwaffe fighters appeared, two FW-190s, which attacked the unit from straight ahead.

A few minutes later, swarms of German fighters, both FW-190s and ME-109s, swept into action. Soon machine guns in every B-17 were firing as the German fighters swooped in from a number of different angles. The Germans came in waves. One US co-pilot looked out of his window and saw two complete squadrons of German fighters; he counted twenty-three, almost level with the bomber stream, with a number of other German squadrons forming below to attack. He then looked to see if there were any American P-47s nearby flying fighter escort, but could not find one. The B-17s were on their own.

For the next hour and a half the bomber stream was attacked by these waves of German fighters, numbering, one pilot guessed, at least two hundred. To the American flyers they seemed "demented."[2] German fighters at this point were equipped with the heavy firepower of excellent 20 mm cannon which started to blow holes in the B-17s. Every so often, an American bomber would be forced out of the protective flying box which they strove so hard to maintain. At this point the plane was doomed, as it would have no other complementary defensive firepower and would be swarmed like a whale attacked by sharks.

Still, German fighter tactics and abilities, even at this stage of the war, showed some marked differences to the those of the Americans.

Fighter tactics were running fairly true to form. Frontal attackers hit the low squadron and lead squadron, while rear attackers went for the high. The manner of their attacks showed that some of the pilots were old-timers, some amateurs, and that all knew pretty definitely where we were going and were inspired by a fanatical determination to stop us before we got there. The old-timers came in on frontal attacks with a noticeably slower rate of closure, apparently throttled back, obtaining greater accuracy than those that bolted through us wide out. They did some nice shooting at ranges of 500 or more yards, and in many cases seemed able to time their thrusts so as to catch the top and bell turret gunners engaged with rear and side attacks. Less experienced pilots were pressing attacks home to 250 yards and less to get hits, offering point-blank targets for the break-away, firing long bursts of 20 seconds, and, in some cases, actually pulling up instead of going down and out. Several FW pilots pulled off some first rate deflection shooting on side attacks against the high group, then raked the low group on the break-away out of a side slip, keeping the nose cocked up in the turn to prolong the period the formation was in their sights.[3]

For a while, members of the 100th thought the entire group would be shot down.[4] They were under constant attack for more than one and a half hours before even reaching Regensburg. However, just before arriving at the target, the fighter pressure eased off and light flak fire took over. Fortunately for the Americans, the skies were clear and the weather ideal, with the ME-109 factories below clearly visible, allowing them to be attacked with relative accuracy. The surviving B-17s then continued to head south, aiming for sanctuary in Tunisia. LeMay had the entire air division circle over Lake Garda in northern Italy, to allow any damaged aircraft that could still fly to try and rejoin the bomber stream. The rest of the flight was uneventful as most German fighters had been removed from the Mediterranean and the tactic of flying on to Africa caught the Germans by surprise. However, every once in a while a B-17 would run out of fuel and drift down into the sea. By 6.15 that evening, what was left of the 100th had landed and the exhausted crew members fell asleep on the earth under the wings of their damaged planes.[5]

In the end, the 100th suffered more than any other 8th Air Force unit during the Regensburg raid, losing nine of its twenty-one B-17s. This was an unsustainable casualty rate, and it is one of the reasons that the Anglo-American strategic air offensive of 1943 is almost universally seen as a failure. And yet, for all its heavy losses, this one raid on Regensburg destroyed far more aircraft than the Germans lost during the Battle of Kursk, perhaps more than they lost on the Eastern Front during all of the summer of 1943. From the point of view of the ultimate destruction of German power, the strategic air campaign was a necessary failure. By the end of 1943, German air and anti-air defenses had been drawn down from the land battlefields and were now focused on protecting Germany, and the stage was set for the German collapse of 1944.

The Combined Bomber Offensive: the war-winning failure

Arthur Harris and Ira Eaker were very different personalities, yet in 1943 they were jointly responsible for implementing the first serious attempt at the strategic destruction of an enemy's production by air power. All previous attempts had been either poorly conceived or provided with far too little equipment to be effective. Now, however, the Combined Bomber Offensive (CBO) of Britain and the United States had available large forces with a considered plan of action. Unfortunately for both Harris and Eaker, the reality still fell far short of the ideal. And this has provided the source of one of the constant, and partially deserved, criticisms of Anglo-American strategic bombing in 1943. A plan that was based on the destruction of German production seems a prima facie failure when that production continues to rise (with a few notable exceptions) throughout 1943 and into 1944 – and many historians have rightly pointed this out.[6] Even those historians who give a more even-handed appreciation of air power during the war tend to view strategic bombing in general as falling short, particularly the campaigns of 1943.[7]

Both men's faith in air power bordered on the religious. Harris, who had been in charge of Bomber Command since February 1942, was convinced that the systematic destruction of German cities by high-level, night-time area bombing, if given priority over all other campaigns, would produce victory quickly and with few Allied casualties. Publicly he liked to be seen as stern and unyielding, though in private he was volatile, emotional and full of disdain. (See Figure 33.) In December 1942, while making one of his regular complaints about the use of strategic bombers against U-boat-based targets, he argued, "Had the entire heavy aircraft resources of the United Nations been employed for the past year in a direct offensive against our enemies, the war would by now have been nearly over."[8] In private, Harris was just as confident. In an April 1943 letter to the British Air Attaché in Washington, DC, Air Commodore H. H. Thornton, Harris boasted that, if just left alone, he could win the war that year. "If things go as we hope and expect that they will, Bomber Command have every prospect of bringing the Germans to the verge of catastrophe by night bombing alone in the next six months."[9]

Eaker was just as convinced about the American plan to destroy specific industries during daylight "precision" bombing. On April 29, 1943, he made an official presentation to the JCS about the upcoming campaign which Leahy recorded in his diary:

> At two thirty p.m. General Eaker, USA, commanding American
> bombers in England made an interesting statement to the Joint
> Chiefs of Staff in which he said that with provision of an
> adequate number of bombers his force and the RAF can in the

33 Arthur "Bomber" Harris, commander in chief of Bomber Command from
1942 until the end of the war. This picture shows how Harris liked to be seen,
as hard and unyielding. However, he could also be emotional and petulant when
crossed.

next year so wreck the German war production as to make an
invasion of Europe not difficult.

He will need by the end of 1943, 2346 bombers, approximately
1000 fighter planes and an eventual American air personnel in
England of 376,000.[10]

The nature of his claims not only seemed grand to Leahy, they raised some profound questions for Marshall. The army chief wrote to Arnold the next day to see if the head of the USAAF was willing to support Eaker's dramatic statements "without qualification."[11] Arnold replied immediately with complete support. If anything, he believed that the commander of the 8th Air Force was being too cautious. "The targets proposed for destruction and continued neutralization have been well selected to produce the maximum depreciation of the German munition potential with the minimum bombing effort. The operational plan submitted for accomplishing this destruction is sound. The yardstick used is very conservative."[12] At the same time, Portal added his prestige to a full backing of the CBO. He not only wrote a formal letter which fully endorsed it, including American claims about precision bombing, he also sent a personal letter on the subject to Arnold.[13] He told the head of the USAAF that he had "carefully examined the plan and discussed it in all its aspects with the Commanding General 8th Air Force. I take this opportunity of saying that I believe it to be entirely sound and that it has my full support."[14]

Proponents of strategic air power had asked for a chance to win the war on their own – and their request was about to be met. The reason for such confidence was partly understandable, even if the depth of the confidence was too dramatic. In the previous six months, the first modern and sophisticated plan for a strategic bombing campaign had been constructed. Instead of relying on the vaguer notions of air power and inferior machinery that existed up until 1941, by this time in the war both the RAF and the USAAF knew what they wanted to do and believed they had the means to do it. (See Map 4.)

Harris' confidence began with the performance of the Lancaster bomber.[15] The Lancaster had become the British bomber of choice in 1942 and in Harris' mind was not only the best British strategic bombing weapon, but the best strategic bombing platform possessed by any country in the world.[16] By Harris' own calculations, each Lancaster was more than twice as effective as one Halifax and more than three times as effective as one Wellington.[17] This faith in the Lancaster persisted even when improved Halifax III bombers were introduced at the end of 1943. At this time, Harris suggested ending all Halifax production and retooling the factories to build Lancasters.[18]

In 1943 it seemed there would finally be enough Lancasters. In 1942 the weekly construction rate of this aircraft was 13.3.[19] Going into 1943, the plan was that this rate would almost triple to 33.3 per week, though even this was raised. Remarkably for a World War II construction plan, the number produced exceeded targets. Between January and September 1943, when it was planned to build 1,248 Lancasters, in the end 1,272 were actually constructed.[20]

The Lancaster was indeed a superb weapon to deliver large amounts of high explosive as part of a night-time bombing campaign. The amount that any bomber could deliver was directly related to the distance that had to be flown, so giving one figure to a bomb load is misleading. In the summer of 1943, however, Harris calculated that one Lancaster flying from Bomber Command bases in the UK could carry 12,800 lb of bombs to Cologne or 11,700 lb of bombs to Hamburg.[21] In his mind that made five or six Lancasters the equivalent of a Prince of Wales Class capital ship, the largest in the Royal Navy. Moreover, the Lancaster could fly at a much higher altitude with this bomb load than any other British bomber, capable of reaching 30,000 feet.[22] This not only afforded it greater protection (the Halifax could barely reach 20,000 feet), it allowed the Lancaster to make use of two important advances, one technical and one tactical. The former was Oboe, a directional beam that became operational in January 1943, which could place British bombers over their targets, and worked better at higher altitudes. The second was increased use of the highly trained and skilled pathfinder units which, in conjunction with Oboe, gave the RAF a good chance of directing a force of Lancasters over a city-sized target.[23]

The Lancaster did have some drawbacks that became more apparent as 1943 went on, in particular its vulnerability to German fighters. It was relatively slow and under-armed with protective machine guns, especially compared with its American counterparts. Attack from below a formation of Lancasters (they were not originally equipped with machine guns that could fire straight downwards) was one German tactic that could be particularly effective. Yet, large numbers of Lancasters, guided by pathfinder units and directed by Oboe, could now do what Harris was convinced would win the war.

What he wanted was concentration of large flights of bombers over a single target, which he believed could cripple cities and wear down Germany's war-making potential. In 1942 the British had moved more and more towards a bombing plan based around the destruction of German cities. In March 1942, Lord Cherwell, who had particular influence with the Prime Minister because he remained close to Churchill in the 1930s when the former was out of office, claimed that the systematic bombing of Germany's fifty-eight largest cities would be decisive. Cherwell, who was wrong more than right throughout the war, based his argument on a problematic reading of the impact of German bombing on British cities.[24] Still, his arguments had impact, particularly as they were followed not long after by the famous thousand-bomber raid over Cologne on May 30–31, 1942. This raid, which Harris believed had a "staggering" effect on the Germans, was in his mind responsible for almost eliminating the city from German war production for months with at least the partial destruction of 250 factories. "Briefly, half the inner City was wiped out. Cologne, the third greatest German city and capital of the Rheinland with over three-quarters of a million inhabitants received a wound from which even partial recovery was a matter of months. It would be useless to catalogue the devastation."[25]

With many more Lancasters, Cologne-type raids, or even larger, would be regular events in 1943. In fact, raids by four hundred Lancasters were capable of dropping as many bombs in fifteen minutes as were dropped on Cologne by a thousand aircraft in one and a half hours.[26] The only thing that could keep Harris from winning the war would be foolish dispersals to other theaters such as Coastal Command or the Mediterranean.

> ... given sufficient bomber force it would be possible in the next few months to raze substantially to the ground 30–40 of the principal German cities, and it is suggested that the effect upon German morale and German production of so doing would be fatal to them and decisive as encouragement and direct assistance to Russia.[27]

Harris' confidence in his methods was matched by those in the USAAF. In 1942 the impact of American bombers based in the UK was minimal. Diversions to the Pacific and North Africa kept the size of the 8th Air Force strictly limited, which severely restricted its operational usage.[28] However, beginning in 1943, the 8th Air Force was made the primary destination for American four-engine bombers. Like Harris with the Lancaster, leaders of the USAAF had great confidence in the B-17 and B-24, particularly the former, to deliver high explosives accurately on targets deep inside Germany. Instead of relying on night-time darkness for protection, the Americans relied on a large amount of defensive firepower, to be supplied by the bombers themselves. In this area the B-17 was unsurpassed. The B-17G, the best type of the war, had thirteen 50-caliber machine guns. Some of the smaller raids launched by the USAAF from the UK in 1942 had persuaded senior air force officers, including Eaker and Spaatz, that the aircraft could defend itself well against German fire.[29] Of rugged construction, the B-17 could also take a great deal of damage and keep flying. Like the Lancaster, it was also a very steady platform able to carry a heavy bomb load. Arnold had great faith in the aircraft, at one point arguing that twenty would have been enough to keep the Japanese out of Java in 1942.[30] The key for defending the B-17 was considered close formation flying in a defensive box. Together, eighteen to twenty-one bombers were considered an optimal number to provide combined defensive firepower which, it was hoped, would be able to protect the force from German fighters.[31]

The B-24 was actually a more modern design than the B-17, though, as it turned out, less suited for the daylight bombing of Germany. Possessing a longer range and with an ability to carry a heavier load than the B-17, the B-24 was suitable for many different operations. It was, as mentioned earlier, the ideal aircraft to provide long-range air patrol over the Atlantic, which made convoys almost invulnerable in 1943.[32] Yet the B-24 turned out to have two handicaps when compared with the B-17. First, it did not have the weight of defensive firepower of the B-17.[33] Also, its construction was not quite as sturdy and it was therefore more easily damaged by German firepower. (See Figure 34.) For that reason, even though large numbers of B-24s were used to bomb Germany (more were built during the war than B-17s), the B-17 became the preferred weapon of the 8th Air Force – in particular when later designs of the bomber increased both its range and its payload. From that point on, B-24s were usually sent to the Mediterranean first.

Like the Lancaster, the B-17 and B-24 in 1943 were set to start coming off the production line in numbers sufficient to launch a large strategic bombing campaign. Franklin Roosevelt's dramatic intervention in favor of aircraft construction in 1942 paid almost immediate dividends in the first quarter of 1943. In 1942, US four-engine bomber construction came in well below expectations, with 2,576 B-17s and

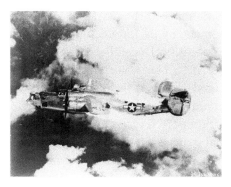

34 The B-24 had excellent range and could carry a heavy bomb load. However, it was not well defended and was vulnerable to German air and ground fire, particularly if caught unescorted. Here a B-24 attacking a target over Austria explodes into flames.

B-24s built during the entire year.[34] In the first quarter of 1943, however, their combined construction was 1,329. At that time the plan for the entire year was to build 4,456 B-17s and 5,928 B-24s for a massive total of 10,384.[35]

The great unanswered question about American bombers was whether, even with their greater defensive firepower, they could survive for long without fighter escort. In 1942 their ability to do this had not been realistically tested. Almost all American strategic bombing raids from the UK had occurred over France, Belgium or the Netherlands and included strong fighter support. These attacks, usually aimed at German U-boat facilities, did relatively little damage.[36] There were a few instances where B-17s were discovered by German fighters and acquitted themselves well, but they were much closer to their UK bases than they would be in 1943.[37]

In 1943 American strategy was based around the destruction of certain key German productive industries. There has been some historical discussion about just how different British and American ideas on strategic bombing really were.[38] Certainly both campaigns were aimed at damaging German production, and both assumed that German civilians would die as part of this process. However, that does not mean that they were the same – the differences might not be black and white, but they were strongly different shades of grey. For instance, there were certain Americans, such as Lovett, who favored direct attacks on German cities, while others, including Eaker, resisted.[39] The American campaign was, in many ways, the far more intellectually cogent of the two (far more than any of the works of Douhet, Mitchell or Trenchard). The key moment in its intellectual development had been Arnold's decision to appoint, in December 1942, the Committee of Operations Analysts (COA).[40] The non-military members of the committee were a sophisticated group of businessmen: Edward Earle, Fowler Hamilton, Thomas Lamont, Edward Mason, Elihu Root, Jr.

The committee, which reported its recommendations in March 1943, provided an intellectual structure to American bombing strategy. The USAAF had favored the notion of industry bombing since the 1930s, but in many ways had not advanced much beyond that in terms of actual priorities. The war plan drawn up under Arnold's supervision in response to Roosevelt's direct request in August 1942 was still based on having too many targets and assumed that too much could be destroyed far too easily.[41] That plan called for the destruction of a whopping 177 specific targets that were thought necessary for the shutting down of the German economy. These were made up of Germany's fighter and bomber airframe production (twenty-five targets), aircraft engine production (seventeen targets), submarine production (twenty targets), transportation system (primarily railway yards) (thirty-eight targets), power industry (thirty-seven targets), oil production and refinement (twenty-three targets), aluminum production (fourteen targets) and rubber industry (two targets). To achieve this incredibly ambitious plan, it was believed an operational bomber force of 1,512 B-17s and 720 medium bombers (B-25s and B-26s) was needed.

When the COA reported its findings in March 1943, a considerably more focused strategy was put forward, with an understanding that even this would take many more aircraft.[42] Instead of trying to wreak havoc across the entire German war economy, they argued for the destruction of a few key industries. For instance, instead of attacking all German aircraft manufacture, the COA targeted single-engine fighter production. Within this, they argued that rather than attacking all parts of the process, it was better to focus on twelve targets where German fighter aircraft went through their final assembly process.[43] The target lists for other industries were slashed (or in some cases completely removed). German oil industry targets were narrowed down to thirteen hydrogenation plants (plants that created fuel oil from coal) and the Ploesti facilities in Romania.[44] Overall, compared with the 177 targets that were mentioned in the September 1942 plan, the COA listed only 66 major sites to be destroyed.[45]

Perhaps the COA's most famous, and controversial, industrial target, which heretofore had rarely been mentioned in USAAF war plans, was the German anti-friction bearing (ball-bearing) industry.[46] Ball-bearings appealed to the COA for a number of reasons. They were indispensable elements for all modern war equipment (aircraft, submarines, tanks, artillery). Most importantly, however, most of Germany's ball-bearing production was concentrated in the vicinity of the town of Schweinfurt. By the COA's estimation, at least 40 percent of all ball-bearing production within Germany and German-occupied Europe was in three facilities around this town. The actual figure was even larger, with the three Schweinfurt plants in August 1943 accounting for 57 percent of German manufacturing capacity in anti-friction bearings, and when it came to ball-bearings of the crucial size of between 8 and 150 mm, they produced 95 percent.[47] Destroying them and a handful of other targets, it was hoped, would send shock-waves throughout all Germany's munitions production.

> Destruction of the ball bearing plants would have a pervasive effect on the Western Axis [Germany] war effort in view of the fact that all the high speed moving parts are dependent upon ball bearings for their operation. This effect cannot be timed with accuracy but it is believed that it would begin to be felt within a month and that, thereafter, the situation would become progressively acute.[48]

The COA's report provided the intellectual ammunition for Eaker's presentation that April. Certainly, its conclusions remain controversial – and the COA made their share of mistakes. Their downgrading of transportation attacks and their focus on aircraft assembly as opposed to engine production are two choices that now seem less than prescient. However, in understanding the more limited number of targets that could possibly be attacked, they provided the first realistic plan for the use of American strategic air power. Eaker's problem was that he took this plan and guaranteed that it could be implemented – and this was a completely different issue.

British reaction to the COA report was mostly positive, with one important doubt. The Ministry of Economic Warfare reported back to Portal that they agreed with the COA that the highest priority industries for destruction should be fighter aircraft and engines, ball-bearings and petroleum products.[49] However, Portal, who also supported most of the COA's findings, was still wary about implementing the plan. To him, the targets might be right, but the ability to destroy them using unescorted bombers remained questionable. He made a pointed comment about this when he first reported on the plan drawn up by Arnold in September 1942 – a plan that Portal also believed was right conceptually, but lacking in realism. "I have seen this plan and – while in some respects academic and unduly optimistic – it is a very impressive bit of work and, always assuming it *is* possible to bomb Germany by day, I believe it is a war winner."[50]

And so, by the spring of 1943, the British and American air forces had come up with the first coordinated plan for strategic bombing in history. Their combined vision was released in the Combined Bomber Offensive (CBO), which in May 1943 was officially approved by the Combined Chiefs of Staff during Trident.[51] The CBO listed six German industrial systems as having high priority for destruction, representing combined British and American evaluations of what needed to be attacked: submarine construction yards and bases, the aircraft industry, ball-bearings, oil, synthetic rubber and tires, and military transport vehicles – with a combined target list of seventy-six. It did, however, lay down another specific target that needed to be removed before these could realistically be destroyed, and that was Germany's fighter aircraft strength – which it singled out as the first priority. It was known that the Luftwaffe was beginning to deploy more fighters to defend the skies over the Reich and this force had to be neutralized, either through destruction in the production phase or through relentless combat, before the CBO could really come into force. "If the growth of the German fighter strength is not arrested quickly, it may become literally impossible to carry out the destruction planned and thus create the conditions necessary for the ultimate decisive action by our combined forces on the Continent."[52] This notion of making Germany's fighter aircraft the number one priority was actually further developed a few weeks later when the Pointblank directive was released.

For almost all major Anglo-American air commanders (with the crucial exception of Harris), Pointblank became the key test of the CBO's progress for the rest of 1943. Harris' exception did matter, of course. All the activity that underlay the COA, CBO and Pointblank barely altered his strategic vision of bombing. He continued to do what he had been planning to do since 1942, relentlessly level German cities, kill Germans of all kinds and break the survivors' will to resist. His skepticism about the CBO was born of his overconfidence in his own ideas and his doubts about the survivability of the American bombers in daylight raids as well as the intellectual pretension that the destruction of one or two specific industries would somehow cripple the German economy in total (he called such focused plans "panacea" targets).

When the CBO was first agreed, Harris was already heavily involved in the process of bombing German industrial towns in the Ruhr.[53] However, in late July 1943, he was able to launch a series of the kind of concentrated and seemingly destructive raids that he believed would prove the success of his notions beyond a reasonable doubt – the raids on Hamburg. Hamburg was a perfect target for Harris. Germany's second largest city, it was an industrial hub which played a particularly important role in U-boat construction. Also it was close to the sea, so British bombers would not have to fly over hundreds of miles of German-controlled territory to reach their target. On July 24, Harris opened the assault, which he termed the Battle of Hamburg, in which he sent 791 bombers against the city, bombers which not only were directed by Oboe but were aided significantly by the development of Window, the dropping of large quantities of aluminum strips which caused chaos in the German radar system.[54] Over the following eight nights, five more large raids were launched against Hamburg, culminating in a 740-bomber raid on August 2, which led to apocalyptic devastation.[55] In the end much of Hamburg collapsed into a sea of rubble and up to 50,000 people died, many caught in a vortex of flames that turned their bodies to ashes.[56] (See Figure 35.)

The immediate reaction to the raids seemed to vindicate Harris. The Germans were stunned. Albert Speer told Hitler in August 1943 that "six more attacks as successful as the attack on Hamburg would bring armament production to a standstill."[57] Later, when trying to reassure the Japanese ambassador in Berlin about Germany's future, he admitted that his immediate reaction to the bombing of Hamburg had been exceedingly pessimistic.[58] Harris could point to a number of supposed successes. Photo reconnaissance of the devastation led him to claim that 6,200 acres of Hamburg had been destroyed – a figure that he was soon comparing with the 600 acres of London or the 135 acres of Coventry that the Luftwaffe had leveled during the course

35 A charred German corpse after the firebombing of Hamburg in 1943. The RAF's raids against Hamburg caused short-term panic in the Nazi state; however, production recovered surprisingly quickly, even after tens of thousands died.

of the war.[59] Moreover, RAF losses during the Hamburg raids had been low. A total of 3,095 sorties were launched as part of the operation, but only eighty-six bombers (a 2.8 percent loss rate) were shot down.[60] It did seem that an important, if horrible, new phase in the air war had begun.

The 8th Air Force took longer to be able to fully launch the kinds of raids that it believed were central to the CBO. On June 22, 1943, it launched what could be termed the first raid against a real target of German production, the synthetic rubber plant in Huls, which alone supplied almost one-third of Germany's rubber needs.[61] This small raid seemed to provide vindication of the American conception of bombing. Not only was the accuracy of the bombing high, the plant was shut down for a month after the operation. In August, however, a more ambitious operation was undertaken: the first attacks on German ball-bearing production at Schweinfurt and ME-109 production in Regensburg.[62] This time the attacks, particularly at Regensburg, were thought to have caused great industrial damage, but came at a sobering cost, as both towns were beyond Allied fighter escort range at the time (see Map 4).[63] At Schweinfurt, about 50 percent of the ball-bearing manufacturing equipment was damaged and production in September was only 40 percent of pre-raid levels.[64] However, the 8th Air Force lost thirty-six B-17s attacking Regensburg and another twenty-four attacking Schweinfurt, the combined total of which represented 16 percent of the 376 bombers sent out on the operation.[65] These losses were so high that the Americans would not attempt so ambitious a raid again deep into Germany for two more months.

When they did return, the results were much the same, though on a grander scale. Beginning in the second week of October, the 8th Air Force launched a number of raids deep into Germany, not only returning to Schweinfurt, but attacking FW-190 production at a series of facilities in eastern Germany. There were some extremely important successes. In particular, one factory, the FW-190 assembly plant at Marienburg, was entirely destroyed. Portal was particularly impressed and wrote to Churchill:

> This is about the best high altitude bombing we have seen in this war. You asked yesterday whether they could put their bombs into the area of St. James Park. As a matter of interest, I have attached to the photograph a tracing of St. James Park on the same scale from which you will see that almost all the bombs would have gone into the area.
> Only one building of the factory is not destroyed, and that one is damaged. It was a magnificent attack.[66]

The attacks on Schweinfurt were not as immediately damaging in October as those in August. But they continued to limit ball-bearing manufacture at these plants to 45 percent of the pre-August attack level.[67] However, if these raids caused some real damage to German production, they did so at a terrible cost. The Schweinfurt raid was particularly devastating. Of the 291 B-17s sent out to attack Schweinfurt that October, only 228 reached the target because of weather and the fog of war.[68] At the end of the day, 60 had been shot down and a further 17 so badly damaged that they could not be effectively repaired, a loss rate of 26 percent. To show just how much firepower the attacking force had been subjected to, another 121 of the B-17s were hit in different ways, though they could still limp home. German fighters showed a strong ability to find the weak-spots in B-17 and B-24 defensive firepower. They had discovered that both American bombers had blind-spots firing forward, so a fighter coming straight at a bomber (a very tricky maneuver) was much safer than one attacking from the side or above.[69]

Such a loss rate was politically unacceptable in a western democracy, and was far higher than the proponents of strategic bombing had led people to believe would occur. Eaker had earlier talked about loss rates of no more than 4 percent during his raids.[70]

Almost immediately after the Schweinfurt raid, Arnold came in for such fierce criticism that he was worried it would have damaging political repercussions. RAF representatives in Washington, DC reported to Portal on October 19 that Arnold was "having a very difficult time at present. Next year's presidential election affords the opportunity to certain sections of the press and public to attack anyone in office and anything they do. The Eighth Air Force casualties are the excuse to shoot at Arnold. As an example the loss of 60 Heavy Bombers in the Schweinfurt Raid was given great prominence in the press ..."[71]

What these American raids demonstrated more than anything was that, for all its defensive firepower, the unescorted B-17 was too vulnerable to German fighter planes. Eaker, who had earlier spoken of the ability of the B-17 to protect itself, now blamed the Schweinfurt and Regensburg losses squarely on the lack of long-range fighter escort.[72] The best American fighter of the time, the P-47 Thunderbolt, with its enormous (and therefore fuel-guzzling) engine, could not, even with drop tanks, escort bombers deep into Germany.[73] During the Schweinfurt raid, the furthest the P-47 with drop tanks could reach was Aachen, 240 miles from the English Channel.[74] From that point on, the B-17s were on their own, and the Luftwaffe was able to attack them in force during the additional 150 miles to Schweinfurt (and then, even more damaging, the hundreds of miles they traveled back without escort). The range of the P-38 Lightning, the famous two-engine fighter that was not considered quite as good against the FW-190s or ME-109G as the P-47, could be extended a little further, but even then it could not stay with the bombers until they reached the target.[75]

Until the United States had access to a fighter that could stay with the bombers for the entire mission, its philosophy of bombing was never going to succeed. For what 1943 showed is that one raid on a target, even a successful one, was not enough to comprehensively damage a production system. What was needed was a number of continuous, high-intensity raids to continually batter a productive target into submission. Had that been possible at Schweinfurt, particularly after the August raid, it could have had a very damaging impact on German production. However, for the British and Americans at least, the losses suffered were so great as to make it too damaging to return quickly, and the opportunity was lost.

In 1944, however, the appearance of the famous P-51 Mustang with its great range would change the situation and allow for a fuller implementation of the policy. Until the Mustang was available in sufficient numbers, however, American planning would have to change drastically. Arnold made that perfectly clear in a November 1 memorandum for the JCS calling for a revision of the air plan to defeat Germany.[76] Instead of focusing on a range of productive targets, Arnold believed that American (and British) air power in Europe should have one priority – destroying Luftwaffe aircraft. This could be done through direct combat, or through raids on aircraft production, but until it happened, no other targeting system could have higher priority.

If American confidence in the ability of air power to decisively damage Germany at this time had been subverted, this was certainly not the case for Harris. In November 1943, as the United States was ending all deep penetration raids into Germany, he was starting a new and ambitious air campaign that once again he argued would bring Germany to its knees. This was his attempt to wipe Berlin from the map, and it would be the focus of Bomber Command operations from November 1943 to March 1944.[77] Harris cockily claimed that the attacks would cost the Allies 400–500 aircraft, but in return it "will cost Germany the war."[78]

Harris also stated publicly that the Berlin attacks would go on "until the heart of Nazi Germany ceases to beat."[79] It was one of the first public statements that British bombing was directed against German society, including civilians, and it caused some disquiet in British circles. The large-scale bombing of Berlin was something that Harris had been dreaming about since early 1942. In late 1943, however, he now possessed the kind of force that could implement these dreams, almost entirely without any cooperation with the 8th Air Force. The long nights of late fall and winter also promised to give British bombers greater protection and time to reach their target and return safely.[80] And so British bombers, primarily Lancasters, were sent on the extremely long journey to Berlin and back during thirty-five major missions involving 20,244 sorties, in what Harris called "The Battle of Berlin".

Berlin was the ideal target for Harris. It was the capital and largest city in the Reich, which for morale purposes would have made its destruction more important than any other target. Moreover, it was an area where a great deal of manufacturing capacity had been concentrated during the war, as its greater distance from the UK meant that it was much safer from air attack than the Ruhr or northwest Germany. Many different elements of German aircraft construction were concentrated around the city, so Harris could argue he was directly targeting the Luftwaffe, making the Battle of Berlin a major part of Pointblank.[81]

However, Harris was also exposing his bombers to greater risk than ever before. The German night-fighter force had many more miles in which to attack unescorted bombers. They could attack them both on their way to the target and on their way back to base. Moreover, Berlin was now ringed by German flak batteries, along with some of the strongest and costliest concrete towers in the world, which became a major construction priority in 1943. The more the Lancasters returned to the same target, the more the Germans were ready for them. The result was massive losses. Harris had talked about losing 400–500 planes when the campaign started. However, by the end of March 1944, 1,047 bombers had been shot down and a further 1,682 had been damaged.[82]

The loss rates also meant that it was more likely than not that a British bomb crew would be shot down while on active duty. In 1943 the normal Bomber Command crew expectation was thirty missions for active service, and this could be defined to mean even more.[83] During the Battle of Berlin, which was divided into three different series of operations, the loss rates per raid were 4.7 per mission, 4.1 per mission and then 5.2 per mission.[84] This was by far the longest period of high loss rates for Bomber Command during the war.[85] Having to do thirty missions with an average loss rate of 4.6 percent per mission are odds with which only Japanese soldiers defending cut-off islands could really empathize. It was no wonder that by April Harris stopped sending his bombers back to Berlin.

Before leaving the CBO, a mention should be made of the strategic bombing campaign from the Mediterranean in 1943. Once the Luftwaffe was significantly reduced in the Mediterranean theater, those aircraft that remained were actually mostly concerned with fighting the bombers. The growth of a large bombing force in the Mediterranean was not without its critics. Both Harris and Eaker (before the latter was sent there) complained loudly that too many four-engine bombers were being diverted from the UK for what they considered to be a secondary theater of operations. Numerically they had a point. Though the 15th Air Force was not formally created until November 1943, significant strategic bombing raids had been launched from the region from August onwards. On June 12, 1943, when there were 879 four-engine American bombers in the United Kingdom, there were 270 in North Africa.[86] However, once bases became available in Sicily, and then crucially southern Italy, there was a very large build-up of forces. On November 1, 1943, when the 15th Air Force came into being, there were 939 four-engine bombers attached to it.[87]

This was an almost entirely American-driven affair, which goes a certain way towards undermining Churchill's notion that he saw the Mediterranean as a theater from which to seriously damage German power. Indeed, he fought against the deployment of American strategic bombers in this area just as their numbers were being increased. This build-up seemed to be driven by both technological concerns and strategic ideas. On the one hand, the Mediterranean was considered a much more suitable environment for the B-24, which had already been shown to be less rugged than the B-17. Of the 939 large bombers on hand, 739 were B-24s. Moreover, the monthly allocation to the 15th Air Force from that time onwards was to be 171 B-24s and 60 B-17s. Arnold believed that American bases in the UK were practically at full capacity as it was, and therefore separating out the B-24s in this way was only logical.

Beyond the question of aircraft suitability, the American air force did see the Mediterranean as a theater with a few prime strategic bombing targets that would be well suited for "precision" bombing. Unlike the British, who paid lip-service to the notion of large strategic bombing raids in the region, Arnold and Spaatz both believed that there were a few choice targets that could be attacked from bases in southern Italy. In particular, they focused on German aircraft manufacture in southern Germany and Romanian oil production.[88] Also, they saw the build-up of a large Mediterranean bombing force as a useful means of drawing German fighters, which were exacting such a toll on American aircraft flying from the UK, away from the Reich.

That there were some targets that could cause Germany real productive problems was clear from the relatively small number of raids that were launched from the Mediterranean in 1943. There was the attack on August 12, by sixty-one B-24s flying from North Africa against the Messerschmitt plant at Wiener Neustadt in present-day Austria, one of the five largest aircraft construction facilities under German control.[89] Along with the attacks launched on Regensburg by the 8th Air Force, this Wiener Neustadt raid was one of the most damaging to Messerschmitt production in 1943.[90] However, the raid benefited greatly from the element of surprise, as there were at that time no German fighters prepared to repel strategic bombing raids on Germany launched from North Africa. In response, a new German fighter command, "Ostmark," was established near Vienna.

The second attack of some note occurred on August 1, 1943, when 177 B-24s were sent to bomb the Ploesti oil facilities near Bucharest in Romania, which supplied 60 percent of Germany's crude oil supplies. The high value of the target meant that even though no raid had been attempted before, the attacking force came under serious German resistance. In the end, fifty-four aircraft were lost, forty-one due to German action, which was a crippling loss rate of 30 percent.[91] The results of the raid had actually been impressive and showed the value of such a target, with 42 percent of Ploesti's refining capacity put out of action.[92] For Speer, the attack came as another shock, and once again he feared for the future of German production.[93] However, as with the Hamburg raids, he was surprised by how quickly production could be restored. In this case the real problem for the Germans was that the Romanians seemed reluctant to repair the works, as they didn't want to have them targeted again.

So the experience of strategic bombing from the Mediterranean reinforced the lessons learned from the UK. Destroying a facility like Ploesti required repeated bombardment, and this was not going to happen because of the high loss rate. Indeed, no further attempt was made to bomb Ploesti until the spring of 1944. Like the strategic bombing of Germany itself, 1943 showed what needed to be done to damage the German economy, but it also showed there was one major hurdle that needed to be surmounted before that damage could be made devastating.

The German reaction: the dominance of the air war

The general indices of German munitions production more than doubled between July 1942 and July 1944. Between January 1943 and January 1944, overall munitions production went up by approximately one-third. (See Figure 36.)[94] According to both the British and American air power supporters, this should not have

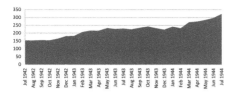

36 German finished munitions output, July 1942–July 1944.
Source: USSBS, European Report 1, Appendix Table 100.

happened, particularly once the CBO began in earnest in the summer of
1943. Those with the greatest knowledge of the German war economy
were certainly very worried when the bombs started to drop. The first
raids on ball-bearing production came as a shock, according to Speer.

> The first time you bombed a bottleneck with considerable energy
> was when you attacked Schweinfurt in your first big daylight
> attack. This was the first time that in my opinion we were brought
> into extraordinary danger. I have to include here a criticism
> inasmuch as the further attacks were not carried out with necessary
> energy. Had you repeated your attack within a short time,
> reconstruction and dispersal would have been impossible and we
> might have been unable to continue armaments after three or four
> months."[95]

Instead of being a permanently crippling attack, however, the Schweinfurt ball-bearings raids showed the difficulty of winning the war
through direct attacks on production installations. As Speer pointed
out, and the lessons of the war would reinforce regularly, a few raids
were generally not sufficient to fully destroy a factory. Simply destroying buildings, for instance, did not destroy production. Heavier
machine tools often survived bombing even if the buildings in which
they were housed were hit. This seemed to be a particular problem after
American raids, as American bombs were less powerful than their
British counterparts.[96] Surviving machine tools could be used to restart
production quite quickly. The Germans, and Japanese, were also able
to make use of alternative products or different techniques to keep
production going while the recovery of a factory was taking place.
The Germans discovered after the Schweinfurt raids that they could
make do with considerably fewer ball-bearings in each piece of equipment. In the case of aircraft, they calculated that they could make do

with only 40–50 percent as many ball-bearings per plane as they were using before the Schweinfurt raids. They were thus able to make their stockpile of bearings last considerably longer than anticipated. Also, partly because of the issue of the surviving machine tools mentioned above, construction could be dispersed to a new location and restarted with great speed (if less efficiently than before).

Of all the reasons, however, maybe the most important was that human beings held up better under bombardment than expected and were able to restart production far more quickly than anticipated. This really hit home to Speer after the bombing of Hamburg – which at first seemed to him to herald the end of the war. He was amazed and surprised when he saw the speed with which Hamburg industry recovered from the attacks.[97] Moreover, the Schweinfurt raids also highlighted a real problem in American and British coordination. The CBO stated that wherever possible Bomber Command and the 8th Air Force should cooperate to hit the same area so as to maximize destruction. This was something that the Germans expected – but it rarely happened. Instead, Harris and Eaker chose their own targets and went after them almost entirely independently. The 8th Air Force made little effort to support the attacks on Hamburg and Harris did everything possible to avoid supporting the Schweinfurt raids. To the Germans this seemed a major mistake.

The inability of either American or British strategic bombing to cause the type of production collapse they called for was compounded by what can only be termed poor intelligence of the German economy. Going into the CBO, Portal admitted that the Allies had a flimsy notion of how German production would actually be affected by bombing.

> The subject which causes particular difficulty is enemy war production. Intelligence work under three severe handicaps:
>
> (a) We do not know the programme for the output of the different types of weapons and so are unable to estimate the reduction caused by bombing.
> (b) Even when a spectacular success is achieved like the bombing of Vegesack or Renault or Krupps, it is difficult to make a reasonable estimate of the effect on output and information about the rate of repair is very scanty...

(c) Industrial output is affected not only by bombing but by other factors such as the shortage of manpower, raw materials and so on, and it is not possible to disentangle the results of one from the results of the other.[98]

When intelligence reports were eventually produced as the CBO developed, these handicaps worked to create a significant overestimation of the impact of strategic bombing on German war production. In November 1943, the Joint Intelligence Committee (JIC) produced its most detailed study so far.[99] While many of the specific observations were measured and sensible, the overall estimate of the impact of bombing was far too optimistic. It claimed that German production at the end of September 1943 was 10–15 percent lower than it had been at the beginning of the year.[100] The reality was that German production in September 1943 was almost 30 percent higher than in January. The March 1944 report was equally over-optimistic. While it stated that bombing since November had not caused a collapse in German production, it still argued that there had been no improvement.

> Although the rate of decline in Germany's overall industrial production registered during the previous quarter was not maintained, the normal winter recovery in production was for the first time prevented. The hardships of everyday life in Germany were further aggravated, and the capacity of the German people to support Germany's war effort was further weakened. Despite every effort that the German leaders are making, there are no signs of their being able to arrest the decline in the productivity of labour.[101]

When this was being written, German munitions production was in fact 50 percent larger than January 1943.

And yet, while the CBO was definitely a failure if judged by both its proponents' bombast and the assumed effects it was having at the time, it can still be seen as the most important development in 1943 anywhere in the war in Europe. While it did not destroy Germany's ability to produce, fighting against it became the focus of the most important sections of the German economy, and at the same time it was probably responsible for destroying more finished German production then were the land battles, which are usually seen as the arenas in which German power was defeated.

It was in 1943 that the Luftwaffe's real priority was determined for the rest of the war. The German air force went into the year with three major areas of deployment: the Eastern Front, the Mediterranean and the air over Germany itself. These forces were fighting quite distinct battles and for the first eight months of the year there was a significant deployment to each. On the Eastern Front, at the beginning of 1943, the Luftwaffe was primarily concerned with supplying the 6th Army at Stalingrad. After its surrender, a large force made up of one-quarter fighters and three-quarters ground-attack or transport aircraft was built up to support the Citadel (Kursk) Offensive in July. In the Mediterranean, a force that was about equally split between fighters and bombers was maintained, first to try to protect German troops in North Africa, and later to try to halt the invasion of Sicily. In the Reich and on the Western Front, there was a force that was overwhelmingly composed of fighters, which was deployed primarily to fight against Anglo-American strategic bombing. (See Figure 37.)[102]

However, the summer of 1943 was the last moment when the Luftwaffe dispersed itself so equally. Confronted with Russian successes on the Eastern Front, an invasion of Sicily and Italy, and a Combined Bomber Offensive against German cities and industry, a decision was made that the last was by far the greatest threat to German power. It began a decisive shift in deployment towards fighting American and British strategic bombing.[103] By December 30, 1943, 54 percent of all aircraft were in Germany or on the Western Front, and

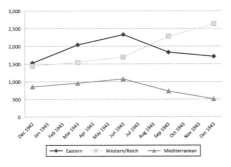

37 Luftwaffe aircraft deployment by front, December 1942–December 1943.
Source: Air 40-1207.

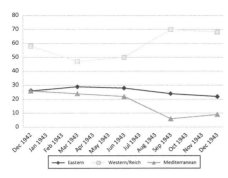

38 Luftwaffe fighter deployment (all types), December 1942–December 1943 (percent).

when it came to fighters, the figure was almost 70 percent. Adolf Galland, probably Germany's most famous fighter ace during the war and from 1941 also overall commander of its fighter forces, admitted that by the end of 1943, the Luftwaffe had only eleven weak fighter *Gruppen* on the entire Eastern Front.[104] (See Figure 38.)

The prioritizing of fighter deployment to defend the Reich is crucial. First, starting in 1943, there was a decisive shift that would see German fighter production become the focus of much of the war economy.[105] During 1943 as a whole, the Germans built 9,626 single-engine and 2,112 twin-engine fighters, while total bomber construction was 8,589. This ratio of 1.36 fighters built to every bomber was a marked shift from 1942, when the Germans built 5,213 fighters and 6,569 bombers, a ratio of 1.26 bombers for every fighter.[106] In 1944 bomber production would all but cease. Secondly, this stripping of fighter cover from the battlefields would prove devastating in 1944. German troops in the field were left without any force capable of holding air superiority over their lines. On the Eastern Front, the Germans left a force that was geared towards ground attack, often containing older aircraft such as HE-111s and JU-87s. There were so few fighters relatively speaking that when the Soviets sent a far larger air force to attack German positions, there was no way to resist them.

In that sense, German strategy for the land war was dictated by what was happening in the skies over the Reich. The army would have to get by with modest air support for the rest of the war while home defense became the overriding focus of German production. There was an assumption that the armies in the field could not receive first call on production until the skies over Germany had been secured.

Aircraft deployment tells only part of this shift in the war. The number of aircraft lost fighting against Anglo-American strategic bombing was much higher than in any other theater. When combined with Luftwaffe losses over the Mediterranean, the air war against the British and Americans became the single greatest equipment drain on German production. Although the Russians had improved the effectiveness of the Red Air Force since 1941, it was still not a force that was qualitatively up to German, British or American standards. In 1943, this meant that from January through November, 69 percent of German aircraft lost in combat were fighting the British and Americans and 31 percent were on the Eastern Front.[107] By the second half of 1943, the gap between deployment percentages and loss percentages for the Luftwaffe was even larger. (See Table 29.)

It is particularly interesting to note how comparatively dangerous it was for the Germans to fly in the Mediterranean. These extreme losses happened when a large number of Luftwaffe units, including many of Galland's best fighter groups, were switched to the Mediterranean to fight against the Anglo-American landings on Sicily which began on July 9, 1943.[108] The 711 German aircraft lost in July 1943 in the Mediterranean comprised the single highest monthly loss suffered by the Luftwaffe in any theater during the year. In comparison, 558 aircraft were lost on the Eastern Front during July 1943 when the Kursk Offensives were at their most intense. The danger for the Luftwaffe in fighting in the Mediterranean, coupled with the overriding need to protect the skies over German production, was so severe that it signalled a great withdrawal of the Luftwaffe from the Italian battlefield and a rapid decline in the percentage deployed in the Mediterranean.[109] Anglo-American air dominance was considered too dangerous to challenge, and the majority of fighters sent to the

Table 29 *Germany: aircraft average deployment and total losses by front, July–November 1943*

	Deployed	Percent	Lost	Percent
Eastern Front	1,957	40	1,841	28
Mediterranean	771	16	2,000	30
Defense of Reich	2,201	44	2,732	42

Note: The deployment figures are an average of the deployment numbers for June 30, September 30 and December 31, 1943.

Mediterranean region were concerned with protecting the Romanian oilfields from strategic bombing attacks.

The great concentration of German air power in the Reich from the late summer of 1943 meant that the air war over Germany was fought with a much greater intensity than that over the battlefields. The Luftwaffe often opposed Anglo-American bomber raids with mass formations. As early as August 1943, during the first American daylight raid on Regensburg, more than three hundred German fighters were scrambled to intercept.[110] When the 8th Air Force sent 228 bombers against Schweinfurt in October, 340 Luftwaffe aircraft were sent up to meet them.[111] By December 1943, single raids could be met by up to 500 fighters, more than there were in the entire Mediterranean or approximately as many as were stationed on the entire Eastern Front.[112]

So, looking at the air war solely from a battlefield perspective, 1943 witnessed a dramatic shift as the Luftwaffe, quantitatively and qualitatively, was basically drawn down from the land war and deployed against the CBO. And the high losses incurred by them in fighting the CBO were responsible for neutering the value of the great increases in German production. In 1943 the Germans built 20,330 fighters and bombers of all types, almost double the 11,782 built in 1942. However, the force that the Luftwaffe was able to deploy during the course of the year was remarkably static.[113] In fact, overall deployment peaked in June 1943 when the Luftwaffe had 5,097 aircraft deployed on the different fronts. By December 1943, this figure had actually been reduced to 4,849.

However, just looking at the air battles on the different fronts tells but part of the story. When one adds pre-production, production and deployment losses to the story, the strategic bombing campaign's crucial role in the destruction of German power becomes clearer, even in 1943. For instance, in 1943 German aircraft deployment and non-operational losses began to grow considerably. One of the key factors in this was inadequate pilot training. A combination of a lack of fuel and the need for ever more pilots meant that training hours were reduced, sometimes unofficially, in 1943.[114]

Up until 1942, German pilot and non-operational aircraft losses were manageable. However, in late 1943 and early 1944 losses resulting from poor pilot training grew significantly. According to Galland, a German fighter pilot had a 5 percent chance of being killed or wounded badly per month in 1942. By 1944, this had reached 30 percent per month, with the great acceleration being in the second half of 1943.

> Q. When did the quality of the fighter pilots start to grow worse?
> A. When our losses increased to such an extent that insufficient experienced pilots had to be trained on the front. This curtailed training was only tolerable when the losses on the front were so small that the pilots could gain experience there. However if they were shot down prior to that, and that was the case starting the middle of 1943, where our fighters experienced such great losses that these pilots did not gain any experience...[115]

For Galland this decline in training standards was particularly ominous, as the new German pilots had to confront Anglo-American aircraft being flown by pilots who had received detailed and superb training. In the second half of 1943, British and American pilots generally received twice as many hours of real flight training as their German counterparts.[116] (See Figure 39.) According to Galland, "In 1943, insufficient training of our fighter pilots in the West became obvious, and also in the defense of the Reich, as a matter of fact, it became obvious when the American fighters entered the picture."[117]

The poor training was particularly problematic when the new pilots were asked to fly in bad weather and had to rely on their instruments.[118] German fighter pilots, who had to climb to meet the Anglo-American bomber streams, often had to fly through difficult

39 USAAF enlisted men doing bomb-spotting training, Roswell Army Flying School, Roswell, New Mexico. By 1943 there was a growing divergence between excellent British and American air force training and that of Germany and Japan.

meteorological conditions to reach the planes that were cruising above in clearer skies, and they suffered accordingly.[119] Overall accident rates, which the Luftwaffe believed were acceptable earlier in the war, accelerated greatly at the end of 1943 – almost entirely due to the rushed pilot training and poorer quality pilots that had to be produced because of the increased losses.[120]

The view from German industry was similar. The chief technical director of the Focke-Wulf Company believed that shortcomings in 1943 pilot training caused very large non-combat losses by the beginning of 1944.

> In February 1944, at the time of the decision to launch a vast fighter aircraft expansion program Goering expressed great concern about obtaining the necessary personnel to go with it. Lack of pilots was a great handicap. Not only were pilots lacking in numbers, but the state of their training deteriorated constantly. A situation was reached where the training schedule was reduced to 40 hours. The direct result was an aircraft wastage rate of 25 percent, caused by pilot error.[121]

Statistically, something quite significant did occur in German aircraft and personnel losses, particularly in the second half of 1943, which further supports this point. Luftwaffe pilots trained after the CBO began experienced a much higher rate of non-operational aircraft losses than earlier in the war. Between 1939 and 1941, the Luftwaffe lost 2,066 aircraft of all types while on non-operational duties and had an additional 2,453 damaged.[122] These figures include losses in training, but do not include training aircraft, as their loss would damage the Luftwaffe's strength indirectly. In 1942 the loss rate was higher, but considering the general increase in Luftwaffe production, it was not completely unexpected. In 1942, 1,655 aircraft were lost on all non-operational duties and another 2,152 were damaged. In 1943, however, the rate of non-operational losses soared, 2,988 aircraft being lost and 4,215 damaged. This rate was almost twice the earlier one. (See Figures 40 and 41.) Moreover, there was a significant acceleration of these losses in the second half of 1943, when the need to produce more fighter pilots to combat the CBO first became a high priority. It was also a time when Luftwaffe production was not increasing because of the first successes of the

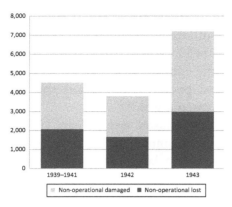

40 German aircraft lost and damaged on non-operational duties, 1939–43.
Source: Spaatz MSS, 116. GAF Aircraft and Aircrew Losses, September 1939 to January 1945.

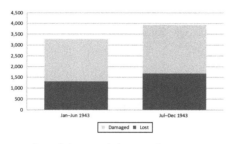

41 German aircraft lost and damaged on non-operational duties, 1943, in six-month intervals.
Source: Spaatz MSS, 116. GAF Aircraft and Aircrew Losses, September 1939 to January 1945.

CBO, which makes the acceleration that much more indicative of a problem in pilot training.

In the end, the wastage meant that between one-quarter and one-half of the increase in 1943 aircraft construction was lost or damaged in non-operational actions. These were planes that had actually been built. At the same time, the CBO also played a major role, through pre-production losses, in significantly reducing German aircraft numbers and in affecting patterns of production in other areas after July 1943. This has sometimes been forgotten because of the fact that production did rise significantly in 1943 as a whole. However, this rise, impressive as it was, was actually considerably lessened because of

Anglo-American strategic bombing. Field Marshal Milch, who was in charge of German aircraft production until March 1944, calculated that output in the second half of 1943 was cut by 25 percent because of American raids on different German aircraft facilities.[123] He stated that German fighter output was expected to have reached 2,000 units a month by the end of 1943, but was kept to approximately 1,000 by the raids on German airframe production. It was the best example in 1943 of a significant amount of German equipment being destroyed before it reached the field of battle.

> During June/July [1943], however, the heavy raids – mainly
> American, but also English – started, which had as their chief
> target the air-frame industry. As a result we were not able to
> produce more than those 1000 fighters a month from August
> 1943 until February 1944. The additional number which we would
> have produced was destroyed. According to the programme, by
> January 1944 we should have reached the figure of 2000 fighters
> a month ...[124]

The view from within the German fighter aircraft industry supports Milch's outlook. The August attacks on ME-109 production at Regensburg destroyed more aircraft than an entire average month's losses on either the Mediterranean or the Eastern Front. Messerschmitt claimed that they "only" suffered a 30–40 percent loss of production for one month.[125] This would have been equal to at least three hundred aircraft.[126] Furthermore, he claimed that the dispersal plan that was put in place after the August raids reduced Germany's potential output by 50 percent until well into 1944.[127] Even assuming this is slightly overstated, the total effect of the CBO on German output of ME-109s in the last six months of 1943 would have been about two to three thousand aircraft.

The Focke-Wulf production losses, even with the complete destruction of the Marienburg plant, were probably less dramatic. As Marienburg was a final assembly yard, the main destruction was of aircraft actually being assembled at the moment of the raid.[128] It seems that approximately a hundred aircraft were destroyed directly during the raid, and that no assembly could take place for another four months. Dr. Kaether, the chief technical director of the company, endorsed this notion.[129] On the other hand, Tank echoed

Messerschmitt in saying that the American daylight attacks of July 1943 were responsible for Germany implementing its industrial dispersal program with the corresponding loss of production.[130]

Dispersal caused real problems for the Luftwaffe in more than just lost production.[131] A major problem was that the new factories, built with great haste, produced aircraft with more structural flaws.[132] Goering believed that this was a particular problem that plagued the Luftwaffe in 1944. The quality of aircraft built in the dispersed factories "suffered considerably. It happened, for instance, that the fittings at the assembly were not accurate enough, and similar things. Sometimes it was just that the fittings on the wing section were rough, in other cases the two landing wheels were different."[133]

There were, of course, aircraft losses in other production areas as well. In 1943 bombing damaged German aluminum production modestly. In July of that year, the Giulini aluminum processing factory in Ludwigshafen was hit.[134] This one attack reduced German annual production of alumina by 27,000 tons (or of finished aluminum by 13,000 tons). As aluminum was the life-blood of aircraft construction, this loss of production would have been another reason aircraft building fell far below targets after July 1943. Hans Kehrl, one of Speer's most important deputies and someone who played a great role in the allocation of raw materials throughout the German war economy, claimed that a 7,000 unit aircraft program required a finished aluminum allocation of 28,000–30,000 tons.[135] As such, the Giulini raid deprived Germany of enough aluminum to build more than 3,000 aircraft.

Using Milch's calculations above, supported by the evidence from the different industrialists, it would be conservative to say that the total number of German aircraft, mostly fighters, destroyed before production because of factory destruction, relocation and aluminum losses in 1943 was somewhere between five and six thousand. This estimate is in line with Strategic Bombing Survey calculations and the differences between German intended and actual outputs. The USSBS estimated that between July 1943 and December 1944, German aircraft production was reduced by 18,492 units because of strategic bombing, of which 14,353 were fighters.[136] This all makes sense when one looks at how the rise in German aircraft construction stopped immediately in July 1943, and leveled off (with some noticeable declines) until February 1944. (See Figure 42.) This leveling off in

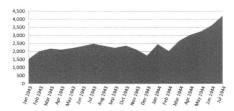

42 German aircraft construction (by unit), January 1943–July 1944.
Source: USSBS European Report 1, Appendix Table 102.

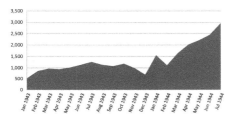

43 German fighter production (by unit), January 1943–July 1944.
Source: USSBS European Report 1, Appendix Table 102.

production happened almost entirely because of fighter production losses – which one can see visually by comparing their production to German aircraft production as a whole, as shown in Figure 43.

Beyond aircraft, which suffered most from all these attacks, the other area of German production to dip at this time was naval construction. This, however, had little to do with strategic bombing. The U-boat failure in the Battle of the Atlantic in the spring of 1943 led to an overhaul of production. The Type VII and IX boats, which had been the backbone of the war to this time, were drastically cut back as newer models were designed, most famously the Type XXI. This change, however, meant that construction fell until the design process for the newer models was complete. Side by side, it is interesting to see how aircraft production dipped and naval construction fell significantly in the second half of 1943. (See Figure 44.) On the other hand, all other war construction did rise, with the sole exception of motor vehicles. (See Figure 45.) The German railway network was able to cope relatively efficiently with Anglo-American strategic bombing in 1943 and had perhaps its best year of the war.[137] Finally, German production for the land war which came out of the Ruhr did not seem to be greatly affected by Harris' city attacks.[138]

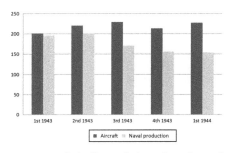

44 German quarterly indices of aircraft and naval production, 1943 and first quarter 1944.
Source: USSBS European Report 1, Appendix.

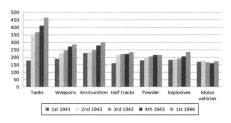

45 German quarterly indices of production (other types), 1943 and first quarter of 1944.
Source: USSBS European Report 1, Appendix.

It should be kept in mind that there were other areas where German production was destroyed in 1943 before it reached the battlefield. The most important of these was finished metal production, particularly steel. The USAAF estimated after the war that German steel ingot production in 1943 was reduced by 13.7 percent and in 1944 was reduced by 25.2 percent.[139] In 1944, Speer's ministry estimated that crude steel production in the previous year was reduced by 6.4 percent by the combined impact of all bombing.[140] This reduction set a ceiling on the increase of German army munitions (which was where most steel was used) in 1943.[141]

Other industries also suffered declines in production due to the dispersal policies that were put in place. The dispersed factories constructed for the German chemical industry, which was one of the CBO's priority targets, were 20 percent less efficient than pre-dispersal facilities.[142] Finally, bombing hit other industries by interfering with their retooling. In 1942 it was decided that the Opel Corporation would retool its truck factories to make a new three-ton truck.[143] Production was supposed to reach a thousand vehicles per month in October 1943 and two thousand a month by April 1944. However, because of the pressure being placed on the system, the first of the new trucks did not appear until August 1944.

The strategic air war also became the dominant front in areas such as the deployment of the German-controlled workforce. The production of aircraft always had the plurality of industrial workers in Germany.[144] Now, however, hundreds of thousands, perhaps millions, of extra workers were switched into different positions to help fight the bombing campaign. Maybe the greatest shift in the workforce was in workers assigned to repair and maintain bomb-damaged industries. According to Dr. Emil Fischer, commercial manager of IG Farben and president of the German Oil and Oil Products Association, there were 350,000 workers who could be assigned to repair damage to Germany's internal fuel production system in 1943.[145] When it came to those whose full-time occupation was repairing bomb damage, the figure at the end of 1943 was 330,000, of whom 138,000 were skilled craftsmen.[146]

Construction materials were also diverted to protect against strategic bombing. German concrete allocation may be the best example of this. In the second half of 1943, more concrete was devoted to the construction of protected aircraft factories in Germany than to preparations for a D-Day landing in northwest Europe or building fortifications on the Eastern Front. At that time, on average 90,000 tons of concrete per month were being used to build fortifications in the east, and 100,000 tons per month were being used in France and Belgium (and an additional 50,000 tons per month in the Netherlands).[147] Concurrently, 130,000 tons per month were being used to build protection just for aircraft production. And this was only part of the concrete being used domestically to prepare for Anglo-American air attacks. For instance, another 20,000 tons of concrete per month were being used to build facilities to protect Hitler from air assault. Speer calculated that by 1944, 28,000 workers were devoted to building constructions to protect Hitler from British and American bombs.[148] The Führer was so terrified by the prospect of being killed in an air raid that the concrete roof thickness of these structures ultimately reached 16.5 feet, or more than 5 meters.[149] However, Hitler's personal safety only tells part of the story.

The impact of preparing for and then repairing bomb damage in the Reich beginning in 1943 was massive. To prepare for air attacks, a huge German effort was put into constructing new and sturdy concrete structures. These modern fortresses range from the Führerbunker and flak towers in central Berlin to the U-boat pens that populated the western European coast. (See Figure 46.) They were built to and did withstand multiple direct bomb hits. To this day many of them remain indestructible, such as the U-boat pens constructed in Trondheim, Norway, which have proved too difficult and expensive to dismantle even after repeated attempts.

The effort that Germany put into these anti-air-raid construction efforts is sometimes overlooked in the histories of the war. The Anglo-American air offensive from 1942 onwards became a major preoccupation of Organization Todt (OT), the largest construction department in the German government and builder of everything from the Westwall (Siegfried Line) to fortifications on the Eastern Front, to airports and protected factories for the V-2. Organization Todt documents captured after the war claimed that by 1944 there were 1,495,623 workers on their different projects.[150] Of these, 972,371 were employed in Germany proper. This was the same number of workers as were employed on all finished army munitions production.

The cost of these constructions was also enormous. Xavier Dorsch, the head of Organization Todt from 1943 until the end of the war, claimed that in 1943, 4–4.5 billion Reichsmarks were spent on construction. This figure was more than 10 percent of the spending on German war production as a whole, which in 1943 was approximately 35 billion Reichsmarks.[151] The driving force behind this enormous sum was Hitler's desire to respond to the threat of Anglo-American bombing. (See Figures 47 and 48.)

> The OT came into the Reich in April or May 1943, when the Mohne dam was bombed by the RAF. Speer felt that others could have done the repair and reconstruction work that was necessary in the Ruhr, but wanted the OT to undertake it, because of the OT's flexibility and because the OT could do it fastest. Then, about September 1943, Hitler became concerned about the danger to which dispersed industry was exposed through attack on transportation. He therefore wanted bombproof factories of great

46 The famous flak tower at Berlin Zoo. The Germans had to divert great
resources and manpower to building these types of anti-air-raid structures. This
picture was taken in 1946 and the tower was eventually blown up in 1947. It took
three attempts, the last involving 35 tons of dynamite.

47 Hitler, Goering and Speer in 1943 as the Luftwaffe was being redeployed into the battle for control over German airspace. Fortunately Hitler had only a limited understanding of the uses of air power, while neither Goering nor Speer could cope with American and British dominance of the skies.

48 Speer with Erhard Milch and Professor Willy Messerschmitt. These three men were crucial to the German air production effort in the last two years of the war. Milch actually controlled most air production until 1944 when it was transferred to Speer's ministry. Messerschmitt's company was well known for producing some of Germany's most famous aircraft such as the ME-109 and ME-262.

size where an entire product could be manufactured from raw materials. In this way, it would be possible to avoid the dangers of attacks on transportation which would interfere with the assembly of parts produced in dispersed underground plants. For this purpose, Hitler proposed one or more thick concrete roofs over narrow valleys within which production could go on safely.[152]

Finally, there were two other areas of German production that received extra impetus beginning in the second half of 1943: the building of flak and the push for the V-2/A-4 rocket system. Both were strongly linked to fighting or retaliating against the CBO and both were particularly important to Hitler. The V-weapons became a way of striking back at the British for the bombing of German cities, as the dictator made clear in July 1943. "Terror must be broken by terror. It doesn't disturb me that they attack airfields, but when they destroy towns in the Ruhr Area! ... We can eliminate it only by affecting the people over there. Otherwise our people will go crazy in time."[153]

The building of anti-aircraft weaponry, which was overwhelmingly used to fight Anglo-American strategic bombing, was also given increasing precedence.[154] Hitler believed that fighters were actually a less efficient means of combating strategic bombing than anti-aircraft guns.[155] During 1943, the construction of anti-aircraft guns made up 28 percent of German weapons production, or almost 3 percent of overall munitions output.[156] These weapons also consumed a massive amount of German ammunition production, which was the second highest category of munitions production in Germany after aircraft. Between January 1943 and September 1944, anti-aircraft ammunition made up about 17 percent of overall German ammunition production.[157] As ammunition production made up approximately 30 percent of German munitions output, producing ammunition for anti-aircraft guns in 1943 would have been almost 5 percent of overall output – so that building and arming anti-aircraft weaponry in 1943 would have been approximately 7 percent of overall German munitions output. This would have put it almost exactly on a par with German AFV production (not including ammunition) for the year.

This output was aimed at combating the CBO. In November 1943, after flak forces had been built up numerically in terms of both units and personnel, there were approximately 13,500 heavy guns, 37,500 light guns and 1,365,585 personnel deployed in flak services throughout German-held territory including Luftwaffe field divisions, SS divisions and naval flak. (See Table 30.) The forces in Germany, France, Belgium and Holland were almost all directed towards Anglo-American strategic bombing. Most of the forces in the Balkans were there to protect Germany's oil supplies from air attack. Those in Italy and Norway/Denmark were also partly involved in combating the bombing. Overall, about 80 percent of Germany's operational flak weaponry and more than a million German personnel were focused on fighting off American and British strategic air attacks.

Table 30 *German flak in all services deployed on November 1, 1943*

Area	Heavy flak	Light flak	Personnel
Germany	7,000	17,500	678,075
France/Belgium/Holland	2,500	9,000	259,015
Norway/Denmark	700	2,500	65,605
Eastern Front	1,850	6,200	261,100
Italy	900	1,200	53,020
Balkans	550	1,100	48,770

Source: Arnold MSS, Reel 190, The Contribution of Air power to the Defeat of Germany, Appendices, Section 2.

Manning all these new flak guns also caused an important shift in manpower. According to Speer, 100,000 skilled workers were taken out of the factories and made to man anti-aircraft guns in the Reich in 1943.[158] Worker numbers assigned to different anti-aircraft tasks became so high that Saur and Buhle believed that it was a major element in depriving the front of extra troops.[159]

Finally, the CBO caused a significant change in German production when the A-4 (better known as V-2) rocket system was given precedence over all other weapons programs. In 1943, as the bombing of German cities intensified, Hitler, who had earlier been a skeptic about the potential of rockets to bombard Britain, called for a massive investment to build the V-2 as soon as possible. Speer also supported heavy investment in this system in 1943, as it was an army program and therefore came under his control as he had yet to take over Luftwaffe production.

The V-2 was the single most expensive weapon system that Germany ever attempted and its purpose was almost entirely to strike back at the British for the bombing of German cities. During one of his post-war interrogations, Speer corrected an interrogator who thought other reasons might have mattered.

Q: The development of V weapons, especially V-2, took up a significant part of your total production. Was its goal a preparation for a German invasion of England, or to stop our own preparations for invasion?

Sp: Neither one. Its purpose was to counter British night attacks with something similar, without the expensive bombers and practically without losses. The main reason was therefore a psychological one for the benefit of the German people.[160]

The specific cost of the V-2 was discussed earlier. However, in driving the Germans to invest so much of their money and effort in the weapons system, which in the end delivered relatively small results, Harris achieved something valuable, if unexpected, through the area bombing of German cities in 1943.[161]

Comparing land and air in 1943

Unlike the strategic bombing campaign, which is seen as a failure in 1943, German losses in land battles occurring at the same time are generally considered much more damaging blows to Nazi power. These German defeats in 1943 are some of the best-known battles of the war. In North Africa there was the defeat of the Afrika Corps, which culminated with the surrender in Tunisia in May 1943. Following from that, there were the successful Anglo-American invasions of Sicily and then Italy. Yet, these successes are seen as relatively small affairs compared with what happened on the Eastern Front at the same time. The surrender of the 6th Army in Stalingrad in February 1943, followed by the failure of the Citadel Offensive in central Russia (known more often as the Battle of Kursk) in July are seen as much more important blows to German power.

The general assumption that these land battles were all more damaging for Germany stems from the supposition that the losses suffered by the German army in these encounters made up a significant share of German production. Actually, destruction in all of them was modest. The amount of equipment lost was at no time larger than what was being produced and, more often than not, as in the case of German AFV, it was equipment of growing obsolescence. The battles were not devastating blows to Germany's ability to wage war.

The battle for Stalingrad, which was part of the German summer offensive of 1942 designed to seize Soviet oilfields in the Caucasus, is often portrayed as a decisive, war-changing defeat for Germany. The story of the campaign is well known. On June 28, 1942 the German army launched Operation Blue (*Fall Blau*) in which a major armored spearhead would plunge southwards into the oil-producing Caucasus region of the USSR. The 6th Army, the fate of which became the focal point of the campaign, was given a crucial, supporting role in the operation. It was to protect the northern flank of the main assault by seizing and holding a crossing on the Volga.

The first part of Operation Blue went well for the Germans. The main thrust into the Caucasus advanced hundreds of miles and was nearing control of the oilfields. The 6th Army also advanced rapidly at first, encountering light resistance, until it reached Stalingrad, a major town on the Volga. There Soviet resistance stiffened considerably and the 6th Army was sucked into a street-by-street urban quagmire. When on the verge of taking Stalingrad, the 6th Army was hit by a hammer-blow Soviet counterattack from north and south of the city, against weaker units mostly composed of German allies such as Italians and Hungarians. The counterattacks entombed the 6th Army in a pocket, nicknamed the Cauldron (*Kessel*), from which any break-out was specifically forbidden by Hitler. Instead, the Luftwaffe was sent in to supply the army by air, while a relieving force was assembled to fight its way into the Kessel. These efforts failed: the Luftwaffe was unable to deliver enough supplies to keep the 6th Army functioning and the relieving force was unable to reach Stalingrad. On February 2, 1943 the 6th Army's commander, Field Marshal von Paulus, bowed to the inevitable and defied Hitler's orders by surrendering to the Soviets.

It was certainly a major defeat in the traditional sense for the Germans. Symbolically, the Wehrmacht's air of invincibility was broken for the first time. In material terms, the surrender of an entire German army represented a real, if moderate, loss of equipment and manpower. However, it was also a loss that German production could replace easily. According to General Thomas, OKW's armament chief, during the entirety of Operation Blue (seven months including the thrust into the Caucasus and the Stalingrad debacle), the German army lost the equivalent of equipment for forty-five divisions.[162] At the same time, Dr. Karl Hettlage, who was one of Speer's key financial advisers, estimated that in 1942–3, Germany produced every month on average enough material to supply twenty-three divisions.[163] He also argued that complete equipment losses during the first two winters of the war in Russia equaled supplies for a combined sixty divisions, so he supports Thomas' claim as to the general level of losses during Operation Blue. Hettlage's figure seems roughly correct, as in 1944 Speer estimated that in one year Germany produced enough equipment to equip 290 divisions – 250 of which would be infantry and 40 armored.[164] As a whole, production in 1944 was only a little higher than that in 1943 because while there was a steep rise in production up until July, there was a steep decline afterwards. Another way of putting into context the total losses from Operation Blue, not just Stalingrad, is to compare them with German losses on the Eastern Front from the start of Barbarossa until the launch of the 1942 summer offensives. During that period, the German army lost fifty divisions' worth of equipment.[165] This shows that actual wastage of equipment was far more a result of actual attrition than of losing or winning a battle.

Specific German losses of panzers and aircraft during Stalingrad were also not particularly high. Separating German armor losses at Stalingrad from those lost in other theaters is not simple. We do know that between July 1 1942 and January 31 1943, which covers all but four days between the launch of Fall Blau and the surrender of the 6th Army, the German army lost 1,278 Panzer Mark IIIs (an increasingly obsolete AFV), 421 Panzer IVs, 20 Panzer VIs and 191 75 mm assault guns in all theaters of the war, for a total loss of 1,910 AFV.[166] The overall losses on the Eastern Front would have made up a large majority of these, maybe as many as 1,500. On the other hand, during that same period, the Germans accepted into service 2,788 AFVs (1,312 Mark IIIs, 795 Mark IVs, 111 Mark VIs and 570 75 mm assault guns). Both quantitatively and, maybe more importantly, qualitatively, the German army would have had a considerably more powerful armored force on February 1 1943 than on July 1 1942.

This loss of aircraft was surprisingly light as often the narrative of the battle stresses Germany's large commitment of aircraft in support of the 6th Army.[167] Luftwaffe aircraft losses during the last seventy-one days of the battle, when they were trying to ferry in supplies to the 6th Army and taking great risks, have been estimated at 488.[168] This would have equaled less than 2 percent of German aircraft production for 1943. Actually, Luftwaffe deployment on the Eastern Front as a whole in the winter of 1942–3, was lower than in other theaters. On December 30, 1942, when the battle for Stalingrad was entering its most horrible phase and the 6th Army was in need of total resupply by air, the Luftwaffe had 1,528 aircraft on the entire Eastern Front (802 bombers and dive-bombers, 445 single- and twin-engine fighters, 254 support aircraft and coastal patrol planes).[169] At the same moment, the Luftwaffe had 2,300 aircraft deployed against the British and Americans in western Europe or the Mediterranean (873 bombers and dive-bombers, 1,295 single- and twin-engine fighters, 23 support aircraft and 109 coastal patrol planes). The fact that the Eastern Front as a whole had less than 40 percent of the Luftwaffe's deployed aircraft at the time was considered by their own historian as the reason Germany lost the Battle of Stalingrad.[170]

The final thing to mention here is the dangerous tendency by historians to fetishize an individual battle by over-rating the importance of a specific unit. This is often done by describing the unit as the "cream" of an army – something that occurs regularly in books about Stalingrad and the 6th Army. In World War II, using such a phrase is unhelpful romanticism. The 6th Army was an excellent unit, better than many, not as good as others. The German army fought extremely tenaciously before Stalingrad and it fought just as ferociously afterwards. The difference was in the relative balance of munitions production and equipment between it and its opponents – not the loss of a somehow superior fighting unit.

That can be seen in the next great encounter on the Eastern Front, what has come to be known as the Battle of Kursk. In July 1943, the German army launched its last major offensive in the east, Operation Citadel, the aim of which was to cut off a heavily defended salient which bulged into the center of the German front line. To achieve this, the Germans massed two large armored spearheads, one on either side of the salient, but the Soviets, who were expecting an assault, poured in even larger forces of their own. When the Germans began their attack, they had 2,451 AFV in the area of operations, while the Red Army had 5,128.[171] Not only were these armored forces large, they represented some of the newest and most powerful units in either army. One of the reasons that Citadel took so long to be launched was that Hitler was waiting to deploy significant numbers of the new Panzer V (Panther) tank for the first time.

The resulting slugfest is often described as the largest battle of World War II, and the German failure to cut off Soviet forces, and then subsequent withdrawal, as a great defeat. However, in this case there is far less reason to consider Kursk a great defeat for the German army in production terms. German armor losses were surprisingly light. Estimates of German AFV destroyed during the first twelve days of the Citadel Offensives (July 5–16, 1943) range between 250 and 350.[172] David Glantz and Johnathan House have calculated that the Wehrmacht lost 323 AFV during the Citadel Offensives,[173] while Niklas Zetterling and Anders Frankson claim a smaller number were lost, with

Army Group South losing 190 AFV from July 5 to 17, while Army Group Centre losses were very small indeed.[174] Richard Evans has described these overall German losses in AFV and artillery pieces as "relatively light."[175] When these losses are placed into their overall context within German production, it can be seen that their impact was quite manageable. The 1,331 AFV lost everywhere on the Eastern Front in July and August 1943, which included the Battle of Kursk, were equal to 11 percent of that year's annual production of such vehicles.[176] When it came to overall German munitions production, the value of the AFV losses on the entire Eastern Front during July and August 1943 was less than 1 percent.

Moreover, a significant plurality of the panzers lost at Kursk were the increasingly obsolescent Mark IIIs, while few were the newer Mark Vs (Panthers) or Mark VIs (Tigers).[177] Total losses of Panthers in all theaters of the war were 83 in July 1943 and 41 in August.[178] Tiger losses were considerably less as the Germans lost only 33 in July and 40 in August, again in all theaters of operations, not just central Russia. On the other hand, combined losses for Mark IIIs were a very large 367. The next closest comparison was Mark IV losses, at 345, and 75 mm assault gun losses at 303. So, much of the German armor destroyed in both central Russia and the Mediterranean in the summer of 1943 was already obsolete – indeed, the last Mark IIIs ever accepted into army service became available in August 1943. It should also be kept in mind that, during July and August of 1943, the German army accepted into service 20 Mark IIIs, 527 Mark IVs, 322 Mark Vs, 125 Mark VIs and 572 75 mm assault guns. These 1,566 AFV represented a far more powerful force quantitatively and qualitatively than the 1,331 losses that were being replaced.

In fact, the most serious losses for the Germans on the Eastern Front during the summer of 1943 were aircraft losses. To support Citadel, they deployed the largest air force that they would ever have in the east in 1943. On June 30, there were 2,330 aircraft throughout the Eastern Front – the large majority of which were prepared to support the offensive. This number included 1,354 bombers and dive-bombers, 664 single- and twin-engined fighters, and 274 support aircraft.[179] The high rate of operations that went on with this force led to a comparatively high rate of loss in comparison with normal Eastern Front Luftwaffe deployments. During July and August 1943, the Luftwaffe lost 1,030 aircraft on the entire Eastern Front, or

4 percent of its annual aircraft production that year (trainers not included).[180] So, in combination, the armor and operational aircraft losses on the Eastern Front in July and August 1943 represented a little less than 3 percent of Germany's weapons output for the year.

It must always be borne in mind, however, that the Anglo-American victories in land battles in 1943 destroyed less German production of ground equipment than those on the Eastern Front. Interestingly, the fighting towards the end of the North Africa campaign resulted in greater German losses than those which occurred later in the year in Sicily. We know from German shipping records that between November 1942 and May 1943, a total of 142,407 German troops were shipped into North Africa, almost all of whom were killed or eventually surrendered. To support this force, 544 tanks, 8,173 vehicles and 1,093 different artillery pieces were landed in North Africa in the same period, with another 79 tanks, 2,546 vehicles and 320 artillery pieces sunk in ships trying to make the perilous journey across the Mediterranean.[181] This total force of 623 tanks, 10,719 vehicles and 1,413 artillery pieces represented a commitment of force not dissimilar to that of the 6th Army when it began its offensive as part of Operation Blue in the summer of 1942. Of course, in overall German production terms the loss was modest. Combining German AFV losses and acceptances for key classes such as the Panzer IV and all 75 mm assault guns during these crucial months in 1942 and 1943, it is clear that the German army was still growing substantially in strength, regardless of the outcome of the battles. (See Figure 49.) In this period the German army received 294 more Panzer IVs than it lost, and 421 more 75 mm assault guns.

Losses of German AFV during the fighting in Sicily were also inconsequential within the overall context of German production. When Anglo-American forces landed on the island on July 10, 1943, the two

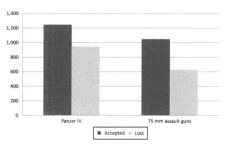

49 Major German AFV accepted into service and lost, June 1942–March 1943.
Source: Cab 146/197, published as Winter (ed.), *Defeating Hitler*, Appendix VII.

main German divisions on the island, the Hermann Goering Division and the 15th Panzer Grenadier Division, had between them approximately 150 panzers.[182] During the course of the fighting, elements of another panzer division, the 29th Panzer Grenadier, were also sent to the island. The total commitment of German panzers to the defense of Sicily in 1943 represented a little over a week's production from German industry. And it should also be kept in mind that 51 German tanks and 163 guns were successfully evacuated to Italy in August.[183]

In the Mediterranean during 1942, German aircraft losses were also moderate. In the first two weeks of the Battle of El Alamein (October 23 through November 5), the Luftwaffe lost 114 aircraft.[184] On the other hand, the Luftwaffe loss rates against the British and Americans in the Mediterranean became much more significant in 1943 as was shown earlier. Combined, the great land battles on all fronts in 1943, in terms of AFV and aircraft destroyed, were responsible for the destruction of somewhere between 15 percent and 20 percent of German weapons output.

Finally, a word should be said about human casualties. Even though this book argues that equipment allocation and production are more important indications of how a war is developing than casualties, the latter were not unimportant. Taken as a whole, these land defeats in 1943 were responsible for an increase in German battle deaths, but not a decisive one. The year from September 1, 1942 to August 31, 1943, which included almost all the battle deaths of Stalingrad, Kursk, North Africa, Sicily and countless other small engagements, saw 735,554 Germans die in all the armed services.[185] That is fewer than in three consecutive months in 1944 (June through August) and two months in 1945 (January and February).

What the evidence points to is that concentrating on the destruction of German equipment on the battlefields alone, even when including aircraft losses, gives an incomplete picture of how German production was being destroyed in 1943 and how German power was being broken. In fact, combining pre-production, production, deployment and non-operational losses by the Luftwaffe in 1943, with their aircraft lost fighting the CBO, will result in a higher figure than the total combined AFV and aircraft losses of the Eastern Front and the Mediterranean. These can be seen in Table 31.

Of course, aircraft and AFV production tells only part of the story of war munitions in 1943. Those who believe that the land war was more important could point to artillery, ammunition, trucks, etc.

Table 31 *German equipment destroyed (equivalencies)*[a] *in 1943*

	Land battles (Eastern front/ Mediterranean)		Air war over Germany/ Western front	
	Percent produced[b]	Percent overall production[c]	Percent produced	Percent overall production
AFV	78[d]	5.5[e]	0	0
AFV pre-production	0	0	4[f]	0.3
Aircraft	31.5[g]	12.6[h]	19.7[i]	7.9
Aircraft pre-production/produced	0	0	23.4[j]	9.4
Non-operational aircraft	0	0	7.3[k]	2.9
Total		18.1		20.5

Sources: Figures drawn from Cab 146/197, published as Winter (ed.), *Defeating Hitler*, Appendix VII. USSBS, European Report 3, Appendix Table 104, and pp. 144–5.

Notes:

[a] The word equivalencies is used here because the table includes some pre-production losses.

[b] This is the percentage destroyed of the overall amount produced of that class in 1943. It is based simply on unit number and takes into account no differences in types of aircraft or AFV.

[c] This is the percentage of overall German munitions output that was lost in this category.

[d] We know that a total of 7,315 AFV were listed as lost in 1943. This figure is the combination of 1943 losses of Panzer VIs (275), Panzer Vs (376), Panzer IVs (2,400), Panzer IIIs (2,682) and 75 mm assault guns (1,582). However, it does not include self-propelled guns, which made up 22.7 percent of German AFV production for the year (2,744 units of 12,063 produced. See USSBS, European Report 3, Appendix Table 104). For the sake of overall estimation I am calculating the self-propelled gun losses at the same rate as those for all other AFV.

[e] Based on a calculation that AFV made up 7 percent of overall German munitions production in 1943.

[f] This figure is based on the 6.4 percent of German steel production that was destroyed through strategic bombing in 1943.

[g] We know that aircraft losses from January through November on the Eastern Front and in the Mediterranean were 6,777. To calculate for the year, I added an additional one-eleventh of this amount, for a grand total of 7,395. This number is almost probably a little higher than the real figure because in December there was usually relatively less Luftwaffe activity in either land theater.

[h] Based on aircraft construction for the year being 40 percent of German annual weapons production. USSBS, European Report 3, pp. 144–5. This figure probably underestimates the amount of effort put into aircraft construction in 1943.

[i] Luftwaffe operational aircraft losses over Germany and the Western Front were 4,227 between January and November 1943. If another month is added at the same rate, the annual figure would be 4,611.

ʲ This is an equivalence figure, based on 5,500 aircraft not being produced in
  1943 because of air attacks. This is halfway between 5,000 and 6,000, which were
  estimates given, and, considering the losses in aluminum production mentioned
  earlier, is certainly a conservative estimate.
ᵏ This is just the additional rise in wastage (aircraft lost or damaged) above and
  beyond the normal rise expected in deployment. The number of aircraft used is
  1,705, of a total lost and damaged in 1943 of 9,156.

On the other hand, those who view the air and sea war as more
important could point to anti-air production, V-weapon production,
U-boat production, and the hundreds of thousands, maybe millions, of
workers who were redeployed. The basic point remains unaltered – that
the Combined Bomber Offensive was tying down or destroying more
production than any part of the land war, the Eastern Front included.

If one adds in the sea fighting in 1943, the area of air–sea
fighting also dwarfed that of the land war. (See Map 1.) The land war
in 1943 took place in two well-defined areas. In the USSR, fighting
during the year was focused in a large southern area between Stalingrad
in January and the Dnepr River by the end of the year. At its greatest
length (between Stalingrad and Kiev, as an example), it covered about
600 miles in depth. The fighting in the Mediterranean covered an area
that started in North Africa, and later took in Sicily and southern Italy
to a line just north of Naples – a few hundred more miles of distance.
The air and sea war, however, sprawled across an area of many
thousands of miles. Looking at areas of high-intensity sea fighting,
combat occurred from the Gulf of Mexico through the convoy routes
to Murmansk and Archangel. The strategic air war reached from southern France to eastern Germany, from Scandinavia to northern Italy.

Meanwhile, the air–sea super-battlefield had come into
existence. (See Map 2.) With the exception of front-line infantry, it
became the focus of national effort. Its weaponry was the most advanced
and expensive, both to design and to build. It ended up destroying
equipment in a multi-layered process from the time before production
occurred to the battlefield itself. It engaged industrial workers and bur-
eaucrats, scientists and sailors and airmen more than did the land war.
And it witnessed the engagement of equipment in an area vastly larger. Its
outcome would determine the course of the end of World War II.

9 THE WAR IN EUROPE IN 1944

In 1944 Panzer Lehr was one of the most powerful divisions in the German army. It was completely mechanized and had twice the number of AFV of a normal panzer division. Having been created from the best instructors in the German panzer corps, Panzer Lehr was made up of 60 percent veterans of Russia and North Africa, with the rest eager recruits, so that the average age of a soldier in the division was only 21.5 years old.[1] Not only that, it was one of the few units in the German army with a large complement of motorized flak vehicles.[2] At full force, its fighting strength was reckoned to be equal to that of four standard panzer divisions.

Panzer Lehr was to be one of the key German units in the defense of France against the expected Allied invasion. General Heinz Guderian told the commander of Panzer Lehr, Fritz Bayerlein, that the division "alone must hurl the English back into the Channel. Your goal is not the coast; it is the sea."[3] However, until May 1, because of fear of air attack, the division was based near Budapest. When it was thereupon moved to France, it was stationed near the town of Nogent-le-Rotrou, about halfway between Le Mans and Chartres, only 80–90 miles from the town of Caen which lay just behind the Normandy beaches. On June 6, as soon as the first reports came in about Allied airborne troops landing in Normandy, Panzer Lehr was ordered to concentrate near Caen and drive the invasion into the sea. Such a journey would normally take a motorized division a few hours. However, Panzer Lehr had to fight its way along the roads of Normandy against constant air attack. Because it was desperately needed if the Germans were to have any chance of victory, Panzer Lehr couldn't take the precaution of moving only at night. The result was that it had to crawl along slowly by day, watching out for and receiving constant attacks from Anglo-American aircraft. Its speed was drastically reduced to somewhere between 6 and 8 miles per hour.[4] During its advance, Panzer Lehr suffered losses from air attacks of "84 half-tracks, prime movers and SP guns out of 700; 130 trucks (more than 1/10th of the original complement of 1000) and 5 out of 150 tanks."[5] It was therefore in no fit state to join in the fighting until June 9 at the earliest, and much of the division was not in action until the 10th.

Seven weeks later, Panzer Lehr was still in Normandy, fighting around the town of Saint-Lô when, on July 25, it was hit by Operation Cobra. This was the use of overwhelming air power to decimate a small section of the German lines across from the American 1st Army. Large flights of fighter-bombers were sent up to continually hit anything that moved and, crucially, the heavy bombers of the 8th Air Force would deliver the largest blow, carpet-bombing an area only 6,000 yards wide and 2,400 yards deep. This was exactly where Panzer Lehr was stationed.

The carnage inflicted on the division over two days of bombardment destroyed it completely. The bombing on the evening of July 25th left the division's sector looking like "a landscape on the surface of the moon, all craters and death."[6] Approximately 70 percent of Panzer Lehr's personnel had been knocked out of action – either "wounded, crazed or dead." All of its AFV in the front line were lost, some having been flipped over and lying on their turrets, while others found themselves so deep in bomb craters that they could not be extricated. The process was repeated on the next evening.[7] By July 27, only fourteen AFV could be mustered by the division to try to stop the attack of the US 1st Army. Bayerlein was forced to flee on foot from his divisional command post just before it was overrun by American armor. He fled through the woods to the village of Percy, where he found a German mobile radio operator who allowed him to report to his corps commander that of the "Panzer Lehr Division nothing remained. Its armor was almost completely destroyed, its combat personnel killed, wounded, captured or scattered, all the headquarters records, papers and equipment were lost."[8]

The story of this powerful unit encapsulated the fate of the German army and the German war economy in 1944. While it still had raw materials, munitions and soldiers enough to resist, it was inexorably losing the ability to move. This loss of mobility meant the loss of the war.

The growth in the understanding of strategic air power

In July 1944, after rising markedly over the previous eighteen months, German war production reached a wartime peak, and thereafter declined. By January 1945, armaments production was back at an identical level to that of December 1943, having declined by one-third. (See Figure 50.) If World War II had been defined by the results of the land war this would not have happened. Even though Germany was clearly losing territory in 1944, almost all its munitions factories remained in German hands throughout the year. Also, it was ruthlessly exploiting the territory it did control by stripping it of resources.[9] Crucially, German stockpiles of raw materials meant that there was more than enough on hand to keep munitions production at its peak level for years, even with no access to outside trade. In September 1944, Albert Speer ordered a study of the raw material situation for Germany if the country was limited to its present stockpiles and what it could draw from just Germany itself, the Italian Alps, and parts of Croatia and Hungary.[10] It was discovered that the present high level of production, if left undisturbed by air attack, could continue into 1946 – and only then would decline progressively.[11]

Stocks of chrome, the material in shortest supply at present rates of usage, would be the first to come under pressure and begin to run out in January 1946. Until that time, steel production could continue at its present high pace. Other raw materials were stockpiled in even greater quantities. Nickel would last at present rates until June 1946, wolfram and molybdenum (an important element in

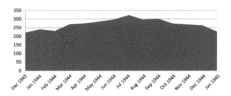

50 German munitions production, 1944.
Source: USSBS, European Report 3, Appendix 100, p. 275.

strengthening steel) until April 1946, zinc until August 1948, copper until July 1947 and manganese until June 1946. Aluminum, the vital metal for aircraft construction, would continue in full supply until January 1946, after which time a 25 percent reduction would take place.

The decline in war production could not be blamed on the loss of fuel because of the land war either. By 1944 imported fuel was already a relatively small part of German output. One of the most important successes of the German economy during the war was the growth of domestic, synthetic oil manufacturing.[12] Domestic production was particularly crucial for the supply of high-octane aviation fuel, almost all of which was being created inside Germany by 1944. The Soviet capture of the oil regions of Romania in August 1944 made almost no difference in the economic calculation of German production. Finally, the decline in German armaments production cannot be blamed on a lack of workers. The Nazi empire in 1944 was ruthlessly exploiting Europe for labor, and at the same time was making use of millions of its women as workers, who heretofore had been exempted from full participation in the wartime economy.[13] Between September 1943 and September 1944, the total of those employed in all of German industry increased slightly from 10,803,300 to 10,858,100.[14] This occurred even as more and more men were being taken from the factories and sent into military service.

The reason that German production deteriorated so sharply in the second half of 1944 was that air power, in its totality, for the first time in history, was used effectively. The lessons of 1943 had been digested and (some of) the right conclusions had been drawn. Most famously, when the P-51 Mustang started appearing in substantial numbers during the first half of 1944, bombers could now be escorted all the way to their targets in Germany.[15] First designed by North American Aviation for the British in 1940, the P-51 was a disappointment when it came off the assembly line. Its American-built Allison engine was underpowered and the aircraft's top speed and performance were substandard. However, the airframe, which was wonderfully light and aerodynamic, held out great potential, and in 1942 the RAF equipped some Mustangs with the Rolls-Royce Model 61 Merlin engine.[16] The P-51 was then a revelation, capable of high performance in all flying aspects and, because of its relatively light weight, great range.[17] In 1943 and 1944, its range was further increased through

51 This is a picture of the first P-51 Mustang ever to land and be serviced on
the east bank of the Rhine. It sits before the ruined airframe of a German fighter, an
apt metaphor for the course of the air war over Germany in 1944 and 1945.

modifications and the adding of fuel drop tanks, so that by March
1944, it could fly far into eastern Germany or over Czechoslovakia.[18]
(See Figure 51.)

   Arnold, to his great credit, did everything possible to make
sure that as many Mustangs as possible were used as long-range escorts
for bombers.[19] Originally thought of as a ground-attack plane, in the
run-up to the Normandy landings, Mustangs were switched from this
role in place of P-47s.[20] The Mustang was a superior dogfighter
compared with any German plane then flying; it would not be matched
until the ME-262 went into operational deployment, and being flown
by better-trained American and British pilots, at this stage of the war
exacted a heavy toll on German fighters. During the first six months
of 1944, 2,800 Mustangs were built, giving it the second highest
production total for the USAAF – behind the P-47 at 3,756, but more
numerous than the P-38 at 2,031.[21] The Mustang's great range meant
that it could fly ahead of the bomber streams and disrupt the
Luftwaffe's attempts to form large attacking groups of its own fighters.
Taking advantage of this ability, in early 1944 the new commander of
the 8th Air Force, James Doolittle, ordered his fighters to concentrate
on shooting down German fighters, and not to stay anchored to the
bomber stream.[22] The result was higher losses that seriously damaged
German morale.

   Earlier in the air war, the American air force kept its escorts
close to the bombers, which allowed the Luftwaffe fighters to climb to
the right altitude, assemble and even attack the bomber streams before
encountering stiff resistance. Starting in late 1943, however, attacks on
the Germans as they were assembling showed real promise. In 1944,

when the Mustang, with its longer range, was made available in significant numbers, these attacks could be significantly increased and allowed the American bombers some protection when attacking almost all of the Reich's key industries. (See Map 5.) From that point great effort was put into dispersing German fighters as they were trying to assemble. The most effective tactic used by the American fighters was to make extremely broad sweeps in front of the bomber streams, which inevitably discovered German formations lurking ahead waiting for an opportunity to attack.[23]

To Adolf Galland, this was the first time that the spirit of the German fighter pilot began to break. He even coined a phrase for their fear of engaging with the Mustangs: "Jägershreck" or "fear of fighters."[24] When Goering ordered that all Luftwaffe fighter pilots fly two missions a day in reaction to increasing Anglo-American air attacks, a silent revolt took place and the orders for the extra mission were often not given.[25]

Moreover, there was now a far more sophisticated understanding of just how focused a strategic air campaign needed to be and which targets needed to be given priority. The Committee of Operations Analysts (COA), in reconfiguring its plan at the end of 1943, now argued that just four industries should be attacked, ones that were "vital to Germany's ability to continue the war, vulnerable to aerial bombardment and within the capacity of our available force – aircraft production, anti-friction bearings, oil and rubber."[26] The COA had now made oil one of its four main targets, though it resisted attempts to give it a special priority.[27] It continued to advocate for ball-bearing attacks as a high priority and argued that German aircraft construction was always the paramount target.

The key person driving this revision forward from the American end was General Carl Spaatz, and his focus was squarely on oil. Spaatz was one of the most intellectually engaged and reliable senior American air force officers of the war.[28] He also got along well with many RAF officers, and formed a friendship with Slessor in 1940.[29] A favorite of Arnold and Eisenhower, Spaatz controlled American air forces in North Africa and the Mediterranean until January 1944, when he was named the overall commander for American air forces in the European theater of operations. At the same time, Eaker was transferred to the Mediterranean to take over the 15th Air Force and Doolitte was named his replacement as commander of the 8th Air Force. Arnold gave Spaatz complete authorization to run the American strategic bombing campaign however he saw fit.[30]

By March 5, Spaatz had redrafted the American part of the Combined Bomber Offensive.[31] It was now intellectually aimed at destroying just two kinds of targets. Once again, German fighter production was given a high priority (although, interestingly, it was only second on this list). However, the other group of targets to be attacked were all related to stopping German mobility – from the pre-production phase all the way to the battlefield. The first priority, and Spaatz's personal favorite, was German oil production. This was followed by the third priority, rubber production, in particular Germany's ability to produce and stockpile tires, and then general transportation targets such as railways.[32] As this was written in the run-up to D-Day, Spaatz chose to stress the effect of restricted mobility on the German army most of all. Thus the campaign against oil production would keep German troops from reacting efficiently on the battlefield; in particular, it would greatly hinder any major withdrawal (which was a prophetic statement considering the situation only a few months later).[33] A successful attack on German rubber and tire production would impose "a spreading crisis" on the German army "which would progressively limit its mobility."[34] Combined with a continuing successful campaign against German fighter aircraft, it would mean that the German army would be without fighter cover in both the west and the east which would further limit its ability to move.

Spaatz also went ahead and downgraded a number of targets that had been high priority in 1943. Some of these were sensible, others less so. He started by reinforcing and strengthening the American opposition to morale bombing, but all on practical not ethical grounds.

> Morale in a totalitarian society is irrelevant so long as the control patterns function effectively. The Nazi party controls have functioned well. Air raids have produced temporary local outbreaks, but opposition has had little opportunity to take advantage of the breakdown of communications, transport and services in these periods. Social control is required to re-establish the conditions where life is possible. This the Nazi party has been sufficiently adaptable to provide.[35]

As well as not attacking morale directly, the plan argued against any more attacks on German submarine pens, grinding-wheel production and truck production, mostly sensible omissions.[36] On the other hand, it continued to argue against attacks on aircraft engine production and, within transport targets, viewed attacks on railways as the least effective. Yet, for all its flaws, this kind of thinking represented a further step in the understanding of the use of strategic air power in the war.

The idea of focusing on Germany's oil supplies and its ability to move goods and military equipment was something that many in Britain had been arguing for years. When writing the history of the air war in 1944, it can be implied that oil and rail/transport attacks were somehow oppositional.[37] In early 1944 this might even have been the view of Spaatz himself.[38] There was certainly a fight over which should receive the highest priority – but that tells only part of the story. The most important thing was that both were aimed at mobility as opposed to attacking specific production points. This meant that, rather than them being distinct campaigns intellectually, it was possible for someone like Portal to move easily to support attacks on both.

In 1944, along with Air Marshal Arthur Tedder, Portal played the crucial British role in allocating some resources to these mobility attacks. Portal had been a strong supporter of attacks on Germany's transport system in 1941 and early 1942, and this had remained in his mind ever since. He supported Harris' campaign against German cities in 1943 and the first few months of 1944 because it was a campaign that the RAF could realistically undertake, and it seemed at first, according to the intelligence reports, that such a campaign was having an impact on German morale and production. Portal was aware that British bombing in 1944 would be governed by the capabilities of the Lancaster and that British production of those bombers had a natural ceiling that could not be expanded greatly.[39] However, he was also never dogmatic on the subject of area bombing and had shown earlier in the war that he believed "precision" bombing was actually the most effective way forward – if it could actually be implemented.

Tedder, on the other hand, was perhaps the strongest believer in a campaign against Germany's transportation system – its railways, roads and bridges. His position in 1943 and 1944, first as head of the Mediterranean Air Command and then as Eisenhower's Deputy Supreme Commander at SHAEF, meant that his actual command decisions were more in regard to the tactical use of air power – at which he steadily improved from El Alamein to Normandy.[40] Even in late October 1943, he was listing his priorities in the Mediterranean as ground support first and Pointblank second.[41] His influence over British strategic bombing, on the other hand, was muted, sadly, for his general instincts were often sensible. Like Portal, Tedder believed that precision attacks held out great promise; he just had strong but realistic doubts that American bombers could survive unescorted in the face of powerful German fighter opposition. He therefore stressed coordinated targeting between the British and Americans. In January and March 1943, he strongly argued that Bomber Command and the 8th Air Force be required to act in tandem to attack similar areas and targets on similar days.[42] This was typical of Tedder, one of the most cooperative of the Anglo-American senior commanders in Europe. Unlike someone like Harris, he did his best to look at the Anglo-American war effort as a united whole. Because of this, he became one of Eisenhower's most trusted British or American associates.[43]

Until well into the summer of 1944, Tedder remained focused on tactical air support over strategic bombing, helping to plan and coordinate the enormous air effort over the battlefields of France. However, this gave him real influence over the latter as both strategic air forces were ordered to place themselves at Eisenhower's disposal starting on April 1, 1944.[44] Tedder used his power at this time from the start to try to force coordination on Anglo-American day and night efforts.[45] The first direction he gave when devising the overall air effort in support of Overlord was that all efforts must be coordinated.

> If we are to derive full value from the immense air power available, the selected target system should:
>
> (a) be based on one common object towards which all available Air Forces can be directed. We would waste much of our power if the US Strategic Air Forces were to operate against one system of objectives, Bomber Command against another, and the AEAF [Allied Expeditionary Air Force] against yet another.
> Concentration against one common system, by both day and night, is essential.

When the strategic air forces were released from their primary obligation of supporting the land armies in July, Tedder's views on the importance of concentration remained unchanged, and he came strongly to believe that the real focus of a highly coordinated Allied air effort should be German communications, in which he linked German transport networks, rail, roads and canals, and fuel supplies into one large target group. "In my opinion our primary Air objective should be the enemy's communications. Road, water and rail are interdependent and complementary and our Air operations should play on that fact. The present Oil plan is the key to movement by road and air, and, moreover, directly affects operations in the Battle area."[46]

The gradual merging of the thinking of Spaatz, Portal and Tedder throughout 1944 in favor of a campaign against German mobility was one of the important reasons so much damage was eventually inflicted on Germany's production and armed forces. However, there remained one convinced skeptic, Arthur Harris. He regularly blustered against, ignored or subverted all plans to try to make him use Bomber Command in a coordinated campaign against oil or transportation targets. The abovementioned memorandum from Tedder was the kind of advice that was sure to attract a rebuke from Harris, who immediately complained to Portal.[47] He would only allow Bomber Command to take part in any such effort as part of its ongoing area attacks against German cities. Harris' unwillingness to accept direction or suggestion was one of the reasons this campaign was only partially underway by the time Anglo-American armies were ashore in France. For the first three months of 1944 he was wedded to his ongoing Battle of Berlin, and devoted whatever he could to that endeavor.[48] However, most others in control of the application of Anglo-American air power had a far better understanding of how to proceed in the destruction of German war production.

The first step: the destruction of the Luftwaffe as a fighting force

The strategic bombing of Germany in 1944 proceeded along a route, partially planned, occasionally by accident, which ended up destroying German production in a series of steps. The first, crucial step in that process was the de-fanging of the Luftwaffe as a force that could disrupt the Anglo-American air forces as they attacked German targets.

As had been demonstrated repeatedly in 1943, the Luftwaffe was still capable of shooting down large numbers of expensive British and American bombers. Moreover, in 1944 the Luftwaffe was based in Germany as never before, as the land battlefield increasingly became a secondary concern.

In 1944 German aircraft production was turning out almost exclusively fighters as production of bombers was either scaled back or halted altogether. Because of this change, German fighter production jumped by more than 150 percent when compared with 1943 (28,926 versus 11,738). The best pilots were also always sent to the fighter wings, including those who had originally been trained to fly bombers. However, when it came to deploying these new fighters, the battlefield became subsidiary – in both real and percentage terms. In June 1944, only 27 percent of German fighters were on the Eastern Front or the Mediterranean, and by December this figure was down to 15 percent. German fighter losses were equally, and at times more so, skewed away from the Eastern Front and the Mediterranean.[49] Of these, a disproportionately small number would have come from the Eastern Front. In 1944 as a whole, the monthly loss rate for the Luftwaffe when flying against the RAF and USAAF was on average a crippling 82 percent of its effective strength in single-engine fighters. On the Eastern Front, the loss rate for single-engine fighters was 42 percent.[50]

The air war over Germany and France at this time reached the kind of scale that put it out of proportion with all other air conflicts in World War II. American, British and German production of aircraft peaked in 1944, which meant that the numerical size of the forces involved was unprecedented. The Luftwaffe, for instance, increased the normal size of each Geschwader based in Germany by one-quarter, giving them each an allocated strength of 288 aircraft.[51] By the summer of 1944, the average number of Luftwaffe fighters opposing just the American daylight raids was 300.[52] The Germans, however, found it impossible to reap any advantage from this build-up of large forces, because their loss rates over Germany were going up even faster than their increases in construction.

The most extreme example of this was the skyrocketing losses of German daylight fighters and the toll inflicted by the longer-range escort fighters such as the Mustang. Starting with "Big Week" (see below), German pilot losses became unsustainably high.[53] The average monthly lost/damaged rate for Luftwaffe aircraft jumped from an already high 52.4 percent in January 1944 to a completely unsustainable 96.3 percent in June.[54] The main Luftflotte in charge of defending German home industry, Luftflotte Reich, which was founded in February 1944 out of Luftwaffenbefehlshaber Mitte, saw losses which went up by 150 percent between the end of 1943 and the first half of 1944. In the last quarter of 1943, it lost 671 aircraft destroyed or damaged (almost all of them fighters) opposing just the daylight raids.[55] In the first quarter of 1944, this number jumped to 1,555. This extreme loss rate opposing daylight raids was almost exactly the same in the second quarter of 1944, when another 1,551 aircraft were lost – again 99 percent of them fighter aircraft.[56]

The only comparative losses were those suffered by the Luftwaffe during its attempts in June and July to intervene in the land battle in France after the D-Day landings. During these two months, the fighter forces based in Germany were for all practical purposes combined with those fighting in France, and were sometimes used to try to intervene over the land battles in large formations. Yet, for all their size, they made little impact and suffered extreme losses. Except for these two months, however, what occurred was a massive air-on-air conflict which tied down four to five times as much German fighter aircraft production as the supposedly large battles on land.

By this stage, the air war over Germany, in terms of equipment deployed and equipment destroyed, was, for the Nazi state, by far the largest battle in Europe during World War II. (See Figure 52.) The land battlefields, with the exception of the engagements over Normandy, played a very small role in the destruction of German air power in

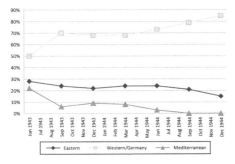

52 German fighter deployment (all types), June 1943–December 1944 percentage by front.
Source: Air 40-1207, Luftwaffe Deployment Chart compiled October 1945.

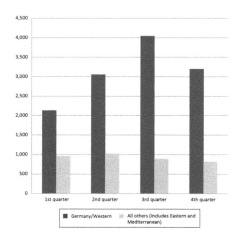

53 German single-engine fighter losses, 1944, by front.
Source: USSBS, European Report 59, "The Defeat of the German Air Force," p. 2.
The exact figures are not given for the fourth quarter so they are estimates from
the chart on that page.

1944. (See Figure 53.) These fighter aircraft losses dominated all
German aircraft losses for the year. In the end, the Luftwaffe lost
15,327 combat aircraft on operational duties in 1944.[57] Of these
12,430, or 81 percent, were single-engine fighters.[58]

So, just as the Luftwaffe was reaching the peak of its production in the middle of 1944, it was being destroyed in ever greater
numbers by Anglo-American air power. Of course, that tells only part
of the story of the destruction of the Luftwaffe. These losses were only
those of aircraft on combat operations. The pressure placed on Germany also destroyed a great deal of its air power in pre-production,
deployment and non-operational stages. Up to 15,000 German aircraft
were "lost" this way in 1944.

To begin with, there were the continuing attacks on the
German aircraft industry. The 8th Air Force made the most famous
series of attacks of this type in early 1944. Starting on February 20, in
what was termed "Big Week," they launched a series of raids on a
range of Messerschmitt, Focke-Wulf and Junkers aircraft facilities.[59]
There were some successes, in particular through the destruction of
German airframe production. Dr. Karl Frydag, the head of air frame
industry, estimated that Germany lost the production of 4,000 aircraft
in these raids.[60] Furthermore, he believed that these raids were
the real impetus behind another expensive and massive dispersal of

aircraft production.[61] (See Map 6.) According to Speer, the 1944 plan was eventually to have 3 million square meters of aircraft construction space underground.[62] By the time Germany surrendered, about 1 million square meters of this plan had been constructed. Of this, 200,000 square meters was being used for actual production, so that much had been spent, but as of yet relatively little had been built.[63]

This dispersal effort helps further illustrate the great gap that existed in efficient man-hour aircraft productivity between Germany, a country that had to produce its aircraft under constant threat of strategic air attack, and the United States and the United Kingdom, which could plan more rationally. As mentioned earlier, the United States and Germany employed approximately the same number of workers building aircraft in 1943 and 1944 – 2 million.[64] It is even possible that the Germans, who were desperately trying to find additional workers for their ME-262 program, were using more by 1944. However, the Germans suffered through great inefficiencies – many owing to the pressures of building aircraft under the threat of air attack. The physical process of dispersing production to the east itself caused production declines just because of transportation. These were such a problem that Tank did his best to keep any important Focke-Wulf plants from being dispersed.[65] Some plants which were structured to build bombers had to be completely reconfigured to build fighters, losing a great deal of their productivity while the process was ongoing.[66] Messerschmitt believed that this 1944 dispersal caused a 50 percent loss of production while it was undertaken.[67] In the end, much of German aircraft production was for its own safety placed in distant, out of reach facilities, some in caves, where the workers had to do their jobs in difficult conditions when compared with the large and orderly American factories churning out aircraft at the same time. (See Figures 54 and 55.)

Returning to Frydag's estimate of 4,000 aircraft lost as a result of the impact of Big Week, the figure seems possible but rather high, partly because of the panic that ensued which forced the Germans to channel greater efforts into recovering lost production. According to Saur, the immediate reaction to Big Week was a crisis that threatened to cause a German "erschuetternd" or shattering.[68] Almost 75 percent of major German factory buildings in which airframes were built suffered damage – though, as usual, many of

54 Production of the most advanced aircraft Germany would produce during the war, the ME-262, often took place in cramped underground facilities such as this – a whole different world from American or British production (see Figures 4–7).

55 V-weapon production also often took place in underground facilities, such as this for the V-1 cruise missile, with the added horror of slave labor.

the vital machine tools survived the destruction of their buildings as only 25–30 percent of them were lost.[69] These attacks were one of the prime reasons that aircraft production was finally taken away from the Luftwaffe and made part of Speer's industrial empire. The creation of the Jaegerstab on March 1 1944 resulted, according to Saur, in a dramatic rationalization of aircraft production which mitigated the potentially damaging impact of Big Week. More recently, however, a number of different historians have argued that the production increases that occurred at this time owed little to Speer's or Saur's efforts. Tooze ascribed the increases more to Speer and Saur's coercive and oppressive production methods than any rationalization.[70] Meanwhile Budrass, Scherner and Streb give credit to the aircraft industry itself, which they believe increased production because of steps put in place long before the Jaegerstab or Speer had anything to do with aircraft construction.[71]

Regardless, the Jaegerstab took control of all single-engine and twin-engine fighters, fighter-bombers, close-range reconnaissance and ground-strafing aircraft, primarily the ME-109, 110, 210 and 410, the FW-190 and the JU-88 and 388.[72] For whatever reason, there was a significant increase in the production of German fighters on a unit, if not a quality, basis. According to Speer, who claimed that the original estimates were that Big Week would reduce monthly fighter construction to somewhere between 30 percent and 60 percent of the previous level, three major repair and rationalization steps were taken which kept the production losses under control.

(a) ... all building facilities in the neighborhood of damaged plants were immediately mobilized for repair work.
(b) The evacuation and dispersal program then in progress was temporarily suspended to avoid production losses due to relocation.
(c) A purge of the Luftwaffe production programs was initiated in order to reduce the number of types and sub-types then in production, which numbered about 200.[73]

In February the overall production loss when compared with January was 18 percent. By the end of March, production, in terms of units, had recovered so swiftly that the monthly output was 25 percent higher than in February. For the next four months production rose as almost all types of aircraft other than fighters were discontinued. However, even the temporary loss of production in February and March 1944 was important because in May a new series of attacks began which caused the Luftwaffe even more problems than the direct attacks on their aircraft manufacturing facilities.

On May 12, an event occurred that seemed particularly ominous to those with knowledge of the German economy. The first large raid on German oil production, as part of the revamped CBO, was launched. A total of 935 four-engine bombers, a very large force by the standards of the previous year, were sent to attack Germany's synthetic oil plants.[74] Crucially, this attack was supported by hundreds of long-range fighters. However, the Luftwaffe was also there in force. To fight this one attack, at least 200 German fighters were scrambled. They attacked the bombers and fighter escorts in large groupings of up to 30 fighters at a time. Ultimately, 800 four-engine bombers were able to reach the target, where they severely damaged the oil plants, although in the end almost 50 bombers were shot down.

For the Americans under Spaatz's direction, this marked the beginning of regular attacks on German fuel supplies. Although the attacks were never as frequent as Spaatz would have liked, they made up a regular part of the strategic bombing targeting process. Particular attention was paid to Germany's hydrogenation plants. Hydrogenation was the process by which tar from anthracite coal was converted to fuel using high pressure, heat and extremely toxic chemicals. Because of the enormous growth in American aircraft construction, these raids in 1944 were considerably more powerful than those launched by the Americans and British in 1943, even when they were being launched as secondary priority operations after supporting the Normandy landings and attacking Crossbow targets (see below). In 1944 as a whole, the British and Americans dropped four times the tonnage of bombs on German production as they had in 1943: 921,990 tons to 235,075 tons.[75] This includes tonnage that was specifically dropped on German production, including British area attacks and American "precision" bombing, but exempts all bombs dropped on the V-weapon sites, airfields, German troop concentrations and in support of Anglo-American armies. (See Figure 56). The real shift when it came to strategic bombing was away from the targets of 1943, such as submarine yards and German cities, towards a more focused attack on fuel production and other mobility targets, such as rail yards and bridges. (See Figures 57 and 58.)

For the Germans this was an extremely depressing development.[76] The coordinator of German airframe production, which itself was heavily bombed in 1943 and 1944, believed that the oil attacks made a greater contribution to the German defeat than the attacks on his own industry.[77] Speer's reaction to these first heavy attacks in May

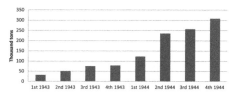

56 Anglo-American bombs dropped on economic targets by quarter, 1943–4, in thousands of tons.
Sourc: Arnold MSS, Reel 190, "The Contribution of Air Power to the Defeat of Germany," Appendix K.

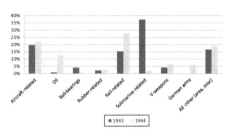

57 USAAF strategic air forces, selected targets for bombing, 1943 and 1944 (first nine months), percentage.
Source: Air 40-1120, Strategic Bombing of Axis Europe, January 1943–September 1944, pp. 10–11.

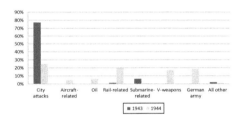

58 UK strategic air forces, selected targets for bombing, 1943 and 1944 (first nine months), percentage.
Source: Air 40-1120, Strategic Bombing of Axis Europe, January 1943–September 1944, pp. 10–11.

1944 was a momentary despair similar to that after the attack on Hamburg in 1943. He went directly to Hitler to ask for special support for the oil industry, as he told his interrogators after the war.

> When you attacked several hydrogenation plants on 12 May 1944 it became clear to me that a continuation of these attacks would be the deadly danger to us. I flew to Poelitz on the same day in order to look at the bombed plants. I continued my journey the following night to Obersalzberg to get a special authorization which I transferred to Geilenberg who carried through the reconstruction of the hydrogenation plants with special effort. The happenings of the 12th of May had been a nightmare for us for more than two years.[78]

Just as with the first ball-bearing attacks in 1943, these attacks were not followed up immediately. This gave the Germans some time for partial recovery – though at a huge cost in manpower.[79] Edmund

Geilenberg, whom Speer mentioned, soon had an army of 350,000 workers whose job it was to repair damaged oil installations.[80] However, unlike in 1943, the bombers did return to the targets before all the repairs had been finished. On June 20, one evening's raids on a set of oil installations involved 1,361 four-engine bombers escorted by 729 fighters.[81] In July the bombers returned and caused considerably more damage, so much so that this time German production of synthetic oil never came close to recovering. By the end of the summer, twenty-four synthetic oil plants and sixty-nine refineries had been seriously damaged.[82]

This was a particular disaster for the Luftwaffe. The May raids by the 8th Air Force had been specifically aimed at German synthetic production plants in Bruex, Poelitz, Leuna, Boehlen, Luetzkendorf, Magdeburg, Zeitz and Ruhland.[83] These plants produced almost all Germany's high-octane aviation-grade fuel. In the first quarter of 1944, Germany produced 546,000 tons of aviation fuel, of which 503,000 tons came from hydrogenation.[84] Hans Kehrl said that the May attacks had resulted in the loss of about 20 percent of this monthly production, while further attacks in June reduced April production levels by half.[85] By September, aviation fuel production was down to 10,000 tons a month. (See Figure 59.)

Of course, aviation fuel was only part of the problem. These attacks also destroyed German production of fuel for vehicles and power generation, though not quite as dramatically to begin with. Overall German fuel production also went into a serious decline in May and June 1944. (See Figure 60.)

There is a mistaken notion that the loss of Romania as part of the land war made a significant difference in this. In 1944, imported oil made up a relatively small percentage of German fuel products even before the largest oil-producing areas were captured by land armies. Ploesti, the large Romanian oil facility near Bucharest which was the largest exporter of fuel products into Germany, fell to the Red

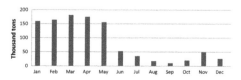

59 German monthly production of aviation fuel, 1944, in thousands of tons. *Source:* USSBS, European Report 3, p. 79.

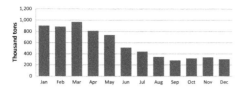

60 German monthly production of oil products (all sources), 1944, in thousands of tons.
Source: USSBS, European Report 3, p. 79.

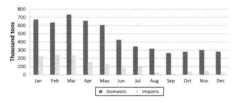

61 German monthly domestic and imported oil production, 1944, in thousands of tons.
Source: USSBS, European Report 3, p. 79.

Army on August 10, 1944. However, between January and July 1944, imported oil made up only 22 percent of German oil products, and imports had already declined significantly since March. (See Figure 61.) In fact, what the production figures show is that by the time Ploesti was physically captured, Germany had already lost access to most of its fuel production because of strategic bombing. Ira Eaker, now commander of the 15th Air Force in the Mediterranean, had made attacking Ploesti one of his highest priorities. (See Figure 62.) Beginning in April 1944, the 15th Air Force launched a series of raids that were so effective (if costly in American aircraft) that imported fuel imports into Germany dropped by two-thirds between February and June of that year. The key for Germany in terms of continuing to fight the war in 1944 was not protecting oil imports, but trying to protect its domestic hydrogenation plants. Had that been done, then the German armed forces and economy would have been able to continue resisting.[86]

The impact of the loss of domestically produced aviation fuel made things many times worse for the Luftwaffe. From June onwards, production was wholly inadequate to meet its needs, so the only way operations could be maintained was to draw down stockpiles.[87] To maintain optimal operational performance, the Luftwaffe needed at least 300,000 tons of aviation fuel per month.[88] However, they were

62 A formation of B-24s attacking Romanian oil production at Ploesti, May 1944. These raids, part of a growing offensive against German access to fuel, helped deprive Germany of most of its fuel before the oilfields were physically captured by the Red Army in August.

able to cope, though reducing flying time, with the production of about 160,000 tons, which was available through May 1944. When production dropped below that, it had a very damaging impact on operations and helped lead to a growing loss rate in the second half of 1944. British intelligence noted that beginning in the summer of 1944, the number of sorties flown per German aircraft declined, so that the Luftwaffe was getting significantly reduced value from its increased production of aircraft.[89] As Goering said rather plaintively after being captured, "without fuel, nobody can conduct a war."[90]

The effects of this shortage of fuel could be felt throughout the Luftwaffe. One of the other reasons losses mounted in the second half of 1944 was even more seriously degraded pilot training. Even as the need for more and more pilots became pressing owing to increased production and increased losses, the Luftwaffe had no fuel to train them. In July 1944 the number of hours a German pilot trainee needed before being sent on operations was reduced to approximately 100.[91] Of this, only 30 were spent in aircraft with the power of operational fighters. At the same time, both the RAF and USAAF required at least 300 hours before operations, and almost all the flying time was in aircraft with engines as powerful as they would have when on operations.[92] However, it does seem that in certain cases the Germans couldn't even supply enough fuel to give their pilots the 100 hours of training. Lt General Gerd von Massow, who directed German pilot training in 1944 and 1945, admitted that as fuel ran low, he simply stopped training certain pilots. "Eventually I arrived at the state where, with the small amount of petrol still remaining to me, I trained only those who were instructors with me and those who were half finished – all the rest, thousands and thousands of them, I handed over, men of the very best material whose training I simply couldn't complete anymore."[93]

The qualitative difference of this inferior flight training exacerbated the already growing disparity in combat loss rates between the Germans and Anglo-American air forces. The German idea starting in 1943, when the air domestic war became the crucial front in German production, was that a loss rate of one German fighter plane for one American or British bomber would actually lead to a victory for the Luftwaffe in the skies over Germany.[94] This was quite sensible. They had calculated that one B-17 or Lancaster used nine times as much aluminum as one FW-190 or ME-109. As combined Anglo-American production of aluminum, the vital metal for aircraft construction, was thought to be four times larger than German production, a one to one loss ratio between German fighters and Allied bombers would quickly become too expensive for the Allies to maintain.

In 1943, the Germans believed, this is precisely what happened. By their calculations, the Allies were losing at least one bomber for every German fighter, and for the 8th Air Force, even for all the damage that it was inflicting, such a loss rate became unbearable. However, all the calculations proved useless in 1944 when Luftwaffe losses soared. According to Galland:

(Q) What were your loss rates before we attacked Central Germany with fighter-escort?

Galland: Before you used fighter-escort our losses were amazingly small. According to our reports – from which one naturally has to deduct a few – we shot down fifteen to twenty four-engine bombers and only lost an equal number of fighters at *the very most* and only six or seven pilots...

(Q) What were your highest losses in a month?

Galland: I used to keep exact count and graphs regarding that as daily losses were of less interest to me ... I only compiled the data and used them to make my dispositions for the following month. Our highest monthly total loss from all fronts was 1800 aircraft and not quite 700 pilots – consisting of losses due to enemy action, technical breakdown, smashes, etc. – only day fighters.

(q) Did that include night-fighters?

Galland: No.

(Q) When was that?

Galland: During the main fighting months, either July/August or September 1944.

(Q) Wasn't air activity on the Eastern Front very slight then?

Galland: Relatively slight. Above all, our losses there were extraordinarily light.[95]

Galland's memory was correct. Losses over Germany in the summer of 1944 were unbearable for the Luftwaffe. Between January and May 1944, the Anglo-American and Luftwaffe loss rates had started diverging sharply. The Allies were losing only 1.4 percent per sortie while German fighter losses leapt to 10.7 percent.[96]

Luftwaffe aircraft, when they were given enough fuel to fly operations, were being damaged at a much higher rate. In 1944, on average, the Luftwaffe lost 73 percent of its single-engine fighter aircraft strength every month.[97] For the British and Americans, the opposite occurred and their chances of being shot down plummeted. At the height of the war in 1943, bombers of the 8th Air Force had an 18.2 percent chance of being damaged by a German aircraft while on operations. In the second half of 1944, after the hydrogenation campaign had started to damage Luftwaffe operations, the rate dropped to below 1 percent.[98] Soon the Americans felt so safe that they started increasing the standard number of flights that they expected each bomber crew to do from twenty to thirty.

At the same time that operational losses were soaring for the Luftwaffe, non-operational losses became very large. During the year, 24,285 aircraft were lost or damaged on operational duty, while at the same time, 9,872 were lost or damaged on non-operational duty.[99] (See Figure 63.) To put those non-operational losses into context, the Luftwaffe had 8,498 aircraft lost or damaged in operational duties in all theaters in 1942.[100] Now, in 1944, they were losing as many aircraft in non-operational ways as they lost in all operations in the year of El Alamein, Torch and Stalingrad. Finally, the fact that the Luftwaffe lost approximately 40 percent as many valuable aircraft in non-operational actions as it did in operations does help lend credence to the statement of Speer and others than in 1944, 25 percent of aircraft were being lost on the way to their deployment areas.

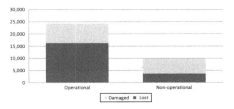

63 German aircraft, lost and damaged on operational and non-operational
duty, 1944.
Sourc: Spaatz MSS, 116, GAF Aircraft and Aircrew Losses 1939–1945.

So, by the end of the summer of 1944, the Luftwaffe had been
neutered. Its construction rate, even though it had risen since February,
was thousands of units behind its potential. Completed units, because
they were often being built in hastily constructed, inefficient plants to
protect them from Anglo-American bombing, were often poorly made
and malfunctioned quickly. Those planes that were built and could fly
well were being shot down in unsustainably high numbers in the skies
over Germany and France by better Allied planes. A lack of aviation
fuel because of the strategic bombing attack on their hydrogenation
plants meant German operations were being progressively limited.
Moreover, the lack of fuel meant that those pilots going through
training were so inexperienced with their aircraft that they posed
relatively little threat to the Allies. From now on, the RAF and USAAF
could fly over the Reich with the knowledge that their chance of being
shot down or damaged was very small. The crucial first step in the
strategic bombing campaign had been taken, and what was left to do
was to shut down movement in the German economy and for German
armed forces as a whole.

Crossbow: one of the greatest battles of World War II

Before addressing the rest of the strategic bombing campaign in 1944,
it would be worthwhile discussing a separate campaign that was one of
the greatest "battles" of World War II. The standard narrative of the
air war in Europe focuses on the switch of Anglo-American air
resources from strategic bombing to support of the impending D-Day
operations beginning in March 1944. What is perhaps less well known
is that this switch was only partial. It was not that many aircraft were

still regularly bombing Germany as part of a strategic bombing campaign. It was that large numbers of Allied aircraft in the next few months were used in operations that had nothing to do with the D-Day landings, namely those employed as part of Operation Crossbow.

In 1965 a major movie was made about Operation Crossbow which epitomizes everything that is wrong about the daring-do vision of World War II. Starring George Peppard and Sophia Loren, it tells the story of an American secret agent being infiltrated into an underground German V-2 factory that looks more like the lair of a James Bond villain than the real caves of misery and death in which the rockets were built. From the inside, this brave secret agent proceeds to sabotage German rocket production. However, within the context of winning World War II, the real problem with the movie is that it hardly mentions the real Operation Crossbow, which was the enormous allocation of air resources against German V-1 and V-2 production and launch facilities.[101]

Crossbow involved considerably more production, on both the German and Allied sides, than far more famous engagements such as El Alamein and Kursk. On both sides, it represented an enormous expenditure of expensive and technologically advanced resources. For the Germans, it was an investment which began in 1934 when early rocket experiments began on the island of Peenemunde on the Baltic coast of eastern Germany. In 1943, in response to the strategic bombing of Germany, Hitler's interest in the program grew markedly, and in that summer it became the single highest-priority weapons program for the Nazi state.[102]

Overall, the V-2 was the most expensive weapon system the Nazis ever undertook. The USSBS estimate was that the effort that went into the project in 1944 and 1945 alone was equal to the cost of production of 24,000 aircraft.[103] Another estimate is that the development and production of the V-2 cost Nazi Germany RM 2 billion.[104] In that case it would have cost Germany in relative terms as much as the Manhattan Project cost the United States. Actually this latter estimate might be too low, as production costs alone would have reached that level. In per unit costs, according to Speer, the first V-2s cost RM 1 million each.[105] Later, when production became more efficient, the per unit cost dropped to somewhere between RM 250,000 and RM 300,000.[106] The actual number of V-2s built was between 6,000 and 7,000. At the end of the war, documents from Speer's ministry claimed that in 1944, 4,145 were completed, with an additional 2,165 finished in 1945.[107] However the director of the main assembly plant, the Mittelwerke at Niedersachswerfen claimed that a larger number was built, more than 7,000.[108] Even if we accept the lower estimate on production and cost, more than 6,000 V-2s were built, at an average cost of something close to RM 300,000 each, which alone would have cost close almost RM 2 billion. If the higher estimates for number and cost are right, the overall cost could easily have reached 3 billion RM.

In terms of construction man hours, producing the V-2 represented one of the great investments of the German war economy between 1943 and 1945. Frydag believed that putting so much effort into the V-2 seriously limited aircraft production in 1944, and he wanted to kill off the V-2 completely to build more fighters. Once production of V-2s became relatively efficient, the smallest estimate is that it still took 20,000 man hours to build one unit.[109] This figure was still far above that expected if the plant had been able to operate normally.[110] Milch, by way of comparison, said that he heard it took between 40,000 and 50,000 hours for each V-2.[111] The reality was probably closer to 20,000 than 40,000. Speer claimed that when production was up and running, one V-2 took the equivalent effort of six or seven fighters.[112] As one FW-190 took 3,700 man hours to build in 1944, if Speer was correct, one V-2 would have taken between 22,200 and 25,900 man hours to construct.[113]

The V-1, on the other hand, was the Luftwaffe's attempt to develop a pilotless weapon in response to the attention being lavished on the V-2. Design started before the war began, but it was after the Battle of Britain that the V-1 was really pushed forward, with the first successful test launch occurring in 1942. Speer, who was a prime backer of the V-2 as it was under his control, was rather dismissive of the V-1, which he called "primitive."[114] An early form of cruise missile, the V-1 carried 1,870 pounds of explosive attached to its own pulse-jet engine and was guided to its target by a gyroscope-based system.[115] It was extremely inaccurate: basically pointed in a straight line at a target, its specific hitting point was determined by when it ran out of fuel and plunged to earth. Its cost was relatively cheap, however, with the production of every V-1 costing approximately 5 percent in materials and 2 percent in labor of the cost of a V-2.[116] Professor Tank, who oversaw a great deal of work on the engine development for the V-1s and who was critical of both V-weapon projects – believing that their high priority was a result of Hitler's "romantic" notions about how to run the war – claimed that one V-1 took 300 man hours to construct.[117] Milch confirmed the 300 man hour estimate after the war.[118] However, as far more V-1s were built than V-2s – 30,257 compared with 6,000–7,000 – the final man hours differential was large but not as extreme as the unit cost might indicate.[119] It should also be kept in mind that the support cost of these weapons was very high. As early as September 1943, 40,000 Organization Todt workers were building the launch facilities in Holland, Belgium and northern France for the V-1 alone.[120]

If the German commitment to V-weapons was enormously costly in all respects, the reaction that it created amongst the British and Americans, particularly the former, was dramatic and also expensive. In early May 1943, the British government became worried about reports it was receiving about weapons development, specifically rockets, on the island of Peenemunde. A combination of different intelligence sources, including photography, prisoners of war and agents, led to a fascinating internal discussion over just what the Germans were doing.[121] In what was probably the most impressive example of intelligence analysis anytime in the war, on June 29, 1943 an expanded War Cabinet met to discuss this set of evidence. Not only was the strategic leadership present – Churchill, Brooke, Pound and Portal – but they were joined by Attlee, Eden, Herbert Morrison, Stafford Cripps, Lord Cherwell and Duncan Sandys, who had done a great deal of work preparing the intelligence.[122] Cherwell did not distinguish himself or his scientific credentials by arguing that any rocket was probably a German hoax.[123] If not, he argued, then it would only be able to fly for approximately 40 miles and would not do much damage. Most of those in the room, on the other hand, took the report seriously and gave approval to a large raid on the Peenemunde facility whenever the RAF believed it could be done effectively.[124]

On the evening of August 17, a large force of 597 four-engine bombers was dispatched by Bomber Command to attack Peenemunde.[125] Although they damaged a number of buildings and killed a handful of technical experts, as well as some prison laborers, work on the V-2 development was not affected as the missile was ready to go into production.[126] However, in response to the attacks, V-2 work was switched to more secure locations and the production facilities were moved into expensive underground factories. The expense of such a move added a great deal to its already exorbitant production costs. One of the reasons that it took so long, relatively, for the V-2 to be launched was the complexity of its manufacture and the great expense of having to relocate its production efforts. For instance, 3,000 V-2s had to be test-fired before it was thought prudent to start stockpiling models for an eventual offensive.[127]

In the next few months after the Peenemunde raid, the British became even more convinced that Germany was pressing ahead with a long-range weapons program. In October 1943, Sandys published an updated summary of the situation which assumed that an attack could start as soon as early 1944.[128] Just a few days later, photographic intelligence discovered a series of fixed ramps being constructed by the Germans, all facing towards the United Kingdom. These "ski-slopes," as they were nicknamed, were intended for the V-1 and not the V-2, but were quickly singled out as an important target for air attack. The British officially requested that the USAAF make attacking them one of their highest priorities. Large raids by medium and heavy bombers in November and December 1943 damaged many of these seriously and forced a delay in the overall launch of the V-1.[129] Considering how late in the year these attacks occurred, they ended up making up a creditable amount of the year's bombing totals. During 1943, the 8th Air Force dropped 4.1 percent of its total weight of bombs on flying-bomb sites.[130] That might not sound impressive, but it was actually the same amount as was dropped on all ball-bearing targets the same year, which is seen as one of the main foci of the American effort. It was also more than five times as many bombs as were dropped on all oil targets.

These attacks were also some of the most successful of the Crossbow campaign and caused a rethink by the Germans on how to launch their weapons.[131] Instead of relying on just a small number of fixed sites, a range of different launch systems were developed. New sites had to be assembled which were far better camouflaged and different mobile launching options, including temporary ramps and air-launched V-1s, were developed. By the time the first V-1s were launched, more than 160 possible targets had been identified by the Anglo-American air forces in France, Belgium and Holland alone and most had been attacked.[132] It was an example of the overall complexity of a campaign such as Crossbow when compared with a standard land battle. There was a basic lack of knowledge on each side of what the other knew. Systems like these first fixed launching ramps could be attacked and destroyed, but they were then replaced by alternative systems. In that way the battle between the Allies and Germany became a fully layered form of warfare, with a cycle of moves and counter-moves. It also forced the British and Americans to come up with many different ways of defeating these weapons, from attacking factories which made their fuel, to bombing their launch mechanisms, to, for the V-1 only, actually attacking the weapon in flight. As such, an extraordinary range of aircraft was sent on Crossbow operations.[133] Fighters such as the P-47 Thunderbolt and the Spitfire patrolled along the French, Belgian and Dutch coasts hoping to observe different launch preparations. Light bombers such as the Mosquito and mediums such as the B-25 and B-26 were sent to attack specific targets identified by aerial intelligence. The heavies such as the B-17s and the Lancasters were sent to attack large development and industrial targets thought vital to V-1 and V-2 production.

For the first five months of 1944, Crossbow operations were a regular factor in Anglo-American air planning. Between February and June 1944, there were 11,550 Crossbow-directed sorties which dropped 16,500 tons of bombs.[134] In April 1944, General Eisenhower, who as supreme commander had been given control over all British and American aircraft in the ETO, designated Crossbow attacks as temporarily the single greatest priority for the RAF and USAAF, higher in importance even than the attacks to be launched in preparation for the D-Day landings.[135] On May 26, during a meeting of the combined Air Staffs in preparation for D-Day, a meeting attended by Tedder, Spaatz, Harris and Doolittle, it was stated that 10 percent of all the American and British air efforts at this time were being directed towards Crossbow targets and would continue to be so until the landings.[136] At that point, it was hoped, Crossbow attacks could be downgraded. However, the exact opposite occurred.

The first V-1s were launched towards London on the evening of June 12. Twenty-three were launched, but only four made landfall.[137] On the evening of June 15, things became much more serious when 122 V-1s were launched, 44 of which landed in London. From then until September 3, the UK was attacked almost every day. When faced with this new threat, a decision was made to divert a massive amount of Anglo-American air power from the battlefields of Normandy to take part in Crossbow operations. In particular, four-engine heavy bombers, which had made a minority of Crossbow sorties to this point, now became by far the most involved aircraft. The importance given to Crossbow targets was so great that, when strategic bombers were permitted to be used for other tasks than the preparations for D-Day, they were sometimes not allowed to attack oil targets, Spaatz's preference, but instead were sent against possible V-1 and V-2 targets.[138]

Because of this, the amount of bombs dropped and the number of sorties flown as part of Crossbow until the end of August was immense. For instance, at this time more RAF Bomber Command daytime sorties were directed at Crossbow targets than were made in support of the British armies fighting in France.[139] What made this more impressive was that Harris was forced to do this when he personally lobbied against having to spend much effort on Crossbow targets.[140] From the beginning of June until the end of August, approximately 81,000 tons of bombs were dropped by the RAF and USAAF on Crossbow targets.[141] This is a remarkable figure, as many of these attacks were made by medium bombers and fighters, which carried considerably smaller payloads than the heavies, against smaller, more difficult to hit targets. (See Figure 64) Additionally, these 81,000 tons represented 3 percent of the bombs dropped by the British and Americans in all theaters by all aircraft *during the entire war*.[142] As a point of comparison, only 32,000 tons of bombs were dropped on Germany itself during all of June, July and August 1944.[143] Also, the amount of bombs dropped in support of the British and American armies fighting in France during these three months was, at most, 67,000 tons.[144]

At this point, the RAF started shouldering the majority of the load as part of Crossbow. Driven obviously by the need to try to protect the British population, it dropped 17 percent of its bomb tonnage on suspected V-1 launch sites during the first nine months of 1944.[145] On June 19, less than two weeks after D-Day, when the Anglo-American armies were making slow headway in Normandy, Eisenhower wrote Marshall specifically about the V-1s, and said that every heavy American and British bomber was prepared to launch two consecutive attacks on V-1 sites as soon as the weather made that possible.[146] In the end this was a major diversion of British and American strategic bombing resources, as a British intelligence report calculated in October 1944.

64 An indication of how Crossbow was one of the "biggest" battles of the war. To destroy the small target in the center of the picture in 1944, many thousands of bombs were dropped in multiple attacks.

> Defensive operations against launching and supply sites used for flying bomb attacks against England required the diversion of a considerable part of the strategic bombing effort. About 106,400 tons of bombs were dropped by Allied strategic forces in this campaign. During the first nine months of 1944, about 7 percent of USAAF tonnages and 17 percent of RAF tonnages were dropped on such installations. As a result of these attacks construction was delayed and numerous sites rendered unusable, including four very large installations intended for heavy rockets.[147]

The number of sorties launched as part of Crossbow grew just as relentlessly as the weight of bombs dropped. Between March and August 1944 alone, the British and American air forces launched an astonishing 35,000 attacks on different Crossbow targets.[148] Just scouting for possible V-1 launches became a huge operation. British and American aircraft were often sent on speculative patrols over the roads of suspected launch sites on the chance that a target would appear. Between September 1944 and April 1945, more than 4,300 aircraft were sent on such reconnaissance missions.[149] It should be said that these extraordinary efforts support the notion that the V-1 was by far the more cost-effective of the two weapons systems. Although Speer was dismissive of it as a weapon, it was much cheaper than the V-2, but, if anything, caused even more of a reaction in air power by the British and Americans. The most intense period of Crossbow air activity was June, July and August 1944, when the V-1 was the great target.

After September 1944, when the threat of the V-1 subsided and the V-2 appeared, Crossbow missions became less numerous. The V-2 could not be intercepted in flight, and its production facilities were underground and were therefore almost impossible to attack. Moreover, as the British and American armies pushed westward, the focus of V-1 and V-2 attacks moved from the UK to harbors and cities in western Europe from which British and American armies were gathering supplies. Hitler specifically ordered that all V-2s be aimed at the west, particularly London and the Belgian port of Antwerp.[150] Still in 1945 attacks continued. In April and May as the war was ending, there were a combined 4,000 attacks on Crossbow targets.[151] In an attempt to make a general summary of the extent of the operation, an internal USAAF study said immediately after the war:

> Total tonnage of bombs dropped on and sorties flown against German long-range weapon program are difficult to obtain... It is estimated, however, that altogether 124,000 tons of bombs were directed against the V-weapons. It is more accurately estimated that of the total Allied heavy bomber effort for 1944/5 5.6 per cent of all tonnage dropped was against this program. In the month of July 1944, heavy bombers devoted 22.4 per cent of all their tonnage to these targets. Among all target systems attacked by heavy bombers, the tonnage against oil and rails only the exceeded the amount expended on long range weapons.[152]

And yet, Crossbow as a battle is hardly discussed in the general literature of the great battles of World War II. Almost certainly, Crossbow is never mentioned in the same breath as Kursk or

El Alamein because, except for the great suffering of the slave laborers building the weapons, human casualties were light. Even though the Allied air effort put into Crossbow was superior to its efforts in the fighting in France from the middle of June 1944 until the end of August, relatively few airmen died. The United States, for example, lost only 610 military personnel in Crossbow operations.[153] British civilian casualties were also relatively light, considering the immense efforts that the Germans put into the weapon. The V-1 was responsible for 5,864 deaths in the UK, with another 17,200 people being seriously injured.[154] The V-2 was considerably less damaging than this, which, thankfully, makes the enormous cost of its construction one of the least efficient examples of military spending in human history in terms of damage inflicted (albeit not in terms of the reaction it caused). In the UK, 2,865 people were killed by V-2s, with another 6,286 seriously injured. On the continent, in particular around the port of Antwerp, thousands more died. The V-1 was responsible for 4,676 deaths and 10,072 serious injuries in Europe excepting the UK.[155] The V-2 was responsible for about 2,000 more deaths in the same area. On the other hand, tens of thousands of other workers, overwhelmingly slave laborers, were forced to build the new underground factories needed to construct the V-2. It seems that at least 60,000–70,000 slave workers were forcibly put to work at the main production facilities for the V-2.[156] Tragically, 10,000 of these workers perished from the extraordinary brutality they were shown by their Nazi captors, making them the single largest group of human victims killed by the V-weapons.

Within the context of World War II civilian casualties, these combined figures are very small. Individual air raids on Hamburg and Tokyo killed many times more civilians than all the V-1s and V-2s together. One of the reasons for this relatively limited loss of life was the effectiveness of Crossbow, especially against the launch sites. Xavier Dorsch, the head of the Organization Todt, immediately after the war claimed that in the construction of "V-1 and V-2 launching sites, there was very heavy damage, and some of the sites were never finished on this account. The first V-2 launching site was completely destroyed."[157] In the case of both weapons, the first launch and production rates were seriously retarded by Crossbow. And the fact that Germany put so much effort into the V-1 and V-2 as the war was entering this phase considerably lessened what it could build for the

battlefield. By all estimates, the Germans spent more on the V-1 and
V-2 in 1944 than they spent constructing vehicles of all types for the
army, perhaps many time more. In terms of aircraft, the 4,000 V-2s
built in 1944 had a labor value of more than 20,000 FW-190s. In that
sense the battle between the V-1/V-2 and Crossbow operations ended
up destroying far more German production than any land battle that
year, not even counting George Peppard's valiant efforts.

The loss of movement and the decline of German production

Once the Luftwaffe was rendered impotent to stop Anglo-American
strategic bombing, the campaign was broadened to target German
production and mobility as a whole. The attack against oil was maintained, so that German fuel production continued to decline until
September and then flattened out for the year. The average monthly
production at the end of 1944 of around 300,000 tons was one-third
of that in the beginning of the year. The German army found its fuel
supplies severely limited for the rest of the war, as the Ardennes
Offensive in December 1944 would demonstrate. Moreover, the
amount available for the domestic economy was itself wholly
inadequate.

Beginning in September 1944, a new campaign started against
German mobility, involving the heavy bombing of railway centers,
bridges, trains and canals within the Reich. In this, both strategic and
tactical air forces were used to great effect.[158] There had been a great
deal of railway bombing in the first half of 1944, but that had almost
all been in France as the RAF and USAAF were sent out to cut all rail
links into the landing beaches.[159] Once that was accomplished, and the
Luftwaffe was so damaged it couldn't resist, it was now the German
rail network's turn. At this time Tedder's arguments for a campaign
against transport made a significant difference.[160] While Spaatz still
remained focused on his campaign against oil production and Harris
continued to view anything other than his campaign of destroying
German cities as a waste of time and effort, Tedder, as Eisenhower's
most senior deputy, pressed for more regular attacks on German rail-
roads. He certainly seemed to get his way. In September 1944, there
were seventy attacks on German railway centers which involved the
dropping of 17,000 tons of bombs.[161] Transportation bombing, like

area bombing, was not solely directed towards destroying equipment in a pre-production mode. By ripping up Germany's transport net, primarily its rail network but also its river and canal traffic, equipment could be destroyed in the pre-production, production and deployment phases. (See Figures 65–7.)

On September 19, 1944, just a few weeks after concentrated attacks on Germany's transport network had commenced, Speer told Hitler that these attacks were stopping munitions production before it could begin.[162] The crucial issue was the shipment of coal throughout

65 A direct bomb hit on an ammunition train in a small railyard south of Hof, Germany, sends great billows of smoke up thousands of feet. An example of an attack that destroyed both German rail communications and equipment before it could reach the battlefield.

66 Another sign of an attack that accomplished two important aims – destroying German access to fuel and their transportation system – in order to shut down their mobility. These are oil-carrying train carriages blown on top of each other during an attack by P-47 Thunderbolts of the XIX Tactical Air Command (TAC), April 1945.

67 This two-deck, rail and road bridge which crossed the Moselle at Bullay was destroyed by a flight of four P-47 Thunderbolts on February 10, 1945.

the German productive process.[163] Attacking these coal shipments was always seen as one of the key benefits of a transportation campaign.[164] By destroying rail and canal transport facilities, only a tiny portion of the coal needed to power Germany's factories could be delivered from the mines to the power stations. Between September and October 1944, the amount of coal shipped in the Ruhr fell from 19,900 wagons daily to 7,700.[165]

Speer's arguments certainly seemed to register with the German dictator. Hitler actually referred to the devastation of the transport attacks in late December 1944. In a speech to German army divisional commanders on December 28, he urged them to support aggressive action. His main reason was that if Germany stood on the defensive, Anglo-American air supremacy would wreck its rail network and have a catastrophic impact on the home front and battlefield.[166]

Many others were also aware of what was happening to German transport at the time. Dr. Walter Schieber, an SS general as well as being a senior official in the Armaments Ministry with particular interest in heavy industry, believed that shipments of coal, which he termed "all-important," were the key determinant in all German munitions production. Only with a regular supply of coal could the factories of the Ruhr keep working. During the height of the air raids of 1943 and early 1944, even after being attacked from above, the factories were able to continue producing. However, as soon as they had their coal shipments cut, they withered and died.

> The air attacks of this area [Ruhr] from the spring of 1942 to
> the early summer of 1944 were not able to reduce its great
> contribution to the German war effort. On the contrary, it reached

its highest output in the autumn of 1943, and the early spring of 1944. This can be seen straight away from the supply figures for coal ... From the Summer of 1944, reaching a climax in October and onwards, the Ruhr and its transport network was subjected to the heaviest raids and by the end of the year had ceased to be industrially important to the Reich, from a war point of view.[167]

One of the great problems for the Germans was that they had not properly prepared for a strategic bombing campaign directed against their transportation system. Their experience in 1943 and the first part of 1944 was that, when it came to attacking economic targets, the British continued to favor the attack on cities while the Americans targeted specific systems such as oil production, aircraft production and ball-bearings. As such, the rationalization that had been undertaken for Germany's production had not been undertaken for its transportation. For instance, coal shipments across the Reich were not logically planned. In some cases coal for the plants in the Ruhr was supplied from Upper Silesia, while at the same time coal from the Ruhr was being sent to factories in far eastern Germany.[168] The result was that the weaknesses in the system were immediately revealed. One of the best historians of Speer and the air war has concluded that it was the combination of these transport attacks coming on the heels of the synthetic oil campaign that was the most important factor in persuading Speer that the war was lost.[169] Certainly Speer's writings at the time did become far more pessimistic in tone.

> Did the possibilities for mass production suffer because of air attacks?
>
> (Speer). As long as transport was alright we paid no attention to the errors in mass production and rationalization. We brought about special armaments production until 1944 without considering the problem of transport, and that was our mistake. Later, because of the lack of transport we were not able to function.[170]

Speer was so alarmed that he started writing increasingly dramatic memoranda for Hitler's attention. On October 5, he sent Hitler this memorandum:

353 / The decline of German production

The employment of all available progressing staff for the safeguarding of home production is, however, urgently necessary because the transport situation in the Ruhr Area has deteriorated extraordinarily.

Whilst in September 1943, an average of 19,900 wagons of coal were transported daily in the Ruhr Area, this allocation of wagons has fallen in the last few days to 8700 and 7700 wagons due to air attacks. Consequently, after about 8 to 12 weeks the industrial stocks, which are based on 4 weeks' supply, will be exhausted.[171]

By November the situation was so serious that much of German industry, which still had stockpiles of raw materials sufficient for at least another year, was on the verge of losing its sources of power. In early November, Speer sent a series of memoranda to Hitler and Keitel about the transport problems that had arisen because of bombing, in particular the problem of power generation in Germany. Lack of coal had forced a number of power plants to close and others were down to just a few weeks of reserves. Meanwhile, the transport campaign was systematically cutting Germany's industrial heart, the Ruhr, off from the rest of the country.

For over 6 weeks, there has been literally an increasing effect of isolating the Ruhr from its markets. Although it seemed that temporarily the number of wagons allocated for coal in the Ruhr had again improved from 7000 a day to at least 11000 or 12000, the number has actually sunk at the present time to the record low figure of 4000 to 5000 wagons daily.

The daily wagon allocation in the Ruhr area for coal would have to amount to 18000 to 21000 in order to cover both the Ruhr's own requirements for coal and the deliveries to the north, south, west and central German areas. The number of wagons provided daily at present, however, is not even adequate to begin to satisfy the internal traffic of the Rhine-Westphalian industrial area which had a normal demand amounting to 10000 wagons...

In view of the overall economic structure of the Reich, it goes without saying that a stoppage in the Rhine-Westphalian industrial area *would be intolerable for the entire German economy and for the successful continuation of the war over any period of time.*

In fact, except for that production still continuing on a local basis, the Ruhr is at present a total loss to the German economy.

There is no point in discussing the consequences for the entire Reich of a long-term stoppage in the Ruhr. (Emphasis in original)[172]

And the Ruhr did slowly grind to a halt. Railway activity throughout the Reich was reduced by almost 40 percent between August and December 1944.[173] When it came to coal, the factories of the Ruhr used up their stocks and existed in a hand-to-mouth state, with production restricted to times when they had access to fuel. The allocation of railway cars for the Ruhr coal trade dropped by 22 percent between July and September 1944, and by October was down 60 percent.[174] This rate of loss was then maintained for the rest of the year.[175]

If there was one crucial industry that was particularly hit by this slowdown in coal deliveries, it was Germany's iron and steel producers. Steel needed the intense heat generated by coal to be purified from pig iron. Either coal had to be brought to the steel plants or the steel plants needed to be built near to coal production. In 1944 those plants built close to German coal mines saw their production of steel stay high.[176] On the other hand, those that were built near the iron ore deposits and had to rely on coal shipments, which declined significantly in the last four months of 1944, saw much larger drops in production. The fact that these losses were due to the transport campaign is supported by the discovery after the war that, in most cases, the refining equipment within the German steel industry was mostly undamaged.[177]

This transportation campaign, coming after the earlier attacks on German oil production, led to a mobility crisis for the German economy and army. It stopped raw materials from moving to factories, reduced production, then hindered this reduced production from reaching the battlefield. It had a particularly damaging impact on the Luftwaffe, severely restricting Luftwaffe training so that large numbers of aircraft were put out of action owing to poor landings or flying errors. Those that made it to the battlefield were shot down more easily.

The combined impact of the oil and transport campaigns on both German labor allocation and armaments output was devastating. Hundreds of thousands of workers were moved from producing jobs to repairing jobs as the campaigns developed. One estimate after the war was that between September 1943 and October 1944 between 1.5 and

2 million workers were shifted from "productive" to "unproductive" work in response to the bombing campaigns.[178] That would have been at least equal to the number of workers who were employed on all German army munitions at the same period. Such an estimate is supported by other evidence. We know that 350,000 workers were assigned to repair bombing damage to different German oil facilities. Another 250,000–300,000 were undertaking similar repairs in the German chemical industry.[179] On the other hand, Milch, who a few months after losing control over aircraft construction to Speer was appointed to oversee the repair of bombed German railway lines, claimed that one million workers were taken out of factories to support his work.[180]

> There are two targets which are vulnerable in Germany: the synthetic oil plants, and communications. The invasion in the North of France would never have been so successful if communications had still been working properly. Then the Allies completely destroyed the area to the left of the Rhine in Germany, then completely destroyed the area to the right of the Rhine as far as the Ems, then as far as the Weser, then as far as the Elbe, and did it so systematically that we could no longer carry on any transport. We took a million workers out of the armament factories in order to put them on repair of communications, but it was too late to win the race. We already had 800,000 people on the job and wanted to repair the lines again with 1,800,000.[181]

Taken together these worker diversions meant that, even when Germany reached its highest output of armaments in the summer of 1944, real production was significantly below possible production. For the National Socialist regime, one of the most troubling aspects of this shift was that it was felt necessary to assign reliable German workers to repair work – foreign or slave workers were considered neither reliable nor motivated enough for such a responsibility. On August 3, Speer addressed a conference of Gauleiters in Posen, and mentioned how shifting workers away from direct construction was harming output.

> For it is obvious that, in this complicated, individualized work of removing air raid damage, it is unfortunately necessary to employ for the most part only German workers. We estimate the loss of armament potential due to air attacks at an average of 30 percent

of our total armament capacity. In other words, we should be able to produce 30 percent more than the figures already given to you, if we could regain air superiority at home...[182]

One final thing should be mentioned about the oil and transport campaigns in 1944 and their impact in shutting down the German economy, and that is the successful and entirely unplanned chemical campaign. German manufacture of certain vital chemicals such as nitrogen and methanol was grouped in the same complexes and owned by the same firms as many of its synthetic oil plants. According to Hans Kehrl, when the attacks started on their oil production the Germans did not know whether oil or chemical production was the real target. "The attacks on the chemical and oil industry cannot be separated, because the firms, e.g. Ludwigshafen, Oppau, Linz and so on were mixed firms, so that we did not know what product was meant to be attacked."[183]

The unintended destruction of these chemical plants had a damaging effect on a number of crucial areas of the German economy. Huge quantities of nitrogen, for instance, were needed both for ammunition production and for fertilizer to increase food production. Yet, because of the attacks on the hydrogenation plants, German nitrogen production was seriously affected.

By the end of 1944 strategic air power had shown itself, finally, to be very effective through this attack on German industrial and military mobility. What it also showed was that it was not necessary to find specific industries and try to destroy their factories. If you could shut down their power and their ability to receive raw materials or ship out finished goods, that would be even more damaging. In fact, in 1944 and 1945 targeting specific industries, other than aircraft manufacture, was a relatively unimportant part of Anglo-American strategic bombing operations. (See Figure 68.) When it came to specific targets, they were now afterthoughts. In the end, the campaigns against oil targets and transport must be seen as linked efforts which brought about the collapse of the German economy before the land war had reached the centers of German production.

Milch, trying to ingratiate himself with his captors at the end of the war, even suggested that this was how the Americans should attack Japan.

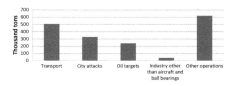

68 Tonnage dropped in European theater of operations by heavy bombers (RAF and USAAF), 1944–5, by target categories.
Source: Arnold MSS, Reel 190, "The Contribution of Air Power to the Defeat of Germany," Appendix K, The Attack on General Industry.

> If I had the American Air Force at my disposal, I should now use it against Japan just as it was used against Germany, after having learned a lesson as regards the choice of targets. That is, it should attack right from the beginning those targets which in Germany were attacked at the end. There are two targets the bombing of which brings everyone to their knees: fuel and communications.[184]

According to Speer, the oil and transport campaign not only destroyed production, it determined the outcome of the battlefield as well.

> Summarizing the situation I have to say that seen from my side of the picture the American attacks with the effect as of May 1944 brought about the decision of the war. The attacks on the hydrogenation plants were so extensive that our troops at the front could not be supplied with the necessary amount of fuel. Even without supply from Rumania [*sic*] we would have been in position to keep the troops supplied with fuel, possibly this material would have been a little scarce. Without the attacks we could have maintained a constant flow of fuel to the front.
>   At the same time it has to be pointed out that the breakdown of the armament [*sic*] was brought about on a broad basis through the destruction of transportation.[185]

The German army and the cataclysm of 1944

The 276th and 277th Divisions of the German army were much less famous than Panzer Lehr. Examples of infantry divisions that were raised relatively late in the war, neither had a particularly distinguished

358 / The war in Europe in 1944

career. However, like Panzer Lehr, in 1944 they were assigned to defend the coast of France to repel the expected Anglo-American invasion. Before D-Day they had two of the most pleasant assignments in the German army, as both were stationed in southwest France, the 276th near Bayonne and the 277th near Narbonne. A week after D-Day, German High Command decided that they needed to be moved to Normandy in a desperate attempt to concentrate enough German force in the area to throw the invaders into the sea. The 276th left first, on June 11.

> the 276 Inf Div travelled as far as the Loire by train. Part of the division detrained north of the Loire, leaving 75 miles to be travelled by road. The rest detrained south of the river to journey 130 miles by road. Thereafter both parts proceeded in broken elements, some with the aid of motor vehicles but most on foot or bicycle. Their arrival was piecemeal after a variety of experiences. One unit on foot made the road journey in eight days while a motorized company took 11 days...All units of the division observed the now customary precautions, avoiding main thoroughfares and travelling only at night in small groups. Added to the delays this form of travel imposed, all experienced difficulty in crossing the Loire. One battalion was twice attacked by Allied aircraft at its detraining point, Cholet, during daytime rest periods.[186]

On June 16, the 277th was put in motion.[187] Until the division reached the Loire it was also able to travel by train. At that point, however, it entered a completely different transportation universe. Not only did it find that most of the railway bridges over the Loire had been destroyed by bombing, the threat of daylight attack by patrolling Allied fighters and bombers meant that it was safer for the division to be broken up into smaller units and travel mostly by foot at night. What should have taken a few hours by rail turned into a tortuous journey by road that took parts of the 277th Division two weeks to complete. The 277th "moved in broken elements, and for the road journey employed a variety of vehicles, including buses, bicycles and horse-drawn wagons. The usual efforts were made to conceal movement by travelling at night on the side roads. Nevertheless PWs [prisoners of war] report numerous strafing attacks by Allied aircraft. The division's arrival was spread over several days, and it was not identified in battle until the 9th of July."[188]

The experience of these two divisions was not unusual in the German army at this time in the war. When on both the Eastern and Western fronts mobility was crucial, the German army found the skies over their positions empty of Luftwaffe aircraft. Moving from place to place had become a time-consuming and dangerous task.

One of the best examples of how air power reduced mobility, which would have been particularly apparent to the men of the 276th and 277th, was the campaign of destruction waged on the French rail network in the run-up to the Normandy invasion. On March 25, General Eisenhower made one of his most important decisions in preparations for D-Day.[189] He ordered that American and British strategic air forces in the UK should be used, where possible, to destroy the transportation system in France, Belgium and Holland. This transportation plan, which was partially the brainchild of the British scientist Solomon (Solly) Zuckerman, came to be hotly debated in early 1944. Spaatz and Harris both opposed it as a less than optimal way to employ their heavy bombers. Eisenhower, however, persuaded by Tedder and Air Marshal Trafford Leigh-Mallory, the overall commander of Anglo-American air forces for D-Day, ordered that the destruction of all rail communications to the coast receive precedence. These attacks, particularly the destruction of the bridges over the Seine and the Loire and the wrecking of certain large railyards such as that in Le Mans, played a significant role in retarding German movement before the landings.[190] By forcing German troops off the railway lines, they deprived them of the most efficient means of mobility open to a European army in the war.[191]

Together, all of these attacks on German army mobility resulted in a cataclysm of losses that dwarfed those of earlier in the war. As mentioned previously, German casualties before 1944 were actually manageable and running at a pace below that of World War I. In 1944, however, casualties became catastrophic. In just two months of 1944, July and August, the Germans reported 563,973 deaths in their armed services.[192] This was equal to the number of deaths in all of 1942 and 70 percent as many deaths as suffered by the Germans in all of 1943.[193] German ground equipment losses followed suit and, for the first time in the war, progressed at a rate far higher than replacement production. In Chapter 2 Figures 10 and 11 showed how the two most numerous panzer classes (the Panzer IV and Panzer V) first saw destruction pass production in the summer of 1944. The same situation

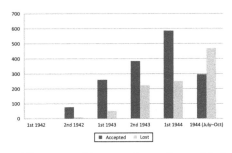

69 Panzer VIs accepted into service and monthly losses, 1942–October 1944, in six-month intervals.
Source: The figures for the chart come from a Joint Intelligence Committee Report compiled in 1946 and based on different translated German documents and wartime intelligence reports. These specific figures come from the Wehrmacht's QMG office. A copy of the report is kept in Cab 147/497. See Winter, *Defeating Hitler: Whitehall's Secret Report on Why Hitler Lost the War*, p. 254.

occurred for all other German AFV including the Panzer VI (Tiger), the most famous heavy tank of the war. (See Figure 69.)

The reasons for these losses on land were intimately connected to the evolving air war. One of the ways the strategic air campaign achieved this was through the success of the campaign against German oil production which became a major factor by July 1944. In a September memorandum to Hitler, Speer described how these attacks on Germany's fuel reserves were making the German army immobile – even if he couched the warning in faux-optimistic language about offensives. "The basis for army movements at the Front is getting so slight that planned operations can no longer take place in October. In the present fuel situation, it is no longer possible to gain offensive successes, as the fuel quantities required for the supplies necessary for an offensive are no longer available."[194] Speer's solution was to devote the entire Luftwaffe to protecting the German economy. Yet, by this time there were hardly any German fighters left over the battlefields.

The Mediterranean, for instance, saw almost all fighters withdrawn by the end of September 1943.[195] Before that, what fighters were sent were mostly concerned with defending the airspace over the Romanian oil fields and refineries. The situation on the Western and Eastern fronts was not in actuality that different, because the fighters that were committed on these fronts were unable to provide any meaningful protection for the German army. In the east, the

Luftwaffe still deployed 20–30 percent of its numerical strength, but in
a way that made it impossible to protect German forces. There were
simply too few fighters and too few anti-aircraft guns.

Those in charge of the Luftwaffe seem remarkably uninterested
in the number of aircraft that were deployed or lost in the east at this
time. When Milch was asked about losses on the Eastern Front as a
result of Soviet action, he basically said the figures were low enough
that he did not track them, but that Galland and his staff would have a
better idea.[196] When Galland was asked a similar question, he did not
have an exact figure, but claimed that "our losses there were extraordinarily light."[197] This ignorance is not that surprising considering that
the Luftwaffe had decided a year previously that the Eastern Front was
a secondary theater to be populated by less-skilled pilots flying inferior
aircraft. At the time that Operation Bagration began (see below), there
were approximately six hundred single- and twin-engine fighters
deployed on the entire Eastern Front. Luftflotte 6, which had the
specific job of protecting Army Group Center, had only a hundred
single-engine fighters ready for action.[198] However, as the Luftwaffe
on the Eastern Front was a low priority for resources, only forty of
these were fighters in working order, and even they lacked enough
petrol to keep them flying.[199] As Army Group Center collapsed, the
air reinforcements sent to stem the tide were extremely limited, with
between 200 and 270 aircraft sent from other fronts.[200]

These small numbers meant that German fighters were so
relatively few in number that they could not be sent out in large enough
formations to fight for air control. At the same time many of the planes
in the east were antiquated dive and two-engine bombers, such as
the JU-87 and HE-111, which had shown themselves unable to fight
effectively against the British during the Battle of Britain. The HE-111,
for instance, was only kept in production until the end of 1944 because
it could still be effective in the east,[201] and as late as March 1945,
HE-111s were still being used to support German army units there.[202]
(See Table 32.)

The German fighters still in the east were so relatively small in
number that they could only be used in support roles such as ground
attack, and could not attempt to control the airspace over Army Group
Center. Whereas over Germany the Luftwaffe would deploy hundreds
of fighters in specific operations, in the east fighters would be deployed
in formations of two or four.[203] General Koller bemoaned the fact that

Table 32 *Luftwaffe distribution on the Eastern Front, June 30, 1944*

Aircraft type	No.
Long-range bombers	480
Reconnaissance aircraft	162
Dive-bombers	569
Single-engine fighters	513
Twin-engine fighters	88
Army cooperation (transport)	237
Coastal patrol	26

Source: Air Ministry (UK) 40–1207, "German Air Force First Line Strength during the European War 1939–1945," October 1945.

in the Soviet Union the Luftwaffe was really a form of mobile artillery and could not exercise air superiority.[204] Galland described how the fighter force there had evolved from 1942 to 1944:

> Fighter forces in Russia were much weakened. Two Geschwader had been sent to the Mediterranean in 1942, and in 1943 various units came back to participate in the defense of the Reich. Strategic bombing carried out in the Balkans by American bombers from Italy forced the deployment of some units in Roumania [sic], Yugoslavia and Austria. By the end of 1943 there were about eleven weak Gruppen on the entire Eastern Front...
>
> It [the fighter force on the Eastern Front] flew well the few escort missions which were ordered and for the rest of the time engaged in low level attacks. Bombs were not usually dropped by fighter units, since there were an ample number of Schlachtflieger [ground-attack aircraft] on hand for this function. Fighters flew in small formations of two or four and felt able to cope with whatever Russian fighters they encountered. Each unit flew several missions a day, and the best pilots flew every mission.

The only thing that could be said about this way of fighting was that it kept aircraft losses down for the Germans. Including the reinforcements sent in from other areas, the Luftwaffe on the Eastern Front lost a total of between 550 and 600 aircraft of all types in those two months – though only part of this would have come from the collapse of Army Group Center. The USSBS calculated that single-engine fighter aircraft losses by the Luftwaffe everywhere but in the fighting over Germany and the Western Front between June 1, 1944 and August 31,

1944 totalled 893.[205] Specific losses on just the Eastern Front would probably have been between 600 and 700.[206] Therefore, using these ratios, one could assume that the total number of aircraft lost on the Eastern Front in those three months was approximately 1,000.

To compound the problems for the German army in the east, they were also receiving a decreasing percentage of German anti-aircraft support. The great increase in anti-aircraft production made it one of the fastest growing elements in the German war economy between 1942 and 1945. Defending the Reich, and the Reich's productive resources, was always the first priority of Germany's flak forces – in particular protecting fuel production and Berlin. On June 21, 1944, it was decided to protect Germany's main hydrogenation plants using a combined total of 1,720 anti-aircraft guns of different calibers.[207] A few months before, on January 1, 1944, Berlin alone was covered by 104 heavy flak batteries.[208] The entire Eastern Front at the same time had only 273 heavy flak batteries and 28 medium flak batteries.[209] In percentage terms, this force in the east represented 10 percent of Germany's deployed heavy batteries and less than 2 percent of its medium batteries. This lack of protection from the air led to one of the greatest disasters for the German army, the collapse of Army Group Center, in response to the Red Army's offensive Operation Bagration.

This is often seen as the most crushing defeat that Germany suffered in 1944. In the five weeks following the start of the Soviet assault on June 22, exactly three years after Germany launched Barbarossa, the Germans were pushed back by 300 miles.[210] At the start of the offensive, when Army Group Center was being protected by 40 operational fighters, the Soviet Air Force deployed 5,417 aircraft, including 2,528 fighters, just to the fronts that took part in Bagration.[211] With such preponderance, the Soviet Air Force could attack German troops with relative ease, flying 153,545 sorties between June 22 and August 29.[212] In comparison, during the first two weeks of the Citadel Offensive the Luftwaffe flew 27,221 sorties.[213] German units were either pinned down immobile, or when they tried to move, they were regularly attacked by Soviet ground and air forces.[214] Major General Erich Dethleffsen, who was a leading staff officer for the Wehrmacht's 4th Army, which suffered the most as a result of Operation Bagration, claimed that this was the moment when Soviet air power moved from being an annoyance to the Germans to being a battle-winning weapon. In earlier operations the Wehrmacht had maintained mobility in the face of Soviet aircraft, but by the second half of 1944 it was stuck. "In 1943 the Russian Air Force was a negligible factor, and did not bother us much. Strategic moves at Smolensk were carried out without our sustaining heavy losses at the hands of the Russian Air Force. In 1943 it was a negligible factor, in 1944 an unpleasant one and in 1945 a decisive one."[215] Later, when asked specifically about the importance of the Soviet Air Force in preventing German troops from staging successful retreats in the face of Russian offensives, he was more specific. "Not in 1943, in 1944 only in the case of badly beaten up troops; since Fall 1944 the [USSR] Air Force played an essential part and contributed largely to their success."[216]

The corresponding German losses in manpower during the collapse of Army Group Center were large. For the first time on the Eastern Front, with the exception of Stalingrad, large German formations were surrounded and captured en masse. About 400,000 Germans were said to have been captured during the fighting.[217] Another estimate is that Army Group Center lost 450,000 men killed, wounded and missing during the battle.[218] German manpower losses on the Eastern Front as a whole during June, July and August 1944 were an extremely high 589,000.[219] When it comes to AFV, finding specific losses for Army Group Center is not that easy, but they seem to be more moderate. When the Red Army began its assault, the German 4th Army, the largest part of Army Group Center, had only 402 AFV of all types on its books.[220] The 9th Army, a far less powerful force, only had 76 AFV.[221] So, at most, Army Group Center would have had about 500 AFV when the Soviets attacked.[222] Even if they had lost all of the AFV with which they started the campaign, which is unlikely, it did not represent an unmanageable loss because German AFV strength on the Eastern Front actually grew from 2,608 on June 1 to 3,658 on August 1.[223]

The reason that the Luftwaffe could do nothing to protect German soldiers in Army Group Center was that it was overwhelmingly engaged in a two-headed death struggle against the Anglo-American air forces. Both the ongoing strategic bombing campaign and German attempts to provide some air support for their troops fighting against the D-Day landings in Normandy ended up sucking the life out of the Luftwaffe.[224] In the run-up to the D-Day landings, the Germans did develop plans to deploy large formations of fighters against the expected invasion. However, because of the pressure of

70 By 1944 it was extremely dangerous for the Germans to base aircraft in France because of Anglo-American air dominance. This FW-190 had to be camouflaged extensively for its own safety.

the Allied air campaign against German airfields in France, these aircraft had to be stationed far away from the beaches. Even using extremely heavy camouflage, it became unsafe for the Luftwaffe to base aircraft close enough to the fighting that they could intervene quickly and for longer periods. (See Figure 70.) Instead, it was decided to base most German aircraft in Germany itself and the plan was to rush them to France when the invasion commenced. Except for a few units that would be left so that German airspace was not completely empty, the Luftwaffe was preparing to throw every fighter it had in Germany against the landings.[225] Major General Eckhard Christian, who was particularly close to Hitler and had access to complete figures, believed that the Luftwaffe had put aside 1,200 fighters to contest the D-Day landing.[226] According to Goering, who interestingly was not so sanguine, there were only 50 aircraft in France to face the Normandy invasion when it started, but approximately 800 fighters were immediately deployed to meet the new threat.[227]

On the day of the landings, there were 815 German aircraft based in France, Belgium and Holland, of which 315 were single- or twin-engine fighters.[228] In the next few days more than 300 additional fighters were sent in from Germany.[229] The Germans eventually reached a deployed figure of 1,000 aircraft. However, constant attacks against German airfields, and the overwhelming presence of Allied aircraft in the skies, meant that hardly any German aircraft reached the battlefield.[230] Goering estimated that, of the 850 German aircraft sent to oppose the landings, only about 200 survived their initial encounters.[231] Christian believed that the fact that they had to be redeployed from Germany itself played a huge role in their ineffectiveness and loss. Galland described how the totality of the pressure placed on the Luftwaffe by the Anglo-American air forces meant that, even using all of the aircraft available to defend Germany itself, the Luftwaffe could not influence what happened in France.

> When the Invasion finally came, the carefully made preparations immediately went awry. The entire transfer of the Fighter Arm into France was delayed for 24 hours because the Oberkammando West would not give the order, expecting a heavier landing attempt in the Pas de Calais. The Luftwaffe finally issued the order on its own authority and the transfer began.
>
> Most of the carefully prepared and provisioned airfields assigned to the various fighter units had been bombed out and the units had to land at other hastily chosen landing grounds...
>
> The poor navigating ability of most of the pilots and even the formation leaders, used only to flying under expert fighter control systems in Germany, brought many units down on the wrong fields. The confusion and lack of facilities made only a few missions possible, and the pilots were not good at the type of tree top war fought over the Normandy beach-heads.
>
> The poor airfields prepared for alternative use by Luftflotte 3 were too few in number, poorly camouflaged and badly supplied. There were few airfields near the Normandy beach-head and most units had to operate from the vicinity of Paris. The transfer flight from Germany to France was east to west, exposing the flank on transferring German formations to prolonged attacks by roving Allied fighters. Supplies came through very slowly over the bombed out railways.[232]

This Luftwaffe attempt to make a mass incursion over the French battlefields was repeated twice more, incidents that Galland termed (derisively) "big blows."[233] Some Luftwaffe units were wiped out, completely rebuilt and then wiped out again.[234] After the Allied breakout in Normandy and the disastrous German defeat in the Falaise pocket, the Germans once again decided to make a mass injection of fighter aircraft over France to gain some semblance of air control. In July Hitler ordered that the entire Luftwaffe fighter reserve, a force of 800–900 new aircraft, be committed to the fray over the Western Front.[235] It was destroyed in a few days. "The transfer of the reserve

367 / The German army and the cataclysm of 1944

to France was accomplished under circumstances much worse than those of June. Units became lost, landed on fields already bypassed by Allied armor, found no fuel, and had to destroy their aircraft...Galland is certain that the entire 800 aircraft of the reserve did not destroy two dozen Allied aircraft."[236] This German force consisted of almost twice the number of German fighters that were on the entire Eastern Front at the same moment – where they would have made a major difference protecting the skies over Army Group Center.

In total, the Luftwaffe losses over Normandy were massive. In the first few days alone they probably averaged a hundred per day. Separating the specific losses attributable to the Normandy battlefields from those suffered in the skies over Germany is not simple. Speer estimated that the Luftwaffe sent approximately two thousand aircraft in different deployments to Normandy, the large majority of which were lost.[237] This figure seems about right. The 3rd Air Fleet was the unit specifically directed to supporting the German armies in France. It was heavily reinforced by fighters from the Luftflotte Reich as soon as the landings commenced. Together these forces lost 3,656 aircraft between the D-Day landings and the end of August 1944.[238] We know that the 3rd Air Fleet alone lost 2,127 on operational duty. Non-operational losses would have pushed this figure much higher. A further 1,016 aircraft were lost in operations by Luftflotte Reich at the same time, many of them during their commitment to the fighting in France. The Strategic Bombing Survey paints a similar picture, claiming that the Germans lost 4,043 single-engine fighters over Germany and the Western Front between June 1 and August 31, 1944.[239]

One of the pilots to experience this massacre was the famous Luftwaffe ace Gunther Rall. Rall is credited with shooting down 275 aircraft during the war, 272 on the Eastern Front. In April 1944 he was transferred to Germany to fight against the British and Americans, and the situation he found there was completely different. "No longer did we go out hunting for the enemy all day ... shooting down as many as we could, returning to base to refuel and rearm again, then taking off again."[240] On one of his first missions, he was shot down by a flight of P-47 Thunderbolts, losing his thumb and being forced out of combat. He then started training pilots for the Luftwaffe, but discovered that there was no way that they could supply the needed men, considering the massive losses over Germany and in the fighting in France. In September 1944, when Luftwaffe production was near its

71 Anglo-American air dominance in France meant that even though the Germans often had superior ground equipment, they were frequently overwhelmed from the air. Here a Panzer Mark V (Panther) of approximately 45 tons has been flipped completely over after an air attack – possibly by RAF Typhoons.

peak, he was told that the entire German air force had only 680 fighter pilots capable of flying missions.[241]

So, even though the Germans made some mass efforts to try to intervene with aircraft over the battlefields of the Western Front in 1944, unlike their efforts in the east or the Mediterranean, the constraints placed on their air power by the Anglo-American effort meant that, despite a huge number of planes, the land battles were fought by the German army under conditions of grave disadvantage. (See Figure 71.) The Germans fighting on land in Normandy actually possessed many advantages that should have made it almost impossible for the Allied armies to break out.[242] In Normandy, thanks to the limited geographic extent of the fighting in the first month, each German division was given a fighting frontage many times smaller than that on the Eastern Front, in fact smaller than that of the German army on the Western Front in World War I. German ground equipment was, in qualitative terms, at least as good if not better than that of the western Allies. The superiority of German panzers like the Panther and Tiger over the American Sherman or British Churchill is well known.[243] During the Normandy campaign, this superiority even led to some skittishness on the part of Allied armored crews.[244] The Germans also possessed the best machine gun in the world, the Type 42. The countryside of Normandy, with its thick hedges, known as Bocage, made coordinated armor movements difficult and provided the defender with excellent unprepared cover. Finally, as the German army would be able to reinforce over land and the Allies would have to come by ship, the Germans ostensibly had the ability to move troops to the landing area more quickly.

However, as the Luftwaffe was constantly thwarted in its attempts to provide air cover for the German troops in Normandy, the great advantages afforded the German army were lost. Throughout the fighting the Luftwaffe was outnumbered in the skies by between 16 and 20 to 1.[245] German aircraft were subjected to constant attacks by Anglo-American aircraft and could operate only with the greatest of difficulty. A great deal has been written about the Allied use of tactical air power in France. For the first time in Europe, the totality of air power was unleashed on a defending army. For two months before the landings started, all types of aircraft had been used to try to cripple the rail network in France, to make German resupply and reinforcement of the battle area as difficult as possible.[246] There were attacks on almost all major bridges across the Seine and all major French railyards.[247] Some of these attacks, including early carpet bombing in front of the British positions near Caen, did not destroy much German equipment.[248] Others, such as Operation Cobra, did put large amounts of equipment out of action.[249] While it could have been better coordinated in certain areas, even those who point out the flaws in Anglo-American tactical air power in France believe it was crucial to victory.[250] Important lessons had been learned in North Africa beginning in 1942, so that by 1944 Allied troops were much better served on the battlefield.[251] When Allied armored forces eventually broke through the German lines, their coordinated action with aircraft kept them moving at a high rate and never allowed the Germans to settle.[252]

Even when it did not directly destroy equipment, Anglo-American air power kept German troops immobile and destroyed their defensive coherence.[253] General Buhle, who while still in charge of allocating German military personnel went to France to witness the fighting, believed that if only the Germans had been able to contest Anglo-American air supremacy over the battlefield, then the Normandy invasions would have failed. "General Buhle stated that the Germans' ground force operations were made impossible by our tactical air power. Movement was virtually impossible during the day and in view of their [German] lack of motor transport, it could only be by foot at night. It was his opinion that 700 to 800 German fighters would have made our invasion impossible."[254] Had the Germans been able to transport that force to the Normandy beachhead quickly, they would have had a very good chance of driving the invading forces into the sea, as Field Marshal von Rundstedt, the commander of German forces in the west, stated at the war's end.

> Had I been able to move the armored "Divisionen" which I had behind the coast, I am convinced that the invasion would not have succeeded. Always assuming your air force ... (word missing) ... away. If I had been able to move the troops, then my air force would also have been in a position to attack your ships. You would first of all have sustained losses on disembarkation and you would not have been able so undisturbed to bring up your large battleships so near the coast to act as floating gun batteries. This is all a question of air force, air force and again air force.[255]

It is striking how long, when the mobility destruction that was inflicted before the invasion was combined with the constant Anglo-American domination of the skies over France, it took German reinforcements to reach the Normandy fighting. Even divisions close to the fighting, such as those stationed in Brittany, found it extremely difficult to get into action.[256] Anglo-American air power meant that they couldn't travel by road or rail by day, and had to wait for the short summer nights to try to move.[257] Other German divisions were dispatched to the Normandy beaches from throughout the German empire, although, because of air power, far fewer than the British and Americans expected. Going into the landings, there was an assumption that up to sixteen German divisions would be dispatched from outside France: six from Italy, five from the Balkans and five from Scandinavia.[258] As it was, only two large formations, the 9th SS Panzer and 10th SS Panzer divisions were able to be dispatched from the east. Because of the intensive attacks on the French rail network, German forces, if they were lucky, could only travel by rail to within 100–150 miles of the fighting. At that point they were forced off the trains and had to struggle on by foot or by improvised vehicle convoys. Those divisions coming from the south were forced to detrain near the Loire; those coming from the east would usually detrain before reaching Paris as all rail lines to the west and north of the city were out of action.[259] Some troops and supplies bound for Normandy even had to be detrained in Germany to protect them on their way to combat.[260]

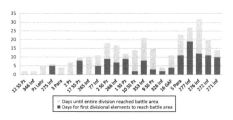

72 Days of travel for German divisions between dispatch and reaching the Normandy battlefields.
Source: Arnold MSS, Reel 190, "The Contribution of Air Power to the Defeat of Germany," Appendix H, The Attack on Enemy Roads.

Therefore, instead of the German army unleashing one hammer-blow to try to drive the Allies back into the sea, its units were slowly fed into a meat grinder from which they could not withdraw. The 2nd SS Panzer Division, which was sent from Toulouse, was originally expected to be able to attack the landing areas by June 9 or 10, but was not able to assemble in the battle area until June 23, seventeen days after departing. The 10th SS Panzer Division was sent from Russia. It had an easy railway journey until it was detrained between Paris and Bar Le Duc between June 16 and 22. From that point it took until July 1 for the division to travel the 150 miles or so to the Normandy fighting. (See Figure 72.) Even divisions being sent from as close as Holland had bizarre circuitous journeys before they could reach the fighting. One from the 15th Army could not go by the direct route: it ended up being sent by rail hundreds of miles behind Paris from Rheims to Dijon and then to Tours before being sent up to Normandy.[261] It could only be sent in eight trains daily when it usually took between forty-eight and sixty to move a division. Moreover, divisions were often heavily damaged en route and, thanks to travel chaos, arrived piecemeal without cohesion.

For the commanders in charge of German forces in Normandy, the overall impact of Anglo-American air power was irresistible. Erwin Rommel, who commanded Army Group B, had personal experience of Allied air power when he was strafed and almost killed by RAF Spitfires on July 17, 1944. Just before that he had written a despairing report on the situation in Normandy. After blaming the unprecedentedly high German losses on Anglo-American air power, which he said "commands the battlefield unchecked," he went on to describe how difficult it was to get supplies and men into the battle area.

The supply situation is so difficult, through the disruption of the railway network and the great danger of the major and minor roads up to 150 kilometers behind the front through the enemy airforce, that only what is most essential can be brought up and above all artillery and werfer (mortar) ammunition must be spared everywhere to the utmost. These conditions are unlikely to improve in future, as the supply area is perpetually being decreased by enemy action and enemy air activity is likely to become still more effective by reason of their occupation of the many air-fields in the bridgehead.[262]

With Rommel out of action and Field Marshal von Rundstedt, the overall commander of German forces in the west, also despairing of achieving anything against British and American air power, Hitler sent Field Marshal Gunther von Kluge to take command. Kluge, who had only fought on the Eastern Front since the launching of Barbarossa, was stunned by the air power he found arrayed against his forces. Within two weeks of taking over, he wrote to Hitler endorsing Rommel's views and adding his own, deeply pessimistic, melodramatic description of the situation.

in our present position – including the material position – there is no way by which, in the face of the enemy air force's complete command, we can find a strategy which will counterbalance its annihilating effect without giving up the field of battle. Whole armored formations, allotted to the counter-attack were caught up in bomb-carpets of the greatest intensity so that they could be got out of the torn up ground only by prolonged effort and in some cases only by dragging them out ... The psychological effect of such a mass of bombs coming down with all the power of elemental nature on the fighting force, especially the infantry, is a factor which has to be given specially serious consideration. It is immaterial whether such a carpet catches good troops or bad. They are more or less annihilated and above all their material is shattered. If that occurs frequently then the power of endurance of the force is put to the highest test. In fact, it becomes dormant and dies.[263]

Kluge was right to be panicked, as German ground equipment losses were extreme during the fighting in France, considerably higher even than in the collapse of Army Group Center. In *Germany and the*

Second World War, it is claimed that 648 German AFV were found abandoned either in the Falaise pocket or during the final evacuation over the Seine.[264] This was augmented by another 5,625 different motorized vehicles of all types and 421 artillery pieces. When it comes to overall losses of AFV from D-Day through August and the full-scale German withdrawal over the Seine, numbers vary from 1,500 on the low side to 2,000 on the higher end.[265] Manpower losses also became extreme, and beginning in August, those in the west surpassed those in the east for the first time in the war.[266]

The fighting in France destroyed about 9 percent of German 1944 AFV production and 7.5 percent of German aircraft production. Within the overall context of annual German armaments production for 1944, the losses on the Eastern Front during Bagration were equal to approximately 1.6 percent of Germany's output, while AFV and aircraft losses in France were equivalent to 4.3 percent.[267] It is interesting to see how much more equipment was damaged in France at this time. It was, in terms of production, the most intensive air–land battle of the war to that time, one that the Germans had feared for decades. The German army had realized that if it became involved in a full-fledged "*materialschlact*," or material battle, with the United States and Britain combined, it could not compete.[268] That is precisely what happened. In the summer of 1944, Anglo-American air power determined the course of the land war. General Jodl summarized this situation when he was asked at the end of the war why Germany lost. He answered that it had little to do with what happened on land, and a great deal to do with what happened in the air. It was the totality of pressure put on Germany and the German army at the front that caused German defeat.

> Not taking into consideration the Russian air force, which was of no great importance, I would say in general that in the end the winning of the complete air superiority in the whole area of the war has altogether decided the war. I would go as far as to say that our power on the land was numerically and, from the point of view of armament, sufficiently strong, if not to win, at least to hold our own on all fronts, if our air force had kept up on the same level.[269]

10 THE AIR AND SEA WAR AGAINST JAPAN, 1942-4

In 1944 the Imperial Japanese Navy controlled one of the largest striking forces available to the Axis. When a census was taken of the aircraft on hand for operations on April 1, it was found that the IJN had 1,854 fighters, 930 bombers and 1,104 assorted other support aircraft.[1] Qualitatively, many of these aircraft were superior to those produced months earlier. Starting in late 1943, the Zero Type 52 was sent to the navy in large numbers.[2] This updated model of Japan's most famous fighter, considered its most effective variation, had been re-engineered to meet the American navy's F-6F Hellcat and F-4U Corsair carrier-based fighters. In shipping terms, the Japanese navy still retained a large fleet with an impressive mix of ships. Admiral Ozawa, who commanded the Mobile Fleet when the Battle of the Philippine Sea commenced, had nine different aircraft carriers which could launch a combined 473 aircraft.[3] As well as the carriers, this striking force had the two largest battleships in the world (*Yamato* and *Musashi*), four other battleships, eleven excellent heavy cruisers and thirty destroyers.[4]

The number one priority for this force of aircraft and ships was the defense of the Mariana Islands, most famously Saipan, Tinian and Guam. By way of comparison, the Japanese navy had access to many times more aircraft than the Luftwaffe had assigned to the defense of Army Group Center in the summer of 1944. The Marianas were the linchpin of Japan's defensive perimeter and had been the focus of Japanese planning for months.[5] The Japanese navy realized that their striking force would still be smaller than the approaching American fleet possessing seven fleet aircraft carriers and eight light carriers which could launch a combined 900 aircraft. To counterbalance this inferiority, the Japanese stationed an additional 540 land-based aircraft within range of the Marianas.[6] In numerical terms, therefore, the Japanese defending the Marianas were approximately equal to the American aircraft that were attacking. The Japanese should also have been able to move reinforcements to the area quickly. When news arrived that the Americans had appeared off Saipan, between 120 and 130 aircraft in Japan were redeployed to Iwo Jima, which put them within range of the American landing forces. Another 100 naval aircraft were also ordered to redeploy from the Dutch East Indies to Yap and Palau where they could attack the American fleet. As the United States was relying on carrier-borne aircraft, reinforcing its navy quickly from outside the theater would be more difficult.

This large Japanese effort shows how the Combined Fleet was well aware of the gravity of the situation facing Japan. If the Marianas fell, the great majority of the Japanese population would come within the range of the new American long-range bomber, the B-29. The telegram that was read out to all the sailors and airmen on the eve of fighting for once spoke the truth when it said that "the rise and fall of the empire depends on this one battle."[7] And yet, when the IJN sent this powerful force out to fight during the greatest air–sea battle of World War II – the Battle of the Philippine Sea which reached a climax on June 19–20, 1944 and was two to three times as large as the Battle of Midway – something extraordinary happened. Though waves of Japanese planes were sent into action and fought with suicidal devotion, the American fleet suffered almost no damage. Instead, Japanese flyers, extremely brave but amateurish, were massacred.

During the two worst days of fighting, what came to be known as the Marianas Turkey Shoot, the Combined Fleet lost 426 aircraft of all types, or 90 percent of its force.[8] The land-based aircraft fared little better. More than half the aircraft sent from Japan to Iwo Jima were quickly shot down or crashed because of insufficient pilot training. According to Captain Akira Sasaki, who was a staff officer at the Yokosuka naval air base, their impact on the battle was negligible.

> As soon as the Saipan landing developed, attempts were made to get together the maximum number of planes for an early strike against the United States landing force. At Yokosuka they were

able to scrape about 120–130 miscellaneous naval aircraft including Betty's [the Allied codename for the Mitsubishi G-4M land-based bomber], carrier bombers, torpedo planes and fighters. Of the pilots employed, only about one-third were experienced, the others being students. This conglomerate attack was launched on 18 June 1944 with the specific objective of attacking the landing beaches or the landing craft. En route, however, they became involved with United States carrier aircraft with result that few, if any, reached the assigned target.

Practically all attacking aircraft were lost either through being shot down or as a result of forced landing and landing crashes . . .[9]

The aircraft sent from the Dutch East Indies fared even worse. Again, their pilots were not up to the task. Of the hundred aircraft sent, half disappeared or were damaged en route. Of the fifty that remained, only one, in the opinion of Captain Toshikazu Ohmae, the Chief of Staff to the 3rd Fleet, was capable of contributing meaningfully to Japanese operations. When the fighting around the Marianas ended, Rear Admiral Toshitane Takata, who was brought in to reorganize Japanese naval aviation, claimed that hardly any of the Japanese pilots who were on duty when the Marianas attacks started had survived the fighting.[10] During the entire month of June, the IJN lost 789 aircraft in combat, by far the highest number they would lose in any month during World War II.[11] At the same time, they lost another 449 aircraft in operational non-combat actions.

Even after all this sacrifice and effort, very few Japanese planes got close enough to see American vessels. The USN estimated that between June 11 and 20, 1944, only 150 Japanese aircraft were able to make it through the American fighter screen protecting the Marianas landings.[12] Of these, more than fifty were shot down by ship-based anti-aircraft weapons, so that fewer than a hundred were able to attempt an attack run at any time over the ten days. (See Figures 73 and 74.) At the end of operations, their total accomplishment was the sinking of one landing craft.[13]

The story of how the United States recovered from the defeats of early 1942 and had established the platform for total victory over Japan in the Marianas is the greatest American triumph in the air and sea war. It saw the integration of different technologies and logistic capacity to perform the kinds of operations that were not imaginable

73 The Battle for the Marianas. A Japanese aircraft being shot down while attacking the USS *Kitsun Bay* in June 1944. Japanese aircraft were massacred during the fighting around the Marianas, often as a result of the inferiority of their training brought on by the strain of the air–sea war.

74 US troops landing on Saipan, June/July 1944. Air–sea dominance meant that the American army was able to land a force approximately as large as that which assaulted Normandy, at the same time with almost no damage from Japanese attacks.

before the war. On the other hand, the strategic process that ended up with the Marianas operation also supported two other, expensive and to a large degree redundant, drives towards Japan. It revealed both the best and worst of democratic air and sea war-making.

For many of those with a real knowledge of Japan's strategic situation, the Marianas disaster represented the practical end of the war for Japan. Immediately after the Battle of the Philippine Sea ended, Admiral Matome Ugaki, who commanded the 1st Battleship Division and who would later lead the navy's kamikaze corps, penned this poem whilst on the deck of *Yamato*.

Utterly awakened from the dream of victory,
Found the sky rainy and gloomy
Rainy clouds will not clear up,
My heart is the same
When the time for battle's up.[14]

Guadalcanal sets the stage

Less than two years before this, in October 1942, the United States was locked in a struggle with Japan over Guadalcanal that was a very different, far more equal conflict.[15] Franklin Roosevelt was particularly concerned. On October 24, when he first received news about a major battle raging around the crucial airfield on Guadalcanal, he took the unusual step of dispatching a private order to the Joint Chiefs to make sure the United States committed everything that it could to hold on to the island.[16] He considered the letter so important that he specified that it be given directly to Leahy, King, Marshall and Arnold – and no one else.

> My anxiety for Southwest Pacific is to make sure that every
> possible weapon gets into that area to hold Guadalcanal, and that
> having held it in this crisis that munitions and planes and crews are
> on the way to take advantage of our success. We will soon find
> ourselves engaged on two active fronts and we must have adequate
> air support in both places even though it means delay in our other
> commitments, particularly to England. Our long-range plans could
> be set back for months if we fail to throw our full strength in our
> immediate and impending conflicts.[17]

This direct order received an instant response from the Joint Chiefs.[18] Four major warships, including the battleship *Indiana* and the cruiser *Columbia*, were transferred from the Atlantic to the Pacific.[19] Also at least a hundred aircraft and twenty submarines were sent from other areas of operations, and the supply of replacement aircraft to the southern Pacific was increased sharply – even as the fighting in North Africa was growing in intensity. Before Roosevelt wrote this letter, Guadalcanal was already the focus of a huge amount of American production. On October 14, 1942, a census was taken of the location of all USAAF aircraft. At that time there were 1,055 in just the South Pacific and Australia, while there were 1,192 in North Africa, the Middle East and the United Kingdom.[20] By adding USN aircraft, which were heavily committed to the Guadalcanal campaign, there would easily have been more aircraft in this one area than in the entire European theater of operations (ETO). Combined, the United States Navy and Air Force commitment to Guadalcanal would have made it the largest air–sea operation the United States had ever launched to that point.

This was indicative of many things at the time. It was another sign that at this point the United States was willing to prioritize the war in the Pacific over that in Europe. It was also a sign that for Roosevelt the strategic die had been cast in 1942 away from a build-up in Britain and a direct assault on Germany, and to more peripheral campaigns such as those in North Africa and the Solomon Islands. The decision to invade Guadalcanal was one to which Roosevelt had only limited input and was, like so much of the war in the Pacific, the brainchild of Ernest King.[21] After the Battle of Midway, King pushed for some action in the Pacific that would keep his forces active. He selected Guadalcanal because the Japanese were about to activate an airstrip on the island, which would have allowed them to threaten the sea lanes to Australia. As King described his thinking in 1950:

> Just as soon as the news of the Battle of Midway [June 4–5, 1942] was checked over, I began to move and made out orders to Nimitz and told him to tell Ghormley to get ready with everything we could muster as soon as the battle of Midway was decided and that the time had come to take a stand in the South Pacific Area because the "enemy" would have had a great defeat which would take them time to get over; it is my own tenet of war to now hit the "enemy" and keep hitting them to try to keep them off balance and keep on making them stay off balance.

One of the other reasons King settled upon Guadalcanal was because it was the furthest extent of the Japanese empire in the South Pacific and therefore the most vulnerable.[22] However, even though it was the most vulnerable, it ended up being an incredibly tough nut to crack. Guadalcanal was the most "even" battle that the United States would fight in the war, and in terms of equipment deployed and lost, the most expensive American commitment of 1942. American troops landed on August 7, 1942 and Japanese troops were not withdrawn until more than six months later, on February 9, 1943.[23]

After landing, the first thing American troops did was seize the Japanese airstrip (renamed Henderson Field). That was crucial. The American invasion force first went into action with air cover completely provided by the USN's remaining aircraft carriers. This was not something foreseen before the war, but had to be improvised because of the lack of airbases within range to cover the American assault. However, the threat to the American carriers caused their commander, Admiral Frank Jack Fletcher, controversially to pull them away from Guadalcanal on the third morning after the landing. Without the carriers, the only way that the Marines on Guadalcanal could have held out is by maintaining their hold on Henderson Field.

The Japanese also decided from the beginning that they were going to commit as many resources as possible to retake the airstrip and throw the Americans off Guadalcanal. They had a series of other bases in the Solomons from where air attacks could be launched on the island. Moreover, their largest base in the southern Pacific, Rabaul, was close enough to Guadalcanal that the Japanese navy could be stationed nearby to pose a constant threat to the Americans who were trying to cling to their airstrip. The Japanese decided quickly to redeploy two strong infantry divisions to the island, the 2nd which was based in Java and the 38th from Hong Kong.[24] The problem they would face was getting them there – they were both thousands of miles away. It illuminates the way in which the war in the Pacific required greater effort than that in Europe. By the summer of 1942, the Japanese had to move forces over an area far larger than that from, for example, Berlin to Stalingrad. (See Map 7.) Moreover, they had to do this with only the barest minimum of support from an advanced rail network, the most efficient means of supply at the time. In the end it would take months before these divisions were fully in place and they would suffer large losses in transit.

At first, the balance between the Americans and Japanese even extended to the times of the day.[25] Technologically the Americans had important advantages in radar, but the Japanese had a more sophisticated understanding of night-fighting – which they used to devastating effect.[26] Their superiority at night allowed them to bring in supplies and reinforcements to their troops on the island and even bombard the American forces around Henderson Field. The Americans generally controlled the skies and seas around Guadalcanal during the day, which they used to their advantage. Both the American and Japanese navies suffered serious losses. In less than four months after the initial Guadalcanal landings, there were six major naval battles: Savo Island (August 9, 1942 and the greatest defeat at sea that the United States Navy would suffer in its history), the Eastern Solomons (August 24), Cape Esperance (October 11–12), Santa Cruz (October 26–27), Guadalcanal (November 12–15) and Tassafaronga (November 30), as well as countless smaller engagements between naval vessels and aircraft. The toll taken on the US Navy was historic. Between just August 8 and November 15, 1942, the American navy lost 40 percent of all the fleet carriers (two of five) it would lose in the war, 57 percent of the heavy cruisers (four of seven), 67 percent of the light cruisers (two of three) and a remarkable 17 percent of the destroyers (twelve of sixty-nine) in the waters near Guadalcanal.[27] This last figure is particularly telling. Destroyers were the ubiquitous naval vessel of World War II, serving in all theaters and performing a host of roles. That the United States lost twelve of the sixty-nine destroyers it would lose in the entire war (both Pacific and Atlantic) off the coast of Guadalcanal in three months speaks to the intensity of the combat. Guadalcanal, rather like Gettysburg in 1863, had changed from a relatively unknown location that no one had thought of as important, to the scene of historic destruction.

However, it was a balance that couldn't last unless the Japanese were able to retake the airfield or destroy American equipment at a much higher rate than the Americans could destroy Japanese forces. The longer the campaign went on, the more secure the American hold on the island became. The fighting reached a climax between October 24 and 27 when the Japanese threw their ships, aircraft and land forces into a concerted attempt to capture Henderson Field. A force made up of 20,000 men attacked the airstrip in a series of bloody (for the Japanese) night assaults. At sea the Japanese Combined Fleet, commanded by the famous Admiral Isoroku Yamamoto, believing that the airstrip was about to fall, committed much of its strike power, including its two largest remaining aircraft carriers, *Shokaku* and *Zuikaku*, to aid the assault and, hopefully, destroy the remaining American support system for the Guadalcanal garrison.[28] The United States Navy, commanded in the theater by Admiral William "Bull" Halsey, responded with two of its remaining large carriers, *Enterprise* and *Hornet*. The ensuing Battle of Santa Cruz, a confused and evenly balanced affair, saw the United States lose the *Hornet*, but in exchange, Japanese losses in carrier aircraft and pilots were high. When the dust settled, the United States still held Henderson Field. Even though the fighting on Guadalcanal would go on for more than three more months, the Japanese had lost their best chance to retake the island.

After the war, King's decision to launch the invasion of Guadalcanal, which turned out to be such a long and destructive affair, was criticized, particularly by army partisans who believed that it would have been better to support Douglas MacArthur in a more direct assault on New Britain which was closer to Rabaul – at this time considered the necessary first step towards the defeat of Japan. King's decision to fight on the periphery seemed rather cautious to those who would later become used to bypassing many Japanese positions as the United States island-hopped towards Tokyo.[29] The historiography of the past few decades has taken this question and often folded it into the larger issue of the Central Pacific thrust versus the Southwest Pacific thrust, or to personalize it, Douglas MacArthur versus Ernest King. After Guadalcanal, the Pacific was divided into two quite distinct campaigns for the United States. There was MacArthur's Southwest Pacific campaign, heavy on army and air force power, which moved up through New Guinea to the Philippines. Then there was the Central Pacific campaign, the brainchild of King, which was led by Nimitz and used a series of island assaults from the Gilbert/Marshalls to the Marianas to reach Japan.

There does seem to have been little need, except for domestic and inter-service politics, for two separate lines of advance. By dividing the campaigns, Roosevelt was able to give MacArthur, a potential presidential rival in 1944, his own theater of operations. The navy, on the other hand, was allowed to dominate the Central Pacific thrust and have its area of glory. Those who argue in favor of the Southwest Pacific thrust believe that MacArthur's campaign to take the Philippines played the vital role in defeating Japan.[30] It avoided the bloody beach landings such as Tarawa, Saipan and Iwo Jima which typified Nimitz's thrust. On the other hand, others criticize MacArthur for his pomposity and attack his campaigns for being considerably more expensive than his public relations efforts led the American people to believe.[31]

At the time, Arnold, for one, believed that the entire Guadalcanal operation was a King-inspired waste and it would have been better to support MacArthur. In September he grudgingly went to the Pacific to examine the situation and make sure that the Americans would hold Guadalcanal. As he wrote in his travel diary, "King for some time has tried to get more planes for the South Pacific. Tries subterfuge and cunning. Navy is trying to run a land war, relying upon Army Air and Marines to put it across ... Navy wants to send in more and more planes, apparently with view of making that their main theater by employing most of our aircraft."[32] Arnold was not wrong. King was trying desperately to carve out an independent role for the navy beyond any authority that MacArthur would be given in the South Pacific.[33]

The question remains as to whether it was worth it for the United States to have fought on Guadalcanal. This can only be seen through looking at the campaign's impact on the Japanese. In terms of just battlefield destruction, Guadalcanal represented a serious loss of production, though actually one that was still in Japan's favor when compared with US losses. The Japanese lost two battleships, three large cruisers, one light cruiser and eleven destroyers in the waters around Guadalcanal between August 1942 and February 1943.[34] The battleship losses stand out – but as the Japanese did not lose any aircraft carriers around Guadalcanal and the United States lost two, the real striking power of the American navy was considerably more reduced than that of the Imperial Japanese Navy.

When it came to aircraft losses, the consistent damage sustained during the Guadalcanal fighting in head to head combat was significant, but in and of itself manageable in production numbers. The aircraft that Japan lost in operations were something that its economy could replace. The Japanese navy, which did the vast majority of the air fighting around Guadalcanal, lost 901 naval aircraft fighting the Americans between August 1 1942 and January 1 1943.[35] This figure was little more than 10 percent of Japanese aircraft production for the year. (See Figure 75.)

Actually, had the Japanese withdrawn from Guadalcanal after the battles of Henderson Field and Santa Cruz, the overall balance of destruction would have clearly been in their favor. They would have extracted a higher ratio of equipment losses from the Americans and been able to continue to protect the core of their naval air strength. However, they seemed reluctant to accept the reality of the situation

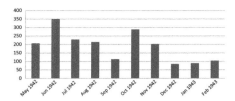

75 Japanese naval aircraft combat losses, May 1942–February 1943.

and continued to try and reinforce Guadalcanal for another three months, and the losses they suffered then were actually the most serious. For instance, their non-combat aircraft losses rose considerably after October. Fighting a large military campaign in the Solomons was an extraordinary undertaking for Japan, one that was greater than anything attempted by Germany during the war. The distance between Tokyo and Guadalcanal is 3,395 miles as the crow flies – an equivalent distance from Berlin would have taken the Germans into the American state of Maine or into India. Of course, the Japanese had to use a long series of staging posts, so the actual distance to be traveled was hundreds or thousands of miles more. Deploying equipment over such a great range was one of the most difficult tasks of the war. This task was compounded by the fact that during the fighting in the Solomons, the Japanese started moving away from using aircraft carriers to deploy aircraft. At the beginning of the campaign, one of the preferred reinforcement methods was to use carriers to physically carry aircraft to Truk.[36] At this point they had only one flight to make to Rabaul, which was a relatively safe way to deploy aircraft. In early December 1942, however, the Japanese carrier *Ryuho* was deploying aircraft when it was torpedoed, but not sunk.[37] At that point, the decision was made that during deployment army aircraft would more often fly themselves to their forward bases. This meant that some recently trained flyers, to reach facilities such as Rabaul, would have to undertake three long-distance overseas flights.

The Japanese navy lost 680 aircraft in non-combat operations during the same period that it lost 901 in combat. As the fighting in Guadalcanal went on, non-combat operational aircraft losses became significantly larger than those from combat. (See Figure 76.)

Japanese naval aviators became worn down by the constant combat in the Solomons. Deprived of adequate leave and asked to fly too many missions, mistakes and accidents became a greater problem

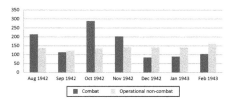

76 Japanese naval aircraft losses, combat and operational non-combat, August 1942–February 1943.

than combat losses. Unlike in previous operations, such as Midway, the Japanese found it more difficult to rescue their downed pilots, and so the fighting represented a much greater blow to the fundamentals of Japanese naval air power. Slowly but surely, the superbly trained, pre-war generation of Japanese naval aviators, some of the finest pilots on the planet, were being exterminated. It was an ominous shift that would continue with only a few monthly exceptions for the rest of the war, and eventually altogether undermined Japan's system of pilot training.

Beyond the question of aircraft and pilot losses, the Japanese defeat on Guadalcanal brought home the crucial question of shipping. The Japanese had such a large empire that they had to ship supplies into Guadalcanal at extreme distances. Both the 38th and 2nd Division had to be transported more than 3,000 miles to reach their destination.[38] Tellingly, the 38th was attacked while in transit, and only 2,000 of the division's 12,000 men made it ashore on Guadalcanal.[39] The rest disappeared into the oceans, in the first of what would turn out to be many successful American attacks to destroy Japanese power before it reached the battlefield. Once Japanese troops were ashore, they had to be resupplied, and this became an enormous effort which tied down Japanese merchant and naval shipping. Their convoys, which were given the nickname "Tokyo Express," became particularly vulnerable to American air attack, and as the battle turned in the United States' favor, Japanese attritional losses became serious.[40] In many Japanese eyes, it was the toll taken on the convoys heading to Guadalcanal, not the fighting on the island, which really decided the course of the battle. Re-examining the statement made by Lt General Shuichi Miyazaki, Chief of Staff to the Japanese 17th Army during the fighting on Guadalcanal, it is interesting to see how shipping was considered to be the crucial issue.

> The biggest problem was the loss of ships. Actually the bombing of troops and troop concentrations on the ground were not much of a hindrance because, although the bombing scared everybody and made lots of noise and had an effect on morale, the actual destruction was not great. The biggest problem was the loss of our capacity to move these troops to the fighting areas.[41]

By December 8, Nimitz was so satisfied with these attritional losses that he wrote in a memorandum describing his future plans for operations in the Solomons that he sincerely hoped the Japanese would continue to fight for Guadalcanal.[42] In the end he was probably sad when they left.

The pattern of equipment losses on Guadalcanal further reinforces the point that focusing on battles alone gives at best a partial and at worst a misleading perception about how Japan and Germany were defeated. In terms of naval vessels and aircraft lost in combat, the battles around Guadalcanal were balanced or even slightly in Japan's favor.[43] However, it was the effects of the campaign beyond the battles, from the growing losses of aircraft and pilots outside combat to their impact on pilot training, which were particularly damaging to Japan. The attritional strain of fighting to hold Guadalcanal began a process that would restrict the Japanese ability to resist American thrusts in 1943 and, more importantly, 1944. In that sense it was a crucial step in paving the way for Japanese defeat.

Deciding on the three-pronged advance to Japan

When the fighting on Guadalcanal began winding down in December 1942, it paved the way for discussions that would determine United States' strategy to bring the war to Japan. This is often seen as resulting in a two-pronged campaign: an advance through the Central Pacific and one through the Southwest Pacific. This is only partly true. There was another campaign, strongly supported by the USAAF, to defeat Japan through a strategic air campaign from China – which was eventually labelled Matterhorn. The launching of Matterhorn was always a major consideration in American policy and entailed enormous logistical considerations, so it is only proper to discuss the three quite distinct visions of how best to defeat Japan. (See Map 8.)

The way in which the United States determined its war-fighting strategy against Japan showed the best and worst aspects of American war-making. On one side, there was a vibrant debate between very different conceptions of modern warfare. Intellectually it allowed for the development of some farsighted and ambitious air–sea projections of power that completely superseded pre-war notions. Unfortunately, it was also deeply politicized and wasteful, and resulted in a number of competing efforts which cost extra lives and resources. Ultimately the American system was excellent at creating options, but considerably less successful at choosing between them.

Getting American power into China was something that almost everyone, with the possible exception of King, believed was an extremely high priority at the time of Guadalcanal. For Roosevelt, keeping a supply route into China was "essential."[44] The great problem was how to achieve this. As soon as the war started, Roosevelt ordered Marshall to draw up a strategy memorandum which made maintaining a land route into China from Malaya the highest Anglo-American priority in the Pacific.[45] When this route was closed, however, he ordered Arnold to study all possible air supply routes into China and report back to him quickly. The President wanted to keep China fighting for three main reasons.[46] The first two were military: to tie down as many Japanese troops as possible in China and to launch a major bombing campaign of the Japanese homeland from Chinese soil. The last was Roosevelt's geopolitical vision. He believed that China would increasingly matter in the future and that it was in the American interest to help guide that process.

The only problem with believing that China would be crucial both to deciding the war in the Pacific and the future was how to get in supplies. The preferred American option was to aid a British effort through Burma, to stabilize the situation and reopen an overland route into China. However, when this proved impossible, the other option, which was considered necessary until mid-1944, was for the United States to drive through the Pacific until it reached the Chinese coast. The real choice from the perspective of late 1942, when the American hold on Guadalcanal became secure, was how to cover such a vast distance. This was the genesis of Marshall's and the army's support of the Southwest Pacific campaign. It was to head up through the Bismarck Islands with its first objective being the Japanese fortress-base at Rabaul. After Rabaul had been taken, the push would be to retake the

Philippines (at this point the assumed starting point would be Mindanao). Once that had been done, it was off to the Asian mainland and China.

Such a plan appealed to Marshall for two main reasons. The first was his honest and strong conviction that bases in China were a necessity for the defeat of Japan. The second was the need to give Douglas MacArthur a major command that would appease his enormous ego. Marshall had many prima donnas to deal with during World War II, but MacArthur was especially gilded. He was desperate for glory in general, but specifically focused on leading a major campaign to retake the Philippines. In March 1942, after having led a mostly incompetent defense of the Philippines, he had been ordered to leave by Roosevelt who believed that his capture would be too large a public relations disaster. After pocketing $500,000 from the Filipino government, MacArthur left his troops for Australia, from where he planned his personal vindication.

However, while MacArthur remained focused on the Philippines as an end in their own right, for Marshall and pretty much everyone else in the army, they were a means to reaching China. This was made clear in the preparation for Trident, when the army developed a step-by-step plan for an advance to defeat Japan.

> Phase I, (1) Assist in the recapture of Burma and reopening of the Burma Road. (2) Open a line of communications to the Celebes Sea by a westward advance from Pearl Harbor through the Central and South Pacific, with the main effort in the central Pacific.
> Phase II. Recapture the Philippines.
> Phase III. (1) Secure control of the northern part of the South China Sea. (2) Assist in the capture of Hong Kong.
> Phase IV. Assist in the seizure of suitable air bases in China from which to bomb Japan.
> Phase V. Conduct an intensive air offensive against Japan in preparation for the final invasion of Japan.[47]

The specific locations for these bases were well to the north of Hong Kong. It was thought necessary to secure a line of major facilities heading due west from Shanghai.

If the army was coalescing behind a Southwest Pacific campaign in 1942 and 1943, Ernest King was developing a different plan.

The Central Pacific thrust towards the Mariana Islands was very much his personal brainstorm. It is interesting to see how little, in the run-up to American entry into the war, the Marianas figured in American war planning against Japan.[48] Even after Pearl Harbor, they hardly appeared as a strategic goal for the first year. It was in December 1942, during preparations for the Casablanca Conference, that King started toying with the notion of reorienting American strategy in taking the war to Japan. In the series of notes in which he first mentioned that Roosevelt wanted somewhere between 20 and 35 percent of the American effort sent to the Pacific, King started reimagining the different ways to move forward in the Pacific.

> December 12 [1942]...
> 5. Would it be profitable to move westward in central Pacific, perhaps through Marshalls. Jap air forces there have been strengthened. If divided, how proceed? CinCPac says reverse of Midway, Jap airfields fairly close – frontal attack – not as profitable as continuation of campaign where now in contact. Discussion of Marianas and strategy ... Alternate plans – Truk – Saipan. This cutting communications to Dutch East Indies, *or* frontal as per McA's apparent conception. All this after Rabaul falls – three possible approaches to Far East. Promised on surface (C?) – North, South and Middle. War College problems via South, Cominch favors the Northern.
> After Rabaul,
> British insistence on air cover
> Discussion of Strategic Considerations
> Air Superiority
> CominCh sees no point in frontal attack on Malay Barrier
> Raid on Wake? Should be immediately preceding some other operation – not good by itself –
> What about Gilberts – funa futi – Canton
> Attack on Samoa awkward for us –
> Saturate airfields with planes – good protection.

The next day his notes on the subject continued.

> December 13 [1942]...
> If push is at New G – we support by solidifying Tulagi – situation in reverse – command of Navy LST's etc will pass to

McA – A new directive will probably be necessary to clarify –
reorientation to a degree
. . .
After Rabaul – where – 1 2 and 3 get us there, new offensive-
defensive – strength in air, weakness on surface – lack of docks and
repair facilities – will we have a naval superiority – hope so
Frontal through Marshalls
Partial advance through Truk
    Both involve capturing bases
If elsewhere, we get bases but also cut off raw materials.
If through Ph or Dutch East Indies – shorter jumps –
infiltration.[49]

There was a great deal going through King's mind at the time, some of
which was petty, some farsighted. He was well aware that any campaign directed towards New Guinea and Rabaul would inevitably be
dominated by MacArthur. More interestingly, he was now toying with
the notion of making large leaps towards Japan. One was the extraordinary leap from the Gilberts directly to Canton, which would have
raised island-hopping to rarefied air. Of all these notations, maybe the
most important was his meditation about Truk. This large base in the
Caroline Islands was considered by the Japanese navy as their defensive
bastion after the withdrawal from Guadalcanal. Truk possessed a
superb natural harbor and lay 600 miles south of the Marianas, which
the Japanese viewed as the single most vital series of islands for their
home defense. Nimitz believed that the taking of Truk, which he
termed the "cojones" of the Japanese empire, was a necessary operation.[50] It certainly would have been a major campaign. In May, during
the preparations for Trident, a study was made of the forces needed to
take Truk.[51] It was decided that at least three full amphibious divisions
supported by 12 battleships, 10 fleet aircraft carriers, 7 smaller carriers,
31 cruisers of different size, 108 destroyers and 2 long-range ground-
based air groups would be needed to take the atoll. It was a force
approximately equal to that which did take the Marianas in the
summer of 1944.

Taking Truk was considered the necessary precursor to taking
the Marianas, by almost everyone in early 1944.[52] However, as early as
December 1942, King was wondering whether such an operation was
necessary. As he wrote in his notes, if Japanese raw materials could be
cut off without taking Truk, was such an operation really necessary?

It was the first time that he seriously seemed to consider a separate Central Pacific strategy that would go straight for the Mariana Islands, bypassing both Truk and Rabaul. Now it took a time for this strategy to crystallize in his mind. In the first case, from the vantage point of late 1942 or early 1943, these operations were still more than a year away. Any such operations would be based on having enough carrier-borne air power to support them outside the range of land-based aircraft. This would not be possible until well into 1944.

Those who talk rather simplistically about the war in the Pacific sometimes forget how small American naval air striking power – the key to any successful island-hopping campaign – was until relatively late in the war. During the first year of the war, the United States only lost carrier strength, having four fleet carriers, *Lexington*, *Yorktown*, *Wasp* and *Hornet,* sunk between May and October 1942. The first of the famous Essex Class carriers, which would form the backbone of the fleet that would vanquish Japan, was not ready for service until December 1942. It was not until May 1943, six months later, that another three had entered service – which meant that American naval air power in terms of launch capacity was only back to where it had started in December 1941. It took until January 1944 for the next four Essex Class carriers to enter service – and it took longer before they were combat ready.[53] (See Figure 77.) Because of this, American carrier doctrine did not really come of age until 1943.[54] That presented a real dilemma and opportunity for King. Long-range campaigns, during which air support for the landing troops would have to be provided by aircraft carrier, could not be attempted until 1944 at the earliest. Until that time, it would certainly have been safer to advance up through the Southwest Pacific, which was within range of land-based air support the entire way. However, as King came to realize, such a campaign offered no advantages that would not be obtained from a Central Pacific campaign (as well as one that would leave the

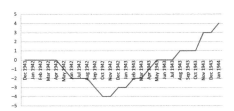

77 USN fleet carrier losses and gains, December 1941–January 1944.

392 / The air and sea war against Japan

USN under army control). The reason that it would offer no advantages was that both would eventually sever Japanese supply lines with the Dutch East Indies and their vital supplies of oil and aluminum.

However, if both campaigns offered the same benefits in terms of cutting Japanese access to raw materials, the Central Pacific campaign offered a number of crucial advantages that would be completely missed with a Southwest Pacific campaign that was directed at recovering the Philippines. A Central Pacific campaign that captured the Marianas would bring Japan into range of direct air attack using the new B-29 bomber. (See Map 8.) Air power could be used not only to bomb Japan directly but, just as importantly, to cut off trade between Japan and its empire in China. King's conviction of the importance of basing the B-29s in the Marianas grew steadily. While Arnold was more interested in putting these aircraft in China, and MacArthur wanted to use them to support his campaigns in the Southwest Pacific, King wanted to see them sent to the Marianas as soon as possible once the islands had been seized.[55]

Furthermore, from bases in the Marianas both air and sea power could be used effectively to sever trade in the Sea of Japan. The United States, in seizing the Marianas, would then have a forward staging post that would allow it to jump directly towards Japan without another major operation (the taking of Iwo Jima was definitely optional). None of these advantages would have been gained had just the Philippines been retaken. Instead, the United States would have had to launch another major operation, either towards the Asian mainland, Formosa or even the Marianas after the Philippines. It would still be a long way from Japan.

The centrality of the Marianas in King's mind grew throughout the first six months of 1943. Morison mentions that in January 1943, King first brought up the importance of the Marianas during the Casablanca Conference.[56] However, during the meeting he still talked far more about the need to have a campaign up through the Southwest Pacific to retake Rabaul – and from there head to the Philippines and China. Yet, soon afterwards King started pressing for a clear division in the Pacific, between a MacArthur-led drive through New Guinea and a navy-dominated operation through the Central Pacific. First, he met with Nimitz before Trident to hammer home the importance of this drive. Then he set about persuading the JCS to divide the Pacific – which was always something about which Marshall, who instinctively supported regional supreme commanders, was unsure. Previously, all operations in the Pacific had been joint army–navy tasks where the services were expected to "cooperate" for the common good.[57] However, on March 28, the JCS separated the Central and Southwest Pacific into distinct theaters. Leahy played an important role in this development. While he believed that China was crucial for geopolitical reasons (and because of Roosevelt's intense interest), he really believed that the US Navy and American air power would bring defeat to Japan. He did not want to see the navy put under MacArthur's thumb in the Southwest Pacific, but wanted to give it freedom of action to destroy the Japanese fleet.[58] As Leahy described the decision in his diary for March 28, Nimitz and the Pacific Fleet were to have enormous freedom of action:

> In the forenoon held a special meeting of the Joint Chiefs of Staff to decide upon command in the South and Southwest Pacific for immediately future operations against the Japanese invaders of that Area. We decided that General MacArthur is to have full command of operations in New Guinea and the adjacent islands, and that the Commander in Chief, Pacific Fleet, will have full command in other Pacific areas with full responsibility for defeating Japanese Fleet.[59]

Under JCS 353, the navy was given the go-ahead to plan for an invasion of the Marshall Islands in November 1943.[60] This allowed King to develop his ideas during Trident. He made a persuasive presentation on May 21 on the need to take the Marianas, which even impressed Alanbrooke.[61] Almost immediately after Trident, King had one of his regular meetings with Nimitz during which the Central Pacific was staked out as the navy's number one priority. King's notes survive from a meeting on May 30. It is clear how much he wanted to separate out MacArthur and the Southwest Pacific from the navy in the Central Pacific.[62] The key thing was to keep freedom of action in the Central Pacific – so that whatever Marine Corps forces became available could be used to take the Gilbert and Marshall Islands. Then the plan was to go for the Marianas, and King and Nimitz discussed which harbor in those islands could best support a large fleet, Saipan or Guam.

Finally, beyond the Southwest and Central Pacific campaigns, there was Arnold's and the USAAF's plan, Matterhorn, to use long-range B-29 bombers based in China to destroy Japanese production through strategic bombing. This is why in late 1942 Arnold earmarked all B-29 production to be sent to fight the Japanese.[63] Launching Matterhorn had been a particular passion of Arnold's from the moment the United States entered the war. As early as the Arcadia Conference, he was claiming that American policy was to move heavy bombers into China as soon as possible.[64] In late January 1942, he told Roosevelt that a bombing campaign from China was the most feasible way for the United States to bring the war to Japan.[65]

In 1943 Arnold worked doggedly to turn this plan into a reality. Not long after the Casablanca Conference, he visited China where he discussed basing heavy bomber units with Chennault and Stillwell.[66] The problem was one of supply. With the overland supplies cut off by the Japanese occupations of Burma and Malaya, everything needed to launch a strategic bombing offensive would have to be flown into China. Even for American air power, this was an extraordinarily expensive proposition. Throughout 1943 the United States worked on a plan to increase deliveries by air into China to 10,000 tons a month. Even a much reduced version of Matterhorn would have taken 70 percent of this, leaving precious little over for anything else.[67]

This issue of supply was one of the key reasons that American and British decision-makers clashed repeatedly in 1943. For every part of the American decision-making structure, with the exception of King, an offensive into Burma to open up a land route into China was a very high priority. The JCS plan for the defeat of Japan which was handed to the British before Quadrant made sure to give special mention to the strategic importance of China.

> The Strategic Plan for the Defeat of Japan ... envisages the actual invasion of Japan following overwhelming air offensive from bases in China. This requires the opening of lines of communication to China which, in turn, involves the early capture of Burma and the seizure of a port in China. This requires a westward advance by the United States through the Central and South-Southwest Pacific.[68]

However, British reluctance to put forces into Burma left the Americans having to decide how to get to China on their own, and that was one of the main considerations behind the tortuous internal American decision process about the war in the Pacific in 1944.

For that reason it makes sense to examine the different views that eventually led to the famous face-to-face meeting between Roosevelt and MacArthur – which resulted in one of the less seemly political deals in American history.

Going into 1944, no strategic choice in the Pacific was preordained, either a thrust towards the Philippines or one towards the Marianas. The only definite assumption was that Matterhorn would commence sometime in the coming year. Even though the Marianas were being talked about as an American destination, the USAAF still believed that bases in China would be far more effective.[69] The army, at least Marshall and those around him, talked about an advance to the "China–Formosa–Luzon" area, which in and of itself is an extremely large region.[70] What worried Marshall was that this effort was being subverted by King taking too many resources for his Central Pacific campaign.

A January 1944 joint army–navy conference in Pearl Harbor, not attended by King or MacArthur, but involving Nimitz and senior army and navy commanders in the Pacific, endorsed a route to China through the Philippines.[71] The conference's results were reported to Marshall, with the Marianas deliberately downgraded as a priority for the strange reason that the B-29s would not be effective if launched from them.

> The consensus of opinion seemed to be that the best plan for the Pacific campaign for this year included the completion of the Marshalls operations including the capture of Eniwetok; the Kavieng–Manus operation; Truk to be by-passed and the next jump through the Central Pacific to the Pilaus; in the meantime the advance would continue up the New Guinea coast, and after the Pilaus were captured, the move into Mindanao would be made. It was felt that, if all forces were concentrated on the above operations, the Philippines might be entered by the end of 1944. There seemed to be general agreement that Truk should be bypassed and that there was little to be gained from going to the Marianas. Although the B-29s could attack Japan proper from the Marianas, the range is long, thus cutting down the bomb load; and the operation would in no way be decisive.
>
> As far as I can see, Admiral Nimitz did not express himself directly on this plan, although he did say it was his view that Japan could only be defeated from bases in China.[72]

This was only one indication that the army and much of the navy did not see the Marianas as particularly important and remained focused on reaching China. In March Arnold, who was increasingly frustrated by what he saw as a lack of priorities in Pacific strategy, called for the JCS to make a clear decision on the way forward. He assumed, like Marshall, that the ultimate goal of all operations was the "China–Formosa–Luzon" area, which was much more important than the Marianas.[73]

King, however, was planning for a different war. He seems to have become convinced at the start of 1944 that Truk could be neutralized by air assault and bypassed. While he had started contemplating this in late 1942, the general assumption by everyone else throughout 1943 was that Truk would have to be assaulted. At the end of Quadrant, the CCS reported to Roosevelt and Churchill that in 1944 Truk needed to be taken so that the Allies could establish a large fleet base from where they could launch further attacks.[74] At the same time, Nimitz was telling King that he wanted to take Truk in 1944.[75] The army also assumed that Truk would be invaded.[76] King, however, was starting to push for a move directly to the Marianas. When he first heard of the results of the January 1944 meeting which called for attacking the Philippines over the Marianas, he rebuked Nimitz and demanded that the commander of the Pacific Fleet come to Washington to confer.[77]

In early February, in a fascinating memorandum that he sent to Marshall, King ranged widely over the Pacific war.[78] He expressed his normal skepticism about MacArthur and stated his determination to keep the Central Pacific drive separate from the former's command. He also specifically mentioned the need to place B-29s in the Marianas as soon as those islands were taken. When it came to Truk, he openly broached the notion of not taking the Japanese fortress. He ended his meditation on strategy in the Pacific by saying that it was his "opinion that we must either seize Truk or interdict it by seizing part of the Marianas."[79]

Soon events would help support King's hunch that Truk could be bypassed. A series of carrier-based assaults on the Japanese base on February 16–17 damaged it so much that it was no longer a great threat.[80] American carrier aircraft devastated the atoll, reducing the effectiveness of the Japanese aircraft stationed there by 80 percent and sinking every Japanese naval combat vessel at anchorage, which included three cruisers and three destroyers, plus thirty-one merchant ships.[81] Truk was left helpless.

Marshall seems to have been in two minds about canceling the invasion of Truk.[82] He was clearly becoming frustrated by all the conflicting ideas and pressures he was receiving. On February 21, he brought to the rest of the JCS his desire to have both the navy and MacArthur state their ideas clearly by submitting concrete plans for the best way forward.[83] The navy opted for a major amphibious operation to be launched on June 15, the ultimate destination of which, Truk or the Marianas, would be decided closer to the time. MacArthur smelled a rat, as can be seen in the following summary of the navy plan as drawn up by his chief of staff, Major General R. K. Sutherland. It showed no strategic grasp of the importance of the Marianas.

> Admiral Nimitz proposes to prepare all available forces for a major effort on 15 June, but to postpone the decision as to the objective. His alternate lines of action contemplate:
>
> (1) The attack on Truk 15 June, southern Marianas 1 September and the Palaus 15 November
> (2) The by passing of Truk to the northward, the attack on the southern Marianas 15 June, Woleai 15 July, and the Palaus 10 October.
>
> The Central Pacific plan contemplates actions in the enemy's outpost area during all of 1944 and will not secure any major strategic effect during the year. It does not include the capture of Luzon. . .[84]

In the short term it was a victory for King and the navy. Marshall was persuaded by Nimitz's arguments for the change.[85] On March 12, the Joint Chiefs finally approved a plan to head straight for the Marianas, bypassing Truk.[86] However, that did not end things; rather it set the stage for the most famous grand-strategic summit meeting of the Pacific war. With the Marianas safely under American control, there was now no need to retake the Philippines. This was realized not only by King and Nimitz, but also by Marshall and Arnold. Taking the Philippines would inflict no extra damage on the Japanese economy and would delay any further move forward to Japan until 1945. King had started to believe that MacArthur's drive towards the

Philippines was unnecessary in 1943. His suggestion in favor of an attack on Formosa, if that indeed is what he really would have done, would have been equally as difficult and unnecessary. However, his proposal to attack Formosa rather than the Philippines caused one of the most intense American upper-echelon strategic battles of the war.

With the Marianas operation proceeding smoothly, and the Japanese navy so clearly damaged by the Battle of the Philippine Sea, King moved to cancel any operation against the Philippines and instead to invade Formosa or even go straight for China or Japan. This was obviously a move that was going to antagonize MacArthur. His personal stake in the Philippines was something that he had stressed to Marshall in February 1944, when discussions about what could be bypassed on the way to China first began to simmer. MacArthur threatened blackmail.

> It is quite evident that the ultimate issue in question is the control of the campaign in the Pacific, and immediately, that for the initial major objective, the Philippine Islands which have always been in my area. This has been entrusted to me from the very beginning and has been reiterated in directives from the Joint Chiefs of Staff and the Secretary of War. While I do not for a moment believe that this will be changed, my professional integrity, indeed my personal honor would be so involved that, if otherwise, I request that I be given early opportunity personally to present the case to the Secretary of War and to the President before finally determining my own personal action in the matter.[87]

It was both an astute and an appalling letter. MacArthur knew that in a presidential election year, in which he was already being talked about as a possible Republican candidate, the administration would have to take his threat to resign seriously. And they did. Leahy, who had a finely tuned political sense which only became more acute every day he spent with Franklin Roosevelt, made a remark in his diary when MacArthur finally was smoked out by the press and made an ambiguous statement that he did not "covet" the presidency.[88] However, it was also indicative of the destructive ego of MacArthur. The only thing that he should have been concerned with was determining the best route to Japan. Getting to the Philippines was not a strategic necessity for the United States.

Suspicion of MacArthur's intentions was widespread amongst the Joint Chiefs and other senior commanders. King, who was distrustful by nature, believed that MacArthur did not understand modern air and sea war and tried to keep as much of the USN away from him as possible. After the war he claimed that, when Marshall tried to make MacArthur supreme commander in the Pacific, he refused because the latter "knew very little about sea-power and also not very much about air-power."[89] King also wrote an unsolicited letter to an author who had written a positive article about MacArthur in *Cosmopolitan*, expressing his displeasure that the general had been praised so heavily and his "regret" that the author's "contacts with the Navy and the Marine Corps should have made you feel so positive in regard to the general views about McArthur [sic]."[90]

Of course, King disliked so many people that his particular disdain for MacArthur on its own might not mean much. Much more telling was others' estimations. Interestingly, on a number of occasions Arnold could be particularly damning about MacArthur. When he went to the Pacific and met with the general in September 1942, Arnold thought MacArthur had lost touch with reality and wondered if he was suffering from shell-shock.[91] Nimitz's estimation of the man in 1944 is frightening. The quiet Texan was not prone to strong emotional dislike. However, in 1944 he clearly believed that MacArthur was fighting for personal glory. After the JCS asked Nimitz and MacArthur to refine their plans for moving forward, the two commanders met to discuss the process. Nimitz wrote a description of the meeting that was so sensitive that he refused to send it by cable. Instead he put it in a handwritten letter which he gave to the Marine General Arthur Vandegrift to deliver to King personally. According to Nimitz, when he and MacArthur first met the general was all charm.

> Everything was lovely and harmonious until the last day of the conference when I called attention to the last part of the JCS directive which required him and me to prepare alternate plans for moving faster and along shorter routes towards the Luzon–Formosa–China triangle if deteriorating Japanese strength permitted. Then he blew up and made an oration of some length on the impossibility of bypassing the Philippines, his sacred obligations there – redemption of the 17 million people – blood in his soul – deserted by American people – etc, etc – and then a

criticism of "those gentlemen in Washington" who – far from the scene – and having never heard the whistle of bullets etc – endeavor to set the strategy of the Pacific War – etc.[92]

If Nimitz is to be believed, then MacArthur at this point was not fit for command. No general in a constitutional democracy should ever base his strategy on a supposed personal and "sacred" obligation. Even Marshall started to lose patience with MacArthur at this time. He, who had to cope with MacArthur's petulance more than anyone, could easily have agreed to bypass the Philippines if it would have gotten the United States to China more quickly. Moreover, he was worried that Japanese defensive preparations in the Philippines and the Palau Islands meant that MacArthur would be dragging the United States into a campaign that was bound to be bloody as well as unnecessary.[93] He began to look favorably on heading directly for Formosa or, even more ambitiously, striking directly for Kyushu if the Japanese fleet could be dealt a devastating defeat. On June 23, he drafted a letter for MacArthur which both scolded the latter for his personal ambition and asked him to consider these alternatives to an invasion of the Philippines. It was Marshall at his finest.

> [T]here is a further consideration in this matter that presents a pressing problem to the Chiefs of Staff and that is the collapse of resistance in China which is already threatened by the Japanese activity of the past month. A successful culmination of the war against Japan undoubtedly will involve the use of a portion of the China coast. Therefore we cannot afford to stand by and see this region completely overrun and consolidated by the Japanese.

He added a page later:

> Whether or not the Formosa or the Kyushu operation can be mounted remains a matter to be studied but neither operation in my opinion is unsound in the way you indicate. Whether or not such operations should be carried out before a heavy blow is struck at the Japanese fleet is also of course a serious consideration. There is little doubt in my mind, however, that after a crushing blow is delivered against the Japanese Fleet that we should go as close to Japan as quickly as possible in order to shorten the war, which means the reconquest of the Philippines.

> With regards to the last, it seems to me that you are allowing
> your personal feelings and Philippine political considerations to
> override our great objective which is the early conclusion of the
> war with Japan. Also that you confuse the word "by-pass" with
> "abandonment", the two are in no way synonymous in my
> view . . .[94]

The problem that the Joint Chiefs of Staff had with MacArthur,
however, was that Roosevelt, unlike Truman a few years later, was
unwilling to call the general's bluff. And the President had a chance.
King's call for the invasion of the Philippines to be cancelled and the next
attack be directed to Formosa caused another eruption by MacArthur.
It was so serious that it was decided that Roosevelt would head out to
Hawaii to meet with Nimitz and MacArthur to personally decide where
the next American offensive in the Pacific should be directed.

The Joint Chiefs, with the exception of the ubiquitous Leahy,
were deliberately kept away from the proceedings which took place on
July 27–29. This meant that the quieter Nimitz and not the more
forceful King had to argue against a major operation in the Philippines.
King had clear views on the subject.

> The President, as Commander in Chief of the Army and Navy, had
> been called upon to make the decision, not as to the Philippine
> Campaign per se, but as to the Philippines *or* Formosa. Plans were
> ready in outline for either campaign. The chief merits of the
> Formosa plan were (1) that it definitely cut all Japanese
> communications southward of Formosa, and (2) that it afforded
> immediate opportunities for a seaway into China, whereby to
> equip and supply Chinese manpower . . .[95]

However, Nimitz was clearly less willing to be confrontational and
instead argued that Mindanao, the southerly and second largest island
in the Philippines, could be invaded but that taking Luzon, the main
island on which the capital Manila was located, was unnecessary.[96]
MacArthur, on the other hand, dazzled Roosevelt with tales of easy
victories and grateful Filipinos and American voters. The general was
certainly wildly optimistic about how easy it would be to retake Luzon.
He told Roosevelt during the conference and Marshall right after
that all of Luzon could be captured in a maximum of six weeks.[97]
Furthermore, he promised that soon after the liberation of Luzon, he

could have a string of operating air and sea bases from which the war could be taken to Japan. On the other hand, he painted a very damaging "political" picture for Roosevelt if for some reason Luzon were not liberated and stories started emerging about mass starvation on the island.[98]

It really was too much for the President, whose health was failing, to resist.[99] MacArthur's promise of a quick and painless victory that would result in great political benefit persuaded him to approve an invasion of the Philippines including Luzon.[100] Even Leahy, who had not committed himself either way before this, seems to have been won over by MacArthur's sweeping vision. For those who have written positively about MacArthur, this victory was crucial. They believe not only that the Philippines campaign was a damaging blow to Japan, but that by liberating the Philippines the United Stated repaid a moral obligation.

The first of those questions will be discussed later, but the second deserves some comment now. By taking the war into the Philippine islands in late 1944, MacArthur almost certainly caused the deaths of hundreds of thousands of Filipino civilians who would not have died otherwise. During World War II, as might be expected, civilian deaths were considerably higher where fighting was intense as opposed to places where combat was rare. During MacArthur's campaign to retake the Philippines, fighting was particularly brutal around Manila, which was not liberated until late February.[101] During the fighting, it is estimated that 100,000 Filipino civilians were killed, mostly as a result of Japanese atrocities.[102] As fighting was still going on in Luzon at the time of the Japanese surrender, during the rest of the liberation it has been estimated that hundreds of thousands more Filipino civilians died.[103] Even admitting the brutality of Japanese rule, it is unlikely that anything like this number of Filipino civilians would have died had fighting not been so severe on the islands. In order to end Japanese rule a few months sooner, the Filipinos paid a steep price.

The numerical rise and qualitative fall of Japanese air power, 1942–4

In 1941 and 1942 Japanese torpedo plane pilots were some of the best-trained and most tactically capable flyers in the world. They had inflicted major damage on the American Pacific Fleet in Pearl Harbor and they went on to sink the aircraft carrier *Lexington* in the Battle of the Coral Sea. Later, they were partially responsible for sinking the carrier *Hornet* off Guadalcanal. The key to successful torpedo attacks was known to be approaching American warships in concentrated formations, which could overwhelm anti-air defenses. However, this required great skill, and Japanese pilots in 1944 were not trained well enough. Instead, Japanese torpedo bombers were then instructed to attack in small units whenever they felt ready. Captain Mitsuo Fuchida, who was the IJN's senior staff officer on the 1st Air Fleet which was responsible for defending the Marianas, described the change:

> Until February 1944 a method of coordinated attack was used in which all torpedo planes attacked from one side as soon as proper illumination had been provided by illuminating planes which dropped flares ... This type of coordinated attack required skilful pilots.
>
> In February 1944 the method was changed to one in which the illuminating planes circled the ships to be attacked at a radius of 3000 to 5000 meters and dropped flares at 20 minute intervals. The attacking planes also circled the ships but at about 10,000 meters radius. When the flare illumination was correct and one section was in position to attack, that section went in without further orders. This method did not require a high degree of coordination and, therefore, not nearly as many skilful pilots.[104]

This change in pilot tactics and ability was clear to the Americans assaulting the Marianas who witnessed the massacre of Japanese naval aircraft as they tried in vain to attack the American fleet. In an after-action summary report on naval anti-aircraft perform-ance, it was stated that during the battle Japanese air attacks were "poorly coordinated, with no attempt to coordinate strafing-torpedo attacks or dive-bombing torpedo attacks. Although many of the enemy pilots showed their usual suicidal tendency by fanatically pressing home their attacks, they failed to take evasive action or use their potential high speed to best advantage. Approaches were straight and there were no deflection shots at low altitude."[105]

The Japanese were aware of the poor performance of their pilots in the Marianas. Admiral Ozawa, commander of the IJN's Combined Fleet during the Battle of the Philippine Sea, singled out poorly trained pilots, along with Japanese radar weaknesses, as the reason for the debacle.[106] Rear Admiral Toshitane Takata, a naval air expert who helped reorganize the IJN's air service after Midway, when asked if he knew how many pilots were lost fighting for the Marianas, replied that as far as he knew it "was almost a total loss."[107]

This deterioration in Japanese pilot training helps underscore the complexity and interdependence of many parts of the air–sea war. In 1942 and 1943 almost all of the fighting in the war in the Pacific, unlike that in Europe, occurred thousands of miles away from Japan itself. With the exception of the famous, but possibly counterproductive, Doolittle Raid, the islands of Japan remained as untouched by the war as California or New York. Because of this, and the fact that aircraft production was given special status in the Japanese economy, the number of planes produced rose dramatically, actually matching the targets set by the Japanese army and navy through the end of 1943.[108] Neither the United States nor Germany was able to meet its production targets at this time. Moreover, after the first few months of fighting in Guadalcanal, aircraft combat losses for the Japanese navy also remained relatively stable, until the heavy losses around Rabaul between September and November 1943 (after which they declined again). (See Figure 78.) This meant that the aircraft on hand for the Japanese navy increased substantially by April 1944. (See Figure 79.)

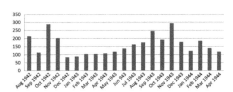

78 Japanese naval aircraft lost in combat, August 1942–April 1944.

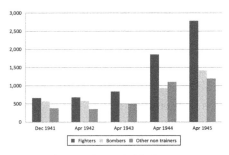

79 Japanese naval aircraft available for operations, December 1941–April 1945.

Japanese aircraft production grew markedly in 1943 and 1944. Because the USN was not yet ready to launch the massed aircraft carrier operations which it would make famous in 1944 and 1945, the number of planes available to the Japanese navy doubled between April 1943 and April 1944, at which point it controlled a force about two and a half times as large as that which the Luftwaffe had deployed on the Eastern Front. US intelligence actually had a good idea how large a force of aircraft the Japanese navy had its disposal in 1944. Earlier they had significantly underestimated Japan's productive prowess and assumed that Japanese air power would soon dwindle. However, in early 1944, American intelligence estimated that in total the Japanese navy had 2,550 aircraft ready for operations.[109] In April the IJN had 2,784 fighters and bombers available, so the intelligence estimate was close to reality. It was one of the reasons that such a large American force was considered necessary to take the Marianas. During this period, Japan's navy was given at least half the country's aircraft production and its complete focus was on fighting the United States. The army, which received the other half, throughout 1942 and 1943 basically split its allocation between aircraft fighting the United States (which became increasingly concentrated in New Guinea and the Dutch East Indies) and those on the Asian mainland, which were operating in China, Manchuria or as far away as Burma. For the Navy there was no such dispersion of effort.

However, the power of this force was severely restricted and, when tested in combat in June 1944, it performed poorly. The reasons for this performance had everything to do with how the war had developed over the previous two years, as much in terms of what happened away from the traditional notion of the battlefield as what happened on it. The major problem was inferior pilot training, but poor maintenance and deployment procedures all combined to mean that this numerically large force fought valiantly but ineffectively.

The poor pilot training that beset first the Japanese navy and then the army was caused by a combination of factors. At the beginning of the war, Japanese naval air training was some of the best in the world, though it stressed quality over quantity.[110] It certainly produced pilots who could more than match their American counterparts and were thought considerably better than those of the Japanese army.[111] Their numbers were, however, modest. The IJN possessed between 3,000 and 4,000 trained pilots at the start of the war, only 1,500 of

406 / The air and sea war against Japan

whom were trained to fly from aircraft carriers.[112] Losses of trained pilots in the first eight months of the war were light and the navy felt that it had their pilot situation well in hand. Before the Battle of Midway, it had lost only about seventy pilots, and during the battle itself lost a further hundred.[113] Luckily for the Japanese, however, they were able to save more than two-thirds of the pilots whose planes were shot down or crashed during Midway.[114]

However, losses suffered during Guadalcanal led to significant reductions in trained pilot numbers. The extreme need for pilots caused the Japanese to rush back many of the pilots who had been injured at Midway, even if they were desperately in need of time to rest and recover.[115] Eventually, the navy even had to use its best carrier pilots from land-based airfields, as it was considered too dangerous to deploy aircraft carriers in the area. Often these pilots, trained especially for use from ships such as Saburo Sakai (see Chapter 2), were wasted flying numerous missions at the extreme end of their effective range between Rabaul and Guadalcanal.

During fighting in the Solomons, the recovery of downed pilots, which had been efficient earlier, became increasingly difficult. Moreover, those Japanese pilots fighting in the Solomons were usually denied leave as the need to keep them in action was considered too great. The result was a serious decline in morale which led to even higher wastage.[116] Pilot losses soon became severe. During the Battle of Santa Cruz on October 26, 1942, the IJN lost 150 pilots, 50 percent more than during Midway.[117] Yet this was one of only six major naval battles and countless smaller engagements that occurred in the Solomons. It further highlights the attritional importance of power destruction over the focus on battles or events.

Commander Tadashi Yamamoto, an IJN officer who served in the Solomons during the entire Guadalcanal battle, believed that these attritional losses were far more important in destroying Japanese naval air power than Midway had been. "Almost all of the Navy's first class pilots and a few of the Army's were lost in the Solomon Operations. The greatest portion of these was lost against Guadalcanal. At one time we had three of four squadrons at Rabaul but they were sent down one at a time. The constant attrition was expensive. The 21st, 24th, 25th and 26th air groups were lost."[118]

So combat losses definitely became a strain on Japanese pilot numbers, but that was only part of the story. Non-combat aircraft

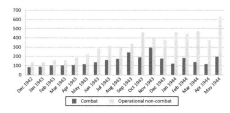

80 Japanese naval aircraft losses, in combat (dark) and non-combat (light) operations, December 1942–May 1944.

casualties also caused the loss of a great number of pilots. In Figure 80 it is striking just how many more aircraft the Japanese navy lost outside combat than in, but maybe more important was the enormous relative increase in non-combat losses when compared with those in combat.

Between November 1942, when combat losses declined once the peak of fighting in Guadalcanal had passed, and June 1944, when the fighting erupted around the Marianas, the gap between those Japanese naval aircraft lost in combat and those lost outside grew from a small difference to a massive one. During the entire period, the navy lost 5,889 aircraft in non-combat operations and only 2,754 in combat. Of these non-combat losses, 2,393 occurred between just January and May 1944 when combat losses were only 763 – a ratio of more than three to one. It meant that many pilots, who might very well have ended up being excellent flyers, were lost to the Japanese air forces in accidents before ever gaining any combat experience.

Many of these aircraft were those that never made it to their deployment areas. Throughout 1942 Japanese naval aircraft losses in the deployment stage were manageable. Pilot error, bad weather and mechanical error meant, in one estimate, that about 5 percent of Japanese naval aircraft were lost during transfer from their depots in Japan to their tactical units.[119] However, in 1943 and into 1944, these deployment losses rose sharply. One of the major reasons for this was that more and more pilots had to fly themselves to their first posting.[120]

Among the most difficult of these deployment flights, for both navy and army pilots, were those that had to be made to Rabaul or New Guinea. (See Map 7.) To deploy aircraft to the large air facilities at Rabaul on the island of New Britain, new army pilots had to fly from the southern island of Kyushu to Formosa and then to the Philippines, and from there to Rabaul.[121] Many of the new pilots never even completed the first leg, disappearing before reaching Formosa. Major

C. Takahasi of the Japanese army's aircraft supply section and Captain T. Takeuchi, who was in charge of keeping the statistics for a major supply center, both claimed that from early on in the war, 50 percent of Japanese army aircraft were not reaching their deployment points capable of flying.

> Q. You have stated that ferrying losses averaged 50 percent throughout the war. Was the figure really that high during the early stages?
> A. Yes, early in the war the haul down to the southern areas was much longer and any number of things occurred enroute. Later, when the haul became shorter, engine failures between Kyushu and Formosa accounted for heavy losses. Another factor was the decline in effectiveness of maintenance personnel. Virtually all the best technicians were sent to forward areas, got stuck there and could not return.[122]

The Japanese navy, maintaining the strict separation of the services that was such a problem for Japanese war-making, had an equally difficult deployment phase. For their new pilots to reach Rabaul, the IJN usually had them first fly from the Yokusuka base in Honshu to Saipan with a possible stop in Iwo Jima. If they were lucky enough to complete this route, next they had to fly over completely open ocean to the large fleet base at Truk in the Caroline Islands and from there to Rabaul.[123] Even the last leg, by which time the pilot had shown that he could handle his aircraft and the plane had demonstrated that it was moderately well built, could lead to losses. Captain C. Kanai, who was in charge of the IJN's Southeast Air Depot based in Rabaul, said that 5 percent of the aircraft which took off from Truk never reached Rabaul. In June 1943, one flight of army aircraft left Truk for Rabaul with twenty-four aircraft, but only two arrived.[124]

There was one other element which, when added to high Japanese pilot losses, further compounded the training problem, and that was fuel shortages. The submarines of the United States Navy during 1943 began choking off much of Japan's supply of oil. It was the start of World War II's most successful trade destruction campaign. By the end of 1943 and early 1944, even Japan's army and navy, who always had the highest priority for fuel that made it past the submarine blockade, were starting to feel the pinch.

Combined with combat and non-combat pilot losses, this fuel shortage set up a catastrophic situation for Japanese pilot training. New Japanese pilots in both the navy and army were given hundreds

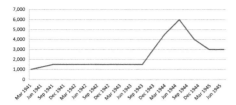

81 Japanese Army Air Force, number of pilot graduates per month

of fewer hours to learn their craft, both on the ground and in the air. Rear Admiral Seizo Katsumata was the head instructor of the navy's technical school in Yokosuka in 1941 and 1942, before serving in a number of other senior positions in charge of naval aircraft for the rest of the war.[125] He stated that losses through the Battle of Midway had actually run at pre-war estimates. However, the fighting around Guadalcanal and Rabaul was so costly in aircraft, because of both operational and non-operational losses, that Japanese pilot training had to be greatly accelerated to produce the pilots necessary to make up the losses.[126] (See Figure 81.) That could only be achieved through reducing the number of flying hours that each new pilot was given.

According to Yamamoto, the effect of the Guadalcanal losses and the pilot training reductions was a real blow to Japanese power. "This loss was keenly felt in the defense of the Empire during the Marshall–Gilbert campaign. In 1943 our training program began to be restricted so we were never able to replace these losses although we still had a number of carriers."[127] Before the Guadalcanal losses, Japanese naval pilots received 800 hours of different flight training, both classroom and in aircraft, before being sent on operations.[128] By the end of that campaign, training had been cut to 600 hours. By 1944 the number of hours was reduced even further to 500 or less. It also seems that the expected training hours were often not being met. Commander Masatake Okumiya, who flew out of Rabaul before the evacuation and served on the *Ryuho* during the Marianas operation, claims that by early 1944 the fighter pilots there were being sent into action after only 300 hours of training and the dive-bombers between 300 and 400 hours.[129] These new pilots were particularly weak when flying at dusk and during hours of darkness. At times they even had to be forbidden from flying except in daylight. At the same time, American naval aviators were receiving ever more sophisticated and detailed training before being sent on operations.

The Japanese army also began cutting back its training at this time. At first, the fuel shortage presented a greater problem for the Japanese Army Air Force than an immediate shortage of pilots. As the Army Air Force had only part of its force deployed in the Pacific in 1942, its pilot losses were more moderate. For the army the real need for more pilots only became serious in the second half of 1943.[130] Two things contributed to this change. The first was the wholesale redeployment of Army Air Force units from the Asian mainland to the Pacific, primarily New Guinea, the Dutch East Indies and Rabaul.[131] The army's Manchurian Air Force, which had been one of its largest, first started sending large numbers of planes to Rabaul in February 1943.[132] Soon this regular supply became a flood, as by 1944 the army was forced to strip China and Manchuria of aircraft to deploy to the Pacific.

These redeployments, however, resulted in massive losses. Japanese army pilots, who were used to flying overland on mainland Asia and were flying aircraft with considerably shorter ranges than the Zero and other Japanese naval aircraft, often disappeared or were seriously damaged doing a series of hazardous over-water leaps to get to the area of combat. Those units that were redeployed, particularly those sent to New Guinea which were based around Wewak, suffered heavy attritional losses in the period between March and October 1943.

The response by the army was also to reduce training schedules starting in October 1943.[133] Before the war it was believed that an army pilot needed about two years of training before he was ready for operations. By 1944 this was down to nine months and in 1945 reduced to just over four months.[134] In terms of hours of training, army pilots by the end of 1943 were often down to 500 hours. These pressures from oil shortages not only caused the Japanese army to shorten its training regimen, it also caused them to move the training from Japan down to the Dutch East Indies to be closer to the sources of fuel. Ultimately, much of the training therefore occurred in operational units near to combat areas. The new pilots ended up in action long before they were ready.[135]

Just as importantly, those reduced hours of flying were used to train pilots to do specific tasks, so that the routine but crucial steps of learning to take off and land were increasingly marginalized. The army eventually changed its entire flight curriculum. Before the war, its flight training had focused on tactical attacks in support of Japanese ground forces. Now, training had to focus on attacks on American shipping. Because of that, the percentage of time devoted to the routine mechanics of flying was cut severely. Before 1943, the flying time for a Japanese army pilot was divided between take-off and landing – 20 percent; maneuvering in flight – 28 percent; navigation – 12 percent; and bombing practice – 40 percent.[136] Nearer to the end of the war, the percentages had been altered to take-off and landing – 15 percent; maneuvering in flight – 20 percent; navigation – 8 percent; and attacks on shipping – 57 percent. Like the navy, by 1944 the Japanese army was producing pilots who spent significantly less time learning their craft before deployment and who were receiving in percentage terms far less training in the fundamentals of flight. They were accidents waiting to happen. Combined, these navy and army training cut-backs were part of a vicious circle that led to even greater non-operational aircraft losses.

Lt General Iwa Kawabe, the head of the army's Bureau of Aeronautics in 1943 and 1944, believed that the strain of the air–sea war meant that Japan could not provide adequate maintenance to the aircraft that were being deployed. Even as Japanese production of aircraft was reaching new and impressive heights, the strain of maintaining these planes while on their way to deployment meant that, at times, only 10 percent were able to enter combat once they arrived at base.

> At that time, although we didn't have any to spare, I feel that the production was more or less adequate. But of the planes produced in the home country, we couldn't have one-hundred percent of them in action at the destination.
>
> Q. What percent could you have, normally?
> A. I can't express it exactly in figures, but it was a very small figure. One of the reasons for the low percentage of planes reaching the destinations which were operational was that, unlike the United States, the maintenance of bases enroute was very poor. Had we been able to set up good bases fast like the United States did, our losses would have been much smaller; but as it turned out, only a very small percentage actually became operational at the destination.
> Q. Well, roughly 10 or 25 percent?
> A. The ones that actually engaged in combat ... I would guess around 10 percent.[137]

These deployment losses made up a large percentage of Japanese war production. They materially affected a number of major engagements. In the spring of 1944, when the Japanese started preparing to fight for the Marianas, their navy started rushing aircraft to Saipan, Tinian and Guam. Captain Toshikazu Ohmae, who served on the staff of the First Mobile Fleet during the battle, recounts how, at one point, a hundred aircraft were diverted from operations in the Dutch East Indies to the Marianas.[138] However, owing to poor pilot training, only half of them actually arrived at their destination.

Even those aircraft that arrived were confronted by a real difficulty that meant they could quickly be put out of action by small problems. In the first place, navy and army maintenance procedures were completely separate, and since the services used different aircraft that had been developed independently of one another, they usually did not have spare parts to repair the other's planes. Even within the services, divisions in responsibilities meant that relatively minor damage could keep an aircraft out of action for long periods. Within the navy, for instance, the mechanics who oversaw aircraft delivery were completely separate from those who did operational aircraft maintenance.[139] This meant that if planes arrived damaged, they could not be repaired if the delivery service lacked the right spare parts. Eventually a specialist bureau, called 101 Kokusentai, was set up to centralize the procedures. However, by the time it became operational, the decline in pilot training standards had become so severe that non-combat losses, if anything, became worse. The air and sea war against Japan had gone a long way towards neutering Japanese air power before it could be sent into battle.

Fighting the three campaigns towards Japan

The losses that the Japanese suffered around Guadalcanal in aircraft and naval vessels caused them to severely reduce their defensive perimeter, which brings us back to the question of the different American thrusts to Japan. Up through the winter of 1942–3, the Japanese were planning on holding an ambitious defensive line stretching from the Solomons and New Britain (based around Rabaul) to the Gilbert and Marshall Islands. However, losses had been so high in the Solomons that this line was retracted by hundreds of miles back to the Mariana

Islands, Truk and the northern tip of New Guinea.[140] The garrisons on the Marshall and Gilbert Islands would be left in place as obstacles, but were not to be reinforced or protected if assaulted.

With the delineated areas of responsibility decided by the JCS in March 1943, MacArthur and Nimitz could start moving forward in their respective areas towards this new line. The navy's first major move was exactly what the Japanese had been hoping, the seizure of the Gilbert and Marshall Islands. These islands had actually figured in American and British pre-Pearl Harbor planning, when it was assumed that they would be taken to provide a buffer against Japanese expansion while overwhelming force was applied to Germany.[141] Some of these islands, particularly Tarawa which was assaulted on November 19, 1943 but also Kwajalein which was hit on January 31, 1944 (and was where Harry Hopkins' son was killed), became household names in the United States because of the brutality of the fighting that they witnessed.

The landing of the Marines on Tarawa was the one example during the war when an American amphibious assault was almost pulled off the beaches. Though the island of Betio, where the main landings occurred, had been well scouted with aerial photographic reconnaissance, the Americans had no charts on the expected tidal situation. This was a major blunder. When the Marines started landing, the tide was very low and turned many of the landing craft into immobile, easy targets for the Japanese defenders. They became stuck on exposed coral formations and the assaulting troops were often dropped a long way from the beaches. Having to swim for long distances to reach the shore, the troops were then cut down by the Japanese who were dug in well, almost all of then having survived the too-short and poorly planned pre-landing bombardment.

The casualties experienced on this first day were far higher than expected. When the Marines landed on Guadalcanal, they had caught the Japanese by surprise and it took a few days for the defenders to recover and launch serious military operations. At Tarawa, however, the Japanese were ready. In just a few days' fighting, the Marines and the navy suffered 1,009 deaths and 2,101 wounded.[142] This casualty rate of 17 percent of the combat troops involved was extremely high by United States' standards in World War II, and was used by those who favored the Southwest Pacific thrust to argue that King was needlessly sacrificing his Marines in a campaign that wasn't needed to defeat Japan.

This flagged up a legitimate point. The taking of Tarawa, and really all of the Gilberts and Marshalls, was not necessary to defeat Japan. Though there were Japanese airfields on the islands, supplying them adequately for offensive operations was beyond Japan's capabilities in 1943. By attacking the islands, the United States Navy was doing what the Japanese had hoped – exerting effort assaulting fortified islands on the far periphery of their defensive zone.[143] However, it is very hard to criticize the decision to make these attacks. Without overwhelming carrier air power, the Gilbert and Marshall Islands represented the only safe targets in the Central Pacific, as they were too far from Japanese bases to be protected by Japanese air power. Also, the assaults provided valuable lessons for the much larger air–sea assaults of 1944 and 1945.

If Tarawa was a bloodbath, the rest of the landings in the Gilberts and Marshalls were much less costly. The taking of Kwajalein, which was a much larger operation involving 41,446 troops, had a casualty rate of less than 5 percent (372 killed/missing and 1,582 wounded).[144] Much better pre-landing intelligence, and the fact that the beaches did not have the same coral reefs as Tarawa, meant that the landing troops could get ashore faster and more safely. Also, the American assault, which was now supported by naval air power, provided much greater fire-support. In some ways, this was the main success of the whole campaign. Between Tarawa and Kwajalein the Americans had learned some important lessons about what was needed to launch successful amphibious assaults. Marshall, for one, believed that these lessons were important. He passed along a report to Eisenhower on the subject, and added that Tarawa was an example of an error-strewn assault, whereas Kwajalein provided a model for future operations.[145]

For King, not taking the islands was probably politically impossible. As the navy did not yet possess the carrier force needed to launch long-distance amphibious assaults, his alternative would have been to wait and let MacArthur's campaign in the Southwest Pacific gain all the attention. For while the Gilberts and Marshalls were being taken, MacArthur was pushing up the coast of New Guinea.

This campaign was one that tactically forced MacArthur to learn the same lessons that the navy was learning in the Central Pacific.[146] While this analysis is not kind to MacArthur (though it is not quite as harsh as some others), his campaign along the New Guinea coast showed important intellectual adaptation.[147] His early landings were often made against well-defended Japanese positions, and his troops suffered large casualties, not only from Japanese firepower, but also from a host of tropical diseases that made the jungles of New Guinea one of the least healthy environments in the world. Compared with the fighting on Guadalcanal, these early campaigns were actually more expensive.[148] One historian has argued that it was MacArthur's eagerness for personal vindication and a return to the Philippines that caused him to overestimate the capacity of his troops and place them in dangerous situations.[149]

As the campaign developed, however, MacArthur did start directing his assaults at what were thought to be less well-defended outposts, bypassing more strongly held areas. This notion, which MacArthur's supporters called "hitting them where they ain't," was hardly novel, but it did show some initiative in the face of rather limited naval support. Ernest King provided MacArthur a regular naval force of only cruisers and destroyers, which would only occasionally be supplemented by carrier task forces. On the other hand, MacArthur's advance was screened by the navy which was fighting its way through the Solomons after the taking of Guadalcanal, neutralizing the string of Japanese airfields that covered the islands. MacArthur was also extremely lucky to be so well served by perhaps the most successful theater air commander that the USAAF produced during the war, Lt General George Kenney. Kenney was able to use his land-based air forces both to attack Japanese shipping and to provide support for MacArthur's forces as they moved up the New Guinea coast.

While MacArthur's campaigns seemed to be growing less expensive, this was partly because Australians often made up a majority of those fighting and dying under his command – and they didn't really count when it came to American public opinion. Still, by the end of 1943 he seemed to be advancing towards his short- and medium-term objectives – the taking of Rabaul and then the Philippines – faster than the Central Pacific drive which was still in the Gilberts and Marshalls. This was when the strategic debate over just how to continue the assault on Japan reignited back in Washington. By this point, the idea of bypassing the great Japanese bases on Rabaul and Truk had become feasible. It was part of the combined, and not surprising, lesson that became apparent in both the Central and Southwest Pacific drives. Success in any amphibious operation, even those such as Tarawa where the landing forces encountered unexpected problems and suffered high casualties, would be ensured by combined air and sea control in the area of the fighting. There were no more repeats of Guadalcanal. The United States was reaching the point of aircraft and naval vessel production where it could concentrate enough force both to provide excellent firepower support to American landing forces and, maybe more importantly, to make it impossible for the Japanese to reinforce or resupply their troops. Therefore, if the Japanese lost air and sea control over an area, even if it was one of their major bases such as Truk and Rabaul, those facilities became functionally unimportant. This is precisely what occurred in late 1943 and early 1944. Heavy carrier strikes on both facilities destroyed large amounts of Japanese air power and made it clear that the Japanese fleet would be unable to contest the seas around them.

On the other hand, after the bypassing of Truk and Rabaul, the notion of hitting the Japanese where they "ain't" was over. Why the decision over where the United States would attack in 1944 was so important was that, whatever was attacked – the Marianas, the Philippines, Formosa or even the Chinese mainland – was now well defended by Japanese forces. There would be no "easy" campaigns in 1944 and 1945.

The string of reverses that the Japanese had suffered since 1943 meant that by the following year, the Japanese army had joined the navy in throwing almost all of its resources into the war against the United States. The army started reinforcing and beefing up its garrisons throughout the Pacific, including many of the islands that would become famous in the coming year and a half. This redeployment, often of forces on the Asian mainland, was fraught with peril. Major General Inichiro Sanada, who served on the army's General Staff and in the War Ministry from 1941 to 1945, said that in 1943 a plan was made to withdraw almost all the artillery pieces in Manchuria to supply army forces fighting in the Pacific. Most of this equipment was eventually assigned to the Philippines, Iwo Jima or Okinawa. However, a majority of it was lost in transit.[150] In the specific case of Iwo Jima, 75 percent of the equipment dispatched never reached the island.

Much of this was down to the successful American submarine campaign. (See Figure 82.) By 1943 the United States Navy had built and, crucially, armed a dangerous long-range submarine force which, based in Pearl Harbor, could patrol the vital shipping routes between Japan and its southern empire. Until air power joined with them,

82 The launching of the submarine USS *Robalo*, May 1943. GATO Class submarines like the *Robalo* played a crucial role in severing Japanese shipments of oil and bauxite from the Dutch East Indies to Japan, thereby destroying much Japanese equipment before it could be produced. The *Robalo* was actually sunk by the Japanese off the Philippines in July 1944.

American submarines were the most effective weapon that the United States had in the trade war, and they did extract a large toll on Japanese merchant shipping.[151] However, it seems difficult to reach a consensus on their value. Morison paid only a small amount of attention to this trade campaign, giving only eleven pages in one of his volumes.[152] On the other hand, others imply that they could almost have won the trade war by themselves and shut off Japanese trade throughout the empire.[153] This is almost certainly an exaggeration. While US submarines continued to do damage, it was in the second half of 1944, when air power joined them, that the catastrophic losses occurred in Japanese shipping.[154] This view also assumes that the Japanese would not have improved their anti-submarine weapons and tactics in 1944. Anti-submarine warfare was not a great concern of the IJN heading into the war; it was considered decidedly defensive in a service that prided itself on offensive action.[155] However, by 1944 there were signs that the Japanese had learned some of the same lessons that the British learned years earlier in the Atlantic, and were running larger convoys with more escorts.[156]

The submarine campaign did show how vulnerable Japan's supply from the south could be, especially considering that its attack on Pearl Harbor was prompted by the need to have access to southern raw materials. In 1942 and the first part of 1943, Japan's strategic economic needs were well met. The oil installations in the Dutch East Indies were captured almost entirely intact in early 1942, giving Japan access to more oil than it would need to fight the war.[157] In 1942 it was able to ship 1,779,000 kiloliters from the Dutch East Indies to Japan, a figure that rose to 3,534,000 kiloliters in 1943.[158]

In the same way that oil could be cut off by either a Southwest Pacific or a Central Pacific thrust, so could crucial Japanese imports of bauxite, which were needed to maintain their impressive increase in aircraft production that occurred between 1942 and the middle of 1944. The original plan of the Japanese government was to import a million tons of bauxite a year from the Dutch East Indies and the Palau Islands, almost entirely to support aircraft construction in the home islands.[159] In 1943 they were well on their way, as 820,430 tons were successfully imported.[160] Had the eventual target figure been reached – and the issue was never one of access to the raw materials, it was one of shipping – Japanese aluminum production would have come close to matching Germany's. Japan had the capacity to produce approximately 400,000 tons of aluminum a year if the bauxite was available for refining, but owing to the shipping crisis, in the end it only produced 225,000 tons.[161]

The success of the American submarine campaign highlighted one of the great strategic failings of the Japanese – their inability to attack American supply-lines with their own submarines. For a military that went to war to secure the flow of raw materials, the Japanese army and navy had a very battlefield-centric conception of power. Though they entered the war with some fine, long-range submarines armed with excellent and reliable torpedoes (unlike the Americans), they failed to use them in one of their most effective roles.[162] They could have attacked American trade much farther from land-based air support than could the Germans, as American ships crossed the thousands of extra miles in the Pacific. However, luckily for the United States, the Japanese stuck rigidly to their pre-war naval doctrine which called for submarines to play a strictly tactical role, either acting as protective weapons for Japanese surface vessels or searching out American warships to attack. Even after the Germans started urging them to use their submarines to attack American trade routes, the Japanese obstinately refused to change. Had they done so, with relatively small cost to themselves, they could have destroyed or at least diverted a large amount of American production.

King couldn't understand why the Japanese, who in his mind had sixty-five to seventy high-quality submarines, never used them to attack US supply. During his late May 1943 summit with Nimitz, he expressed his concern that the Japanese might actually start using their submarines effectively, and in his notes wrestled with just why the Japanese might be behaving the way that they were.

> Jap sub operations – not very effective or at least not maximum use – what does CinCPac [Nimitz] think Japs have in mind – Japs have about 65–70 subs – have lost some – they are in a fix to supply their troops by subs – good for us because it takes the subs out of offensive war – Japs short of torpedoes – also need other things …[163]

King also correctly guessed that the Japanese were having trouble developing an effective underwater radar system for submarines, although he wondered why they hadn't received help from the Germans in this area. Regardless, the two campaigns show how concentrating just on the "battlefield" as the Japanese usually did, meant that one's understanding of how to fight in World War II was seriously limited.

The American submarine campaign also drives one of the final nails into the coffin of those who believe that MacArthur's drive into the Philippines was strategically necessary. As trade was already being heavily restricted between the Dutch East Indies and Japan by American submarines, the one great benefit that the United States could add into the mix in 1944 was interjecting American air power closer to Japan itself. That had been accomplished by the summer of 1944 when the Marianas were taken. This operation, from the American end, showed just how overwhelming a combined air–sea striking force could be in that year. The Marianas invasion was launched at the same time that troops were going ashore in Normandy, but was in many ways a more complex operation. The United Kingdom was close enough to the Normandy beaches so that continual, overwhelming air support could be provided by forces numerically vastly larger than those the Luftwaffe could throw into combat. However, while assaulting the Marianas the United States Navy had to launch every plane it would need from the deck of an aircraft carrier.

This meant that the naval force involved in the Marianas was one of the most expensive collections of equipment ever assembled during the war. The major warships of Spruance's 5th Fleet had a combined building cost, conservatively calculated, of approximately $2.5 billion. (See Table 33.)[164] This $2.5 billion of warships at sea

Table 33 *The costs of major warships during the assault on the Mariana Islands, June 1944*

	Cost per ship (million US $)	Total (million US $)
Aircraft carriers		
6 Essex Class	73[a]	438
1 other (*Enterprise*)	25[b]	25
Light aircraft carriers		
8 Independence Class	35[c]	280
Battleships		
2 Iowa Class	100[d]	200
5 earlier classes	77[e]	385
Cruisers		
3 Baltimore Class	40[f]	120
5 earlier classes	10[g]	50
Light cruisers		
3 San Diego Class	23	69
9 Cleveland Class	31[h]	279
Destroyers		
67 Fletcher Class (mostly)	11[i]	737
Total		2,583

Source: Jane's Fighting Ships of World War II (London, 1989), pp. 259–61, 267–9, 272–4, 276–7, 281.

[a] Essex Class carriers were originally estimated to cost almost $69 million each, but some came in at $76 million; the *Kearsage* (not at the Battle of the Philippine Sea) cost about $90 million. The sum of $73 million was chosen because it is halfway between the expected cost and the recorded cost of some of the vessels.

[b] The *Enterprise* was completed in 1938, by which time it cost $25 million.

[c] It is extremely difficult to find a production cost for the Independence Class. This figure is an estimate based on the cost of the Essex Class.
Each Independence Class vessel was just over half the tonnage of an Essex Class vessel (14,000 tons compared with 27,500 tons), but as they were less complex vessels, I have estimated their cost at less than half that of an Essex.

[d] The costs of each Iowa Class battleship were estimated to "exceed" $100 million, so the figure used here is actually conservative.

[e] These other five battleships came from the South Dakota and Washington Classes, which each cost approximately $77 million.

[f] The Baltimore Class vessels are estimated at $39 million each.

[g] Earlier classes of cruisers were all built in the 1930s so the $10 million figure is actually a conservative one (estimated for 1933) and doesn't include upgrading or modernization.

[h] The Cleveland Class could actually cost up to $42 million, so the figure given here is conservative.

[i] Again this is a conservative estimate; the original Fletcher Class destroyers cost $11 million each, but some of the later variants were more expensive.

would have paid for the United States' entire spending on ground forces in 1942. It is approximately the same, though probably larger, than the cost of building every Sherman tank (of all variants) constructed during the war.[165]

Of course, this figure leaves out a number of other extremely large expenses associated with these naval task forces. The total number of ships in Spruance's fleet, including landing craft, was actually 535, so this figure of $2.5 billion for the 109 largest covered numerically only 20 percent of the ships involved.[166] The carriers were equipped with almost a thousand aircraft of different types and had a huge supply network that had to stretch back for thousands of miles.[167] The fuel needed for the battle would have powered the entire German war machine for a month in 1944. Forty-six different tankers were used to ferry fuel to the fleet, and they ended up delivering 4,496,156 barrels of standard oil, 8,000,000 gallons of aviation fuel, and 275,000 barrels of diesel (overall supply being equal to 715,000 metric tons).[168] In 1944 the highest monthly fuel production for Germany was around 1 million metric tons of all fuel types, 180,000 of which was aviation grade.

What this force allowed the United States to do was take the Marianas with a relatively small number of ground troops – something which was typical of the entire Central Pacific drive.[169] By this time in the war, American support systems were overwhelming. Naval air power not only kept the Japanese from providing any support to their troops, it was now able to supply excellent tactical air cover to American soldiers fighting on the islands.[170] After securing the beaches, the Americans were able to move supplies ashore without any real fear of Japanese air or sea attack. While US casualties could be high in terms of percentage of troops deployed, they were actually quite modest when one considers the importance of the territory being conquered. Taking Saipan, Tinian and Guam cost the Americans 5,250 dead and 20,563 wounded.[171] This figure was approximately equal to the combined casualties suffered during the Battle of Antietam, on one day of the American Civil War.[172] On the other hand, approximately 60,000 Japanese defenders lost their lives. That an attacker in the industrial age, facing a defensive force with modern weapons which was actually being supported by one of the largest air striking forces anywhere in the world at the time, suffered so few casualties as the USA in relative terms is remarkable. For a British observer who was sent to watch the Marianas landing and report back, the most impressive thing was how few troops were needed to take islands in which the Japanese had prepared defenses.

> In invading the Marianas the Americans followed their usual procedure in the Central Pacific. First of all the complete neutralization of enemy air forces within striking distance followed by the application of overwhelming air in that larger land masses were involved. The American ground forces, well trained and of excellent morale, were not in overwhelming numbers when they faced the sum total of the enemy opposition. This opposition was stubborn and casualties were heavy but for the Japanese they looked like being entire.[173]

The other reason why this cost can be judged as relatively small is that, in taking the Marianas, the war was over strategically.[174] For those with knowledge of Japan's strategic situation, the loss of the Marianas meant defeat. It forced the Japanese government to tell something about the real war situation to their people. To the German naval attaché in Tokyo, Admiral Paul Wenneker, it was the decisive moment when the government's charade about Japan's prospects of victory collapsed. "Saipan was really understood to be a matter of life or death. About that time they started telling the people the truth about the war. They began preparing them for whatever must happen. Before that, they had been doing nothing but fooling the people."[175]

Many within the Japanese power structure also realized that the loss of the Marianas was so profound that, had it been politically possible, Japan should have sued for peace at that time.[176] Rear Admiral Soichi Takaga began studying the potential impact of the loss of the Marianas on Japanese power in 1943. What he discovered was that losing the islands, regardless of any further operations to take the Philippines or Singapore, would effectively end Japanese trade with their southern empire.[177] He claimed that he passed this verbal analysis on to his superiors, but was too afraid to commit it to paper. One of those he claimed he spoke to was Admiral Mitsumasa Yonai. Yonai was one of the most sophisticated Japanese sailors and politicians of his era. A former Navy Minister, he served as Prime Minister for seven months in 1940 before he was forced to resign because of his opposition to Japan's commitment to the Axis powers. Yonai did not want to see Japan blunder into a war with the United States, and because of his moderate opinions, he was brought back into government as Deputy

Prime Minister and Navy Minister in July 1944 during the political shake-up that followed the loss of the Marianas. His analysis was that the loss of the islands was so devastating that Japan should have made peace at that time.[178] Fleet Admiral Osami Nagano was also one of the most powerful Japanese admirals during the war. An adviser to the emperor, he served as commander of the 1st and Combined Fleets from 1941 to February 1944. His reaction to the loss of the Marianas was a great shock and a feeling that for Japan "Hell is on us."[179] It was so powerful an emotion that he said it was "neither scientific nor calculated."

Both men were right. Within months of the American landings on the Marianas, the first B-29 raids were launched on the Japanese homeland. (See Figure 83.) The American capture of the islands also immediately stepped up the destruction of Japanese merchant shipping by opening up more areas for those vessels to be attacked from the air. During the last year of the war, the airplane was the most effective weapon of war against Japanese trade.[180] American carrier task forces now could sail near the China coast, pulverizing all shipping they encountered.

The effects of this were dramatic. The taking of the Marianas was the most important event in undermining the dominant narrative to that point – which was that a large foothold in China was necessary to defeat Japan.[181] It made any invasion of the Philippines unnecessary. In fact, bypassing the Philippines would have been the most sophisticated example in the war of "island-hopping." With the fall of the Marianas, the Japanese guessed, because of MacArthur's bombast, that

83 B-29s in action in 1945. The seizure of the Marianas allowed the USAAF to use B-29s efficiently against most of the Japanese homeland. It helped fully sever Japanese trade with the south, leading to a collapse in Japanese production in late 1944 and early 1945.

the Philippines were next. Admiral Kichisaburo Nomura had as good an understanding of American intentions as anyone inside the Japanese government. He had served as ambassador to Washington during the year leading up to Pearl Harbor. When he returned to Japan, he was put on the shelf at first, possibly because he was considered too sympathetic to the United States. However, when Japan reached the crisis stage he was brought back as a member of the Privy Council. After the war, when asked whether the Japanese government believed that the United States might go straight for the Chinese coast after the capture of the Marianas, he had this response:

> Q. Why go to the Philippines, did you still feel we would go to the Philippines?
> A. Yes. There was much talk by one of your Generals that he would recapture the Philippines. He gave much praise to the Filipinos and said that he would come back to the Philippines. Therefore, it was our opinion that you had to go there.[182]

To truly see how MacArthur's campaign was a waste, it is best to start with the landings on Peleiu on September 15. The key island of the Palau chain, Peleiu was south of the Marianas, and could easily have been left behind if the Americans had wanted to head closer to Japan after the capture of Saipan, Tinian and Guam. There was, however, a Japanese airbase on Peleiu which made MacArthur nervous. His demands for Peleiu to be taken led to one of the finest combat divisions in the entire American armed forces, the 1st Marines, to be allocated to this unnecessary task.

The intense combat experienced by the 1st Marines on Peleiu was one of the major battles featured in the recent Steven Spielberg–Tom Hanks television series *The Pacific*. One of the Marines, Private Eugene Sledge, wrote a gripping and depressing recollection of what happened.[183] The Japanese garrison, knowing that it had no ability to drive the Americans from the island once they landed, held out in caves and fortifications for weeks, trying to extract as many casualties as possible before they, inevitably, gave up their own lives. The last serious combat took place on the island more than two months after the landings, a final Japanese banzai charge on the evening of November 24.[184] The 1st Marine Division was so damaged by the fighting on Peleiu that it was unable to enter active operations again until the invasion of Okinawa in April 1945. In the first week of fighting on the island the Marines suffered 3,946 casualties (killed and missing).[185] By the time the 1st Marines had been relieved by the 81st Infantry Division, they had suffered 6,336 casualties, and expended 1,600 rounds of ammunition for every Japanese soldier killed.[186]

Almost immediately after Peleiu, was taken, it was realized that the effort was unnecessary. Admiral Halsey for one claimed it was a waste of time and they should have been bypassed, even if the Americans were going to the Philippines.[187] Avoiding Peleiu would have saved many American lives, for instance on Iwo Jima. That famous island was defended by just a small number of unprepared Japanese troops when the Marianas fell. Saburo Sakai, when he made his emergency deployment to Iwo Jima after the news of the invasion of Saipan broke, was surprised to see how poorly the island was protected. American air attacks on Iwo as part of the Marianas operations left the forces on the island unable to react, and in his view it would have been conquered easily at that time. However, the diversion of effort to the Philippines saved the island for Japan, for now.

> It was obvious to all of us that we could only offer token resistance, that after an hour or two after the landing the Americans would control Iwo. Who then, of all the men on the forsaken hump of volcanic ash, with its bubbling sulphur springs could have foreseen the actual turn of events? Who among us too would have dared to prophesy that the Americans would throw away their priceless opportunity to take the island with minimum casualties on their side? We felt we had but a few days in which to remain alive...We did not know, of course, that the Americans had already turned for the Philippines.[188]

Also, by attacking Peleiu, the Americans only confirmed to the Japanese that their next step would be the Philippines. Lt General Seizo Arisue served on the General Staff during most of the war, with a special role in army–navy liaison. He described after the war how the move to Peleiu caused the Japanese to send even more forces to the Philippines. "After the landing on Saipan, it was felt that the next attack would come in the Philippines, although it might come on Iwo Jima ... The landings on Morotai and Palau confirmed us in the view that the next move was to Mindanao, and planes were brought to the Philippines from Southeast Asia." In the end, not only did the Americans attack first where they were expected, they allowed the

Japanese to strengthen Iwo Jima, leading to the very high casualties there when the Americans finally showed up in February 1945. Arisue added later, with what seems to be a hint of satisfaction, "After the Philippines campaign we expected a landing on Iwo Jima at about the time when it actually took place and were ready for it."[189]

MacArthur's bombast had made bypassing the Philippines even more important. Not only was Iwo Jima turned into a death-trap, the Japanese flooded the Philippines with equipment, making the invasion far bloodier than MacArthur had assured Roosevelt it would be. Eventually the Japanese built up an impressive air force on the islands. The Japanese navy's 6th Base Air Force, which was then made available to reinforce the Philippines, had 737 aircraft, 223 of which were fighters, available for action on October 10, 1944.[190] These were quickly joined by another 688. The navy's 5th and 4th Air Base Air Forces on the Philippines, even after suffering large losses in American attacks preceding the invasion of Leyte, had a combined total of 440 aircraft on October 10. The navy also sent an additional 500, then 600 new aircraft to the Philippines in the two months after MacArthur landed.[191]

The Japanese army aircraft deployment, while more difficult to measure exactly, was probably larger than that of the Navy. Lt General Ija Kawabe, the chief of the army's General Affairs section of the Bureau of Aeronautics until 1943 and then commander of the army's air forces in China, believes that by October 1944, the army had more aircraft assigned to the defense of the Philippines than to any other task.[192] Most of these aircraft were based in Luzon. From May 1944 to January 1945, Colonel M. Matsumae was the senior staff office of the army's 4th Air Army which was based in Manila.[193] To keep a deployed strength of 400 aircraft with an operational strength of 200, the 4th Air Army was sent a remarkable 2,200 aircraft between October 20 and December 31 1944.[194] Other theaters were basically denuded to defend the Philippines against the expected attack. Lt General Ryosuke Mamakishi, who was chief of staff to the army's 5th Air Army in China, claimed that by late summer 1944 he only had five or six operational fighters under his command.[195] This Japanese build-up, which was matched by increases in army troops, meant that when MacArthur arrived off Leyte, he did not embark on a swift march to victory, but ended up in a nasty attritional slugfest which was still ongoing when the Japanese surrendered. Japanese troops exacted a heavy toll on MacArthur's men, often slowing down or even decimating much larger American formations.[196] The American cost in casualties was almost three times that incurred in taking the Marianas.[197]

Finally, not long after the Marines went ashore on Saipan, Arnold's vision of winning the war with strategic air power from China went into action. By this time, it had become almost a personal crusade for the head of the USAAF.[198] His assumption at the start of 1944 was that, since the invasion of the Marianas wouldn't be until October at the earliest, B-29s could be more effectively used from China.[199] He therefore pressed forward with an American deployment to China. The first B-29 raid from the mainland, the bombing of the Yawata steelworks, the most important plant of its type in Japan, took off on June 15.[200]

Had the Marianas not been taken, this would have marked the start of perhaps the most expensive campaign waged anywhere during the war. The Matterhorn Plan that Arnold assembled on August 20, 1943 was unprecedented. He imagined operations starting in October 1944, with preparatory efforts starting one year before.[201] For the operations he envisaged using almost all of the United States' B-29s. By October 1944, he wanted to have ten groups operational, a force that would double to twenty groups by May 1945.[202] At that point in time, a B-29 group was composed of ten aircraft, with four groups combined into one bombardment wing. The logistical tail for such a force was stunning. By October 1944, Arnold planned to have 2,800 B-24s (far more than there were in the entire ETO) running supplies to the B-29s, and by May 1945 that figure would reach 4,000. Furthermore, Arnold expected that there would be 127 separate airfields in operation in China and India, 20 for the B-29 groups actually bombing Japan and the remaining 107 to fly in supplies.[203] Of these 127, only 14 actually existed when Arnold made his plans.

Yet, this airlift capacity would provide only 20,000 tons of supplies a month, just a small part of the enormous amount of support that the B-29s would need. Arnold also planned that the road into China from Burma would be reopened in 1944 and an oil pipeline would be constructed from India to China to supply fuel. This pipeline would provide 18,000 tons of fuel a month, while an additional 65,000 tons of supplies would be coming in by road in 1945.[204] Had this plan been put into place, it would have dwarfed any other campaign of the war in terms of cost. To put it into context, Arnold was planning on supplying his B-29s by early 1945 with 103,000 tons of supplies per month. During the 72-day period of the Stalingrad airlift, the Germans were able to deliver just over 8,000 tons to the surrounded 6th Army, a rate per day of 117 tons.[205] The German estimate was that the 6th Army needed 300 tons per day, or 9,000 tons per month, to be adequately supplied. So Arnold was planning on supplying the equivalent of more than eleven German armies to launch twenty groups of American B-29s against Japan. Statistics like this go a long way to show just why the Marianas campaign was strategically so important. Not only did it bring the B-29s into operation far more effectively than Matterhorn, it was far less costly, as supplies could be brought directly from the United States by ship.

However, Matterhorn was the impetus behind the first serious analysis of targets in Japan. On March 23, 1943, Arnold formally directed the COA to prepare an analysis of the Japanese economy. Their report, which was ready in early November, like the similar document prepared for the CBO against Germany in 1943, was an important intellectual step forward.[206] The industrial targets that the COA thought should receive the highest priority were Japan's merchant ship, steel, aircraft, ball-bearing and electronic equipment production. However, they also broadened out their recommendations in two important areas. They wanted a focused campaign against already-constructed merchant ships that were either at sea or in port. And they specifically endorsed more general attacks to destroy Japanese cities, attacks which they opposed in the case of Germany.

However, right from the beginning, B-29s from China had trouble doing any of this. Though thanks to Arnold's support, a force was ready to go into action in June instead of October, its enormous logistic demands ended up limiting the B-29s' effectiveness.[207] Just reaching to China was such an effort that, even with the United States' highly advanced support network, many of the B-29s needed significant repairs when they arrived. To give an idea of the great logistic trail, the B-29s themselves were first dispatched from Salinas, Kansas, where they were based. The route they took just to get to India, their last stop before deployment to China, was 11,530 miles and involved five major flights:[208]

(1) Salina, Kansas to Gander Lake, Newfoundland	2,580 miles
(2) Gander Lake to Marrakech	2,700 miles
(3) Marrakech to Cairo	2,350 miles
(4) Cairo to Karachi	2,400 miles
(5) Karachi to Calcutta	1,500 miles

Once they reached China, their new bases presented some real problems. The location of the first B-29 airstrips, around the city of Chengtu, meant that even with their great range, they could only hit the southern Japanese island of Kyushu and a relatively small part of the main island Honshu. (See Map 8.) As such the Matterhorn raids ended up revealing more the substantial teething problems associated with the B-29 than doing any real damage to the Japanese economy. Moreover, by locating the bases in China, the USAAF had played into one of the few remaining strengths of the Japanese, namely their large land army. They were able to advance on Chengtu as a result of the chaos in Chiang Kai-Shek's Nationalist Chinese army, putting the expensive new bombers at risk. In the end, only by pulling out the B-29s was it thought that the Chinese could be provided the aid they needed to help them resist Japanese advances. As there had been no road built or pipeline into China, by November 1944 the B-29s, even operating on a much reduced scale compared with Arnold's grand 1943 plan, were consuming the majority of all supplies that could be flown into the theater.[209] At the same time, the B-29s based in the Marianas, which could hit far more Japanese industry, were completely safe and relatively easy to supply. Soon Matterhorn was scaled down, having made little impact on Japanese production.[210]

So the story of the three drives across the Pacific in 1944 ended clearly and decisively. The drive across the Central Pacific to the Marianas had destroyed Japanese hopes and opened up the island homeland to direct assault. It allowed the United States to deploy the full panoply of its air and sea weaponry to sever trade between Japan and its southern empire, and would lead to an economic collapse in 1945. The campaign in the Philippines had seen the Americans launch attacks against well-prepared Japanese forces and gave the United States no strategic advantage that it did not already possess. At the same time, it prevented the United States from striking straight to Iwo Jima or even the Chinese coast much nearer to Japan until the Japanese were able to prepare for those eventualities. This ended up causing historic levels of casualties. Finally, the strategic air campaign from China showed how air power could be too clever and expensive for its own good. In order to work, it needed better bases, better logistics and a much better Chinese ally.

11 THE END OF THE WAR

Chugi Kawamura was the luckiest unlucky man in World War II. He had the most dangerous job in any theater of the war, except for perhaps a kamikaze pilot. He was the captain of a Japanese oil tanker.[1] On December 31, 1944 he set sail from Japan in the *San Diego Maru* bound for Singapore to bring back a load of desperately needed oil for the faltering Japanese war machine. It was a select convoy of ten merchant ships, most of them tankers, with a very large escort of eight anti-submarine vessels. The convoy, because it was made up of such prized vessels, was also able to travel at a high speed of 12 knots, a pace which had shown itself to be of great value in the Battle of the Atlantic.

For safety, the convoy hugged the Chinese coast. Upon reaching Shanghai, it was routed to Formosa. It was on this leg of the journey that the first tanker was sunk, torpedoed by a US submarine. The convoy then took refuge in the port of Takao, but it was spotted by American carrier aircraft and three more of the precious ships were destroyed on January 9. Three hundred carrier aircraft attacked in four waves, diving low so that they were only 200 yards above the huddling ships. At least ten bombs dropped close to the *San Diego Maru*, some only feet away, and another vessel nearby was sunk. Kawamura himself manned the anti-aircraft guns which were now standard equipment on all Japanese tankers, and he believed that he and the other gunners were responsible for shooting down a number of the American attackers. Miraculously, the *San Diego Maru* was not damaged.

The next day what was left of the convoy departed Takao and headed south until they heard that Task Force 38, Bull Halsey's force of seventeen carriers, was in the region, so again they took refuge in harbor, this time at Hong Kong. However, American carrier planes found the convoy once more, and for the next two days subjected it to repeated assault with devastating effect. When the attacks were over, the *San Diego Maru* was the only merchant ship left afloat. The commander of the escort vessels suggested that Kawamura fill the oil containers of the tanker with water, to make it look like the ship was sinking in case any more American aircraft approached, but Kawamura decided to press on as was.

So, with what amounted to a personal protection force of the four surviving escort vessels, his lone tanker again went south. For a while they avoided attack, by hugging the coast from southern China to Indochina and then Malaya. Along the coast of Malaya, one of the remaining escort vessels was hit by a torpedo from an American submarine, and had to leave the convoy. Finally, on January 26, Kawamura and three escorts, all that remained of the original eighteen-ship convoy, entered the Singapore straits. However, they were in no way safe. That night B-29s appeared over Singapore and mined the harbor. The next morning, as the *San Diego Maru* was entering port, it hit one of the new mines and was forced into dry-dock, where it had to stay until emergency repairs once again made it seaworthy.

With the ship now laden with diesel oil, Kawamura had to try to take his desperately needed cargo back to Japan. A new convoy was put together, including two other tankers and three other merchant vessels which were protected by six escort vessels. On March 19, not long after the *San Diego Maru* left Singapore, it struck another mine, which blasted an enormous hole in the engine room. On the verge of sinking and with no other option, the ship was towed to shore and beached to keep it from going under. This was another stroke of luck for Kawamura, for in the next few days every ship of the convoy disappeared somewhere along the coast of Indochina.

Captain Kawamura, however, still had plans to get back to Japan. After spending one night on the ruined *San Diego Maru*, he was rescued by the Japanese navy and taken back to Singapore. Rather miraculously, on April 1 he was put on the last Japanese vessel to safely leave Singapore during the war, the hospital ship *Kazuura*, for which he was named assistant chief officer. Even though the *Kazuura* was constantly shadowed by US aircraft, its status as a hospital ship was respected and it found its way safely to Japan.

That Kawamura survived this ordeal was remarkable. His was the only one of sixteen different tankers and merchant ships in two convoys not to have been sent to the bottom – and even then, it was heavily damaged. It was indicative of the air and sea stranglehold that had been clamped on Japan's economic neck by the end of 1944. American carrier- and land-based air power and submarines meant that the Japanese empire, even while it still had all the resources needed for a powerful war economy, was helpless.

This one story helps to summarize the state of both Japan and Germany during the last few months of the war. By this time, their productive and military systems were being engaged over a super-battlefield of extreme length and breadth. Anglo-American air power could now attack targets everywhere in the Reich, obliterating the notion of there being a clear "front line" for battle. In the Pacific the Japanese were stuck trying to defend an even larger area, and were overwhelmed in the process. Perhaps the most telling sign of the dominance of Anglo-American air and sea power is that a major discussion among historians concerns whether there was in fact too much dominance. Whether the Allies needed to, or were even morally right to, attack cities such as Dresden, Tokyo or Hiroshima, all of which were still being defended with as much force as Germany or Japan could muster. The victory was so total that the Germans and Japanese have often been reduced to victims in the historical argument.

The air and sea strangulation of Japan

On the surface, Japan and Germany seemed very different powers. The latter, mostly landlocked in the center of Europe, had rail access to most of the raw materials that it needed to produce, with the exception of some high-grade iron ore shipments from Sweden. Where Germany had to keep its rail network moving to maintain production, Japan had to do the same with its sea lanes. As discussed earlier, in 1943 the US submarine offensive first started sinking Japanese merchant ships in large numbers. However, in the second half of 1944 and early 1945, when both carrier- and land-based aircraft were added to the mix, Japanese merchant shipping was cleared from most of the seas.

This change is important because often the end of the war in the Pacific is seen as one in which the firebombing of Japanese cities played a major role. While it certainly contributed, it was actually a development that occurred late in the day. The first heavy incendiary raid on Tokyo was launched during the evening of March 9, 1945. By that time, Japanese production was already in a state of terminal decline as their ability to move raw materials and finished goods around their empire had ground to a halt.[2]

Between July 1943 and May 1944, before the Marianas were assaulted, the tonnage of Japanese merchant ships on hand had dropped by more than 1 million tons. (See Figure 84.) However, by concentrating on vital necessities, the effect of this tonnage loss was partly mitigated. This was particularly the case when it came to oil shipments from the southern empire to Japan, which were given the highest priority. In 1943, Japanese access to oil tanker tonnage actually grew, as more and more effort was put into their construction or the conversion of other vessels into tankers. Overall, in 1943 and 1944 Japan built 2,469,008 tons of merchant shipping, 879,217 of which was oil tankers.[3] (See Figure 85.) This was one of the most impressive industrial production stories of the war. It was only made possible by a

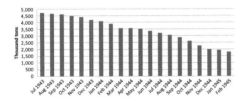

84 Japanese merchant tonnage afloat, by month, in thousands of tons.
Source: USSBS, Pacific Report 53, p. 181.

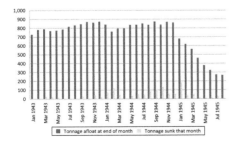

85 Japanese oil tanker tonnage, 1943–5.
Source: USSBS, Pacific Report 53, p. 181.

great increase in Japanese steel production, one that made Japan the equal of the USSR in 1943 and the first six months of 1944. In many ways Japanese production of merchant shipping and tankers was, for them, the equivalent of AFV production for the USSR.

By putting so much effort into tanker construction, the Japanese were able to keep supplying their army and navy with just enough fuel for operations, though training had to be significantly cut back (with the disastrous implications discussed in Chapter 10). It was not until September 1943 that the American submarine attacks on fuel supplies were considered serious.[4] Until the summer of 1944, at least, the combined Japanese army and navy inventory of aviation fuel was still more than 2 million barrels. (See Figure 86.) Although stocks were going down, there was still some kind of contingency. However, the great cost in terms of aviation fuel of fighting for the Marianas, followed by the combined air and sea campaign against the supply of fuel from the south, meant that this contingency disappeared in the second half of 1944. Rear Admiral Yoshiro Yamamoto, who from February 1942 was attached to the Bureau of Military Affairs and had detailed knowledge of Japan's oil importation problem, described the change.

> We had bigger convoys so that we could supply more escorts,
> from the beginning of 1944. But such measures were not effective
> because of the US superiority of the submarine and in air attacks. It
> was very overwhelming. But in the first half of 1944, although we
> had many difficulties in the convoys, in the south the factories
> and oilfields were not damaged so we had no difficulty in the
> supply of oil.[5]

It was the combination of air power with submarines that made the great difference. The Japanese by 1944 actually had come

86 Japanese army and navy inventories of aviation fuel, in thousands of barrels. *Source:* USSBS, Pacific report 53, p. 138.

to understand some of the main lessons of trade warfare that had already been learned in the Atlantic. They realized that convoy speed played an important role in maximizing the chances of survivability, and started using smaller, faster vessels such as the *San Diego Maru*.[6] However, while speed might provide some protection against submarines, it did not against air power. Without the Marianas as a bulwark, American carrier aircraft could venture into the South China Sea which heretofore had been relatively safe for Japanese shipping. The first large carrier air attacks made possible by the seizure of the Marianas occurred in October 1944, when Japanese shipping around Formosa and the Chinese coast was hit hard. These attacks, which involved ten large carriers and eight light carriers as part of what was designated TF 38 (as Halsey was in command), launched thousands of sorties against Japanese shipping in the waters around Okinawa, Formosa and the northern Philippines.[7] They started a massacre of Japanese merchant shipping that would go on into 1945. In just three days around Formosa, approximately 40 Japanese merchant ships were sunk and more than 500 Japanese aircraft were lost.[8] Soon, land-based bombers added their weight to the campaign to stop Japanese trade. Japan's southern empire was effectively severed from the economy of its home islands.

Rear Admiral Shigetada Horuichi, who commanded both Japanese surface and air escort forces along the Chinese coast, described the process. Even though the escorts for Japanese fuel convoys were considerably strengthened, and the speed increased, the triple threat from submarines, carrier-based and land-based aircraft meant that by early 1945 no fuel was getting through.[9] Lt General Tadakazu Wakamatsu, who served on the staff of the Southern General Army in 1944 which was waiting for the fuel and was made vice-minister in the War Department just before the atomic bomb was dropped on Hiroshima, claimed that in January 1945, in one series of attacks (probably those that involved Chugi Kawamura's convoy) American carrier aircraft sank twenty-four tankers.[10] Plenty of oil was available for shipment to Japan; there were simply too few surviving tankers that could make the journey.[11]

The disruption of Japanese fuel shipments in late 1944 and 1945 led to drastic changes in the way that the Japanese fought. It meant that flight training for new Japanese pilots, which had already been cut seriously, now involved almost no time actually flying in aircraft. Mogami Sadao, who was a Japanese army fighter pilot forced into staff work because of ill-health, described the disastrous decision.

> Our pilots were being killed one after the other in great numbers. Aviation fuel reserves were very limited. We calculated total national domestic production of aviation fuel, combined with fuel made from pine roots, was only ten thousand kiloliters a month. If we used our reserve every month exclusively for training, we'd have no reserve at all in just four months. Training of pilots in the homeland virtually ceased.[12]

The lack of fuel also provided a spur to the wide-scale introduction of kamikaze (suicide) pilots who were specifically tasked with crashing their aircraft into American warships. The connection between the shortage of fuel, poor pilot training and the switch to suicide attacks existed in both the army and navy.[13] Some in the IJN started pressing for suicide operations as soon as the Marianas were lost.[14] The first attacks during the fighting in the Philippines persuaded the Japanese of the economic benefits of this grisly method of warfare. One of the "advantages" of the kamikaze was that poorly trained pilots could be expected to do much more damage than they would otherwise. (See Figures 87 and 88.) New pilots who could only be given a few hours of flight training had a chance to do considerably more damage in their one, and only, mission. Lt Colonel Naomichi Jin, who specialized in army intelligence and played a major role in determining tactics for the Tokkotai, the army's version of the kamikaze, wrote a paper just after the Japanese surrender which listed the four main "benefits" of this new form of war.

1. There was no prospect of victory in the air by employment of orthodox methods.
2. Suicide attacks were more effective because the power of impact of the plane was added to that of the bomb, besides which the exploding gasoline caused fires – further achievement of the proper angle effected greater speed and accuracy than that of normal bombs.
3. Suicide attacks provided spiritual inspiration to the ground units and to the Japanese public at large.
4. Suicide attack was the only sure and reliable type of attack at the time such attacks were made as they had to be with personnel whose training had been limited because of shortage of fuel.[15]

87 The loss of the Mariana Islands was an impetus behind Japanese "kamikaze" attacks, as they were a way to cope with dwindling fuel supplies and inferior pilots. Here is a picture of the USS *Bunker Hill* not long after it was hit by a kamikaze off Okinawa in May 1945. The ship was put out of commission until the war ended.

The kamikaze, however, was only one part of an overall change. While suicide attacks were being increased to try to cope with declining fuel supplies, non-suicide operations were drastically reduced. For long periods the Japanese stopped using conventional

88 The British aircraft carrier HMS *Formidable*, on fire after a kamikaze hit in May 1945. Though the damage looks serious in this picture, the *Formidable*'s armored flight deck meant that the ship was back in operations not long after.

air power except for convoy escort duties. When American forces landed on both Iwo Jima and Okinawa, Japanese air power, except for suicide attacks, was almost nowhere to be seen.[16] These reductions were particularly catastrophic for Japan's home air defenses. By 1944 the country was producing a significant number of potentially excellent fighters such as the KI-84, nicknamed "Frank" by the Americans. The KI-84 was fast: some Japanese pilots said it could out-fly the Mustang, and could shoot down a B-29.[17] However, severely restricted fuel shipments meant that a decision was made to strictly limit its flying time. At different moments, the Japanese even stopped trying to intercept the enormously destructive B-29 raids being launched from the Marianas.[18] In April 1945, only a month after the most devastating air raid launched on any city during World War II, the firebombing of Tokyo on the evening of March 9, the Japanese army ordered its aircraft to stop opposing the B-29 raids.[19] As the navy had suffered so many pilot losses during the Marianas and Philippines campaigns, the army played the dominant role in Japanese home air defense in 1945, and this order meant that the B-29s did not have to worry about fighter opposition for long periods. The policy was not changed until July.

The extreme fuel shortage also contributed to the already large non-combat aircraft losses in other ways. With fuel scarce, newly constructed aircraft engines were only test run for a short time. When the war started, the Japanese army mandated that every new engine be given a test-run of 7 hours and 20 minutes.[20] By 1945 each engine was only run for a total of 2 hours and 56 minutes. Combined with the raw material shortages which meant that Japanese airframes and engines were now being made with inferior materials, this meant far fewer flaws were found before a Japanese aircraft was sent on deployment.[21]

The rationale behind this decision shows how the Japanese economy had so completely been cut off. The Japanese idea of resistance had shifted from trying to stop any American advance to making such an advance extremely costly. One plan was to provide the resources for an extraordinary effort to attack American forces when they first appeared to invade the main islands. At this point, the Japanese were to commit everything they had left – suicide planes, boats, soldiers and civilians – to extract the maximum in American losses. The fantastic efforts that they went to to provide fuel for this *Götterdämmerung* was best typified by one of the most unusual fuel stories of World War II: the Japanese pine needle extraction plan. More than 34,000 small stills were set up throughout the Japanese home islands to distil the oil from pine needles into aviation fuel. By heating the needles for 18 hours at high temperature, it was found that a relatively high-quality fuel (91–94 octane) could be extracted. Eventually enough oil for 7,000 aircraft missions was produced this way, though it was labor intensive and expensive.[22] It was planned to use this fuel in a massive suicide operation when the Americans started landing on Kyushu.

If these crippling fuel shortages, which affected almost every level of Japanese resistance, were the most devastating example of American air and sea power in action, there were others. The most important of them was a collapse in Japanese metals production, most importantly steel and aluminum. To make steel, Japan had to have a workable transportation system that could bring iron ore and coal from northern China and Manchuria to its factories. The Japanese plan to keep increasing steel production was based around the idea of shipping raw materials from China to Japan's southern island, Kyushu, where they would then be moved by boat to the heavy rail lines on the main island of Honshu. With the Marianas in Japanese hands, the only effective way to attack this trade was with submarines. However, after the fall of the Marianas, carrier air power could now venture along the north Chinese coast, while strategic air power could start mining harbors and attacking Japanese rail lines. Admiral Teijiro Toyoda, who served as Minister of Foreign Affairs in 1941 and then chairman of the Japan Steel Company from late 1941 until 1945, when he became Minister of Munitions, described the change.

> The route that runs from Tokyo to Kobe is Japan's most important railroad. Here the curvature is slight, grades are gradual and the weight of the rails is heaviest. We have a railroad system covering southern Honshu, running from Osaka to Shimonoseki. This stretch is largely owned by private companies. There are steep grades and wide turns and the rails are extremely light. As we originally planned, all steel and coal from Kyushu would come by ship through the Inland Sea up to Osaka; however with the increased weight of air attacks and submarine attacks on our shipping we found it impossible to carry out this plan. We were forced to transfer a great deal of the tonnage to this inferior system in South Honshu. Even under the best conditions this would have been unsatisfactory; however your air attacks made the situation almost fatal. Track was destroyed, water facilities were ruined and moreover the firebombing of cities along the way, such as Fukuyama, Tokoyama, Shimonoseki and Hiroshima made the situation impossible. Transportation facilities were reduced 75 percent along this line.[23]

Because of this collapse of movement around Japan and the Japanese empire, by the end of 1944 steel production had been cut almost in half. (See Figure 89.)

The transportation disruption to Japanese metal production was so dramatic that a plan was put in place to switch the refining process for iron ore from Japan to Korea, China and Manchuria to be closer to the ore and coke deposits. Japanese steel companies constructed seventeen blast furnaces in these countries with a combined refining capacity of 1 million tons of iron ore a year.[24] This

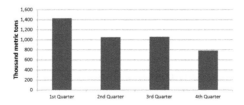

89 Japanese steel production, 1944 by quarters, thousands of metric tons. *Source:* USSBS, Pacific Report 53, p. 30.

was to be done even though these smaller furnaces were considerably less efficient than the larger ones in Japan itself – the need to "economize transportation" meant that the Japanese were willing to sacrifice production quality to protect their shipping resources.[25] In the end it seems that attacking the transportation system had already led to the ultimate collapse of Japanese steel production before the direct attacks on the factories that made the steel themselves.[26] By early 1945, Japanese steel production was down to one-fifth of what it had been just a few months earlier. When asked what was more important in this collapse, attacks on the transport system or on the factories themselves, Admiral Toyoda quickly selected transportation.[27]

This crippling of steel production was similar to the collapse in Japanese aluminum production discussed earlier.[28] From a potential capacity to refine 400,000 tons a year for increased aircraft production, they were reduced to little more than half that amount.[29] Once again it was the loss of the Marianas that heralded the collapse in Japan's economic position. In the first half of 1944, when aluminum was still getting through, Japanese aircraft construction rose. However, a catastrophic shortage of the metal started to develop in the second half of 1944 after the Marianas came under American control.[30] (See Figure 90.) The mobility of the Japanese to ship resources around their empire fatally undermined their war output.

The figure allocated to aircraft represented 99 percent of all the aluminum Japan had available for its home industry. For Kiysohi Goko, who was the head of Mitsubishi Heavy Industries, one of Japan's largest aircraft manufacturers, the loss of the Marianas spelled the end of Japanese aircraft production.[31] At first, because fewer raw materials were reaching Japan, construction of war material, including

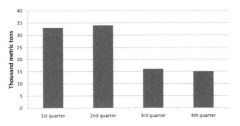

90 Aluminum allocated to Japanese aircraft construction, 1944.
Source: USSBS, Pacific Report 53, p. 25.

aircraft, had to be done with inferior grade ores and finished materials. The result was equipment that could not perform up to standard, which weakened the defense against air attacks. In the end, Japan's metal problem became so severe that it stopped using different ores to make everyday items such as coins, and resorted to porcelains and clays.

Beyond attacking raw materials before production, there were also raids on the production centers themselves. The first of these industrial targets was airframe building factories – similar to American strategic bombing attacks against the German economy in 1943 and early 1944. Admiral Soemu Toyoda, who became commander in chief of the Combined Fleet in May 1944 after Admiral Koga was killed, believed that this bombing was one of the factors, but certainly not the most important, in the halving of naval aircraft construction between 1944 and 1945.[32] In the case of Mitsubishi, the builder of the Zero fighter and many other types of aircraft from bombers to trainers to reconnaissance planes, the bombing of two plants reduced production significantly. Their main airplane engine factory in Nagoya was heavily damaged on December 13 and their main airframe factory was hit on December 19. These raids were crucial in cutting all Mitsubishi aircraft production by one-third.[33] For those in charge at the company, the raids were devastating to their perceptions about the future of the war; for the first time there were feelings of "helplessness and hopelessness."[34]

These Nagoya raids also set off a chain reaction within Japanese munitions production which reduced construction across the board. According to Teijiro Toyoda, they caused a dispersal of industry into smaller plants which was not a success – because of the increased bombing of small towns.

> The destruction of the two Mitsubishi plants in Nagoya was remarkably complete and the loss of those plants was very important to us. You know that the growth of the Japanese aircraft industry had been remarkably rapid and as a result relies heavily on small and home industries. Besides the precision attacks, your destruction of the little plants in the smaller cities hit by bombing reduced our productive power greatly.
>
> Q. What steps did you take to overcome the destruction of the little plants and industries?

A. The small plants were scattered all over the country in an attempt to avoid destruction. However, when you attacked our transportation facilities and bombed the small cities in which so much transportation had been established, our production was dealt a fatal blow.[35]

Another success in the bombing of aircraft factories occurred in China. As the transportation of raw materials around the Japanese empire became increasingly more perilous, a decision was made to try to produce Japan's superb KI-84 Frank in Mukden, so as to negate the need to ship the materials across the China Sea. In the summer of 1944, however, B-29s flying from China were able to hit this plant and other industrial centers in China and Manchuria. The KI-84 factory was bombed just as it was starting production.[36] In reaction, it was decided to again disperse production for greater safety, and the KI-84 was never successfully constructed outside Japan.

In the end, all these efforts led to a steep and quick fall in Japanese aircraft production. By the end of 1944, mostly because of the dramatic decline in aluminum supplies, plane production was down by one-third and aircraft engine production had declined by more than half. (See Figure 91.)

By the end of 1944, the rot had already set in to the Japanese economy as American air and sea power had dealt a killer blow to the country's production in much the same way that the RAF and USAAF had to Germany's. Attacks on Japan's fuel supplies and its transportation system, including extremely high shipping losses and the mining of Japanese ports, meant that even though the Japanese empire had within its different areas all the raw materials needed to continue producing at a high level, it could not bring the different elements together. Japanese war production was only able to continue by drawing on stockpiles

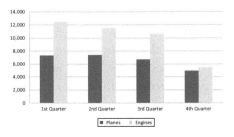

91 Japanese aircraft construction, planes and engines, 1944 by quarters.
Source: USSBS, Pacific Report 53, p. 24.

which were quickly running out. Industrial collapse was imminent – before the USAAF turned to the bombing of Japanese cities.

Strategies for coping with failure in the air–sea war

As World War II moved towards its horrible conclusion, the land fighting undertaken by Germany and Japan became a grotesque parody of modern warfare as both tried to compensate for their failures in the air and sea war. Though they continued to resist with ferocity, their armies engaged their enemies as if they had stepped back in time. Both countries maintained some strong air assets in 1945; however, these were used almost entirely against American and British air and sea power, leaving almost nothing to support their ground forces. Even more damaging, the toll that the air and sea war had taken on their whole chain of production and deployment meant that only a small percentage of what was built ever did any fighting.

Take, for instance, the most advanced operational fighter in the world in 1944 and 1945, the German jet-powered ME-262. This aircraft was one of the highest priorities of the German war economy, and it was planned to devote more workers to its construction than to any other piece of equipment. It was thought of as one weapon that might pose a realistic threat to the heavily escorted British and American bombers, and for this reason resources were poured into its construction. As a result, the number of units built continued to rise, albeit much more slowly than expected, until relatively late in the war.

The ME-262 alone could never have won the war in the skies over Germany – that was beyond all German technology and production at this time. However, what stands out is how few of the ME-262s that were built actually entered combat.[37] Insufficient pilot training, a lack of fuel and maintenance shortfalls meant that approximately half of the 1,400 ME-262s that Germany was able to build were destroyed outside combat.[38] Those that were lucky enough to enter active service continued to suffer because of these faults, with insufficient pilot training a real problem. As a consequence of these shortfalls, and other reasons, ME-262s that did become active suffered from a very high daily loss rate of 13 percent.[39]

A similar story can be told about Nazi Germany's last great hope for the war at sea, the Type XXI U-boat.[40] After the collapse in

1943 of German attempts to sink Allied merchantmen, Doenitz realized that the key to restarting the campaign was to develop a new U-boat which could operate for long periods, and at high speed, under water.[41] In early 1944 he told Hitler how the earlier submarine campaign had failed because the boats had to remain submerged all day for safety, and they lacked the speed to get into position to attack. He then went on to describe how the new boats would change the war at sea.

> With this type [XXI] it would have been possible to shift the location of the boats sufficiently *while submerged*, even on the day preceding the night of the attack. Besides, these boats would not have been immobilized after the attack, but would have continued operations under water.
>
> Our general tendency to change to underwater tactics is thus correct in every respect. We will always be at a disadvantage on the surface due to the enemy's air superiority and his surface location-finding devices, so we must avoid them by submerging
>
> Taking everything into account, a fundamental defense by the enemy against a submarine operating while submerged is hard to imagine. Of course, it could possibly be detected by listening devices, but their range is not anywhere near as great as that of the high-frequency location-finding equipment used in aircraft against submarines operating on the surface. It is still true that a ship is sunk if the submarine is able to close in. The difficulty lies in getting close enough to the target, because this still has to be done on the surface. With the new submarine it is possible *under* the water.
>
> Since the new submarine has a great chance of success, the intended construction program must be accelerated in every way possible.
>
> *The Fuehrer* agrees wholeheartedly.[42]

Hitler continued to have great hopes in the effectiveness of the Type XXI until the moment when he put a bullet into his head. One of the reasons that the German dictator ordered German forces in the Courland pocket to hold their positions (thus depriving Germany of many troops that could have been stationed in front of Berlin) was because the navy needed a safe area along the Baltic coast in which it could test the Type XXI.[43] In his last clear instruction for armaments priorities, given in January 1945, the Type XXIs were given the highest rating.

In the end, one of the least appreciated contributions of the strategic air campaign was the severe delays that it imposed on the production of these new U-boats. Even with Hitler's consistent and strong backing, by the time the war ended, Type XXI construction had been seriously retarded – and this was a consequence of how Anglo-American air power had delayed its entire production process. The Type XXI was constructed in individual sections, which were only to be transported by rail to the more vulnerable assembly yards on the coast for final construction. The original construction plans developed in the summer of 1943 had to be cut by more than 50 percent by November 1944 because of the cumulative effect of Anglo-American air power.[44] At different times the production of steel plates and electric engines was hit hard. From the fall of 1944, the attacks on Germany's transportation system, as well as direct attacks on the Type XXI's main assembly yards, also delayed production or destroyed outright many boats in the process of being constructed.[45] Because of this, only one Type XXI was able to start operations before Germany surrendered – when the original plan had been to have thirty to forty boats attacking Allied shipping at that time.[46]

The destruction of Japanese air power before it could be used on the battlefield might be an even better example of how battles were won long before they occurred, or how air and sea power determined so much more than did land battles. The cumulative effect of American sea and air power meant that by 1945, Japan suffered enormous aircraft losses long before they ever engaged American aircraft. The Japanese navy lost 3,293 aircraft in combat between December 1944 (after the air fighting over the Philippines began to wind down) and August 1945, and 5,981 aircraft in various non-combat operations. Even without counting the additional aircraft that were lost in deployment before they became operational, it is remarkable how small a percentage of the Japanese aircraft that were built were lost fighting the enemy. By 1945 the battlefield was receiving less than half of the aircraft Germany and Japan were able to build, and if one factors in the destruction of units before they were built, the figure is considerably smaller.

In consequence, the land battles that Germany and Japan fought near the end resembled engagements between World War I armies and those of World War II. The German offensive in the

Ardennes begun in December 1944, known as the Battle of the Bulge, was in many ways the most dramatic attempt by the Germans to turn back the technological clock to a time before air power existed. They were praying for the weather gods to protect the German army. After his capture, Keitel admitted rather pathetically that the Germans were hoping that clouds would decide the battle. "The time of the Ardennes offensive was so chosen that we could expect a series of days during which the Anglo-American air force was unable to play a decisive part. We were clear in our own minds that an offensive was entirely impossible in those days if the enemy fighter-bombers and the rest of the air force were permitted to bear full pressure."[47]

For the offensive, the Germans assembled a large striking force of AFV, which Hitler envisaged would split the American and British armies, cause the capture of Montgomery's 21st Army Group and compel the United States to make peace. According to Fritz Bayerlein, the commander of Panzer Lehr,

> He [Hitler] said that he had scraped together everything available for this effort; if it did not succeed, the war was lost. Manteuffel [commander of the 5th Panzer Army] was to take Antwerp, Dietrich [commander of the 6th SS Panzer Army] Liège. Montgomery's 21st Army Group was to be nearly bagged. The political consequences would be that Canada would withdraw from the war, the US would not stand for the loss of a whole Army Group and would be as discouraged and then be a negligible factor thereafter. They need have no worry about Allied fighters; 3000 German fighters would clear the air for the Wehrmacht.[48]

It was a fantastical view of the war, and those who were in charge of the Ardennes Offensive knew its goals were unachievable.[49] The greatest flaw in the plan, and there were many, was that it needed weeks, maybe months, of bad weather to have any hope of success. Hitler's boast about making a difference with 3,000 Luftwaffe aircraft, which was even part of the Nazi propaganda effort to persuade their own soldiers that the offensive stood a chance of success, was also known to be a chimera.[50] As von Rundstedt was well aware, Anglo-American air power would be decisive as soon as the clouds parted.[51] The Luftwaffe was rarely seen over the battlefield during the opening stages of the battle, and when it did try to interfere, its planes were often engaged by American or British aircraft well behind the front line.[52]

For the first week of the offensive, the weather gods did favor the Germans, with heavy rain and such deep overhead cloud that air power could not be used effectively. Those planes that could try to attack the Germans had to rely on air-to-ground radar which made their sorties ineffective. On December 23, however, the weather changed completely, and cold clear air opened the skies and allowed air power to be used.[53] On the 24th, the weather was even better and Allied air power was deployed in even greater depth, both to stop the German advance and also to attack the movement of their supplies behind the lines.[54] On that day, every 8th Air Force plane that could fly, 2,046 bombers, dropped 5,052 tons of bombs on German targets they could see.[55] Air power was used in a layered way to attack German troops at the front, those in the rear and even to halt German aircraft trying to resupply their units by air.[56] At the same time, air power could now deliver supplies to American units behind the German front lines, most famously in the town of Bastogne. (See Figure 92.) The German advance stopped in its tracks that day and went into irretrievable reverse. For all of Hitler's talk of using the Luftwaffe over the battlefield, they seem to have made no impression except for an attack on Anglo-American air bases on New Year's Day. At that one moment, incredulous German ground troops saw hundreds

92 Bastogne, December 26, 1944. Once the skies cleared during the Battle of the Bulge, supplies could be delivered to American troops, as in this picture, and air power could be used to attack German ground troops. At that point, the German offensive stopped in its tracks and historical interest in the campaign wanes.

of Luftwaffe aircraft overhead.[57] However, even though the Germans did catch many Allied air units by surprise, their own losses were even higher than those they inflicted, and for the rest of the war the Luftwaffe was finished as a tactical force.

In addition to relying on storms and clouds to push back the technological clock, the other way that the Germans were fighting a primitive campaign was in their use of and access to fuel. Another terrible movie about World War II is the Henry Fonda blockbuster *The Battle of the Bulge*.[58] In this film, which is riddled with errors, the German units go into battle without adequate fuel supplies, planning to capture what they need from the Allies, like some grand guerrilla army with tanks. This was not the case – entirely. By concentrating almost all of the Reich's remaining fuel supplies, there was enough fuel to support the offensive, at least to begin with.[59] However, the air campaign meant that it became impossible to move the fuel forward in the needed quantities. The most famous example of this was Joachim Peiper's *Kampfgruppe* which was to exploit the offensive for the 1st SS Panzer Division. Peiper's halting and relatively minor advance, which seems to have been the inspiration for the offensive of Robert Shaw's astonishingly bleached-blond Colonel Hessler in the movie, figures prominently in most narratives of the battle. It is hard to figure out why. After a few days of running around in circles, the Germans were unable to get any fuel to Peiper, who thereupon had to abandon almost all of his vehicles less than 20 miles from where the German offensive was launched – and walk back to the German lines. Peiper's fate encapsulates what is wrong about a battle-centric view of the war. Almost all the books on the Battle of the Bulge concentrate overwhelmingly on the period from December 16 to 24, when the weather was overcast and air power could not be used effectively over the battlefield.[60] It is as though once the reality of what the war had become reasserted itself, it becomes less interesting.

If the Battle of the Bulge is important, it is in showing how unimportant superiority in ground equipment was at this time in the war. When it came to equipping their ground forces, the Germans were still widely acknowledged to be superior to the Americans in many areas. Allan Millett has claimed that apart from artillery, the Germans were superior to the United States in most areas of land-war equipment.[61] The German hand-held anti-tank weapons, reloadable bazooka and single-shot panzerfaust, were considerably more destructive than their American counterparts. Most famously, German armor had shown itself to be much more effective in individual units, when running properly and supplied. The bulk of American armor throughout the fighting in Europe in 1944 and 1945 was made up of different variations of the famous M-4 Sherman tank or different open-topped, lightly armored tank destroyers such as the M-10 Wolverine. While the Sherman had many admirable qualities, being rugged and maneuverable, it was also relatively under-gunned when compared with most German AFV.[62] Except for some later models, such as the M-4A3E8 Sherman (known as the Easy Eight and equipped with a better suspension and a more powerful 76 mm gun), which only went into production in 1944 and were therefore available only in relatively small numbers until late in the war, American AFV were considerably less powerful than German.[63] One of the other persistent problems with American armor, including the Sherman, was that their guns were regularly outranged by German AFV, not just the Panther and Tiger, but also the more numerous Panzer IV.[64]

As much of British and Canadian armor was earlier-version Shermans, they were hardly in a better position. Interestingly, the United States had a tank under design years earlier, the M-26 Pershing, which could have at least equalled the Panthers and Tigers.[65] However, developing such a superior land vehicle was not considered that important by many in the US Army, and thus the easier decision to keep producing Shermans in different variations was made. Eisenhower, who had actually tried to play down American armor deficiencies earlier in the war, eventually admitted to Marshall that the Shermans were no match for German AFVs and that the American army needed Pershings.[66]

If American land equipment was often inferior to that of the Germans, it has also been argued, more controversially, that the American army was also less well led and administered than the German.[67] However, the fact that the basic American inferiority in AFVs and training did not change the outcome on the battlefield shows how air power, when properly used, was the key variable. Tactical air power not only allowed for direct attacks on German armor (attacks to which the Germans could mostly not respond), its presence also severely limited German mobility, so that inferior American armor or excellent American artillery could triumph. According to General Maurice Rose, whom Eisenhower considered one of his "finest" division commanders, this was what made the difference in the land war. Eisenhower was so impressed by Rose's analysis that he sent it on to Marshall with great praise.

> It is my personal conviction that the present M4 and M4A3 tank is inferior to the German Mark V. I recognize the problem of shipping our equipment over long distances, but am basing my remarks purely from the point of view of comparing our medium tank with the German tank that we are constantly meeting on the battlefield. The fact that the M4 and M4A3 were inferior to the Mark V is borne out by the excessive number of losses we took while fighting in Belgium in December and January. The question naturally arises as to how I can account for the fact that in all of our operations against German armor we have been successful if the statements I have heretofore made are to be accepted. The answer is that we compensate for our inferior equipment by the efficient use of artillery, air support, and maneuver ...[68]

By the time of the Battle of the Bulge, spending on vehicles of all types for the American army made up a relatively insignificant part of overall American munitions production. For 1944 as a whole, only 8 percent of the USA's military production budget was spent on producing land vehicles of all types for the army, navy and air force (from AFV to trucks to jeeps).[69] At the same time, 30 percent of American munitions construction was made up of just basic aircraft (not including all the ammunition, guns, communications and electronic equipment that went into the aircraft) and 22 percent was spent on ships. Thus, by the end of 1944, the building of land weaponry was an afterthought in American production priorities.

If the Germans were still trying to pretend that they could fight a modern battle at the end of 1944, the Japanese had realized that this was no longer possible. Their tactics changed to trying to lose land battles – painfully.[70] The Japanese knew that they could not hold anything beyond the main islands if the Americans attacked in force, so their plans changed to sacrifice the defending troops outside Japan, and use this sacrifice to try to destroy American warships and aircraft while causing politically damaging levels of American casualties. The official army and navy defense plans as outlined on January 20, 1945, which had imperial approval, read: "While the enemy penetrates the defense zone, a campaign of attrition will be initiated to reduce his preponderance in ships, aircraft and men, then obstruct the establishment of advance bases, to undermine enemy morale, and thereby to seriously delay the final assault on Japan ..."[71] The two famous island assaults that took place in 1945, the invasions of Iwo Jima (landings commenced on February 17, 1945) and Okinawa (landings commenced on April 1, 1945), were just such attritional campaigns. They were two of the bloodiest battles that the United States would fight during the war, especially considering the relatively small areas to be captured. The assault on Iwo Jima cost the United States 6,821 killed and 19,217 wounded.[72] This tiny island, which was only 4.5 miles long and 2.5 miles wide at its widest point, has become famous for this bloodshed.[73] The cost was so high that the value of taking the island has been questioned.[74] (See Figure 93.)

The major reason it was so bloody was that the Japanese were under no illusions that they could throw the American landing force off the beaches or hold the island. The Japanese commander, Lt General Tadamichi Kuribayashi, did not expose his troops by having them fight against the landing, but instead placed them in well-concealed and defended positions from which they exacted this terrible toll – one of the few times in World War II when American casualties killed and wounded were higher than those of the force they were fighting. Although only 200 of the 22,000 Japanese troops on Iwo Jima when the Americans landed survived the fighting and were made prisoners,

93 Destroyed US equipment on Iwo Jima in February/March 1945. Having lost the air–sea war, all the Japanese garrison on Iwo Jima could do was sacrifice itself while causing high American losses – something which they achieved.

the fact that they actually killed and wounded more Americans shows how significantly their strategy had changed.

What the Japanese troops on Iwo lacked was any meaningful air and naval support. Before the battle, few supplies actually made it to the island. One estimate is that only 25 percent of the supplies for Kuribayashi's forces made it through American air and sea power.[75] Once the American landings commenced, even this pitiful supply was stopped. The aircraft that were sent were overwhelmingly kamikaze, not attacking to try to save the garrison or the island, but to sacrifice themselves like the soldiers on Iwo, to cause damage which might politically improve Japan's situation when it came to peace negotiations. The first kamikaze sweeps, on February 21, which involved waves of eighteen to twenty Japanese aircraft, were directed at American naval air power, the great goal being to hit as many carriers as possible.[76]

If the Japanese had believed they could, they certainly would have tried to hold Iwo Jima. An airbase almost exactly halfway between the B-29s in the Marianas and Tokyo, Iwo Jima was perfectly placed to try to interfere with American raids. It had been one of the largest Japanese airbases during the Marianas fighting, regularly accommodating more than two hundred aircraft.[77] However, this vital spot, which would prove extremely valuable in saving many damaged B-29s by providing them respite while returning from attacking Japan, was written off.

The fighting on Okinawa resembled that on Iwo Jima – on a larger scale. The largest of the Ryukyu Islands, fertile and with a warm climate, Okinawa supported a civilian population of 463,000 in 1940.[78] Lying only a few hundred miles from Japan itself, Okinawa was an ideal staging point for the land invasion that was being seriously debated in the spring of 1945. The approximately 100,000 Japanese troops on Okinawa made no attempt to defend the beaches; in fact, the Americans could find no defenders at all for the first day.[79] However, when they moved inland, the Americans discovered that the entire south of the island had been turned into a brutal series of defensive positions, each one of which had to be conquered at great cost. American casualties in the end were a combined 49,151, of which 12,520 were killed or missing.[80] (See Figure 94.)

The Japanese used this sacrifice to launch the largest waves of kamikaze assaults seen so far in the war. They even used the greatest

94 A USN carrier-borne Corsair launching attacks on Japanese ground forces resisting in Okinawa. This was the costliest battle of the Pacific war.

battleship ever built, the *Yamato*, weighing 64,000 tons and carrying 18-inch guns, as a kamikaze. The *Yamato* was dispatched to ground itself off Okinawa, from where it was supposed to serve as an artillery platform until its inevitable destruction. As it was, it was destroyed not long after leaving port, and never fired a shot at an American warship. However, Japan's kamikaze efforts combined did exact a heavy toll on the USN: ninety American vessels were either sunk or damaged so severely that they had to be removed from the campaign.[81] Japanese losses were also extreme. One estimate is that they lost approximately 7,800 aircraft fighting the American navy around Okinawa, and had twenty more ships (of an increasingly denuded Japanese navy) sunk or damaged.[82]

But, again, the Japanese made no attempt to save the island of Okinawa. The head of their army's kamikaze efforts (Tokkotai), Lt General Torashiro Kawabe, admitted as much about the Okinawa campaign after the war: "our strategy was aimed solely at the destruction of your fleet and transport fleet when it landed here in Japan, that was our view as to our strategy to destroy your fleet at landing."[83]

Interestingly, Kawabe then went on to comment on the great weakness in Japanese aircraft construction at the time (which was just as LeMay's fire raids were starting; see below). The issue of poor metal quality, including the decline in aluminum supplies, meant that Japanese factories were now producing poor-quality machines. When asked whether it was worth it for the Japanese to sacrifice a pilot with every plane, which in American calculations would have led to a disastrous decline in air power, Kawabe said it wasn't that great a problem because at that time, Japan was only able to make cheap, second-rate aircraft: "It was not very difficult to manufacture second-rate planes – that is make-shift planes – and it was not difficult to train pilots for such a duty."[84]

In many ways the manner in which the battles on Iwo Jima and Okinawa were fought shows how the incendiary raids were considerably less important in Japanese defeat than the layered campaigns against movement. The Japanese knew what they wanted to do: they were preparing for a giant battle when the Americans landed on Kyushu. They had already put aside the equipment needed for a mass suicide operation to cause as many American casualties as possible. The equipment that was produced after March 1945 was an extra bonus to this plan, but it did not change the fundamentals of Japanese strategy.

Strategic air power, ethical choices, atom bombs and victory

In June 1945, Hap Arnold paid a visit to the Marianas and marveled at the enormous effort that was going into the destruction of Japan from the air. When it came to the killing of the Japanese, Arnold expressed no remorse.

> Apparently the atrocities by the Japs have never been told in the U.S. – babies thrown up in the air and caught on bayonets – autopsies on living people – burning prisoners to death by sprinkling them with gasoline and throwing in a hand grenade to start a fire. If any tried to escape they were killed by machine guns as they came through the door. More and more of the stories which can apparently be substantiated.
> There is no feeling of sparing any Japs here – men, women or children – gas, fire, anything to exterminate the entire race exemplifies the feeling.[85]

Arnold was giving voice to the feelings of many, maybe most, of those serving in the US armed forces in the Pacific. American flyers believed that they were operating in a theater where any notion of decency had been suspended – and they had a point. The Japanese had stated publicly that they were executing many of the B-29 crewmen who were shot down over Japan. For the airmen, it was a grisly sign of how successful they believed their campaign was against Japan, and they seemed to show no remorse for the destruction of Japanese cities.

Nor was this notion limited to the USAAF. The idea was widespread that the Japanese, as a people, could or should be killed, not just to win the war, but as a form of retribution.[86] John Dower has written an important book arguing that the racial component was decisive in determining American behavior in the war against Japan.[87] More recently, there has been a challenge to race as an all-encompassing notion in this way.[88] If American war-making against Japan was not entirely driven by race, there certainly seemed to have been less squeamishness about killing Japanese civilians. The war in the Pacific saw Americans behaving with, and treated with, far greater brutality than in the war in Europe. Certainly, American propaganda, when directed against the Japanese, often talked about punishing or crushing the Japanese people. (See Figure 95.)

Franklin Roosevelt was keen that the bombing of Japanese cities should take place as soon as possible – and he seemed completely

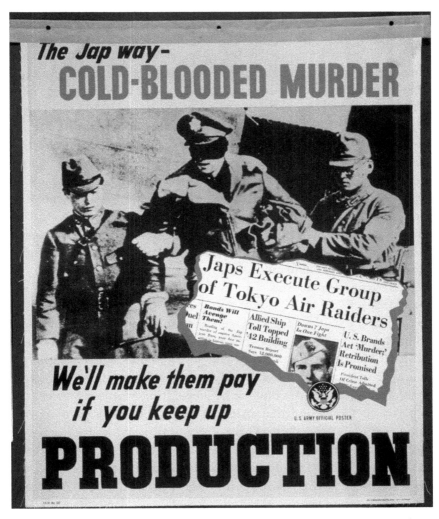

95 Many Americans believed that the Japanese were a more brutal enemy who deserved to be bombed mercilessly from the air. This kind of propaganda poster promised little mercy.

uninterested in making sure that civilians inside those cities were avoided. For instance, he followed the development of Matterhorn and, in March 1944, in an unusual move for the time, wrote to Chennault explaining that he wanted all the B-29s that were sent to China to be kept under command in Washington, DC, as opposed to in theater.[89] One of the things that the President was keen to see happen was a B-29 raid on Tokyo as soon as possible, in particular in time for the second anniversary of the 1942 Doolittle Raid.

That did not mean that the United States developed its strategic bombing campaign with the overriding goal of killing Japanese civilians; it is just that it was easier to adapt to that when the time came. Throughout late 1944 and early 1945, there was a sustained build-up of B-29s in the Marianas as it quickly became apparent that Saipan, Tinian and Guam were far superior to China as a location from which to launch a strategic bombing campaign. The bases in China were too vulnerable to Japanese land forces, far too expensive to supply, and by late 1944 were being phased out.[90] The wholesale reorientation of the strategic air campaign away from China to the Marianas was recognized when the USAAF 20th Air Force was established on Guam. Previously, there had been two separate commands, the 20th Bomber Command in China and the 21st in the Marianas, but as the Chinese operations were halted, the former was folded into the latter.

By 1945, the Marianas were among the most crowded places on earth. Arnold, during his visit, was told that there were at that time 170,000 American military personnel and 30,000 vehicles of different kinds just on Guam.[91] It also quickly became apparent how much more economical it was to run the bombing operation from the Marianas as opposed to China. By the spring of 1945, 25,000–30,000 tons of supplies were unloaded into Guam every day, which was considerably more than had been able to reach the B-29s in China during any month of the war.[92] When LeMay arrived in the Marianas, he was pleasantly surprised to see how much easier it was to receive supplies there than in China.[93] As they became the dominant place of deployment for the incredibly expensive bombers, these small islands may also be said to have had the most valuable store of equipment anywhere on earth. They were covered in massive supply dumps. (See Figure 96.)

Between November 1944 and August 1945, the number of B-29s on hand in the Marianas increased from 119 to 986.[94] And they dropped huge tonnages. By June 1945 flights of more than five hundred B-29s were hitting targets in Japan daily. One raid on Osaka involved 520 B-29s which dropped approximately 3,000 tons of bombs. This was a weight of attack two hundred times larger than the Doolittle Raid, or more than twice as large as the thousand-bomber raid on Cologne in that same year.[95]

96 A huge supply dump in Saipan in March 1945. The Marianas were some of the most crowded islands in the world during the bombing of Japan. This long line of crates held just belly tanks to extend the range of escorting fighters, in particular P-51 Mustangs.

The history of this bombing campaign often revolves around a shift in tactics that started in March 1945. Before then, the B-29s had been used mostly against specific industries, particularly Japanese aircraft production, as well as transport attacks on ports and harbors. This high-level, daytime bombing was close in philosophy to that which the USAAF had used, most of the time, against Germany in 1943 and 1944. As part of the general campaign to throttle Japanese trade and transportation, these raids were a useful element in a war-winning policy as Japanese production had already gone into terminal decline before March 1945. However, such a role did not meet the more glamorous expectations set out for the largest air force in the world in control of the most expensive airplanes ever built. For instance, the USAAF was reluctant to enter into one of the most effective campaigns open to it, using the B-29s to mine Japanese ports.[96] Most in the air force were very grudging about the effort, and had to be persuaded to take part.[97] LeMay himself only took mining up in late March 1945 and seemed uninterested in it in his memoirs.[98] However, this mining of Japanese waters, which before March 1945 was only sporadic, immediately started paying dividends. Had the mining of Japanese harbors started in earnest in late 1944 instead of late March 1945, Japanese production would have collapsed even sooner than it did. The great range of the B-29s meant that they could mine harbors throughout much of Japan and down the Chinese coast to Malaya and Singapore. Mining not only destroyed ships, it forced diversions of Japanese cargo from major ports to minor ones, with their inadequate facilities and poor rail communications.

Even though heavy mining around Japan did not start until March, in 1945 as a whole it was responsible for sinking more tonnage than US submarines.[99]

But mining harbors didn't provide good copy and this was not enough for the USAAF, which wanted as much individual credit as possible for the victory over Japan. There was growing USAAF dissatisfaction as the early raids by the B-29s were not as awesomely destructive as hoped. These earlier "failures" occurred for a number of reasons. The original raids were much smaller than those from March onwards, often involving fewer than a hundred bombers. Also, the Japanese were still flying interception missions at this time.[100] Finally, the weather in the winter of 1944/5 over Japan was particularly cloudy, so that many times the bombers were unable to see their specific targets and drop their bombs. Even though the overall impact of strategic bombing was having a significant impact on Japanese production, it seemed from photographic evidence that they were not blowing things up spectacularly enough.[101]

These factors combined to lead Arnold to change the commander of the 21st Bomber Command, removing General Haywood Hansell, who he clearly believed lacked the necessary drive.[102] This was a personal decision for Arnold. He had kept for himself the overall command of the 20th Air Force, instead of giving it to someone in theater.[103] He was thus on the hook for their perceived achievements or failures. In Hansell's place he selected General Curtis LeMay, who had made a great name for himself as a leader in the bombing of Germany in 1943. He had led one of the formations against Regensburg that August, and had been decorated for his fearlessness in the face of enemy fire.[104] In August 1944 he was sent to take over B-29 operations in India and China as commander of the 20th Bomber Command, where he seemed to provide some spark to what was tuning into a secondary theater. In January 1945 Arnold appointed him to take over all B-29 operations from the Marianas, and the newly appointed commander of the 21st Bomber Command moved to Guam. In many ways LeMay resembled an American version of Arthur Harris. He was absolutely convinced that he could cripple the enemy with the use of air power, and drove his men hard. Like Harris, he also looked after his forces, keeping them at a high state of readiness and in excellent mechanical condition. This allowed him to mount ever larger raids as more and more B-29s flooded in. At first he continued to bomb specified industrial targets by day, but like his predecessor, he seemed to achieve only modest results. Feeling the pressure, he opted, if only to please Arnold, to change course.[105]

LeMay drastically cut the number of high-level precision attacks on Japanese factories, and replaced them with incredibly destructive low-level incendiary raids on Japanese cities.[106] Not only had the weather over Japan been extremely disruptive in early 1945, LeMay noticed that the Japanese had deployed few, if any, low-altitude flak batteries.[107] He sent the B-29s at night, stripped of weight and much of their advanced machinery, and loaded with incendiary bombs to set fire to Japan's heavily wood-based cities and cause firestorms considerably larger than those that broke out in Hamburg in 1943. The first large-scale raid of this type occurred on the evening of March 9, when 334 B-29s left to bomb a densely populated and industrially important part of Tokyo.[108] The change in attacks caught the Japanese by surprise. The B-29s, appearing so low in the sky and at night (a clear one at that), were able to drop their loads on target with minimum interference. The result was a hideous firestorm which obliterated everything that was sucked into its wide path.[109] At least 80,000 civilians, and potentially more than 100,000, died.

The dramatic impact of the great fire allowed the raid to be considered a triumph and the firebombing of Japanese cities now became the highest priority of LeMay's command. Ever larger raids were launched, some heading back to destroy other parts of Tokyo and some to other large Japanese cities. The destruction meted out in the next three months surpassed anything that Germany had experienced from aerial bombardment in such a short period of time. Before these raids, Japanese civilians, while suffering deprivation from the war, had not been killed in large numbers. In Tokyo, for instance, approximately 1,300 had been killed before March 9th. By the time Japan surrendered in August, half a million of its civilians were dead from aerial attack

The destruction was so great that by June, when bombers started returning to cities attacked earlier, they often discovered that there was nothing left to burn.[110] The question remains whether it was necessary to do this to defeat Japan – and this brings up a moral or ethical problem that this study has so far avoided: namely, the use of strategic air power in operations that were bound to kill civilians in large numbers. While this is not the place for a detailed discussion of the question, a few comments should be made, as the use of air power in the war remains a widely discussed issue up until today. As Richard Overy says in his recent history of the bombing war, each time there was a major escalation in the use of strategic air power during the war, there was a realization that a new ethical boundary was being crossed.[111]

During the war, in both the United States and United Kingdom there was regular discussion about whether the bombing of (mostly German) cities in area attacks was something that western democracies should undertake. The targeting of civilians, in particular industrial workers, was considered an important way to win the war by many, such as Portal, who were not devoted to the concept of area bombing. He admitted as much in a letter to Eaker in which he described the area bombing of German towns connected to the aircraft industry: "The purpose of night area attacks on the towns listed ... is the destruction of workers' homes, the killing of skilled workers and the general dislocation of public services and administrative services ..."[112]

Once the British had turned to the wholescale destruction of German cities, a number of prominent voices within the country started questioning the ethicality of such a policy, even calling for the suspension of area bombing.[113] In November 1943, Lord Salisbury wrote to the head of the Air Ministry, Archibald Sinclair, after hearing Harris say that Bomber Command's attacks on Berlin would go on until the "heart of Nazi Germany ceases to beat."[114] Salisbury claimed the statement undermined Britain's claim for moral superiority in the war and ran counter to the government's stated position that the UK was only bombing military and industrial targets. Sinclair, in response, said that German civilians would have to die to win the war. "I have never pretended in the House of Commons or elsewhere that it is possible to pursue this aim without inflicting terrible casualties on the civilian population of Germany."[115] (See Figure 97.)

However, as the destruction mounted near the end of the war and it was clear that Germany was defeated, a less assertive tone was taken about the ethics of city bombing. The most prominent catalyst for this change was the bombing of Dresden in February 1945.[116] This attack, in which the USAAF joined the RAF to destroy one of the most beautiful baroque cities in Europe, killed approximately 25,000 civilians and created immediate disquiet in some quarters.[117] Winston Churchill actually described the attacks as "terror" raids and questioned whether they were necessary.[118]

97 The civilian toll from strategic bombing: rows of corpses after an air raid in Berlin, 1944.

Since the war ended, this debate has blossomed. Some have even gone to the point of calling strategic bombing in the war "genocide" and comparing it to the holocaust.[119] There have been two different debates, though they are interrelated. The first is whether the attacks on civilian-heavy targets were ethically justified and the second is whether they were effective in ending the war more quickly than would have been the case otherwise.[120] Ronald Schaffer is perhaps the most important critic of American policy. In his history of American air power and other writings, he has described how at different times the leaders of the USAAF, including Arnold, Spaatz and Eaker, all accepted the reality of bombing civilians as legitimate targets.[121] Schaffer's view elicited a strong response from other air power historians.[122] One of the fundamental differences between these visions is the degree to which American bombing tactics were materially different from those of the British.[123] In a way it comes down to whether, in the European war, American participation in the raids on Dresden should be seen as an exception to American air strategy, or as the culmination of a change that was made possible by the wide-scale acceptance by those in charge of American air power that civilians could be targeted.[124] On the other hand, there are those who argue that war is war, and that civilians were going to die.[125] In this case, the German and Japanese civilian deaths were perhaps regrettable, but certainly not too high a price to pay for victory against two such horrific states.

The two Axis powers have rather different views of their roles as targets of the Anglo-American strategic bombing. In Germany, there has been an interesting, at times heated, but also sophisticated discussion of the ethics of strategic bombing.[126] The tension that exists concerns whether the bombing, as horrible as it was, remained a needed method of war to rid the world of Nazi Germany. Joerg Friedrich seems to accept at face value an ethical difference between British city bombing and American "precision" strikes.[127] In Japan, on the other hand, the stress is often on the role of the Japanese people as victims, with little linkage between the experience of bombing and the totality of Japanese participation in the war. This is particularly the case with regard to the bombings of Tokyo, Hiroshima and Nagasaki.

I do believe, though some people reject this link, that the question of victory and civilian deaths in combination is important in forming a judgment about the policy of city bombing.[128] One of the problems of the debate in general is the widely held assumption that strategic bombing was a failure.[129] This is for two reasons: both of the arguments on the extremes, that any civilian deaths are wrong or that all were acceptable as the price of fighting the terrible regimes of Nazi Germany or imperial Japan, are unconvincing. Civilian deaths were going to occur in large numbers in World War II, regardless of policy. In World War I, approximately 6 million civilians died (if you take into account indirect deaths caused by famine and deprivation), hardly any because of air attack.[130] Civilians were going to die in their many millions during World War II (and actually within the context of World War II, the percentage of civilians who died as a result of strategic bombing was less than 5 percent), with the *length* of the fighting being far more important in determining the overall losses than the type of bombing employed. As the war went on, all deaths rose at a far higher pace, so that ending the conflict even a few months earlier through bombing would have saved a large number of lives on all sides.

On the other hand, the notion that somehow strategic bombing was acceptable simply because of the regimes and the people who supported the regimes being attacked has unsettling implications, even if it was the feeling of many who dropped the bombs.[131] The United States and the United Kingdom believed they were fighting for a different set of values than Germany or Japan. Basing an air policy on killing civilians of the latter as a form of retribution undermines this case. Moreover, no one in charge of the bombing campaign saw the war so neatly. Though many believed that the bombing of Axis cities was more than justified by German and Japanese behavior, they were also convinced that this policy would shorten the war significantly and save many lives (including those of their enemies).

Therefore, the effectiveness of bombing does have important ethical implications. What if Arthur Harris had been right? Had Albert Speer's first instincts come to pass, and six more attacks like Hamburg had led to a collapse of German munitions production, then "Bomber" Harris would have saved more lives than almost any military leader in human history. To argue that such a policy which would have saved millions of lives was wrong because Harris hated Germans and was intent on retribution seems decidedly self-indulgent.[132]

Trying to determine the relative motivation of those in charge between feelings of revenge and cold-headed reasoning about victory is impossible in men like Curtis LeMay and Arthur Harris. Both clearly believed that their campaigns, which necessarily involved the killing of hundreds of thousands of civilians, also involved the destruction of Germany and Japanese productive capacity and were going to end the war much more quickly with fewer casualties. Harris repeated this point throughout 1943 and 1944, when he felt that his bombers were being diverted to less crucial campaigns. When Arnold came to the Marianas, LeMay and his staff believed that their bombing was aimed at destroying Japanese production and that it would be able to drive Japan out of the war in just a few months. "Back to the house where LeMay's staff showed how industrial facilities would be completely destroyed by October 1st. 30 large and small cities, all to go, then Japan will have none of the things needed to supply an Army, Navy or Air Force. October 1st – we will see."[133]

It is hard to find anyone in a position of authority in the United States or the United Kingdom who did not believe that civilians could be targeted if it was part of a war-winning strategy. With the notable exception of James Doolittle, who passionately argued against the USAAF taking part in the bombing of Dresden because it represented a betrayal of American values, most Americans who had a say over the bombing of Germany and Japan took a practical view of the issue.[134] For much of the war, American bombing strategy was determined more by technology than by conscience. If this American strategy spared civilians, that was less by deliberate choice than by happy coincidence. In March and April 1943, there was actually a flurry of discussion about this, as the American strategic bombing campaign was getting ready to begin. The widespread view was that the 8th Air Force should be able to attack whatever targets it believed it needed to attack to win the war. Lovett, who made an investigation into the subject, believed that there was widespread opposition to bombing targets that would cause too high a death rate amongst civilians in German-occupied Europe, but not within the Reich itself.[135]

Arnold made that perfectly clear in April 1943, before the American strategic bombing campaign had really started, when he heard that there was a protest being circulated against the killing of German civilians in bombing raids. He was worried that USAAF theater commanders might hesitate to attack civilian targets, so he circulated a direct order throughout the upper echelons of the USAAF explaining his stance on the subject.

> He [Arnold] wants the Air Staff to realize that this is a brutal war and that the way to stop the killing of civilians is to cause so much damage and destruction and death that the civilians will demand that their government cease fighting. This does not mean that we are making civilians or civilian institutions a war objective, but we cannot "pull our punches" because some of them may get killed. There will be no concurrence given by any member of the Staff to any message to any theater indicating that we reduce our efforts in any way.[136]

When, in late 1944 and early 1945, the USAAF was given the opportunity of taking part in a campaign against German morale and German civilians, it adjusted quite well and took part in some major raids against German cities.[137]

The use of incendiaries to destroy Japanese cities was also something that was well discussed within American air power circles long before LeMay's first raid. However, it was still usually seen as a way of destroying production by burning down large industrial areas with the open admission that many civilians would die. In 1943, the COA, when it drew up its main report for the air war against Japan, discussed the possibility of destroying Japan's cities through incendiary attack – though like the British in the war against Germany, they couched their arguments in terms of causing dislocation and de-housing rather than killing civilians.

> Urban industrial areas in Japan are few, concentrated and vulnerable to incendiary attack. A relatively small weight of

incendiaries effectively placed is believed adequate to cause great damage through destruction of industrial housing, essential public services and a significant number of industrial installations … Maximum industrial disruption in an urban area will be attained by attacks of a magnitude sufficient to overwhelm the firefighting resources of the area in question; simultaneous attacks on many urban areas may well overwhelm the relief and repair facilities of the country as a whole.[138]

Later, the COA departed from the production argument and, in rather British language, argued that such attacks could also play a damaging role in weakening Japanese morale. "Although the greater number of the more important industrial plants lie outside the specific areas suggested for incendiary attack, some of the large plants contained in these areas are important objectives. In addition incendiary attacks of the above nature should have a substantial detrimental effect on the morale of the population."[139]

This kind of discussion in 1943 was understandable, if somewhat sobering. Both Germany and Japan still controlled large areas of the world with great deposits of natural resources and both were in the process of increasing production rapidly. The true ignorance about the use of air power meant that no one could say with any assurance what would work or what wouldn't. Bombing on the scale about to be unleashed by the British and Americans had never been tried.

However, the second half of 1944 was different, when it had become clearer which elements of the strategic air campaign were effective in damaging German power and which were marginal. Obtaining convincing intelligence on the impact of strategic bombing had always been a great problem.[140] However, by the middle of 1944 it was becoming increasingly clear that area attacks on German cities were not producing anything like the decisive results that Harris had expected.[141] The Joint Intelligence Committee (JIC) reports became increasingly brief and less engaged when discussing the effects of area bombing on German morale, production or even "de-housing" workers. The JIC submitted a report on the impact of Anglo-American air power during the first half of 1944 with particular attention paid to its role in supporting the D-Day landings.[142] Its summary of the impact of the bombing on German morale and production damned with the faintest of praise: "By destroying houses, interrupting public services, straining nerves and drastically reducing the supply of goods available to the public, the bombing offensive has *probably* made German morale less able to withstand the effects of military disasters which threaten Germany herself with invasion." (Emphasis added.)[143]

As the year went on, reports became even less complimentary. On November 15, 1944 a consolidated estimate of specific damage inflicted on targeted German systems was produced by the RAF.[144] What was interesting was how little mention was made of area attacks. There was a stated belief that the bombing of German cities was contributing somewhat to a decline in German production, but it was also acknowledged that within the overall scheme of Anglo-American bombing, it was not very important.

> The industrial output lost through area attacks has included vital armaments and military equipment, as well as civilian and industrial supplies. Overall losses of production have been distributed over many types of industry, and have thereby supplemented the specific shortages of aircraft, oil and bearings. Although no industry has been damaged to a critical degree by area attacks, the general losses of industrial output have weakened the Wehrmacht and contributed thereby to military successes of the Allies.[145]

This rather vague assessment stood in stark contrast to the accompanying analysis of the effectiveness of the campaign against German oil production, which was seen as having concrete and decisive results. The report was astonishingly accurate as to the damage to German oil supplies – stating that monthly German fuel production between April and November 1944 averaged 49 percent of that in March, which was the highpoint of the year.[146] The actual total was 48.7 percent.[147] Such losses had been confirmed by both a lack of fuel given to German combat units and a reduction of Luftwaffe activity. Moreover, they had forced the Germans to draw heavily on their reserve fuel stocks, action which was soon bound to bring on a major mobility crisis. The specific analysis of just why the Luftwaffe was able to make so little impact on the war, when its production of fighters had risen substantially, tied together the different pressures being put on the German air force. The reasons given were the bombing of factories, repair facilities and airfields, the heavy combat losses of the Luftwaffe and the steep reduction of aviation fuel supplies.[148]

Both Portal and Arnold seemed convinced that the oil campaign was causing great dislocation within the German war effort.[149] Portal actually put together a thick dossier of all the intelligence reports that he could find on the subject, including from Ultra.

> The strongest evidence of the soundness of the oil plan is to be found in the enemy's own reactions to our oil offensive. Since this was launched there has been an unceasing flow of reliable intelligence showing the immense effect which the resulting shortage of oil is having upon the enemy's fighting ability. In the JIC dossier I have included copies of the JIC reports, from June 1943 to January 1945, upon the attacks on the oil situation in Europe. I am sending you also a dossier of "ultra" information on the same subject covering the period from May to December. These reports give strong confirmation of the soundness of the oil policy and suggest that the effects which have already been achieved might be much increased if we press on with the offensive with all determination.
>
> If additional evidence were needed one has only to look at the extraordinary measures which have been taken to protect the plants by means of flak and smoke screens. There are more heavy guns round Leuna and Lutzkendorf than at Berlin, more at Politz and Brux than at Munich and more at Zeitz and at Blechhammer than at Leipzig. The prodigious efforts which the enemy is making to repair plants as soon as they have been damaged, so that he can obtain *some* production before they are damaged again, further confirm his desperate anxiety about his oil output.[150]

This forthright letter was sent to Arthur Harris, and came at the end of a long and increasingly bitter exchange between Portal and the head of Bomber Command.[151] For more than two months the Chief of the Air Staff had tried to persuade Harris of the importance of switching the bulk of his attack to German fuel supplies while at the same time decreasing the amount spent destroying cities. Harris would have none of it. He bristled at what he saw as Portal's slights about Bomber Command's contribution to the victory over Germany and continued his usual attacks about bombing individual "panacea" targets.[152] When he received Harris' response, Portal seemed to lose the will to continue the fight, though he criticized the head of Bomber Command strongly in the first paragraph of his last letter on the subject.

> I am sorry to see from your letter...that I have failed to convince you of the soundness of the Oil Plan. I do not think it is any good my going over all the evidence again since you have really not rebutted it.

He then added closer to the end:

> We must agree to differ. You apparently believe in putting all your efforts into area attacks. We recognise that area attacks have been extremely valuable but we are convinced that in order to be decisive in themselves or in the near future they would require a very much larger force than we possess, the main reason for this being that an industrial area recovers much of its productive capacity in 4 or 5 months, as you yourself have stated in the past. We are further convinced that the devotion of a part of your effort to reducing the enemy's supply of a vital commodity of which he is now desperately short, gives the best chance of an early end to the war.[153]

It was an exchange ripe with ethical implications. Harris, as Portal stated, seemed to have switched from being a rational supporter of one form of strategic air power to a man of faith. At this time, then, the ethicality of strategic bombing of cities can be very much called into question. Now there was evidence about what was working and what was not. From the autumn of 1944 onwards, it becomes difficult to justify any of the area attacks on German cities as important in winning the war. However, removing Harris, which might have allowed for such a change, was beyond the Churchill government's courage.[154]

Turning to the Pacific, the first raids against Tokyo came months after Portal started trying to persuade Harris. Within the USAAF, the belief in the importance of attacking oil targets had only grown since the spring of 1944.[155] It does seem, therefore, that LeMay's change was partly motivated by the need to seem to be doing something dramatic. On the one hand, his attacks did have a real effect on the Japanese. The president of the Mitsubishi heavy industry division, who was constantly monitoring the output from his factories, believed American morale attacks against Japanese cities did more damage to production than their attempts to target individual factories. He claimed right after the war that "Morale stood up as long as plants only were bombed, but when homes and towns were bombed and deaths occurred in the family, absenteeism increased and morale became very low."[156] This sentiment was echoed by Admiral Teijiro Toyoda, chairman of the Japan Steel Company from 1941 and Minister of Munitions in 1945. He came to believe that attacks on Japanese cities, which undermined morale, were actually more important than the severing of sea lanes in the ultimate collapse of Japanese production.

Q. In Admiral Toyoda's opinion did the real bottleneck in the shortage of materials and the decrease of production stem from the loss of shipping or the B-29 raids?

A. I think that the air raids were much more effective than the gradual war of attrition by the submarines. The terror of these raids undermined the mentality of the people, reduced their working effectiveness and moreover the destruction of a great mass of small industry disrupted the whole economy.

Q. And submarine warfare?

A. Of course submarine warfare affected everything in the Japanese economy, but at no time did it have an immediate effect on policy. It was a great factor in stopping production and as such weighed heavily in the overall planning. But the stability of the populace was directly upset by the fire raids.[157]\

However, the overall production argument seems even less convincing for Japan than for Germany. As Japan relied on shipping for its raw materials, attacking cities was going one step further down the production process – whereas it was more efficient to concentrate on keeping the resources away from the centers of production.

The US Strategic Bombing Survey is in many ways distinctly unconvincing when it comes to its claims about Japanese production – or at least, its claims do not always correlate well with the data that it collected. It made detailed studies of the impact of LeMay's firebombing campaign on Japan's major industrial cities.[158] In the introduction to this study, it claimed that production in these cities was "drastically reduced."[159] Yet, the individual sections on the cities, which are very detailed on the destruction caused, have few, if any, actual production figures which would show the situation before or after the attack. For instance, two of the most important cities were Nagoya and Tokyo. Nagoya's aircraft industry was seriously damaged long before LeMay's switch. The report details the destruction of buildings (113,460 were claimed to have been destroyed), dead civilians (7,724) and people made homeless (522,951).[160] Yet, there are no specifics on the impact on Japanese aircraft production. That might be because no data could be found, but it might also be because Japanese aircraft production had already been in steep decline for eight months before the attacks occurred.

The Tokyo section is even more detailed as regards destruction, but remains relatively vague on the actual impact. The operative section states:

> No over-all figures for production loss were available since not all the plants in the area were visited. However, an estimate of the loss of production to the damaged area resulting from the 9–10 March attack was made by the local managers of 10 of the larger plants. Building and equipment damaged in these plants ranged from five to 100 percent and loss of production was estimated at 50 percent.[161]

It sounds dramatic (if rather vague and in no way scientific), but makes no reference to the extremely large declines in Japanese production prior to the attack. And this Tokyo section was among the only ones to actually try to measure the results. The sections on smaller industrial towns, such as Hachioji, Oita, Aomori, Akashi and Ube, were even vaguer. Also, as many of these attacks occurred in July 1945, it is hard to see how they would have inflicted any meaningful damage on Japanese production. It is also interesting to note – and this is something that LeMay and those who support the incendiary campaign fail to acknowledge – that the civilian casualties suffered during these raids appeared to be decreasing the longer they went on. One of the reasons that the Tokyo attack was so damaging was that the Japanese were not prepared. They had not faced a low-level incendiary attack like that before, and neither the civilians nor the fire-fighting forces knew how to react. Just a few months later, when LeMay's incendiary attacks were commonplace, the Japanese had adapted somewhat. Buildings still burned, but fire-fighting seemed more effective and the loss of life from the raids was much reduced – at least in the cities that the USSBS studied in detail. Nagoya, the population of which in December 1944 was 1,160,000, but had been reduced to something closer to 600,000 by the earlier raids on its aircraft factories, was attacked four times by incendiaries after the Tokyo bombing.[162] The combined loss of life in these four raids was 3,866.[163] Ube, a city of 100,000 which was attacked on July 2, suffered 230 killed and missing; Akashi, an industrial town of 100,000 attacked on July 6, suffered 386 killed and missing; Aomori, which also had a population of 100,000 and was attacked on July 28, suffered 736 killed and missing; Imbabari, a center of textile production with a population of 60,000 attacked on August 5, suffered 484 persons killed; Hachioji, a city of 68,000 attacked on August 2, suffered 305 killed.[164] In the smaller towns, casualties totaled 0.5 percent. These raids caused damage, but in many ways the Japanese lesson reinforced something which the Germans realized. Early raids, such as those on Hamburg, are usually the most damaging when it comes to loss of life. As time goes on, casualties per raid are reduced as preparations are put in place and the population is not caught by surprise. This seems also to be the case for Tokyo, which was subjected to four more large incendiary raids, two in April and two in May. Considerably less of the city burned in each one in relative terms to the weight of incendiary bombs dropped, and while specific casualty levels are difficult to determine, they were far less than those of March 9–10.[165] So, those who believe that LeMay's incendiary raids were going to drive the Japanese out of the war because of civilian casualties need to explain how that would be the case when the loss of life was decreasing significantly. Certainly, from the Japanese point of view, in which human death in service to the country was not something to be feared, the level of casualties being suffered by the summer of 1945 seems to have been manageable.[166]

In the end, LeMay's campaign was one of awesome destruction, the real impact of which on Japanese production remains difficult to quantify.[167] LeMay referred to the impact of his campaigns on Japanese production in vaguer terms than did the USSBS. In his autobiography, a strange work of disjointed thoughts and impressions, there is no discussion of the specific impact of incendiary bombing on Japanese production. Instead, he justifies the importance of the raids in terms of damaging Japanese morale – relying on a short *Air Force* article.[168] His proof of Japanese morale breaking was the decline in Tokyo's supposed population, not production – though the population in cities being bombed almost always went down as production was relocated after raids. To LeMay, however, this seems to have been proof enough. "All my logic, my reasoning, had told me that this would come about. But it still remained to be *proved*, until the operations had actually taken place. We could have been surprised; but thank God we weren't." (Emphasis in original.)[169] When it came to production, he argued that basically all Japanese were targets because all Japanese were involved in production. His evidence for that was that when he saw burned-out Japanese cities after the war, many of the civilian houses had small drill presses. Anything that helped the enemy forces, however small, was therefore a military target to LeMay. "There's nothing new about this massacre of civilian populations. In ancient times, when an army laid siege to a city, everybody was in the fight. And when that city had fallen, and was sacked, just as often as not every single soul was murdered."[170]

By LeMay's standard, the Japanese got off lightly. However, he was absolutely wrong when it came to past standards – at least those of the early United States. From the moment the country was founded, there was an attempt to regulate what the United States would or would not do in combat. During the Revolution, George Washington tried to act in accord with Enlightenment ideals, which worked towards the protection of civilians.[171] Abraham Lincoln explicitly called the killing of non-combatants (as well as vanquished foes) "barbarous and cruel" and claimed no civilized country would do such a thing.[172] LeMay's view of warfare was definitely a step backwards – and possibly self-defeating. His notion of causing justified destruction with little evidence beyond the physical action of destruction added an unnecessary air of irrationality to the American campaign. His bombing doubtless damaged some production, but it was less effective than the attacks on targets that shut down the enemy's economic mobility. Like Harris, he would not have known that in 1943, but one could say that he should have known it by 1945.

Of course, this leaves one final issue: the dropping of the two atomic bombs on Hiroshima and Nagasaki. (See Figure 98.) The American decision to use these new weapons was debated at the time, and continues to be today.[173] On the one hand, these bombs might not deserve all the special attention. The number of civilians killed, within the context of all civilians killed by air attack during the war, was only moderately high. The number of dead from both bombs is still the

98 Nagasaki in ruins after the atom bomb attack of August 9, 1945. One of the only recognizable landmarks is the ruined Roman Catholic cathedral on the hillside. The necessity of this bomb was debated in 1945 and is still being argued about today.

subject of some discussion, but certainly most estimates set the combined figure of those killed almost immediately at somewhere between 100,000 and 110,000.[174] The impact of radiation, however, continued to take its toll for years, so that the eventual total of those killed would have climbed significantly. Again, finding a total figure is extremely difficult, and the process has been partly politicized with those trying to support the attacks as morally justified opting for lower figures and those trying to point out the especially horrible nature of them choosing some much higher. The final range therefore could be anywhere from 130,000 to well over 200,000.

As it is, strategic bombing as a whole killed more than a million German and Japanese civilians combined, so that the atomic bomb figures, while high, were not exceptional. The individual raids on Tokyo and Hamburg killed comparable amounts to those on Hiroshima and Nagasaki. However, the fact that the latter raids were clearly political, and not intended to damage Japanese production, and that they kept on killing for many years afterwards, has added an ethical twist, in two different ways.

The political argument concerns just how important these weapons were in compelling the Japanese to surrender. This has led to a bitter disagreement. One camp, highly critical of the decision to drop the bombs, believes that in doing so the Truman administration was motivated not by a desire to defeat Japan, but by a desire to warn the Soviet Union and halt any potential Soviet expansion into East Asia. They also believe that the Japanese government was already determined to seek an end to the war, and would have capitulated sooner rather than later, even without the dropping of the bombs. Another view is that in forestalling a US invasion of Japan, many hundreds of thousands of Japanese lives were spared. Any invasion of Japan promised to be a particularly horrible affair. The Japanese would have committed almost everything in the fight – possibly including the most advanced stockpile of biological and chemical weapons in the world. During the war, in large part as a result of a grotesque policy of using humans for live experiments, the Japanese had developed some of the deadliest chemical and biological weapons in existence.[175]

Answering this political question clearly is difficult. Even right after the war, the USSBS had trouble saying just how important the dropping of the atom bomb was in compelling Japanese capitulation.[176] Under this analysis, the Japanese state was looking for a way out of the war to save itself. Some have also argued that it was worried by the appeal of communism to the Japanese people, especially once the Soviet Union had been shown to be a victor in Europe and then attacked Japan.[177] Certainly the Soviet invasion of Manchuria and declaration of war made it clear to the Japanese government that there was no further room for negotiation and contributed to the decision to surrender when they did.[178] Also, that Japanese morale was showing real signs of weakness and desperation is clear.[179] People who outwardly seemed to be backing the war effort were inwardly depressed and desperate for the war to end.[180] Some Japanese diplomats and business leaders were also keen to see the war ended as soon as possible.[181]

However, this growth in defeatism did not seem to pose a treat to the Japanese government's immediate hold on power.[182] It remained extremely unlikely that the Japanese state would surrender in weeks or even months. In Germany, for instance, morale went into serious decline in September 1944 with defeat on all fronts, east, west and in the air.[183] Yet the Nazi state continued to resist, and suffer growing and horrific casualties, for another nine months.[184] It is hard to imagine that Japanese civilians could have compelled the army or navy to end the war, without at least one atomic bomb. In that sense, the atomic bombs almost certainly saved many thousands of lives, both Japanese and American. However, for the most important critic of the atomic bomb, this was still not reason enough to use the weapon. He wrote:

My own feeling was that, in being the first to use it, we had
adopted an ethical standard common to the barbarians of the Dark
Ages. I was not taught to make war in that fashion, and wars
cannot be won by destroying women and children...

These new concepts of "total war" are basically distasteful to
the soldier and sailor of my generation. Employment of the atomic
bomb in war will take us back in cruelty towards non-combatants
to the days of Genghis Khan.[185]

These were the thoughts of William Leahy, written a few years after
World War II ended. There often exists a crude caricature of military
men which has them wanting to use all weapons at all times. When it
came to the atomic bomb, this was not the case for Leahy, who during
the war tried hard to keep it from being dropped.

It was a sign of how discreet Leahy was that he never even
mentioned the existence of the atomic bomb project in his diary until
October 1944, and even then he only used the code name for it,
referring to it as the "tube alloy" plan.[186] In May 1945, he started
mentioning the Manhattan Project by name. He was skeptical about
using the weapon (which he mentioned had cost the USA $2 billion to
this point), on both practical and moral grounds. He had serious
doubts about whether it would actually work,[187] but what really
bothered him were the ethical implications. He believed that if the
United States used this new weapon, it would be a "barbaric" act that
would usher in a new and potentially apocalyptic era of warfare. To
him, the closest comparison was with the use of poison gas.[188]

So Leahy was more than willing to spare the Japanese people
from being attacked by atom bombs. However, and this poses the great
question, in doing so he would have chosen a policy that most probably
would have led to even greater numbers of Japanese dying – and that
was because of Leahy's understanding of the air and sea war. As well as
opposing the dropping of the atomic bomb, he was opposed to any
invasion of Japan. He believed that any invasion was unnecessary and
would involve extreme American casualties. He was more than willing
to let American air and sea power drive Japan out of the war, a position
that he had come to believe in the summer of 1944.

A large part of the Japanese Navy was already at the bottom of the
sea. The same was true of Japanese merchant shipping. There was
every indication that our Navy would soon have the rest of

Tokyo's warships sunk or out of action. The combined Navy surface and air force action even by this time had forced Japan into a position that made her early surrender inevitable. None of us knew at this time the potentialities of the atomic bomb, but it was my opinion, and I urged it strongly on the Joint Chiefs, that no major land invasion of the Japanese mainland was necessary to win the war. The JCS did order the preparation of plans for an invasion, but *the invasion itself was never authorized*. (Emphasis in original)[189]

It was the great conundrum posed by the fantastic growth of air and sea power. By the summer of 1945, the United States controlled movement in the seas and air in and around Japan, and on much of the land as well. It thus had the ability to win the war without setting foot on Japanese soil; it could have done this by shutting down practically all Japanese mobility. Such a move would not have required an invasion which, as Leahy very well knew, would have killed many tens of thousands of American military men – at the least. On the other hand, unless the Japanese state had capitulated relatively quickly, the country would have descended into starvation and decay, being constantly bombarded by air and sea.

One's response to that dilemma sums up the whole ethical argument about the growth of sea, but particularly air power. It did allow for an extraordinary broadening of warfare away from the battlefield. As such, it allowed for enormous destruction, of both people and equipment, far away from the traditional area of combat. As for the ethical question, for both the atom bomb specifically and strategic bombing in general, it ultimately comes down to a question of ends versus means. Both shortened the war and saved many thousands of lives, Allied, German and Japanese. Air and sea power allowed for a swifter and more decisive Allied victory.

CONCLUSION: THE SUPREMACY OF AIR AND SEA POWER AND THE CONTROL OF MOBILITY

Adolf Hitler spent the last few weeks of his life deep underground in a very expensive complex of bunkers built to protect him from Anglo-American air attacks. (See Figure 99.) While entombed, he oscillated between episodes of rage and depression, with occasional bursts of fantastical bravado as he tried to persuade those around him, and maybe even himself, to keep up the useless struggle. On April 28, he had one of the last formal meetings that he would hold as dictator of the German state. He met with Luftwaffe Field Marshal Ritter von Greim.[1] Hitler had just named Greim as the head of the German air force, replacing Hermann Goering who Hitler believed had tried to oust him as head of state. Greim, who remained a true believer to the end and would commit suicide not long after Germany's surrender, listened devotedly as Hitler analyzed the Luftwaffe's performance during the war. According to Greim, Hitler stated that the personnel of the Luftwaffe had fought with greater bravery than other members of the German armed forces, but they had simply been outclassed by the British and Americans. Although, or so Hitler claimed, many senior commanders had tried to hide the truth from him, he eventually realized that German aircraft and supporting technologies were simply not good enough to contend with those of the USAAF and RAF.

Two days later, Hitler shot himself.

Hitler's belated comprehension of Germany's inferiority in the air war showed that, in this one area at least, he had not altogether taken leave of his senses. However, German surrender still had to wait until after Hitler killed himself, and in many ways the last few months

99 In the last stages of the war, Anglo-American air power was so dominant that much of the leadership of the Reich as well as the state's valuables were stuck underground for their own safety. This is a picture of a cache of Reichsbank gold and other treasures discovered by American infantry in salt mines near Merkers, Germany.

of completely unnecessary fighting were a dirty slog to extend his physical existence. Japan's surrender, coming two days after the second atomic weapon was dropped on Nagasaki, was scarcely less self-interested – as neither the Japanese army nor the navy wanted to admit that they had led the country into such a disaster. Like the Germans, they had been outclassed in the air–sea war years earlier.

Thus, German and Japanese capitulation in May and August of 1945 occurred long after each had "lost" World War II. That their leaders, to try to prolong their political authority, would not take the honorable step that the leaders of imperial Germany took in 1918 speaks volumes about both the horrible and yet grotesquely petty nature of both regimes. The fate of Germany and Japan was sealed much earlier by the many-layered application of Anglo-American air and sea power. The totality of this pressure, from the home front to the battlefield, eventually choked off Axis mobility. Starting in 1943, when Germany and Japan still possessed all the basic prerequisites of great powers, their growing inability to move goods and armies led inexorably to catastrophic collapses in both Europe and the Pacific. This then is what separates air and sea power from traditional notions of land power. Air and sea power could operate throughout the productive process, not only to affect the battlefield, but to determine how much and what kinds of military equipment were produced and deployed.

The fate of Germany was determined in the summer of 1943. Its inability to stop trade across the Atlantic, the one campaign that the

Nazi state could wage that held out the prospect of an efficient destruction of Allied resources, coupled with the decision to strip the battlefield of Luftwaffe fighter cover, sent the war into an unstoppable tailspin. From that point onwards, the destruction of German war equipment from the pre-production process up until the battlefield grew almost exponentially – so that by the summer of 1944, when German armaments production was reaching its apex for the war, destruction of equipment drastically outstripped German production for the first time. From that time, equipment losses before the battlefield actually outpaced those of the battlefield, as the crippling of Germany's fuel production coupled with an assault on its rail network meant that considerably more than half of the country's potential and actual production was lost before firing a shot. Late 1943 also witnessed the start of the first serious assault on Japanese mobility. Until that time, Japan had shown itself to be an economic and technological power at least equal, and probably superior, to the USSR. However, from that point it came under an air and sea blockade that transformed how it could fight the war. The American submarine campaign reached deep into the western Pacific, and started the process of sinking Japanese merchant shipping faster than it could be replaced. It was in 1944, however, after the American capture of the Mariana Islands, that Japanese mobility was fully crippled. The use of both land-based and carrier aircraft along with the submarine isolated Japan from its large, resource-rich empire.

This reduction in mobility determined the course of the war for both German and Japanese war production and for German and Japanese armies in the field. When engaged in battle, both countries' armies were denied effective air cover. The skies over their positions were dominated by British, American and Soviet aircraft. German and Japanese soldiers could fight with brutal determination from defensive positions and inflict high casualties, but when their lines were broken, their reactions and options were severely limited. They could either be killed in place, surrender (much more in the case of Germany than of Japan), or abandon their equipment and try to walk to safety. Forward movements became an increasing rarity, and were attempted only under exceptional conditions. The one great example of an Axis offensive in 1944 and 1945 was the Ardennes Offensive, which was only made possible because cloudy skies kept Anglo-American air power away from the battlefield for a week. When the skies cleared, the

German advance stopped immediately. Japanese attacks on Allied material only became feasible through the kamikaze, the acceptance that the person making the attack would have to die to have any chance of fulfilling his mission.

It is in broadening our understanding of just how German and Japanese equipment was destroyed that the true impact of air and sea power can best be seen. Both Japanese and German armaments construction went into a terminal decline in the summer of 1944, when their empires still possessed all the raw materials needed to keep production rising. One of the main reasons for this was the inability of both to transport raw materials from their sources to the refining factories, and then from those factories to the place of finished munitions production. The Japanese lost the ability to bring oil and bauxite from the Dutch East Indies and iron ore from the Asian mainland. Germany's increasing difficulty in transporting coal throughout the country led to increasing power shortages and declining munitions output.

At the same time, the plant used to construct German and Japanese equipment came under direct assault. Centers of German aircraft construction such as Regensburg and Wiener Neustadt were first destroyed in 1943. This caused the dispersal of aircraft production which retarded construction for many months. Even when the new factories were up and running, they often produced inferior equipment because of their hasty construction and awkward layouts. Japanese aircraft production around Nagoya was heavily damaged in late 1944, which contributed to the steep falls in aircraft output. Beyond aircraft, there were important examples of industrial plant being destroyed by direct air attack. German finished metal production was hit in the second half of 1943, leading to the first restrictions in the growth of German land equipment. In 1944, direct bombing attacks on construction facilities, such as the U-boat assembly pens, led to a high level of construction losses and delayed the introduction of the more advanced Type XXI U-boat until the end of the war.

However, even completed German and Japanese weapons suffered massive losses through the pressure of the air and sea war. One of the least understood ways in which this happened was through deployment losses. By 1944, Germany and Japan were losing between one-quarter and one-half of their produced aircraft trying to deploy them to their operating areas. These extraordinary losses show how air and sea power operated on a far more profound level than land warfare. One of the main paths to these losses was laid in 1943, when the pressure of the air and sea war forced both countries to try to produce many more pilots while severely reducing their access to fuel. The upshot was that both began a process of reducing the flight time allocated to trainee pilots. By 1944, the cutbacks became severe and many of their new pilots were incapable of successfully executing basic tasks such as flying in bad weather, landing or even taking off in their expensive machines. The result was that they often damaged or completely destroyed their aircraft in the process of deployment or on other non-operational duties. Such aircraft losses represented far more equipment than was lost by the Germans and Japanese during the famous land battles of the war. This is just one example.

German and Japanese equipment for the land war also started disappearing in large quantities in 1944 before it could be used in combat. The Japanese were desperately trying to reinforce the islands which blocked the American path to their homeland, such as the Marianas, the Philippines and Iwo Jima. Much of the manpower and equipment for these reinforcements came from the Japanese armies in China and Manchuria. However, up to three-quarters of the reinforcements, including parts of Japan's most advanced chemical and biological weapons unit, were lost en route. The German army also lost trainloads of equipment in the second half of 1944, as the German rail network for the first time came under sustained attack. Before that, air attacks on the German-controlled rail network in France had significantly slowed the ability of the Wehrmacht to reinforce Normandy after D-Day and made possible an Anglo-American landing that could have failed had it been based on land power. The destruction of the Seine and Loire bridges meant that almost all the units that were rushed to the fighting had to be de-trained at least a hundred miles from the beaches. From that point they could only safely travel at night, when they would not be spotted by patrolling Anglo-American aircraft. Instead of overwhelming the landing forces, which they might have done had they had complete freedom of movement into Normandy, German units ended up being drip-fed into a meat grinder of their destruction.

Understanding this role of air and sea weaponry should lead to a redefinition of what was a great "battle" in World War II. Throughout the war, the economies of Germany, Japan, the United Kingdom and the United States were geared by very large majorities towards the manufacture of air and sea weaponry. In every case, the construction of aircraft was the single greatest priority for each economy, composing at a minimum one-third of output, as for the United States, to more than half, as for the United Kingdom. When the equipping and arming of the aircraft was added to the mix, these figures were increased. Because of this, during the war the Luftwaffe received more than half of German production. When one adds to this the enormous German effort in anti-aircraft construction from 1943 onwards, the vast majority of which was for the air war over Germany, approximately 60 percent of German production was made up of armed aircraft and anti-air weaponry when munitions output reached its peak.

Naval construction, both war and merchant, was smaller in Germany, usually around 10 percent of output, but could be approximately one-third in the cases of the United States and Japan. Combined, however, air and naval weaponry left only a small percentage for the land armies. The German army received approximately 30–35 percent of German construction, when it was lucky. The British, American and Japanese armies had to get by with much less. What this meant was that many of the "great" battles of World War II, such as El Alamein or Kursk, actually resulted in the destruction of negligible percentages of overall munitions output. Air-to-air battles, on the other hand, could be considerably more expensive. The German V-1 and V-2 campaigns, which the Anglo-Americans tried to counter with enormous air assets under the codename operation Crossbow, represented a far greater economic exertion on both sides than did land battles such as Stalingrad or the invasions of Sicily and Italy. The design and construction of the V-2 rocket, for instance, probably cost as much as all German AFV construction between 1939 and 1945. On the other hand, the RAF and USAAF actually dropped more ordnance on Crossbow targets in the summer of 1944 than they dropped in support of Allied armies in Normandy – in the end it represented 3 percent of the Anglo-American air effort in all theaters throughout the entire war.

This brings us back to the question of victory and defeat in the war. While the overwhelming consensus of historians is that Germany was defeated primarily through the interaction of the large land armies on the Eastern Front, this is only true if one believes that the number of soldiers deployed was the best indicator of national effort. On the other hand, if economic, technological, and overall domestic allocation of resources is a better measurement, the air–sea war between the

Germans and the British and Americans was the defining campaign of the war – by a considerable measure. This contest was by far the more modern of the two, involving the most advanced, expensive machinery, in the largest quantities and controlled by the best-trained warriors. It cost the most, destroyed the most, and determined strategy for the last three years of the war. That the Eastern Front was responsible for the greater human suffering is undeniable. But this human suffering should not obscure the fact that it was a secondary theater in terms of production and technology, where force was actually used in a far more limited front-based manner which caused considerably fewer choices to be made and smaller amounts of equipment to be utilized and destroyed.

Understanding the modern potentialities of air and sea power was therefore one of the great tests of Anglo-American grand strategy. The men in charge of the process – Churchill, Roosevelt, Hopkins, Alanbrooke, Portal, Pound, Marshall, Arnold, King and Leahy – often had different agendas. The soldiers, Alanbrooke and Marshall, usually had the most limited understanding of warfare, were focused on the battlefield and viewed the war almost entirely from that context. To them, air and sea power mostly existed to service the land armies, and they viewed the war in terms of engaging the German and Japanese divisions and production in the field. Roosevelt and Churchill provide a more interesting contrast. Although Churchill had served as First Lord of the Admiralty, and early in the war spoke of the potential of strategic bombing, when it came to the war in Europe he moved more towards a battlefield-centric understanding as the war progressed. Not only did he become less interested in strategic air power, his focus on the Mediterranean was plainly more backward-looking than forward. He was concerned with preserving the British Empire and as such actually ignored some of the more advanced campaigns that could have been waged on German production from the region. Roosevelt provides quite a different picture. He entered the war determined that the United States would gain total dominance in the air and sea. He was not particularly clear on how air power should be used – but then again, that was not his job. His greatest contribution to grand strategy was his decisive intervention in the second half of 1942, overruling Marshall, and making sure that the United States gave a dominant priority to aircraft construction. Had he not done this, the USAAF would have been considerably smaller in 1943 and 1944 (as would the RAF and USSR air force, both of which flew many planes manufactured in the United States). German resistance might therefore have gone on for far longer, as the Luftwaffe would have been able to play a major role in the European land war in 1944 and German production would have been even higher.

Though it might be assumed that the sailors and airmen had a greater grasp of the potentialities of air and sea power, this was only partially true. Arnold tended to view air power in isolation from sea power and Pound the opposite. Arnold believed that the role of the American navy was to provide service to the USAAF, for instance arguing that Japan could be knocked out of the war from airbases in China. Pound, meanwhile, believed that air power's first usage was in helping the British win the Battle of the Atlantic.

Leahy, King and Portal had a more well-rounded understanding of modern warfare. Portal, though he focused overwhelmingly on air power, was one of the first believers in the importance of attacks on German transportation and mobility. In 1941, when the issue first came to the fore, he worked hard to make the bombing of the German rail network a high priority. Unfortunately, such a campaign was beyond the capacity of any air force at this time. In 1944, however, when the Anglo-American air forces now had the means of destroying different targets in Germany, Portal once again pushed for mobility attacks, particularly those on German oil production. It was tragic, however, that he could not compel the head of Bomber Command, Arthur Harris, to go along with these plans.

Ernest King and William Leahy had balanced understandings of the integration of air and sea power. King, in fact, was the first and most effective advocate of the plan that would most efficiently defeat Japan. More than anyone else, he came to understand the crucial importance of the Mariana Islands, the taking of which would allow the United States to sever Japan's links to its empire through the combined use of air and sea power, from the new B-29 bombers to the massive carrier strike forces. That the American decision-making process only partially supported his plan ended up causing far greater losses, and costing far more in treasure, for the United States. On the other hand, if King had the most sophisticated understanding of how the war would be won in the Pacific, his wilful refusal in early 1942 to send enough American escort vessels to the Caribbean and Atlantic seaboard ended up costing the Allies huge amounts in unnecessary escort vessel construction in 1943 and 1944.

Leahy's vision of air and sea power was the most straight-forward. He believed that if the Allies established dominance in both against Germany and Japan, they would win the war. When it came to the war in Europe, he arrived too late to make much of a difference in the U-boat war, and he was more than happy to allow Arnold and the USAAF to decide their own campaign priorities for strategic bombing. When it came to the Pacific, he made perhaps his most interesting interjection on the subject of air and sea power near the end of the war. In his view, Japan's defeat was guaranteed the moment the United States had established air and sea superiority around the Japanese home islands. He believed it unnecessary either to invade Japan, which he believed would lead to the loss of far too many American lives, or to drop the atom bomb, which he believed was a barbaric weapon akin to poison gas. To Leahy, victory had already been achieved, and the United States should simply continue to use air and sea power until the Japanese were compelled to accept reality.

Before ending this book, a few words should be said about the importance of mobility in warfare in general. World War II might seem exceptional because air and sea power allowed the British and Americans to attack German and Japanese production in so many ways before this equipment was used on the battlefield. This does not mean, however, that the lessons of these campaigns are not applicable today (or would have been applicable long before World War II). Crushing an enemy on the battlefield, the favored notion of both real and armchair generals everywhere, is an extremely difficult thing to do. This is true even in the great asymmetric campaigns of the late twentieth and the early twenty-first century. American military power, which can be overwhelming in any area of battle, usually has not ended up providing a clear-cut political victory for the United States. In wars such as those in Vietnam and Afghanistan, even "winning" engagement after engagement has resulted in the United States losing the political war. In both of those wars, killing the enemy in large numbers did not result in success.

That is because, except for killing every one of the combatants fighting against you, the only way to "win" a war is to stop your enemy

100 During the surrender ceremony in Tokyo Bay on September 2, 1945, as a sign of victory American air and sea power was put on full display.

from moving. Particularly in asymmetric wars, the less-advanced enemy will always be able to regroup and re-equip if he or she can maintain mobility. They will then come back year after year. The lesson of this is the same as that for World War II. Only by stopping an enemy's movement can you hope to win a war.

NOTES

Introduction

1 The period of late 1942 and early 1943, through the surrender at Stalingrad, is often seen as the pivotal moment for the destruction of the German army. See Citino, *Death of the Wehrmacht: The German Campaigns of 1942* (Lawrence, KS, 2007), pp. 303–9.

2 *Daily Telegraph*, October 19, 2012; *Daily Mail*, October 27, 2012, http://www.dailymail.co.uk/news/article-2224077/Battle-El-Alamein-Veterans-bloody-gather-heartfelt-70th-anniversary-memorial-service.html. For a BBC television report on the commemoration; see http://www.bbc.co.uk/news/world-20014747 (accessed September 9, 2014).

3 For examples of reports about Stalingrad's seventieth anniversary from the UK, France, India and USA, Australia see www.scotsman.com/news/international/stalingrad-victory-marked-by-dictator-s-rehabilitation-1-2772805; www.france24.com/en/20130202-russia-marks-70th-anniversary-battle-stalingrad-world-war-two; www.ibtimes.com/stalingrad-70-years-after-decisive-world-war-ii-battle-another-war-over-citys-name-1055562; www.telegraphindia.com/1130205/jsp/opinion/story_16500625.jsp; www.theaustralian.com.au/news/world/old-foes-remember-horror-of-stalingrad-70-years-on/story-fnb64oi6-1226566992385; www.nytimes.com/2013/02/01/world/europe/volgograd-named-stalingrad-again-at-least-sometimes.html?_r=0. (accessed September 9, 2014).

4 Clairmont, "Stalingrad, Hitler's Nemesis," *Economic and Political Weekly* (July 2003), 2819–23.

5 Kimball, "Stalingrad: A Chance for Choices," *Journal of Military History*, vol. 60, 1 (Jan. 1996), 89–114. Kimball argues not that Stalingrad was a decisive

victory in the war, but that it changed the tenor of US–USSR relations, making it necessary for the USA to start judging what the USSR would be in the future.

6 www.history.com/this-day-in-history/largest-tank-battle-in-history-ends.

7 See Chapter 8.

8 See Chapter 8.

9 Playfair, *The Mediterranean and Middle East, vol. IV: The Destruction of Axis Forces in Africa* (London, 1966), pp. 9–11. Adding in Italian tanks pushes this number up a little. One estimate is that Panzerarmee Afrika had 600 tanks in total at the start of the battle, and ended up losing 450 of these. See Fred Majdalany, *The Battle of El Alamein: Fortress in the Sand* (Philadelphia, 1965), p. 143.

10 Playfair, *The Mediterranean and Middle East, vol. IV*, p. 34.

11 See chapter 8.

12 Parshall and Tully, *Shattered Sword: The Untold Story of the Battle of Midway* (Dulles, VA, 2007). Appendix 10 has a list of the Japanese pilots and their fates; it is striking to see that the overwhelming majority of them survived and were recovered by the Japanese.

13 In 2000 I published an article which argued that, just taking into account battlefield effort, the Germans were expending more effort fighting the British and Americans in 1943 than they were fighting the Russians. See O'Brien, "East versus West in the Defeat of Nazi Germany", *Journal of Strategic Studies*, vol. 23, 2 (2000).

14 Historians who focus on the Eastern Front like to accuse western historians of ignoring the USSR's contribution to the defeat of Germany. David Glantz, who has written a series of superb and detailed histories of the war in the east, is perhaps the most important to make this charge. In his 2005 history of the Red Army between 1941 and 1943 he accuses other western historians of World War II of "masking" the Soviet contribution to victory. "Ironically, despite its massive scale, scope, cost and global impact, the Soviet Union's Great Patriotic War remains in large part obscure and imperfectly understood by Westerners and Russians alike. Worse still, this obscurity and misunderstanding has perverted the history of World War II overall by masking the Red Army's and Soviet state's contributions to ultimate allied victory" (Glantz, *Colossus Reborn: The Red Army at War, 1941–1943* (Lawrence, KS, 2005), p. xv. A similar statement was recently made in another solid book written about Operation Barbarossa. In it David Stahel accuses western historians of "belittling" the Soviet contribution to victory. "Many western representations of World War II therefore offer a slanted perspective which belittles the contribution of the Soviet Union and consequently hinders our understanding of the eastern front in World War II" (Stahel, *Operation Barbarossa and Germany's Defeat in the East* (Cambridge, 2009), p. 21).

15 Kennedy, *Engineers of Victory: The Problem Solvers who Turned the Tide in the Second World War* (London, 2013), p. 183.

16 Burleigh, *The Third Reich: A New History* (London, 2000), p. 485.

17 Burleigh, *Moral Combat: A History of World War 2* (London, 2010), p. 187.

18 Roberts, "Stalin's Victory? The Soviet Union and World War II," *History Ireland*, vol. 16, 1 (Jan.–Feb. 2008), 42. This article is a textbook example of the extraordinary assumptions that some people make about the centrality of combat on the Eastern Front. Roberts claims that the USSR was responsible for destroying 77,000 enemy aircraft (one presumes the vast majority of which were German). I have no idea where he has obtained this figure, but it bears no resemblance to reality.

19 Lowe, *Inferno: The Devastation of Hamburg, 1943* (London, 2007), p. 323.

20 It is interesting to see that even books devoted solely to Anglo-American campaigns feel the need to point out how relatively small these events were when compared with the fighting on the Eastern Front. For just one example, see Rick Atkinson, *An Army at Dawn: The War in North Africa 1942–43* (New York, 2002), p. 539.

21 Beaumont, "The General History of the Second World War," *International History Review*, vol. 14, 4 (Nov. 1992), 758.

22 Weinberg, *A World at Arms: A Global History of World War II* (Cambridge, 1994), p. 608; Calvocoressi, Wint and Pritchard, *Total War: The Causes and Courses of the Second World War* (London, 1995), p. 510.

23 Murray and Millett, *A War to be Won: Fighting the Second World War* (Cambridge, MA, 2000), pp. 410, 483.

24 Hastings, *Armageddon: The Battle for Germany 1944–45* (London, 2005), p. 508.

25 Roberts, *The Storm of War: A New History of the Second World War* (London, 2008).

26 Roberts, *Masters and Commanders: How Four Titans Won the War in the West* (London, 2010), p. 573.

27 O'Brien, "East versus West in the Defeat of Nazi Germany," 91–2.

28 Pape, *Bombing to Win: Air Power and Coercion in War* (London, 1996), pp. 157, 311–12; see also Pape, "The True Worth of Air Power," *Foreign Affairs* (Mar./Apr. 2004), 117. In this later piece, Pape dismisses strategic air power and claims that it was really only effective in a tactical role in wars before the 1980s.

29 Gentile, *How Effective is Strategic Bombing? Lessons Learned from World War II to Kosovo* (New York, 2001), pp. 55, 64–5; Ellis, *Allied Strategy and Tactics in the Second World War* (New York, 1990), pp. 213–21; Ross, *Strategic Bombing by the United States in World War II: The Myths and Facts* (London, 2003).

30 Milward, *The German Economy at War* (London, 1965), pp. 162–3;
   Edward R. Zilbert, *Albert Speer and the Nazi Ministry of Arms* (Rutherford,
   NJ, 1981), p. 18.
31 Beaumount, "The General History of the Second World War," p. 757.
32 Kennedy, *Engineers of Victory*, p. 85.
33 Corrigan, *The Second World War: A Military History* (London, 2010),
   pp. 451–2; Beevor, *The Second World War* (New York, 2012).
34 Beevor, *The Second World War*, provides no significant analysis of the
   strategic air war in 1943 and ignores huge issues such as the
   Crossbow campaign versus the V-2 rocket (neither of which is listed in
   the book's index).
35 Zeiler, *Annihilation: A Global History of World War II* (Oxford, 2011),
   pp. 235–6.
36 Hastings, *Bomber Command* (London, 1979), pp. 231–4.
37 Biddle, *Rhetoric and Reality in Air Warfare: The Evolution of British and
   American Ideas about Strategic Bombing* (Princeton, 2002), pp. 223–6.
38 Schaffer, *Wings of Judgement: American Bombing in World War II* (Oxford,
   1985), pp. 64–7.
39 Sherry, *The Rise of American Air Power: The Creation of Armageddon*
   (London, 1987), p. 158.
40 Weinberg, *A World at Arms*, pp. 577–8; Murray and Millett, *A War to be Won*,
   pp. 310–16. More recently, Williamson Murray has made a strong argument in
   favor of both the impact of area bombing and the increase of RAF bombing
   accuracy from 1943 to 1945. See Murray, *War, Strategy and Military
   Effectiveness* (Cambridge, 2011), pp. 242–56.
41 Tooze, *The Wages of Destruction: The Making and Breaking of the Nazi
   Economy* (London, 2007), pp. 597–602.
42 Gentile, *How Effective is Strategic Bombing?*, pp. 1–9.
43 It is interesting to see how often USSBS estimates appear throughout World
   War II historiography. Joerg Friedrich uses it throughout his history of
   bombing, and even accepts at face value its estimate that German production in
   1943 was reduced by 9 percent due to strategic bombing. Friedrich, *The Fire:
   The Bombing of Germany 1940–1945* (New York, 2006), p. 89. When it
   comes to Japanese data, it seems that, as with Germany, that which was
   collected was broadly correct, though there were some areas of omission, and
   the analyses, as always, could be questioned. See Pauer (ed.), *Japan's War
   Economy* (London, 1999), pp. 189–90.
44 Horowitz, "Were there Strategic Oil Targets in Japan in 1945?" *Air Power
   History* (Spring 2004), 34.
45 Gentile, "Advocacy or Assessment? The United States Strategic Bombing
   Survey of Germany and Japan," *Pacific Historical Review*, vol. 66, 1 (Feb.
   1997), 79.

46 Arnold, *Allied Air War and Urban Memory: The Legacy of the Strategic Bombing in Germany* (Cambridge, 2011), pp. 7–8.

47 USSBS, European Report 1, pp. 15–16.

48 Gian Gentile has written a great deal about the USSBS in the past twenty years, and he strikes a decidedly skeptical tone. He believes that the USSBS on the whole discovered what the USAAF wanted it to discover. Gentile, *How Effective is Strategic Bombing?*, p. 78.

49 A copy of the UK Strategic Bombing Survey (UKSBS) has been published as *The Strategic Air War against Germany 1939–1945*, introduction by Sebastian Cox (London, 1998).

50 See also Zuckerman, *From Apes to Warlords: The Autobiography (1904–1946) of Solly Zuckerman* (London, 1978), pp. 343–4.

51 Werrell, "The Strategic Bombing of Germany in World War II: Costs and Accomplishments," *Journal of American History*, vol. 73, 3 (Dec. 1986), 702–13. Werrell, one of the best and most measured historians of American strategic air power, still hedges his bets on just how crucial strategic air power was in 1944. He believes it was extremely important, but also qualifies his conclusions quite substantially (see pp. 712–13). For more of those who believe that strategic bombing in 1944 and 1945 made a real impact in defeating Germany, see Ehlers, *Targeting the Third Reich: Air Intelligence and the Allied Bombing Campaigns* (Lawrence, KS, 2009). The importance of Anglo-American strategic bombing in 1944 in destroying German production and leading to a swifter end to the war is also part of some general histories of that period, such as Kershaw, *The End: Hitler's Germany 1944–45* (London, 2011), pp. 79–80.

52 Craven and Cate (eds.), *The Army Air Forces in World War II*, vol. 3 (Washington, DC, 1983), pp. 303–4; Davis, *Carl A. Spaatz and the Air War in Europe* (Washington, DC, 1993).

53 Mierzejewski, *The Collapse of the German War Economy: 1944–1945* (Chapel Hill, NC, 1988), pp. 180–7.

54 Buckley, *Air Power in the Age of Total War* (Bloomington, IN, 1999), pp. 166–8.

55 Overy, *Why the Allies Won* (London, 1995), p. 98.

56 Overy, *Why the Allies Won* (London, 1995), pp. 1–2.

57 Overy, *The Air War 1939–45* (New York, 1991).

58 Overy, *War and Economy in the Third Reich* (Oxford, 2002), pp. 373–4.

59 Overy, *The Bombing War: Europe 1939–1945* (London, 2013), pp. 343–4, 616, 619.

60 Spector, *Eagle against the Sun: The American War with Japan* (New York, 1985), pp. 504–6; Weinberg, *A World at Arms*, pp. 869–70.

61 Schaffer, *Wings of Judgement*, p. 148.

62 There is an excellent article which explores the different pressures placed on the USSBS in its analysis of Japanese defeat which anyone interested in the subject

should read: Gentile, "Shaping the Battlefield, 'For the Future': The United States Strategic Bombing Survey's Evaluation of the American Air War against Japan," *Journal of Military History*, vol. 64, 4 (Oct. 2000), 1085–112.

63 USSBS, Pacific Report 1, pp. 20–2.

64 USSBS, Pacific Report 1, pp. 13–5.

65 USSBS, Pacific Report 1, Anderson Appendix, July 11, 1946.

66 Craven and Cate (eds.), *The Army Air Forces in World War II*, vol. 5, pp. 752–4.

67 Sherry, *The Rise of American Air Power*, pp. 285–7.

68 Biddle, *Rhetoric and Reality*, pp. 267–70.

69 Frank, *Downfall: The End of the Imperial Japanese Empire* (New York, 2001), pp. 306–7.

70 Murray and Millett, *A War to be Won*, pp. 507–8.

71 See Chapter 10.

72 Sadkovich, "Understanding Defeat: Reappraising Italy's Role in World War II," *Journal of Contemporary History*, vol. 24, 1 (Jan. 1989), 50.

1 The dominance of air and sea production

1 *Germany and the Second World War*, vol. V/II (Oxford, 2003), p. 597.

2 The word "panzer," which has become widely used, actually referred only to German tanks – vehicles with a rotating turret. These included the famous Mark IVs, Mark Vs (Panther) and Mark VIs (Tiger). However, panzers of this type made up only approximately half of German armored vehicle construction. The other half were self-propelled guns, armored vehicles with guns with similar calibers to the panzers, but with a non-rotating turret. The gun could swivel a small amount from its forward firing position, but it was up to the tank driver to position the self-propelled gun in such a way that they could hit the target. As self-propelled guns did not have to be engineered so heavily, they were easier to construct. Many of them also became well known, such as the Jagdpanther and Jagdtiger. Throughout this book I will use the term AFV (armored fighting vehicles) to refer to overall armored production which includes both types.

3 For a while it was very common to portray Speer as an economic genius who came in and helped transform the German armaments industry. See Joachim Fest, *Speer, the Final Verdict* (London, 1999), pp. 138–42. However, Speer's reputation as an economic organizer has come under increasing attack during the past few decades; see Budrass, Scherner and Streb, *Demystifying the German "Armament Miracle" during World War II: New Insights from the Annual Audits of German Aircraft Producers*, Yale University Economic Growth Center, Discussion Paper 905, Jan. 2005. For a more pro-Speer view, which was more common in the earlier historiography, see Zilbert, *Albert Speer and the Nazi Ministry of Arms*.

4 King, *The Two Worlds of Albert Speer: Reflections of a Nuremberg Prosecutor* (New York, 1997). King was one of Speer's prosecutors during the war crimes trials and clearly became fascinated with and attracted to the personality of the German. During the interviews with Speer conducted by the USSBS team in May and June 1945, he was extremely cooperative and seems to have impressed his questioners. During these interviews he even went out of his way to advise the Americans how best to bomb Japan so as to do maximum damage to his erstwhile ally (in this case he advised attacking Japanese power production). See Spaatz MSS, Reel 135, Speer Interview, May 20, 1945, p. 1.

5 An interesting and even-handed analysis of this attempt can be found in Billson, "Inside Albert Speer: Secrets of Moral Evasion," *The Antioch Review*, vol. 37, 4 (Autumn 1979), 460–74. For another view that attempts to deconstruct the picture of Speer constructed by the man himself, see Schmidt, *Albert Speer: The End of a Myth* (London, 1985).

6 Albert Speer, *Infiltration: How Heinrich Himmler Schemed to Build an SS Industrial Empire* (New York, 1981). From the beginning of the work Speer describes himself as a "technocrat" (p. 10) who was not directly guilty of German atrocities – though he does apologize profusely for not trying to discover more about them.

7 Speer, *Infiltration*, p. 237. He also describes the process in one of his post-war interviews. See Spaatz MSS, Reel 135, Speer Interview, May 20, 1945, p. 3.

8 Speer, *Infiltration*, p. 35. Speer does not seem to have any reason to inflate the Luftwaffe's dominant position in German arms production as he was most concerned at this point in proving relative efficiency between his factories and those of the SS.

9 USSBS, Goering Interview, June 29, 1945, p. 2.

10 Goldsmith, "The Power of Victory: Munitions Output in World War II," *Military Affairs*, 10 (Spring 1946), 72. This article, which unfortunately has been used a number of times in more recent work, was written before the details of German and Japanese production were known. Its erroneous assumption that 60 percent of the German war economy was producing for the land war is the most glaring mistake, but it also significantly overestimates ground production for the USA, the UK and Japan.

11 Harrison, "Resource Mobilization for World War II: The USA, UK, USSR, and Germany, 1938–1945," *Economic History Review*, vol. 41, 2 (May 1988), 171–92. This article uses Goldsmith throughout. Also see Ranki, *The Economics of World War II* (Vienna, 1993), p. 227, for another use of Goldsmith that would lead to an overvaluing of land armaments.

12 For one of the best challenges to the Blitzkrieg economy idea, see Overy, "Hitler's War and the German Economy: A Reinterpretation," *Economic History Review*, vol. 35, 2 (May 1982), 290–1.

13 Overy, *War and Economy in the Third Reich*, pp. 311–14.

14 Gregor, *Daimler-Benz in the Third Reich* (New Haven, CT, 1998), p. 119. In this analysis, much of the groundwork for the increase in production was laid before Speer took office, though he did help things along.

15 Below, *At Hitler's Side: The Memoirs of Hitler's Luftwaffe Adjutant 1937–1945* (London, 2004), see pp. 198, 230.

16 *Germany and the Second World War*, vol. V/II, p. 602.

17 Overy, *War and Economy in the Third Reich*, pp. 356–7.

18 Abelshauser, "Germany, Guns, Butter and Economic Miracles," in Harrison (ed.), *The Economics of World War II: Six Great Powers in International Competition* (Cambridge, 1998), p. 172.

19 FO 1031-148, Speer Interview Notes, May 28, 1945, p. 2.

20 USSBS, Saur Interview, May 23, 1945, p. 3.

21 USSBS, Christian Interview, May 19, 1945, p. 4.

22 FO 1031-148, translated document from Speer Ministry, "On the German Economic Situation 1943–44," p. 12.

23 *Germany and the Second World War*, vol. V/II, p. 598.

24 USSBS, European Report 3, p. 162. The panzer calculation in this section includes tanks, assault guns and self-propelled guns, not just tanks.

25 FO 1031-148, translated document from Speer Ministry, "On the German Economic Situation 1943–44," p. 11.

26 This is because of the impact of strategic bombing on German aircraft production in the second half of 1943. See Chapter 8.

27 FO 1031-148, translated document from Speer Ministry, "On the German Economic Situation 1943–44," p. 11.

28 USSBS, European Report 3, p. 145.

29 Below, *At Hitler's Side*, see pp. 148, 169–70, 182.

30 USSBS, Keitel Interview, May 2, 1945, p. 4.

31 USSBS, Fleisher Interview, May 19, 1945, p. 6.

32 USSBS, Fleisher Interview, May 19, 1945, p. 7.

33 Arnold MSS, Reel 190, The Contribution of Air Power to the Defeat of Germany, Appendix L.

34 Hitler knew how important Milch was. Along with only a handful of other senior officers, he received one of Hitler's largest cash bribes for loyalty during the war: RM 250,000. See Norman and Goda, "Black Marks: Hitler's Bribery of his Senior Officers during World War II," *Journal of Modern History*, vol. 72, 2 (June 2000), 433.

35 WO 208-4340, Milch Interview Report, July 9, 1945, p. 5.
36 USSBS, Fleisher Interview, May 2, 1945. In this folder there is a copy of the letter Speer sent out on January 26, 1945 listing the thirteen highest priority weapons systems (all of equal priority) which would last until the end of the war. Panzers were not listed but assault guns were. On the other hand, all the major air–sea weapons were on the list.
37 USSBS, European Report 92, p. 18. The subsequent percentages all come from this citation.
38 Herwig, "Germany and the Battle of the Atlantic", in Roger Chickering, Stig Foerster and Bend Grevier (eds.), *A World at Total War: Global Conflict and the Politics of Destruction, 1937–1945* (Cambridge, 2005), p. 80.
39 Roskill, *The War at Sea 1939–45*, 3 vols. (London, 1954–61), vol. III, pt 1, pp. 17–18. See also Barnett, *Engage the Enemy More Closely: The Royal Navy in the Second World War* (London, 1991), pp. 802–4.
40 USSBS, European Report 92, pp. 1–2. Until 1943 submarine construction only received 36 percent of the labor force working on all naval construction. At that point, submarine construction was given its own divison.
41 USSBS, Saur Interview, May 23, 1945, p. 3.
42 Speer, *Infiltration*, p. 35. Speer does not seem to have any reason to inflate the Luftwaffe's dominant position in German arms production as he was most concerned at this point in proving relative efficiency between his factories and those of the SS. Alan Milward has a figure of 1.94 million men working in all army production at this point and 780,000 working for the navy/shipbuilding. Milward, *The German Economy at War*, p. 114.
43 See the discussion in Chapter 9 on dispersal of German production.
44 Webster and Frankland, *The Strategic Air Offensive against Germany 1939–1945*, 4 vols. (London, 1961), vol. IV, p. 345.
45 Gregor, *Daimler-Benz in the Third Reich*, p. 115.
46 FO 1031-148, Speer Interview, June 26, 1945, p. 7.
47 FO 1041-148, Speer Interview, May 28, 1945, p. 2.
48 USSBS, Fleisher Interview, May 19, 1945, p. 4.
49 USSBS, Tank Interview, translated Tank letter, July 7, 1942.
50 USSBS, Frydag Interview, July 9, 1945, p. 7.
51 For the early design history of the HE-177, see Griehl and Dressel, *Heinkel, HE 177, 277, 274* (Shrewsbury, 1998), pp. 9–16.
52 Griehl and Dressel, *Heinkel, HE 177, 277, 274*, pp. 92–3.
53 Heiber and Glantz (eds.), *Hiter and his Generals: Military Conferences, 1942–1945* (New York 2003), p. 414.
54 USSBS, Freydag Interview, May 19, 1945, p. 3.
55 USSBS, Tank Interview, April 17 and 24, 1945, p. 15.

56 Spaatz MSS, Reel 134, Milch Interview, May 23, 1945, p. 8. It is interesting to see Milch being so critical of Daimler-Benz engines. The Air Ministry had constant problems with aircraft engine building during the war. In 1943 and 1944, BMW production of engines fell well behind its expected target, and the Luftwaffe ended up changing the management of the company. See James, *The Nazi Dictatorship and the Deutsche Bank* (Cambridge, 2004), pp. 204–5.

57 Below, *At Hitler's Side*, see pp. 182–3.

58 Spaatz MSS, 134, Goering Interview, May 10, 1945, p. 9.

59 *Germany and the Second World War*, vol. V/II, pp. 639–42.

60 Spaatz MSS 134, Seiler Interview, May 16, 1945, p. 1.

61 Spaatz MSS 134, Seiler Interview, May 16, 1945, p. 1.

62 Some of the facilities still exist, such as those that were buried in Walpersberg.

63 Spaatz MSS 135, Speer Interview, May 21, 1945, p. 6.

64 At one point Speer claimed a V-2 was equal to six or seven fighters and at another to five or six, so I have opted to describe it as six. See Spaatz MSS 135, Speer Interview, May 21, 1945, p. 6; FO 1031-141, Speer Interview, May 28, 1945, p. 5.

65 Neufeld, *The Rocket and the Reich: Peenemunde and the Coming of the Ballistic Missile Era* (New York, 1995), pp. 190–1.

66 Neufeld, *The Rocket and the Reich*, pp. 272–3.

67 King and Kutta, *Impact: The History of Germany's V-Weapons in World War II* (Rockville Center, NY, 1998), p. 249. The only V-2s targeted somewhere else were those fired at the Remagen Bridge in 1945 to try to destroy it before the Americans were able to send many forces across.

68 Murray, *Luftwaffe: Strategy for Defeat, 1933–1945* (London, 1985), p. 96.

69 Shachtman, *Laboratory Warriors: How Allied Science and Technology Tipped the Balance in World War II* (New York, 2003), p. 39.

70 *Germany and the Second World War*, vol. V/II, p. 743.

71 Hancock and Gowing, *British War Economy* (London, 1949), p. 282.

72 Postan, *History of the Second World War: British War Production* (London, 1952), p. 12.

73 Millett and Murray, *Military Effectiveness*, vol. III, p. 114.

74 See figure 88 for an example of a British aircraft carrier that was able to survive and quickly return to action after a direct kamikaze hit because of its armored flight deck.

75 Ferris, "The Symbol and Substance of Seapower: Great Britain and the United States and the One-Power Standard," in McKercher (ed.), *Anglo-American Relations in the 1920s* (London, 1991); McKercher, "Wealth, Power and the New International Order: Britain and the American Challenge in the 1920s," *Diplomatic History*, vol. 12, 4 (1988).

76 Webster and Frankland, *The Strategic Air Offensive against Germany 1939–1945*, vol. IV, Appendix 41, p. 440.

77 Ellis, *Victory in the West*, 2 vols. (London, 1962, 1968), vol. II, Appendix VII, p. 407.

78 Hancock and Gowing, *British War Economy*, p. 285.

79 Hancock and Gowing, *British War Economy*, p. 452.

80 Air 8/692, "Labour for Aircraft Programme," July 10, 1942.

81 Rolfe, "Manpower Allocation in Great Britain during World War II," *Industrial and Labor Relations Review*, vol. 5, 2 (Jan. 1952), 188–9. The high wages were important to Rolfe: the main argument of this article is that using wage differentials was a far better way to channel worker numbers than forced allocation.

82 Postan, *British War Production*, p. 225 and Hancock, *British War Economy*, p. 453 for two different discussions of this issue.

83 Postan, *British War Production*, pp. 159–60.

84 In 1941 and 1942 Beaverbrook was one of the few British war leaders, other than Winston Churchill, who had regular inside access to Franklin Roosevelt, mostly through Harry Hopkins. Hopkins, like Beaverbrook, believed that aircraft construction was the most important element in World War II production and the two became very close during this time.

85 Edgerton, *Britain's War Machine: Weapons, Resources and Experts in the Second World War* (Oxford, 2011), pp. 126–7.

86 Gilbert (ed.), *The Churchill War Papers* (London, 1993–2000), vol. III, p. 994.

87 Gilbert (ed.), *The Churchill War Papers*, vol. III, p. 998.

88 Postan, *British War Production*, p. 161.

89 Webster and Frankland, *The Strategic Air Offensive against Germany 1939–1945*, vol. IV, Appendix 49, p. 496.

90 See Chapter 3.

91 Hurstfield, *The Control of Raw Materials* (London, 1953), pp. 346–8. The Air Ministry played a very large role in the workings of Britain's light alloy industry throughout the war; see pp. 373–5.

92 Sandys MSS, 2-2-12, Memorandum, March 24, 1943.

93 Sandys MSS, 2-2-12, Tank Supply Memo, July 8, 1943.

94 Sandys MSS, 2-2-12, War Cabinet Minutes, May 3, 1943.

95 Sandys MSS, 2-2-12, Minutes of Ministry of Supply Meeting, December 23, 1943.

96 Sandys MSS, 2-2-12, Tank Policy Memo, January 12, 1944.

97 Air 8/693, War Cabinet Minutes, January 7, 1943.

98 Postan, *British War Production*, p. 304.

99 Postan, *British War Production*, p. 304.

100 *Statistical Digest of the War*, p. 135.

101 See Chapter 7.

102 Edgerton, *Britain's War Machine*, p. 212.

103 Among the production stories from the dominions, Canada's is the one that needs some comment. During the war 16,000 aircraft were built in Canada, of which almost 4,600 went to the RAF. Of these, the most important were 1,051 Hurricanes, 307 Catalinas, 395 Lancasters and 961 Mosquitoes. Between 1943 and 1945, all UK purchases from Canada (including munitions, food and raw materials) totalled about $1.6 billion. Hall, *North American Supply* (London, 1955), pp. 25, 242.

104 Lash, *Roosevelt and Churchill 1939–1941: The Partnership that Saved the West* (London, 1976), pp. 40–51.

105 Craven and Cate, *The Army Air Forces in World War II*, vol. I, p. 107.

106 USSBS, European Report 4, Figure VI-6. The annual production rate for 1941 was approximately 20,000.

107 Craven and Cate, *The Army Air Forces in World War II*, vol. VI, p. 352.

108 Much of the discussion of American production in the war dwells on the vast quantities and tends not to delve into the idea of having to make hard choices. See Kennedy, *The Rise and Fall of the Great Powers* (New York, 1988), pp. 457–9; Showalter, "Global Yet Not Total: The US War Effort and its Consequences," in Chickering *et al.* (eds.), *A World at Total War*, pp. 110–16; Ranki, *The Economics of the Second World War*, pp. 212–16.

109 Craven and Cate, *The Army Air Forces in World War II*, vol. VI, p. 345. The official histories put the number of workers building American aircraft at 2.1 million.

110 Craven and Cate, *The Army Air Forces in World War II*, vol. VI, p. 315.

111 FDR PSF 10, FDR to Stimson, January 3, 1942.

112 See War Progress Report, May 8, 1942, in FDR PSF 172-2. This report has monthly updates as well as cumulative totals of expenditure from July 1941. The cumulative expenditure on munitions between July 1, 1940 and March 31, 1942 was $102,308 million of which aircraft construction had received $28,619 million (28 percent). The specific monthly expenditures varied due to production cycle. During the one for February 1942, 34 percent was spent on the aircraft construction program.

113 Werrell, *Blankets of Fire: US Bombers over Japan during World War II* (Washington, DC, 1996), pp. 56–74.

114 Werrell, *Blankets of Fire*, p. 82.

115 Boyne, "The B-29's Battle of Kansas," *Air Force Magazine*, vol. 95, 2 (Feb. 2012), 95.

116 Hopkins MSS, "Summary Data of Military Objectives," April 1942.

117 According to Nelson, in February 1942 aircraft were given an A-1-a rating to prioritize their production, a move that had a real "psychological" impact. See FDR PSF 7-8, Nelson to Hopkins, April 20, 1942.

118 *The Papers of Dwight David Eisenhower: The War Years*, vol. I (Baltimore, 1970), Eisenhower to Marshall, February 20, 1942, 122–3.

119 Rockoff, "The United States: From Ploughshares to Swords," in Harrison, *The Economics of World War II*, p. 117.

120 Herman, *Freedom's Forge: How American Business Produced Victory in World War II* (New York, 2012), p. 279. See also Chapter 7 for aluminum losses.

121 FDR PSF 3-4, Nelson to FDR, August 1942.

122 FDR PSF 3-4, FDR to Marshall, August 24, 1942.

123 FDR PSF 3-4, Marshall to FDR, April 1, 1942.

124 FDR PSF 3-4, FDR to Marshall, August 27, 1942.

125 Hopkins MSS, 125, Memorandum for the president, October 1942.

126 Hopkins MSS, 125, Somervell to Hopkins, October 21, 1942.

127 Hopkins MSS, 125, Hopkins to FDR, October 20, 1942.

128 Hopkins MSS, 125, FDR to Nelson, October 29, 1942.

129 Leighton and Coakley, *United States Army in World War II: Global Logistics and Strategy, 1940–1943* (Washington, DC 1955), pp. 632–3.

130 Leighton and Coakley, *United States Army in World War II: Global Logistics and Strategy, 1940–1943*, p. 302.

131 FDR PSF 172-2, War Progress Report, October 2, 1943, p. 12.

132 FDR PSF 172-2, War Progress Report, January 15, 1944, p. 4.

133 Hopkins MSS, 24, War Progress Report, February 1944, p. 5.

134 Hopkins MSS, 24, War Progress Report, February 1944, p. 5.

135 Hopkins MSS, 24, War Progress Report, July 1944, p. 2.

136 FDR, PSF 11, War Progress Report, January 1945, p. 10.

137 The War Progress Report of November 20, 1942, given to FDR and his inner circle, was focused on tanks (see copy kept in FDR PSF 172-2). "Tank production constitutes only about 5 percent of total munitions output as now scheduled."

138 FDR PSF 172-2, War Progress Report, September 18, 1943, p. 7.

139 FDR PSF 11, War Progress Report, February 24, 1945, p. 9.

140 Craven and Cate, *The Army Air Forces in World War II*, vol. VI, pp. 239–40.

141 FDR PSF 11, War Progress Report, February 24, 1945, p. 9.

142 See Chapter 11.

143 See Chapter 7.

144 Hopkins MSS, 24, War Production File, US War Production, Review of 1942 and Prospects for 1943, p. 22.

145 *US Navy at War 1941–1945*, Official Report by Ernest King (Washington, DC, 1946), Appendix B, available at http://www.ibiblio.org/hyperwar/USN/USNatWar/index.html.

146 FDR PSF 11, Commodity Chart Book, May 18, 1942.

147 FDR PSF 172-2, War Progress Report, November 20, 1942, p. 2.

148 FDR PSF 6, Combined Productions Program Report, July 1, 1944, p. 6.

149 FDR PSF 6, Combined Productions Program Report, July 1, 1944, p. 5.

150 FDR PSF 172-2, War Progress Report, October 2, 1943, p. 16.

151 FDR PSF 172-2, War Progress Report, May 13, 1944, p. 3.

152 FDR PSF 172-2, War Progress Report, May 13, 1944, p. 3.

153 USSBS, Kawamura Interview, November 23, 1945, p. 7.

154 NAUSA, USSBS, Sanada Interview, November 2, 1945, pp. 3–4.

155 USSBS, Yoshizumi and Sato Interview, October 15, 1945, p. 2.

156 USSBS, Yoshizumi and Sato Interview, October 15, 1945, p. 3.

157 Morgan, "The Japanese War Economy: A Review," *Far Eastern Quarterly*, vol. 8, 1 (Nov. 1948), 65.

158 USSBS, Goko Interview, October 29, 1945, p. 7.

159 USSBS, Endo Interview, November 3, 1945, p. 3.

160 Cohen, *Japanese Economic History 1930–1960*, vol. II (London, 2000), pp. 209–14.

161 Keegan, *World War II* (London, 1989).

162 Beevor, *The Second World War* (New York, 2012). Only ten of fifty chapters are concerned with the war in Asia or the Pacific.

163 See Chapter 10.

164 Nakamura and Odaka (eds.), *The Economic History of Japan: 1600–1900* (Oxford 1999), p. 291. For an analysis of the increase in shipbuilding, see pp. 267–9.

165 USSBS, Pacific Report 53, p. 215.

166 *Statistical Digest of the War*, p. 133.

167 USSBS, Pacific Report 54, p. 55.

168 *Statistical Digest of the War*, p. 135.

169 FDR PSF 172-2, War Progress Report, November 27, 1942.

170 HW 1/3177, Japanese Ambassador, translated report of conversation with Speer, August 11, 1944.

171 Sherwood, *The White House Papers of Harry L. Hopkins*, vol. I (London, 1948), p. 329.

172 FDR, PSF 6, Combined Production Program, December 31, 1943. The USSR received 145 million pounds of ingot aluminum in 1943, while the United States Navy received 121 million pounds.

173 Weeks, *Russia's Life Saver: Lend-Lease Aid to the USSR in World War II* (Lanham, MD, 2004), p. 150.

174 Muller, *The German Air War in Russia* (Baltimore, 1992), pp. 192, 221.

175 See Galland Interview in Spaatz MSS 134.

176 Morgan, "The Japanese War Economy," 69.

2 The air and sea war and the phases of equipment destruction

1 Sakai with Gaidin, *Samurai!* (New York, 2001), pp. 207–34 gives a detailed description of the combat Sakai went through on August 8, 1942.

2 Sakai, *Samurai!*, p. 278.
3 Sakai, *Samurai!*, p. 279.
4 USSBS, Kawabe Interview, November 26, 1945, p. 3.
5 Spaatz MSS, Box 135, Speer and Baumbach Interview, May 18, 1945, p. 11.
6 USSBS, Kaether Interview, April 24, 1945, p. 1.
7 Parshall and Tully, *Shattered Sword*, p. 420.
8 USSBS, Pacific Report 15, "The Japanese Aircraft Industry," p. 155.
9 USSBS, Fukamizu Interview, Appendix B. Fukamizu had access to excellent statistics of Japanese naval aircraft losses, and reproduced some invaluable charts for the USSBS, including a monthly breakdown of losses for the entire war.
10 USSBS, Fukamizu Interview, Appendix B.
11 Morison, *History of United States Naval Operations in World War II*, vol. VIII, p. 319.
12 USSBS, Fukamizu Interview, Appendix B.
13 USSBS, Pacific Report 15, "The Japanese Aircraft Industry," p. 168.
14 USSBS, Fukamizu Interview, Appendix B.
15 USSBS, Army and Navy Oil Operations and Overall Allocations, October 27, 1945, p. 4.
16 USSBS, Army–Navy Production of Oil and Overall Allocation, October 29, 1945, p. 4.
17 USSBS, Yamamoto Interview, November 3, 1945, p. 3.
18 USSBS, Army–Navy Production of Oil and Overall Allocation, October 29, 1945, p. 5.
19 USSBS, Army–Navy Production of Oil and Overall Allocation, October 29, 1945, p. 4.
20 USSBS, Yamamoto Interview, November 3, 1945, p. 8.
21 USSBS, Goko Interview, October 25, 1945, p. 8.
22 USSBS, Pacific Report 53, p. 25.
23 USSBS, Pacific Report 53, p. 25. Germany produced 480,000 tons of aluminum in 1944.
24 See Chapter 11.
25 *The Strategic Air War against Germany 1939–1945*, p. 93.
26 *The Strategic Air War against Germany 1939–1945*, p. 96.
27 See Chapter 9.
28 See Chapter 9.
29 See Chapter 9.
30 FO 1031-148, Documentary Extracts, p. 8.
31 FO 1031-148, Documentary Extracts, p. 8.
32 WO 208-4340, Report from Captured Personnel, July 9, 1945, p. 7.
33 See Chapter 8.

34 See Chapters 8–9. A brief word should be said about the abbreviation of the Messerschmitt 109. This aircraft, one of the most famous of the war, should technically be referred to as the BF-109. This is because the company that constructed the fighter was called Bayerische Flugzeugwerke, and it was the abbreviation that the Germans used during the war. However, since the war the plane has more commonly been referred to as the ME-109, after the name of its most important creator, Willi Messerschmitt. I have decided to stick with ME-109 in this book as that is the abbreviation used in *Germany and the Second World War*.

35 *Germany and the Second World War*, vol. VII, p. 171.

36 WO 208/4340, Milch Report, July 9, 1945, p. 9.

37 USSBS, Messerschmitt Interview, May 11 and 12, 1945, p. 9.

38 USSBS, Messerschmitt Interview, May 11 and 12, 1945, p. 10.

39 USSBS, Tank Interview, May 19, 1945, p. 14.

40 USSBS, Kaether Interview, April 24, 1945, pp. 2–3.

41 USSBS, Tank Interview, May 19, 1945, p. 14.

42 FO 1031-141, Saur Interview, Report 11, June 10, 1945, p. 2.

43 WO 208-4340, Report from Captured Personnel, July 9, 1945, p. 9.

44 USSBS, Goering Interview, June 29, 1945, p. 2.

45 Arnold MSS, reel 190, "The Contribution of Airpower to the Defeat of Germany," Appendices, Section 1.

46 FO 1031-148, Translated Document, "On the German Economic Situation 1943/44," June 29, 1944, p. 2.

47 Arnold MSS, reel 190, "The Contribution of Airpower to the Defeat of Germany," Appendices, Section 2.

48 Arnold MSS, reel 190, "The Contribution of Airpower to the Defeat of Germany," Appendices, Section 1.

49 USSBS, European Report 4, p. 82.

50 See Chapter 11.

51 USSBS, Toyoda Interview, November 13–14, 1945, p. 18.

52 USSBS, Endo Interview, November 3, 1945, p. 7.

53 USSBS, Endo Interview, November 3, 1945, p. 7.

54 USSBS, Toyoda Interview, October 5, 1945, p. 6.

55 See Chapter 11.

56 Spaatz MSS, Box 134, Intelligence Summary of Goering, June 1, 1945, p. 14.

57 USSBS, Kanai Interview, October 26, 1945, p. 2.

58 USSBS, Takahashi and Takeuchi Interview, October 24–26, 1945, p. 2.

59 USSBS, Takahashi and Takeuchi Interview, October 24–26, 1945, p. 3.

60 USSBS, Takahashi and Takeuchi Interview, October 24–26, 1945, p. 2.

61 USSBS, Kanai Interview, October 26, 1945, p. 2.

62 Mellenthin, *Panzer Battles* (Stroud, 1956), p. 275.

63 USSBS, Dethleffsen Interview, May 20, 1945, p. 6.

64 USSBS, Peters Interview, June 3, 1945, p. 1.
65 USSBS, Peters Interview, June 3, 1945, p. 3.
66 USSBS, Toppe Intervew, May 17, 1945. p. 6.
67 USSBS, Keitel Interview, June 2, 1945, p. 18.
68 USSBS, Miyazaki Interview, December 3, 1945, p. 4.
69 USSBS, Miyazaki Interview, December 3, 1945, p. 4.
70 Prados, *Combined Fleet Decoded: The Secret History of American Intelligence and the Japanese Navy in World War II* (New York, 1995), pp. 560–1.
71 Tillman, *Clash of Carriers: The True Story of the Marianas Turkey Shoot* (New York, 2005), p. 42.
72 USSBS, Sanada Interview, November 2, 1945, p. 3.
73 Mellenthin, *Panzer Battles*, p. 270.
74 Mellenthin, *Panzer Battles*, p. 275.
75 Sources include Bechtold, "A Question of Success: Tactical Air Doctrine and Practice in North Africa, 1942–43," *Journal of Military History*, vol. 68, 3 (Jan. 2004), 821–51.
76 Robert Pape is one of those who denigrate strategic air power in World War II and afterwards, and at the same time believes that tactical air power is a far more effective tool. Pape, "The True Worth of Air Power," 116–30. See also Dater, "Tactical Use of Air Power in World War II: The Navy Experience," *Military Affairs*, vol. 14, 4 (Winter 1950), 192–200.
77 Bechtold believes that tactical air power in North Africa still suffered from some real shortcomings, but the lessons learned there made it very effective in the fighting in northwest Europe in 1944. Bechtold, "A Question of Success." Thomas Hughes believes that while tactical air power made Allied land victories possible, it still suffered from major weaknesses in 1944, particularly as regards coordination between the different national air forces. Hughes, "Air-Lines: Anglo-American Tactical Air Operations in World War II," *Air and Space Power Journal*, vol. 18, 4 (2004), 43–4.
78 Gooderson, *Air Power at the Battlefront: Allied Air Close Support in Europe 1943–1954* (London, 1998). Gooderson gives a mixed verdict on tactical air power, pointing out its developmental issues but also ascribing to it a great deal of psychological damage. Also see Hall, *Strategy for Victory: The Development of British Tactical Air Power, 1919–1943* (London, 2008). Hall argues that early tactical use of air power in North Africa, at least through Torch, was patchy. However, by 1944, he believes that the British forces in Normandy were receiving some of the most effective support found anywhere in the world (pp. 146–51).
79 Overmans, *Deutsche Militärische Verluste im Zweiten Weltkrieg* (Munich, 2004), p. 239.
80 The exact figure of German military deaths during the war is unclear, but seems to be at least 2 million. During the war itself the Germans recorded 1,808,546 battle deaths. Tucker (ed.), *The European Powers and the First*

World War: An Encyclopedia (New York, 1996), p. 173. At the same time, another 1,152,000 were listed as either missing or captured – and many of these were dead. As such the figure of 2 million war dead (at least) is often stated. Winter, *The Experience of World War I* (New York, 1989), pp. 206–7.

81 Megargee, *Inside Hitler's High Command* (Lawrence, KS, 2000), pp. 118, 144–5.

82 USSBS, Buhle Interview, June 1, 1945, p. 2.

83 Morison, *History of United States Naval Operations in World War II*, vol. V, p. 372.

84 Morison, *History of United States Naval Operations in World War II*, vol. V, p. 370.

85 Morison, *History of United States Naval Operations in World War II*, vol. VII, pp. 146–74.

86 There were 31,629 Japanese military personnel on Saipan on June 15 when the American troops began landing. About 1,700 of these eventually surrendered, with the rest killed or missing. See Morison, *History of United States Naval Operations in World War II*, vol. VIII, pp. 168, 339.

87 Cab 147/497. See Winter (ed.), *Defeating Hitler: Whitehall's Secret Report on Why Hitler Lost the War* (London, 2012) pp. 254–6.

88 See Chapter 9.

89 Heiber and Glantz, *Hitler and his Generals: Military Conferences 1942–1945*, p. 446.

90 USSBS, European Reprt 3, p. 277.

91 Overy, *Interrogations: Inside the Minds of the Nazi Elite* (London, 2002), p. 303.

92 Overy, *Interrogations*, p. 301.

93 Overy, *Interrogations*, p. 303.

3 The air and sea war to November 1940

1 Roskill, *Hankey: Man of Secrets*, 3 vols. (London, 1974), vol. III, pp. 422–3.

2 Hankey MSS, 10-9, 10, 11, Letter to Hankey, December 9, 1940.

3 Hankey MSS, 10-9, 10, 11, Letter to Hankey, December 9, 1940.

4 Hankey MSS, 10-9, 10, 11, Letter to Hankey, December 9, 1940.

5 Hankey MSS, 10-9, 10, 11, Letter to Hankey, December 9, 1940.

6 The most important works that put stress on the militarization of the interwar period are Maiolo, *Cry Havoc: The Arms Race and the Second World War* (London, 2011); Edgerton, *Britain's War Machine: Weapons, Resources and Experts in the Second World War* (London, 2012); Edgerton, *Warfare State: Britain, 1920–1970* (Cambridge, 2005). Edgerton is concerned with the military in the UK while Maiolo covers the great powers.

7 Scherner, "Nazi Germany's Preparation for War: Evidence from Revised Industrial Investment Series," *European Review of Economic History*, vol. 14 (2010), 433–68.

8 Steiner, *The Triumph of the Dark: European International History 1933–1939* (Oxford, 2011), pp. 605–6; Imlay; *Facing the Second World War: Strategy, Politics and Economics in Britain and France, 1938–1940* (Oxford, 2003), pp. 77–8.

9 O'Brien, *British and American Naval Power: Politics and Policies, 1909–1936* (Westport, CT, 1994), pp. 19–21.

10 Historic exchange rates can be found at www.miketodd.net/encyc/dollhist.htm.

11 O'Brien, *British and American Naval Power*, pp. 65, 111, 221. An argument could be made that this extra base spending in peacetime paid some dividend during the war as the USA went into the conflict with a larger number of facilities.

12 Stockings and Fernandes, "Airpower and the Myth of Strategic Bombing as Strategy," *ISAA Review*, vol. 5, 2 (2006), 6–18. Stockings and Fernandes take this point to what I believe is too much of an extreme, arguing that there has never been a real air power strategy, because there cannot be – on its own. It's a provocative point but overdone, unless one also believes that there could never be a sea power strategy.

13 Douhet, *The Command of the Air* (1921), republished in English translation in Jablonsky (ed.), *The Roots of Strategy: Book 4* (Mechanicsburg, PA, 1999), see pp. 290–1.

14 Douhet, *The Command of the Air*, in Jablonsky (ed.), *The Roots of Strategy*, p. 294.

15 Douhet, *The Command of the Air*, in Jablonsky (ed.), *The Roots of Strategy*, p. 330.

16 Douhet, *The Command of the Air*, in Jablonsky (ed.), *The Roots of Strategy*, p. 340.

17 Mitchell, *Winged Defense: The Development and Possibilities of Modern Air Power – Economic and Military* (New York, 1925), republished in Jablonsky (ed.), *The Roots of Strategy*.

18 Craven and Cate (eds.), *The Army Air Forces in World War II*, vol. I, p. 12.

19 This documentary, which was released in 1943, argued that Japan and Germany could be brought to collapse through strategic bombing and that land campaigns were a thing of the past. It began with a tribute to Mitchell for his farsightedness. It can be viewed in its entirety on YouTube: https://www.youtube.com/watch?v=J7NjJ59bfoM.

20 Mitchell, *Winged Defense*, in Jablonsky (ed.), *The Roots of Strategy*, pp. 465–76. Also see Craven and Cate (eds.), *The Army Air Forces in World War II*, vol. I, p. 25.

21 Mitchell, *Winged Defense*, in Jablonsky (ed.), *The Roots of Strategy*, pp. 502–7.

22 Mitchell, *Winged Defense*, in Jablonsky (ed.), *The Roots of Strategy*, p. 508.

23 Meilinger, "Trenchard and 'Morale Bombing': The Evolution of Royal Air Force Doctrine before World War II," *Journal of Military History*, vol. 60, 2 (Apr. 1996), 255.

24 Templewood (Hoare) MSS, Part XI, File 2, Diary Notes, September 1939.

25 Air 20-4069, Minutes of Meeting held by CAS, June 2, 1941, p. 1.

26 Clodfelter, "Aiming to Break Will: America's World War II Bombing of German Morale and its Ramifications," *Journal of Strategic Studies*, vol. 33, 3 (2010), 404–8; also see Overy, "Allied Bombing and the Destruction of German Cities," in Chickering *et al.* (eds.), *A World at Total War: Global Conflict and the Politics of Destruction, 1937–1945*, p. 278.

27 Craven and Cate (eds.), *The Army Air Forces in World War II*, vol. I, p. 68.

28 Craven and Cate (eds.), *The Army Air Forces in World War II*, vol. I, pp. 598–9; also see McFarland, *America's Pursuit of Precision Bombing: 1910–1945* (Washington, DC, 1995). Even though McFarland concludes that American strategic bombing during the war experienced real problems with accuracy, he discusses how the air force believed in its accuracy before the war.

29 Mowbray, "Air Force Doctrine Problems 1926–Present," *Airpower Journal* (Winter 1995).

30 Craven and Cate (eds.), *The Army Air Forces in World War II*, vol. I, p. 131.

31 Air 9/15, Air Power and Imperial Defence, pp. 3–4.

32 Slessor MSS, Air 75-5, Western Plans, September 1, 1939.

33 Webster and Frankland, *The Strategic Air Offensive against Germany 1939–1945*, vol. I, p. 129.

34 See Chapter 8.

35 An interesting argument has been made that the coordination between American science and the military was too close during the war, as it led to the militarization of too much research afterwards. Owens, "The Counterproductive Management of Science in World War II: Vannevar Bush and the Office of Scientific Research and Development," *Business History Review*, vol. 68, 4 (Winter 1994).

36 WO 208-4340, "Information GAF Policies and Experience with Opinions," June 3, 1945, p. 3. This document contains a summary of Milch's opinions right after the war. While he could be described as protecting his own position, Milch blamed the relative failure of Luftwaffe technological innovation on Goering's lack of interest. He also claimed that Hitler had little comprehension of air technology. Also see *Germany and the Second World War*, vol. V/II, p. 719.

37 Hartcup, *The Effects of Science on the Second World War* (New York, 2000) p. 20.

38 Brown, *A Radar History of World War II: Technical and Military Imperatives* (Philadelphia, 1999), pp. 51–2.

39 This figure comes from the RAF Museum's website www.rafmuseum.org.uk/ research/online-exhibitions/history-of-the-battle-of-britain/radar-the-battle-winner.aspx (accessed December 2013).

40 Edgerton, *Britain's War Machine*, p. 40.

41 Brown, *A Radar History of World War II*, p. 145.

42 Edgerton, *Britain's War Machine*, p. 254.

43 Hartcup, *The Effects of Science on the Second World War*, p. 26.

44 For an interesting take on the failure of the German navy to understand its purpose in the interwar years, see Herwig, "The Failure of German Sea Power, 1915–1945: Mahan, Tirpitz and Raeder Reconsidered," *International History Review*, vol. 10, 1 (Feb. 1988), 86–94.

45 Roskill, *Naval Policy between the Wars*, 2 vols. (London, 1968, 1976), vol. pp. 345–7. See also Franklin, *Britain's Anti-Submarine Capability 1919–1939* (London, 2003), pp. 58–65.

46 Roskill, *Naval Policy between the Wars*, vol. II, pp. 452–3.

47 Hartcup, *The Effects of Science on the Second World War*, p. 62; Roskill, *The War at Sea*, vol. 1 (London, 1976), p. 34.

48 Franklin, *Britain's Anti-Submarine Capability*, pp. 186–8.

49 See below, Chapter 7.

50 See Chapter 7.

51 Roskill, *Naval Policy between the Wars*, vol. I, pp. 581–2.

52 Roskill, *Naval Policy between the Wars*, vol. I, pp. 582–3.

53 Roskill, *The War at Sea, 1939–1945*, vol. III, pt 2, pp. 346, 352.

54 Roskill, *The Navy at War 1939–1945* (London, 1960), p. 25.

55 Roskill, *The Navy at War 1939–1945*, p. 28; Till, *Air Power and the Royal Navy 1914–1945: A Historical Survey* (London, 1979) includes an excellent survey of the problems of British naval aircraft development in the interwar period; see pp. 85–103.

56 Till, *Air Power and the Royal Navy 1914–1945*, pp. 137–45.

57 Morison, *History of United States Naval Operations in World War II*, vol. I, p. 214.

58 Home, Friedman and Mandeles, *American and British Aircraft Development 1919–1939* (Annapolis, MD, 1999), p. 81.

59 Kuehn, *Agents of Innovation: The General Board and the Design of the Fleet that Defeated the Japanese Navy* (Annapolis, MD, 2008), pp. 142–3, 165.

60 Kuehn, *Agents of Innovation*, p. 160.

61 Hone, "Replacing Battleships with Aircraft Carriers in the Pacific in World War II," *Naval War College Review*, vol. 66, 1 (Winter 2013), 56–8.

62 The USN's own historical division contains a clear description of all the battleships (and other major vessels) laid down in these years. See www.history.navy.mil/photos/usnshtp/bb/bb.htm.

63 The Montana Class would have been the largest capital ships laid down by the USN.

64 Morison, *History of United States Naval Operations in World War II*, vol. I, pp. l–li (Introduction).

65 Murray and Millett, *Military Innovation in the Interwar Period*, vol. III (Cambridge, 1996), p. 220.

66 Peattie, *Sunburst: The Rise of Japanese Naval Air Power 1909–1941* (Annapolis, MD, 2001), p. 161.

67 Parshall and Tully, *Shattered Sword*, p. 65.

68 Bekker, *Hitler's Naval War* (London, 1974), p. 372.

69 There is a slight difference of opinion on the numbers. Morison, *History of United States Naval Operations in World War II*, vol. I, p. 5 and Assman, "Why U-boat Warfare Failed," *Foreign Affairs*, vol. 28, 4 (July 1950), 664.

70 Murray, *Luftwaffe*, pp. 21–2.

71 Templewood MSS, Part XI, File 2, Diary Notes, September 1939–May 1940.

72 Templewood MSS, Part XI, File 2, Diary Notes, September 1939–May 1940; see entry for September 14, 1939.

73 Templewood MSS, Part XI, File 5, Hoare to Lothian.

74 Webster and Frankland, *The Strategic Air Offensive against Germany 1939–1945*, vol. I, pp. 129–32.

75 Webster and Frankland, *The Strategic Air Offensive against Germany 1939–1945*, vol. I, pp. 134–40.

76 USSBS, *Summary Report, European War*, p. 39.

77 USSBS, *Summary Report, European War*, p. 40.

78 Hankey MSS, 10/6. Hankey maintained a regular stream of reports on Germany's oil supply situation from the beginning of the war. Before the invasion of France there were three major reports, in November 1939, January 1940 and April 1940.

79 Hankey MSS, 10/6, Hankey to Churchill, May 1, 1940.

80 Hankey MSS, 10/6, Hankey to Churchill, May 1, 1940.

81 Air 9/129, Memo, "Attack on the German Oil Industry," April 1940.

82 Air 9/129, Memo, "Attack on the German Oil Industry," April 1940, Annex V.

83 Roskill, *The Navy at War 1939–1945*, p. 40.

84 Roskill, *The Navy at War 1939–1945*, p. 45.

85 Roskill, *The Navy at War 1939–1945*, p. 41.

86 The invasion of Norway has been covered in a number of works other than Roskill's. A more German-centric view can be found in Haarr, *The German Invasion of Norway, April 1940* (Barnsley, 2009). For a short but strong argument on Churchill's negative influence see Roskill, *Churchill and the Admirals* (London, 1977), pp. 283–99; Brown, "Norway 1940: The Balance of Interference," in Salmon (ed.), *Britain and Norway in World War II* (London, 1995), pp. 26–32.

87 Levy, *The Royal Navy's Home Fleet in World War II* (Basingstoke, 2003), pp. 52–3.

88 The complexity of using naval aircraft off Norway can be seen in a very useful set of primary sources put together by the Naval Records Society: Jones (ed.), *The Fleet Air Arm in World War II*, 3 vols. (Farnham, Surrey, 2012), vol. I. pp. 121–61, offers after-action reports of the various uses of HMS *Ark Royal's* air arm during the fighting in Norway.

89 Ellis MSS, 1-1, Air Ministry to Admiralty, May 5, 1940.

90 *The Rise and Fall of the German Air Force, 1933–1945*, pp. 66, 165.

91 *The Rise and Fall of the German Air Force, 1933–1945*, p. 66.

92 Jackson, *The Fall of France: The Nazi Invasion of 1940* (Oxford, 2003), pp. 20–1. This book on the fall of France is important, and to some degree controversial. See Jackson, "Returning to the Fall of France: Recent Work on the Causes and Consequences of the 'Strange Defeat' of 1940," *Modern and Contemporary France*, vol. 12, 4 (2004).

93 Webster and Frankland, *The Strategic Air Offensive against Germany*, vol. I, pp. 144–6.

94 Jackson, *The Fall of France*, p. 21.

95 Corum, "The Luftwaffe's Army Support Doctrine, 1918–1941," *Journal of Military History*, vol. 59 (Jan. 1995), 53–76.

96 Corum, "The Luftwaffe's Army Support Doctrine, 1918–1941," p. 41.

97 Robineau, "French Air Policy in the Inter-War Period and the Conduct of the Air War against Germany from September 1939 to June 1940," in Boog (ed.), *The Conduct of the Air War in the Second World War* (New York, 1992) pp. 627–57.

98 Chapman, *Why France Collapsed* (London, 1968), pp. 351–4; Horne, *To Lose a Battle: France 1940* (London, 1969), pp. 244–50.

99 Air 20/4076. Statement A, July 26, 1940.

100 Air 20/4076, Statement A, July 26, 1940

101 Air 20/4076, "Germany: The Aircraft Industry," May 6, 1940.

102 USSBS, Aircraft Division, Industry Report, p. 41.

103 Bungay, *The Most Dangerous Enemy*, pp. 419–26.

104 Air 20/4094, Statement of Aircraft Position, October 11, 1940.

105 Murray, *Luftwaffe*, p. 57.

106 Butler, *Grand Strategy*, vol. II (London, 1957), p. 285.

107 Hankey MSS, Handwritten Home Defence Memo.

108 Templewood (Hoare) MSS, Part XI, Cadogan to Hoare, September 13, 1940.

109 Templewood (Hoare) MSS, Part XI, Hankey to Hoare, July 19, 1940.

110 Campion, *The Good Fight: Battle of Britain Propaganda and the Few* (London, 2010), pp. 1–4.

111 There is a translated copy of the German plan in Spaatz MSS, 289, "General Directive for the Air Force Campaign against England," June 30, 1940, p. 2.

112 Spaatz MSS, 289, "General Directive for the Air Force Campaign against England," June 30, 1940.

113 See Chapter 9.

114 Higham, *Unflinching Zeal: The Air Battles over France and Britain, May–October 1940* (Annapolis, MD, 2012), p. 218.

115 Campion, *The Good Fight*, p. 53.

116 Bungay, *The Most Dangerous Enemy*, pp. 368–71

117 Postan, *British War Production*, Appendix 4; USSBS, European Report 3, p. 277.

118 Bungay, *The Most Dangerous Enemy*, p. 201.

119 Murray, *Military Adaptation in War: With Fear of Change* (Cambridge 2011), pp. 176–7. Murray believes that Britain's overall advantage in military adaptation was crucial to its victories in the war in the air and at sea in 1940–1; see pp. 193–4 for a summary. He also makes the case strongly in Millett and Murray, *Military Effectiveness*, vol. III, pp. 97–8, 114.

120 Addison and Crang (eds.), *The Burning Blue: A New History of the Battle of Britain* (London, 2000), pp. 59–62.

121 See Chapter 11.

122 Templewood (Hoare) MSS, Part XI, Beaverbrook to Hoare, August 30, 1940.

123 Templewood (Hoare) MSS, Part XI, Halifax to Hoare, 14 October, 1940.

124 This can be seen in many of the histories of the U-boat war including Terraine, *Business in Great Waters: The U-boat Wars 1916–1945* (London, 1989).

125 See Chapter 7.

126 Grove (ed.), *The Defeat of the Enemy Attack on Shipping 1939–1945*, Navy Records Society, 137, 2 vols. [vols. Ia and Ib] (Aldershot, 1997), vol. Ib, Table 13.

127 Grove (ed.), *The Defeat of the Enemy Attack on Shipping 1939–1945*, vol. Ib, Table 13.

128 Roskill, *The War at Sea*, vol. I, pp. 47–8.

129 Alexander MSS, 5-4-60, Some Notes on U-boat Warfare by Admiral Sir Frederick Dreyer [undated, but written in 1940], p. 12.

130 Alexander MSS, 5-4-60, Some Notes on U-boat Warfare by Admiral Sir Frederick Dreyer, p. 13.

131 Grove (ed.), *The Defeat of the Enemy Attack on Shipping 1939–1945*, vol. Ia, p. 59.

132 Grove (ed.), *The Defeat of the Enemy Attack on Shipping 1939–1945*, vol. Ib, Table 13.

133 Grove (ed.), *The Defeat of the Enemy Attack on Shipping 1939–1945*, vol. Ib, Table 12 (ii).

134 Roskill, *The Navy at War 1939–1945*, p. 93.

135 Roskill, *The War at Sea*, vol. I, Appendix F, pp. 588–9.

136 Anyone who wants to start delving into the historiography could begin by reading Doenecke, "Historiography: US Policy and the European War, 1939–1941," *Diplomatic History*, vol. 19, 4 (Fall 1995). Doenecke breaks down much of the historiography into pro- and anti-Roosevelt groupings.

137 Templewood MSS, Part XI, File 5, Lothian to Hoare, September 15, 1939.

138 Templewood MSS, Part XI, File 5, Lothian dispatch, February 1, 1940.

139 FDR MSS, PSF 2. The letters from Bullitt to FDR regularly discussed German air attacks on civilian and military targets. See Bullitt to FDR, May 20, 1940 (two letters on this date speak of air attacks on civilians); May 14, 1940 discusses German air attacks in combination with tanks against military targets.

140 FDR MSS, PSF 2, Bullitt to FDR, May 14, 1940.

141 FDR MSS, PSF 2, Bullitt to FDR, May 14, 1940.

142 FDR MSS, PSF 2, Bullitt to FDR, May 14, 1940.

143 Loewenheim, Langley and Jonas (eds.), *Roosevelt and Churchill: Their Secret Wartime Correspondence* (London, 1975), p. 94, Churchill to FDR, May 15, 1940.

144 Loewenheim *et al.* (eds.), *Roosevelt and Churchill*, p. 97, Churchill to FDR, May 20, 1940.

145 Craven and Cate (eds.), *The Army Air Forces in World War II*, vol. I, p. 107.

146 Templewood MSS, Part 13, File 7, Moore-Brabazon to Hoare, May 29, 1940.

147 Reynolds, *The Creation of the Anglo-American Alliance 1937–41: A Study of Competitive Cooperation* (London, 1981), pp. 113–31.

148 Reynolds, *The Creation of the Anglo-American Alliance 1937–41*, p. 131.

4 Grand strategists and the air and sea war

1 Leahy MSS, Diary, April 12, 1945.

2 Leahy MSS, Diary, April 15, 1945.

3 In Dallek's *Franklin Roosevelt and American Foreign Policy 1932–45* (New York, 1995), Leahy has eight index entries while Marshall has sixty-one.

4 Even though Alanbrooke was not ennobled until the war ended, so should properly be referred to as Sir Alan Brooke before 1945 (he had been knighted), he will be referred to as Alanbrooke in this text as that is how he is best known.

5 Anyone interested in the direct Churchill–Roosevelt relationship should start with Warren Kimball, who has produced a number of important works on the subject including: *Forged in War: Churchill, Roosevelt and the Second World War* (London, 1997) and *The Juggler: Franklin Roosevelt as Wartime Statesman* (Princeton, 1991). Kimball has also produced an invaluable edition of the correspondence between the two: *Churchill and Roosevelt: The Complete Correspondence*, 3 vols. (Princeton, 1984). There are a number of other books

on the relationship between the two men including Lash, *Roosevelt and Churchill 1939–1941, The Partnership that Saved the West* (London, 1976); Sainsbury, *Churchill and Roosevelt at War: The War They Fought and the Peace They Hoped to Make* (London, 1994). One work which adds Stalin into the mix is Feis, *Churchill, Roosevelt, Stalin: The War They Waged and the Peace They Sought* (Princeton, 1957).

6 Examples of tension are discussed is Costigliola, *Roosevelt's Lost Alliances: How Personal Politics Helped Shape the Cold War* (Princeton, 2012), pp. 56–7; Charmley, "Churchill and the American Alliance," *Transactions of the Royal Historical Society*, Sixth Series, vol. 11 (2001), 353–71.

7 There is an online copy of the short address in which Churchill made this comment maintained by the Churchill Society of London: www.churchill-society-london.org.uk/EndoBegn.html (accessed August 29, 2014).

8 Leahy, *I Was There: The Personal Story of the Chief of Staff to President Roosevelt and Truman Based on his Notes and Diaries at the Time* (London, 1950), p. 156.

9 Thorne, *Allies of a Kind: The United States, Britain, and the War against Japan, 1941–1945* (London, 1978), pp. 233–48, 358–62; Aldrich, *Intelligence and the War against Japan; Britain, America and the Politics of the Secret Service* (Cambridge, 2000), pp. 115–32.

10 FDR MSS, PSF, FDR to Winant, February 1942; Hopkins to FDR, April 1942; Johnson to FDR, April 1942.

11 Hopkins MSS, 24, FDR to WSC, March 10, 1942.

12 The effect of the British desire to keep casualties low and rely on machines had a mixed impact on the combat performance of the British army. See French, *Raising Churchill's Army: The British Army and the War against Germany 1919–1945* (Oxford, 2000), pp. 243–6, 277.

13 Stettinus, *Lend Lease: Weapon for Victory* (New York, 1944), p. 57.

14 FDR MSS, PSF, 1, Marshall to FDR, December 22, 1941.

15 FDR MSS, PSF, 3-4, Hopkins to Marshall, July 1942.

16 FDR MSS, PSF, 3-4, Marshall to FDR, February 1942.

17 FDR MSS, PSF, 3-4, Roosevelt–Marshall correspondence, May 1942.

18 FDR MSS, PSF, 3, FDR to Hopkins, July 1942. Amos Perlmutter has argued that FDR went so far to please Stalin that he ended up as an enabler of the greatest tyrant of the twentieth century. Perlmutter, *FDR and Stalin: A Not So Grand Alliance 1943–1945* (Columbia, MO, 1993), pp. 3–7.

19 FDR MSS, PSF, 3, FDR to Hopkins, Marshall and King, August 1942.

20 Hopkins MSS, 24, Mountbatten to Hopkins, June 1942.

21 FDR MSS, PSF, 62, FDR to Knox, May 4, 1942.

22 FDR MSS, PSF, 83, FDR to JCS, Stimson and Hopkins, May 6, 1942.

23 Emerson, "Franklin Roosevelt as Commander-in-Chief in World War II," *Military Affairs*, vol. 22, 4 (Winter 1958–9), 193.

24 Gilbert, *Winston S. Churchill, vol. VII: The Road to Victory* (London, 1986), pp. 548–9.

25 Bateman, "Observations of President Roosevelt's Health during World War II," *Mississippi Valley Historical Review*, vol. 43, 1 (June 1956), 86.

26 *The Cunningham Papers*, vol. II, Navy Records Society 150 (Aldershot, 2006), Dill to Cunningham, October 18, 1943.

27 *The Cunningham Papers*, Cunningham Diary, May 29, 1944. Cunningham started having his doubts about Churchill's strategic understanding long before taking over as First Sea Lord. Roskill, *Churchill and the Admirals*, p. 188.

28 Wingate, *Lord Ismay: A Biography* (London, 1970) pp. 44–6.

29 Cherwell is a very interesting case in point. His close personal relationship with Churchill gave him great power during the war, but his understanding of war and technology was often flawed. For the best book on the relationship between the two men, see Wilson, *Churchill and the Prof* (London, 1995).

30 Ben-Moshe, "Winston Churchill and the 'Second Front': A Reappraisal," *Journal of Modern History*, vol. 62, 3 (Sep. 1990), 535.

31 Brian Farrell has argued that the German invasion of the USSR helped push Churchill into an even more Mediterranean-centric policy as a way of engaging the German army as quickly as possible. Farrell, "Yes, Prime Minister: Barbarossa, Whipcord, and the Basis of British Grand Strategy, Autumn 1941," *Journal of Military History*, vol. 57, 4 (Oct. 1993), 604–7. Martin Kitchen presents him as increasingly frustrated by Soviet pressure for a second front in France, which was one of the reasons for his growing skepticism about Stalin. Kitchen, "Winston Churchill and the Soviet Union during the Second World War," *Historical Journal*, vol. 30, 2 (June 1987), 426–7.

32 In 1950 the USSR released one of its most spectacular films about the war, *The Fall of Berlin*. Churchill comes across as a villain almost equal to Hitler. Roosevelt, on the other hand, is presented as well meaning but weak.

33 Triumph is a double-edged sword here. From a shipping point of view, Churchill actually undermined Britain's long-term vision by concentrating on the Mediterranean in 1943. He certainly delayed Operation Bolero, and through that the amount of shipping made available to bring supplies to the UK. See Smith, *Conflict over Convoys: Anglo-American Logistics Diplomacy in the Second World War* (Cambridge, 1996), pp. 133–76.

34 Churchill, *The Second World War*, 6 vols. (London, 1948–53), vol. IV. p. 435.

35 Churchill, *The Second World War*, vol. V, pp. 321, 327–8.

36 See Chapter 8.

37 WD 165, History File, Book 18, Wedemeyer to Handy, April 13, 1944.

38 Leahy, *I Was There*, pp. 11–12.

39 Samuel Morison, for example, seems to overlook Leahy almost completely. Morison, *American Contributions to the Strategy of World War II* (London, 1958), mentions Leahy on only four pages. Most books that discuss the grand

strategy of the Roosevelt administration discuss Leahy much less frequently than they do Marshall or King. For example, see Larrabee, *Commander in Chief: Franklin Delano Roosevelt, his Lieutenants, and their War* (New York, 1987), which has individual chapters on every major military commander (including Stilwell), but does not have one on Leahy.

40 Mark Stoler has written two excellent books which discuss American grand strategy, except for the fact that Leahy rarely figures in the narrative, especially when compared with Marshall. In *Allies in War: Britain and America against the Axis Powers 1940–1945* (London, 2005), Leahy has three mentions in the index, while Marshall has twenty eight. In *Allies and Adversaries: The Joint Chiefs of Staff, the Grand Alliance, and US Strategy in World War II* (London, 2000), Stoler goes further than anyone in discussing Leahy's enormous influence. On page 91 he writes about Leahy being FDR's representative to the JCS. However, Marshall still seems a much larger presence in the book, with approximately three times as many index entries.

41 Leahy, *I Was There*, p. 12.

42 More work needs to be done on Leahy's period as ambassador to Vichy France. For some information, see Jackson and Kitson, "The Paradoxes of Vichy Foreign Policy 1940–42", in Adelam (ed.), *Hitler and his Allies in World War II* (New York, 2007).

43 Leahy MSS, Diary, August 3, 1942 and October 6, 1942.

44 Danchev, *Establishing the Anglo-American Alliance: The Second World War Diaries of Brigadier Vivian Dykes* (London, 1990), p. 154.

45 Leahy MSS, Diary, September 4, 1942.

46 Leahy MSS, Diary, September 10, 11 and 12, 1942.

47 Marshall MSS, JCS Anvil File, Leahy to FDR, June 28, 1944.

48 Leahy MSS, Diary, June 21, 1943.

49 Leahy MSS, Diary, April 23, 1943.

50 Skates, *Invasion of Japan: Alternative to the Bomb* (Columbia, SC, 1995), pp. 24–5.

51 Leahy MSS, Diary, January 9–10, 1943.

52 King MSS, Box 35, "Mr. Roosevelt versus the Philippines and Formosa."

53 Leahy MSS, Diary, September 9, 1942.

54 Leahy MSS, Diary, September 20, 1942. In this entry Leahy is "inclined to agree" that America should direct its effort at the present time against Japan first and foremost.

55 Sarantakes, "One Last Crusade: The British Pacific Fleet and its Impact on the Anglo-American Alliance," *English Historical Review*, vol. 121, 491 (Apr. 2006), 439–40; Coles, "Ernest King and the British Pacific Fleet: The Conference at Quebec, 1944 (Octagon)," *Journal of Military History*, vol. 65, 1 (Jan. 2001), 105–29.

56 King MSS, Box 35, Random Notes, p. 1.

57 King MSS, Box 35, Random Notes, pp. 2–3.

58 Sarantakes, *Allies against the Rising Sun: The United States, the British Nations and the Defeat of Imperial Japan* (Lawrence, KS, 2009), pp. 125–6, 211–12.
59 Buell, *Master of Sea Power: A Biography of Fleet Admiral Ernest J. King* (Annapolis, MD, 1980), p. 105.
60 Buell, *Master of Sea Power*, pp. 153–4.
61 For more details, see Chapter 6.
62 Alanbrooke Diary, April 15, 1942, p. 249.
63 King MSS, Box 35, Random Notes, pp. 4–7.
64 Slessor MSS, Air 75-52, Slessor Notes, 1941, p. 4.
65 Cray, *General of the Army: George C. Marshall, Soldier and Statesman* (New York, 1990), pp. 148–9.
66 Cray, *General of the Army*, p. 144.
67 FDR MSS, PSF 3-4, Marshall Memo for FDR, undated but sometime in first half of 1942.
68 *The Papers of George Catlett Marshall*, vol. III (Baltimore, 2003), p. 276.
69 *The Papers of George Catlett Marshall*, vol. III, pp. 516–17.
70 *The Papers of George Catlett Marshall*, vol. III, pp. 668–9.
71 FDR MSS, PSF 3-4, Marshall to FDR, April 1, 1942.
72 See Chapter 1.
73 FDR MSS, PSF 3–4, Marshall to FDR, May 6, 1942.
74 See Chapter 10.
75 Daso, *Hap Arnold and the Evolution of American Airpower* (Washington, DC, 2000), pp. 89–95.
76 Leahy, *I Was There*, p. 105.
77 Slessor MSS, Air 75-52, Slessor Notes, 1941, p. 8. Slessor believed that Arnold was energetic, but not in possession of a first-class brain. A recent work that argues that Arnold was very hands-on and in control of USAAF operations is Wolk, *Cataclysm: General Hap Arnold and the Defeat of Japan* (Denton, TX, 2010).
78 Meilinger, "US Air Force Leaders: A Biographical Tour," *Journal of Military History*, vol. 62, 4 (Oct. 1998), 839–40.
79 Daso, *Hap Arnold and the Evolution of American Airpower*, p. 167.
80 Daso, *Hap Arnold and the Evolution of American Airpower*, p. 163.
81 Arnold MSS, Reel 2, Diary, September 16, 1942, p. 2.
82 Prioritization of the war against Germany was a regular refrain in Arnold's diary. See Arnold MSS, Reel 2, Diary, April 21, 1941, p. 15; Reel 203, Arnold to Marshall, July 29, 1942.
83 Craven and Cate, *The Army Air Forces in World War II*, vol. II, pp. 349–55.
84 FDR MSS, PSF 2, Arnold to FDR, January 1942.
85 Leahy, *I Was There*, p. 105.
86 Sherwood, *The White House Papers of Harry L. Hopkins*, p. 5.
87 Cray, *General of the Army*, pp. 139, 144.

88 Marshall MSS, Hopkins File, Marshall to Hopkins, February, April 1944 and May 1945.

89 For an interesting overview of how the British utilized Hopkins to influence Roosevelt and Truman, see Harbutt, "Churchill, Hopkins and the 'Other' American: An Alternative Perspective on Anglo-American Relations 1941–1945," *International History Review*, vol. 8, 2 (May 1986), 236–62. For a larger work on Hopkins' role in setting up the wartime alliance, see Roll, *The Hopkins Touch: Harry Hopkins and the Forging of the Alliance to Defeat Hitler* (Oxford, 2013).

90 Slessor MSS, Air 75-52, Slessor Notes, 1941, p. 2.

91 Stettinus, *Lend-Lease: Weapon for Victory*, p. 95.

92 Hopkins MSS, 24, Churchill to Hopkins, May 1942.

93 Sandys MSS, 2-2-12, see March 1943 memo on new tank construction.

94 Sherwood, *The White House Papers of Harry L. Hopkins*, pp. 324–6.

95 FDR, PSF 3-4, Marshall Folder, Litvinov to Hopkins, March 1942.

96 FDR, PSF 3-4, Marshall Folder, Burns to Hopkins, April 1942.

97 Hopkins MSS, 24, MAB papers, has an interesting collection of MAB minutes.

98 Hopkins MSS, 24, MAB minutes, October 14, 1942, pp. 3–4.

99 Hopkins MSS, 24, MAB minutes, appendix to minutes, p. 2.

100 King MSS, Box 20, memorandum for CNO, August 18, 1941, p. 3.

101 FDR MSS, PSF 82, Hopkins to FDR, October 14, 1941.

102 Hopkins MSS, 125, Hopkins to FDR, October 1, 1942.

103 Hopkins MSS, 125, FDR to Nelson, October 1, 1942.

104 Thorne, *Allies of a Kind*, pp. 156–7.

105 Cab 122-1035, Law to Churchill and Eden, October 7, 1943.

106 Harbutt, "Churchill, Hopkins and the 'Other' American," 250–2; Roll, *The Hopkins Touch*, p. 340.

107 Costigliola, "Broken Circle: The Isolation of Franklin D. Roosevelt in World War II," *Diplomatic History*, vol. 32, 5 (Nov. 2008), 680. Also see Costigliola, *Roosevelt's Lost Alliances*, pp. 83–4, 206.

108 Fraser, *Alanbrooke* (London, 1997), pp. 13–14.

109 In Washington, Dill served with great skill and became a particular favorite of George Marshall. When he died in 1944, he was given the special honor of being buried in Arlington National Cemetery and his contributions to the war effort were recognized by a joint resolution of Congress. See Danchev, *Very Special Relationship: Field Marshal Sir John Dill and the Anglo-American Alliance* (London, 1986).

110 Harris, *Bomber Offensive* (London, 1947) p. 155. Harris remarked in his memoirs on the fact that Alanbrooke did not once come to visit Bomber Command to find out more about the war from their perspective.

111 Alanbrooke Diary, July 24, 1943, p. 433.

112 Alanbrooke Diary, August 23, 1943, p. 447.

113 Cab 121/53, Notes Chiefs of Staff Committee, May 9, 1943, p. 2.

114 Cab 121/53, COS Committee, Record of Meeting Held in North Africa between May 29, and June 3, 1943, p. 4.

115 Alanbrooke Diary, October 22, 1942, p. 332; October 13, 1943, p. 460.

116 Alanbrooke Diary, January 14, 1943, pp. 358–9.

117 Alanbrooke Diary, May 24, 1943, pp. 410–11.

118 Churchill, *The Second World War*, vol. II, p. 19.

119 Richard, *Portal of Hungerford* (London, 1977), pp. 36–70.

120 Leahy, *I Was There*, p. 163.

121 Arnold MSS, Reel 2, contains the diary from Arnold's trip and Portal is mentioned positively a number of times.

122 Arnold MSS, Reel 2, Diary, May 29–30, 1942, pp. 12–13.

123 Air 20-4069, Minutes of Meeting, June 2, 1941.

124 Air 20-4069, Minutes of Meeting, June 2, 1941, p. 4.

125 Air 20-4069, Churchill Minute, September 27, 1941.

126 Air 20/4069, Portal to Prime Minister, re minute of 27.9.41.

127 Air 8/292, Minutes, COS Meeting, May 31, 1941, p. 2.

128 Air 8/292, COS Memo, June 21, 1941, p. 2.

129 Cab 120/26, Transcripts of Arcadia Conference, Record of Meeting, December 24, 1941, p. 10.

130 Cab 121/153, COS Minutes, May 8, 1943, pp. 1–2.

131 Cab 121/153, COS Minutes, May 9, 1943, p. 1.

132 Harris MSS, Portal to Harris, October 10, 1942.

133 Harris MSS, Portal to Harris, December 22, 1944.

134 Alanbrooke Diary, February 3, 1942, p. 226; January 17, 1943, p. 357 – just two of the occasions on which it is mentioned.

135 Leahy, *I Was There*, p. 195.

136 King MSS, Box 35, Random Notes, unnumbered page.

137 Rodger, *The Admiralty* (Lavenham, Suffolk, 1979), p. 152; Stephen Roskill generally portrays Pound as rather passive in his dealings with Churchill. Roskill, *Churchill and the Admirals*, pp. 118, 124–5.

138 King MSS, Box 20, King notes of August 1941 meeting with the British (Argentia); Box 24, Pound to King, February 1943.

139 Roskill, *The War at Sea 1939–1945*, vol. II, pp. 79–89.

140 Roskill, *The War at Sea 1939–1945*, vol. II, p. 80.

141 Roskill, *The War at Sea 1939–1945*, vol. II, p. 89.

142 Cab 120-26, Annex I, American and British Strategy. This type of summary strategy memo after the Arcadia Conference placed the highest priority on maintaining the direct lines of communication between the USA and the UK.

143 See Chapter 1.

144 *The Cunningham Papers*, vol. II, Cunningham to Pound, August 12, 1942.

145 King MSS, Box 35, Memorandum for the Record, April 12, 1951.

146 Initially, during the assault on Okinawa, the British Pacific Fleet was actually kept away from the main body of American carriers, and given the job of attacking Japanese bases on Formosa-which was not a central mission. Roskill, *The War at Sea: 1939–1945*, vol. III/2, p. 348.

5 Understanding the air and sea war from December 1940 to March 1942

1 The best descriptions of the first Stalin–Hopkins meetings are found in Sherwood, *The White House Papers of Harry L. Hopkins*, vol. I, pp. 326–44.

2 Ulam, *Stalin: The Man and his Era* (London, 1989), pp. 260–1.

3 Sherwood, *The White House Papers of Harry L. Hopkins*, vol. I, p. 332.

4 Sherwood, *The White House Papers of Harry L. Hopkins*, vol. I, pp. 328–9.

5 Sherwood, *The White House Papers of Harry L. Hopkins*, vol. I, p. 338.

6 Sherwood, *The White House Papers of Harry L. Hopkins*, vol. I, p. 329.

7 Weeks, *Russia's Life Saver*, see tables on pp. 144, 150. During the war the United States delivered more than 14,000 aircraft under lend-lease, and supplied the USSR with almost 75,000 tons of processed aluminum and more than 194,000 aluminum ingots and bars.

8 Sherwood, *The White House Papers of Harry L. Hopkins*, vol. I, pp. 339–40.

9 Wilson, "The First Summit, FDR and the Riddle of Personal Diplomacy," in Brinkley and Facey-Crowther, *The Atlantic Charter* (London, 1994), p. 16; Cashman, *America, Roosevelt and World War II* (New York, 1989), pp. 66–7.

10 Anyone interested in reading about the economic/financial pressures placed on Japan could start with Miller, *Bankrupting the Enemy: The US Financial Siege of Japan before Pearl Harbor* (Annapolis, MD, 2007). For an overview of some other scholarship, see Ienaga, *Japan's Last War: World War II and the Japanese* (Oxford, 1979), pp. 132–4; Iguchi, "The Secrets behind Japan's Ability to Cope with US Economic Sanctions, 1940–1941," *Diplomatic History*, vol. 34, 1 (Jan. 2010), 177–82.

11 Kimball, *Forged in War*, p. 104. Kimball believes that FDR was still looking for ways to keep the USA out of full participation in the war in the second half of 1941. Another very nuanced view of FDR, showing how his positions changed during the course of 1941 until, in September, he seemed set on the USA entering the war relatively soon, can be found in Heinrichs, *Threshold of War: Franklin D. Roosevelt and American Entry to World War II* (Oxford, 1988), pp. 178–9.

12 Meilinger, "The Historiography of Airpower: Theory and Doctrine," *Journal of Military History*, vol. 64, 2 (Apr. 2000), 485–6. Meilinger believes strongly that Slessor was intellectually very important for the RAF and that more work needs to be done on his impact before and during the war.

13 Slessor MSS, Air 75/52, Slessor to Portal, November 11, 1940.

14 Slessor MSS, Air 75/52, Slessor to Portal, November 11, 1940.
15 Slessor MSS, Air 75/52, undated Slessor memorandum.
16 Slessor MSS, Air 75/52, undated Slessor memorandum.
17 Slessor MSS, Air 75/52, Record of Conversation with President Roosevelt, April 7, 1941.
18 Slessor MSS, Air 75/52, undated Slessor memorandum.
19 Slessor MSS, Air 75/52, undated Slessor memorandum.
20 Sherwood, *The White House Papers of Harry L. Hopkins*, vol. I, pp. 231–2.
21 Hopkins MSS (FDR Library) 24, WSC to FDR, January 13, 1941.
22 Harbutt, "Churchill, Hopkins and the "Other" American,", 239.
23 Hankey MSS, 5/4, Hankey to Halifax, April 29, 1941. Also see Hankey to Halifax, March 19, 1941.
24 Hopkins MSS, 24, Campbell to Hopkins, September 22, 1941.
25 FDR Papers, PSF 2, Beaverbrook to FDR, December 1941.
26 Hopkins MSS, 24, handwritten note, Beaverbrook to Hopkins.
27 Welles MSS, 151–2, Welles to FDR, January 9, 1941.
28 Macleod, "'All for Each and Each for All': Reflections on Anglo-American and Commonwealth Scientific Cooperation 1940–1945," *Albion*, vol. 26, 1 (Spring 1994), 83–8.
29 Air 9/168, for the full final report issued in March 1941 after the conclusion of the talks which commenced on January 29, 1941. For an interesting discussion of these talks from the naval perspective; see Leutze, *Bargaining for Supremacy: Anglo-American Naval Cooperation, 1937–1941* (Chapel Hill, NC, 1977), pp. 209–15.
30 Air 9/168, United States–British Staff Conversations (ABC-1), March 27, 1941, p. 1. it includes a full list of the delegates.
31 Air 9/168, United States–British Staff Conversations (ABC-1), March 27, 1941, p. 3.
32 Air 9/168, United States–British Staff Conversations (ABC-1), March 27, 1941, p. 3.
33 Air 9/168, United States–British Staff Conversations (ABC-1), March 27, 1941, Annex 3, pp. 4–6, 9.
34 Air 9/168, United States–British Staff Conversations (ABC-1), March 27, 1941, Annex 3, p. 12. The exact American force that would be moved to Gibraltar included three battleships, one aircraft carrier, four 8-inch gun cruisers and thirteen destroyers.
35 FDR MSS, PSF 4, Knox to FDR, March 20, 1940, p. 2.
36 King MSS, Box 20, "Brief of ABC Agreements," pp. 1–2.
37 King MSS, Box 20, "Brief of ABC Agreements," p. 2.
38 WD, History File, 165, Notes of Conference, February 6, 1941.
39 WD, History File, 165, Notes of Conference, February 6, 1941. See also Stimson to Smith, April 3, 1941; Brown to Marshall, March 31, 1941.
40 FDR MSS, PSF 3, Memorandum for FDR, January 17, 1941.

41 Slessor MSS, Air 75-52, Record of Conversation with President Roosevelt, April 7, 1941.
42 FDR MSS, PSF 82, FDR to Stimson, May 4, 1941.
43 *Statistical Digest of the War*, p. 152. In 1941 the British built 498 heavy bombers in total and in 1944 they built 5,507.
44 USSBS, European Report 4, Aircraft Division Industry Report, pp. 41–2.
45 FDR MSS, PSF 82, Hopkins to FDR, October 14, 1941.
46 FDR MSS, PSF 82, FDR to Stimson, October 14, 1941.
47 Hopkins MSS, 24, undated [1941] notes of meeting between Dowding and FDR.
48 Slessor MSS, Air 75-52, Record of Conversation with President Roosevelt, April 7, 1941.
49 Hankey MSS, 11-5/4, "The Second German War after Eighteen Months: An Appreciation," p. 3.
50 Halifax MSS (microfilm kept at Churchill College Archives), Reel 1, Halifax Memo, June 13, 1941.
51 Caruana and Rockoff, "An Elephant in the Garden: The Allies, Spain and Oil in World War II," *European Review of Economic History*, vol. 2 (2007), 175.
52 Payne, *Franco and Hitler: Spain, Germany and World War II* (London, 2008), pp. 69–70.
53 Templewood MSS, XIII, part 16, Hoare to WSC, February 18, 1941.
54 Hankey MSS, 5-4, Halifax to Hankey, July 15, 1940, June 22, 1941.
55 Kimball, *The Juggler: Franklin Roosevelt as Wartime Statesman*, pp. 21–41.
56 FDR MSS, PSF 62, Knox to FDR, June 23, 1941.
57 FDR MSS, PSF 62, Knox to FDR, July 23, 1941
58 FDR MSS, PSF 62, FDR to Knox, July 9, 1941.
59 Templewood MSS, Bracken to Hoare, August 16, 1941.
60 Arnold MSS, Arnold Diary (Microfilm reel 2), Diary Entry for August 9, 1941, p. 6. McJimsey, *Harry Hopkins: Ally of the Poor and Defender of Democracy* (Cambridge, MA, 1987), pp. 184–5.
61 Arnold MSS, Reel 2, Arnold Diary, August 12, 1941, p. 11.
62 See Hankey MSS, 11 5/6, Memorandum on State of War, September 1941; Harris MSS, 84, Harris to Freeman, September 1941.
63 WD, History File, 165, Sherman Memo for CNO, August 18, 1941.
64 WD, History File, 165. In this folder there is a memorandum in which Sherman kept a record of the meetings of the service chiefs in which their discussions were recounted. They spent a great deal of time discussing a possible Anglo-American occupation of the Azores, as well as the process through which equipment would be transferred to the UK. However, no exact agreements about transfer amounts were reached.
65 Sumner Welles, who was very close to Roosevelt, wrote a summary of the meetings, and a copy of his memorandum ended up in the King Papers. See

King MSS, Box 20, Memorandum of Conversation, August 11, 1941. It is fascinating recollection of the discussions, with Roosevelt regularly trying to avoid making new public commitments and expressing worry about the domestic opposition in the United States to aggressive action.

66 Heinrichs, "President Franklin Roosevelt's Intervention in the Battle of the Atlantic," *Diplomatic History*, vol. 10, 4 (Oct. 1986), 330–1.

67 For an example of an article that argues that, at this time, Roosevelt was still not entirely convinced that the USA would enter the war, and that his naval actions must be seen in this light, see Clifford and Ferrell, "Roosevelt at the Rubicon: The Great Convoy Debate of 1941," in Piehler and Pash (eds.), *The United States and World War II* (New York, 2010), pp. 10–37. For an argument that says he was convinced, see Ross, *How Roosevelt Failed America in World War II* (London, 2006), pp. 15–22. This work is particularly vitriolic on the role of the President.

68 Arnold MSS, Reel 2, "The President's Announced Policy." After the recollection, Arnold writes that these thoughts were given by Roosevelt while waiting for Churchill's arrival in Newfoundland, and were given in front of all military men.

69 Lowe, "War and War Plans in the Far East," *International History Review*, vol. 21, 1 (Mar. 1999), 128–9.

70 FDR MSS, PSF 4, Stark to FDR, September 9, 1941 and FDR to Stark, September 12, 1941. In his letter Stark included a map with the new American protection zone.

71 ADM 1-14994, Knox to Alexander, October 16, 1941.

72 FDR MSS, PSF 4, Beardall to FDR, September 9, 1941.

73 Heinrichs, *Threshold of War*, pp. 166–8.

74 Heinrichs, *Threshold of War*, pp. 205–6.

75 Doenecke, *Storm on the Horizon: The Challenge to American Intervention, 1939–1941* (New York, 2003), p. 268.

76 Baer, *One Hundred Years of Seapower, The United States Navy 1890–1990* (Stanford, 1994), pp. 162–3.

77 Barnhart, *Japan Prepares for War: The Search for Economic Security, 1919–1941* (Ithaca, 1987), pp. 263–4. Even the statement that Roosevelt made embargoing Japanese oil was somewhat confused. See Feis, *The Road to Pearl Harbor: The Coming of the War between the United States and Japan* (Princeton, 1950), pp. 236–7.

78 Hatano, "The Japanese Navy and the Development of Southward Expansion," in Best (ed.), *Imperial Japan and the World, 1931–1945*, 2 vols. (London, 2011), vol. II, pp. 238–47.

79 Barnhart, "Japan's Economic Security and the Origins of the Pacific War," in Best (ed.), *Imperial Japan and the World, 1931–1945*, vol. II, pp. 228–32.

80 Barnhart, *Japan Prepares for War*, pp. 237–62.

81 Barnhart, "Japan's Economic Security and the Origins of the Pacific War,"
   pp. 233–4. See also Graebner, "Hoover, Roosevelt and the Japanese", in Borg
   and Okamoto (eds.), *Pearl Harbor as History: Japanese–American Relations
   1931–1941* (New York, 1973), pp. 49–52.
82 Roskill, *The War at Sea*, vol. I, Appendix R, pp. 615–16.
83 Roskill, *The War at Sea*, vol. I, p. 528.
84 Grove (ed.), *The Defeat of the Enemy Attack on Shipping 1939–1945*, vol. Ib,
   Table 10.
85 Grove (ed.), *The Defeat of the Enemy Attack on Shipping 1939–1945*, p. 70;
   for a chronological list of German U-boats sunk in this period, see Roskill,
   The War at Sea, vol. I, Appendix K, p. 599. Five U-boats were lost between
   March 7 and 23 1941.
86 Grove (ed.), *The Defeat of the Enemy Attack on Shipping 1939–1945*, pp. 101–3.
87 WD, History File, Britain 1941.
88 Cab 120–409, Dominion Office to Canadian Government, September 6, 1941.
89 Cab 120–409, First Lord of the Admirally to CNO, December 2, 1941.
90 Harris MSS, Harris Memorandum on Status of Bomber Command, July 1942.
91 Roskill MSS, 4–19, Directive by the Minister of Defence, March 6, 1941.
92 See Chapter 7.
93 Air 9/129. In this file there are two discussions from December 1940 of a
   strategic bombing campaign against German oil supply. See "The Oil Supply
   and Demand Position in Axis Controlled Europe, with Special Reference to Air
   Target Priority," undated, though Appendix C is dated December 29, 1940;
   Plan WA 6 (ii), "The Attack on Germany's Oil Resources," December
   31, 1940.
94 There is a very helpful eight-page chronology of this 1942 internal British
   discussion over strategic bombing in Slessor MSS, Air 75-52, "Bombing
   Policy," undated.
95 Webster and Frankland, *The Strategic Air Offensive against Germany
   1939–1945*, vol. IV, Appendix 40, pp. 431–9. The Appendix has a breakdown
   of daytime and night losses for Bomber Command during the entire war.
96 Webster and Frankland, *The Strategic Air Offensive against Germany
   1939–1945*, vol. I, pp. 219–20.
97 Webster and Frankland, *The Strategic Air Offensive against Germany
   1939–1945*, vol. I, pp. 299–300.
98 Webster and Frankland, *The Strategic Air Offensive against Germany
   1939–1945*, vol. I, pp. 163–5.
99 Slessor MSS, Air 75-52, "Bombing Policy," undated. Ismay is recorded as
   expressing serious doubts on March 17, 1941.
100 Air 8/929, "The Present War Situation Mainly in So Far as it Relates to Air,"
   Trenchard Memorandum, May 19, 1941.
101 Air 8/929, "The Present War Situation Mainly in So Far as it Relates to Air,"
   Trenchard Memorandum, May 19, 1941, pp. 2–3.

102 Trenchard MSS, Trenchard to WSC, September 25, 1941. This is one of Trenchard's most impassioned pleas against the diverting of British bombers away from attacks on Germany, and he included attacks on assumed German preparations for the invasion of the UK as diversions.

103 Air 8/929, Extract from Minutes of COS Meeting, May 30, 1941.

104 Air 20/4069, Minutes of Air Staff Meeting, June 2, 1941.

105 Hankey MSS, 11–5/4, "The Second German War after Eighteen Months: An Appreciation," p. 2.

106 Hankey MSS 10-12, Notes on Morale, August 15, 1941, p. 5.

107 Hankey MSS 10-12, Notes on Morale, August 15, 1941, pp. 6–7.

108 Hankey MSS 10-12, Notes on Morale, August 15, 1941, p. 13.

109 Halifax MSS, Reel 1, Hankey to Halifax, May 1941.

110 Slessor MSS, Air 75-52, "Bombing Policy," p. 4. Portal announced to the War Cabinet on September 4 that the bombing of oil targets in Germany had been "suspended" and instead attacks would be directed against communication systems.

111 Air 8/929, Extract from Minutes of COS Meeting, May 30, 1941, p. 2.

112 Air 8/929, Extract from Minutes of COS Meeting, May 30, 1941, p. 2.

113 Air 8/929, Bombing Policy, Dill, Portal and Pound to WSC, June 7, 1941.

114 Slessor MSS, Air 75-52, "Bombing Policy," p. 2.

115 Churchill, *The Second World War*, vol. III, p. 451. There is also a copy of the minute in Air 20-4069.

116 For a more detailed discussion of why the Luftwaffe was so much smaller when it took part in Barbarossa, see Murray, *Lufwaffe*, pp. 74–8.

117 See Chapter 3.

118 Air 40/1207. This is a chart on Luftwaffe deployment based on official Luftwaffe Quartermaster General Reports. There were 2,404 bombers of all types and 1,583 single- and twin-engined fighters.

119 Air 40/1207.

120 Hill, "British Lend Lease Aid to the Soviet War Effort, June 1941–June 1942," *Journal of Military History*, vol. 71, 3 (July 2007), 773–808.

121 Slessor MSS, Air 75-52, "Bombing Policy," p. 4.

122 Webster and Frankland, *The Strategic Air Offensive against Germany 1939–1945*, vol. I, pp. 185–6.

6 Grand strategy in action: prioritizing the air and sea war

1 King MSS, Box 20, Handwritten Notes Dated December 12 [has to be 1942 because of the context].

2 Adm 205/19. See two memoranda: "Future British Naval Strategy" and "Disposition of Naval Forces." These are both undated, but must have been written in either December 1941 or January 1942. The latter was specifically

listed as being authored by Pound and contains a list of the battleships and aircraft carriers to be sent into the war against Japan.

3 WD, History File, RG 165, "Joint Planning Committee Report to Chiefs of Staff," January 13, 1942.

4 Baxter, *The Great Power Struggle in East Asia, 1944–50: Britain, America and Post-War Rivalry* (Basingstoke, 2009), p. 176.

5 A great deal has been written about the Anglo-American relationship and the Pacific war, discussing both the agreements and the areas of difference – in particular the differences over the importance of China. Some of the most important books on the subject are: Thorne, *Allies of a Kind*; Aldrich, *Intelligence and the War against Japan*; Sarantakes, *Allies against the Rising Sun*.

6 Kirby, *The War against Japan*, 5 vols. (London, 1957–65), vol. V, p. 543.

7 Roskill, *The War at Sea*, vol. III, pt 1, p. 219.

8 Roskill, *The War at Sea*, vol. III, pt 1, pp. 221–2.

9 Kirby, *The War against Japan*, vol. III, p. 387.

10 Harris MSS, Harris to Portal, October 29, 1943.

11 FDR MSS, PSF 1, Marshall Memorandum drawn up under FDR direction, December 22, 1941.

12 See Cab 120/26, Transcript of Washington War Conference (Arcadia), December 23, 1941. Here the assumption is that Japanese aircraft production would be between 200 and 300 units a month.

13 Emerson, "Franklin Roosevelt as Commander-in-Chief in World War II," 195.

14 Hastings, *All Hell Let Loose: The World at War: 1939–45* (London, 2011), pp. 253–4.

15 Stoler, *Allies and Adversaries*, pp. 90–7. Stoler also discusses the 1942 situation well in *Allies and War*, pp. 68–70. For an early article on the subject see his "The 'Pacific-First' Alternative in American World War II Strategy," *International History Review*, vol. 2, 3 (July 1980), 432–52.

16 Spector, *Eagle against the Sun*, pp. 298–9.

17 See WD History Files, RG 165, Eisenhower to Marshall, April 1942, "Strategic Conceptions and their Application to the Southwest Pacific."

18 *The Papers of Dwight David Eisenhower*, vol. I, Eisenhower to Somervell, February 19, 1942, pp. 118–19; Eisenhower to Marshall, March 6, 1942, pp. 169–70.

19 Lubin MSS, Stevens to Lubin, February 25, 1943.

20 Lubin MSS; there are reports in this for troop shipments for most months in 1943.

21 Lubin MSS, Stevens to Lubin, November 17, 1944.

22 Lubin MSS, Stevens to Lubin, March 24, 1945.

23 Lubin MSS, Stevens to Lubin, March 24, 1945.

24 See Chapter 1.

25 FDR MSS, PSF 172-2, War Production Report, August 12, 1944, figure for June 1944, p. 5.

26 Arnold MSS, Reel 203, Air War Plan, August 24, 1942. See also Arnold to Marshall, July 29, 1942, for a plea from Arnold directly to Marshall to make sure that the striking power of the Army Air Force be directed primarily towards the UK for the strategic bombing of Germany.

27 Hopkins MSS, 125, "Location of Combat Airplanes of the Army Air Force," October 14, 1942.

28 Lubin MSS, Chart: US Army Air Forces: Planes in Principal Theaters during 1943, Heavy Bombers.

29 Craven and Cate (eds.), *The Army Air Forces in World War II*, vol. VI, p. 208; the original contracts were completed in September 1940.

30 Hopkins MSS, 126, Arnold Report to FDR about American Strategy in 1943.

31 Hopkins MSS, 126, Arnold Report to FDR about American Strategy in 1943; see "Recapitulation of Combat Units of Army Air Forces as of 31 December 1943," dated September 9, 1942.

32 Wilt, "The Significance of the Casablanca Decisions, January 1943," *Journal of Military History*, vol. 55, 4 (Oct. 1991), 528.

33 Cab 121/152, Combined Chiefs of Staff, Minutes of Meeting, January 14, 1943, p. 1.

34 Cab 121/152, Combined Chiefs of Staff, Minutes of Meeting, January 14, 1943, p. 1.

35 Alanbrooke Diary, p. 359.

36 King MSS, Box 35, King to Dobyns, January 12, 1951.

37 Arnold MSS, Reel 2, Diary Entry, January 14, 1943.

38 In 1943 Leahy started remarking in his diary about how the air/sea combination was the crucial one. He was particularly impressed by how it determined the land fighting in North Africa. See Leahy MSS, Diary, May 11, 1943.

39 Thorne, *Allies of a Kind*, p. 289.

40 There is an interesting memorandum on the subject that Leahy sent to Roosevelt just after Casablanca which is quoted in Kimball (ed) *Churchill and Roosevelt: The Complete Correspondence*, vol. II, p. 696.

41 Brower, *Defeating Japan: The Joint Chiefs of Staff and Strategy in the Pacific War, 1939–1945* (New York, 2012). There is a good description of the importance of China in the American JCS mind before Trident on pp. 28–9.

42 The Japanese had a difficult time understanding just how important China was in the American mind. There is an interesting discussion of this issue in terms of the Japanese view of the war since 1945 in Matsuda, Takeshi, "The Coming of the Pacific War: Japanese Perspectives," *Reviews on American History*, vol. 14, 4 (Dec. 1986), 643–6.

43 Leahy MSS, Diary Entry, September 9, 1942.

44 Leahy MSS, Diary Entries, September 20 and October 1, 1942.

45 Leahy MSS, Diary Entry, February 2, 1943.

46 Leahy MSS, Diary, April 23, 1943.

47 Leahy MSS, Diary, April 6, 1943.

48 Leahy MSS, Diary, May 2, 1943.

49 Leahy's conviction regarding the supremacy of air and sea power was reinforced at this time by the German surrender in Tunisia, which he considered proof of their decisive influence on modern warfare. See Leahy MSS, Diary, May 11, 1943.

50 FDR MSS, PSF 2, Memorandum from JCS to FDR, May 8, 1943.

51 Churchill, *The Second World War*, vol. IV, p. 702. Also see Cab 121/153, Aide Memoire for Opening Conversations with US Chiefs of Staff, May 8, 1943. In this, the British admit that they have no intention of attempting Anakim in 1943.

52 Cab 121/153, Transcripts of Trident Meetings, Conference Held in White House, May 12, 1943, starting at 2.30 p.m.

53 Alanbrooke Diary, Entry for May 20, 1943, p. 407.

54 Leahy MSS, Diary, December 31, 1943.

55 Roskill, *The War at* Sea, vol. III, pt 1, p. 18.

56 There is an online copy of the official end of war report that King compiled, available at www.ibiblio.org/hyperwar/USN/USNatWar/ (accessed August 29, 2014). which includes a greak deal of useful data on ship losses. The exact quote about the Marianas comes from p. 108.

57 Morison, *History of United States Naval Operations in World War II*, vol. VIII, p. 233.

58 Morison, *History of United States Naval Operations in World War II*, vol. VIII, p. 160.

59 Morison, *History of United States Naval Operations in World War II*, vol. VIII, p. 180.

60 Friedman, "The Quiet Warrior Back in Newport: Admiral Spruance and the Lessons of the Pacific War, 1946–1947," *Naval War College Review*, vol. 64, 2 (Spring 2011), 122.

61 Roskill, *The War at Sea*, vol. III, pt 2, p. 191.

62 Morison, *History of United States Naval Operations in World War II*, vol. VIII, p. 233.

63 Craven and Cate (eds.), *The Army Air Forces in World War II*, vol. VI, p. 352.

64 Craven and Cate (eds.), *The Army Air Forces in World War II*, vol. VI, p. 352.

65 WD, Historical File, RG 165, Handy Memorandum for the President, November 23, 1943.

66 Hopkins MSS, 126, Review of the Aircraft Resources of the United Nations, September 30, 1943.

67 Morison, *History of United States Naval Operations in World War II*, vol. X, p. 44.
68 Prem 3/420/3, Churchill to War Cabinet, January 17, 1943.
69 Cab 120/26, Arcadia Transcripts, see meeting on December 23, 1941. See also Sainsbury, *Churchill and Roosevelt at War*, pp. 179–80.
70 FDR MSS, PSF 3-4, FDR to Hopkins, Marshall and King, July 24, 1942.
71 WD, RG 165, Marshall notes in preparation of meeting with FDR, "Object: To prevent, prior to the Quadrant conference, the making of commitments, verbal or written, affecting operations now under way or future operations."
72 WD, RG 165, Analysis of the Trident and ANFA Conference.
73 Cab 121/153, Final Report (Trident) to the President and Prime Minister, May 25, 1943.
74 Alexander MSS (Churchill College Cambridge), Pound to Alexander, August 25, 1943.
75 Kimball (ed.), *Churchill and Roosevelt: The Complete Correspondence*, vol. II, pp. 443–5.
76 Cab 121/155, Churchill to Eden, *c.* October 19, 1943.
77 Prem 3/165/5, Sextant meeting transcript, December 4, 1943.
78 Leahy MSS, Diary, Entry for November 28, 1943.
79 Sainsbury, *The Turning Point: Roosevelt, Stalin, Churchill and Chiang-Kai-Shek, 1943: The Moscow, Cairo and Teheran Conferences* (Oxford, 1985), pp. 225–7; Feis, *Churchill, Roosevelt, Stalin: The War They Waged and the Peace They Sought*, pp. 259–65.
80 There is a full discussion of his condition at this time in Gilbert, *Winston S. Churchill*, vol. VII, pp. 603–12.
81 Hopkins MSS, 24, Bedell-Smith to Marshall, November 9, 1942.
82 Prem 3/443/2, Meeting with Dominions, May 20, 1943.
83 Alanbrooke Diary, August 6, 1943, p. 437.
84 Air 8/1146, Operations in the European Theater of War, Aide Memoire (by COS), August 6, 1943.
85 Cab 121/154, Quadrant Transcripts; Meeting on August 15, 1943, p. 23.
86 Alanbrooke Diary, October 13, 1943, p. 460.
87 Air 8/1146. This file contains the internal British discussion/opposition to Arnold's proposal.
88 Air 8/1146, WSC Note, November 24, 1943.
89 Air 8/1146, COS Note, November 21, 1943.
90 Cab 121/153, Transcript of COS Meeting on *Queen Mary*, May 9, 1943, p. 1.
91 CAB 121/153, Transcript of Trident Meeting, May 12, 1943, p. 2.
92 Cab 121/154, Quadrant Transcript, Meeting on August 15, 1943, p. 22.
93 See Chapter 8.
94 Air 8/1146, Portal Note, November 2, 1943. See also Portal Memorandum, October 12, 1943.

95 The most assertive argument for a 1943 invasion is Dunn, *Second Front Now, 1943* (Birmingham, AL, 1980). A critique can be found in Weinberg, *Germany, Hitler and World War II* (Cambridge, 1995), pp. 257–8.

96 Roskill, *The War at Sea*, vol. III, pt 2, p. 18.

97 Roskill, *The War at Sea*, vol. III, pt 1, p. 121.

98 Morison, *History of United States Naval Operations in World War II*, vol. VII, pp. 114–18. Morison does not have one table, but breaks the overall force down into its different components (landing forces, strike forces, etc.). The figures given in the text are reached by adding up the different vessels mentioned as part of each force.

99 Roskill, *The War at Sea*, vol. III, pt 2, p. 19. LSTs are landing ship, tanks and LCTs are landing craft, tanks.

100 Roskill, *The War at Sea*, vol. III, pt 1, p. 121.

101 NARA, WD, RG 165. There is an excellent memorandum written for Marshall in preparation for Trident which shows just how US strategy in terms of landing craft allocation had been affected by Casablanca.

102 NARA, WD, RG 165.

103 Roosevelt, PSF 2. There is an almost complete set of the memoranda which the JCS prepared for Trident in these files. See Operations in the Pacific and Far East in 1943–44, p. 31 for the data on landing craft allocation.

104 Morison, *History of United States Naval Operations in World War II*, vol. VII, Appendix 2.

105 Playfair, *The Mediterranean and the Middle East*, vol. IV (London, 1966), p. 400.

106 Playfair, *The Mediterranean and the Middle East*, vol. IV, see pp. 248, 306–7 for a discussion of the formation and operation of the Northwest Air Command.

107 Molony, *The Mediterranean and the Middle East*, vol. V (London, 1973), p. 46.

108 Molony, *The Mediterranean and the Middle East*, vol. V, p. 225.

109 Playfair, *The Mediterranean and the Middle East*, vol. IV, Appendix 8 has a breakdown of the British and American squadrons with plane types.

110 WD, RG 165, see Chart: Status of Aircraft by Theater, Prepared for Operations Division, April 27, 1943.

111 Lubin MSS, Chart: US Army Air Forces: Planes in Principal Theaters during 1943, Heavy Bombers.

112 Arnold MSS, Reel 121, AAF Aircraft Losses and Attrition Rates, May–December 1942.

113 Arnold MSS, Reel 121, AAF Aircraft Losses and Attrition Rates, May–December 1942.

114 WD History File, RG 165, Wedemeyer to Handy, April 13, 1944.

115 Hopkins MSS, 126, Review of the Aircraft Resources of the United Nations, September 30, 1943. This supports the notion about the 8,000 aircraft that

were mentioned by Wedemeyer being available to support an invasion in
1943 only coming from the USAAF and RAF. It is exactly one-third of all the
aircraft that they had on hand, which would allow for a front-line strength of
8,000 with constant reinforcements to make up losses.
116 Ellis, *Victory in the West*, vol. I, p. 72.

7 Winning the shipping war

1 Marc Milner has written a great deal about SC 42, including an entire article
that can be accessed online. See Milner, "The Fate of Slow Convoy 42," *Legion
Magazine*, vol. 18 (June 2009), available at http://legionmagazine.com/en/
index.php/2009/06/the-fate-of-slow-convoy-42-navy-part-33/ (accessed
August 29, 2014). See also his *North Atlantic Run: The Royal Canadian Navy
and the Battle for the Convoys* (Toronto, 1985), pp. 66–76; and *The Battle of
the Atlantic* (Stroud, 2003), p. 73. For other works see Van der Vat, *The
Atlantic Campaign: World War II's Great Struggle at Sea* (New York, 1988),
pp. 208–9, 213; Barnett, *Engage the Enemy More Closely*, p. 270.
2 Roskill, *The War at Sea*, vol. I, p. 599.
3 Roskill, *The War at Sea*, vol. I, p. 468.
4 Roskill, *The War at Sea*, vol. I p. 469.
5 Van der Vat, *The Atlantic Campaign*, p. 208.
6 Milner, *North Atlantic Run*, pp. 72–3.
7 Cab 120-409, Churchill to Hopkins, March 12, 1942.
8 Churchill also pressed Roosevelt directly on this a number of times. See Kimball
(ed.), *Churchill and Roosevelt: The Complete Correspondence*, vol. I, pp. 515.
9 Roskill, *The War at Sea*, vol. II, p. 486. Also see Morison, *History of United
States Naval Operations in World War II*, vol. I, p. 412.
10 Adm 223-220, "The Battle of the Atlantic 1939–1943," March 10, 1944, see
chart attached to p. 24.
11 In the first five months of 1943, British, American and neutral shipping losses
throughout the world comprised 365 ships with a combined weight of 200,918
tons. After that the U-boats were withdrawn from the Atlantic so losses became
minimal (Roskill, *The War at Sea*, vol. II, p. 486).
12 Churchill, *The Second World War*, vol. V, p. 6.
13 Ross (ed.), *US War Plans 1938–1945* (Boulder, CO, 2002). There is a full copy
of Rainbow 5 here, with the paramount importance of sea trade stated on
p. 138.
14 Cab 120/26, Annex I, "American and British War Strategy," for a summary of
Arcadia's strategic conclusion.
15 *The Papers of George Catlett Marshall*, vol. III, Marshall to FDR, June 10,
1942, p. 231.
16 Hopkins MSS, 24, WSC to Hopkins, July 4, 1942.

17 Slessor MSS, Air 75-52, Slessor Memo, April 1941, p. 6.
18 Cab 120-409, Churchill to Hopkins, March 12, 1942
19 Kimball (ed.), *Churchill and Roosevelt: The Complete Correspondence*, vol. I, p. 407.
20 Chalmers, *Max Horton and the Western Approaches* (London, 1954), pp. 149–50.
21 Adm 205/19, Pound Memo, undated but sometime after Pearl Harbor and before the loss of Singapore.
22 Buell, *Master of Sea Power*, p. 139.
23 King MSS, Box 35, King to All Holders, US Atlantic Fleet Operation Plan, December 20, 1941.
24 Morison, *History of United States Naval Operations in World War II*, vol. I, p. 200.
25 Roskill, *The War at Sea*, vol. II, p. 99.
26 Buell, *Master of Sea Power*, pp. 286–9.
27 Murray and Millett, *A War to be Won*, p. 337.
28 Miller, *War at Sea: A Naval History of World War II* (New York, 1995), pp. 296–7. Also see Allard, "A United States Overview," in Howarth and Law (eds.), *The Battle of the Atlantic, 1939–1945: The 50th Anniversary International Naval Conference* (Annapolis, MD, 1994, pp. 568–70.)
29 King MSS, 35, "Notes about the First Draft of the Two Brief Subsections ..." p. 2.
30 King MSS, 35, Random notes.
31 Morison, *History of United States Naval Operations in World War II*, vol. I, p. 235.
32 Morison, *History of United States Naval Operations in World War II*, vol. I, p. 131.
33 Morison, *History of United States Naval Operations in World War II*, vol. IV, p. 83.
34 He also fought against a combined army–navy command structure in the Caribbean, which would have allowed for greater coordination of air assets against the U-boats. See *The Papers of Dwight David Eisenhower: The War Years*, vol. I, Eisenhower to Marshall, March 20, 1942, p. 197.
35 King MSS, 35, "Notes about the First Draft of the Two Brief Subsections ..." p. 2.
36 FDR MSS, PSF 3, King to FDR, March 5, 1942.
37 FDR MSS, PSF 3-4, King Memorandum for JCS, undated but probably early May 1942.
38 FDR MSS, PSF 3-4, see FDR to Marshall, May 5, 1942 and Marshall Memorandum, May 1942.
39 FDR MSS, PSF 4, King–Nimitz Correspondence (Cominch to Cincpac), February 1942.

40 FDR MSS, PSF 4, King–Nimitz Correspondence (Cominch to Cincpac), February 1942.

41 Marshall MSS, Eisenhower File, Eisenhower to Marshall, March 3, 1942

42 Padfield, *War Beneath the Sea: Submarine Conflict during World War II* (New York, 1995), p. 212.

43 Van der Vat, *The Atlantic Campaign*, p. 245.

44 Kimball (ed.), *Churchill and Roosevelt: The Complete Correspondence*, vol. I, p. 452.

45 Cab 120-409, Air Ministry to British Delegation, May 26, 1942.

46 Cab 129-409, WSC Notes for Ismay, March 21, 1942.

47 Kimball (ed.), *Churchill and Roosevelt: The Complete Correspondence*, vol. I, p. 434.

48 Cab 120-409, Air Ministry to Britman (WDC), May 26, 1942.

49 Craven and Cate (eds.), *The Army Air Forces in World War II*, vol. I, pp. 522–3.

50 Arnold Reel 121, Extract of King Memo, July 21, 1942.

51 Arnold MSS, Reel 121, Memorandum for Chief of Staff, June 29, 1942.

52 Morison, *History of United States Naval Operations in World War II*, vol. I, pp. 131.

53 Hopkins MSS, 125, "Location of Combat Airplanes of Army Air Force Planes," August 21, 1942.

54 Milner, *The Battle of the Atlantic*, p. 97.

55 *The Papers of George Catlett Marshall*, vol. III, Marshall to FDR, February 18, 1942, p. 106.

56 *The Papers of George Catlett Marshall*, vol. III, Marshall to FDR, June 19, 1942, pp. 241–2.

57 King MSS, Box 14, FDR to King, July 7, 1942.

58 Morison, *History of United States Naval Operations in World War II*, vol. I, p. 142.

59 Morison, *History of United States Naval Operations in World War II*, vol. I, pp. 130–1.

60 Roskill, *The War at Sea*, vol. II, p. 96.

61 Morison, *History of United States Naval Operations in World War II*, vol. I, p. 121.

62 Grove (ed.), *The Defeat of the Enemy Attack on Shipping 1939–1945*, Ia, p. 84.

63 Morison, *History of United States Naval Operations in World War II*, vol. I, p. 257.

64 See Till, "The Battle of the Atlantic as History," in Howarth and Law (eds.), *The Battle of the Atlantic, 1939–1945*, pp. 584–5. For another discussion of the importance of Ultra, see Terraine, *Business in Great Waters*, pp. 400–1. Barnett provides a more mixed picture, definitely praising Ultra intelligence, but also

claiming that other aspects mattered. Barnett, *Engage the Enemy More Closely*, pp. 268–72.

65 Harry Hinsley's arguments have had a great impact on the historical discussion over the Battle of the Atlantic. Hinsley, *British Intelligence in the Second World War: Its Influence on Strategy and Operations*, vol. II (London, 1981), p. 169. What he says exactly is that, even with Ultra, the war at sea was only won by the "narrowest" of margins. This alone is a debatable claim.

66 Hinsley, "The Enigma of Ultra," *History Today* (Sep. 1993), 19.

67 Grove (ed.), *The Defeat of the Enemy Attack on Shipping 1939–1945*, vol. Ib, Table 13.

68 A useful corrective to Hinsley is Gardner, *Decoding History: The Battle of the Atlantic and Ultra* (London, 1999). Gardner argues that Ultra, while important, was not nearly as decisive as Hinsley and others have said (see p. 172). It is interesting to see people attack Gardner for provocative revisionism. Murfett, *Naval Warfare 1919–1945: An Operational History of the Volatile War at Sea* (London, 2009), p. 467.

69 See Chapter 1.

70 FDR MSS, PSF 3-4, FDR to Marshall, August 24, 1942.

71 Danchev, *Establishing the Anglo-American Alliance*, p. 213.

72 Kimball (ed.), *Churchill and Roosevelt: The Complete Correspondence*, vol. I, p. 603.

73 Kimball (ed.), *Churchill and Roosevelt: The Complete Correspondence*, vol. I, pp. 615, 631.

74 Hopkins MSS, 24, WSC to Hopkins, October 31, 1942.

75 Postan, *British War Production*, p. 287.

76 Postan, *British War Production*, p. 291.

77 Leahy MSS, Diary, October 23, 1942.

78 Arnold Reel 198, "Recommended Priorities for 1943," undated but probably November 1942 as it mentions FDR order of October 1942.

79 FDR MSS, PSF 6, Third Report of the Combined Production and Resources Board, p. 5.

80 Hopkins MSS, War Production File, Report "Review of 1942 and Prospects for 1943," p. 22.

81 Hopkins MSS, War Production File, Report "Review of 1942 and Prospects for 1943," p. 29.

82 FDR MSS, PSF 172-2, War Progress Report, December 4, 1942, p. 16. Spending per quarter on destroyers, when added to the other anti-submarine vessels, goes even further in showing just how dominant this production became in American minds in the second half of 1942. Spending on destroyers in 1942 was $67 million in the first quarter, $75 million in the second and $76 million in the third. It should always be kept in mind, however, that most of these destroyers were not intended for anti-submarine warfare in the Atlantic.

83 Hopkins MSS, War Production File, Report "Review of 1942 and Prospects for 1943," Table 4, p. 31.

84 Leighton and Coakley, *United States Army in World War II*, p. 607, Table 18.

85 Hopkins MSS, War Production File, Report "Review of 1942 and Prospects for 1943," Chart III, p. 19.

86 WD History File, RG 165, "Notes Pertaining to Long Term Planning...," p. 7.

87 Leighton and Coakley, *United States Army in World War II*, pp. 302, 632–3.

88 *US Navy at War 1941–1945*, Official Reports by Fleet Admiral Ernest King USN, Appendix B, "Major Combatant Ships Added to the United States Fleet." Available online at www.ibiblio.org/hyperwar/USN/USNatWar/index. html (accessed February 2014).

89 Craven and Cate (eds.), *The Army Air Forces in World War II*, vol. I, p. 557.

90 Craven and Cate (eds.), *The Army Air Forces in World War II*, vol. II, p. 242.

91 Kimball (ed.), *Churchill and Roosevelt: The Complete Correspondence*, vol. I, p. 434.

92 Arnold MSS, Reel 113, Eaker to Arnold, November 26, 1942.

93 Arnold MSS, Reel 203, Arnold Memo for JCS, "Strategic Policy for 1943," November 16, 1942.

94 Harris MSS, Harris to Portal, November 21, 1942.

95 Air 20/4069, Harris to Eaker, April 15, 1943.

96 Harris MSS, "The Strategic Control of our Anti-Submarine Campaign," Harris Memorandum, December 19, 1942.

97 Harris MSS, "The Strategic Control of our Anti-Submarine Campaign," Harris Memorandum, December 19, 1942, p. 4.

98 Air 40-1120, "Strategic Bombing of Axis Europe, January 1943 to September 1944," p. 25.

99 See Chapter 1.

100 Hopkins MSS, 24, War Production Board, Monthly Report, February 1944, p. 35.

101 FDR MSS, PSF 7-8, Forrestal to FDR, September 21, 1943.

102 Postan, *British War Production*, p. 295.

103 Grove (ed.), *The Defeat of the Enemy Attack on Shipping 1939–1945*, vol. Ib, Table 13.

104 Grove (ed.), *The Defeat of the Enemy Attack on Shipping 1939–1945*, vol. Ib, Plan 16 (5).

105 Mulligan, "German U-boat Crews in World War II: Sociology of an Elite," *Journal of Military History*, vol. 56, 2 (Apr. 1992), 280.

106 Bekker, *Hitler's Naval War*, p. 307.

107 Kimball (ed.), *Churchill and Roosevelt: The Complete Correspondence*, vol. I, p. 649.

108 Cab 120-409, "Fast Ships for Britain," March 31, 1941.

109 Roskill MSS, 4-19, Directive of Ministry of Defence (Churchill), March 6, 1941.

110 Adm 116-5456, "Effect of Speed on the Safety of Convoys and Independents," July 24, 1943.

111 Cab 121-153, Transcripts of Trident Meeting, Chiefs of Staff Committee, May 12, 1943, p. 4.

112 King MSS, 25, Land to Stark, March 6, 1942.

113 King MSS, 25, King to Stark, March 10, 1942.

114 Adm 116/5456, "Standing Committee to Investigate Reason for Lack of Speed ..." June 1, 1943.

115 Morison, History of United States Naval Operations in World War II, vol. I, pp. 293–5.

116 Adm 116/5456, The Effect of Speed on the Safety of Convoys and Independents, July 16, 1943.

117 Adm 116/5456, "Size of Convoys," March 8, 1943, Note from Director of Trade Division.

118 Adm 116/5456, "Size of Convoys," March 16, 1943.

119 Schofield, "Defeat of the U-boats during World War II," Journal of Contemporary History, vol. 16, 1 (Jan. 1981), 119–29. Admiral Schofield became the head of the Admiralty's trade division in 1941 and he is firmly convinced that the move towards the larger convoys made a dramatic difference in the war with the U-boats. Another British admiral, Sir Peter Gretton, supports the general point about Blackett's importance. See Gretton, Crisis Convoy: The Story of HX 231 (London, 1974), pp. 164–5.

120 There is an excellent article on this subject which sadly is quoted not nearly enough in major histories of the war at sea: Water, "The Mathematics of Convoy," Navy International (May 1978). The copy that I consulted is kept in Roskill MSS, 4-27. The article offers particularly good insights into how the understanding of convoy size helped thwart the U-boats. Interestingly, Maurice Hankey was one of the first people to comment on the importance of convoy size. See Hankey MSS, 13-4, Hankey Appreciation of the War Situation, summer 1943.

121 Adm 116/5456, "Size of Convoys," undated note, after March 8 and before March 16, 1943.

122 Adm 116/5456, "Size of Convoys," Convoys and Escorts, undated (March 1943) remarks from ANA to ANCS. See also "Size of Convoy and Escorts," Whitehead Memo.

123 Kimball (ed.), Churchill and Roosevelt: The Complete Correspondence, vol. II, p. 173.

124 Roskill, The War at Sea, vol. II, Appendix G, pp. 457–60.

125 Grove (ed.), The Defeat of the Enemy Attack on Shipping 1939–1945, vol. Ia, Appendix 5, p. 298.

126 *US Navy at War 1941–1945*, Official Reports by Fleet Admiral Ernest King USN, Appendix B, "Major Combatant Ships Added to the United States Fleet," available online at www.ibiblio.org/hyperwar/USN/USNatWar/index. html (accessed February 2014).

127 For an excellent chart with a timeline of the technological changes from 1939 to 1943 see Adm 116/5456, Review of the Development of Tactics and Weapons in the U-boat War, January 19, 1944.

128 The Germans soon upgraded the Metox set.

129 Roskill, *The War at Sea*, vol. II, pp. 369, 371, 375. Also see Barnett, *Engage the Enemy More Closely*, pp. 256–7, 479–80, 580–3.

130 Doenitz, *Memoirs: Ten Years and Twenty Days* (London, 1990), p. 339.

131 Roskill, *The War at Sea*, vol. II, pp. 205, 369.

132 Milner, *The Battle of the Atlantic*, pp. 156–7.

133 Marc Milner has written some excellent analyses of the Battle of the Atlantic with particular attention to the Canadian contribution. He often puts stress on how the enormous responsibilities placed on the RCN kept it from improving and updating its equipment and training during the war. He is particularly fair-minded when it comes to looking at the distressing British decision to remove the Canadians from convoy duties in early 1943. See Milner, *North Atlantic Run*, pp. 243–68.

134 Milner, "Convoy Escorts: Tactics, Technology and Innovation in the Royal Canadian Navy, 1939–1943," *Military Affairs*, vol. 48, 1 (Jan. 1984), 22–4.

135 Milner, *The Battle of the Atlantic*, pp. 129–30.

136 Assman, "Why U-boat Warfare Failed," 667–8.

137 Cab 120-409, Air Ministry to British Delegation, May 26, 1942.

138 Buckley, "Air Power and the Battle of the Atlantic," *Journal of Contemporary History*, vol. 28, 1 (Jan. 1993), 155.

139 Roskill, *The War at Sea*, vol. II, p. 372, Map 40.

140 There is an excellent collection of articles on the subject of the German air force and the war at sea, which discusses the shortcomings in great detail. See Isby (ed.), *The Luftwaffe and the War at Sea, 1939–1945* (London, 2005). There were problems in aircraft range, coordination of tactics, and high politics. The navy's general view was that the Luftwaffe was not interested enough in devoting the resources needed to develop the proper equipment and tactics for a war at sea.

141 Roskill, *The War at Sea*, vol. II, p. 485.

142 Roskill, *The War at Sea*, vol. II, pp. 365–6.

143 Roskill, *The War at Sea*, vol. II, p. 363.

144 Grove (ed.), *The Defeat of the Enemy Attack on Shipping 1939–1945*, vol. Ia, p. 92.

145 Roskill, *The War at Sea*, vol. II, p. 372.

146 Grove (ed.), *The Defeat of the Enemy Attack on Shipping 1939–1945*, vol. Ia, p. 95. There were forty-nine very long-range Liberators assigned to convoy protection throughout the North Atlantic by May 1943.

147 Roskill, *The War at Sea*, vol. II, p. 486, Table II.

148 Roskill, *The War at Sea*, vol. II, pp. 486, 377.

149 Doenitz, *Memoirs*, p. 340.

150 Adm 116/5456, Admiralty's Appreciation of U-boat Trend, June 24, 1943.

151 See Chapter 11.

8 The war in Europe: strategic bombing and the land war

1 WD, Historical File, RG 165, Book 13, Personal Report on Regensburg Mission, August 17, 1943.

2 Turner, *Fight for the Air* (Annapolis, MD, 2000).

3 WD, Historical File, RG 165, Book 13, Personal Report on Regensburg Mission, August 17, 1943, p. 5.

4 WD, Historical File, RG 165, Book 13, Personal Report on Regensburg Mission, August 17, 1943, p. 4.

5 WD, Historical File, RG 165, Book 13, Personal Report on Regensburg Mission, August 17, 1943, p. 6.

6 See Smith, "The Strategic Bombing Debate: The Second World War and Vietnam," *Journal of Contemporary History*, vol. 12 (1977), 175.

7 Werrell, "The Strategic Bombing of Germany in World War II." This is quite a balanced look at the campaign, but even it has a more critical outlook on the results. In particular, it believes the 1943 campaign was a complete failure (p. 705).

8 Harris MSS, "The Strategic Control of our Anti-Submarine Campaign," December 19 1942

9 Harris MSS, Harris to Thornton, April 13, 1943.

10 Leahy MSS, Diary, April 29, 1943.

11 WD, History File, RG 165, Arnold to Marshall, April 30, 1943.

12 WD, History File, RG 165, Marshall to Arnold, May 1, 1943.

13 Air 20-4069, Eaker to Dean, April 15, 1943.

14 Air 20-4069, Portal to Arnold, April 15, 1943.

15 Perhaps the best summary document on Harris' view of the air war going into 1943 is an overview report on 1942, the construction of which he oversaw. There is a copy in his private papers: Harris MSS, "Bomber Command: 1942."

16 Harris, *Bomber Offensive*, pp. 102–3.

17 Harris MSS, "Bomber Command: 1942," p. 3. In this calculation each Lancaster destroyed meant the loss of 68.5 tons of bombs dropped on Germany, while the equivalent figure for the Halifax was 30.1 and the Wellington was 21.6.

18 Harris MSS, December 21, 1943, "Final Minutes of Meeting Held on December 21st to Consider Future Use of Halifax in Bomber Command." Harris was adamant that even the improved Halifax bombers could not reach a high enough altitude to be effective.

19 Air 8/693, Sinclair to WSC, undated program for 1943 aircraft production plan.

20 Air 8/693, Heavy Bomber, Production Compared with Planned Programme, October 16, 1943.

21 Harris MSS, Harris to Trenchard, September 22, 1943.

22 Webster and Frankland, *Strategic Air Offensive against Germany*, vol. III, p. 307.

23 Harris MSS, "Bomber Command: 1942," p. 14; Oboe was the "new navigational aid" referred to on this page. See also Harris MSS, Dispatch on War Operations, February 23, 1942 to May 8, 1945, p. 3.

24 Biddle, "Bombing by the Square Yard: Sir Arthur Harris at War, 1942–1945," *International History Review*, vol. 21, 3 (Sep. 1999), 636.

25 Harris MSS, "Bomber Command: 1942," p. 7. See also Harris MSS, Harris to Lovett, December 24, 1942.

26 Spaatz MSS, 289, "The War in the Air," post-war study, pages unnumbered.

27 Harris MSS, "Future Main Strategy of the War," December 3, 1942, p. 3.

28 Jacobs, "Strategic Bombing and American National Strategy, 1941–1943," *Military Affairs*, vol. 50, 3 (July 1986), 133–9.

29 Arnold MSS, reel 113, Arnold to Marshall, August 22, 1942.

30 FDR MSS, PSF 82, Memorandum from Arnold to FDR, March 23, 1942.

31 Craven and Cate (eds.), *The Army Air Forces in World War II*, vol. II, pp. 266–7.

32 See Chapter 7.

33 Craven and Cate (eds.), *The Army Air Forces in World War II*, vol. VI, pp. 207–8.

34 Hopkins MSS, 126, Lubin to Hopkins, Review of the Aircraft Position of the United Nations as of March 31, 1943.

35 Hopkins MSS, 126, Lubin to Hopkins, Review of the Aircraft Position of the United Nations as of March 31, 1942.

36 Konvitz, "Bombs, Cities and Submarines: Allied Bombing of the French Ports, 1942–1943," *International History Review*, vol. 14, 1 (Feb. 1992), 39–41.

37 Craven and Cate (eds.), *The Army Air Forces in World War II*, vol. II, pp. 217–21.

38 Biddle, "Bombing by the Square Yard," 646.

39 Konvitz, "Bombs, Cities and Submarines," 43–6.

40 There is a copy of the letter Arnold sent setting up the COA in Spaatz MSS, 67, Arnold to Assistant Chief of the Air Staff, December 9, 1942.

41 Hopkins MSS, 126, Combat Aircraft which Should be Produced in the United States in 1943, September 9, 1943.
42 The preliminary COA report can be found in Spaatz MSS, 67, COA to Arnold, March 8, 1943. There is also a bound copy with charts in the JCS file, RG 218.
43 See COA March 1943 Report (no page numbers), "Single-Engine Fighter Aircraft Targets in Greater Germany."
44 See COA March 1943 Report (no page numbers), "Petroleum Production Targets in Axis Europe."
45 This was the number that was agreed to under the CBO in May 1943; see Cab 121/153, Plan for Combined Bomber Offensive from the United Kingdom, May 14, 1943.
46 See COA March 1943 Report (no page numbers), "Ball-Bearing Production in Axis Germany."
47 USSBS, Klingler Interrogation, May 2, 1945, p. 1.
48 See COA March 1943 Report (no page numbers), "Ball-Bearing Production in Axis Germany."
49 Spaatz 67, MEW report to Portal, April 3, 1943.
50 Air 9-424, Portal Response to Secretary of State for Air, September 26, 1942.
51 Cab 121/153, Plan for Combined Bomber Offensive from the United Kingdom, May 14, 1943.
52 Cab 121/153, Plan for Combined Bomber Offensive from the United Kingdom, May 14, 1943, p. 87.
53 Webster and Frankland, *Strategic Air Offensive against Germany*, vol. II, pp. 108–37.
54 Webster and Frankland, *Strategic Air Offensive against Germany*, vol. II, pp. 146–7.
55 Webster and Frankland, *Strategic Air Offensive against Germany*, vol. II, p. 154.
56 For a good popular history of the Hamburg raids, see Lowe, *Inferno*. Unlike some of the current historiography, Lowe does not view the raids solely as a humanitarian disaster or a war crime. In terms of its effect on German production, he uses the USSBS to claim that it had a significant, if short-term, impact on German war-making. See pp. 318–23.
57 FO 1031/148; see documentary extracts of Speer quotes in November 8, 1945 memorandum, p. 3.
58 HW 1/3177, translated intelligence of Japanese cables, Japanese Ambassador Reports, August 18, 1944.
59 Harris MSS, Speech made May 15, 1944 in preparation for Overlord operation.
60 Webster and Frankland, *Strategic Air Offensive against Germany*, vol. II, p. 155.

61 Craven and Cate (eds.), *The Army Air Forces in World War II*, vol. II, p. 671.

62 Craven and Cate (eds.), *The Army Air Forces in World War II*, vol. II, pp. 682–3.

63 Air 8-1109, JIC Memo, Effects of Bombing Effort on German War Economy, November 12, 1943, p. 7.

64 USSBS, Klingler Interrogation, May 2, 1945, pp. 2–3.

65 Craven and Cate (eds.), *The Army Air Forces in World War II*, vol. II, p. 683.

66 Air 8/711, Portal to WSC, October 12, 1943.

67 USSBS, Klingler Interrogation, May 2, 1945, p. 3.

68 Craven and Cate (eds.), *The Army Air Forces in World War II*, vol. II, pp. 703–4.

69 Craven and Cate (eds.), *The Army Air Forces in World War II*, vol. II, pp. 264–5.

70 Craven and Cate (eds.), *The Army Air Forces in World War II*, vol. II, p. 236.

71 Air 8/1146, Welsh to Portal, October 19, 1943.

72 Eaker MSS, Eaker to Portal, October 1943.

73 Arnold MSS, Reel 2, Diary entry, September 3, 1943. The need for more drop tanks was obvious to Arnold at this point, as was the value of the P-47. Eaker claimed that with more drop tanks for his P-47s, at least twenty more bombers would have been saved. Eaker-MSS, Eaker to Portal, October 1943.

74 Craven and Cate (eds.), *The Army Air Forces in World War II*, vol. II, p. 700.

75 See Arnold MSS, Reel 125, Lovett to Arnold, June 18, 1943 for an interesting discussion of using the P-47 or P-38 for long-range escort. The P-47 was definitely considered the better fighter plane, but the P-38 could travel further.

76 NARA, WD History File, RG 165, "Air Plan for the Defeat of Germany," Arnold Memorandum, November 1, 1943.

77 Webster and Frankland, *Strategic Air Offensive against Germany*, vol. II, pp. 190–212. There are a number of different histories written about the "Battle of Berlin." Among the best is Searby, *The Bomber Battle for Berlin* (Shrewsbury, 1991). Searby, who would later reach the rank of air commodore in the RAF, was a squadron leader in a Pathfinder force during the war. He certainly views the losses suffered by the RAF during the battle as extremely high considering the return (see pp. 8–9).

78 Webster and Frankland, *Strategic Air Offensive against Germany*, vol. II, pp. 190.

79 Harris MSS, Letter from Salisbury to Sinclair, November 26, 1943.

80 Harris MSS, Dispatch on War Operations, February 23, 1942 to May 8, 1945, p. 10.

81 Harris MSS, Harris to Lovett, January 24, 1944.

82 Webster and Frankland, *Strategic Air Offensive against Germany*, vol. II, pp. 197.

83 Francis, *The Flyer: British Culture and the Royal Air Force, 1939–1945* (Oxford, 2008), pp. 117–18.

84 Webster and Frankland, *Strategic Air Offensive against Germany*, vol. II, p. 194.

85 Harris MSS, Dispatch on War Operations, February 23, 1942 to May 8, 1945, "Diagram Showing Bomber Command Loss Rate on German Targets." During the bombing of Germany there was only one other period when losses matched the Battle of Berlin and this was during the heavy operations for a few days during the D-Day landings.

86 Lubin MSS, USAAF, Principal Planes in Principal Theaters in 1943. Exact data given for June 12, 1943.

87 Craven and Cate (eds.), *The Army Air Forces in World War II*, vol. II, p. 568.

88 Air 8-1146, Memo from US Chiefs of Staff, October 19, 1943.

89 Spaatz MSS, 289, "The War in the Air," post-war study, pages unnumbered. Also see USSBS, European Report 4, p. 18a. Wiener Neustadt had the fifth largest number of workers attached to the plant as well as the fourth largest floorspace.

90 USSBS, Messerschmitt Interview, May 11 and 12, 1945, p. 9.

91 Craven and Cate (eds.), *The Army Air Forces in World War II*, vol. II, p. 477. For a relatively negative appraisal of the August 1943 raids on Ploesti, see Rein, *The North African Air Campaign: US Army Air Forces from El Alamein to Salerno* (Lawrence, KS, 2012), pp. 168, 190.

92 Craven and Cate (eds.), *The Army Air Forces in World War II*, vol. II, p. 478.

93 Spaatz MSS, 135, Speer Interview, May 19, 1945, p. 8.

94 The data in Figure 36 comes from Speer's ministry. It was first given to Arnold as part of an internal USAAF history of the role of air power in the defeat of Germany. See Arnold MSS, Reel 190, The Contribution of Airpower to the Defeat of Germany, Appendix K.

95 Spaatz MSS, Box 135, Minutes of Speer Meeting, May 19, 1945, p. 1.

96 The relative lack of power of American bombs when compared with those manufactured by the British was mentioned a number of times in post-war German interrogations.

97 FO 1031-141, Speer Interrogation Notes, May 30, 1945, p. 4.

98 Harris MSS, Portal to Harris, April 10, 1943.

99 Air 8-1109, Effects of Bombing Offensive on German War Effort, November 12, 1943.

100 Air 8-1109, Effects of Bombing Offensive on German War Effort, November 12, 1943, p. 3.

101 Air 8-1109, Effects of Bombing Offensive on German War Effort, March 4, 1944, pp. 2–3.

102 In October 1945, the Air Ministry compiled a chart of Luftwaffe deployment by type of aircraft and area.

103 USSBS, Junck Interview, May 19, 1945, p. 5.

104 Spaatz MSS, 134, Galland Report, The Birth, Life and Death of the German Day Fighter, p. 39.

105 *Germany and the Second World War*, vol. VII, pp. 284–9.

106 USSBS, European Report 4, German Aircraft Industry, p. 94.

107 An almost complete edition of the Luftwaffe's loss register from the beginning of the war through November 1943 survived. Copies can be found both in the National Archives in College Park, Maryland and in the Imperial War Museum, London. Williamson Murray used these registers to compile a number of extremely useful tables. The one showing aircraft lost by theater is in Murray, *Luftwaffe*, p. 138. Unfortunately, the loss register has a major gap from November 1943 until February 1945, at which point it becomes more difficult to divide losses between theaters. However, the USSBS was able to find the figures for single-engine fighters, which it included in some of its reports.

108 Spaatz MSS, 134, Galland Report, The Birth, Life and Death of the German Day Fighter, pp. 38–9. Galland was first sent to the Mediterranean in May to await an expected invasion somewhere in Italy.

109 *Germany and the Second World War*, vol. VII, p. 215.

110 *Germany and the Second World War*, vol. VII, p. 65.

111 Spaatz MSS, 289, Reich Air Defense 1939–1945, Internal USAAF history written August 1946 (no page numbers).

112 *Germany and the Second World War*, vol. VII, p. 179.

113 USSBS, Koller Interview, May 23 and 24, 1945, p. 6.

114 USSBS, Summary Memorandum, Interrogation of Officers of the Luftwaffe, June 21, 1945, p. 2.

115 USSBS, Galland Interview, June 4 and 7, 1945, pp. 5–6.

116 USSBS, European Report 1, pp. 21–2.

117 USSBS, Galland Interview, June 4, 1945, p. 2.

118 USSBS, Galland Interview, June 4 and 7, 1945, p. 6.

119 *Germany and the Second World War*, vol. VII, p. 176.

120 USSBS, Summary Memorandum, Interrogation of Officers of the Luftwaffe, June 21, 1945, p. 4.

121 USSBS, Kaether Interview, May 24, 1945, p. 1.

122 Spaatz MSS, 116, GAF Aircraft and Aircrew Losses, September 1939 to January 1945. These are overall losses taken from translated German Luftwaffe documents captured after the war.

123 *Germany and the Second World War*, vol. VII, p. 171.

124 WO 208/4340, Milch Report, July 9, 1945, p. 9.

125 USSBS, Messerschmitt Interview, May 11 and 12, 1945, p. 9.

126 USSBS, Messerschmitt Interview, May 11 and 12, 1945, p. 5. He said that the average monthly production figure in 1943 was 700.

127 USSBS, Messerschmitt Interview, May 11 and 12, 1945, p. 10.

128 USSBS, Tank Interview, May 19, 1945, p. 14.

129 USSBS, Kaether Interview, April 24, 1945, pp. 2–3.

130 USSBS, Tank Interview, May 19, 1945, p. 14.

131 One area that the USSBS seems to have misinterpreted is the concentration of German aircraft construction (which they argued was significant). It seems now that the war led to a fragmentation of the industry into more separated units, which would support the notion of dispersal inefficiencies. See Reichardt, "Industrial Concentration and World War II: A Note on the Aircraft Industry," *Business History Review*, vol. 49, 4 (Winter 1975), 498–503.

132 USSBS, European Report 4, pp. 88–9.

133 USSBS, Goering Interview, June 29, 1945, p. 2.

134 Arnold MSS, Reel 190, The Contribution of Airpower to the Defeat of Germany, Appendices, Section 2.

135 USSBS, Kehrl Interview Summary, June 11, and July 18, 1945, p. 10.

136 USSBS, European Report 4, p. 82.

137 Mierzejewski, *The Collapse of the German War Economy, 1944–1945*, p. 52.

138 Unfortunately, in the bombing of the Ruhr it seems that the foreign workers suffered even more than the German population, as many were staying in camps that had only primitive means of protection. Herbert, *Hitler's Foreign Workers: Enforced Foreign Labor in Germany under the Third Reich* (Cambridge, 1997), pp. 317–19.

139 Arnold MSS, Reel 190, The Contribution of Airpower to the Defeat of Germany, Appendices, Section 1.

140 FO 1031-148, Translated Document, On the German Economic Situation 1943/44, June 29, 1944, p. 2.

141 USSBS, Kehrl Interview, June 8, 1945, p. 6.

142 USSBS, Martin and Hagemann Interview, June 5 and 9, 1945, p. 7.

143 Gregor, *Daimler-Benz in the Third Reich*, pp. 144–9.

144 See Chapter 1.

145 USSBS, Fischer Interview, undated, p. 2.

146 FO 1031/48, Economic and Financial Branch Memo based on German documents, November 8, 1945, p. 4.

147 USSBS, Endros Interview, June 23, 1945, p. 2.

148 Speer, *Inside the Third Reich* (New York, 1995), p. 720.

149 Speer, *Inside the Third Reich*, p. 304.

150 USSBS, Dorsch Interview, July 29, 1945, p. 14. Dorsch actually thought that the figure from the document was high, saying that he believed that the total number of workers involved in construction was approximately 1.25 million.

151 FO 1031-148, translated report on German war economy, authored by Kehrl and dated June 29, 1944, p. 1.

152 USSBS, Dorsch Interview, July 29, 1945, pp. 5–6.

153 Heiber and Glantz (eds.), *Hiter and his Generals*, p. 189.

154 USSBS, Fleisher Interview, May 19, 1945, p. 6.

155 Hitler started demanding greater flak protection for Berlin in 1942. See Heiber and Glantz (eds.), *Hiter and his Generals*, p. 49. Also see USSBS, Keitel Interview, June 2, 1945, p. 2.

156 USSBS, European Report 3, pp. 182, 284. In 1943 weapons production was approximately 8 percent of output; see pp. 144–5.

157 USSBS, European Report 3, pp. 183, 284.

158 Spaatz MSS, 135, Speer Interview, May 20, 1945, p. 10.

159 USSBS, Buhle and Saur Interview, May 18, 1945, p. 5.

160 Spaatz MSS, 135, Speer Interrogation, May 21, 1945, p. 5.

161 Murray, *Luftwaffe*, pp. 271–2.

162 USSBS, Thomas Interview, July 4–5, 1945, p. 3.

163 USSBS, Hettlage Interview, June 16, 1945, p. 4.

164 FO 1031-41, Speer Interrogation, May 30, 1945, p. 2.

165 USSBS, Thomas Interview, July 4–5, 1945, p. 3.

166 Cab 146/197, Some Weaknesses in German Strategy and Organization, internal UK study based on German primary sources which has recently been published as Winter (ed.), *Defeating Hitler*; the charts on AFV losses are in Appendix VII.

167 Citino, *Death of the Wehrmacht: The German Campaigns of 1942* (Lawrence, KS, 2007), pp. 299–300.

168 Hayward, *Stopped at Stalingrad: The Luftwaffe and Hitler's Defeat in the East, 1942–1943* (Lawrence, KS, 1998), p. 310. During 1943, Germany built 25,527 aircraft.

169 Air 40-1207, Luftwaffe Deployment Chart compiled October 1945.

170 Spaatz MSS, 134, Rohden Interrogation Report, May 22, 1945, p. 2.

171 Zetterling and Frankson, *Kursk 1943: A Statistical Analysis* (London, 2000), pp. 18–20. See also Citino, *The Wehrmacht Retreats: Fighting a Lost War* (Lawrence, KS, 2012), pp. 130–4.

172 *Das Deutsche Reich und der Zweite Weltkrieg*, vol. VIII (2007), p. 151, supplies figures unavailable in the English translation (*Germany and the Second World War*, 9 vols. (Oxford, 1990–2008).

173 Glantz and House, *The Battle of Kursk* (Lawrence, KS, 1999), p. 276.

174 Zetterling and Frankson, *Kursk 1943: A Statistical Analysis*, pp. 120–2.

175 Richard J. Evans, *The Third Reich at War: How the Nazis Led Germany from Conquest to Disaster* (London, 2008), p. 489.

176 A number of sources mention that the Germans lost 1,331 tanks on the Eastern Front in July–August 1943. Divide this number by the sixty-two days in the two months and on average you have a loss daily rate of 21.6.

177 There is a very interesting chart which shows the difference between losses and production of German AFV throughout the war in *Germany and the Second World War*, vol. V, pt 2, p. 615.

178 Cab 146/197, published as Winter (ed.), *Defeating Hitler*, Appendix VII.

179 Air 40-1207, Luftwaffe Deployment Chart compiled October 1945.

180 In 1943 Germany produced 25,527 aircraft of all types, including trainers. USSBS, European Report 3, p. 156.

181 Howe, *United States Army in World War II: Northwest Africa, Seizing the Initiative in the West* (Washington, DC, 1993), Appendix B, pp. 682–3.

182 Molony, *The Mediterranean and the Middle East*, vol. V (London, 1973), pp. 41–2.

183 DiNardo, *Germany and the Axis Powers: From Coalition to Collapse* (Lawrence, KS, 2005), p. 177.

184 This is my calculation from the Luftwaffe loss charts for October 23 through November 5 and includes the entire Mediterranean area, so a number of these losses had nothing to do with the fighting around El Alamein. It is interesting to note that Rommel believed it was British air superiority that really made the difference during the battle, and it seems to have shaken his confidence greatly. See Kitchen, *Rommel's Desert War: Waging World War II in North Africa, 1941–1943* (Cambridge, 2009), pp. 349–51.

185 Overmans, *Deustche Militärische Verluste im Zweiten Weltkrieg*, Table 38, p. 238.

9 The war in Europe in 1944

1 Spaatz 134, Enemy Intelligence Summaries, May 29, 1945, p. 1.

2 Spaatz 134, Enemy Intelligence Summaries, May 29, 1945, p. 2.

3 Spaatz 134, Enemy Intelligence Summaries, May 29, 1945, p. 2.

4 Spayd (ed.), *Bayerlein: After Action Report of the Panzer Lehr Division Commander from D-Day to the Ruhr* (Atglen, PA, 2005), p. 22.

5 Spaatz 134, Enemy Intelligence Summaries, May 29, 1945, p. 3.

6 Spaatz 134, Enemy Intelligence Summaries, May 29, 1945, p. 7.

7 Spaatz 134, Enemy Intelligence Summaries, May 29, 1945, p. 8.

8 Spaatz 134, Enemy Intelligence Summaries, May 29, 1945, p. 9.

9 Mazower, *Hitler's Empire: Nazi Rule in Occupied Europe* (London, 2008), pp. 288–90 for a description of the policy of expropriating food.

10 FO 1031-141, Speer Interview, May 30, 1945, p. 2.

11 FO 1031-148, Documentary Extracts Showing Effects of Aerial Warfare and Allied Military Success on German War Production, November 8, 1945, pp. 10–11.

12 Stokes, "The Oil Industry in Nazi Germany," *Business History Review*, vol. 59, 2 (1985), 255.

13 By 1944 a large percentage of the workers in many German industries were from outside Germany. Herbert, *Hitler's Foreign Workers*, p. 248. Also see Klemann and Kudryashov, *Occupied Economies: An Economic History of Nazi-Occupied Europe, 1939–45* (London, 2012), p. 122; they claim that, in 1944, Germany had 7,126,000 foreign or POW labourers employed throughout their economic system, 19.3 percent of the total workforce.

14 *Germany and the Second World War*, vol. V/II, p. 914.

15 Harris MSS, Lovett to Harris, October 31, 1943.

16 Webster and Frankland, *Strategic Air Offensive against Germany*, vol. II, pp. 80–1.

17 It is interesting to see how quickly the possibilities of the newly powered Mustang reached the top of the American decision-making structure. In June 1942, Arnold told Hopkins in a letter about the British experiment with the Rolls-Royce engine which had created an "exceptional" aircraft and pressed him to increase the production of Merlin engines in the USA. See Hopkins MSS, 125, Arnold to Hopkins, June 1942.

18 USSBS, European Report 59, pp. 8–9.

19 Arnold MSS, Reel 125, Arnold to Eaker, December 16, 1943.

20 Craven and Cate (eds.), *The Army Air Forces in World War II*, vol. III, p. 112.

21 FDR MSS, PSF 6, Combined Production Report, July 1, 1944, p. 7.

22 Thomas and Jablonski, *The Life of James H. Doolittle: Bomber Commander* (London, 1977), p. 281.

23 Spaatz MSS, 134, "The Birth, Life and Death of the German Day Fighter," 1945, as related by Adolf Galland, pp. 47–8.

24 Spaatz MSS, 134, "The Birth, Life and Death of the German Day Fighter," 1945, p. 36.

25 Spaatz MSS, 134, "The Birth, Life and Death of the German Day Fighter," 1945, p. 37.

26 Spaatz MSS, COA Revision as Circulated by Arnold, December 10, 1943.

27 Spaatz MSS, 67, COA Memoranda, January 12 and 18, 1944.

28 Meilinger, "US Air Force Leaders," 846.

29 Davis, "Carl A. Spaatz and the Development of the Royal Air Force–US Army Air Corps Relationship, 1939–40," *Journal of Military History*, vol. 54, 4 (Oct. 1990), 471.

30 Marshall MSS, Arnold Memorandum, January 24, 1944.

31 Spaatz MSS, 144, Plan for the Completion of the Combined Bomber Offensive, March 5, 1944.

32 The plan to attack German tire production was astute. The German army regularly suffered through tire shortages in the war, such as during Barbarossa. In 1944 in France, the tire issue was problematic because the Anglo-American air campaign against French railways meant that German vehicles had to travel many more miles than anticipated, leading to high levels of wastage. See DiNardo, *Germany's Panzer Arm* (Westport, CT, 1997), p. 19.

33 Spaatz MSS, 144, Plan for the Completion of the Combined Bomber Offensive, March 5, 1944, p. 3.
34 Spaatz MSS, 144, Plan for the Completion of the Combined Bomber Offensive, March 5, 1944, p. 4.
35 Spaatz MSS, 144, Plan for the Completion of the Combined Bomber Offensive, March 5, 1944, Part 1, p. 1.
36 Spaatz MSS, 144, Plan for the Completion of the Combined Bomber Offensive, March 5, 1944, Supplement, p. 1.
37 Meilinger, "A History of Effects-Based Operations," *Journal of Military History*, vol. 71, 1 (Jan. 2007), 151–7.
38 Davis, *Carl Spaatz and the Air War in Europe*, p. 353.
39 Harris MSS, Portal to Harris, January 28, 1944 and April 7, 1944.
40 Hall, *Strategy for Victory*, pp. 141–3.
41 Air 8/1146, Tedder to CAS (Portal), October 31, 1943.
42 Air 8/711, Note by Air C-in-C Med, January 30, 1943; see also Portal to WSC, March 14, 1943.
43 *The Papers of Dwight David Eisenhower: The War Years*, vol. III, Eisenhower to Marshall, March 3, 1944, pp. 1758–9.
44 Eisenhower even wrote in his diary how he wanted to make sure that Tedder was superior to Spaatz during this period. *The Papers of Dwight David Eisenhower: The War Years*, vol. III, Memorandum for Diary, April 12, 1944.
45 Spaatz 144, Tedder Memo, Employment of Allied Air Forces in Support of Overlord, March 24, 1944.
46 Harris MSS, Tedder Memo, Notes on an Air Policy to be Adopted with a View to the Rapid Defeat of Germany, October 25, 1944
47 Harris MSS, Harris to Portal, November 1, 1944.
48 See Chapter 8.
49 Of the 16,127 fighters lost, 3,697 were on the Eastern Front/Mediterranean and 12,430 were in operation from Germany or over the Western Front.
50 USSBS, European Report 59, Figure 7.
51 Spaatz MSS, Box 134, Galland Report, "The Birth, Life and Death of the German Day Fighter," p. 40. A *Geschwader* was the largest individually mobile unit fielded by the Luftwaffe in the war. Its American equivalent would be a "wing." A "*Luftflotte*" was a larger strategic command taking in all the *Geschwader* in a certain geographical area or on a combat front. The closest comparison to a *Luftflotte* would be an Army Group.
52 Isby, *Fighting the Bombers: The Luftwaffe's Struggle against the Allied Bomber Offensive* (London, 2003), p. 154.
53 For two excellent descriptions of the decimation of the Luftwaffe as a fighting force in the first six months of 1944, with a great deal of evidence on pilot losses, see Murray, *Luftwaffe*, pp. 214–19; Caldwell and Muller, *The*

Luftwaffe over Germany: The Defence of The Reich (London, 2007), pp. 162–89.

54 *Germany and the Second World War*, vol. VII, p. 126.

55 Caldwell, *Day Fighters in Defence of the Reich: A War Diary 1942–45*, p. 450.

56 Caldwell, *Day Fighters in Defence of the Reich: A War Diary 1942–45*, p. 450.

57 Spaatz MSS, 116, GAF Aircraft and Aircrew Losses, 1939–1945. These figures are for aircraft that were written off, which was defined as suffering damage of 60 percent or greater. The figure is reached by taking that for all aircraft lost on operational duties and subtracting the number of trainers that were part of that number (which is listed below the main numbers in brackets in the document).

58 USSBS, European Report 59, "The Defeat of the German Air Force," p. 2.

59 "Big Week" also demonstrated how expensive the air war was for the Allies. The 8th Air Force needed access to a huge number of supplies to fly almost 4,000 sorties as part of the campaign. For a more detailed description of the logistics, see Sutterfield, "How Logistics Made *Big Week* Big: Eighth Air Force Bombing, 20–25 February 1944," *Air Force Journal of Logistics*, vol. 24, 2 (Summer 2000), 96–112.

60 USSBS, Frydag Interview, Report, July 9, 1945, p. 20.

61 USSBS, Frydag Interview, Report, July 9, 1945, p. 29.

62 FO 1031-148, Report on Interview of Speer, p. 2.

63 FO 1031-148, Report on Interview of Speer, p. 1.

64 See Chapter 1.

65 USSBS, Tank Interview, April 17 and 25, 1945, p. 14

66 USSBS, Frydag Interview, June 21, 1945, p. 1.

67 USSBS, Messerschmitt Interview, May 11, 1945, p. 10.

68 USSBS, Saur Interview, May 18, 1945, p. 2.

69 FO 1031-141, Saur Interview Report, June 10, 1945.

70 Tooze, *The Wages of Destruction*, pp. 627–8.

71 Budrass *et al.*, *Demystifying the German "Armament Miracle" during World War II: New Insights from the Annual Audits of German Aircraft Producers*, Yale University, Center Discussion Paper 905 (Jan. 2005), p. 27. An online version is available at www.econ.yale.edu/growth_pdf/cdp905.pdf (accessed September 9, 2014.)

72 FO 1031-141, Saur Interview Report, June 10, 1945.

73 FO 1031-141, Speer Interview Report, May 28, 1945, p. 5.

74 Craven and Cate (eds.), *The Army Air Forces in World War II*, vol. III, p. 176.

75 Arnold MSS, Reel 190, "The Contribution of Airpower to the Defeat of Germany," Appendix K, "The Air Attack on General Industry."

76 It does seem that even with city attacks receiving a reduced percentage of Anglo-American bombing, the effect that they had on German morale in the last year of the war was more profound, leading to the growth of a post-war

feeling of victimhood amongst the German people. See Bessel, *Nazism and War* (London, 2004), pp. 152–5.

77 USSBS, Frydag Interview, Report, July 9, 1945, p. 23,

78 Spaatz MSS, 135, Speer Interview, May 19, 1945, p. 2.

79 FO 1031-141, Speer Interview, May 30, 1945, p. 3.

80 Craven and Cate (eds.), *The Army Air Forces in World War II*, vol. III, p. 287.

81 Craven and Cate (eds.), *The Army Air Forces in World War II*, vol. III, pp. 284–5.

82 Air 40-1120, Strategic Bombing of Axis Europe, January 1943–September 1944.

83 *The Strategic Air War against Germany 1939–45* (UKSBS), p. 146.

84 USSBS, European Report 3, p. 76.

85 USSBS, Kehrl Interview, June 11, 1945, p. 23.

86 *Germany and the Second World War*, vol. V/II, pp. 473–4.

87 *Germany and the Second World War*, vol. V/II, p. 295

88 Spaatz 134, Goering Intelligence Summary, June 11, 1945, p. 18.

89 Air 40-1120, Strategic Bombing of Axis Europe, January 1943–September 1944, p. 17.

90 Spaatz 134, Goering Intelligence Summary, June 11, 1945, p. 18.

91 USSBS, European Report 59, Figure 3.

92 USSBS, European Report 59, Figure 8.

93 Spaatz MSS, 134, von Massow Interview, May 14, 1945, p. 5.

94 FO 1031-48, Speer Interview, June 13, 1945, p. 2.

95 Spaatz 134, Galland Interview, May 20, 1945, pp. 2–3.

96 *Germany and the Second World War*, vol. VII, pp. 300–1.

97 USSBS, European Report 59, Figure 7.

98 USSBS, European Report 59, Figure 6.

99 Spaatz MSS, 116, GAF Aircraft and Aircrew Losses 1939–1945. These figures are for aircraft that were written off, which was defined as suffering damage of 60 percent or greater; those classified as damaged were less than 60 percent.

100 Spaatz MSS, 116, GAF Aircraft and Aircrew Losses 1939–1945.

101 For a comparison of V-1 and V-2 construction, see Murray, *Luftwaffe*, pp. 175–6.

102 Neufeld, *The Rocket and the Reich*, pp. 190–1. See also USSBS, Saur Interview, May 23, 1945, p. 3; Spaatz MSS, Speer Interview, May 21, 1945, p. 7A.

103 Murray, *Luftwaffe*, p. 272.

104 Neufeld, *The Rocket and the Reich*, p. 273.

105 Spaatz MSS, 135, Minutes of Meeting with Speer, May 21, 1945, p. 6.

106 Speer confirmed the low end of these cost estimates to British interrogators, saying that the early models of the V-2 cost 800,000 RM each and the later ones 250,000 RM. FO 1031-141, Speer Interview, May 28, 1945, p. 5.

107 Arnold MSS, Reel 190, "The Contribution of Airpower to the Defeat of Germany," Appendix J, "The Attack on German Long-Range Weapons."

108 USSBS, European Report 4, p. 120a. This report has the director saying that 6916 V-2s were built, though at another time at the end of the war he said that a total of 7,500 were built. See: Arnold MSS, reel 190, "The Contribution of Airpower to the Defeat of Germany", Appendix J, "The Attack on German Long-Range Weapons."

109 USSBS, Frydag Interview, Report, July 9, 1945, p. 9.

110 USSBS, European Report 4, p. 120.

111 WO 208-4340, Report on Interviews with Milch, July 9, 1945, p. 12.

112 FO 1031-141, Speer Interview, May 28, 1945, p. 5.

113 Based on one V-2 equaling 6.5 FW-190s.

114 Spaatz MSS, 135, Minutes of Meeting with Speer, May 21, 1945, pp. 2, 4.

115 Arnold MSS, Reel 190, "The Contribution of Airpower to the Defeat of Germany," Appendix J, "The Attack on German Long-Range Weapons."

116 Spaatz MSS, 135, Minutes of Meeting with Speer, May 21, 1945, p. 6.

117 USSBS, Tank Interviews, V-Weapons Memoranda, p. 2.

118 WO 208-4340, Report on Interviews with Milch, July 9, 1945, p. 12.

119 Arnold MSS, Reel 190, "The Contribution of Airpower to the Defeat of Germany," Appendix J, "The Attack on German Long-Range Weapons." The total figures given for V-1 production are 23,748 by the end of 1944 and 30,257 by the time of the German surrender. See also USSBS, European Report 4, p. 114a.

120 *The Rise and Fall of the German Air Force*, p. 341.

121 Sandys MSS, 2-4-1, Air Scientific Intelligence Report, June 26, 1945.

122 Sandys MSS, 2-4-1, War Cabinet Minutes, June 29, 1943.

123 Sandys MSS, 2-4-1, War Cabinet Minutes, June 29, 1943, pp. 3–4. See also Wilson, *Churchill and the Prof*, pp. 47–51.

124 Sandys MSS, 2-4-1, War Cabinet Minutes, June 29, 1943, Annex to Minutes, p. 10.

125 Webster and Frankland, *Strategic Air Offensive against Germany*, vol. II, pp. 158–9.

126 Spaatz MSS, 135, Minutes of Meeting with Speer, May 21, 1945, p. 5.

127 USSBS, European Report 4, p. 120.

128 Sandys MSS, 2-4-3, German Long Range Rocket, October 24, 1943.

129 *Germany and the Second World War*, vol. VII, pp. 426–7.

130 Air 40-1120, Strategic Bombing of Axis Europe, January 1943–September 1944, p. 12.

131 USSBS, Dorsch Interview, July 29, 1945, p. 13.

132 Arnold MSS, Reel 190, "The Contribution of Airpower to the Defeat of Germany," Appendix J, "The Attack on German Long-Range Weapons."

133 Craven and Cate (eds.), *The Army Air Forces in World War II*, vol. III, pp. 104–5.

134 Craven and Cate (eds.), *The Army Air Forces in World War II*, vol. III, p. 106.

135 Craven and Cate (eds.), *The Army Air Forces in World War II*, vol. III, p. 103.

136 Spaatz MSS, 97, Allied Air Staff Meeting Minutes, May 26, 1944, p. 3.

137 Arnold MSS, Reel 190, "The Contribution of Airpower to the Defeat of Germany," Appendix J, "The Attack on German Long-Range Weapons."

138 Webster and Frankland, *Strategic Air Offensive against Germany*, vol. III, p. 46.

139 Harris MSS, 47–50, Addison to Harris, July 8, 1944.

140 Harris MSS, Harris Memo for Tedder and Sandys, July 19, 1944.

141 Arnold MSS, Reel 190, "The Contribution of Airpower to the Defeat of Germany," Appendix J, "The Attack on German Long-Range Weapons."

142 Combined, the British and Americans dropped 2,770,540 tons of bombs during the war.

143 Webster and Frankland, *Strategic Air Offensive against Germany*, vol. III, p. 45.

144 The combined tonnage of bombs dropped on France, Belgium, Holland and Germany from June to August 1944 was 180,000 tons. Webster and Frankland, *Strategic Air Offensive against Germany*, vol. III, p. 45. Of these, 81,000 were dropped on Crossbow operations and 32,000 were dropped on Germany, leaving (at most) 67,000 for all other operations.

145 Air 40-1120, Strategic Bombing of Axis Europe, January 1943–September 1944, p. 42.

146 Marshall MSS, Eisenhower to Marshall, June 19, 1944.

147 Air 40-1120, Strategic Bombing of Axis Europe, January 1943–September 1944, p. 42.

148 Arnold MSS, Reel 190, "The Contribution of Airpower to the Defeat of Germany," Appendix J, "The Attack on German Long-Range Weapons."

149 Arnold MSS, Reel 190, "The Contribution of Airpower to the Defeat of Germany," Appendix J, "The Attack on German Long-Range Weapons."

150 King and Kutta, *Impact: The History of Germany's V-Weapons in World War II*, p. 249.

151 Arnold MSS, Reel 190, "The Contribution of Airpower to the Defeat of Germany," Appendix J, "The Attack on German Long-Range Weapons."

152 Arnold MSS, Reel 190, "The Contribution of Airpower to the Defeat of Germany," Appendix J, "The Attack on German Long-Range Weapons."

153 Craven and Cate (eds.), *The Army Air Forces in World War II*, vol. III, p. 5.

154 Arnold MSS, Reel 190, "The Contribution of Airpower to the Defeat of Germany," Appendix J, "The Attack on German Long-Range Weapons."

155 Arnold MSS, Reel 190, "The Contribution of Airpower to the Defeat of Germany," Appendix J, "The Attack on German Long-Range Weapons."

156 Speer claimed that 70,000 workers were building the V-2 by 1945. Spaatz MSS, 135, Minutes of Meeting with Speer, May 21, 1945, p. 6. Neufeld, *The Rocket and the Reich*, p. 264, puts the number at 60,000.

157 USSBS, Dorsch Interview, July 29, 1945, p. 13.

158 The role of tactical air units such as the XIX Tactical Air Command in this campaign can be overlooked. Dr. Graham Cross is doing some fascinating research, arguing that these tactical attacks were extremely important in shutting down German communications. Certainly some of the best pictures of the transport campaign came from the tactical units making the attacks (see Figures 65–7).

159 Air 40–1120, Strategic Bombing of Axis Europe, January 1943–September 1944, p. 40.

160 Craven and Cate (eds.), *The Army Air Forces in World War II*, vol. III, p. 650.

161 *The Strategic Air War against Germany 1939–45* (UKSBS), p. 123.

162 FO 1031-148, Documentary Extracts, November 8, 1945, p. 12.

163 Mierzejewski, *The Collapse of the German War Economy*, pp. 106–13.

164 Air 8-1109, JIC Report on the Impact of Bombing, July 22, 1943, p. 9.

165 FO 1031-148, Documentary Extracts, November 8, 1945, pp. 14–15.

166 Heiber and Glantz (eds.), *Hitler and his Generals: Military Conferences 1942–1945*, p. 558.

167 FO 1031-141, Report of Written Replies by Speer, Scheiber, Roechling and Saur, October 1, 1945, pp. 4–5.

168 Spaatz MSS, Speer Interview, published May 31, 1945, p. 12.

169 Mierzejewski, "When Did Albert Speer Give Up?" *Historical Journal*, vol. 31, 2 (June 1988), p. 397.

170 Spaatz MSS, Speer Interview, published May 31, 1945, p. 12.

171 FO 1031-141, Report of Written Replies by Speer, Scheiber, Roechling and Saur, October 1, 1945, Documentary Extracts in Appendix 1.

172 FO 1031-148, Documentary Extracts, November 8, 1945, pp. 19–20.

173 *The Strategic Air War against Germany 1939–45* (UKSBS), p. 129.

174 *The Strategic Air War against Germany 1939–45* (UKSBS), p. 127.

175 USSBS, European Report 200, Exhibit 78.

176 USSBS, European Report 200, p. 86.

177 USSBS, European Report 200, pp. 88–9.

178 Arnold MSS, Reel 190, "The Contribution of Airpower to the Defeat of Germany," Appendix K, "The Attack on General Industry"; Appendix M, "Miscellaneous Aspects of Air Power."

179 Spaatz 135, Speer Interview, published May 31, 1945, p. 9.

180 Spaatz 134, Milch Interview, May 23, 1945, p. 2.

181 WO 208-4340, Report from Captured Personnel, July 9, 1945, p. 7.

182 FO 1031-148, Documentary Extracts, p. 8.
183 USSBS Kehrl Interview, June 11, 1945, p. 16.
184 WO 208-4340, Milch Interview, July 7, 1945, p. 7.
185 Spaatz MSS, Speer Interview, May 19, 1945, p. 3.
186 Arnold MSS, Reel 190, "The Contribution of Airpower to the Defeat of Germany," Appendix H, "The Attack on Enemy Roads."
187 Arnold MSS, Reel 190, "The Contribution of Airpower to the Defeat of Germany," Appendix H.
188 Arnold MSS, Reel 190, "The Contribution of Airpower to the Defeat of Germany," Appendix H.
189 There is a superb reconstruction of the events leading up to this decision in Davis, *Carl A. Spaatz and the Air War*, pp. 345–52. See also Overy, *The Bombing War*, pp. 572–3.
190 The effectiveness of this campaign has been the subject of some debate. For a positive summation of the effectiveness of the attacks on French transport, see Murray, *Luftwaffe*, pp. 237–44. Murray uses data to describe the impact on rail movement in France and makes the important point that, because of Ultra, the success of the campaign was understood by the British and Americans. For an overall summary which is less positive, see Overy, *The Bombing War*, pp. 576–7.
191 In 2015 Cambridge University Press will be publishing a three-volume *Cambridge History of the Second World War*, edited by Evan Mawdsley and John Ferris, for which I have written a chapter entitled "Logistics by Land and Air," in which the superiority of railway supply is analyzed.
192 Overmans, *Deutsche Militärische Verluste im Zweiten Weltkrieg*, p. 238.
193 Overmans, *Deutsche Militärische Verluste im Zweiten Weltkrieg*, p. 239.
194 FO 1031-148, p. 10, Exploitation of Speer, German Documentary Extracts, November 8, 1945.
195 Spaatz MSS, Box 134, Galland Report, "The Birth, Life and Death of the German Day Fighter," p. 57.
196 Spaatz MSS, 134, Milch Interview, May 27, 1945, p. 13.
197 Spaatz MSS, 134, Galland Interview, May 20, 1945, p. 3.
198 Murray, *Luftwaffe*, pp. 258–60; Bergstrom, *Bagration to Berlin: The Final Air Battles in the East* (Hersham, Surrey, 2008), p. 58.
199 Ziemke, *Stalingrad to Berlin: The German Defeat in the East* (Washington, 8 DC, 1987), p. 321.
200 Murray, *Luftwaffe*, pp. 260. Murray has the figure at less than 200. *The Rise and Fall of the German Air Force*, p. 358, claims the figure was around 270.
201 USSBS, Tank Interview, May 19, 1945, Memorandum at end.
202 Bergstrom, *Bagration to Berlin*, p. 109.

203 Spaatz MSS, Box 134, "The Birth, Life and Death of the German Day Fighter," p. 39.
204 USSBS, Koller Interview, May 23 and 24, 1945, p. 5.
205 USSBS, European Report 59, "The Defeat of the German Air Force," p. 2.
206 USSBS, European Report 59, "The Defeat of the German Air Force," Figure 16. This is an estimate down from this chart which has a specific category for Eastern Front losses.
207 *Germany and the Second World War*, vol. VII, p. 317.
208 *Germany and the Second World War*, vol. VII, p. 89.
209 *Germany and the Second World War*, vol. VII, p. 322.
210 Mawdsley, *Thunder in the East: The Nazi–Soviet War 1941–1945* (London, 2005), p. 301.
211 Hardesty and Grinberg, *Red Phoenix Rising: The Soviet Air Force in World War II* (Lawrence, KS, 2012), p. 301.
212 Hardesty and Grinberg, *Red Phoenix Rising: The Soviet Air Force in World War II*, p. 306.
213 Zetterling and Frankson, *Kursk 1943: A Statistical Analysis*, pp. 123–4.
214 Bergstrom, *Bagration to Berlin*, pp. 63–6.
215 USSBS, Dethleffsen Interview, May 20, 1945, p. 2.
216 USSBS, Dethleffsen Interview, May 20, 1945, p. 3.
217 Overy, *Russia's War* (London, 1998), p. 243.
218 Glantz and House, *When Titans Clashed: How the Red Army Stopped Hitler* (Lawrence, KS, 1995), p. 214.
219 Mawdsley, *Thunder in the East*, p. 308.
220 Niepold, *Battle for White Russia: The Destruction of Army Group Centre, June 1944* (London, 1987), p. 33.
221 Niepold, *Battle for White Russia*, p. 34.
222 *Germany and the Second World War*, vol. VIII, p. 534.
223 Glantz and House, *When Titans Clashed: How the Red Army Stopped Hitler*, p. 215.
224 USSBS, Dethleffsen Interview, May 20, 1945, p. 7.
225 Spaatz MSS 134, Galland Interview, May 20, 1945, p. 51.
226 USSBS, Christian Interview, May 19, 1945, p. 15.
227 Spaatz MSS, Goering Interview Summary, June 1, 1945, p. 11.
228 *The Rise and Fall of the German Air Force: 1933–45*, p. 329.
229 *The Rise and Fall of the German Air Force: 1933–45*, p. 330.
230 USSBS, Christian Interview, May 19, 1945, p. 16.
231 Spaatz MSS, Goering Interview Summary, June 1, 1945, p. 11.
232 Spaatz MSS 134, Galland Interview, May 20, 1945, p. 51.
233 USSBS, Galland Interview, June 4 and 7, 1945, p. 4.

234 Schmider, "The Last of the First: Veterans of the Jagdwaffe Tell their Story", *The Journal of Military History*. vol. 73, 1 (January 2009), 238.

235 Spaatz MSS, 289, The War in the Air, Reich Air Defence 1939–45, Section V. This estimates that 900 aircraft were sent.

236 Spaatz MSS, Box 134, Galland Report, "The Birth, Life and Death of the German Day Fighter," p. 51. This estimates that 800 aircraft were sent.

237 FO 1031-41, Speer Interview, June 13, 1945, pp. 1–2.

238 Ellis, *Victory in the West*, vol. I, p. 491.

239 USSBS, European Report 59, "The Defeat of the German Air Force," p. 2.

240 Amadio and Rall, *Luftwaffe Ace and NATO General: The Authorized Biography* (Santa Ana, CA, 2002), p. 215.

241 Amadio and Rall, *Luftwaffe Ace and NATO General*, p. 40.

242 For a discussion of some of these advantages and why the Germans did not succeed, see Hart, *Clash of Arms: How the Allies Won in Normandy* (Boulder, CO, 2001), p. 373.

243 See Chapter 11.

244 Buckley, *British Armour in the Normandy Campaign 1944* (London, 2004), pp. 105–10.

245 Ludewig, *Ruckzug: The German Retreat from France, 1944* (Lexington, KY, 2012), p. 22.

246 For an interesting description of the aims of the campaign, see Zuckerman, *From Apes to Warlords*, pp. 216–45.

247 Lytton, "Bombing Policy in the Rome and Pre-Normandy Invasion Aerial Campaigns of World War II: Bridge-Bombing Strategy Vindicated and Railyard-Bombing Strategy Invalidated," *Military Affairs*, vol. 47, 2 (Apr. 1983), 53–8.

248 Huston, "Tactical Use of Air Power in World War II: The Army Experience," *Military Affairs*, vol. 14, 4 (Winter 1950), 176.

249 Craven and Cate (eds.), *The Army Air Forces in World War II*, vol. III, pp. 234–6.

250 Hughes, "Air-Lines: Anglo-American Tactical Air Operations in World War II," 43–4.

251 For two descriptions of the importance of the North African campaign to Allied tactical air power, see Bechtold, "A Question of Success: Tactical Air Doctrine and Practice in North Africa, 1942–43," 850–1; Maycock, "Notes on the Development of AAF Tactical Air Doctrine," *Military Affairs*, vol. 14, 4 (Winter 1950), 186–91.

252 This is very much the view of the official histories, but even if they exaggerated a little, it has been supported in other areas. See Huston,

"Tactical Use of Air Power in World War II," 168–76; Bickers, *Air War Normandy* (London, 1994), pp. 150–68.

253 Actual destruction of German AFV was considerably below the claims made by Anglo-American tactical air forces during 1944. The pilots often viewed a visible explosion as a sign that a German panzer had been destroyed when that was not the case. See Gooderson, "Allied Fighter-Bombers versus German Armour in North-West Europe: Myths and Realities," *Journal of Strategic Studies*, vol. 14, 2 (1991).

254 USSBS, Buhle Interview, June 1, 1945, p. 4.

255 Spaatz 134, Von Rundstedt Interview, September 2, 1945, p. 2.

256 Arnold MSS, Reel 190, "The Contribution of Airpower to the Defeat of Germany," Appendix H, "The Attack on Enemy Roads." There is a superb chart and narrative in this appendix describing the transport issues that confronted every German division that was sent to fight in Normandy.

257 Spaatz MSS, 134, Bodenschatz Interview, May 16, 1945, p. 2.

258 Spaatz 97, Notes of Second Allied Air Commanders' Meeting, May 26, 1944, p. 1.

259 Spaatz 134, Milch Interview, May 23, 1944, p. 4.

260 USSBS, Peters Interview, June 3, 1945, p. 1.

261 Spaatz MSS 134, Hoeffner Interview, April 8, 1945, p. 2.

262 This is a British government translation of a captured copy of Rommel's report. It was released by the Air Ministry after the war. The copy consulted was in Templewood MSS, XIV: 4/6.

263 This is a British government translation of Kluge's letter. It was released by the Air Ministry after the war. The copy consulted was in Templewood MSS, XIV: 4/6.

264 *Germany and the Second World War*, vol. VII, pp. 612–13.

265 Niklas Zetterling is one of those who put the total German losses of AFV in France at this time at 1,500; Zetterling, *Normandy 1944: German Military Organization, Combat Power and Organizational Effectiveness* (Winnipeg, 2000), p. 83. There is also a useful chart of German losses (and replacements) of different AFV in France in June and July 1944 in Hart, *Clash of Arms: How the Allies Won in Normandy*, p. 387.

266 Ludewig, *Ruckzug: The German Retreat from France, 1944*, p. 284.

267 See Chapter 1. July 1944 data shows that 48.3 percent of German war production at this time was aircraft and 7.8 percent was AFV.

268 Meschnig, *Der Wille sur Bewegung: Militärischer Traum und totalitäres Programm. Eine Mentalitätsgeschichte vom Ersten Weltkrieg zum Nationalsozialismus* (Bielefeld, 2008), pp. 161–208.

269 Overy, *Interrogations: Inside the Minds of the Nazi Elite*, p. 281. Jodl was also one of the few Germans to argue that the area attacks on German cities

played a major role in Germany's defeat. In his estimation, they damaged German morale significantly, crucially that of the troops from the areas that were bombed.

10 The air and sea war against Japan, 1942–4

1 USSBS, Production, Wastage and Strength of Japanese Naval Air Force, November 1945. These charts were created using documents supplied by Commander Fukamizu.
2 USSBS, Ohmae Interview, December 6, 1945, p. 7.
3 Morison, *History of United States Naval Operations in World War II*, vol. VIII, p. 233.
4 Morison, *History of United States Naval Operations in World War II*, vol. VIII, p. 219.
5 USSBS, Nakajima Interview, October 21, 1945, p. 4.
6 Morison, *History of United States Naval Operations in World War II*, vol. VIII, p. 219.
7 *Fading Victory: The Diary of Admiral Matome Ugaki, 1941–45* (Pittsburgh, 1991), p. 400.
8 Beyond Morison, there are two enjoyable histories of the Battle of the Philippine Sea. Tillman, *Clash of the Carriers*; Y'Blood, *Red Sun Setting: The Battle of the Philippine Sea* (Annapolis, MD, 1981).
9 USSBS, Sasaki Interview, November 23, 1945, p. 1.
10 USSBS, Takata Interview, November 1, 1945, p. 4.
11 USSBS, Capt. J. Fukamizu Interview, Appendix B.
12 Eaker MSS, 20, Diary of Anti-aircraft Efforts, October 1944, Section 5.
13 Eaker MSS, 20, Diary of Anti-aircraft Efforts, October 1944, Section 5.
14 *Fading Victory: The Diary of Admiral Matome Ugaki, 1941–45*, p. 415.
15 There are some good books that discuss this period in the Pacific war in general, including Willmott, *The War with Japan: The Period of Balance, May 1942–October 1943* (Wilmington, DE, 2002).
16 The Battle of Henderson Field started on October 24, but as Guadalcanal is just over the international date line and starts its day more than twelve hours before Washington, there would have been ample time for FDR to be informed that a battle was taking place.
17 WD RG 165, Historical File, FDR to Leahy, King, Marshall and Arnold, October 24, 1942.
18 WD RG 165, Historical File, Marshall to JCS, October 25, 1942.
19 WD RG 165, Historical File, Memorandum for the President, "Diversion of Munitions, Including Aircraft, to the South Pacific."
20 Hopkins MSS, 125, Location of Combat Aircraft of the Army Air Forces, October 14, 1942.

21 King MSS, 35, draft letter from King to Edson (General USMC) laying out the decision to attack Guadalcanal.

22 King MSS, 35, "Western New Britain and Guadalcanal," August 17, 1950.

23 A great deal has been written about the fighting on and around Guadalcanal. One of the best books on the subject is Frank, *Guadalcanal: The Definitive Account of the Landmark Battle* (London, 1992).

24 USSBS, Miyazaki Interview, December 3, 1945, p. 4. See also Miller, *The United States Army in World War II: Guadalcanal, the First Offensive* (Washington, DC, 1949), pp. 138–9, an official history available, at www. ibiblio.org/hyperwar/USA/USA-P-Guadalcanal/ (accessed September 9, 2014).

25 Spector, *Eagle against the Sun*, pp. 196–7.

26 There is a very interesting article which discusses how the Japanese were able to compensate for what seemed to be a technological inferiority through superior night tactics: Mahnken, "Asymmetric Warfare at Sea: The Naval Battles of Guadalcanal, 1942–1943," *Naval War College Review*, vol. 64, 1 (Winter 2011), 95–118.

27 See *US Navy at War 1941–45*, Appendix C, available at www.ibiblio.org/ hyperwar/USN/USNatWar/USN-King-C.html (accessed September 9, 2014). There is an argument that the figure for aircraft carriers should really be two of four, because the last American aircraft carrier sunk in the war, the USS *Princeton*, was actually a vessel of an intermediate class, only 15,000 tons when fully loaded.

28 Morison, *History of United States Naval Operations in World War II*, vol. V, pp. 206–7.

29 King MSS, 35, King to Isely, March 30, 1950.

30 Examples of those who believe MacArthur's strategic drive to the Philippines was the crucial drive of the war include Willoughby, *MacArthur 1941–1951* (New York, 1954), pp. 6–15; O'Neil, *A Democracy at War: America's Fight at Home and Abroad in World War II* (Cambridge, MA, 1993), pp. 267–300. For another positive description of MacArthur, see. Eichelberger, *Jungle Road to Tokyo* (London, 1951). Eichelberger, who served under MacArthur from New Guinea through to the surrender of Japan, praised his abilities but was also quick to point out his quirks, including his love of publicity (see pp. 20–2). Also see Whitney, *MacArthur: His Rendezvous with History* (New York, 1956), pp. 64–5. For overall analyses of MacArthur's career that are generally positive, though make some important critiques, see James, *The Years of MacArthur*, vol. II (Boston, 1975); Long, *MacArthur as Military Commander* (London, 1969).

31 Spector, *Eagle against the Sun*, pp. 117–19.

32 Arnold MSS, Reel 2, Trip to Southwest Pacific, pp. 1–2.

33 King MSS, 35, "Comments by Fleet Admiral Ernest J. King USN on Chapter VI, Supporting the Guadalcanal Campaign," pp. 4–5.

34 For a list of all Japanese vessels lost in the war, with locations, see *Japanese Naval and Merchant Shipping Losses during World War II by All Causes*, Report by Joint Army–Navy Assessment Committee (USA), Feb. 1947. Available online at www.ibiblio.org/hyperwar/Japan/IJN/JANAC-Losses/JANAC-Losses-3.html (accessed February 2014).

35 USSBS, Capt. J. Fukamizu Interview, Appendix B.

36 USSBS, Genda Interview, September 28, 1945, p. 10.

37 *Fading Victory: The Diary of Admiral Matome Ugaki, 1941–45*, p. 304.

38 USSBS, Miyazaki Interview, December 3, 1945, p. 4.

39 Edgerton, *Warriors of the Rising Sun* (New York, 1997), p. 286.

40 For a very interesting description of the functioning of the Tokyo Express and the overall attritional losses that the Japanese navy suffered off Guadalcanal, see Raizo Tanaka, "The Struggle for Guadalcanal," in Evans (ed.), *The Japanese Navy in World War II: In the Words of Former Japanese Naval Officers* (Annapolis, MD, 1986), pp. 156–211.

41 USSBS, Miyazaki Interview, December 3, 1945, p. 4.

42 WD, History File, RG 165, Nimitz Memorandum, Future Operations in the Solomons Sea Area, December 8, 1942, p. 7.

43 Morison, *History of United States Naval Operations in World War II*, vol. V, pp. 372–3.

44 FDR MSS, PSF 2, FDR to Arnold, May 5, 1942.

45 FDR, PSF 1, "Tentative US Views on Subjects of British Memorandum, 18 December 1941," sent from Marshall to FDR, December 22, 1941.

46 FDR MSS, PSF 83, FDR to Marshall *et al.*, May 6, 1942. This is a fascinating memorandum because it was one of only a few times during the war that Roosevelt wrote a document which summarized his strategic view of the war in detail. Once Leahy was put in place as his Chief of Staff, these kinds of direct writing became much rarer, and after 1942 it is hard to find many at all.

47 WD, RG 165, Strategic Agenda for the Asiatic Conference, May 1943, p. 2.

48 Miller, *War Plan Orange: The US Strategy to Defeat Japan* (Annapolis, MD, 1991), pp. 253–4.

49 King MSS, Box 20, Handwritten Notes Dated December 12 (has to be 1942 because of context).

50 Hoyt, *How They Won the War in the Pacific: Nimitz and his Admirals* (New York, 1970), p. 207.

51 FDR, PSF 2, JCS Memo, "Operations in the Pacific and Far East in 1943–44," May 12, 1943, p. 17.

52 In December 1943, the army was planning on allocating a large number of landing craft for the seizure of Truk in July 1944, which would have delayed an assault on the Mariana Islands until October at the earliest. WD, RG 165, Handy Paper, "Major Landing Ships and Craft, Central Pacific," December 3, 1943.

53 US fleet carrier losses were: USS *Lexington* (May 8, 1942), USS *Yorktown* (June 7, 1942), USS *Wasp* (September 15, 1942), USS *Hornet* (October 26, 1942). The first eight Essex Class carriers entering service were USS *Essex* (December 1942), USS *Lexington* (February 1943), USS *Yorktown* (April 1943), USS *Bunker Hill* (May 1943), USS *Intrepid* (August 1943), USS *Wasp* (November 1943), USS *Hornet* (November 1943), USS *Franklin* (January 1944). For a full list of all American warships lost and built during World War II, see *US Navy at War, 1941–45*, Third Report, Appendices B and C.

54 Hone, "Replacing Battleships with Aircraft Carriers in the Pacific in World War II," 62–4; Levy, "Race for the Decisive Weapon: British, American and Japanese Carrier Fleets, 1942–1943," *Naval War College Review*, vol. 58, 1 (Winter 2005), 138–49.

55 Marshall MSS, King to Marshall, February 8, 1944.

56 Morison, *History of United States Naval Operations in World War II*, vol. VIII, p. 5.

57 Leahy MSS, Diary, March 28, 1943.

58 See WD History, RG 165, Deane to Marshall, March 27, 1943. This letter contained a very interesting series of comments that Leahy had made about King's proposal. The Chief of Staff (as he was called) was very keen that the navy did not became bogged down in MacArthur's Southwest Pacific campaign and could keep freedom of action.

59 Leahy MSS, Diary, March 28, 1943.

60 WD, Historical File, Book 11, RG 165, Future Campaign Operations in the Pacific Oceans Area, Joint Staff Planners Response to JCS 353.

61 Buell, *Master of Sea Power*, pp. 336–7. It was notable that Alanbrooke, who usually took shots at King's strategic vision, seemed to accept without comment his presentation about the need to take the Marianas. See Alanbrooke Diary May 21, 1943.

62 King MSS, Box 20, Handwritten notes of meeting of King and Nimitz, May 30, 1943.

63 Hopkins 126, Memorandum Arnold to Marshall with Strategic Air Plan for 1943 and 1944, September 9, 1942.

64 Cab 120/26, Meeting of American and British Chiefs of Staff, December 24, 1941, Annex VII: p. 14 in this collection of Arcadia documents.

65 FDR PSF 2, Arnold to FDR, January 28, 1942.

66 Arnold MSS, Reel 2, Travel Diary, February 4 and 5, 1943.

67 FDR, PSF 2, JCS Memo, Operations in the Pacific and Far East, 1943–44, May 12, 1943.

68 Cab 121/154, Specific Operations in the Pacific and Far East, 27, August 1943, p. 63.

69 Arnold MSS, 114, White to Arnold, June 5, 1944.

70 Marshall MSS, Leahy Correspondence, Marshall to Leahy and King, February 24, 1944.

71 Potter, *Nimitz* (Annapolis, MD, 1976), pp. 280–2.

72 WD Historical File, RG 165, Undated Memorandum for Marshall, to be sent to Hull for opinion. This is a draft of the memorandum; interestingly the first draft about the bombing from the Marianas said, "Although the B-29s could attack Japan proper from the Marianas, the range is long, thus cutting down the bomb load; and strong fighter opposition could be expected, not only at the target, but enroute thereto." Everything after "bomb load" was scratched out and replaced with the quote included.

73 WD History. Book 16, RG 165, "Basic Decisions Which Will Give Strategic Guidance for the Conduct of the War in the Pacific," Arnold Memorandum, March 8, 1944.

74 Cab 121/154, CCS, Final Report to the President and Prime Minister, August 24, 1943, p. 5.

75 WD Historical File, RG 165, Nimitz to King, "The Seizure of the Marshall Islands," August 20, 1943, p. 8.

76 WD Historical File, RG 165, Status of Landing Craft for Operations in 1944, December 4, 1943.

77 Potter, *Nimitz*, pp. 283.

78 Marshall MSS, Memorandum for Marshall from King, February 8, 1944.

79 Marshall MSS, Memorandum for Marshall from King, February 8, 1944, p. 4.

80 For a short description of the impact of the Truk attacks from the Japanese perspective, see Masataka Chihaya, "Account of the Fiasco of Truk on 27 February 1944," in Goldstein and Dillon, *The Pacific War Papers: Japanese Documents of World War II* (Washington, DC, 2004), pp. 279–82.

81 USSBS, The Reduction of Truk, February 1947, pp. 10–12, available online at http://onlinebooks.library.upenn.edu/webbin/book/lookupname?key=United percent20States percent20Strategic percent20Bombing percent20Survey (accessed September 9, 2014).

82 Marshall MSS, Marshall to King, March 1, 1944.

83 WD Historical File, RG 165, Book 15, Marshall to Leahy, King and Arnold, February 21, 1944.

84 WD, Historical File, Book 16, Sutherland to MacArthur, March 8, 1944.

85 *The Papers of George C. Marshall*, vol. IV, Marshall to King, March 2, 1944, pp. 326–7.

86 Morison, *History of United States Naval Operations in World War II*, vol. VIII, p. 9. See also *The Papers of George C. Marshall*, vol. IV JCS to MacArthur and Nimitz, March 12, 1944, pp. 336–8.

87 Marshall MSS, MacArthur to Marshall, February 27, 1944, p. 3.

88 Leahy MSS, Diary Entry, April 30, 1944.

89 King MSS, Box 35, Comments by King on a Chapter on Guadalcanal, p. 4.

90 King MSS, Box 35, King to Lee, April 29, 1946.

91 Arnold MSS, Reel, 2, Diary, September 25, 1942, p. 15.

92 King MSS, Box 14, Nimitz to King, April 14, 1944.

93 *The Papers of George C. Marshall*, vol. IV, Marshall to MacArthur, June 24, 1944, pp. 492–4.

94 Marshall MSS, Draft of Letter from Marshall to MacArthur, June 23, 1944, p. 2.

95 King MSS, Box 35, King to Lee, April 29, 1946.

96 WD, History File, RG 165, Book 22, Notes for Discussion with General Marshall, ref: President's visit to Hawaii and operations in the Pacific.

97 WD, History File, RG 165, Book 22, Notes for Discussion with General Marshall, ref. President's visit to Hawaii and operations in the Pacific, p. 3.

98 WD, History File, RG 165, Book 22, Notes for Discussion with General Marshall, ref. President's visit to Hawaii and operations in the Pacific, p. 10.

99 Bateman, "Observations of President Roosevelt's Health during World War II," *Mississippi Valley Historical Review*, vol. 43, 1 (June 1956), 90–1.

100 Leahy MSS, Diary, July 27–29, 1944.

101 The campaign to take Manila was a personal obsession for MacArthur, and it does seem to have led to greater risks being taken than were necessary. See Holzimmer, *General Walter Krueger: Unsung Hero of the Pacific War* (Lawrence, KS, 2007), p. 225.

102 Http://necrometrics.com/battles.htm (accessed September 9, 2014).

103 Http://countrystudies.us/philippines/21.htm (accessed September 9, 2014).

104 USSBS, Fuchida Interview, October 27, 1945, p. 3.

105 Eaker MSS, 20, Diary of Anti-aircraft Efforts, October 1944, Section 5.

106 USSBS, Ozawa Interview, October 30, 1945, p. 12.

107 USSBS, Takata Interview, November 1, 1945, p. 4.

108 USSBS, Pacific Report 15, Figure 11-17, p. 36. It is interesting to note that as the fighting was ending on Guadalcanal, the Japanese prioritized five key industries within their economy, all of which were connected to the air and sea war: steel, coal, light metals (including aluminum), shipbuilding and aircraft. See Nakamura and Odaka (eds.), *The Economic History of Japan: 1600–1900*, p. 270.

109 JCS Records, RG 218, "Japanese Aircraft and Shipping Situation," JIC Report, February 29, 1944.

110 Peattie, *Sunburst: The Rise of Japanese Naval Air Power, 1909–1941*, pp. 131–4.

111 USSBS, Oikawa Interview, December 1, 1945, p. 3.

112 USSBS, Genda Interview, November 26, 1945, p. 2.

113 USSBS, Genda Interview, November 26, 1945, pp. 6–7.

114 USSBS, Takata Interview, November 1, 1945, p. 2.

115 USSBS, Takata Interview, November 1, 1945, p. 3.

116 Peattie, *Sunburst: The Rise of Japanese Naval Air Power, 1909–1941*, pp. 180–4.

117 USSBS, Genda Interview, November 26, 1945, p. 11.

118 USSBS, Yamamoto Interview, November 20, 1945, p. 6.

119 USSBS, Kanai Interview, October 26, 1945, p. 2.

120 USSBS, Kanai Interview, October 26, 1945, p. 2.

121 USSBS, Takahashi and Takeuchi Interview, October 24–26, 1945, p. 2.

122 USSBS, Takahashi and Takeuchi Interview, October 24–26, 1945, p. 3.

123 USSBS, Takahashi and Takeuchi Interview, October 24–26, 1945, p. 2.

124 USSBS, Ohmae Interview, October 22, 1945, p. 2.

125 USSBS, Katsumata Interview, October 2, 1945, p. 1.

126 USSBS, Katsumata Interview, October 2, 1945, p. 2.

127 USSBS, Yamamoto Interview, November 20, 1945, p. 6.

128 USSBS, Mieno Interview, November 26, 1945, p. 2.

129 USSBS, Okumiya Interview, November 29, 1945, p. 4.

130 USSBS, Matsumae Interview, October 27–28, 1945, p. 19.

131 USSBS, Takata and Shiba Interview, December 4, 1945, p. 3.

132 USSBS, Kawabe Interview, November 26, 1943, p. 4.

133 USSBS, Matsumae Interview, October 27–28, 1945, p. 15.

134 USSBS, Tamaka Interview, November 10, 1945, pp. 1–2.

135 USSBS, Katsumata Interview, October 25, 1945, p. 2.

136 USSBS, Matsumae Interview, October 27–28, 1945, p. 16.

137 USSBS, Kawabe Interview, November 26, 1945, p. 3.

138 USSBS, Ohmae Interview, December 6, 1945, p. 7.

139 USSBS, Katsumata Interview, October 25, 1945, p. 2.

140 USSBS, Nakajima Interview, October 21, 1945, p. 2.

141 Air 9/168, United States–British Staff Conversations, March 27, 1941, p. 5.

142 Morison, *History of United States Naval Operations in World War II*, vol. VII, pp. 184–5.

143 Murray and Millett, *A War to be Won*, p. 348.

144 Morison, *History of United States Naval Operations in World War II*, vol. VII, p. 278.

145 Marshall MSS, Marshall to Eisenhower, April 1, 1944.

146 Perhaps the best analysis of MacArthur's campaigns in New Guinea is Taaffe, *MacArthur's Jungle Wars: The 1944 New Guinea Campaign* (Lawrence, KS, 1998). On the whole the portrayal of MacArthur is positive and stress is placed on his abilty to adapt to the new situations. However, the author also is willing to engage with the general's critics, particularly on the question of whether the campaign was necessary. These ideas are summarized well in the conclusion, pp. 225–42.

147 For an extremely entertaining and excoriating analysis of MacArthur, see Murray and Millett, *A War to be Won*, pp. 205–6. Also see James, *The Years of MacArthur*, vol. II, pp. 281–6.

148 James, *The Years of MacArthur*, vol. II, pp. 279–80.

149 Holzimmer, "Walter Krueger, Douglas MacArthur and the Pacific War: The Wakde–Sarmi Campaign as a Case Study," *Journal of Military History*, vol. 59, 4 (Oct. 1995), 684.

150 USSBS, Sanada Interview, November 2, 1945, p. 3.

151 Blair, *Silent Victory: The US Submarine War against Japan* (Philadelphia, 1975).

152 Morison, *History of United States Naval Operations in World War II*, vol. VIII, pp. 15–26.

153 Smith, *Wolf Pack: The American Submarine Strategy that Helped Defeat Japan* (Hoboken, NJ, 2003).

154 Parillo, *The Japanese Merchant Marine in World War II* (Annapolis, MD, 1993), pp. 76–9.

155 Evans (ed.), *The Japanese Navy in World War II*, pp. 386–9.

156 Parillo, *The Japanese Merchant Marine in World War II*, p. 107.

157 USSBS, Army and Navy Oil Operations and Overall Allocations, October 27, 1945, p. 4.

158 USSBS, Army–Navy Production of Oil and Overall Allocation, October 29, 1945, p. 4.

159 USSBS, Goko Interview, October 25, 1945, p. 8.

160 USSBS, Pacific Report 53, p. 25.

161 USSBS, Pacific Report 53, p. 25. Germany produced 480,000 tons of aluminum in 1944.

162 Torisu, "Japanese Submarine Tactics and the Kaiten," in David Evans (ed.), *The Japanese Navy in World War II*, pp. 440–4.

163 King MSS, 20, Handwritten notes from May 30, 1943 meeting with Nimitz.

164 Morison, *History of United States Naval Operations in World War II*, vol. VIII. See Appendices II and III, pp. 407–17; *Jane's Fighting Ships of World War II* (London, 1989), pp. 259–61, 267–9, 272–4, 276–7, 281.

165 See http://web.inter.nl.net/users/spoelstra/g104/cost.htm (accessed September 9, 2014). The basic cost of a Sherman in 1942 was a little over $30,000. However, as the war went on, the Sherman was modified extensively and its gun and armor were improved. According to the Armed Forces Services Catalog used here, the average cost of a Sherman in the second half of the war was between $45,000 and $55,000. During the war just over 49,000 Shermans were built (all variants).

166 Morison, *History of United States Naval Operations in World War II*, vol. VIII, p. 160.

167 Friedman, "The Quiet Warrior Back in Newport," 121–2.

168 Morison, *History of United States Naval Operations in World War II*, vol. VIII, p. 345; 7.3 US barrels of oil are the equivalent of one metric ton, so that Spruance on the whole would have had considerably more than half the fuel that Germany produced for its entire war effort during a month.

169 Millett, *Semper Fidelis: The History of the United States Marine Corps* (New York, 1991), pp. 410–1; also pp. 409–15, an excellent short description of the overall Marianas campaign.

170 Dater, "Tactical Use of Air Power in World War II", 198–200.

171 Morison, *History of United States Naval Operations in World War II*, vol. VIII, pp. 339 (Saipan: 3,426 killed or missing, 13,099 wounded), 369 (Tinian: 389 killed or missing, 1,816 wounded), 401 (Guam: 1,435 killed or missing, 5,648 wounded).

172 Combined killed, wounded and missing was listed at 22,720 for both sides.

173 DEFE (UK) 2/667, Report by Group Captain Adams, August 1, 1944, p. 9.

174 This was also a view that was shared by many of the Japanese people. See Edoin, *The Night Tokyo Burned* (New York, 1987), p. 7.

175 USSBS, Weneker [sic] Interview, November 11, 1945, p. 3.

176 USSBS, Nomura Interview, November 8, 1945, p. 15.

177 USSBS, Takagi Interview, November 23, 1945, p. 4.

178 USSBS, Yonai Interview, November 17, 1945, p. 9.

179 USSBS, Nagano Interview, November 20, 1945, p. 8.

180 USSBS, Toyoda Interview, November 13 and 14, 1945, p. 17.

181 Gordon, "Historiographical Essay: The China–Japan War, 1931–1945," *Journal of Military History*, vol. 70, 1 (Jan. 2006), 160.

182 USSBS, Nomura Interview, November 8, 1945, p. 7.

183 Sledge, *With the Old Breed: At Peleiu and Okinawa* (Oxford: 1990).

184 Morison, *History of United States Naval Operations in World War II*, vol. XII, p. 43.

185 Morison, *History of United States Naval Operations in World War II*, vol. XII, p. 41.

186 Millett, *Semper Fidelis: The History of the United States Marine Corps*, p. 423.

187 Morison, *History of United States Naval Operations in World War II*, vol. XII, pp. 46–7.

188 Sakai, *Samurai!*, p. 329.

189 USSBS, Arisue Interview, October 26, 1945, p. 2.

190 Morison, *History of United States Naval Operations in World War II*, vol. XII, p. 68.

191 USSBS, Ohmae Interview, December 6, 1945, p. 10.

192 USSBS, Kawabe Interview, November 26, 1945, p. 4.

193 USSBS, Matsumae Interview, October 27–28, 1945, p. 1.

194 USSBS, Matsumae Interview, October 27–28, 1945, p. 3.

195 USSBS, Mamakishi Interview, November 4, 1945, p. 3.

196 Mann, "Japanese Defense of Bataan, Luzon, Philippines Islands, 16 December 1944–4 September 1945," *Journal of Military History*, vol. 67, 4 (Oct. 2003), 1175–6.

197 It is not easy to find one casualty figure for the United States in retaking the Philippines. However, it does seem that killed, wounded and missing totalled more than 60,000. The US Army Official Histories say that in 1945 the army, independently of the navy, suffered 46,930 casualties (10,380 dead) in Luzon and some other parts of the southern Philippines. However, this figure leaves out those army troops who were casualties in 1944 and in other parts of the Philippines such as Leyte, where the original landings occurred. See Smith, *The United States Army in World War II: Triumph in the Philippines* (Washington, DC, 1993), Appendix H, p. 692. The Wikipedia description of the Philippines campaign gives an American casualty total for the entire campaign of 62,514: http://en.wikipedia.org/wiki/ Philippines_Campaign_ percent281944 percentE2 percent80 percent9345 percent29#U.S._Army_and_Army_Air_Forces (accessed September 9, 2014).

198 JCS Records, RG 218, "Optimum Use, Timing and Deployment of VLR Bombers in the War against Japan," JSP Memorandum, March 2, 1944.

199 JCS Records, RG 218, "VLR Bombers in the War against Japan," JSP Memorandum for JCS, April 6, 1944.

200 Craven and Cate (eds.), *The Army Air Forces in World War II*, vol. V, p. 99.

201 JCS Records, RG 218, Air Offensive from China, JCS Meeting, August 20, 1943, includes Arnold Memorandum, "Air Plan for the Defeat of Japan," which has excerpts from the larger COA report.

202 JCS Records, RG 218, Air Offensive from China, JCS Meeting, August 20, 1943, Arnold Memorandum, "Air Plan for the Defeat of Japan," p. 13.

203 JCS Records, RG 218, Air Offensive from China, JCS Meeting, August 20, 1943, Arnold Memorandum, "Air Plan for the Defeat of Japan," p. 14.

204 JCS Records, RG 218, Air Offensive from China, JCS Meeting, August 20, 1943, Arnold Memorandum, "Air Plan for the Defeat of Japan," p. 15.

205 Www.stalingrad.net/german-hq/the-stalingrad-airlift/airstat.html (accessed September 9, 2014).

206 JCS Records, RG 218, VLR Bombers in the War against Japan, Annex A, COA Report to Arnold, November 11, 1943.

207 Plating, *The Hump: America's Strategy for Keeping China in World War II* (College Station, TX, 2011), p. 189.

208 Craven and Cate (eds.), *The Army Air Forces in World War II*, vol. V, p. 78.

209 Marshall MSS, Wedemeyer to Marshall, November 10, 1944. Wedemeyer was actually trying to argue that the B-29s should be kept in China because they were "only" taking 7,197 tons of the 14,000 flown in.

210 Craven and Cate (eds.), *The Army Air Forces in World War II*, vol. V, p. 175.

11 The end of the war

1 USSBS, Kawamura Interview, November 23, 1945, p. 2.

2 Nakamura and Odaka (eds.), *The Economic History of Japan: 1600–1900*, p. 298. There is a very interesting chart there which lists the percentage of damage inflicted on each area of production within the economy. While the air raids themselves did damage certain areas a great deal, it seems the overall decline in production had more to do with the loss of raw material supply.

3 USSBS, Pacific Report 53, p. 181.

4 USSBS, Yamamoto Interview, November 3, 1945, p. 3.

5 USSBS, Yamamoto Interview, November 3, 1945, p. 4.

6 USSBS, Yamamoto Interview, November 3, 1945, p. 7.

7 Morison, *History of United States Naval Operations in World War II*, vol. XII, pp. 86–103 has a good description of these series of attacks including the number of ships and aircraft involved and the assumed Japanese losses at the time. During the final stages of the war, the USN's fast carrier task force in the Pacific was given a different designation depending on who was in command. When commanded by Spruance, it was formally part of the US 5th Fleet and called TF 58. When commanded by Halsey, it was part of the 3rd Fleet and called TF 38.

8 Morison, *History of United States Naval Operations in World War II*, vol. XII, p. 94.

9 USSBS, Horuichi Interview, October 30, 1945, p. 3.

10 USSBS, Wakamatsu Interview, November 7, 1945, p. 2.

11 USSBS, Army–Navy Production of Oil and Overall Allocation, October 29, 1945, p. 5.

12 Cook and Cook, *Japan at War: An Oral History* (New York, 1992), p. 454.

13 USSBS, Kawabe Interview, November 2, 1945, p. 3; Matsumae Interview, October 27, 1945, p. 15.

14 USSBS, Genda Interview, September 9, 1945, p. 16.

15 USSBS, Jin Interview, October 29, 1945, p. 2.

16 That they were being denied any attempts at air cover so that Japanese planes could be used in suicide attacks on US warships was realized by at least one junior officer on Iwo Jima, who mentioned the fact a number of times in a diary that has fortunately survived. Lofgren, "Diary of First Lieutenant Sugihara Kinryu: Iwo Jima January–February 1945," *Journal of Military History*, vol. 59, 1 (Jan. 1995), 97–133. When the American invasion force reached Iwo Jima, Kinryu followed the sucide attack squadrons eagerly.

17 USSBS, Toki Interview, November 20, 1945, pp. 1–3.

18 USSBS, Toga Interview, October 23, 1945, p. 1.

19 USSBS, Tanaka Interview, December 4, 1945, p. 2.

20 USSBS, Pacific Report 15, p. 91.

21 Cohen, *Japanese Economic History 1930–1960* (London, 2000), vol. II, p. 215.

22 USSBS, Army and Navy Oil Operations and Overall Allocations, October 27, 1945, p. 9.

23 USSBS, Toyoda Interview, October 5, 1945, p. 11.
24 USSBS, Sato Interview, November 20, 1945, pp. 17–19.
25 USSBS, Sato Interview, November 20, 1945, p. 19.
26 USSBS, Sato Interview, November 20, 1945, p. 7.
27 USSBS, Toyoda Interview, October 5, 1945, p. 2; see also Toyoda Interview, October 9, 1945, p. 2.
28 See Chapter 10.
29 USSBS, Pacific Report 53, p. 25.
30 USSBS, Pacific Report 53, p. 25.
31 USSBS, Goko Interview, October 29, 1945, p. 8.
32 USSBS, Toyoda Interview, November 13–14, 1945, p. 18.
33 USSBS, Endo Interview, November 3, 1945, p. 7.
34 USSBS, Endo Interview, November 3, 1945, p. 7.
35 USSBS, Toyoda Interview, October 5, 1945, p. 6.
36 USSBS, Rabu Interview, October 21, 1945, p. 3.
37 Spaatz MSS, 113, Some Notes on the Messerschmitt 262 and the Arado 234, June 26, 1945.
38 Spaatz MSS, 134, Intelligence Summary of Goering, June 1, 1945, p. 14.
39 Spaatz MSS, Some Notes on the Messerschmitt 262 and the Arado 234, June 26, 1945, p. 2.
40 Tooze, *The Wages of Destruction*, pp. 613–16.
41 Doenitz, *Memoirs: Ten Years and Twenty Days*, pp. 354–7.
42 *Fuhrer Conferences on Naval Affairs 1944*, minutes of meeting, February 26, 1944, pp. 14–15, Admiralty (UK) translation of German documents (1947).
43 Grier, *Hitler, Dönitz and the Baltic Sea: The Third Reich's Last Hope* (Annapolis, MD, 2007), pp. 216–17.
44 USSBS, Merker Interview, June 20, 1945, p. 6.
45 USSBS, Blohm Interview, May 7, 1945, pp. 2–3.
46 USSBS, Doenitz Interview, June 28, 1945, p. 6.
47 Overy, *Interrogations: Inside the Minds of the Nazi Elite*, p. 351.
48 Spaatz MSS, 134, A Crack Panzer Division ... May 29, 1945, p. 13.
49 MacDonald, *The Battle of the Bulge* (London, 1984), p. 35.
50 Edward Shils and Morris Janowitz, 'Cohesion and Disintegration in the Wehrmacht in World War II, *Public Opinion Quarterly*, Summer 1948, p. 310. This is an analysis of why the German soldier fought so tenaciously to the end, and what kinds of propaganda were most effective in affecting his outlook. Before the Battle of the Bugle, the Germans attempted to persuade their own soldiers that the Luftwaffe would be there to support them.
51 Spaatz MSS, 134, Von Rundstedt Interview, September 2, 1945, p. 6.
52 Cole, *The United States Army in World War II: Ardennes, The Battle of the Bulge* (Washington, DC, 1993), p. 660.
53 Ellis, *Victory in the West*, vol. II, p. 186.

54 Cole, *The United States Army in World War II*, p. 661.

55 Davis, *Carl A. Spaatz and the Air War in Europe*, p. 532.

56 See Carter, "Air Power in the Battle of the Bulge: A Theater Campaign Perspective," *Airpower Journal* (Winter 1989), available online at www.air power.maxwell.af.mil/airchronicles/apj/apj89/win89/carter.html (accessed September 9, 2014).

57 MacDonald, *The Battle of the Bulge*, p. 608.

58 *The Battle of the Bulge*, released in 1965, was a particularly inaccurate war film, which within the context of World War II movies is quite an achievement.

59 MacDonald, *The Battle of the Bulge*, p. 46. Macdonald argues that the Germans had enough fuel for the offensive, and that any captured from the Americans would be a "bonus."

60 For just one example of how the historiography is overwhelmingly weighted to the period in which air power could not be used, see MacDonald, *A Time for Trumpets: The Untold Story of the Battle of the Bulge* (New York, 2002); in this the intervention of air power is first discussed in narrative form on pp. 521–3 of a 620-page book. See also Mitcham, *Panzers in Winter: Hitler's Army in the Battle of the Bulge* (Westport, CT, 2006).

61 Millett and Murray, *Military Effectiveness. Volume III, The Second World War*, p. 61.

62 Millett and Murray, *Military Effectiveness. Volume III, The Second World War*, p. 73.

63 See Marshall MSS, White to Eisenhower, March 20, 1945. White wrote a detailed and interesting evaluation of American equipment when compared with German, pointing out things such as the bazooka inferiority and the general problems with Shermans. As this letter is in Marshall's file of Eisenhower correspondence, it is safe to assume that Eisenhower sent it on to Marshall for the latter to read. Also see Eisenhower, *The Bitter Woods: The Battle of the Bulge* (Edinburgh, 2001), p. 432.

64 Jarymowycz, *Tank Tactics: From Normandy to Lorraine* (Boulder, Co, 2001). This books tells an interesting story about the general inadequacies of Anglo-American armor when compared with German, in particular stressing the problems faced in the four months after the Normandy landings. It also argues that the shorter-range guns were the major drawback faced by Anglo-American armor in straight-up duels with German AFV of all types (see pp. 263–7).

65 Marshall MSS, Eisenhower to Marshall, March 26, 1944.

66 Marshall MSS, Eisenhower to Marshall, March 26, 1944.

67 Van Creveld, *Fighting Power: German and US Army Performance, 1939–1945* (Westport, CT, 1982), pp. 166–8.

68 Marshall MSS, Rose to Eisenhower, March 21, 1945 (sent to Marshall March 26, 1945). There is also a copy in *The Papers of Dwight David Eisenhower: The War Years*, vol. IV, Eisenhower to Marshall, March 26, 1945, pp. 2543–5.

69 Hopkins MSS, 24, Krug Report, Increased War Production for 1945, January 16, 1945, p. 6.

70 Drea, *Japan's Imperial Army: Its Rise and Fall, 1853–1945* (Lawrence, KS, 2009), p. 246.

71 This is actually a translation of the document that was quoted in Morison, *History of United States Naval Operations in World War II*, vol. XIV, p. 92.

72 Kakehashi, *Letters from Iwo Jima* (London, 2007), p. 11. This is a readable book (translated from the original Japanese) based on the letters written by the Japanese commander of Iwo Jima, Lt General Tadamichi Kuribayashi. Kuribayashi was well aware that Iwo Jima would be seized by the Americans and did not want to expose his forces to their firepower by trying to defend the landing beaches. Instead, he kept them mostly inland, in protected positions, from which they took a frightful toll on the American attackers.

73 The fighting on Iwo Jima is considered extremely important institutionally for the Marine Corps. James Forrestal, Secretary of the Navy, said, "The raising of that flag on Suribachi means there will be a Marine Corps for the next 500 years." Millett, *Semper Fidelis: The History of the United States Marine Corps*, pp. 427–32.

74 Burrell, "Breaking the Cycle of Iwo Jima Mythology: A Strategic Study of Operation Detachment," *Journal of Military History*, vol. 68, 4 (Oct. 2004), 1143–86. Burrell argues two points: the first is that the original reason for taking Iwo Jima was to provide a base for American fighter support, which proved unnecessary. Once this reason was shown to be unnecessary, the American military changed the argument and said that Iwo Jima was crucial as an immediate base between the Marianas and Japan which could be used to save damaged B-29s. Burrell also calls this argument into question (I would argue, much less convincingly than the first part of the article). It should also be noted that Burrell's article quickly elicited a critical response. See Brain Hanley, "The Myth of Iwo Jima: A Rebuttal," *Journal of Military History*, vol. 69, 3 (July 2005), 801–9.

75 USSBS, Sanada Interview, November 2, 1945, p. 3.

76 Morison, *History of United States Naval Operations in World War II*, vol. XIV, p. 52.

77 See Chapter 10.

78 Morison, *History of United States Naval Operations in World War II*, vol. XIV, p. 82.

79 Appleman *et al.*, *The United States Army in World War II: Okinawa, The Last Battle* (Washington, DC, 1993), pp. 84, 91.

80 Appleman *et al.*, *The United States Army in World War II: Okinawa*, p. 473. For a Marine Corps view of the Okinawa campaign, see Millett, *Semper Fidelis: The History of the United States Marine Corps*, pp. 432–8.

81 Morison, *History of United States Naval Operations in World War II*, vol. XIV, p. 272.

82 Appleman *et al.*, *The United States Army in World War II: Okinawa*, p. 474.

83 USSBS, Kawabe Interview, November 2, 1945, p. 3.

84 USSBS, Kawabe Interview, November 2, 1945, p. 3.

85 Arnold MSS, Reel 3, Diary Entry, June 16, 1945.

86 Weingartner, "Trophies of War: US Troops and the Mutilation of Japanese War Dead, 1941–1945," *Pacific Historical Review*, vol. 61, 1 (Feb. 1992), 53–67.

87 Dower, *War without Mercy: Race and Power in the Pacific War* (New York, 1986). When it comes to the specific decision to start bombing Japanese cities in March 1945, Dower is surprisingly terse on the matter (see pp. 40–1).

88 Porter, "Paper Bullets: American Psywar in the Pacific, 1944–1945," *War in History*, vol. 17, 4 (2010), 479–511.

89 FDR MSS, PSF 1, FDR to Chennault, March 15, 1944.

90 Marshall MSS, Wedemeyer to Marshalll, November 10, 1944.

91 Arnold MSS, Reel 3, Diary Entry, June 13, 1945.

92 Arnold MSS, Reel 3, Diary Entry, June 14, 1945.

93 LeMay, *Mission with LeMay: My Story* (New York, 1965), p. 341.

94 USSBS, Pacific Report 66, p. 5.

95 Arnold MSS, Reel 3, Diary Entry, June 15, 1945.

96 Craven and Cate (eds.), *The Army Air Forces in World War II*, vol. V, p. 664.

97 Sallagar, "Lessons from an Aerial Mining Campaign (Operation Starvation)," Rand Committee Report for the US Air Force, April 1974, pp. 25–7. Available online at www.rand.org/pubs/reports/2006/R1322.html (accessed August 15, 2014).

98 Sallagar, "Lessons from an Aerial Mining Campaign (Operation Starvation)," p. 3.

99 USSBS, Pacific Report 54, p. 4.

100 It does seem that the Japanese were relatively inefficient in using their own fighters against American bombers; Barrett Tillman, *Whirlwind: The Air War against Japan 1942–1945* (New York, 2010), pp. 252–6.

101 Craven and Cate (eds.), *The Army Air Forces in World War II*, vol. V, p. 575.

102 Biddle, *Rhetoric and Reality in Air Warfare*, p. 267.

103 Craven and Cate (eds.), *The Army Air Forces in World War II*, vol. V, p. 567.

104 LeMay, *Mission with LeMay: My Story*, p. 347.

105 There are some different views as to how important LeMay as an individual was in causing this change in tactics. While all recognize he played a role, some place him as a member of a team which made the decision partly under pressure from Washington and building on already developed ideas. See Schaffer, *Wings of Judgment: American Bombing in World War II* (Oxford, 1985), pp. 126–7; Frank, *Downfall*, p 336; Crane, *American Airpower*

Strategy in World War II (Lawrence, KS, 1993), pp. 131–3; Werrell, *Blankets of Fire*, pp. 150–4; Tillman, *Whirlwind: The Air War against Japan 1942–1945*, pp. 100–5. Though this summary can be criticized, one might say that Schaffer and Frank tend to put more stress on the context of LeMay's decision, while Crane, Werrell and Tillman put emphasis on his individual actions.

106 LeMay, *Mission with LeMay: My Story*, pp. 345–52, has a rather disjointed internal monologue by LeMay about how he decided to switch to the firebombing of Tokyo. It is clear, at least, that he felt great pressure to please Arnold and received great praise from his superior when the scale of the destruction of Tokyo was first reported.

107 Lemay and Yenne, *Superfortress: The Boeing B-29 and American Air Power in World War II* (Yardley, PA, 2007), p. 127.

108 Craven and Cate (eds.), *The Army Air Forces in World War II*, vol. V, p. 615.

109 Frank, *Downfall*. Frank begins this excellent book with a description of the raid on pp. 2–19. Anyone interested in reading more could start there.

110 Craven and Cate (eds.), *The Army Air Forces in World War II*, vol. V, p. 642.

111 Overy, *The Bombing War*, p. 629.

112 Eaker MSS, Portal to Eaker, October 7, 1943, containing Air Ministry Memorandum.

113 Burleigh, *Moral Combat: A History of World War II*, p. 502.

114 Harris MSS, Salisbury to Sinclair, November 26, 1943.

115 Harris MSS, Sinclair to Salisbury, November 29, 1943.

116 Anyone interested in reading a one-volume collection of essays that discusses not only Dresden, but the general notion of strategic air power and the targeting of civilians in World War II, could start with Addison and Crang (eds.), *Firestorm: The Bombing of Dresden, 1945* (London, 2006).

117 Biddle, "Wartime Reactions," in *Firestorm: The Bombing of Dresden, 1945*, pp. 107–16.

118 Webster and Frankland, *Strategic Air Offensive against Germany*, vol. III, pp. 112–13.

119 Markusen and Kopf, "Was it Genocidal?" in Primoratz (ed.), *Terror from the Sky: The Bombing of German Cities in World War II* (New York, 2010), p. 171. Other authors have made strong, if more measured, arguments against the morality of British area bombing after the spring of 1944. See Garrett, *Ethics and Air Power in World War II: The British Bombing of German Cities* (New York, 1993), pp. 183–4; Hansen, *Fire and Fury: The Allied Bombing of Germany 1942–1945* (New York, 2009), p. 281.

120 For a helpful summary of these views, see Overy, "The Post-War Debate," in *Firestorm: The Bombing of Dresden, 1945*, pp. 123–42.

121 Schaffer, "American Military Ethics in World War II: The Bombing of German Civilians," *Journal of American History*, vol. 67, 2 (Sep. 1980), 318–34.

122 Mierzejewski, Werrell and Schaffer, "American Military Ethics in World War II: An Exchange," *Journal of American History*, vol. 68, 1 (June 1981), 85–92.

123 Crane, *American Airpower Strategy in World War II*, pp. 160–1. Crane puts stress on the idea that the Americans in Europe did have a distinct strategy for precision bombing which they tried to follow.

124 Schaffer, *Wings of Judgment: American Bombing in World War II*, p. 106. Unfortunately many of the writings on the Dresden bombing and other US city attacks are hampered by a relatively poor level of research, which leads to an unhelpful simplifying of the issue. For instance, see Lackey, "The Bombing Campaign: The USAAF," in Primoratz (ed.), *Terror from the Sky: The Bombing of German Cities in World War II*; on p. 40 Lackey poses the question "Is precision bombing inherently clean?" Such a question shows a lack of understanding of what "precision" bombing was from the start.

125 Matthews, *RAF Bomber Command at War* (London, 2009), pp. 220–1 (a particularly robust example of this viewpoint). For a more nuanced defense of Harris and British bombing, see Neillands, *The Bomber War: Arthur Harris and the Allied Bomber Offensive, 1939–1945* (London, 2001), pp. 386–97.

126 Moeller, "On the History of Man-made Destruction: Loss, Death, Memory, and Germany in the Bombing War," *History Workshop Journal*, no. 61 (2006), 103–34.

127 Friedrich, *The Fire: The Bombing of Germany 1940–1945*, pp. 88–9.

128 Walzer, *Just and Unjust Wars: A Moral Argument with Historical Illustrations* (New York, 1977), pp. 261–2. This book, which was influential in certain circles, argues that almost all the bombing of German cities in World War II was morally wrong. As an argument it is stimulating, though it is let down at times by labeling almost all the attacks as "terror" raids and using highly inflated numbers about the deaths in places such as Dresden. For an interesting article critiquing Walzer, see Lammers, "Area Bombing in World War II: The Arguments of Michael Walzer," *Journal of Religious Ethics*, vol. 11, 1 (Spring 1983), 96–113.

129 Smith, "The Strategic Bombing Debate: The Second World War and Vietnam," 175; Garrett, "The Bombing Campaign: The RAF," in Primoratz (ed.) *Terror from the Sky: The Bombing of German Cities in World War II*, p. 36.

130 See http://en.wikipedia.org/wiki/World_War_I_casualties#Classification_of_casualty_statistics (accessed September 9, 2014).

131 Astor, *The Mighty Eighth: The Air War in Europe as Told by the Men who Fought it* (New York, 1997), pp. 459–60.

132 Because of this, I believe it is problematic to base any argument about bombing mostly on intentionality. John Rawls makes a big point of this in his analysis of Truman and the atom bomb, but it assumes the President had simplistic emotions on the subject. See Rawls, "The Moral Duties of Statesmen," in Reichbery *et al.* (eds.), *The Ethics of War: Classic and Contemporary Readings* (Oxford, 2006), p. 639. A. C. Grayling also concentrates on the Hamburg raids in his analysis of why the bombing of civilians was immoral. Grayling, *Among the Dead Cities: Was the Allied Bombing of Civilians in WWII a Necessity or a Crime?* (London, 2006), pp. 271–2. It is interesting to see that Grayling seems to accept USSBS findings without much comment and gives much of the credit for the rise of German production to Speer; pp. 91–7.

133 Arnold MSS, Reel 3, Diary Entry, June 13, 1945.

134 Davis, *Carl A. Spaatz and the Air War in Europe*, pp. 563–4.

135 Arnold MSS, 114, Lovett to Patterson, March 18, 1943.

136 Arnold MSS, 114, Hanley Memorandum, April 30, 1943.

137 Clodfelter, "Aiming to Break Will: America's World War II Bombing of German Morale and its Ramifications," 416.

138 JCS Records, RG 218, VLR Bombers in the War against Japan, Annex A, COA report to Arnold, November 11, 1943.

139 For a full version of the COA report, see JCS Records, RG 218, Report of the COA, November 11, 1943. This second quote is from p. 25.

140 Webster and Frankland, *The Strategic Air Offensive against Germany*, vol. III, pp. 302–3.

141 In his memoirs, Harris ends up admitting that the 1943 campaign achieved considerably less than he thought at the time and that it was only during the last year of the war that bombing really hurt German war production. Harris, *Bomber Offensive*, p. 262. Albert Speer, after the war, claimed that Harris' obstinacy in clinging to area bombing was of great advantage to Germany during the war. Fest, *Albert Speer: Conversations with Hitler's Architect* (Cambridge, 2007), pp. 96–7.

142 Air 8-1109, JIC Report, Effects of the Bombing Offensive on the German War Effort, June 13, 1944.

143 Air 8-1109, JIC Report, Effects of the Bombing Offensive on the German War Effort, June 13, 1944, p. 2.

144 Air 40-1120, Strategic Bombing of Axis Europe, January 1943–September 1944, November 15, 1944.

145 Air 40-1120, Strategic Bombing of Axis Europe, January 1943–September 1944, November 15, 1944, pp. 36–7.

146 Air 40-1120, Strategic Bombing of Axis Europe, January 1943–September 1944, November 15, 1944, p. 23.

147 See Chapter 10.

148 Air 40-1120, Strategic Bombing of Axis Europe, January 1943–September 1944, November 15, 1944, p. 18.
149 Marshall MSS, Arnold to Marshall, February 22, 1945.
150 Harris MSS, Portal to Harris, January 8, 1945, p. 5.
151 Tami Davis Biddle did an excellent job of using these letters in her book, describing the split that emerged not only between Harris and Portal, but between Harris and Spaatz. See Biddle, *Rhetoric and Reality in Air Warfare*, pp. 242–53.
152 Harris MSS, Harris to Portal, January 18, 1945.
153 Harris MSS, Portal to Harris, January 20, 1945.
154 Weinberg, *Germany, Hitler and World War II*, pp. 270–1.
155 Davis, *Carl A. Spaatz and the Air War in Europe*, p. 532.
156 USSBS, Motora Interview, November 3, 1945, p. 3.
157 USSBS, Toyoda Interview, October 5, 1945, p. 6.
158 USSBS, Pacific Report 90.
159 USSBS, Pacific Report 90, p. 4.
160 USSBS, Pacific Report 90, p. 234.
161 USSBS, Pacific Report 90, p. 102.
162 USSBS, Pacific Report 90, p. 231.
163 USSBS, Pacific Report 90, p. 234.
164 USSBS, Pacific Report 90, pp. 13, 143, 169, 197, 216.
165 USSBS, Pacific Report 90, p. 117 has a comparative chart of building damage in Tokyo from the different raids. The damage per 100 tons dropped on the March 9–10 raid was considerably higher than in the later attacks.
166 It has been argued that the USAAF's raids were damaging Japanese commitment to the war; it just remains difficult to tie Japanese morale to a specific way of ending the war. For an example of someone arguing that the raids were making a large difference, see Wolk, *Cataclysm: General Hap Arnold and the Defeat of Japan*, pp. 4–5.
167 Even those who on the whole are sympathetic to LeMay and the bombing effort use vague words when describing how much production was damaged through firebombing. Werrell, *Blankets of Fire: US Bombers over Japan during World War II*, p. 229; Tillman, *Whirlwind: The Air War against Japan 1942–1945*, pp. 263–4.
168 LeMay, *Mission with LeMay: My Story*, pp. 354–5.
169 LeMay, *Mission with LeMay: My Story*, p. 355.
170 LeMay, *Mission with LeMay: My Story*, p. 384.
171 Witt, *Lincoln's Code: The Laws of War in American History* (New York, 2012), p. 20.
172 Witt, *Lincoln's Code: The Laws of War in American History*, p. 139.
173 There is an excellent short introduction to the historical discussion around this in Hasegawa, *The End of the Pacific War: Reappraisals* (Stanford, 2005), pp. 1–7.

174 An investigation group was sent in to study the impact of the bombs not long after they were dropped, which calculated the immediate death toll as 105,000. A copy of their report is available online at the Avalon Project, http://avalon.law.yale.edu/20th_century/mp10.asp (accessed September 9, 2014).

175 Grunden, *Secret Weapons and World War II: Japan in the Shadow of Big Science* (Lawrence, KS, 2005), pp. 190–1.

176 Gentile, "Shaping the Battlefield, 'For the Future,'" pp. 1097–106.

177 Koshiro, "Japan's World and World War II," *Diplomatic History*, vol. 25, 3 (Summer 2001), 438–41.

178 Koshiro, "Eurasian Eclipse: Japan's End Game in World War II," *American Historical Review*, vol. 109, 2 (Apr. 2004), 442–3.

179 Havens, *Valley of Darkness: The Japanese People and World War Two* (New York, 1978), pp. 186–7.

180 Thorne, *The Issue of War: States, Societies and the Far Eastern Conflict of 1941–1945* (London, 1985), pp. 306–7.

181 Iriye, *Power and Culture: The Japanese American War 1941–1945* (Cambridge, MA, 1981), pp. 258–9.

182 Ienaga, *Japan's Last War: World War II and the Japanese*, pp. 221–3.

183 Kershaw, *The End: Hitler's Germany 1944–45*, pp. 60–3.

184 Even until the very end, when German civilian morale seems to have turned solidly against further resistance, some elements of the Nazi state fought on with great violence. Fritz, *Endkampf: Soldiers, Civilians and the Death of the Third Reich* (Lexington, KY, 2004), pp. 116–17.

185 Leahy, *I Was There*, p. 514.

186 Leahy MSS, Diary, October 2, 1944.

187 Leahy MSS, Diary, May 20, 1945.

188 Leahy, *I Was There*, p. 515.

189 Leahy, *I Was There*, pp. 288–9.

Conclusion: the supremacy of air and sea power and the control of mobility

1 The best description of this meeting is second-hand. On May 8, 1945, Greim met with the Chief of the Luftwaffe General Staff, Karl Koller, and described the final meeting with Hitler. Not long afterwards Greim killed himself, and the story of the meeting was relayed by Koller to his USSBS interrogators on May 23. The copy of Koller's interrogation consulted here is in Spaatz MSS 134.

SELECT BIBLIOGRAPHY

The amount written about World War II is vast and constantly expanding. Listing every primary source, book or article consulted for this volume would be excessive, so the items listed below are only those which appear in the endnotes. Apologies are owed to many historians whose books I have read and enjoyed, but for some reason or the other did not make it into the notes.

Archival Primary Sources

United Kingdom

National Archives, Kew (NAUK), Files from the following record groups:

Admiralty Papers (ADM)
Air Ministry Papers (Air)
Cabinet Papers (Cab)
Foreign Office Papers (FO)
Prime Minister's Office Papers (Prem)
War Office (WO)

Private papers

A. V. Alexander Papers, Churchill College, Cambridge
Leopold Amery Papers, Churchill College, Cambridge
Ernest Bevin Papers, Churchill College, Cambridge
Alfred Duff Cooper Papers, Churchill College, Cambridge
R. N. Ellis Papers, Churchill College, Cambridge

Charles Goodeve Papers, Churchill College, Cambridge
P. J. Grigg Papers, Churchill College, Cambridge
Lord Halifax Papers, Churchill College, Cambridge
Maurice Hankey Papers, Churchill College, Cambridge
Arthur Harris Papers, RAF Museum, London
Oliver Lyttelton Papers, Churchill College, Cambridge
Bertram Ramsay Papers, Churchill College, Cambridge
Stephen Roskill Papers, Churchill College, Cambridge
Duncan Sandys Papers, Churchill College, Cambridge
John Slessor Papers, National Archives, UK
Lord Templewood (Samuel Hoare) Papers, Cambridge University Library
Hugh Trenchard Papers, RAF Museum, London

United States

National Archives, College Park, MD (NAUS)
State Department Papers (SD)
War Department Papers, including Historical Files (WAR)
United States Strategic Bombing Survey Papers (USSBS), post-war interviews
    of German and Japanese officials. German interviews are paper copies in
    RG 43. Japanese interviews are kept on microfilm.

Private papers

Henry Arnold Papers, Library of Congress, Washington, DC
Ira Eaker Papers, Library of Congress, Washington, DC
William Halsey Papers, Library of Congress, Washington, DC
Harry Hopkins Papers, FDR Library, Hyde Park, NY
Ernest King Papers, Library of Congress, Washington, DC
Ernest King Papers, Naval Historical Centre, Washington, DC
William Leahy Papers, Library of Congress, Washington, DC
Isador Lubin Papers, FDR Library, Hyde Park, NY
George Marshall Papers, Marshall Library, Lexington, VA
Franklin Roosevelt Papers, FDR Library, Hyde Park, NY
Carl Spaatz Papers, Library of Congress, Washington, DC
Sumner Welles Papers, FDR Library, Hyde Park, NY

Official histories and published/edited primary sources

The United States and the United Kingdom both published extensive official
histories after the war, covering everything from the battlefield to economic

policy. As with secondary sources, the ones listed here are only the ones that actually appear in the endnotes. As such many excellent volumes are left out.

Anyone interested in reading some of these sources should know that many of them are now available online through different portals. They are a great asset to historians interested in the subject and need to be commended. Here are some that are particularly useful (all checked and are active as of February 2013).

All seven volumes of the Craven and Cate history of the USAAF in the war are available online from the US Air Force Historical Society: www.afhso.af.mil/booksandpublications/authorindex.asp.

A number of the British official histories, including the first two volumes by Roskill on the war at sea and those by Postan and Hancock on war production and economics, can be found at: www.ibiblio.org/hyperwar/UN/UK/index.html. This site also has started digitizing a number of the USSBS's post-war interviews with Japanese military personnel: www.ibiblio.org/hyperwar/AAF/USSBS/IJO/.

The US Army's Center for Military History has digitized its official histories, all of which can be downloaded: www.history.army.mil/html/book-shelves/collect/usaww2.html.

United Kingdom

Official histories

Butler, J. R. M., *Grand Strategy, vol. II: September 1939–June 1941* (London, 1957).

Ellis, L. F., *Victory in the West*, 2 vols. (London, 1962, 1968).

Hall, H. Duncan, *North American Supply* (London, 1955).

Hancock, W. K., and M. M. Gowing, *British War Economy* (London, 1949).

Hinsley, F. H., *British Intelligence in the Second World War: Its Influence on Strategy and Operations*, vol. II (London, 1981).

Kirby, S. Woodburn, *The War against Japan*, 5 vols. (London, 1957–65).

Molony, C. J. C., *The Mediterranean and the Middle East*, vol. V (London, 1973).

Playfair, I. S. O., *The Mediterranean and the Middle East, vol. IV: The Destruction of Axis Forces in Africa* (London, 1966).

Postan, Michael M., *History of the Second World War: British War Production* (London, 1952).

Roskill, Stephen, *The War at Sea 1939–45*, 3 vols. (London, 1954–61).

Webster, Charles and Noble Frankland, *The Strategic Air Offensive against Germany 1939–1945*, 4 vols. (London, 1961).

Other

Alanbrooke War Diaries, 1939–1945 (London, 2001).
The Cunningham Papers, vol. II, Navy Records Society 150 (Aldershot, 2006).
Danchev, Alex, *Establishing the Anglo-American Alliance: The Second World War Diaries of Brigadier Vivian Dykes* (London, 1990).
Gilbert, Martin (ed.), *The Churchill War Papers*, 3 vols. (London, 1993–2000).
Grove, Eric (ed.), *The Defeat of the Enemy Attack on Shipping 1939–1945*, Navy Records Society 137, 2 vols. [vols. Ia and Ib] (Aldershot, 1997).
Jones, Ben (ed.), *The Fleet Air Arm in the Second World War*, 3 vols. (Farnham, 2012).
Loewenheim, Francis L., Harold D. Langley and Manfred Jonas (eds.), *Roosevelt and Churchill: Their Secret Wartime Correspondence* (London, 1975).
The Rise and Fall of the German Air Force, 1933–1945, Air Ministry Pamphlet 248 (1948) (republished London, 2008).
Statistical Digest of the War (London, 1951).
The Strategic Air War against Germany 1939–1945, introduction by Sebastian Cox (London, 1998) (UKSBS).
Winter, Paul (ed.), *Defeating Hitler: Whitehall's Secret Report on Why Hitler Lost the War* (London, 2012).

United States

Official histories

Appleman Roy E., James Burns, Russell A. Gugeler and John Stevers, *The United States Army in World War II: Okinawa, The Last Battle* (Washington, DC, 1993).
Cole, Hugh M., *The United States Army in World War II: Ardennes, The Battle of the Bulge* (Washington, DC, 1993).
Craven, Wesley and James Cate (eds.), *The Army Air Forces in World War II*, 7 vols. (Washington, DC, 1983).
Howe, George F., *The United States Army in World War II: Northwest Africa, Seizing the Initiative in the West* (Washington, DC, 1993).
Leighton, Richard M., and Robert W. Coakley, *United States Army in World War II: Global Logistics and Strategy, 1940–1943* (Washington, DC, 1955).
Miller, John, Jr., *The United States Army in World War II: Guadalcanal, the First Offensive* (Washington, DC, 1949).
Morison, Samuel, *History of United States Naval Operations in World War II*, 15 vols. (London, 1948–60).
Smith, Robert Ross, *The United States Army in World War II: Triumph in the Philippines* (Washington, DC, 1993).

Other

Kimball, Warren (ed.), *Churchill and Roosevelt: The Complete Correspondence*, 3 vols. (Princeton, 1984).

MacIsaac, David (ed.), *The United States Strategic Bombing Survey*, 9 vols. (New York, 1976) (USSBS).

The Papers of Dwight David Eisenhower: The War Years, 5 vols. (Baltimore, 1970).

The Papers of George Catlett Marshall, vol. III (Baltimore, 2003).

Ross, Steven T. (ed.), *US War Plans 1938–1945* (Boulder, CO, 2002).

Sherwood, Robert, *The White House Papers of Harry L. Hopkins*, vol. I (London, 1948).

US Navy at War 1941–1945, Official Reports by Fleet Admiral Ernest King (Washington, DC, 1946), Appendix B. An online version is available at: www.ibiblio.org/hyperwar/USN/USNatWar/index.html (accessed February 2014).

Germany and Japan

Fading Victory: The Diary of Admiral Matome Ugaki, 1941–45 (Pittsburgh, 1991).

Fuhrer Conferences on Naval Affairs 1944, Admiralty (UK) translation of German documents (1947).

Germany and the Second World War, vols. I–IX/1 (Oxford, 1990–2008).

Goldstein, Donald M., and Katherine V. Dillon, *The Pacific War Papers: Japanese Documents of World War II* (Washington, DC, 2004).

Heiber, Helmut and David Glantz (eds.), *Hitler and his Generals: Military Conferences, 1942–1945* (New York, 2003).

Japanese Naval and Merchant Shipping Losses during World War II by All Causes, Report by Joint Army–Navy Assessment Committee (USA) (Feb. 1947). Available online at www.ibiblio.org/hyperwar/Japan/IJN/JANAC-Losses/JANAC-Losses-3.html (accessed February 2014).

Overy, Richard, *Interrogations: Inside the Minds of the Nazi Elite* (London, 2002).

Spayd, P. A. (ed.), *Bayerlein: After Action Report of the Panzer Lehr Division Commander from D-Day to the Ruhr* (Atglen, PA, 2005).

Books and memoirs

Addison, Paul and Jeremy A. Crang (eds.), *The Burning Blue: A New History of the Battle of Britain* (London, 2000).

(eds.), *Firestorm: The Bombing of Dresden, 1945* (London, 2006).

Adelam, Johnathan R. (ed.), *Hitler and his Allies in World War II* (New York, 2007).

Aldrich, Richard J., *Intelligence and the War against Japan: Britain, America and the Politics of the Secret Service* (Cambridge, 2000).

Amadio, Jill, *Gunter Rall: Luftwaffe Ace and NATO General: The Authorized Biography* (Santa Ana, CA, 2002).

Arnold, Joerg, *Allied Air War and Urban Memory: The Legacy of the Strategic Bombing in Germany* (Cambridge, 2011).

Astor, Gerald, *The Mighty Eighth: The Air War in Europe as Told by the Men who Fought it* (New York, 1997).

Atkinson, Rick, *An Army at Dawn: The War in North Africa 1942–43* (New York, 2002).

Baer, George, *One Hundred Years of Seapower: The United States Navy 1890–1990* (Stanford, 1994).

Barnett, Correlli, *Engage the Enemy More Closely: The Royal Navy in the Second World War* (London, 1991).

Barnhart, Michael A., *Japan Prepares for War: The Search for Economic Security, 1919–1941* (Ithaca, 1987).

Baxter, Christopher, *The Great Power Struggle in East Asia, 1944–50: Britain, America and Post-War Rivalry* (Basingstoke, 2009).

Beevor, Antony, *The Second World War* (New York, 2012).

Bekker, Cajus, *Hitler's Naval War*, trans. Frank Ziegler (London, 1974).

von Below, Nicolaus, *At Hitler's Side: The Memoirs of Hitler's Luftwaffe Adjutant 1937–1945* (London, 2004).

Bergstrom, Christopher, *Bagration to Berlin: The Final Air Battles in the East* (Hersham, Surrey, 2008).

Bessel, Richard, *Nazism and War* (London, 2004).

Best, Antony (ed.), *Imperial Japan and the World, 1931–1945* (London, 2011).

Bickers, Richard Townsend, *Air War Normandy* (London, 1994).

Biddle, Tami Davis, *Rhetoric and Reality in Air Warfare: The Evolution of British and American Ideas about Strategic Bombing* (Princeton, 2002).

Blair, Clay, Jr., *Silent Victory: The US Submarine War against Japan* (Philadelphia, 1975).

Boog, Horst (ed.), *The Conduct of the Air War in the Second World War* (New York, 1992).

Borg, Dorothy and Shumpei Okamoto (eds.), *Pearl Harbor as History: Japanese–American Relations 1931–1941* (New York, 1973).

Brinkley, Douglas and David Facey-Crowther, *The Atlantic Charter* (London, 1994).

Brower, Charles F., *Defeating Japan: The Joint Chiefs of Staff and Strategy in the Pacific War, 1939–1945* (New York, 2012).

584 / Select bibliography

Brown, Louis, A Radar History of World War II: Technical and Military Imperatives (Philadelphia, 1999).
Buckley, John, Air Power in the Age of Total War (Bloomington, IN, 1999).
British Armour in the Normandy Campaign 1944 (London, 2004).
Buell, Thomas B., Master of Sea Power: A Biography of Fleet Admiral Ernest J. King (Annapolis, MD, 1980).
Bungay, Stephen, The Most Dangerous Enemy: A History of the Battle of Britain (London, 2000).
Burleigh, Michael, Moral Combat: A History of World War Two (London, 2010)
The Third Reich: A New History (London, 2000).
Caldwell, Donald, Day Fighters in Defence of the Reich: A War Diary 1942–45 (Barnsley, 2011).
Caldwell, Donald and Richard Muller, The Luftwaffe over Germany: The Defence of the Reich (London, 2007).
Calvocoressi, Peter, Guy Wint and John Pritchard, Total War: The Causes and Courses of the Second World War (London, 1995).
Campion, Garry, The Good Fight: Battle of Britain Propaganda and the Few (London, 2010).
Cashman, Sean Dennis, America, Roosevelt and World War II (New York, 1989).
Chalmers, W. S., Max Horton and the Western Approaches (London, 1954).
Chapman, Guy, Why France Collapsed (London, 1968).
Chickering, Roger, Stig Foerster and Bernd Greiner (eds.), A World at Total War: Global Conflict and the Politics of Destruction, 1937–1945 (Cambridge, 2005).
Churchill, Winston, The Second World War, vols. I–VI (London, 1948–53).
Citino, Robert, Death of the Wehrmacht: The German Campaigns of 1942 (Lawrence, KS, 2007).
The Wehrmacht Retreats: Fighting a Lost War (Lawrence, KS, 2012).
Cohen, Jerome B., Japanese Economic History 1930–1960 (London, 2000).
Cook, Haruko Taya and Theodore F. Cook, Japan at War: An Oral History (New York, 1992).
Corrigan, Gordon, The Second World War: A Military History (London, 2010).
Costigliola, Frank, Roosevelt's Lost Alliances: How Personal Politics Helped Shape the Cold War (Princeton, 2012).
Crane, Conrad C., American Airpower Strategy in World War II (Lawrence, KS, 1993).
Cray, Ed, General of the Army: George C. Marshall, Soldier and Statesman (New York, 1990).
Dallek, Robert, Franklin Roosevelt and American Foreign Policy 1932–45 (New York, 1995).

Danchev, Alex, *Very Special Relationship: Field Marshal Sir John Dill and the Anglo-American Alliance, 1941–44* (London, 1986).

Daso, Dik, *Hap Arnold and the Evolution of American Airpower* (Washington, DC, 2000).

Davis, Richard G., *Carl A. Spaatz and the Air War in Europe* (Washington, DC, 1993).

DiNardo, Richard L., *Germany and the Axis Powers: From Coalition to Collapse* (Lawrence, KS, 2005).

Germany's Panzer Arm (Westport, CT, 1997).

Doenecke, Justus D., *Storm on the Horizon: The Challenge to American Intervention, 1939–1941* (New York, 2003).

Doenitz, Karl, *Memoirs: Ten Years and Twenty Days* (London, 1990).

Douhet, Giulio, *The Command of the Air* (1921) (republished in English translation in Jablonsky (ed.), *The Roots of Strategy*).

Dower, John, *War without Mercy: Race and Power in the Pacific War* (New York, 1986).

Drea, Edward, *Japan's Imperial Army: Its Rise and Fall, 1853–1945* (Lawrence, KS, 2009).

Dunn, Walter Scott, *Second Front Now, 1943* (Birmingham, 1980).

Edgerton, David, *Britain's War Machine: Weapons, Resources and Experts in the Second World War* (London, 2012).

Warfare State: Britain, 1920–1970 (Cambridge, 2005).

Edgerton, Robert, *Warriors of the Rising Sun* (New York, 1997).

Edoin, Hoito, *The Night Tokyo Burned* (New York, 1987).

Ehlers, Robert S., *Targeting the Third Reich: Air Intelligence and the Allied Bombing Campaigns* (Lawrence, KS, 2009).

Eichelberger, R. L., *Jungle Road to Tokyo* (London, 1951).

Eisenhower, John S. D., *The Bitter Woods: The Battle of the Bulge* (Edinburgh, 2001).

Ellis, John, *Allied Strategy and Tactics in the Second World War* (New York 1990).

The World War II Databook (London, 1993).

Evans, David (ed.), *The Japanese Navy in World War II: In the Words of Former Japanese Naval Officers* (Annapolis, MD, 1986).

Evans, Richard J., *The Third Reich at War: How the Nazis Led Germany from Conquest to Disaster* (London, 2008).

Feis, Herbert, *Churchill, Roosevelt, Stalin: The War They Waged and the Peace They Sought* (Princeton, 1957).

The Road to Pearl Harbor: The Coming of the War between the United States and Japan (Princeton, 1950).

Fest, Joachim, *Albert Speer: Conversations with Hitler's Architect* (Cambridge, 2007).

Speer: The Final Verdict (London, 1999).

Francis, Martin, *The Flyer: British Culture and the Royal Air Force, 1939–1945* (Oxford, 2008).

Frank, Richard B., *Downfall: The End of the Imperial Japanese Empire* (New York, 2001).

Guadalcanal: The Definitive Account of the Landmark Battle (London, 1992).

Franklin, George, *Britain's Anti-Submarine Capability 1919–1939* (London, 2003).

Fraser, David, *Alanbrooke* (London, 1997).

French, David, *Raising Churchill's Army: The British Army and the War against Germany 1919–1945* (Oxford, 2000).

Friedrich, Joerg, *The Fire: The Bombing of Germany 1940–1945* (New York, 2006).

Fritz, Stephen G., *Endkampf: Soldiers, Civilians and the Death of the Third Reich* (Lexington, KY, 2004).

Gardner, W. J. R., *Decoding History: The Battle of the Atlantic and Ultra* (London, 1999).

Garrett, Stephen A., *Ethics and Air Power in World War II: The British Bombing of German Cities* (New York, 1993).

Gentile, Gian, *How Effective is Strategic Bombing? Lessons Learned from World War II to Kosovo* (New York, 2001).

Gilbert, Martin, *Winston S. Churchill*, vols. VI and VII (London, 1986).

Glantz, David, *Colossus Reborn: The Red Army at War, 1941–1943* (Lawrence, KS, 2005).

Glantz, David and Johnathan House, *The Battle of Kursk* (Lawrence, KS, 1999).

When Titans Clashed: How the Red Army Stopped Hitler (Lawrence, KS, 1995).

Gooderson, Ian, *Air Power at the Battlefront: Allied Air Close Support in Europe 1943–1954* (London, 1998).

Grayling, A. C., *Among the Dead Cities: Was the Allied Bombing of Civilians in WWII a Necessity or a Crime?* (London, 2006).

Gregor, Neil, *Daimler-Benz in the Third Reich* (New Haven, 1998).

Gretton, Peter, *Crisis Convoy: The Story of HX 231* (London, 1974).

Griehl, Manfred and Joachim Dressel, *Heinkel, HE 177, 277, 274* (Shrewsbury, 1998).

Grier, Howard D., *Hitler, Dönitz and the Baltic Sea: The Third Reich's Last Hope* (Annapolis, MD, 2007).

Grunden, Walter E., *Secret Weapons and World War II: Japan in the Shadow of Big Science* (Lawrence, KS, 2005).

Haarr, Geirr H., *The German Invasion of Norway, April 1940* (Barnsley, 2009).

Hall, David Ian, *Strategy for Victory: The Development of British Tactical Air Power, 1919–1943* (London, 2008).

Hansen, Randall, *Fire and Fury: The Allied Bombing of Germany 1942–1945* (New York, 2009).

Hardesty, Von and Ilya Grinberg, *Red Phoenix Rising: The Soviet Air Force in World War II* (Lawrence, KS, 2012).

Harris, Arthur, *Bomber Offensive* (London, 1947).

Harrison, Mark (ed.), *The Economics of World War II: Six Great Powers in International Competition* (Cambridge, 1998).

Hart, Russell, *Clash of Arms: How the Allies Won in Normandy* (Boulder, CO, 2001).

Hartcup, Guy, *The Effects of Science on the Second World War* (New York, 2000).

Hasegawa, Tsuyoshi, *The End of the Pacific War: Reappraisals* (Stanford, 2005).

Hastings, Max, *All Hell Let Loose: The World at War: 1939–45* (London, 2011).

Armageddon: The Battle for Germany 1944–45 (London, 2005).

Bomber Command (London, 1979).

Havens, Thomas R., *Valley of Darkness: The Japanese People and World War Two* (New York, 1978),

Hayward, Joel S., *Stopped at Stalingrad: The Luftwaffe and Hitler's Defeat in the East, 1942–1943* (Lawrence, KS, 1998).

Heinrichs, Waldo, *Threshold of War: Franklin D. Roosevelt and American Entry to World War II* (Oxford, 1988).

Herbert, Ulrich, *Hitler's Foreign Workers: Enforced Foreign Labor in Germany under the Third Reich* (Cambridge, 1997).

Herman, Arthur, *Freedom's Forge: How American Business Produced Victory in World War II* (New York, 2012).

Higham, Robert, *Unflinching Zeal: The Air Battles over France and Britain, May–October 1940* (Annapolis, MD, 2012).

Holzimmer, Kevin, *General Walter Krueger: Unsung Hero of the Pacific War* (Lawrence, KS, 2007).

Home, Thomas C., Norman Friedman and Mark D. Mandeles, *American and British Aircraft Development 1919–1939* (Annapolis, MD, 1999).

Horne, Alistair, *To Lose a Battle: France 1940* (London, 1969).

Hurstfield, J., *The Control of Raw Materials* (London, 1953).

Howarth, Stephen and Derek Law (eds.), *The Battle of the Atlantic, 1939–1945: The 50th Anniversary International Naval Conference* (Annapolis, MD, 1994).

Hoyt, Edwin P., *How They Won the War in the Pacific: Nimitz and his Admirals* (New York, 1970).

Ienaga, Saburo, *Japan's Last War: World War II and the Japanese* (Oxford, 1979).

Imlay, Talbot, *Facing the Second World War: Strategy, Politics and Economics in Britain and France, 1938–1940* (Oxford, 2003).

Iriye, Akira, *Power and Culture: The Japanese – American War 1941–1945* (Cambridge, MA, 1981).

Isby, David, *Fighting the Bombers: The Luftwaffe's Struggle against the Allied Bomber Offensive* (London, 2003).

(ed.), *The Luftwaffe and the War at Sea, 1939–1945* (London, 2005).

Jablonsky, David (ed.), *The Roots of Strategy: Book 4* (Mechanicsburg, PA, 1999).

Jackson, Julian, *The Fall of France: The Nazi Invasion of 1940* (Oxford, 2003).

James, D. Clayton, *The Years of MacArthur*, vol. II (Boston, 1975).

James, Harold, *The Nazi Dictatorship and the Deutsche Bank* (Cambridge, 2004).

Jane's Fighting Ships of World War II (London, 1989).

Jarymowycz, Roman J., *Tank Tactics: From Normandy to Lorraine* (Boulder, CO, 2001).

Jones, Ben (ed.), *The Fleet Air Arm in the Second World War*, vol. I (Farnham, Surrey, 2012).

Kakehashi, Kumiko, *Letters from Iwo Jima* (London, 2007).

Keegan, John, *World War II* (London, 1989).

Kennedy, Paul, *Engineers of Victory: The Problem Solvers who Turned the Tide in the Second World War* (London, 2013).

The Rise and Fall of the Great Powers (New York, 1988).

Kershaw, Ian, *The End: Hitler's Germany 1944–45* (London, 2011).

Kimball, Warren, *Forged in War: Churchill, Roosevelt and the Second World War* (London, 1997).

The Juggler: Franklin Roosevelt as Wartime Statesman (Princeton, 1991).

King, Benjamin and Timothy Kutta, *Impact: The History of Germany's V-Weapons in World War II* (Rockville Center, NY, 1998).

King, Henry T., *The Two Worlds of Albert Speer: Reflections of a Nuremberg Prosecutor* (New York, 1997).

Kitchen, Martin, *Rommel's Desert War: Waging World War II in North Africa, 1941–1943* (Cambridge, 2009).

Klemann, Hein and Sergei Kudryashov, *Occupied Economies: An Economic History of Nazi-Occupied Europe, 1939–45* (London, 2012).

Kuehn, John T., *Agents of Innovation: The General Board and the Design of the Fleet that Defeated the Japanese Navy* (Annapolis, MD, 2008).

Lacey, James, *Keep from All Thoughtful Men: How US Economists Won World War II* (Annapolis, MD, 2011).

Larrabee, Eric, *Commander in Chief: Franklin Delano Roosevelt, his Lieutenants, and their War* (New York, 1987).

Lash, Joseph P., *Roosevelt and Churchill 1939–1941: The Partnership that Saved the West* (London, 1976).

Leahy, William D., *I Was There: The Personal Story of the Chief of Staff to President Roosevelt and Truman Based on his Notes and Diaries at the Time* (London, 1950).

LeMay, Curtis E., *Mission with LeMay: My Story* (New York, 1965).

LeMay, Curtis and Bill Yenne, *Superfortress: The Boeing B-29 and American Air Power in World War II* (Yardley, PA, 2007).

Leutze, James R., *Bargaining for Supremacy: Anglo-American Naval Cooperation, 1937–1941* (Chapel Hill, NC, 1977).

Levy, James P., *The Royal Navy's Home Fleet in World War II* (Basingstoke, 2003).

Long, Gavin, *MacArthur as Military Commander* (London, 1969).

Lowe, Keith, *Inferno: The Devastation of Hamburg, 1943* (London, 2007).

Ludewig, Joachim, *Ruckzug: The German Retreat from France, 1944* (Lexington, KY, 2012).

MacDonald, Charles B., *The Battle of the Bulge* (London, 1984).

  A Time for Trumpets: The Untold Story of the Battle of the Bulge (New York, 2002).

McFarland, Stephen, *America's Pursuit of Precision Bombing: 1910–1945* (Washington, DC, 1995).

McJimsey, George, *Harry Hopkins: Ally of the Poor and Defender of Democracy* (Cambridge, MA, 1987).

McKercher, Brian (ed.), *Anglo-American Relations in the 1920s* (London, 1991)

Maiolo, Joseph, *Cry Havoc: The Arms Race and the Second World War* (London, 2011).

  The Royal Navy and Nazi Germany: A Study of Appeasement and the Origins of the Second World War (London, 1998).

Majdalany, Fred, *The Battle of El Alamein: Fortress in the Sand* (Philadelphia, 1965).

Matthews, Rupert, *RAF Bomber Command at War* (London, 2009).

Mawdsley, Evan, *Thunder in the East: The Nazi–Soviet War 1941–1945* (London, 2005).

Mazower, Mark, *Hitler's Empire: Nazi Rule in Occupied Europe* (London, 2008).

Megargee, Geoffrey P., *Inside Hitler's High Command* (Lawrence, KS, 2000).

von Mellenthin, F. W., *Panzer Battles* (Stroud, 1956).

Meschnig, Alexander, *Der Wille sur Bewegung: Militärischer Traum und totalitäres Programm. Eine Mentalitätsgeschichte vom Ersten Weltkrieg zum Nationalsozialismus* (Bielefeld, 2008).

Mierzejewski, Alfred, *The Collapse of the German War Economy: 1944–1945* (Chapel Hill, NC, 1988).

Miller, Edward, *Bankrupting the Enemy: The US Financial Siege of Japan before Pearl Harbor* (Annapolis, MD, 2007).

Miller, Edward S., *War Plan Orange: The US Strategy to Defeat Japan* (Annapolis, MD, 1991).

Miller, Nathan, *War at Sea: A Naval History of World War II* (New York, 1995).

Millett, Allan R., *Semper Fidelis: The History of the United States Marine Corps* (New York, 1991).

Millett, Allan R., and Williamson Murray, *Military Effectiveness, vol. III: The Second World War* (Cambridge, 2010).

Milner, Marc, *The Battle of the Atlantic* (Stroud, 2003).

North Atlantic Run: The Royal Canadian Navy and the Battle for the Convoys (Toronto, 1985).

Milward, Alan, *The German Economy at War* (London, 1965).

Mitcham, Samuel W., *Panzers in Winter: Hitler's Army in the Battle of the Bulge* (Westport, CT, 2006).

Mitchell, B. R., *British Historical Statistics* (Cambridge, 1988).

Mitchell, William, *Winged Defense: The Development and Possibilities of Modern Air Power – Economic and Military* (New York, 1925).

Morison, Samuel, *American Contributions to the Strategy of World War II* (London, 1958).

Muller, Richard, *The German Air War in Russia* (Baltimore, 1992).

Murfett, Malcolm, *Naval Warfare 1919–1945: An Operational History of the Volatile War at Sea* (London, 2009).

Murray, Williamson, *Luftwaffe: Strategy for Defeat, 1933–1945* (London, 1985).

Military Adaptation in War: With Fear of Change (Cambridge, 2011).

War, Strategy and Military Effectiveness (Cambridge, 2011).

Murray, Williamson and Allan R. Millett, *Military Innovation in the Interwar Period*, vol. III (Cambridge, 1996).

A War to be Won: Fighting the Second World War (Cambridge, MA, 2000).

Nakamura, Takafusa and Konosuke Odaka (eds.), *The Economic History of Japan: 1600–1900* (Oxford, 1999).

Neillands, Robin, *The Bomber War: Arthur Harris and the Allied Bomber Offensive, 1939–1945* (London, 2001).

Neufeld, Michael J., *The Rocket and the Reich: Peenemunde and the Coming of the Ballistic Missile Era* (New York, 1995).

Niepold, Gerd, *Battle for White Russia: The Destruction of Army Group Centre, June 1944* (London, 1987).

O'Brien, Phillips P., *British and American Naval Power: Politics and Policies, 1909–1936* (Westport, CT, 1994).

O'Neil, William L., *A Democracy at War: America's Fight at Home and Abroad in World War II* (Cambridge, MA, 1993).

Overmans, Rudiger, *Deutsche Militärische Verluste im Zweiten Weltkrieg* (Munich, 2004).

Overy, Richard, *The Air War 1939–45* (New York, 1991).

The Bombing War: Europe 1939–1945 (London, 2013).

War and Economy in the Third Reich (Oxford, 2002).

Russia's War (London, 1998).

Why the Allies Won (London, 1995).

Padfield, Peter, *War beneath the Sea: Submarine Conflict during World War II* (New York, 1995).

Pape, Robert A., *Bombing to Win: Air Power and Coercion in War* (London, 1996).

Parillo, Mark P., *The Japanese Merchant Marine in World War II* (Annapolis, MD, 1993).

Parshall, Johnathan and Anthony Tully, *Shattered Sword: The Untold Story of the Battle of Midway* (Dulles, VA, 2007).

Pauer, Erich (ed.), *Japan's War Economy* (London, 1999).

Payne, Stanley G., *Franco and Hitler: Spain, Germany and World War II* (London, 2008).

Peattie, Mark, *Sunburst: The Rise of Japanese Naval Air Power 1909–1941* (Annapolis, MD, 2001).

Perlmutter, Amos, *FDR and Stalin: A Not So Grand Alliance 1943–1945* (Columbia, MD, 1993).

Piehler, G. Kurt and Sidney Pash (eds.), *The United States and the Second World War* (New York, 2010).

Plating, John, *The Hump: America's Strategy for Keeping China in World War II* (College Station, TX, 2011).

Potter, E. B., *Nimitz* (Annapolis, MD, 1976).

Prados, John, *Combined Fleet Decoded: The Secret History of American Intelligence and the Japanese Navy in World War II* (New York, 1995).

Primoratz, Igor (eds.), *Terror from the Sky: The Bombing of German Cities in World War II* (New York, 2010).

Ranki, Gyorgy, *The Economics of the Second World War* (Vienna, 1993).

Reichbery, Gregory, Henrik Syse and Endre Begby (eds.), *The Ethics of War: Classic and Contemporary Readings* (Oxford, 2006).

Rein, Christopher M., *The North African Air Campaign: US Army Air Forces from El Alamein to Salerno* (Lawrence, KS, 2012).

Reynolds, David, *The Creation of the Anglo-American Alliance 1937–41: A Study of Competitive Cooperation* (London, 1981).

Richard, Denis, *Portal of Hungerford* (London, 1977).

Roberts, Andrew, *Masters and Commanders: How Four Titans Won the War in the West* (London, 2010).

The Storm of War: A New History of the Second World War (London, 2008).

Rodger, N.A.M., *The Admiralty* (Lavenham, Suffolk, 1979).

Roll, David L., *The Hopkins Touch: Harry Hopkins and the Forging of the Alliance to Defeat Hitler* (Oxford, 2013).

Roskill, Stephen, *Churchill and the Admirals* (London, 1977).

Hankey: Man of Secrets, 3 vols. (London, 1974).

Naval Policy between the Wars, 2 vols. (London, 1968, 1976).

The Navy at War 1939–1945 (London, 1960).

Ross, Stewart Halsey, *How Roosevelt Failed America in World War II* (London, 2006).

Strategic Bombing by the United States in World War II: The Myths and Facts (London, 2003).

Sainsbury, Keith, *Churchill and Roosevelt at War: The War They Fought and the Peace They Hoped to Make* (London, 1994).

The Turning Point: Roosevelt, Stalin, Churchill and Chiang-Kai-Shek, 1943: The Moscow, Cairo and Teheran Conferences (Oxford, 1985).

Sakai, Saburo, with Martin Gaidin, *Samurai!* (New York, 2001).

Salmon, Patrick (ed.), *Britain and Norway in the Second World War* (London, 1995).

Sarantakes, Nicholas E., *Allies against the Rising Sun: The United States, the British Nations and the Defeat of Imperial Japan* (Lawrence, KS, 2009).

Schaffer, Ronald, *Wings of Judgement: American Bombing in World War II* (Oxford, 1985).

Schmidt, Matthias, *Albert Speer: The End of a Myth* (London, 1985).

Searby, John, *The Bomber Battle for Berlin* (Shrewsbury, 1991).

Shachtman, Tom, *Laboratory Warriors: How Allied Science and Technology Tipped the Balance in World War II* (New York, 2003).

Sherry, Michael S., *The Rise of American Air Power: The Creation of Armageddon* (London, 1987).

Skates, John Ray, *Invasion of Japan: Alternative to the Bomb* (Columbia, SC, 1995).

Sledge, Eugene, *With the Old Breed: At Peleiu and Okinawa* (Oxford, 1990).

Smith, Kevin, *Conflict over Convoys: Anglo-American Logistics Diplomacy in the Second World War* (Cambridge, 1996).

Smith, Steven Trent, *Wolf Pack: The American Submarine Strategy that Helped Defeat Japan* (Hoboken, NJ, 2003).

Spector, Ronald, *Eagle against the Sun: The American War with Japan* (New York, 1985).

Speer, Albert, *Infiltration: How Heinrich Himmler Schemed to Build an SS Industrial Empire* (New York, 1981).

Inside the Third Reich (New York, 1995).

Stahel, David, *Operation Barbarossa and Germany's Defeat in the East* (Cambridge, 2009).

Steiner, Zara, *The Triumph of the Dark: European International History 1933–1939* (Oxford, 2011).

Stettinus, Edward, Jr., *Lend Lease: Weapon for Victory* (New York, 1944).

Stoler, Mark, *Allies and Adversaries: The Joint Chiefs of Staff, the Grand Alliance, and US Strategy in World War II* (London, 2000).

Allies in War: Britain and America against the Axis Powers 1940–1945 (London, 2005).

Taaffe, Stephen R., *MacArthur's Jungle Wars: The 1944 New Guinea Campaign* (Lawrence, KS, 1998).

Taylor, Brian, *Barbarossa to Berlin: A Chronology of Campaigns on the Eastern Front 1941 to 1945*, 2 vols. (Staplehurst, Kent, 2004, 2008).

Terraine, John, *Business in Great Waters: The U-boat Wars 1916–1945* (London, 1989).

Thomas, Lowell and Edward Jablonski, *The Life of James H. Doolittle: Bomber Commander* (London, 1977).

Thorne, Christopher, *Allies of a Kind: The United States, Britain, and the War against Japan, 1941–1945* (London, 1978).

The Issue of War: States, Societies and the Far Eastern Conflict of 1941–1945 (London, 1985).

Till, Geoffrey, *Air Power and the Royal Navy 1914–1945: A Historical Survey* (London, 1979).

Tillman, Barrett, *Clash of Carriers: The True Story of the Marianas Turkey Shoot* (New York, 2005).

Whirlwind: The Air War against Japan 1942–1945 (New York, 2010).

Tooze, Adam, *The Wages of Destruction: The Making and Breaking of the Nazi Economy* (London, 2007).

Tucker, Spencer (ed.), *The European Powers in the First World War: An Encyclopedia* (New York, 1996).

Turner, John Frayn, *Fight for the Air* (Annapolis, MD, 2000).

Ulam, Adam B., *Stalin: The Man and his Era* (London, 1989).

van Creveld, Martin, *Fighting Power: German and US Army Performance, 1939–1945* (Westport, CT, 1982).

Van der Vat, Dan, *The Atlantic Campaign: World War II's Great Struggle at Sea* (New York, 1988).

Walzer, Michael, *Just and Unjust Wars: A Moral Argument with Historical Illustrations* (New York, 1977).

Weeks, Albert L., *Russia's Life Saver: Lend-Lease Aid to the USSR in World War II* (Lanham, MD, 2004).

Weinberg, Gerhard, *Germany, Hitler and World War II* (Cambridge, 1995).
  A World at Arms: A Global History of World War II (Cambridge, 1994).
Werrell, Kenneth, *Blankets of Fire: US Bombers over Japan during World War II* (Washington, DC, 1996).
Whitney, C., *MacArthur: His Rendezvous with History* (New York, 1956).
Willmott, H. P., *The War with Japan: The Period of Balance, May 1942–October 1943* (Wilmington, DE, 2002).
Willoughby, Charles A., *MacArthur 1941–1951* (New York, 1954).
Wilson, Thomas, *Churchill and the Prof* (London, 1995).
Wingate, Ronald, *Lord Ismay: A Biography* (London, 1970).
Winter, J. M., *The Experience of World War I* (New York, 1989).
Witt, John Fabian, *Lincoln's Code: The Laws of War in American History* (New York, 2012).
Wolk, Herman S., *Cataclysm: General Hap Arnold and the Defeat of Japan* (Denton, TX, 2010).
Y'Blood, William T., *Red Sun Setting: The Battle of the Philippine Sea* (Annapolis, MD, 1981).
Zeiler, Thomas, *Annihilation: A Global History of World War II* (Oxford, 2011).
Zetterling, Niklas, *Normandy 1944: German Military Organization, Combat Power and Organizational Effectiveness* (Winnipeg, 2000).
Zetterling, Niklas and Anders Frankson, *Kursk 1943: A Statistical Analysis* (London, 2000).
Ziemke, Earl, *Stalingrad to Berlin: The German Defeat in the East* (Washington, DC, 1987).
Zilbert, Edward R., *Albert Speer and the Nazi Ministry of Arms* (Rutherford, NJ, 1981).
Zuckerman, Solly, *From Apes to Warlords: The Autobiography (1904–1946) of Solly Zuckerman* (London, 1978).

Articles and online papers

Assman, Kurt, "Why U-boat Warfare Failed," *Foreign Affairs*, vol. 28, 4 (July 1950).
Bateman, Herman, "Observations of President Roosevelt's Health during World War II," *Mississippi Valley Historical Review*, vol. 43, 1 (June 1956).
Beaumont, Joan, "The General History of the Second World War," *International History Review*, vol. 14, 4 (Nov. 1992).
Bechtold, B. Michael, "A Question of Success: Tactical Air Doctrine and Practice in North Africa, 1942–43," *Journal of Military History*, vol. 68, 3 (Jan. 2004).
Ben-Moshe, Tuvia, "Winston Churchill and the 'Second Front': A Reappraisal," *Journal of Modern History*, vol. 62, 3 (Sep. 1990).

Biddle, Tami Davis, "Bombing by the Square Yard: Sir Arthur Harris at War, 1942–1945," *International History Review*, vol. 21, 3 (Sep. 1999).

Billson, Marcus K., III, "Inside Albert Speer: Secrets of Moral Evasion," *Antioch Review*, vol. 37, 4 (Autumn 1979).

Boyne, Walter J., "The B-29's Battle of Kansas," *Air Force Magazine*, vol. 95, 2 (Feb. 2012).

Buckley, John, "Air Power and the Battle of the Atlantic," *Journal of Contemporary History*, vol. 28, 1 (Jan. 1993).

Budrass, Lutz, Jonas Scherner and Jochen Streb, *Demystifying the German "Armament Miracle" during World War II: New Insights from the Annual Audits of German Aircraft Producers*, Yale University Economic Growth Center Discussion Paper 905 (Jan. 2005).

Burrell, Robert S., "Breaking the Cycle of Iwo Jima Mythology: A Strategic Study of Operation Detachment," *Journal of Military History*, vol. 68, 4 (Oct. 2004).

Carter, William, "Air Power in the Battle of the Bulge: A Theater Campaign Perspective," *Airpower Journal* (Winter 1989).

Caruana, Leonard and Hugh Rockoff, "An Elephant in the Garden: The Allies, Spain and Oil in World War II," *European Review of Economic History*, vol. 2 (2007).

Charmley, John, "Churchill and the American Alliance," *Transactions of the Royal Historical Society*, Sixth Series, vol. 11 (2001).

Clairmont, Frederic F., "Stalingrad: Hitler's Nemesis," *Economic and Political Weekly* (July 2003).

Clodfelter, Mark, "Aiming to Break Will: America's World War II Bombing of German Morale and its Ramifications," *Journal of Strategic Studies*, vol. 33, 3 (2010).

Coles, Michael, "Ernest King and the British Pacific Fleet: The Conference at Quebec, 1944 (Octagon)," *Journal of Military History*, vol. 65, 1 (Jan. 2001).

Corum, James S., "The Luftwaffe's Army Support Doctrine, 1918–1941," *Journal of Military History*, vol. 59 (Jan. 1995).

Costigliola, Frank, "Broken Circle: The Isolation of Franklin D. Roosevelt in World War II," *Diplomatic History*, vol. 32, 5 (Nov. 2008).

Dater, Henry M., "Tactical Use of Air Power in World War II: The Navy Experience," *Military Affairs*, vol. 14, 4 (Winter 1950).

Davis, Richard G., "Carl A. Spaatz and the Development of the Royal Air Force–US Army Air Corps Relationship, 1939–40," *Journal of Military History*, vol. 54, 4 (Oct. 1990).

Doenecke, Justus D., "Historiography: US Policy and the European War, 1939–1941," *Diplomatic History*, vol. 19, 4 (Fall 1995).

Emerson, William, "Franklin Roosevelt as Commander-in-Chief in World War II," *Military Affairs*, vol. 22, 4 (Winter 1958–9).

Farrell, Brian P., "Yes, Prime Minister: Barbarossa, Whipcord, and the Basis of British Grand Strategy, Autumn 1941," *Journal of Military History*, vol. 57, 4 (Oct. 1993).

Friedman, Hal M., "The Quiet Warrior Back in Newport: Admiral Spruance and the Lessons of the Pacific War, 1946–1947," *Naval War College Review*, vol. 64, 2 (Spring 2011).

Gentile, Gian, "Advocacy or Assessment? The United States Strategic Bombing Survey of Germany and Japan," *Pacific Historical Review*, vol. 66, 1 (Feb. 1997).

"Shaping the Battlefield, 'For the Future': The United States Strategic Bombing Survey's Evaluation of the American Air War against Japan," *Journal of Military History*, vol. 64, 4 (Oct. 2000).

Goldsmith, Raymond, "The Power of Victory: Munitions Output in World War II," *Military Affairs*, vol. 10 (Spring 1946).

Gooderson, Ian, "Allied Fighter-Bombers versus German Armour in North-West Europe: Myths and Realities," *Journal of Strategic Studies*, vol. 14, 2 (1991).

Gordon, David M., "Historiographical Essay: The China–Japan War, 1931–1945," *Journal of Military History*, vol. 70, 1 (Jan. 2006).

Hanley, Brian, "The Myth of Iwo Jima: A Rebuttal," *Journal of Military History*, vol. 69, 3 (July 2005).

Harbutt, Fraser, "Churchill, Hopkins and the 'Other' American: An Alternative Perspective on Anglo-American Relations 1941–1945," *International History Review*, vol. 8, 2 (May 1986).

Harrison, Mark, "Resource Mobilization for World War II: The USA, UK, USSR, and Germany, 1938–1945," *Economic History Review*, vol. 41, 2 (May 1988).

Heinrichs, Waldo, "President Franklin Roosevelt's Intervention in the Battle of the Atlantic," *Diplomatic History*, vol. 10, 4 (Oct. 1986).

Herwig, Holger H., "The Failure of German Sea Power, 1915–1945: Mahan, Tirpitz and Raeder Reconsidered," *International History Review*, vol. 10, 1 (Feb. 1988).

Hill, Alexander, "British Lend Lease Aid to the Soviet War Effort, June 1941–June 1942," *Journal of Military History*, vol. 71, 3 (July 2007).

Hinsley, F. H., "The Enigma of Ultra," *History Today* (Sep. 1993).

Holzimmer, Kevin C., "Walter Krueger, Douglas MacArthur and the Pacific War: The Wakde–Sarmi Campaign as a Case Study," *Journal of Military History*, vol. 59, 4 (Oct. 1995).

Hone, Thomas C., "Replacing Battleships with Aircraft Carriers in the Pacific in World War II," *Naval War College Review*, vol. 66, 1 (Winter 2013).

Horowitz, Manny, "Were there Strategic Oil Targets in Japan in 1945?" *Air Power History* (Spring 2004).

Hughes, Thomas A., "Air-Lines: Anglo-American Tactical Air Operations in World War II," *Air and Space Power Journal*, vol. 18, 4 (2004).

Huston, James A., "Tactical Use of Air Power in World War II: The Army Experience," *Military Affairs*, vol. 14, 4 (Winter 1950).

Iguchi, Haruo, "The Secrets behind Japan's Ability to Cope with US Economic Sanctions, 1940–1941," *Diplomatic History*, vol. 34, 1 (Jan. 2010).

Jackson, Peter, "Returning to the Fall of France: Recent Work on the Causes and Consequences of the 'Strange Defeat' of 1940," *Modern and Contemporary France*, vol. 12, 4 (2004).

Jacobs, W. A., "Strategic Bombing and American National Strategy, 1941–1943," *Military Affairs*, vol. 50, 3 (July 1986).

Kimball, Warren, "Stalingrad: A Chance for Choices," *Journal of Military History*, vol. 60, 1 (Jan. 1996).

Kitchen, Martin, "Winston Churchill and the Soviet Union during the Second World War," *Historical Journal*, vol. 30, 2 (June 1987).

Konvitz, Josef W., "Bombs, Cities and Submarines: Allied Bombing of the French Ports, 1942–1943," *International History Review*, vol. 14, 1 (Feb. 1992).

Koshiro, Yukiko, "Eurasian Eclipse: Japan's End Game in World War II," *American Historical Review*, vol. 109, 2 (Apr. 2004).

"Japan's World and World War II," *Diplomatic History*, vol. 25, 3 (Summer 2001).

Lammers, Stephen E., "Area Bombing in World War II: The Arguments of Michael Walzer," *Journal of Religious Ethics*, vol. 11, 1 (Spring 1983).

Levy, James P., "Race for the Decisive Weapon: British, American and Japanese Carrier Fleets, 1942–1943," *Naval War College Review*, vol. 58, 1 (Winter 2005).

Lofgren, Stephen J., "Diary of First Lieutenant Sugihara Kinryu: Iwo Jima January–February 1945," *Journal of Military History*, vol. 59, 1 (Jan. 1995).

Lowe, Peter, "War and War Plans in the Far East," *International History Review*, vol. 21, 1 (Mar. 1999).

Lytton, Henry D., "Bombing Policy in the Rome and Pre-Normandy Invasion Aerial Campaigns of World War II: Bridge-Bombing Strategy Vindicated and Railyard-Bombing Strategy Invalidated," *Military Affairs*, vol. 47, 2 (Apr. 1983).

McKercher, Brian, "Wealth, Power and the New International Order: Britain and the American Challenge in the 1920s," *Diplomatic History*, vol. 12, 4 (1988).

Macleod, Roy, "'All for Each and Each for All': Reflections on Anglo-American and Commonwealth Scientific Cooperation 1940–1945," *Albion*, vol. 26, 1 (Spring 1994).

Mahnken, Thomas G., "Asymmetric Warfare at Sea: The Naval Battles of Guadalcanal, 1942–1943," *Naval War College Review*, vol. 64, 1 (Winter 2011).

Mann, B. David, "Japanese Defense of Bataan, Luzon, Philippines Islands, 16 December 1944–4 September 1945," *Journal of Military History*, vol 67, 4 (Oct. 2003).

Matsuda, Takeshi, "The Coming of the Pacific War: Japanese Perspectives," *Reviews on American History*, vol. 14, 4 (Dec. 1986).

Maycock, Thomas J., "Notes on the Development of AAF Tactical Air Doctrine," *Military Affairs*, vol. 14, 4 (Winter 1950).

Meilinger, Phillip, "The Historiography of Airpower: Theory and Doctrine," *Journal of Military History*, vol. 64, 2 (Apr. 2000).

"A History of Effects-Based Operations," *Journal of Military History*, vol. 71, 1 (Jan. 2007).

"Trenchard and 'Morale Bombing': The Evolution of Royal Air Force Doctrine before World War II," *Journal of Military History*, vol. 60, 2 (Apr. 1996).

"US Air Force Leaders: A Biographical Tour", *Journal of Military History*, vol. 62, 4 (Oct. 1998).

Mierzejewski, Alfred, "When Did Albert Speer Give Up?" *Historical Journal*, vol. 31, 2 (June 1988).

Mierzejewski, Alfred, Kenneth Werrell and Ronald Schaffer, "American Military Ethics in World War II: An Exchange", *Journal of American History*, vol. 68, 1 (June 1981).

Milner, Marc, "Convoy Escorts: Tactics, Technology and Innovation in the Royal Canadian Navy, 1939–1943," *Military Affairs*, vol. 48, 1 (Jan. 1984).

"The Fate of Slow Convoy 42," *Legion Magazine*, vol. 18 (June 2009).

Moeller, Robert G., "On the History of Man-made Destruction: Loss, Death, Memory, and Germany in the Bombing War," *History Workshop Journal*, no. 61 (2006).

Morgan, Alfred D., "The Japanese War Economy: A Review," *Far Eastern Quarterly*, vol. 8, 1 (Nov. 1948).

Mowbray, James, "Air Force Doctrine Problems 1926–Present," *Airpower Journal* (Winter 1995).

Mulligan, Timothy P., "German U-boat Crews in World War II: Sociology of an Elite," *Journal of Military History*, vol. 56, 2 (Apr. 1992).

Norman, R. M., and J. W. Goda, "Black Marks: Hitler's Bribery of his Senior Officers during World War II," *Journal of Modern History*, vol. 72, 2 (June 2000).

O'Brien, Phillips P., "East versus West in the Defeat of Nazi Germany," *Journal of Strategic Studies*, vol. 23, 2 (2000).

O'Neil, William D., *Interwar US and Japanese National Product and Defense Expenditure* (June 2003), available online at www.analysis.williamdoneil. com/CIM_D0007249.A1.pdf (accessed August 15, 2014).

Overy, Richard, "Hitler's War and the German Economy: A Reinterpretation," *Economic History Review*, vol. 35, 2 (May 1982).

Owens, Larry, "The Counterproductive Management of Science in the Second World War: Vannevar Bush and the Office of Scientific Research and Development," *Business History Review*, vol. 68, 4 (Winter 1994).

Pape, Robert, "The True Worth of Air Power," *Foreign Affairs* (Mar./Apr. 2004).

Porter, Patrick, "Paper Bullets: American Psywar in the Pacific, 1944–1945," *War in History*, vol. 17, 4 (2010).

Reichardt, Otto H., "Industrial Concentration and World War II: A Note on the Aircraft Industry," *Business History Review*, vol. 49, 4 (Winter 1975).

Roberts, Geoffrey, "Stalin's Victory? The Soviet Union and World War II," *History Ireland*, vol. 16, 1 (Jan./Feb. 2008).

Rolfe, Sidney E., "Manpower Allocation in Great Britain during World War II," *Industrial and Labor Relations Review*, vol. 5, 2 (Jan. 1952).

Sadkovich, James J., "Understanding Defeat: Reappraising Italy's Role in World War II," *Journal of Contemporary History*, vol. 24, 1 (Jan. 1989).

Sallagar, Frederick M., "Lessons from an Aerial Mining Campaign (Operation Starvation)," *Rand Committee Report for the US Air Force*, April 1974, pp. 25–7. Available online at www.rand.org/pubs/reports/2006/R1322. html (accessed August 15, 2014).

Sarantakes, Nicholas E., "One Last Crusade: The British Pacific Fleet and its Impact on the Anglo-American Alliance," *English Historical Review*, vol. 121, 491 (Apr. 2006).

Schaffer, Ronald, "American Military Ethics in World War II: The Bombing of German Civilians," *Journal of American History*, vol. 67, 2 (Sep. 1980).

Scherner, Jonas, "Nazi Germany's Preparation for War: Evidence from Revised Industrial Investment Series," *European Review of Economic History*, vol. 14 (2010).

Schmider, Klaus, "The Last of the First: Veterans of the Jagdwaffe Tell their Story," *Journal of Military History*, vol. 73, 1 (Jan. 2009).

Schofield, B. B., "Defeat of the U-boats during World War II," *Journal of Contemporary History*, vol. 16, 1 (Jan. 1981).

Shils, Edward and Morris Janowitz, "Cohesion and Disintegration in the Wehrmacht in World War II," *Public Opinion Quarterly* (Summer 1948).

Smith, Melden, "The Strategic Bombing Debate: The Second World War and Vietnam," *Journal of Contemporary History*, vol. 12 (1977).

Stockings, Craig and Clinton Fernandes, "Airpower and the Myth of Strategic Bombing as Strategy," *ISAA Review*, vol. 5, 2 (2006).

Stokes, Ray, "The Oil Industry in Nazi Germany," *Business History Review*, vol. 59, 2 (1985).

Stoler, Mark, "The 'Pacific-First' Alternative in American World War II Strategy," *International History Review*, vol. 2, 3 (July 1980).

Sutterfield, Jon M., "How Logistics Made *Big Week* Big: Eighth Air Force Bombing, 20–25 February 1944," *Air Force Journal of Logistics*, vol. 24, 2 (Summer 2000).

Water, D.W., "The Mathematics of Convoy," *Navy International* (May 1978)

Weingartner, James J., "Trophies of War: US Troops and the Mutilation of Japanese War Dead, 1941–1945," *Pacific Historical Review*, vol. 61, 1 (Feb. 1992).

Werrell, Kenneth, "The Strategic Bombing of Germany in World War II: Costs and Accomplishments," *Journal of American History*, vol. 73, 3 (Dec. 1986).

Wilt, Alan F., "The Significance of the Casablanca Decisions, January 1943," *Journal of Military History*, vol. 55, 4 (Oct. 1991).

INDEX